The Psychology of Meaning

The Psychology of Meaning

Edited by
Keith D. Markman, Travis Proulx, and Matthew J. Lindberg

American Psychological Association • Washington, DC

Published by
American Psychological Association
750 First Street, NE
Washington, DC 20002
www.apa.org

To order
APA Order Department
P.O. Box 92984
Washington, DC 20090-2984
Tel: (800) 374-2721; Direct: (202) 336-5510
Fax: (202) 336-5502; TDD/TTY: (202) 336-6123
Online: www.apa.org/pubs/books
E-mail: order@apa.org

In the U.K., Europe, Africa, and the Middle East, copies may be ordered from
American Psychological Association
3 Henrietta Street
Covent Garden, London
WC2E 8LU England

Typeset in Goudy by Circle Graphics, Inc., Columbia, MD

Printer: Edwards Brothers, Lillington, NC
Cover Designer: Mercury Publishing Services, Rockville, MD

Library of Congress Cataloging-in-Publication Data

The psychology of meaning / edited by Keith D. Markman, Travis Proulx, and Matthew J. Lindberg. — 1st ed.
p. cm.
Includes bibliographical references and index.
ISBN 978-1-4338-1224-8 — ISBN 1-4338-1224-X 1. Meaning (Psychology) I. Markman, Keith D. (Keith Douglas), 1967- II. Proulx, Travis. III. Lindberg, Matthew J.

BF778.P757 2013
153—dc23

2012026880

British Library Cataloguing-in-Publication Data
A CIP record is available from the British Library.

Printed in the United States of America
First Edition

DOI: 10.1037/14040-000

CONTENTS

Contributors .... *ix*

Chapter 1. Introduction: The New Science of Meaning 3
Travis Proulx, Keith D. Markman, and Matthew J. Lindberg

I. The Architecture of Meaning 15

Chapter 2. Three Forms of Meaning and the Management of Complexity 17
Jordan B. Peterson

Chapter 3. An Edifice for Enduring Personal Value: A Terror Management Perspective on the Human Quest for Multilevel Meaning 49
Jamie Arndt, Mark J. Landau, Kenneth E. Vail III, and Matthew Vess

Chapter 4. Beyond Mortality and the Self: Meaning Makes a Comeback 71
Travis Proulx

II. Epistemic Understanding 89

Chapter 5. Truth Motivation 91
E. Tory Higgins

Chapter 6. Lay Theories of Personality as Cornerstones of Meaning 115
Caitlin M. Burton and Jason E. Plaks

Chapter 7. Making Meaning by Seeing Human 135
Adam Waytz

III. Teleological Understanding: A Guide for Living 147

Chapter 8. Autobiographical Memory and the Creation of Meaning From Personally Experienced Events 149
W. Richard Walker and John J. Skowronski

Chapter 9. How Actors, Agents, and Authors Find Meaning in Life 171
Dan P. McAdams

Chapter 10. Meaning and Morality: A Natural Coupling 191
Ronnie Janoff-Bulman

Chapter 11. Wrestling With Our Better Selves: The Search for Meaning in Life 215
Michael F. Steger

IV. Teleological Understanding: Explanations for Events 235

Chapter 12. Searching for and Finding Meaning Following Personal and Collective Traumas 237
Roxane Cohen Silver and John A. Updegraff

Chapter 13. Spirituality and Meaning Making in Cancer Survivorship 257
Crystal L. Park

Chapter 14. Finding Silver Linings: Meaning Making as a Compensatory Response to Negative Experiences 279
Joanna E. Anderson, Aaron C. Kay, and Gráinne M. Fitzsimons

Chapter 15. Finding Meaning in One's Past: Nostalgia as an Existential Resource 297
Clay Routledge, Constantine Sedikides, Tim Wildschut, and Jacob Juhl

Chapter 16. Twists of Fate: Moments in Time and What Might Have Been in the Emergence of Meaning 317
Laura J. Kray, Hal E. Hershfield, Linda G. George, and Adam D. Galinsky

Chapter 17. "It Was Meant to Be": Retrospective Meaning Construction Through Mental Simulation 339
Matthew J. Lindberg, Keith D. Markman, and Hyeman Choi

V. Restoring Meaning 357

Chapter 18. Meaning Making Following Activation of the Behavioral Inhibition System: How Caring Less About What Others Think May Help Us to Make Sense of What Is Going on 359
Kees van den Bos

Chapter 19. The Embodiment of Meaning Violations 381
Sarah S. M. Townsend, Dina Eliezer, and Brenda Major

Chapter 20. Neural and Motivational Mechanics of Meaning and Threat 401
Alexa M. Tullett, Mike S. Prentice, Rimma Teper, Kyle A. Nash, Michael Inzlicht, and Ian McGregor

Chapter 21. Still a Thrill: Meaning Making and the Pleasures of Uncertainty 421
Timothy D. Wilson, Dieynaba G. Ndiaye, Cheryl Hahn, and Daniel T. Gilbert

Chapter 22. What Makes Life Meaningful: Positive Mood Works in a Pinch 445
Marc Halusic and Laura A. King

Chapter 23. Psychotherapy and the Restoration of Meaning: Existential Philosophy in Clinical Practice 465
Peter Zafirides, Keith D. Markman, Travis Proulx, and Matthew J. Lindberg

Index 479

About the Editors.. 507

CONTRIBUTORS

Joanna E. Anderson, PhD, Department of Psychology, University of Waterloo, Waterloo, Ontario, Canada

Jamie Arndt, PhD, Department of Psychological Sciences, University of Missouri, Columbia

Caitlin M. Burton, MA, Department of Psychology, University of Toronto, Toronto, Ontario, Canada

Hyeman Choi, MA, Department of Psychology, Ohio University, Athens

Dina Eliezer, PhD, Department of Psychological and Brain Sciences, University of California–Santa Barbara

Gráinne M. Fitzsimons, PhD, Fuqua School of Business, Duke University, Durham, NC

Adam D. Galinsky, PhD, Kellogg School of Management, Northwestern University, Evanston, IL

Linda G. George, PhD, Institute of Personality and Social Research, University of California–Berkeley

Daniel T. Gilbert, PhD, Department of Psychology, Harvard University, Cambridge, MA

Cheryl Hahn, MA, Department of Psychology, University of Virginia, Charlottesville

Marc Halusic, MA, Department of Psychological Sciences, University of Missouri, Columbia

Hal E. Hershfield, PhD, Stern School of Business, New York University, New York

E. Tory Higgins, PhD, Department of Psychology, Columbia University, New York, NY

Michael Inzlicht, PhD, Department of Psychology, University of Toronto Scarborough, Toronto, Ontario, Canada

Ronnie Janoff-Bulman, PhD, Department of Psychology, University of Massachusetts–Amherst

Jacob Juhl, MS, Department of Psychology, North Dakota State University, Fargo

Aaron C. Kay, PhD, Fuqua School of Business, Duke University, Durham, NC

Laura A. King, PhD, Department of Psychological Sciences, University of Missouri, Columbia

Laura J. Kray, PhD, Haas School of Business, University of California–Berkeley

Mark J. Landau, PhD, Department of Psychology, University of Kansas, Lawrence

Matthew J. Lindberg, PhD, Department of Psychological Sciences, Case Western Reserve University, Cleveland, OH

Brenda Major, PhD, Department of Psychological and Brain Sciences, University of California–Santa Barbara

Keith D. Markman, PhD, Department of Psychology, Ohio University, Athens

Dan P. McAdams, PhD, Department of Psychology, Northwestern University, Evanston, IL

Ian McGregor, PhD, Department of Psychology, York University, Toronto, Ontario, Canada

Kyle A. Nash, MA, Department of Psychology, York University, Toronto, Ontario, Canada

Dieynaba G. Ndiaye, MA, Department of Psychology, University of Virginia, Charlottesville

Crystal L. Park, PhD, Department of Psychology, University of Connecticut, Storrs

Jordan B. Peterson, PhD, Department of Psychology, University of Toronto, Toronto, Ontario, Canada

Jason E. Plaks, PhD, Department of Psychology, University of Toronto, Toronto, Ontario, Canada

Mike S. Prentice, MA, Department of Psychological Sciences, University of Missouri, Columbia

Travis Proulx, PhD, Department of Social Psychology, Tilburg University, Tilburg, Netherlands

Clay Routledge, PhD, Department of Psychology, North Dakota State University, Fargo

Constantine Sedikides, PhD, Centre for Research on Self and Identity, University of Southampton, Southampton, England

Roxane Cohen Silver, PhD, Department of Psychology and Social Behavior, University of California–Irvine

John J. Skowronski, PhD, Department of Psychology, Northern Illinois University, DeKalb

Michael F. Steger, PhD, Department of Psychology, Colorado State University, Fort Collins; North-West University, Potchefstroom, South Africa

Rimma Teper, MA, Department of Psychology, University of Toronto Scarborough, Toronto, Ontario, Canada

Sarah S. M. Townsend, PhD, Kellogg School of Management, Northwestern University, Evanston, IL

Alexa M. Tullett, PhD, Department of Psychology, University of Toronto Scarborough, Toronto, Ontario, Canada

John A. Updegraff, PhD, Department of Psychology, Kent State University, Kent, OH

Kenneth E. Vail III, MA, Department of Psychological Sciences, University of Missouri, Columbia

Kees van den Bos, PhD, Department of Social Psychology, Utrecht University, Utrecht, Netherlands

Matthew Vess, PhD, Department of Psychology, Ohio University, Athens

W. Richard Walker, PhD, Department of Behavioral Sciences and Social Work, Winston-Salem State University, Winston-Salem, NC

Adam Waytz, PhD, Kellogg School of Management, Northwestern University, Evanston, IL

Tim Wildschut, PhD, School of Psychology, University of Southampton, Southampton, England

Timothy D. Wilson, PhD, Department of Psychology, University of Virginia, Charlottesville

Peter Zafirides, MD, Central Ohio Behavioral Medicine, Inc., Columbus; Department of Psychiatry, Ohio State University, Columbus

The Psychology of Meaning

1

INTRODUCTION: THE NEW SCIENCE OF MEANING

TRAVIS PROULX, KEITH D. MARKMAN, AND MATTHEW J. LINDBERG

After reading the introductions to a number of books and volumes, it becomes apparent that authors will commonly begin by commenting on the diversity of the perspectives represented in the various chapters. This is especially true of the sort of volume that deals with a general topic (e.g., relationships) rather than a specific field (e.g., evolutionary psychology) or theoretical perspective (e.g., cognitive dissonance theory). In truth, there may be more variety in volumes that deal with a general topic in psychology, relative to other social sciences, given the natural diversity of research methodologies that characterize our science and the disparate manifestations of human mental life that these methodologies assess. For example, self-reports, scales, experimental outcomes, and EEG readings can all tell us something about "relationships" as this notion is commonly understood. However, when dealing with a notion that shares considerably less in terms of a common understanding (superficially, at least), one might expect this natural diversity to multiply further.

DOI: 10.1037/14040-001
The Psychology of Meaning, Keith D. Markman, Travis Proulx, and Matthew J. Lindberg (Editors)

This brings us to our current volume—dealing with the psychological study of meaning—and we will begin by commenting on the diversity of the perspectives represented in the various chapters. Like any volume in psychology that deals with a general topic, there is a great deal of variety in the research methodologies that are summarized and in the theoretical perspectives that frame these research efforts. However, even for those who make their way through these chapters with the expectation of diversity, the sheer scope of the diversity may nevertheless be surprising. Chapters describing anterior cingulated cortex activation in response to goal frustration (Tullett, Prentice, Teper, Nash, Inzlicht, & McGregor, Chapter 20) are included within the same volume as coping strategies following a cancer diagnosis (Park, Chapter 13). We have vascular constriction following expectancy violations (Townsend, Eliezer, & Major, Chapter 19) and the narratives we construct to imbue our lives with a sense of continuity and purpose (McAdams, Chapter 9). Taken together, it might not be clear to a reader from a different discipline (or even from the same discipline) why it is that these chapters should be taken together at all.

Perhaps this is because the *psychology of meaning*—as a distinct discipline—is just now beginning to coalesce. For the first time, psychologists working from different disciplines are comprehending themselves as working toward a common understanding of how it is that people come to understand themselves, their environment, and their relationship to their environment. Across numerous fields in psychology, there is growing recognition that however meaning is construed, all accounts of meaning converge at *sense making*, and psychologists that have explored sense making from a variety of perspectives are increasingly understanding these efforts in terms of meaning. Once the province of existential philosophy, existential psychology, and the related clinical literature, *meaning* is a word that appears with greater frequency within the social, cognitive, and cognitive neuroscience literatures.

Meaning is now something measurable—or perhaps more to the point, meaning is something that has been measured for decades in experimental psychology, along with the affective consequences of meaning loss and growth. These efforts have taken place in different eras using different nomenclatures, with a more recent recognition that something is to be gained by understanding these efforts in terms of a common psychological phenomenon.

In what follows, we summarize some of the classic theoretical underpinnings of the emerging psychology of meaning, with special emphasis on the existentialist perspective that understood meaning in a way that converges with our present understanding, and provides a blueprint for subsequent efforts. As we go on to describe, all of these perspectives intersect at a central understanding of meaning making: the ways that we *make sense* of ourselves and our environment, the feelings that are aroused when these understandings are constructed or violated, and the common ways in which we respond to these violations. In particular, we focus on a general distinction within the notion of meaning that can often obscure what meaning always is—a sense of *what* is, and a sense of *why* this should be so. To a remarkable extent, the chapters that constitute this volume on meaning mirror this distinction, focusing on both the *what* and the *why* of sense making. In particular, these chapters also describe a strikingly analogous account of the feelings and behaviors that follow from violations of either the *whats* or the *whys* of sense making.

MEANING: THE WHAT

Rene Descartes was looking for certainty. Presaging the existentialist movement by 2 centuries, his epistemic worldview was built on the rubble of what had been recently demolished—a diminished sense that life was something he could *understand*. In his *Meditations*, Descartes (1642/1988) begins by lamenting the "large number of falsehoods" he had previously accepted to be true and the "highly doubtful nature of the whole edifice [he] had subsequently based upon them" (p. 76). To rebuild this edifice, Descartes seeks out a foundation of absolute certainty, which he understands as his *Archimedian Point:* "Archimedes used to demand just one firm and immovable point in order to shift the entire earth; so I too can hope for great things if I manage to find just one thing, however slight, that is certain and unshakeable" (p. 80). So intent is Descartes on locating one suitable certainty that he is willing to "if nothing else . . . recognize for certain that there is no certainty" (p. 80).

Given the intellectual lengths that Descartes is willing to go in this quest for certainty—even accepting nihilism if it provides him one firm point—the alternative must have been something that he was especially keen to avoid. What was this alternative, which prompted him to rebuild his philosophy on the foundation of his own, seeking consciousness (i.e., "I think therefore I am")? Descartes' greatest fear was not ignorance but a kind of fear in itself. For Descartes, *anxiety* was the alternative to understanding, which he expresses with one of the most elegant metaphors in Western philosophy—the Cartesian *drowning* that "feels as if I have fallen unexpectedly into a deep whirlpool which tumbles around me so that I can neither stand on the bottom nor swim to the top" (1642/1988, p. 80).

Centuries later, Descartes' fellow countryman—French pied-noir Albert Camus (1942/2004)—would present a similar psychological account: a fundamental impulse to make sense of our experiences, the ability of anomalous experiences to undermine these understandings, the subsequent feelings of uncertainty and anxiety, and the motivational role of these feelings in altering or adopting new understandings. Like Descartes, Camus laments the seemingly arbitrary construction of our speculative models, along with their endless alteration, abandonment, and adoption in the face of endless disconfirmation ("Have I the time to become indignant? You have already changed theories" [p. 454]). He acknowledges the metaphorical nature of our descriptive knowledge structures, "that resolve uncertainty in a work of art" (p. 454), along with the irrationalities and paradoxes that become apparent when these models become objects of reflection. Our capacity for thoughtful reflection, more generally, is understood as a mixed blessing for Camus, insofar as "Beginning to think is beginning to be undermined" (p. 442).

MEANING: THE WHY

> Rising, streetcar, four hours in the office or the factory, meal, streetcar, four hours in the office or the factory, meal, streetcar, four hours of work, meal, sleep, and Monday Tuesday Wednesday Thursday Friday and Saturday according to the same rhythm—this path is easily followed most of the time. But then the 'why' arises and everything begins in that weariness tinged with amazement. (Camus, 1942/2004, p. 448).

These philosophical theorists describe an epistemic understanding of what *is*—our naïve (or not so naïve) scientist conception of what exists and how these existing things tend to interact with one another. While the violations of these understandings are associated with a "feeling of absurdity" (Camus, 1942/2004, p. 442), this feeling also arises when other understandings are brought into question: a sense of the *why* of any of what *is*, should be. According to Camus, every thinking person has reflected upon the daily activities that constitute their everyday life and asked this fundamental question: what is the *purpose* of these activities? Are these the goals that we should be pursuing? What are those goals, and what other, higher goals might they be instrumental in achieving? And what is the context that provides us with an answer to these questions?

What is perhaps most remarkable about Camus' (1942/2004) understanding of *why*, is the relatively unprompted nature of the question. We don't have to be trapped in an especially tortuous existence to have this question occur to us—it is understood to be innate, and we feel anxiety in the absence of an answer. Moreover, it is a sense of pointlessness that underlies the real "pain" of suffering; it is the "uselessness of suffering" (p. 443) that creates the most anxiety in the face of hardship. When describing his own experiences in a concentration camp, Victor Frankl (1946) confirms this contention with numerous concrete examples of pointless pain and punishment:

> At such a moment it is not the physical pain which hurts the most (and this applies to adults as much as to punished children); it is the mental agony that is caused by the injustice, the unreasonableness of it all. (p. 24)

Given that useless suffering can cause such anguish, it should be no surprise that the anguish of useless suffering is alleviated if suffering is imbued with purpose, even (or especially) by the person enduring the misery. In allegorical terms, Camus (1942/2004) recounts the "Myth of Sisyphus," in which the gods punish the titular rebel by assigning him a miserable, futile, and utterly pointless task: pushing a boulder to the top of a hill, watching it roll down the hill, and pushing it back up (again, for all eternity). More ingenious than an eternity of acute pain or the eternal slumber of death, the gods can imagine no worse torture than an existence with no *why*. However, in truth, the true horror of this fate is felt by Sisyphus only when he thinks to ask *why* and is aware that there is no obvious answer—his fate is "tragic only in the rare moments when it becomes conscious" (p. 491).

Yet even in these moments, Sisyphus is able to abridge this tragedy by imbuing it with a *purpose*. While the gods can forcibly assign his task, they cannot shape his attitude toward this task and the way he can choose to interpret it. The same consciousness that asks *why* can *construct* an answer, can choose what is fated, and even take pleasure in it, reveling in an absurd task which he understands to be beneath him ("There is no fate that cannot be surmounted by scorn" [Camus, 1942/2004, p. 491]). And once again, Frankl (1946) validates this metaphorical prescription against the agony of pointlessness; even in the denigrating miseries of a concentration camp, it was clear that "everything can be taken from a man but one thing: the last of the human freedoms—to choose one's attitude in any given set of circumstances, to choose one's own way" (p. 66). In the face of active suffering, the enduring of suffering can be framed in terms of "a genuine inner achievement." "It is this spiritual freedom—which cannot be taken away—that makes life meaningful and purposeful" (p. 67).

MEANING AND PURPOSE?

Frankl's (1946) tacit distinction between "meaning" and "purpose" is telling: why not simply use a single word for both notions, if they represent the same notion? Or—as this tacit distinction implies—are they actually two different notions, in which "meaning" deals with the *what* and "purpose" deals with the *why*. Camus' (1955) discussion in "An Absurd Reasoning" is typical among existentialist essays in making a distinction between epistemic meaning (an understanding of *what is*) and teleological meaning (an understanding of purposes, and *what should* follow)—and then describing these notions somewhat interchangeably in his account of existential repair and growth. On the one hand, Camus outlines a desire for clarity and familiarity. He presents scientific models—their empirical descriptions and hypothetical conjectures—as efforts to meet this need. Ultimately, he feels these efforts don't quite get at what we really want, insofar as they don't give us that most basic mode of familiarity—an anthropomorphic understanding of our experiences. (What do we understand better than ourselves and other people?) It is no coincidence that our initial efforts to understand reality involve human metaphors of growth, mood, and desire. And while petitioning a pantheon of (phenomena personifying) gods may be an ineffective means of interacting with our environment—relative to scientifically derived models—they remain far more psychologically satisfying than strictly empirical accounts.

On the other hand, Camus (1942/2004) distinguishes between these "scientific truths" and the reasons we use to justify our behaviors and our own existence. This is especially true of situations in which suffering becomes salient—in the absence of a "reason for living," we will commonly judge that enduring our suffering "is not worth the trouble" (p. 443). For those who draw this conclusion for their own lives, the end result is suicide, and while this is a relatively infrequent event, Camus believes that the contemplation of suicide is nearly ubiquitous. As noted, Camus understands the role that teleological reasons can play in ameliorating the psychological impact of suffering, and Frankl provides concrete support for the palliative role of purpose in those situations in which one is unilaterally deprived of active pleasures. In these extreme scenarios, suicide becomes commonplace—even rationally so—in absence of good (enough) reasons to endure.

So far, it sounds like we have two distinct "systems of relations" (Camus, 1942/2004, p. 452): those that *describe* and those that *justify*. But even in the face of this distinction, these different systems of relations are just that: systems of expected relationships that ultimately allow us to make sense of ourselves and the world. For Camus, both of these kinds of reasons—the *what* and the *why*—may serve a broad function. In the absence of *why* reasons, a suicidal act could indicate "that life is too much for you, or that you don't understand it"—a failure to ameliorate suffering and make sense of our existence. ("A world that can be explained even with bad reasons is a familiar world" [p. 454]). For Camus, both of these kinds of expected relationships are formed by the same basic motivation: "a nostalgia for unity," which he situates as the "fundamental impulse of the human drama" (p. 452). And the alteration or adoption of these systems is motivated by the same anxiety that follows their violation, whether it is a violation of our scientific understanding, or our understanding of the reasons for why life is worth living.

THE PSYCHOLOGY OF MEANING: THE WHAT AND THE WHY

If you ask a sampling of top psychological researchers and theorists to pen a chapter on meaning, the convergent picture that emerges is also a snapshot of this broadly philosophical understanding, one that transcends disciplines and eras. In terms of philosophy of science, it could be argued that these broadly analogous themes offer convergent validity for a general account of human meaning making. Or more simply—it suggests that we're all on to something. Whatever that something is, it involves both epistemic understandings and teleological understandings and how violations of either kind of understanding likely bottleneck at the same syndrome of arousal and activation and produce the same series of analogous behavioral responses. When surveying these impressive chapters, the *what* and the *why* intertwine and overlap, in the same ways that these understandings overlap in existentialist theory, and the same ways that means and ends overlap in everyday life.

Meaning: What and Why

Many of the chapters in this volume provide evidence that violations of expected relationships—whether they impact a sense of the *what* or the *why*—provoke common physiological and neurocognitive responses. In turn, these states of arousal likely motivate our efforts to make sense of experiences and restore a sense of meaning when our sense-making efforts fail. Peterson (Chapter 2) provides the widest ranging of these accounts, taking us from sponges to (post) modern humans, as each organism forms patterned responses to their respective environments. The latter organism comes to form schematic representations of what is and what should be, in which these meaning frameworks can be understood in terms of three general domains: the domain of the *known*, the domain of the *unknown*, and a third domain that constitutes their intersection and interaction; it is in this third domain that meaning *making* takes place. Peterson goes on to provide a comprehensive account of the neurocognitive systems that determine how we behave in each of these domains, while later chapters focus their attention on specific systems that play a role in meaning making and maintenance.

Arndt, Landau, Vail, and Vess (Chapter 3) also argue for the motivational role of aversive arousal in meaning-making efforts and offer a broad overview of *what* and *why* meaning structures. Arndt et al. argue that epistemic structures are "not important for their own sake," and occupy a micro, lower level status relative to macro, higher level values that are, in turn, important insofar as they assuage death anxiety. Conversely, Proulx (Chapter 4) offers a more ecumenical picture, in which epistemic and values motivations are understood as distinct and complimentary. From this perspective the violation of *what* and *why* meaning structures evoke aversive arousal in proportion to our level of commitment to a given meaning framework rather than the content of any given meaning framework.

Meaning: What

At the outset of Tory Higgins's contribution to this volume (Chapter 5), he makes a distinction between means, ends, and our sense of efficacy in attaining them—namely, a truth motivation, value motivation, and control motivation. Truth motivation is understood as our general motivation to determine what is real, and Higgins draws from a variety of cognitive consistency perspectives in arguing that epistemic needs are just that—a distinct need. While truth motivation can be understood in terms of value motivation (i.e., we fulfill the goal of establishing the truth), it also constitutes a distinct motivational force that is independent from, and does not reduce to other motivations for, value or control. Higgins argues that truth motivation cannot be understood in typically hedonic terms, insofar as we are motivated to seek truth, even if it undermines values or brings us misery. Nevertheless, Higgins acknowledges that we also feel "confused and bewildered" when our truth motivation goes unsatisfied—not a pain per se but an aversive state that echoes the anxiety and uncertainty that is often understood as pushing us towards "the real."

Burton and Plaks (Chapter 6) also begin their chapter with a similar distinction between the "way things are" and "how things should be," though their focus is on the former: the epistemic lay theories that are "central to one's sense of epistemic comfort and competence." In particular, Burton and Plaks focus on those lay theories that are crucial in guiding our interpretations of and predictions for intentional behavior, both our own and others'. People tend to understand human qualities from generally incremental (a focus on variability and context) or entity (a focus on stable traits) perspectives. Remarkably, people will report feeling anxiety if these naïve theories are violated by unexpected experiences that involve positive behaviors, with positive implications for themselves and others. More generally, inferring agentic behavior in other entities is another core element of the *what* of reality, especially when one is attempting to gain mastery over elements of the external environment. Waytz (Chapter 7) describes the many ways that we anthropomorphize other living (and nonliving) things in order to render them familiar, and as such, have them fall within a domain of predictability and control.

Meaning: Why—A Guide for Living

While a sense of the *what* organizes our epistemic understanding of reality, a sense of the *why* directs us in how we should conduct our lives and provides explanations for the events that constitute our life story. At the outset, we tend to organize the events of our lives in terms of a progress narrative—that fundamental meaning framework that allows us to imagine we are flourishing (rather than declining) and that provides a path down which we will continue to grow and improve. The function of progress narratives is highlighted in Walker and Skowronski's wide-ranging account of autobiographical memory (Chapter 8)—in particular, the imposition of a progress narrative on negative events appears effective in reducing lingering anxiety, that is, the re-recalling of tragedy or failure in such a way that it lays the foundation for future success. So appealing is the progress narrative that people will actually heighten the negativity of their reflections so as sharpen the contrast with their current, improved status.

McAdams (Chapter 9) also emphasizes the importance of progress narratives when we act as authors, "storying" our own lives. Often, these narratives converge on a "redemptive self" that allows us to understand past suffering as ultimately edifying and a precondition for our eventual success. Along the way, people are understood to move through periods in which meaning comes by acting in social roles, and later, through goals that at least *feel* chosen by an "agentic self." Often, these goals are determined by the culturally determined morals described by Janoff-Bulman (Chapter 10). These prescriptions outline an ideal set of social interactions that are intended to propagate our continued "eudaimoniac" flourishing. Steger (Chapter 11) also understands meaning primarily in terms of guiding our life path and offers a homeostatic view of these meaning-making and maintenance behaviors. Steger offers data that suggest there is such a thing as "enough meaning," and with regards to the meaning threat literature, in particular, "maintain or restore" accounts appear to provide the most accurate account of many of the processes described in this volume.

Meaning: Why—Explanations for Events

When unexpected misfortunes undermine our progress-oriented *whys*, we often compensate by generating other functions that may have been served by these events–*reasons* why tragedies and traumas occur. Silver and Updegraff (Chapter 12) review their program of research on the role of meaning making following personally experienced traumatic events (e.g., spinal cord injury, childhood sexual abuse, sudden loss of a loved one) and collective traumas (e.g., natural disasters, the 9/11 terrorist attacks). They discuss how both individual and collective traumatic events can stimulate a search for meaning and note that the extent to which individuals search for and find meaning in negative life events is not clearly explained by the objective circumstances surrounding the event. They address the role of meaning making in adjustment, for individuals both directly and indirectly exposed to trauma.

Continuing this theme, Park (Chapter 13) focuses her chapter on the ways that people make sense of unexpected tragedies—in this case, dealing with a cancer diagnosis. Park makes a distinction between global meaning and situational meaning: *global meaning* consists of the core sense-making commitments we maintain for both beliefs and desires, while *situational meaning* is our online appraisal of a given experience. When there is a mismatch between our situational appraisal and our global commitments, the resulting anxiety is understood to motivate meaning-making efforts; in the face of a cancer diagnosis, religion and spirituality may serve a crucial function in restoring both the *what* and the *why* of our global sense-making assumptions. In a similar vein, Anderson, Kay, and Fitzsimons (Chapter 14) demonstrate the direct impact that unexpected negative life events may have on the perception of meaning in our lives. Anderson et al. discuss the surprising extension of these behaviors, in which even a trivial expectancy violation, such as eating unexpectedly bitter chocolate, appears to motivate efforts to perceive our life as more meaningful.

Conversely, the recollection of meaningful events serves to inoculate us against aversive meaning violations. Routledge, Sedikides, Wildschut, and Juhl (Chapter 15), highlight the vital sense-making function served by nostalgia for salient, positive past events, such that making recourse to prior meaningful experiences appears to provide a palliative effect with regards to negative life experiences. And if significant life events are made to appear random or senseless, we will compensate for this loss of meaning by asserting that these events nevertheless occurred for a reason. Both Kray, Hershfield, George, and Galinsky (Chapter 16) and Lindberg, Markman, and Choi (Chapter 17) describe the outcomes of counterfactual thinking: an awareness that our lives could have easily turned out differently. More often than not, we imagine life events as shaped by some guiding force, a "fate" that led us away from some terrible outcome, in which these reasons follow closely from the progressive narratives we imagine as guiding our lives.

RESTORING MEANING

Meaning violations can be negative or positive events: a terrorist attack (Silver and Updegraff, Chapter 12) or improved test scores (Burton and Plaks, Chapter 6). Meaning violations can be profound or trivial: a reminder of death (Arndt et al., Chapter 3) or bitter chocolate (Anderson et al., Chapter 14). But whatever meaning violations are, they appear to involve a common feature—the violation of expectation. Van den Bos (Chapter 18) highlights the role of the behavioral inhibition system in responding to violations of expectation. The "flabbergasted self" experiences anxiety—even in situations where the expectation violation is advantageous to the self. Townsend et al. (Chapter 19) track the manifestations of this anxiety, as it may follow from any given meaning violation, however trivial.

Working from the biopsychosocial model, any given violation of expectation, however trivial, is understood to provoke a physiological threat response that in turn motivates efforts to restore meaning and reduce negative arousal. According to Tullett et al. (Chapter 20), this anxiety likely follows from general mismatches between expectation and reality, as detected by the anterior cingulate cortex, which continually compares our experiences with our understandings and goals. As with Peterson (Chapter 2), our response to meaning violation is also understood in terms of approach behaviors aimed at actively (re)constructing meaning when our understandings have been violated or our current goals rendered unattainable or irrelevant.

Of course, aversive arousal is not the only emotion associated with meaning—even meaning violation. Wilson, Ndiaye, Hahn, and Gilbert (Chapter 21) are at the forefront of efforts to explore the *positive* emotions that follow from unexpected experiences, insofar as people are able to savor the emotions that follow from positive experiences that are both unexpected and unexplainable. In a similar vein, Halusic and King (Chapter 22) present data that support the direct relationship between the perception of one's meaning in life (significance, coherence and purpose), and the experience of positive affect. Regardless of the given source of meaning (e.g., religious belief, belongingness), these experiences appear to bottleneck at an active experience of positive emotion, in addition to serving a palliate function in response to anxiety that follows from the experience of meaninglessness.

Finally, Zafirides, Markman, Proulx, and Lindberg (Chapter 23) examine how existential psychotherapy can be used to restore meaning for clients who suffer from depression and anxiety. The psychotherapist Irving Yalom (1980) identified four ultimate concerns or anxieties that, presumably, drive human behavior: death, freedom, existential isolation, and meaninglessness. According to Yalom, the principal cause of psychopathology is the interplay between stress and the individual's mechanisms of defense against it. The key to the healing process mandates an authentic and genuine consideration by the individual of their present existential place in the world. The existential approach "means to think not about the way one came to be the way one is, but *that* one is . . . the future becoming present is the primary tense of existential psychotherapy" (May & Yalom, 1995, p. 11).

MAKING SENSE OF MEANING

Insofar as anyone is able to make sense of anything, it is always done by determining a *what* and a *why*; this is just as true for efforts to make sense of sense making. There is always an account of the *what* of sense making: the mental representations that are drawn from and imposed upon our experiences, the positive emotions that follow from constructing and validating these representations, the negative emotions that follow from the violation and dissolution of these mental representations, and the various ways that we can make sense of our experiences, along with the ways that we restore a sense of lost understanding when our expectations are violated.

There is also always a *why* account of sense making: the functional role that these understandings serve in guiding and motivating our efforts, the reward of positive feeling when we make sense of our reality or have these efforts validated, and the palliative role these understandings play in ameliorating the anxiety that follows from the violation of committed expectations. As we have tried to show over the course of this introduction, philosophers and psychologists have made sense of sense making in much the same way—and the convergence of their respective *meaning frameworks* may speak to the veracity and usefulness of their sense-making. It is our sincere hope that colleagues may treat this volume as an Archimedian Point—a solid foundation upon which they can leverage their future research efforts.

REFERENCES

Camus, A. (1955). *An absurd reasoning: The myth of Sisyphus and other essays*. New York, NY: Vintage Books.

Camus, A. (2004). The myth of Sisyphus. In G. Marino (Ed.), *Basic writings of existentialism* (pp. 441–492). New York, NY: Random House. (Original work published 1942)

Descartes, R. (1988). Meditation on first philosophy. In J. Cottingham (Ed.), *Selected philosophical writings* (pp. 73–122). Cambridge, England: Cambridge University Press. (Original work published 1642)

Frankl, V. E. (1946). *Man's search for meaning*. New York, NY: Washington Square Press.

May, R., & Yalom, I. D. (1995). Existential psychotherapy. In R. J. Corsini & D. Wedding (Eds.), *Current psychotherapies* (5th ed.; pp. 262–292). Itasca, IL: Peacock.

Yalom, I. D. (1980). *Existential psychotherapy*. New York, NY: Basic Books.

I

THE ARCHITECTURE OF MEANING

2

THREE FORMS OF MEANING AND THE MANAGEMENT OF COMPLEXITY

JORDAN B. PETERSON

Most psychological models, even those as sophisticated as Gray's (1982), are based on the assumption that the world is made of objects—existing independently and given—or, more abstractly, made of stimuli. That assumption is wrong: The boundaries between objects or stimuli are situation-dependent and subjectively determined. Half our brain is devoted to vision. This indicates that we do not simply see what is there. The "frame problem"—a "new, deep, epistemological problem," according to Daniel Dennett (1984, p. 129), encountered by AI engineers producing sensory systems for machines—provides another indication of perception's complexity.

This profound problem—the infinite search space for perceptual representation—looms over all other current psychological concerns. We live in a sea of complexity (Peterson & Flanders, 2002). The boundaries of the objects we manipulate are not simply given by those objects. Every object or situation can be perceived in an infinite number of ways (Medin & Aguilar,

DOI: 10.1037/14040-002
The Psychology of Meaning, Keith D. Markman, Travis Proulx, and Matthew J. Lindberg (Editors)

1999), and each action or event has an infinite number of potential consequences. Thus, as the robotics engineer Brooks (1991a, 1991b) pointed out, echoing Eysenck (1995), perception is the "essence of intelligence and the hard part of the problems beings solved" (Brooks, 1991b, p. 143). The world does not present itself neatly, like rows of tins on a shelf. Nature cannot be easily cut at her joints. We frame our objects by eradicating vast swathes of information, intrinsically part of those objects and categories but irrelevant to our current, subjectively defined purposes (Norretranders, 1998). How do we manage this miracle of simplification? This chapter addresses this question from a neurodevelopmental and evolutionary perspective.

THE NATURE OF REALITY

> The reality of things consists in their persistent forcing themselves upon our recognition. If a thing has no such persistence, it is a mere dream. Reality, then, is persistence, is regularity.
>
> —C. S. Peirce

> The affordances of the environment are what it offers the animal, what it provides or furnishes, either for good or ill.
>
> —J. J. Gibson

> Nothing exists except atoms and empty space; everything else is opinion.
>
> —Diogenes Laertius

The objects and categories we use are neither things nor labels for things. Instead, *objects* are entities bounded by their affective relationship to a goal.[1] We perceive *meaningful phenomena,* not the objective world. The intuitions that guide us are pragmatic and embodied (Gibson, 1979; Lakoff, 1987). Objects have certain properties that, at the "basic-level" category system, we are biologically prepared to use (R. Brown, 1986). They are solid, opaque, massive, and reasonably permanent—features that become salient because of their consequence for action. Solid objects can be gripped and manipulated. Density and solidity thus seem more real than properties such as color. Our embodied, basic-level intuitions also lead us to understand the constituent elements of the objects we manipulate as bits of matter, increas-

[1]J. J. Gibson (1979) described such entities as *affordances*: "An affordance is neither an objective property nor a subjective property; or, it is both if you like. An affordance cuts across the dichotomy of subjective-objective and helps us to understand its inadequacy. It is equally a fact of the environment and a fact of behavior. It is both physical and psychical, yet neither. An affordance points both ways, to the environment and to the observer" (p. 129).

ingly smaller but similar in kind. Gibson (1979) defined the "ambient optic array at a point of observation" as the central concept of ecological optics (p. 65). This array is a heterogeneous, differentiated arrangement. Such an array necessarily surrounds the point of observation in ecological space. "The structure of an optic array, so conceived, is without gaps . . . completely filled. Every component is found to consist of smaller components. Within the boundaries of any form, however small, there are always other forms" (p. 68). These observations are for forging an understanding of the *real*. Gibson also pointed out that the array is segregated, perceptually, into a perspective structure, changing with every displacement of the point of observation, and an invariant structure, common to multiple points of observation.

Democritus, who formulated ancient atomic theory, noted that the void in which atoms were distributed was just as real as the atoms themselves. This seemingly self-evident observation has many interesting consequences. Atoms can differ in arrangement, given space. This allows for both randomness and ordered pattern, or array. Something random can only be represented by something as complex as the random elements themselves. Ordered arrays, by contrast (where some elements repeat) can be represented by using elements within the pattern to stand for the whole. A square composed of an equally spaced 4×4 array of dots is thus "1 line of 4 dots repeated 4 times." Representation of the whole by the part, akin to G. A. Miller's (1956) chunking, massively decreases computational complexity. Now, modern space is more complex than that of Democritus: It is spacetime, with four dimensions: height, length, width, and time. This means that the constituent elements of things are arranged in a (quantized) four-dimensional array of varying heterogeneity.

Intelligible arrays have been identified at many levels of resolution: from that of the quark, $1/10{,}000^2$ as large as an atom, to the supragalactic, at 10^{25} meters. All things-in-themselves exist simultaneously at all those levels, and partake in multiple arrays, at each level. A perceptible object is thus an array segregated, arbitrarily and for subjective, purposeful reasons, from its participation in endless other arrays. However, some aspect of the original array must be retained. Otherwise, the object cannot be said to truly exist and must be regarded as fantasy. Those aspects of the spacetime array we perceive as objects tend (a) to be homogeneous at some resolution level in some structural aspect against a comparatively heterogeneous background, (b) to persist for a biologically relevant length of time, and (c) to serve as affordances or obstacles in relationship to a goal. Knowledge of these facts help us understand (a) how the object can have a subjective property (e.g., as an affordance), (b) why the object is less than the thing-in-itself, and (c) how the object can still be empirically "real." The perceived object is simpler than the thing-in-itself (a prerequisite to comprehension)—while remaining importantly related to the actual thing. This relationship is the encoding of some genuine regularity across some dimension(s). The perceived object is thus a low-resolution image of the thing-in-itself. The concept, in turn, is an abstracted simplification of the perceived object (but retains some not-entirely-subjective relationship to that object).[2]

The constituent elements of an object, the object itself, and the many objects and situations of which the object itself is a constituent element *are all equally real*. Before a given object can be seen or put to use, all of this extraneous reality must be stripped away by applying a pragmatic framework of reference to the object, specifying its relationship to a goal. Perception simplifies the world without sacrificing functional grip. The perceiver learns what resolution level is relevant to a given operation by interacting pragmatically with the patterns amenable to perception. The pattern that manifests itself at the appropriate level is granted object status. In every act of perception, therefore, entropy at some levels of resolution is reduced to a minimum while at others it is allowed to approach the infinite. Thus, the complexity characterizing the thing-in-itself can be successfully, if temporarily, dealt with.

When we see, we do not see much of what is there (Simons & Rensink, 2005). The fact that each object-pattern is involved in many invisible arrays means that things have many invisible properties. This can be a good thing when new problems emerge. Old objects can be investigated for new properties. However, it can also be a bad thing. Since each object-pattern is involved in many arrays, we can perceive incorrectly. Furthermore, the outcome of a hypothetically finite act cannot be definitively calculated. This means simplified knowledge and constant blindness—but also endless opportunity for error. What we fail to see can manifest itself, unexpectedly, forcing us to traumatically attend to objects of perception that appear utterly new (though they may have been lurking in the background forever).

THE MEANING OF *MEANING*

The world therefore manifests itself to us, as religious thinkers and philosophers alike have insisted, in the form of *meaning*. Such meaning, however, does not take a single form. Instead, it makes itself known in three different classes. The first class includes the most basic, universal and evolved

[2]This implies, as well, that the perceptual object is an axiom of the concept and, conversely, that an object may be nothing more than a well-practiced concept—of the species, the social group, or the individual, following Barsalou (1983). What is axiomatic about the object is that it is a representation of the thing-in-itself, sufficient for some delimited purpose. What is axiomatic about the concept is that it is a sufficient representation of the object.

forms of functional simplifications. This class, *meanings of the known, familiar, or determinate world,* includes the meanings of individual and social identity that simplify and structure the world. The second class includes those that arise to challenge the integrity of our current known or determinate worlds. This class, *meanings of the unknown, foreign, or indeterminate world,* includes the meanings of anomaly or novelty—the unexplored world. The third class includes those that arise as a consequence of the integrated interaction of the first two classes. This class, *meanings of the conjunction of the known and the unknown,* includes the meanings arising in the course of voluntary exploratory behavior. These are the existential meanings intrinsic to individual experience. Consideration of all three classes provides a comprehensive, differentiated portrait of meaning, free from paradox.

THE KNOWN, ORDERLY, EXPLORED, DETERMINATE WORLD: MAP SCHEMAS AND THEIR HIERARCHIES

MAP Schema, Considered as Individual Units

If it is impossible to perceive the world, how do we do it? The simple answer is that we don't. We sense it well enough so that some live long enough to reproduce. We maintain our integrity momentarily while the complexity of the world swirls around us and lays us low. Induction is a scandal because things change—on different time frames and scales, but on every time frame and every scale, eventually. Thus, no solution to the problem of perception is final. In the face of such change, Darwinian hyperproduction of potential solutions, allied with severe postproduction culling, maintains life. Life forms vary, in tandem with the endless transformations of the world. Enough variation exists so that a solution to each deviation from inductive predictability has so far been found. The price paid for this, however, is endless deadly failure. Most genes fail to propagate themselves across the generations. Most species go extinct.

Some forms and strategies, nonetheless, have proved themselves and been conserved. These are evident at different levels of resolution, from the subcellular, where the symbiosis between mitochondria and eukaryotic cell has lasted for several hundred million years, to the individual, comprising the uneasy union between the single-minded personalities of thirst, hunger, sexuality, and aggression, through the social, where the dominance-hierarchy structure governing individual relationships has ruled for at least 100 million years. Such forms and strategies allow us to cope with the slowest changing of patterned complexities: Our biological structures presume air, water, light, and darkness, although some of these things have been and may again become scarce. Shorter term psychological realities are also presumed: social structure, cooperation and aggression, to name a few.

It is motivation that provides the most stable of the psychological strategies. Motivation does not drive behavior, deterministically, nor does it simply set goals. Instead, it provides the current state of being with boundaries and values (Barsalou, 1983). These remain unquestioned if current action produces its desired ends. These bounded states may be conceptualized as *determinate microworlds of experience*—as motivation, action, and perception (MAP) schemas. Just as there are qualitatively different states of motivation, such as hunger, thirst, lust, or aggression (Rolls, 1999; Swanson, 2000), there are multiple MAP schemas, manifesting themselves singly and sequentially. The basic MAP schema consists, first, of perceptions of point *a*—the undesired beginning-state—and point *b*—the desired end-state; and second, of motor actions designed to bring about the transformation of the former to the latter (Peterson, 1999). Individuals perceive objects and events relevant to the current schema; those assumed irrelevant fade into nonexistence. Human beings are low-capacity processors, with an apprehension capacity of fewer than seven objects (Cowan, 2001; G. A. Miller, 1956). Our perceptions, tuned by our motivational systems, are limited by our working memory: A good goal thus requires consideration of no more things than we can track. Perhaps it is in this manner that we determine when to deconstruct a task into subgoals—all goals are *motivated;* all *reasonable* goals are *perceptually and cognitively manageable*.

A given MAP schema arises as a consequence of insufficiency, emerging along a basic motivational dimension. This can be brought about by a decrement in the value of the present or by the imagining of a better future. The emergence of a particular motivation induces a state of radical world-simplification. Someone sexually deprived, for example, increasingly frustrated by the present, increasingly sees the future, single-mindedly, as a place of physical satiation. The motivational significance of beginning-and-end states is given by biology, or secondarily and rapidly derived from biology through learning. We confront the environment with loneliness, playfulness, hunger, thirst, and sexual yearning (Panksepp, 1998). We will work to increase wealth, however, after learning its association with pleasure, satiation, and dominance-hierarchy position.

How, therefore, might motivation be given its proper place in the study of perception? We might start with an analysis of the most basic animal strategies, building in stages from there, seeing how evolution solves the problem. Swanson (2003) described the relationship between the simplest multicellular animal, the sponge, and the complex thing-in-itself. The sponge lacks a central nervous system (CNS), entirely. Instead, it is composed of sensorimotor cells, arranged in an array, all over its body. This array maps limited, detectible environmental patterns directly onto a specialized range of motor actions, with no perceptual intermediation. At this primitive level, it is not objects that evoke responses. Instead, the same cells are used for detection and output, and one pattern evokes another. The hydra, a stage above the sponge, possesses a primitive, differentiated CNS, with sensory, neural, and motor cells. Thus, it can detect a wider range of patterns and map them onto more actions. Neural cell intermediation provides the precursor to perception so that the same "thing" can produce different outputs, but the hydra still essentially pattern-matches.

With such increased flexibility, the hydra appears to have an advantage over the sponge, but it is handicapped in one manner: speed. Information moving across more switches means longer reaction time. This problem becomes acute as the nervous system increases in complexity. Conscious human perception can take .5 seconds (Libet, 1999). Sensory systems therefore retain dual branches: one to the motor system, for reflex-like speed; the other, to the cortex, for slower elaboration of response (Swanson, 2003). As behavior proceeds from reflexive to voluntary among complex animals, it is regulated by an increasingly complex control hierarchy (Swanson, 2000). At the simplest level, somatomotor neuron pools in the spinal cord ventral horn innervate the musculature of the major limbs. At the next level (the locomotor pattern generator), operations are surprisingly sophisticated although still spinally localized and reflexive.[3] Animals with the brain–body connection severed at a higher level, midbrain, are still without spontaneous motor behavior. However, when severely stimulated, they can manifest complex actions, which can be adapted to new situations (Whalen, 1998). This midbrain region is a locomotor pattern initiator—an area producing action to more abstract stimuli than those associated with, for example, a treadmill.

The hypothalamus basically constitutes the next stage of the hierarchy: the locomotor pattern controller. Its presence in an otherwise decerebrate animal allows for spontaneous behavior of the fundamental, survival-oriented kind: ingestive, defensive, and reproductive. Hypothalamic animals are hyperactive

[3]A "spinal" animal (i.e., one that is classically paralyzed as a consequence of surgical severing of the spinal cord from the brain) can still manifest coordinated limb movements characteristic of locomotion if suspended above a moving treadmill, with its limbs in contact with the surface of the treadmill (Swanson, 2000). This means that the spine, in isolation, is essentially capable of walking if sensory input reminiscent of locomotion is received by the spinal pattern generator. However, the spinal animal is not capable of any spontaneous or voluntarily controlled or even complex involuntarily controlled motor behavior. Note that what this means, at least from one viewpoint, is that the "representation" of the treadmill-stimuli is, from the spinal perspective, "move limbs in walking pattern"—without any intermediation of representation independent of or abstracted from the treadmill. The spinal animal is therefore clearly not using an objectlike representation of the treadmill to initiate its locomotion behavior. Instead, the treadmill sensory pattern, or array, is mapped more or less directly onto a walking output motor pattern.

in contrast to midbrain animals, who do not eat, drink, or manifest spontaneous defensive behaviors, and to intact animals, whose behavior is more specifically regulated.[4] It is the hypothalamic medial nuclei that are particularly involved in behavioral control. These may be divided into the rostral segment, governing ingestion, reproduction, and defense; and the caudal segment, governing foraging and exploration. The rostral segment sets particular goals: food, a mate, escape from predation. The caudal segment, by contrast, controls the initial analysis of the unexpected and unexplored. It includes the mammillary body, controlling head direction, the ventral tegmental area, origin of dopaminergic incentive reward circuitry (Legault & Wise, 2001), locomotor behavior, and the reticular part of the substantia nigra, regulating the orienting movements of the eyes, head, neck, and upper limbs (Swanson, 2000). The hypothalamus thus functions as follows: The rostral segment generates a MAP schema, oriented toward some basic end, implementing appropriate perceptions and actions. If the schema succeeds, another, based in a different primary motivation, rapidly supersedes it. If it fails, however, the caudal segment switches to exploratory mode and gathers more information. Thus, at the psychological level of analysis, (a) the external world is mapped onto motor output before it is perceived; (b) such mapping transforms itself into object-perception, as the CNS develops in complexity; (c) a tight connection remains between sensation and action, even when perceptual intermediation arises; and (d)—most important—the schema within which an object is perceived is controlled by hypothalamically grounded, goal-directed motivation.

Identifying some end as valuable means granting it consummatory-reward status, formally, as "end" implies consummation. *Consummatory reward* has well-defined, relevant, and oft-instinctive features (Rolls, 1999). The human capacity for abstraction means, however, that the hypothetical, arbitrary, or symbolic may also come to function as consummatory reward; may serve as goal and indicate satiety so that current behaviors can be terminated; and may come to frame the perception of "objects," evaluated as incentives, threats, and punishments (Peterson, 1999). Such consequences of goal setting are universal, regardless of the specifics of the goal. This means that the cortex modulates archaic motivational systems by substituting abstractions for primordial goals and that goals might be considered, generally, as a class, so that the diversity of potential goals can be ignored and the goals serve as object of discussion. We establish point *b*, the ideal endpoint of our linear activity. We specify and evaluate our starting point *a*, and our

[4]The hypothalamus has developed subsystems providing integrated control of all three subsections of the motor system: somatomotor, governing the operation of skeletal, voluntary muscle; autonomic, innervating smooth muscle, cardiac muscle, and glands; and neuroendocrine, exerting its effects through the pituitary (Swanson, 2000, p. 116). The hypothalamus also regulates temperature and the sleep/wake cycle.

actions, in reference to that ideal. We strive to transform *a* into *b*, testing possible solutions to the now-bounded frame problem. We become anxiety ridden or frustrated as a consequence of our failures, manifold and common. Alternatively, we embody a solution as a consequence of favorable mutation or stumble across an answer, communicate our successes, and move up the dominance hierarchy. Our MAP schema solutions are inevitably evolutionary, phylogenetically (as our successful genes accumulate) and ontogenetically (as we try many useless approaches and conserve those that work).

MAP Schemas Considered in Their Social/Hierarchical Multiplicity

Basic motivation helps solve the problem of pragmatic world simplification, but a multitude of problems remain. First are issues of sequence and time frame: In what order should a set of MAP schemas manifest themselves—over the day or week or year? Second is the related issue of importance: Which MAP schemas should be granted priority of value? Third is the even more complex problem of *social being:* How should I adjust my MAP schemas to those around me (who are facing, and trying to solve, the same problems)? It is identity, the idiosyncratic structure of personal integration, that solves these problems. Thus, personal identity shades into the social; personal and social identity is the emergent, unconscious, automatic consequence of the cooperative/competitive generation, sequencing, and rank ordering of MAP schemas. Such organization manifests itself intrapsychically and socially as the dominance hierarchy. Status is the most important determinant of survival and reproductive success. Establishment of a predictable dominance hierarchy allows for orderly resource access so that every consummatory attempt does not end in competitive violence. Status tracking is so important (Abbott et al., 2003; Virgin & Sapolosky, 1997) that group and neocortical size are tightly correlated among primates (Joffe & Dunbar, 1997), and advancement is worth fighting for. Juvenile chimps, our close cousins (Sibley & Ahlquist, 1984), share many MAP schemas with children, including those related to dominance-hierarchy maneuvering. These manifest themselves first, innocently enough, as teasing (De Waal, 1996). Teasing becomes more serious with age but less frequent. The infant engages in little pushes from behind, jumping away when the adult reacts. The adolescent male manifests full-fledged charging displays, seeking to dominate peers and, eventually, higher ranking adults. Adults form sophisticated coalitions, jockeying for position. Such jockeying can become horrifically violent (De Waal, 1996).

The fact of innate dominance striving, however, buttressed by aggression, does not mean that chimps or humans lack social feeling or that they simply come to inhibit their aggression through fear or forethought. Primates are gregarious as much as aggressive, even in the aftermath of violent encounters

(De Waal, 1989b). Agonistic and cooperative behaviors are not simply opposed to one another. More aggressive social creatures may have to be more affiliative (Abbott et al., 2003; De Waal, 1989b). Interaction can be cooperative at one level and competitive at another. The dominance hierarchy is in fact a form of extended cooperation, establishing the frame for within-hierarchy striving, and aggression is counterbalanced by two powerful regulatory processes. One is innate and internal; the other, emergent and social. The internal process is empathy, the ability to feel another's experiences (Preston & De Waal, 2002)—in addition, of course, to the basic inhibition produced by fear. The maternal circuitry governing empathy is deeply rooted (Panksepp, 1998) and modulates response to those deemed kin.[5]

Chimps are predatory. They hunt monkeys and raid foreign conspecifics (Wrangham & Peterson, 1996). A chimp might even maim or kill a troupe-mate during intensely agonistic disputes. Clearly, there is no inevitable *internal* limit on their aggressive MAP schemas. De Waal (1989a) suggested, instead, that it is the whole troupe that constrains the ambitious individual, becoming agitated en masse when any battle goes too far. Thus, a well-socialized individual may not generally need a superego. That is, as long as the social context constraining his behavior remains stable and appropriate. If the social context destabilizes, however, all hell may break loose (see Chang, 1988). This is something terrifying to consider, given our firm belief in the existence of individual moral choice. If he is acceptable to his peers, the modulating effect of their reactions will remain at hand and effective. When human children are socialized, they learn socialized alternatives to violence, which serve as more effective means to social status. They do not simply inhibit the primal aggressive circuits. Instead, they integrate these circuits into more sophisticated behavioral games. Children organize their primary impulses into higher order, low-resolution MAP schema, within the confines of the dominance hierarchies they inhabit.

Such organization is mediated by empathy and then by play. Play is early social cognition: When children play, they adapt their actions to each other. They produce and then share a perspective and work toward a common goal. They embody the same MAP schema to the benefit of both. The capacity to do so unfolds developmentally, starting with the body, in direct physical contact with others' bodies (P. K. Smith & Boulton, 1990). The maturing child begins by constructing small-scale motor patterns, designed to attain indi-

[5]A wide range of animals exhibit empathic reactions to distressed conspecifics, including rats, hyenas, and rhesus monkeys (Masserman, Wechkin, & Terris, 1964; Rice, 1964; Rice & Gainer, 1962; Yoerg, 1991). Likewise, human infants spontaneously cry when they hear others crying (Zahn-Waxler, Radke-Yarrow, & King, 1979), imitate others' distress, and help spontaneously (P. Miller, Eisenberg, Fabes, & Shell, 1996).

vidually motivated ends. "Play is purely individual" at this stage. "Ritualized schemas" develop—skilled play habits—but no collective patterns, much less rules (Piaget, 1932, pp. 16–18). The child plays alone, practicing a repertoire of functional actions and conceptions, from the spinal bottom of Swanson's (2000) control hierarchy to the cortical top. Before there are stateable rules, there are behavioral patterns. As the child progresses, complex social understanding emerges. The child imitates himself, using procedure to map procedure, at the initial, embodied stage of genuine representation. Any successful MAP schema is immediately replicated, practiced, automatized, and readied for future employment (Piaget, 1932). Imitation then extends to others. Patterned social interactions begin to emerge as the play partners exchange information about which (re)actions are desirable, and a prototypical morality emerges—even among rats.[6] Control over MAP schema formation shifts to emergent systems of more complex control. Hippocampal maturation allows for determination by context (LeDoux, 1996). The orbitofrontal and dorsolateral prefrontal cortices increasingly grant abstractions value-status (Krawczyk, 2002), removing the individual from the short-term horizon of basic motivation (Pochon et al., 2002).

Higher order, more explicit, cooperative morality emerges around age 7 (Piaget, 1932). Each child now tries to win, to dominate the hierarchy of game achievement. At first glance, this appears competitive. However, all disagreements about the game have to be resolved before any attempt to play, let alone win, can begin, and all striving must remain civilized enough that the game can continue. Even these more complex play forms emerge procedurally, rather than explicitly. If the playing children are separated and interviewed individually, they give disparate accounts of the emergent game's "rules." They still need the information provided by the others' presence to maintain the game. Once a game becomes a regular occurrence, however, it can be explicitly codified. Then patterns that constitute the game, and the explicit description of the game, come into alignment. The children map their own socially-modified sensorimotor outputs and become conscious players (Piaget, 1932), able to inhabit fictional, social, dramatic worlds (highly abstracted and communal MAP schemas).

It is the ability to establish these joint schemas that allows for the modulation of motivation and emotion toward some shared end. In a good game, there are many opportunities for joint gain. There is no need to be preda-

[6]When juvenile rats are paired together, repeatedly, in rough-and-tumble wrestling bouts, one rat will end up on top more frequently. However, if the now-dominant rat pins its playmate more than 70% of the time, the subordinate, who initiates play sequences, begins to ignore the victor, and play diminishes (Panksepp, 1998). The dominant rat must learn to respond to the cues of the subordinate if it wishes to keep playing. Such modulation lays the foundation for the higher-order morality, keeping aggression and other potentially antisocial schema properly regulated—even among rats.

tory or defensive, so there is little need for violence. Well-socialized adults add their opinions to the process, insisting that the players play fair and act as good sports: "How you play the game is more important than whether you win or lose." The adults know, implicitly, that life is a sequence of games and that those who play properly during a given game become the popular players of many games, benefitting cumulatively from playing each. Thus, a vital form of meta-morality emerges: *The best player is he who is invited to play the most games*. Sacrificing a future invitation for present victory is a counter-productive long-term strategy.

A purely personal MAP schema specifies starting place, goal, objects of perception, and implication for emotion, dealing with the bits of the world relevant to a particular desire. The joint construction of such schema integrates perception across individuals, placing them in the same world of objects, aligning their emotions. Diverse individuals inhabit the same experiential space, cooperating both to reach a goal and to maintain the space's integrity. This is how fundamental agreements emerge, nullifying the very necessity for aggression—or for terror. For the socialized, within the intact dominance hierarchy, the unbearable present predictably turns into the desirable future. Everyone plays the same game, with the same rules, at the same time. Emotion remains controlled.

The specific circuitry mediating such concordance has been recently outlined. Rizzolatti, Fogassi, and Gallese (2001) described the behavior of certain visuomotor neurons, located in the ventral premotor cortex. Some are motor neurons but also respond to visual stimuli. Some are activated by 3-D objects. The most relevant, however—*mirror neurons*—"require action observation for their activation" (p. 661). Mirror neurons, part of the system that uses motor-output patterning as the basis of perception, have remarkable properties. They do not respond to a motivationally significant object in isolation. Nor do they respond to the sight of a conspecific engaged in context-independent action, such as grasping. But they do respond to the sight of a conspecific grasping in the presence of a motivationally significant object. More to the point, their responses match, when a motivated sequence is observed *and* when it is enacted. This congruence can be strict, coinciding in goal and behavioral sequence. Sometimes, however, the congruence is broader; generalizing "the goal of the observed action across many instances of it" (p. 662). This is akin to a child's playing the role of father, rather than precisely imitating any of father's specific behaviors. A neural mechanism allowing both for imitation and the abstraction of imitation has thus been identified.

Mirror-neuron mediated understanding cascades downward from the abstract, through the emotional, to the physical. The mirror system accepts sensory, cognitive, and circadian state inputs and produces somatic, endocrine, and neuroendocrine output (Swanson, 2000). Area F5 (the premotor area of the cerebral cortex), which contains the mirror neurons, shares connectivity to inferior parietal lobe with area *a* of the superior temporal sulcus—part of a circuit including amygdala and orbitofrontal cortex (Amaral, Price, Pitkanen, & Carmichael, 1992). This implies that mirroring extends beyond action, to its emotional, motivational, cognitive and neuroendocrine concomitants. F5 has other relevant functions, as well. It is the primate homologue of Broca's area, which has come to govern voluntary speech. The development of the mirror neuron system allows a maturing child to embody the action and motivational states of those he directly observes, with greater or lesser fidelity. The linguistic abilities of Broca's area, integrated with the mirror neuron circuitry, allow communicating children to verbally instantiate shared MAP schema, not at the level of precise imitation but at a higher, generalized state. Thus, children engaged in pretend play can coordinate their motivations, emotions, actions, and perceptions.

Such processes of coordination, within such schemas, lay the groundwork for the understanding of imagistic and more abstract semantic thought, including drama and fiction, and the ability to engage in increasingly adult-scale social enterprises. A plan is the projection of a compelling fiction onto agreed-upon objects and contexts. The successful joint establishment of such a plan, motivationally significant, emotionally gripping, eliminates the very necessity for uncertainty, anxiety, and conflict. This all means, as well, that it is not precisely *individuals* who occupy a given position in a given dominance hierarchy. MAP schemas themselves cooperate and compete, within and between individuals. The intrapsychic and social structures that result are the consequences of that process. Thus, in a properly formulated dominance hierarchy, the presuppositions of the individuals match the structure of the group. *This keeps the group stable and the individuals affectively regulated.* Any challenge to this match (and not simply to the intrapsychic or social structures themselves) therefore simultaneously dysregulates motivation and emotion.

THE UNKNOWN, CHAOTIC, UNEXPLORED, INDETERMINATE WORLD: NOVELTY, ANOMALY, AND MAP SCHEMA DISRUPTION

The frame consisting of point *a* and point *b* can well be considered a theory-laden MAP schema. Such a schema is also a story, however, in its simplest form, analogous to the necessary fiction of Vaihinger (1924) and Adler (Ansbacher & Ansbacher, 1956), the life-space/field of Lewin (1935), the Dasein of the phenomenologists (Binswanger, 1963; Boss, 1963) and the normal science of Kuhn (1970).

A MAP schema is also a cybernetic unit (see Wiener, 1948). A broad, interdisciplinary consensus has emerged around the cybernetic framework, based on the assumption that goal-directed, self-regulatory systems constantly compare what is to what should be, while attempting to reduce mismatch. Piaget (1954) adopted many cybernetic preconceptions, including the belief that "all knowledge is tied to action . . . on the most elementary sensory-motor level and all the way up to the highest logical-mathematical operations" (Glasersfeld, 1982, p. 613; 1999). Luria (1960, 1980), Sokolov (1963), and Vinogradova (1961, 1975) were also heavily influenced by Norbert Wiener. All four served as precursors to Gray (1982, 1987; Gray & McNaughton, 2003). G. A. Miller, Galanter, and Pribram (1960) used cybernetic principles, as did Powers (1973) and Schank and Abelson (1977). Similar ideas have emerged with regard to emotions and their role in giving value to objects of apprehension (Damasio, 1994; Jung, 1971, pp. 433–436) and indicating the interruption of goals (Oatley & Jenkins, 1992; Oatley & Johnson-Laird, 1987).

Luria, Sokolov, Vinogradova, and Gray (LSVG) hypothesized, specifically, that complex organisms developed a complete internal model of the world and how it should unfold as a consequence of current actions and continuously contrasted this internal model, this *expectation*, with what was, *in fact*, occurring. When things go according to plan, according to this hypothesis, positive affect rules, ensuring that current goal-directed conceptions and actions dominate (Gray, 1982; Rolls, 1999). When something unexpected occurs, by contrast, the *orienting reflex*, a sequence of rapid preparatory responses, manifests itself. Current goal-directed actions cease (Gray, 1982) when mismatch between desire and world emerges, detected by the septal-hippocampal comparator systems. Lower brain circuit function, including the amygdalic, is disinhibited, activating circuitry in the right hemisphere (Tucker & Frederick, 1989) and, later in the processing chain, inhibiting the frontal and prefrontal systems of the left cortical hemisphere, associated with positive emotion (Davidson, 1992). The autonomic nervous system is engaged. Heart rate rises (Fowles, 1980) in preparation for nonspecific action, and cortisol floods the bloodstream (Gray, 1987). Startle responses, primitive but fast, governed by brainstem circuitry, produce virtually instantaneous physiological defensive postures, designed to protect the body, particularly the head and neck (Yeomans, Li, Scott, & Frankland, 2002). This is followed by activation of circuits in the superior colliculus, which direct the sensory systems of the head toward the environmental locale that quick-and-dirty systems have specified as the source of the anomaly (Dean, Redgrave, & Westby, 1989). Hypothalamic systems, particularly those in the rostral segment, ready fight or flight, another aspect of defensive response, in concert with the pain-sensitive systems of the periaqueductal grey (Swanson, 2000).

Finally, the extended amygdala (the bed nucleus of the stria terminalis) enhances vigilance and provisionally associates the anomalous occurrence with anomalies that in the past have produced negative outcomes (Hooker, Germine, Knight, & D'Esposito, 2006). This comparator theory, advanced most completely by Gray, has become exceedingly influential across wide domains of psychological inquiry. It remains predicated, nonetheless, on four assumptions about perception that can no longer be maintained. Thus, the role that the hierarchical arrangement of MAP schema plays in affect regulation has not yet been fully appreciated.

Sokolov's (1963) subjects responded with an orienting reflex to the tiniest alterations in lab stimuli. He used auditory tones and elicited a galvanic skin response to any alteration in volume, tempo, or irregularity in tone onset or offset. It was this sensitivity that produced LSVG's first error: the hypothesis of complete objective modeling. Later researchers demonstrated that orienting only occurs toward "differences that make a difference" (Bargh & Chartrand, 1999; Simons & Rensink, 2005)—anomalies that interfere actively with current goal-directed activity—and not to all stimulus change. Modeling is thus far from complete. Consciousness attends selectively to the minimum set of elements necessary to bring about the desired transformation. LSVG assumed, secondly, that the CNS compared *incoming objective sensory data* (reality) and *expectation* (construed cognitively). As behaviorists, they presumed that stimuli were objectively real and simply given, and they gave short shrift to motivation.

Living creatures do not so much *expect* things as *desire* them. Desire is motivation, and it is motivational systems that fundamentally give rise to MAP schema. For LSVG, mismatch meant error, error meant anxiety, and anxiety indicated that behavior must be retooled. Mismatch, however, is much more than the problem of erroneous action, but this cannot be understood without due consideration of motivation. If the desired future fails to appear, it is not only current actions that might be wrong: *Current desire might be wrong*, as well. Perhaps the MAP schema is motivated by jealousy, for example, and the situation is such that jealousy merely makes things worse.

It is not *reality* that is compared with expectation (now: *desire*). We are not privy to reality, even in the present. Current "actuality" is modeled, much as future "possibility." Sometimes you cannot get from point "a" to point "b" because you are not actually at point "a." We compare a *motivated model of the present* with a *motivated model of the future*. In the case of error, this means that the very way we perceive things, present *and* future, might be incorrect. Failure re-presents us with the frame problem. This is a very serious problem indeed, given all the different ways that the complex world of things and situations can be perceived. Whatever anxiety might arise at the failure of our actions is nothing compared with the terror of having to recalibrate our perceptions. LSVG were not nearly pessimistic enough about error. When what is desired does not manifest itself, motivation and perception, as well as cognition and action, might all be incorrect—and anywhere in their structure.

This brings us to the fourth and final element missing in the standard account: the implications of *hierarchical* MAP-schema structure (see also Carver & Scheier, 1998). In the absence of such nesting, it would be impossible to disinhibit motivation and emotion at different levels of intensity when anomalies of different significance emerge. All errors would be equally overwhelming or irrelevant. However, varying errors indeed produce various reactions. Each mistake cannot be evaluated cognitively, however. There is insufficient time for that. Instead, potential meaning is bounded, a priori, by the breadth or import of the current MAP schema. Large-scale MAP schemas are built from the bottom up, following Piaget and Swanson, established at spinal levels, organized into more complexly sequenced routines, represented as abstractions, and communicated and verbally organized into long-term plans. A large-scale plan thus consists of smaller plans, which consist of even smaller plans, which eventually ground out in muscle movement itself. Thus, the mind meets the body. Development is simultaneous higher order organization of intrapsychic and social MAP schemas. Affective stability, particularly at higher order levels, is dependent upon the match between them. Imagine an inverted neural hierarchy, representing MAP schema import: Mismatch disruption of schemas closer to the point of the V is more upsetting. The meaning of a high-resolution schema depends on its role as a subelement of a lower resolution schema: Grades in a pre-med class only matter in the broader context of wanting to be a physician.

The objects specified by a given MAP schema are positively valenced—the first dimension of emotion—if their appearance indicates (a) that progress is occurring and (b) *that the structural integrity of the currently operative schema is valid and intact*. A working schema is therefore self-verifying, as well as providing direct, dopaminergically mediated (Gray, 1982) incentive reward. Obstacles, by contrast, are negatively valenced (the second basic emotional dimension). Their appearance indicates a schema-world mismatch, danger to current progress, and the fact that the current MAP schema (or hierarchy) may not be functional. If an obstacle does appear, it should first be evaluated for significance at the narrowest and most specific level possible. Such use of Occam's razor limits the spread of chaotic emotion. Elements of self differ in degree, not in kind: The upheaval produced by an obstacle is proportionate to the area of space and time structured by the erroneous schema. The solution may lie close to hand, if the obstacle is merely something expected under different circumstances. Other times, however, the obstacle is too radically unknown for such easy dealings. Then the complexity of things reemerges, with incomputable consequences. The borders between things become questionable, and everything is up for grabs. This is the problem of chaos versus order—*the* eternal problem and the ultimate reality of the world.

We derive one important form of meaning—security and hope—from the match between our personal MAP schemas and the social world. Such ordered meaning emerges as a consequence of the delimitation of its paired opposite, chaos, whose manifestation produces the second kind of meaning. Maintenance of MAP-schema meaning keeps chaos in check rather than revealing it (or allows it to be revealed in doses small enough to be tolerable). Determinate positive and negative events occur as the world manifests itself as tool and obstacle. Irrelevant things occur, too, of course—but are in some important sense never realized. No one can pay attention to all activity; only to all relevant activity. But what of seriously anomalous events? Some occurrences are neither evidently good nor bad, nor immediately eradicable as meaningless. They are *not* understood, *not* explored. They cannot be placed into the context of the current MAP schema nor encapsulated within that schema's hierarchically ordered, larger scale conceptual surroundings. They violate the frame, interfering with its operation, its integrity, and its relationship to other frames. What must happen in such cases?

What is not comprehended but is still extant must logically be experienced as paradoxical (Gray, 1982; Jung, 1967a, 1967b; Peterson, 1999): negative in potential, positive in potential, or irrelevant in potential—and self and world in potential, as well. That potential, the true complexity of the world, is chaos. Its manifestation, no mere threat, constitutes a challenge to the full adaptive capacity of the individual. The emergence of chaos produces more than mere anxiety; something more like generalized MAP schema disinhibition and competition, as new and potentially appropriate means of framing, war with each other for dominance. Motivation for maintaining meaning is thus not merely desire to reduce anxiety: It is instead desire to avoid the internal and, frequently, external war of competing options—and there is something even deeper about the anomalous event. At some point in psychological development, however hypothetical, *all events* are anomalous, though they may be rapidly constrained by the social surround. This means that the schemas allowing for the determinate utilization of objects, situations, and abstractions are dependent for their construction, initially, on information extracted from the overarching, ever-emerging domain of the unknown. It is for such reasons that chaos is meaningful, a priori, and the mother of determinate being itself.

The appearance of the anomalous involuntarily produces its own specific MAP schema, the orienting reflex, or complex, in more modern terms (Halgren, 1992; Ohman, 1979, 1987). The beginning point of *that* schema is the insufficiency of present knowledge. The desired endpoint is classification of the anomalous phenomenon, and its reduction to specified meaning. Increased sensory processing and exploratory activity is brought to bear on the uncomprehended circumstance, examined from the perspective of varying MAP schemas: Is it relevant to another motivational state? Can it serve as an affordance or obstacle, and at what level? Is it like other irrelevant "objects" and treatable as ground? Such effortful exploration constitutes (a) the process by which identity originally comes to be (Peterson, 1999); (b) the elimination of possibility from the indeterminate domain of the anomalous to the finite domain of a determinate MAP schema; and (c) the reworking of identity, which is the sum total of all such schema.

It is here that Swanson's work on hypothalamic function once again becomes relevant. The hypothalamic rostral behavior control segment establishes narrow, biologically relevant MAP schema, ingestive, reproductive, and defensive. The caudal segment, by contrast, *is the origin point of the ventral tegmental dopaminergic system, which governs approach and exploratory behavior, and whose activation is experienced as incentive reward.* Thus, the hypothalamus has a powerful, primordial backup system, which grips control when its more specific rostral systems fail in their efforts. Exploration in the face of the unknown is thus as ancient as hunger, thirst, sex, and aggression. It is a *primary* drive, manifesting itself in the form of the orienting complex under the control of the septal-hippocampal and anterior cingulate CNS systems.

In 2001, shortly before her death, Vinogradova delivered her final opinions on orienting-complex system function. She described the hippocampus as an interface between primeval brainstem systems and newer, learning-dependent cortical systems. Sensory information from the outside world is fed in a bottom-up fashion through the brainstem systems into hippocampal subarea CA3, providing a quick-and-dirty portrait of ongoing events. After a lag, due to increased complexity of processing, information about what is currently desired is fed downward into the hippocampus, first into area CA1, where it is simplified, and then into CA3, where it is compared with the preprocessed brainstem input. If the two inputs match, CA3 sends a message to the raphe nuclei, in the brainstem. These nuclei, in turn, suppress activity of the ascending, excitatory reticular formation, which is responsible for increasing brain "arousal," intensifying attention, increasing sensory throughput (via the thalamus), placing the body in a state of alertness and preparation for action, disinhibiting motivation, heightening anxiety, and potentiating exploration.

This dissolution into chaos is the nervous system's response to the emergent chaos of nature: As order dissolves and transforms in the natural world, so it must in the intrapsychic and social worlds so that adaptation can continue. A rat's a priori state in a novel environment, for example, is dysregulation of motivation and affect, heightened alertness, and a slowly developing inclination to explore (D. C. Blanchard, Blanchard, & Rogers, 1991). This is a phasic behavioral analog to the state of affairs permanently characterizing an animal, decorticated such that its hypothalamus now occupies the highest level of CNS control remaining.

In a nonverbal animal, such as a rat, the transition from frozen anxiety to active exploration and mapping begins with cautious sniffing under the spell of brain systems that minimize exposure to predators. The animal soon switches to vision, using appropriate head movements, then begins to move, assessing territorial layout and significance as something occurring in response to its own actions (D. C. Blanchard et al., 1991). For an isolated rat in a cage, "territory" is something as simple as spatial layout; hence, the cognitive map or spatial models of hippocampus function (O'Keefe & Nadel, 1978), buttressed by findings of hippocampal "place cells" (O'Keefe & Dostrovsky, 1971). Other researchers, however, have noted hippocampal enabling of "transitive associations" (Bunsey & Eichenbaum, 1996)—relations between arbitrary stimuli (Howard, Fotedar, Datey, & Hasselmo, 2005)—and suggest that place cell function is broader identification of context. Context can also mean "behavioral task demand" or *meaning* (D. M. Smith & Mizumori, 2006). Representation of such context may well be equivalent to episodic memory, another hippocampal function (Milner, 1957).

Investigators assessing "cognitive maps" study the behavior of isolated animals. However, many animals are highly social, and their environment primarily the local dominance hierarchy they occupy. Primates, like rats, develop detailed maps of their social structures as they transform across generations and decades. The "place" mapped by the cognitive map is thus a social structure, not just a geographical locale. This map is precisely the MAP schema hierarchy, grounded in motivation, expanded through individual socialization into complex human culture. Proper understanding of hippocampal function therefore appears dependent on the assessment of certain features of territories currently given no consideration. A PubMed search for "hippocampus and social cognition" revealed a mere 17 articles, only one of which (Spreng & Mar, 2010) is relevant, despite the overwhelming importance of the dominance hierarchy for the mapping of territory. Territories are not places of relatively predictable objects and their interactions, but complex and dynamic social dramas, whose behaviorally associated contextual meanings depend upon on the reactions of potentially unpredictable conspecifics. Most animals solve this problem by consorting only with familiar peers, whose behaviors have already been mapped and which are additionally constrained by their particular positions in the MAP schema hierarchy. The cortex can predict the outcomes of interactions with such conspecifics and work so that they remain positive. These predictions/desires generally match information about a known conspecific's behavior as it occurs and is fed, bottom up, into the hippocampus through the brainstem systems. The hippocampus registers "match," and the arousal systems (e.g., anxiety, aggression, panic, exploration) remain tonically inhibited. No threat is detected. No possibility for damage manifests itself. No disinhibition of motivation and emotion is necessary. No increase in allostatic load (McEwen, 2000), with its stress-induced physiological perturbation and damage, has occurred.

Rats, adapted to a predictable, ecologically valid social and territorial environment, with nesting burrows, social interactions, and roaming space, react with sheer horror to the unexpected sight of a cat in their heretofore safe, predictable environment (R. J. Blanchard & Blanchard, 1989). The animals' behavior changes dramatically for 24 hours (equivalent to a human month). Initial freezing, followed by flight to the chamber system, gives way to a period of immobility, during which the rats, petrified by motivational and emotional dysregulation, emit ultrasonic alarm cries at a high rate. Immobilized crying gradually transforms into "risk assessment," at the place where the cat appeared. The still-stressed but now curious rats poke their heads out of their burrows and scan the previously cat-contaminated open area for hours. When the rats finally emerge, they explore in a manner that reduces their visibility to predators, employing short "corner runs" in and out of the open area. These exploratory risk assessment actions help the rats gather information about the possible danger source. The marshalling of such information provides the rationale for their return to nondefensive behaviors—"normal life."

The sensitivity of animals to disruption of the dominance structure and consequent mismatch can hardly be overstated. Children, much as adults, willingly punish rule-breakers (Piaget, 1932). Analogous behavior pervades the animal kingdom. If a well-loved rat is removed from its familial surroundings, provided with a new odor, and returned, it will be promptly dispatched (Lorenz, 1974). Rats identify one another by smell. A "new" rat constitutes "unexplored territory." His presence is thus regarded, not unreasonably, as a threat to security. Chimps—perfectly capable of killing "foreign devils"—act in the same manner (Goodall, 1990). Why do such reactions occur? Because a conspecific in a known action/meaning context is predictable, even desirable. An unfamiliar conspecific, by contrast, could undermine the entire MAP-schema dominance-hierarchy structure because his capacity for challenge and revolution remains unspecified.

The importance of the MAP schema hierarchy, the utility of conceptualizing it as the structure within which experience manifests itself, and its simultaneous intrapsychic and social existence, may be additionally illustrated by the fact that social status transformation produces functional change in the most basic, serotonergic, neurotransmitter system.[7] High status elevates serotonergic tone, decreasing negative and increasing positive emotion. If your personal schemas come first, in the social group, your "environment" is stable, productive, and safe, and are confident, upright, positive, and emotionally stable. If your schemas come last, however, everything is negative and dangerous, you are confused, anxious, and depressed, hovering close to the edge of chaos and disintegration. It is for such reasons that hierarchy maintenance and protection is so important to animal and human alike and that position within that hierarchy is vital (see Wilkinson & Pickett, 2009).

The consequence of MAP schema shattering, particularly at low-resolution, fundamental levels (Janoff-Bulman, 1992; see also Chapter 10, this volume) can be dramatic, neurophysiologically speaking. Posttraumatic stress disorder produces increased susceptibility to anxiety, depression, obesity, infectious illness, and heart disease, as well as hippocampal shrinkage, as a consequence of chronically elevated cortisol levels (E. S. Brown et al., 2004). Such shrinkage may occur because MAP schema-dependent inhibition of motivation and emotion by the hippocampus should be demolished when the models the hippocampus relies on to "justify" such inhibition have been proven wrong. Recent research indicates that treatment with "antidepressant" selective serotonin reuptake inhibitors—whose biochemical effect essentially mimics the pharmacological state characteristic of stable high-dominance animals (Kravitz, 2000)—allows for hippocampal neurogenesis (S. Becker & Wojtowicz, 2007), as well as improvement in episodic memory function (Vermetten, Vythilingam, Southwick, Charney & Bremner, 2003). This is likely the physiological manifestation of the reconstruction of a functional MAP schema hierarchy.

Vinogradova's (2001) work also sheds light on the neurophysiological instantiation of the MAP schema, allowing, in potential, for a developmental description of the relationship between the development of schema hierarchies and their relationship to the tonic regulation of motivation and emotion, extending beyond that of Swanson (2000) to the very domain of abstraction. She pointed out, first, that "habituation" of the orienting response should be regarded, instead, as "negative learning" and that its disappearance is a consequence of the elaboration of an increasingly detailed model "of the stimulus." This modeling occurs as a consequence of sequential learning in structures that receive CA1 hippocampal field outputs: the mamillary bodies, anterior thalamic nuclei, and, finally, the cingulate limbic cortex. The higher up the neural hierarchy above the hippocampus the structure,

[7]The dominance position "counter" is so archaic that it is fully operative in crustaceans, whose physical posturing is adjusted by serotonergic tone, according to their hierarchical positions. They stand taller, more threatening, when victorious in battle, and shrink when they have been defeated.

the more repetitions of the event are necessary to shape the "response." She believed that this hierarchy may be regarded as a chain of integrators, functioning such that each starts to respond only after reaction develops at the previous link, and as a delay line, "preventing premature fixation of spurious, irrelevant, low-probability signals" (p. 579). The highest links in the system serve as the "ultimate signal for information fixation in the nonprimary areas of the neocortex" (p. 579).

It is probable that the ultimate assumptions of the MAP schema hierarchy, derived from exploration, fixed through repetition, are precisely those governing the rules of social interaction, encoded at the highest level in our explicit conceptions of natural rights (Peterson, 2006). It is these universal "rules," after all, that best specify the nature of peaceful, productive shared territory. Disruption of these most fundamental presumptions—the active breaking of rules or the verbal justification for such breaking—thus presents a threat to the structure that inhibits hippocampal disinhibition of chaotic motivational and emotional responses, corresponding in intensity to the hierarchical import of the MAP schema level such disruption affects. Thus, it is human societies with the largest differences in opinion with regard to "intrinsic human right" that possess the most capability for mutual disruption of presumption and its attendant chaotic psychophysiological and social dysregulation.

THE BALANCE BETWEEN ORDER AND CHAOS: MEANING IN ITS REDEMPTIVE FORM

We have now considered two forms of meaning in detail: that of delimited, pragmatic order, dependent on the match between the intrapsychic and social MAP schemas; and that of chaos, the sum total of all meanings that all phenomena possess, in all the arrays they might occupy. Order structures such chaotic meaning, letting it shine forth in measured doses. When anomaly occurs, by contrast, chaos shines through of its own accord, with sometimes revolutionary and devastating results, and forces the alteration of the structures that delimit and constrain what would otherwise be the overwhelming significance of being.

Many approaches to the maintenance of meaning, including those focusing on terror management (see Chapter 3, this volume), consider individual belief the primary source of meaning and the purpose of belief the restriction of anxiety and fear. Within such conceptualizations, following E. Becker (1973), human life is a futile battle: Death is the ultimate reality; all meaning systems serve to shield their adherents from that fact. Thus, the maintenance of meaning requires rigid allegiance to a structured system, and morality is merely the conventionality and cowardice described by Nietzsche. The fundamental problem of life, however, is not the terror of death, although that is an important subproblem. The fundamental problem of life is the overwhelming complexity of being. Animals, like human beings, have to deal with complexity, although they do not necessarily have to deal with the terrors of mortality, at least in their self-conscious forms. They have, however, evolved means of dealing with chaotic complexity, as embodied in their psychophysiological structures. The same is true of human beings, although we have taken the elaboration of the psychological means of dealing with chaos to unprecedented levels of abstraction (and are uniquely aware of our own mortal limitations). In doing so, we have increasingly come to pursue a third class of meaning.

A human being comes into the world with a set of evolutionarily determined tools, some in the form of the very MAP schemas we have discussed. These general-purpose tools help individuals deal with the constant problems of existence, such as hunger and thirst. The problem of the complexity of being is, however, equally constant or even more so. In consequence, very sophisticated means of dealing with that problem have also evolved. The innovation of social being itself is one such solution. Individuals group themselves into social dominance hierarchies, find their position within the phalanx, and employ the resources of the entire group against the challenges of nature and the unknown. To do so, they rearrange their internal natures so that they can exist in productive harmony within their group. This grouping requires conflict, war, within or between individuals. As the child matures, for example, he has to temper his passions so that they reflect his desires and the desires of the group. Successful negotiation of this conflict of interests is no simple matter of subjugation, either, no mere dominance of the superego. The group wants the individual to manifest the possibilities of his being in the manner most beneficial across different spans of time and place and to the smallest and largest number of individuals, simultaneously. The group thus offers the individual the opportunity to extend his powers, as well as forcing their limitation. In what manner must an individual manifest himself, therefore, in order to address all of these intrapsychic and social demands?

The answer can be found in a more elaborated analysis of exploratory behavior and the communication and integration of its consequences. Consider the game, once again—and then, the game of games. The best player is not necessarily he or she who wins a given game or even a sequence of games. The best player is he who plays such that the game continues and expands so that he and others have the greatest chance to play and to excel. When a child is told to be a good sport, this is how he is instructed to behave. The precise rules composing the meta-game "Be a Good Sport" may yet be implicit, in large part, too complex to be fully formulated. This does not mean they do not exist. We dream continuously of the individual who will manifest that pattern most successfully and search for him—or her—everywhere.

What is the best way to successfully play the largest number of games? The answer is not simply computable. Over time different modes of playing emerge, in the attempt to seek the solution. Each individual wants to be maximally valued. Pure aggression is one possible solution. The physically dominant individual can force others to value him as a player. Sufficient display of negative emotion can have the same effect: Someone may be invited on multiple occasions into different games by appealing to the sympathy of the other players. These are not optimal solutions, however. Even among chimps, rule of the merely strong is unstable (De Waal, 1989a). Rule of the weak, likewise, breeds resentment: Social animals want reciprocity and will not give continually. Such behavior is too costly and easily manipulated. Multiple modes of potential playing compete for predominance during childhood.

Such competition and cooperation extend, in a more sophisticated manner, across adult being. What is the victor among those multiple modes, across many individuals? Extend that question further: What is the victorious mode of play across many individuals, across many groups, over historically significant epochs of time? Consideration of the ancient Mesopotamian myth, the Enuma elish—one of many stories of its type (Peterson, 1999)—helps to answer that question. Two deities exist at the beginning of time, according to the Enuma elish. Tiamat is the goddess of chaos, as chaos is the mother of all things. She is reptilian in nature, for the reptile has constantly threatened our lives and our societies while increasing our vision (Isbell, 2009) for tens of millions of years. Apsu, her husband, is the god of order, the foundation of being. The pair nestles together in the deep, like the two halves of the famous Taoist symbol.

Their sexual, creative union gives rise to the elder gods, the primary motivational states. Their dysregulated and careless behavior results in the death of Apsu, order, and the vengeful reemergence of his bride. Hastily organizing themselves in the face of this threat, the elder gods elect Marduk, god of exploration, vision, and speech, as king, top of the sacred dominance hierarchy, and send him out to voluntarily confront Chaos in the guise of his great-grandmother. Emerging victorious, Marduk cuts Tiamat into pieces and makes the world (Peterson, 1999). *This is the oldest and most fundamental story that mankind possesses*. It echoes through ancient Egypt and that state's conceptions of Horus, the redemptive, attentive eye; Isis, the goddess of chaos; and Osiris, the god of the state. It serves as the source for the creation story in the Hebrew bible and profoundly influences Christianity; it is the story of St. George, and of Christ, the perfect man, the second Adam, and the deadliest enemy of death and the eternal serpent (Peterson, 1999). Its existence and meaning should not be overlooked by psychologists, increasingly cognizant of the evolutionary shaping of being.

It is time to understand these stories, instead of considering them the superstitious enemy of science. The great myths of mankind are not theories of objective existence. They are, instead, imaginative road maps to being. They have emerged, painstakingly, piecemeal, as a consequence of our continual close self-observation, our developing understanding of the patterns of action that are essentially adaptive, and their representation in symbolic, narrative, and dramatic form during the transition from implicit behavioral pattern to explicit communicable form. We tell stories about how to play: not about how to play the game, but about how to play the metagame, the game of games. *When chaos threatens, confront it, as quickly as possible, eyes open, voluntarily*. Activate the neural circuitry underlying active exploration, inhibiting confusion, fear, and the generation of damaging stress responses, and not the circuitry of freezing and escape. Cut the unknown into pieces; take it apart with hands, thumbs, and mind, and formulate or reformulate the world. Free the valuable gold from the dragon of chaos, transform leaden inertia into gilded action, enhance our status, and gain the virgin maiden—just like the first of our tree-dwelling ancestors (Isbell, 2009), who struck a predatory snake with a stick, chased it away, and earned the eternal gratitude of mother and group.

The third form of meaning has little to do with group identity, except insofar as that serves as a precursor to its formation. It is, instead, the story of mankind and the meaning to be experienced when that heroic story is imitated, understood, and embodied. Under the loving tutelage of the ever-virgin mother, guided by the wisdom of his forefathers, the always-threatened nascent hero masters known territory and becomes keenly aware of its limitations and errors. He sees the danger threatening before anyone else because he is willing to see it, while others turn away their eyes: The patriarchal structure has become too rigid and self-serving. The widows and children are being ignored, and God's wrath, in the form of a watery chaos, threatens.

Public morality has become too chaotic, and it is time for a return to the individual and collective values that have always ensured the survival of mankind. The hero sacrifices himself to God, offers up his own petty interests to the greatest possible good, and confronts the too-rigid social structure or the looming chaos with nothing but his own courage and truth. It is very easy to be cynical about such things, but we have many modern examples to consider. Gandhi stopped the British Empire dead in its tracks, following Tolstoy, whose morality was directly informed by Orthodox Christianity. Tough-minded observers have noted that Gandhi's strategies would not have worked against Stalin or Hitler, who would have just had him executed. Nonetheless, single individuals brought down tyrannies of such magnitude in the 20th century as well. Solzhenitsyn's (1975) *Gulag Archipelago*, an amazing example of individual courage—of individual use of the Word—demolished the intellectual and moral credibility of communism, forever. Vaclav Havel performed a similar role in Czechoslovakia. It is not for nothing that we consider the individual of the highest value in the West.

The third form of meaning is not to be found in slavish allegiance to a system of beliefs, nor to specific position in a given dominance hierarchy, nor to incautious and wanton exposure to chaos. It is to be found on the border of chaos and order, Yin and Yang, as the Taoists have always insisted. It is to be found in the voluntary pursuit of interest, that subtle prodding by the orienting complex, which turns our heads involuntary towards the most informative places in our experiential fields and lets us see the glimmers of redemptive chaos shining through the damaged structure of our current schemas. That glimmer is the star that has always guided us, the star that signifies the birth of the hero, and, when followed, is the guardian angel who ensures that the path we trod is meaningful enough so that we can bear the burden of mortal limitation without resentment, arrogance, corruption, and malevolence. Life is not the constant shrinking away from the terror of death, hiding behind an easily pierced curtain of beliefs. Life is the forthright challenging of the insufficiencies that confront us, and the powerful, life-affirming existential meaning that such pursuit instinctively produces (see Chapter 23, this volume). It is that which keeps the spectre of mortality at bay while we work diligently and creatively at work the meaning of which is so powerful and self-evident that the burden of existence seems well worth bearing. Terror management, be damned! The path of the eternal hero beckons, and it is a doomed and dangerous fool who turns his back on it.

REFERENCES

Abbott, D. H., Keverne, E. B., Bercovitch, F. B., Shively, C. A., Mendoza, S. P., Saltzman, W., . . . Sapolsky, R. M. (2003). Are subordinates always stressed? *Hormones and Behavior, 43*, 67–82. doi:10.1016/S0018-506X(02)00037-5

Amaral, D. G., Price, J. L., Pitkanen, A., & Carmichael, S. T. (1992). Anatomical organization of the primate amygdaloid complex. In J. P. Aggleton (Ed.), *The amygdala* (pp. 1–66). New York, NY: Wiley-Liss.

Ansbacher, H. L., & Ansbacher, R. R. (1956). *The individual psychology of Alfred Adler: selections from his writings*. New York, NY: Harper Torchbooks.

Bargh, J. A., & Chartrand, T. L. (1999). The unbearable automaticity of being. *American Psychologist, 54*, 462–479. doi:10.1037/0003-066X.54.7.462

Barsalou, L. W. (1983). Ad hoc categories. *Memory & Cognition, 11*, 211–227. doi:10.3758/BF03196968

Becker, E. (1973). *The denial of death*. New York, NY: The Free Press.

Becker, S., & Wojtowicz, J. M. (2007). A model of hippocampal neurogenesis in memory and mood disorders. *Trends in Cognitive Sciences, 11*, 70–76. doi:10.1016/j.tics.2006.10.013

Binswanger, L. (1963). *Being in the world*. New York, NY: Basic Books.

Blanchard, D. C., Blanchard, R. J., & Rodgers, R. J. (1991). Risk assessment and animal models of anxiety. In B. Olivier, J. Mos, & J. L. Slangen (Eds.), *Animal models in psychopharmacology* (pp. 117–134). Boston, MA: Birkhauser Verlag.

Blanchard, R. J., & Blanchard, D. C. (1989). Antipredator defensive behaviors in a visible burrow system. *Journal of Comparative Psychology, 103*, 70–82. doi:10.1037/0735-7036.103.1.70

Boss, M. (1963). *Psychoanalysis and daseinsanalysis* [Psychoanalysis examined and re-examined]. New York, NY: Basic Books.

Brooks, A. (1991a). Intelligence without reason. *Artificial Intelligence Memo 1293*.

Brooks, A. (1991b). Intelligence without representation. *Artificial Intelligence, 47*, 139–159. doi:10.1016/0004-3702(91)90053-M

Brown, E. S., Woolston, D., Frol, A., Bobadilla, L., Khan, D. A., Hanczyc, M., . . . Cullum, C. M. (2004). Hippocampal volume, spectroscopy, cognition, and mood in patients receiving corticosteroid therapy. *Biological Psychiatry, 55*, 538–545. doi:10.1016/j.biopsych.2003.09.010

Brown, R. (1986). *Social psychology* (2nd ed.). New York, NY: Free Press.

Bunsey, M., & Eichenbaum, H. B. (1996, January 18). Conservation of hippocampal memory function in rats and humans. *Nature, 379*, 255–257. doi:10.1038/379255a0

Carver, C. S., & Scheier, M. F. (1998). *On the self-regulation of behavior*. New York, NY: Cambridge University Press.

Chang, I. (1998.) *The rape of Nanking*. New York, NY: Penguin.

Cowan, N. (2001). The magical number 4 in short-term memory. *Behavioral and Brain Sciences, 24*, 87–184. doi:10.1017/S0140525X01003922

Damasio, A. R. (1994). *Descartes' error: Emotion, reason and the human brain*. New York, NY: Avon Books.

Davidson, R. J. (1992). Anterior cerebral asymmetry and the nature of emotion. *Brain and Cognition, 20*, 125–151. doi:10.1016/0278-2626(92)90065-T

Dean, P., Redgrave, P., & Westby, G. W. M. (1989). Event or emergency: Two response systems in the superior colliculus. *Trends in Neurosciences, 12*, 137–147. doi:10.1016/0166-2236(89)90052-0

Dennett, D. C. (1984), Cognitive wheels: the frame problem. In C. Hookway (Ed.), *Minds, machines and evolution* (pp. 129–151). Cambridge, England: Cambridge University Press.

De Waal, F. (1989a). *Chimpanzee politics*. London, England: Johns Hopkins University Press.

De Waal, F. (1989b). *Peacemaking among primates*. New York, NY: Harvard University Press.

De Waal, F. D. (1996). *Good natured*. Cambridge, MA: Harvard University Press.

Eysenck, H. J. (1995). *Genius: The natural history of creativity*. Cambridge, England: Cambridge University Press. doi:10.1017/CBO9780511752247

Fowles, D. C. (1980). The three arousal model: Implications of Gray's two factor learning theory for heart-rate, electrodermal activity, and psychopathy. *Psychophysiology, 17*, 87–104. doi:10.1111/j.1469-8986.1980.tb00117.x

Gibson, J. J. (1979). *An ecological approach to visual perception*. New York, NY: Erlbaum.

Glasersfeld, E. V. (1982). An interpretation of Piaget's constructivism. *Revue Internationale de Philosophie, 36*, 612–635.

Glasersfeld, E. V. (1999). The cybernetic insights of Jean Piaget. *Cybernetics and Systems, 30*, 105–112. doi:10.1080/019697299125307

Goodall, J. (1990). *Through a window*. Boston, MA: Houghton-Mifflin.

Gray, J. A. (1982). *The neuropsychology of anxiety*. Oxford, England: Oxford University Press.

Gray, J. A. (1987). *The psychology of fear and stress* (2nd ed.). New York, NY: Cambridge University Press.

Gray, J. A., & McNaughton, N. (2003). *The neuropsychology of anxiety: An enquiry into the function of the septal-hippocampal system* (2nd ed.). New York, NY: Oxford University Press.

Halgren, E. (1992). Emotional neurophysiology of the amygdala within the context of human cognition. In J. P. Aggleton (Ed.), *The amygdala: Neurobiological aspects of emotion, memory and mental dysfunction* (pp. 191–228). New York, NY: Wiley-Liss.

Hooker, C. I., Germine, L. T., Knight, R. T., & D'Esposito. (2006). Amygdala responses to facial expressions reflects emotional learning. *The Journal of Neuroscience, 26*, 8915–8922.

Howard, M. W., Fotedar, M. S., Datey, A. V., & Hasselmo, M. E. (2005). The temporal context model in spatial navigation and relational learning: toward a common explanation of medial temporal lobe function across domains. *Psychological Review, 112*, 75–116. doi:10.1037/0033-295X.112.1.75

Isbell, L. A. (2009). *The fruit, the tree and the serpent*. Cambridge, MA: Harvard University Press.

Janoff-Bulman, R. (1992). *Shattered assumptions: Towards a new psychology of trauma*. New York, NY: Free Press.

Joffe, T. H., & Dunbar, R. I. (1997). Visual and socio-cognitive information processing in primate brain evolution. *Proceedings of the Royal Society of London, B, 264*, 1303–1307. doi:10.1098/rspb.1997.0180

Jung, C. G. (1967a). *Alchemical studies. The collected Works of C. G. Jung* (R. F. C. Hull, Trans.), Vol. 12. Bollingen Series 20. Princeton, NJ: Princeton University Press.

Jung, C.G. (1967b). *Psychology and alchemy. The collected works of C. G. Jung* (R. F. C. Hull, Trans.), Vol. 13. Bollingen Series 20. Princeton, NJ: Princeton University Press.

Jung, C.G. (1971). *Psychological types. The collected works of C. G. Jung* (R. F. C. Hull, Trans.), Vol. 5. Bollingen Series 20. Princeton, NJ: Princeton University Press.

Kravitz, E. A. (2000). Serotonin and aggression: insights gained from a lobster model system and speculations on the role of amine neurons in a complex behavior. *Journal of Comparative Physiology, 186*, 221–238. doi:10.1007/s003590050423

Krawczyk, D. C. (2002). Contributions of the prefrontal cortex to the neural basis of human decision making. *Neuroscience and Biobehavioral Reviews, 26*, 631–664. doi:10.1016/S0149-7634(02)00021-0

Kuhn, T. S. (1970). *The structure of scientific revolutions* (2nd ed.). Chicago, IL: University of Chicago Press.

Lakoff, G. (1987). *Women, fire, and dangerous thing*. Chicago, IL: University of Chicago Press.

LeDoux, J. (1996). *The emotional brain*. New York, NY: Touchstone Press.

Legault, M., & Wise, R. A. (2001) Novelty-evoked elevations of nucleus accumbens dopamine: Dependence on impulse flow from the ventral subiculum and glutamatergic neurotransmission in the ventral tegmental area. *European Journal of Neuroscience, 13*, 819–828.

Lewin, K. (1935). *A dynamic theory of personality*. New York, NY: McGraw-Hill.

Libet, B. (1999). Do we have free will? *Journal of Consciousness Studies, 6*, 47–57.

Lorenz, K. (1974). *On aggression*. New York, NY: Harcourt Brace Jovanovitch.

Luria, A. R. (1960). Verbal regulation of behavior. In M. A. B. Brazier (Ed.), *The central nervous system and behaviour: Transactions of the Third Macy Conference* (pp. 359–421). New York, NY: Josiah Macy Jr. Foundation.

Luria, A. R. (1980). *Higher cortical functions in man* (2nd ed.). New York, NY: Basic Books. doi:10.1007/978-1-4615-8579-4

Masserman, J. H., Wechkin, S., & Terris, W. (1964). "Altruistic" behaviour in rhesus monkeys. *The American Journal of Psychiatry, 121*, 584–585.

McEwen, B. S. (2000). Allostasis and allostatic load: implications for neuropsychopharmacology. *Neuropsychopharmacology, 22*, 108–124. doi:10.1016/S0893-133X(99)00129-3

Medin, D. L., & Aguilar, C. M. (1999). Categorization. In R. A. Wilson & F. Keil (Eds.), *MIT encyclopedia of cognitive sciences* (pp. 99–143). Cambridge, MA: MIT Press.

Miller, G. A. (1956). The magical number seven, plus or minus two. *Psychological Review, 63*, 81–97. doi:10.1037/h0043158

Miller, G. A., Galanter, E. H., & Pribram, K. H. (1960). *Plans and the structure of behavior*. New York, NY: Holt, Rinehart & Winston.

Miller, P., Eisenberg, N., Fabes, R. A., & Shell, R. (1996). Relations of moral reasoning and vicarious emotion to young children's prosocial behavior towards peers and adults. *Developmental Psychology, 32,* 210–219.

Norretranders, T. (1998). *The user illusion: cutting consciousness down to size.* New York, NY: Penguin Books.

O'Keefe, J., & Nadel, L. (1978). *The hippocampus as a cognitive map.* Oxford, England: Clarendon Press.

Oatley, K., & Jenkins, J. M. (1992). Human emotions: function and dysfunction. *Annual Review of Psychology, 43,* 55–85. doi:10.1146/annurev.ps.43.020192.000415

Oatley, K., & Johnson-Laird, P. N. (1987). Towards a cognitive theory of emotion. *Cognition and Emotion, 1,* 29–50. doi:10.1080/02699938708408362

Ohman, A. (1979). The orienting response, attention and learning: An information-processing perspective. In H. D. Kimmel, E. H. Van Olst, & J. F. Orlebeke (Eds.), *The orienting reflex in humans* (pp. 443–467). Hillsdale, NJ: Erlbaum.

Ohman, A. (1987). The psychophysiology of emotion: An evolutionary-cognitive perspective. In P. K. Ackles, J. R. Jennings, & M. G. H. Coles (Eds.), *Advances in psychophysiology: A research annual* (Vol. 2, pp. 79–127). Greenwich, CT: JAI Press.

O'Keefe, J., & Dostrovsky, J. (1971). The hippocampus as a spatial map. Preliminary evidence from unit activity in the freely-moving rat. *Brain Research, 34,* 171–175.

Panksepp, J. (1998). *Affective neuroscience.* New York, NY: Oxford.

Peterson, J. B. (1999). *Maps of meaning: the architecture of belief.* New York, NY: Routledge.

Peterson, J. B. (2006). Religion, sovereignty, natural rights, and the constituent elements of experience. *Archiv für Religionspsychologie* [Archives of the Psychology of Religion], *28,* 135–180. doi:10.1163/008467206777832580

Peterson, J. B., & Flanders, J. L. (2002). Complexity management theory. *Cortex, 38,* 429–458. doi:10.1016/S0010-9452(08)70680-4

Piaget, J. (1932). *The moral judgment of the child.* London, England: Kegan, Paul, Trench, Trubner, and Company.

Piaget, J. (1954). The problem of consciousness in child psychology: Developmental changes in awareness. In H. A. Abramson (Ed.), *Problems of consciousness: Transactions of the Fourth Macy Conference.* New York, NY: Josiah Macy Jr. Foundation.

Pochon, J. B., Levy, R., Fossati, P., Lehericy, S., Poline, J. B., Pillon, B., . . . Dubois, B. (2002). The neural system that bridges reward and cognition in humans. *Proceedings of the National Academy of Sciences of the United States of America, 99,* 5669–5674. doi:10.1073/pnas.082111099

Powers, W. T. (1973). *Behavior: the control of perception.* Chicago, IL: Aldine.

Preston, S.D., & De Waal, F.B.M. (2002). Empathy. *Behavior and Brain Sciences, 25*, 1–20.

Rice, G.E.J. (1964). Aiding behaviour vs. fear in the albino rat. *The Psychological Record, 14*, 165–170.

Rice, G.E.J., & Gainer, P. (1962). Altruism in the albino rat. *Journal of Comparative and Physiological Psychology, 55*, 123–125. doi:10.1037/h0042276

Rizzolatti, G., Fogassi, L., & Gallese, V. (2001). Neurophysiological mechanisms underlying the understanding and imitation of action. *Nature Reviews Neuroscience, 2*, 661–670. doi:10.1038/35090060

Rolls, E. (1999). *The brain and emotion*. New York, NY: Oxford University Press.

Schank, R., & Abelson, R. (1977). *Scripts, plans, goals and understanding: An inquiry into human knowledge structures*. Hillsdale, NJ: Erlbaum.

Scoville, W.B. & Milner, B. (1957). Loss of recent memory after bilateral hippocampal lesions. *Journal of Neurology, Neurosurgery and Psychiatry, 20*, 11–21.

Sibley, C.G., & Ahlquist, J.E. (1984). The phylogeny of the hominoid primates, as indicated by DNA-DNA hybridization. *Journal of Molecular Evolution, 20*, 2–15. doi:10.1007/BF02101980

Simons, D.J., & Rensink, R.A. (2005). Change blindness: past, present, and future. *Trends in Cognitive Sciences, 9*, 16–20. doi:10.1016/j.tics.2004.11.006

Smith, D.M., & Mizumori, S.J. (2006). Hippocampal place cells, context and episodic memory. *Hippocampus, 16*, 716–729. doi:10.1002/hipo.20208

Smith, P.K., & Boulton, M. (1990). Rough-and-tumble play, aggression and dominance. *Human Development, 33*, 271–282. doi:10.1159/000276524

Sokolov, E.N. (1963). Higher nervous functions: the orienting reflex. *Annual Review of Physiology, 25*, 545–580. doi:10.1146/annurev.ph.25.030163.002553

Solzhenitsyn, A.I. (1975). *The gulag archipelago, 1918–1956: An experiment in literary investigation* (Vol. 2). (T. P. Whitney, Trans.). New York, NY: Harper and Row.

Swanson, L.W. (2000). Cerebral hemisphere regulation of motivated behavior. *Brain Research, 886*, 113–164. doi:10.1016/S0006-8993(00)02905-X

Swanson, L.W. (2003). *Brain architecture*. New York, NY: Oxford University Press.

Tucker, D.M., & Frederick, S.L. (1989). Emotion and brain lateralization. In H. Wagner, . . . (Eds.), *Handbook of social psychophysiology* (pp. 27–70). Chichester, England: Wiley.

Vaihinger, H. (1924). *The philosophy of "as if:" A system of the theoretical, practical, and religious fictions of mankind* (C.K. Ogden, Trans.). New York, NY: Harcourt, Brace, and Company.

Vermetten, E., Vythilingam, M., Southwick, S. M., Charney, D. S., & Bremner, J. D. (2003). Long-term treatment with paroxetine increases verbal declarative memory and hippocampal volume in posttraumatic stress disorder. *Biological Psychiatry, 54*, 693–702. doi:10.1016/S0006-3223(03)00634-6

Vinogradova, O. (1961). *The orientation reaction and its neuropsychological mechanisms*. Moscow, Russia: Academic Pedagogical Sciences.

Vinogradova, O. (1975). Functional organization of the limbic system in the process of registration of information: facts and hypotheses. In R. Isaacson & K. Pribram (Eds.), *The hippocampus, neurophysiology, and behaviour* (Vol. 2, pp. 3–69). New York, NY: Plenum Press.

Vinogradova, O. S. (2001). Hippocampus as comparator: Role of the two input and two output systems of the hippocampus in selection and registration of information. *Hippocampus, 11*, 578–598. doi:10.1002/hipo.1073

Virgin, C. E., Jr., & Sapolsky, R. M. (1997). Styles of male social behavior and their endocrine correlates among low-ranking baboons. *American Journal of Primatology, 42*, 25–39. doi:10.1002/(SICI)1098-2345(1997)42:1<25::AID-AJP2>3.0.CO;2-0

Whalen, P. J. (1998). Fear, vigilance, and ambiguity: Initial neuroimaging studies of the human amygdala. *Current Directions in Psychological Science, 7*, 177–188. doi:10.1111/1467-8721.ep10836912

Wiener, N. (1948). *Cybernetics: or, Control and communication in the animal and the machine*. Cambridge, MA: Technology Press.

Wilkinson, R., & Pickett, K. (2009). *The spirit level: Why more equal societies almost always do better*. London, England: Allen Lane.

Wrangham, R., & Peterson, D. (1997). *Demonic males*. New York, NY: Houghton Mifflin.

Yeomans, J. S., Li, L., Scott, B. W., & Frankland, P. W. (2002). Tactile, acoustic and vestibular systems sum to elicit the startle reflex. *Neuroscience and Biobehavioral Reviews, 26*, 1–11. doi:10.1016/S0149-7634(01)00057-4

Yoerg, S. I. (1991). Social feeding reverses learned flavor aversions in spotted hyenas. *Journal of Comparative Psychology, 105*, 185–189. doi:10.1037/0735-7036.105.2.185

Zahn-Waxler, C., Radke-Yarrow, M., & King, R. A. (1979). Child rearing and children's prosocial initiations toward victims of distress. *Child Development, 50*, 319–330. doi:10.2307/1129406

3

AN EDIFICE FOR ENDURING PERSONAL VALUE: A TERROR MANAGEMENT PERSPECTIVE ON THE HUMAN QUEST FOR MULTILEVEL MEANING

JAMIE ARNDT, MARK J. LANDAU, KENNETH E. VAIL III, AND MATTHEW VESS

Jon Anderson and Steve Howe of the British progressive rock band Yes developed the idea that would grow into their 1973 concept album, *Tales from Topographic Oceans*, on the basis of ancient Indian Shastric scriptures about the essential elements of existence, and in effect, the meaning of life. But like any work of art, *Tales* is composed of more basic structural elements, in this case an intricately complex series of notes, rhythms, and lyrics. While the album, of course, can be enjoyed in many different ways, each approach requires the individual to parse, categorize, and organize the composition's elements at a basic perceptual level. Yet imposing such perceptual order provides no guarantee that the composition will afford a broad sense of meaning—perhaps the music makes sense and can even be experienced as enthralling, but the emergent Shastric themes may fail to speak to the person's "big picture" questions about the world and his or her place within it.

We use this example to illustrate how the meaning-making process takes place at multiple levels. The multileveled nature of meaning making is

DOI: 10.1037/14040-003
The Psychology of Meaning, Keith D. Markman, Travis Proulx, and Matthew J. Lindberg (Editors)

apparent across many domains. People may derive a profound sense of life's meaning and purpose from close relationships, momentous life events, valued accomplishments, or spiritual encounters. We conceptualize such meanings as existing on a "macro" level, as they pertain to a broader and more encompassing view of what is important in life. But these sources of meaning are predicated on more basic conceptions of the world and one's life as orderly and predictable rather than incoherent and chaotic. People expect, for example, that when the traffic light turns red, cars will stop and they can safely cross the street (unless one is in New York City, where such assumptions are more risky). Meanings such as these reside at a more "micro" level.

Therefore, an important goal for understanding human meaning-making is to explain how (and why) meaning-making processes at both the macro and micro levels interrelate, as well as the underlying motivations they serve. With this broad goal in mind, the current chapter addresses the following questions: (a) What is meaning, and what is the connection between macro- and micro-level meanings? (b) Why do people need (these different types of) meaning? (c) How do people maintain meaning across these different levels? and (d) How does the pursuit of meaning interact with other psychological needs to influence people's social behavior? To address these questions, we adopt an existential perspective (see Chapter 23, this volume) grounded in terror management theory (TMT; Greenberg, Pyszczynski, & Solomon 1986).

MEANING AS THE INFRASTRUCTURE FOR SUSTAINING PERSONAL VALUE

We begin with a broad definition of *meaning* as the organism's perception that its environment affords clearly defined and reliable contingencies for effective action. Any organism that actively navigates its environment relies on at least some meaning to obtain desired outcomes and to avoid undesired outcomes. For a squirrel to effectively gather food, find mates, and avoid predators, it has to perceive that trees, cats, and other environmental stimuli operate in expected ways. A definition of meaning that rests solely on expected relations, however, misses that which renders the human quest for meaning so profound and intricate. Whereas humans share the squirrel's reliance on meaning for the biological goals of survival and reproduction, they are also motivated to navigate their environment in the hopes of establishing a broader sense of effective action: to know that their identity and actions have *value*. With this psychological imperative, humans create and invest in systems of meaning that no squirrel or salamander could recognize or appreciate, namely, reliable contingencies for attaining symbolic value. Note that we are not suggesting that providing a foundation for symbolic value is the only reason that people need or want meaning. Rather, we propose that this is one important (distal) impetus behind humans' creation of meaning systems.

We can categorize uniquely human meaning systems into macro and micro levels. At a macro level, humans create a *cultural worldview*—that is, a set of socially constructed beliefs about reality that provides an account of the origin and nature of existence. The worldview not only provides a canopy under which one makes sense of life on a grand scale, often for some higher purpose, but importantly, it also prescribes principles to live by and standards of value to attain. The individual internalizes the worldview through an immersive socialization process that reinforces prevailing norms, values, and ideals through lifelong participation in collective ceremonies, rituals, and rites of passage, and through constant engagement with cultural products that embody those ideologies. This immersion endows normally socialized individuals with a global picture of which roles, statuses, group affiliations, and accomplishments qualify them for value (and which of these have the opposite effect).

At a more micro level, people seek out well-structured perceptions of their everyday social environment. Using basic social-cognitive tendencies to process information in simple and coherent ways, people can perceive other people, events, and their own experiences as well-defined and predictable. We argue that maintaining these structured perceptions is a necessary precondition for people's efforts to maintain adequate faith in the validity of their worldview, and from there, to live up to the worldview's standards of value. For example, as Goffman (1959) so well articulated, to dependably negotiate social interactions and influence how others regard them, people have to perceive others' characteristics and behaviors as being fairly consistent from one moment to the next. Similarly, to anticipate the consequences of actions and feel secure that their life projects will unfold reliably over time, people must believe that favorable and unfavorable outcomes have clear causes and are not arbitrary or random.

Conversely, if people lacked these structured perceptions—if, for example, other people's behavior seemed contradictory or elusory, if the flow of time appeared disordered, or if events seemed haphazard—they would perceive their environment as a chaotic fantasy world in which any attempt to establish personal value (or accomplish any other goals) would be futile. This helps explain why people react defensively when confronted with even relatively minor threats to structured perceptions (e.g., encountering a red four of clubs in a deck of cards; Proulx & Heine, 2009; see also Chapter 4, this volume). Expectations about even mundane aspects of reality serve at a distal level to buttress the person's confidence that the world is a structured place where goal pursuit, and ultimately the securing of personal value, can be attained.

At a more subjective level, the more people can feel confident that their cultural worldview captures a social environment that is orderly and predictable and prescribes legitimate routes to attain value, the more they can view life as meaning*ful*. Of course, the sense that life is meaningful need not be a radical epiphany. Much of the time people take their cultural worldview and structured social perceptions for granted. They "ride along," accepting the identities and long-term projects which are offered to them by virtue of their membership in certain social groups, and they commit themselves to the arrangements and routines of everyday life, secure in the knowledge that they are doing something significant (Berger & Luckmann, 1967).

However, because these meaning systems are essentially fictional accounts of reality built out of abstract symbols (e.g., rules) that escape empirical verification, they can be threatened by social experiences and environmental conditions, thereby putting people at risk for feelings of *meaninglessness*. For example, when people encounter followers of an alternative worldview, they may question the validity of their own worldview and its prescriptions for value ("If *others* have it right, what happens to *me?*"). Additionally, people run the risk of witnessing or falling victim to randomly occurring hazards that negate all strivings for value, or witnessing the incomprehensible prosperity of those who don't believe in or conform to one's worldview. When the environment seems to allot favorable and unfavorable outcomes to people regardless of their adherence to the worldview's prescriptions for valued action, people may have serious difficulty sustaining confidence that following those prescriptions will secure lasting value.

This brings us to an important question: If people seek meaning from the cultural worldview and their structured social perceptions for the purpose of promoting a sense of personal value (at least in part), then why, at the core, are people motivated to view themselves as valuable?

THE EXISTENTIAL IMPORTANCE OF FEELING VALUED

To understand why people, unlike other creatures, need to obtain symbolic perceptions of personal value—and why they create and adhere to macro- and microlevel meanings that support those perceptions—it is useful to consider the developmental trajectories by which these perceptions—and their importance—emerge. As many have noted (e.g., Becker, 1971; Bowlby, 1969; Mead, 1934), humans are thrust into a most unsettling situation at birth. They can experience tremendous amounts of distress in the presence of threats yet are profoundly defenseless against them. This condition renders the infant almost completely dependent upon primary caregivers to assuage anxiety by providing affection and protection from threats. The caregivers also become the critical conveyors of meaning, delineating those parts of the developing child's perceptual experience that should be welcomed, anticipated, avoided, or ignored. Over the course of socialization, the child begins to form expected relationships between specific ways of behaving and the responsiveness of the care-giver to the child's needs. The result is an understanding that security and anxiety-reduction are contingent upon behaving in accord with parental standards. Thus, from very early on, the child's understanding of what things *mean* is gleaned from a conditional sense of safety and protection from harm.

This early dependency on primary caregivers for physical and psychological security sets the stage for a lifelong commitment to meaning systems and the pursuit of personal value as defined by those systems. However, with the emergence of self-awareness and other sophisticated cognitive capacities comes the distressing recognition that parental protection can do nothing to change the terrorizing fact that death is inevitable (Becker, 1973), introducing a need for a new form of psychological protection. People "solve" the problem of mortality by adhering to a cultural worldview that allows them to view their life as embedded in a symbolic reality transcending the biological reality of death. By living up to the particular standards of value prescribed by the worldview, an individual can acquire a sense of enduring significance (i.e., self-esteem) that signals that they will "live on" in either a literal sense (e.g., by means of an afterlife) or a symbolic sense (e.g., by means of remembrance of one's children, accomplishments, or group affiliations on the statues, monuments, park benches, or tombstones that pervade the cultural landscape). From this view, the lifelong struggle to attain self-esteem stems in part from the need to transcend death and thus mitigate death-related anxiety. The human quest for meaning is fundamentally influenced by a desire for clearly defined, seemingly "real" routes for obtaining lasting personal value. Thus, meaning at both a macro and micro level is, as Becker (1973) put it, "more than merely an outlook on life: it is an immortality formula" (p. 255).

Before turning to some of the many macro- and micro-level strategies through which these processes unfold, let us quickly consider the basic prediction that this analysis generates: that those without a secure investment in a worldview, a strong sense of self-esteem, or well-structured knowledge of the world will be especially vulnerable to feelings of meaninglessness when death-related thought is heightened. In support of this prediction, studies have indeed found that reminders of death decrease perceptions of life's meaningfulness among those low in self-esteem (Routledge, Ostafin, et al., 2010; Taubman-Ben-Ari, 2011) and among those lacking well-structured conceptions of the world (Vess, Routledge, Landau, & Arndt, 2009). These findings illustrate the importance of both macro- (culturally derived perceptions of value) and micro- (epistemic structure) level forms of meaning and thus support the view that multilevel perceptions of meaning contribute to protection from the awareness of death. We turn next to research examining the connections between awareness of mortality and specific macro- and micro-level strategies for seeking and maintaining meaning.

MACRO-LEVEL STRATEGIES FOR MAINTAINING MEANING IN THE SHADOW OF DEATH

So far we have claimed that individuals can hold thoughts of death at bay via confident perceptions that one's life is meaningful and valuable. This analysis yields several hypotheses in addition to the prediction just mentioned. One is that threats to meaning and self-esteem will increase the accessibility of death-related thought. This hypothesis has been examined in a growing set of studies that have targeted worldview-relevant beliefs pertaining to such domains as religion, nationalism, close relationships, and sexuality, as well as other social perceptions that support a sense of value or esteem (see Hayes, Schimel, Arndt, & Faucher, 2010, for a review). Using converging methods, these studies show that threatening these aspects of the worldview elevates the accessibility of death-related thought but not the accessibility of other negative cognitions, suggesting that one function of faith in the worldview is to allay concerns about death in particular.

This work then points to a second hypothesis: If faith in a cultural worldview and self-esteem buffer individuals' concerns with personal mortality, then reminding them of their own death (*mortality salience* [MS]) should increase their identification with, and propensity to defend, their cultural beliefs as well as their efforts to obtain self-worth. Hundreds of studies have tested variants on this broad hypothesis and have shown that MS indeed increases investment in multiple aspects of the cultural worldview, including one's nationality, religion, norms, and leaders (see Burke, Martens, & Faucher, 2010; Greenberg, Solomon, & Arndt, 2008, for more comprehensive coverage). For example, in the first such demonstration, Rosenblatt, Greenberg, Solomon, Pyszczynski, and Lyon (1989) showed that MS increased Christians' positivity toward fellow Christians and negativity toward Jews. The effects of MS have been conceptually replicated cross-culturally and have been shown to differ from the effects of making salient other aversive topics (e.g., intense pain) and uncertain future events. Reminders of death have also been found to instigate various forms of self-esteem striving, leading people to try to do (or at least perceive that they are doing) that which provides them with a sense of self-worth (see Pyszczynski, Greenberg, Solomon, Arndt, & Schimel, 2004).

The assumption of the research just discussed is that cultural systems of meaning are defended (and hold death cognitions at bay) in part because they facilitate the perception that we live in an enduring and meaningful reality. This assumption points to an additional hypothesis that critically connects these effects more directly to perceptions of meaning: Defending or affirming one's cultural worldview after reminders of mortality should carry the existential benefit of bolstering life's perceived meaningfulness, perhaps primarily for those who suffer deficits in meaning, as well as dampening the motivation to further search for meaning.

Simon, Arndt, Greenberg, Solomon, and Pyszczynski (1998) found support for the first facet of this reasoning by exposing those with deficits in meaning, the mildly depressed, to a reminder of mortality (vs. a control topic) and an opportunity (vs. no opportunity) to defend their nationalistic worldview. Depressed individuals not only defended their worldview with particular vigor after MS, but if they were given an opportunity to do so, they reported increased perceptions of meaning in life, suggesting that such defense helped to reengage them in a worldview that provides a canopy of meaning. More recently, Vess, Arndt, Routledge, and Goldenberg (2009) explored the second facet of the reasoning noted above. They showed that giving religious fundamentalists the opportunity to affirm their faith after MS, in this case by advocating for the efficacy of prayer in place of medical intervention for illness, subsequently led to decreased motivation to search for meaning. This suggests that the affirmation of their worldview had sated their thirst for meaning.

MICRO-LEVEL STRATEGIES FOR MAINTAINING MEANING IN THE SHADOW OF DEATH

The studies reviewed in the previous section point to the connection between awareness of death and macro-level meanings defined by one's cultural worldview, such as cultural norms and religious beliefs, which provide the scaffolding for attaining personal value. If, as we claim, faith in the worldview rests on more basic or nonspecific conceptions that the world is a structured place, then MS should also increase people's preference for well-structured interpretations of the people, events, and experiences that make up their social world. Accordingly, a large body of experimental research shows that MS increases the use of social-cognitive processes oriented toward simplicity, clarity, and order.

Consider terror management research on basic dissonance-reducing strategies. As Heider (1958) and Festinger (1957) observed, making sense of other people and the self requires the person to resolve mental conflicts and preserve consistency between cognitions. According to TMT, the penchant for cognitive consistency is not simply a built-in feature of our cognitive system. Rather, it is motivated in part by the underlying need to mitigate mortality concerns. A world in which people and the self act in consistent ways is a world that can be reliably negotiated in an effort to make one's lasting mark, whereas an ambiguous world of conflicting information affords few reliable opportunities for establishing a sense of personal value.

This general line of reasoning led researchers to test whether MS motivates people to maintain consistency between their cognitions and behaviors (Friedman & Arndt, 2005; Jonas, Greenberg, & Frey, 2003). Friedman and Arndt (2005), for example, replicated a traditional dissonance effect in finding that participants who freely chose to write a counterattitudinal statement reported more positive attitudes toward a boring passage compared with participants who were forced to write the statement, presumably bringing their attitudes in line with their behavior. Importantly, participants who had been previously primed with mortality reported even stronger liking for the passage, suggesting that they were especially motivated to reduce dissonance. These findings illustrate how terror management motivation drives people to maintain consistency in even non-specific ways because stating that a boring passage was interesting did not pose an explicit threat to any specific aspect of the participants' cultural worldview.

Of course, some people have a high dispositional preference for well-structured knowledge. Individuals high in *need for closure* (NFC; Kruglanski, Webster, & Klem, 1993) and *personal need for structure* (PNS; Thompson, Naccarato, Parker, & Moskowitz, 2001) are particularly inclined to seek simple and clear interpretations of social information and to respond aversely to complexity and ambiguity. Individuals low in dispositional structure-seeking are, on the other hand, more comfortable with ambiguous, complex, or inconsistent information. How can we account for individual differences in structure-seeking from a TMT perspective? Solomon, Greenberg, and Pyszczynski (1991) argued that each person clings to an individualized worldview for psychological security, and differences in personality traits can reflect different sources of security-providing meaning. Thus, certain people may be especially likely to invest in well-structured conceptions of the world as a preferred means of managing terror, whereas others (i.e., low structure-seeking individuals) may be more comfortable with, and perhaps derive meaning from, epistemic openness and novelty (we revisit this latter possibility below). This suggests that individual difference constructs like NFC and PNS can be useful for predicting the types of people who are especially likely to respond to MS with increased preference for well-structured interpretations of social information.

Accordingly, research shows that MS leads individuals high in PNS, but not those low in PNS, to do the following: seek simple and consistent interpretations of other people; view social events as following a just and benevolent order; prefer order over chaos in visual stimuli; clearly define their personal characteristics and coherently organize their personal experiences, activities, and goals (e.g., Landau, Greenberg, Solomon, Pyszczynski, and Martens, 2006; Landau, Greenberg, Sullivan, Routledge, & Arndt, 2009; Landau et al., 2004). A full review of this work is beyond this chapter's scope (for a more complete presentation, see Greenberg, Landau, Arndt, in press), but let's take look at one line of research.

As noted earlier, the belief that social events follow a just and benevolent order constitutes a fundamental building block of terror-assuaging meaning. If people perceived that randomly occurring hazards could negate all their strivings for value, then they would have difficulty sustaining confidence that following the worldview's prescriptions for value will facilitate their death transcendence. This suggests that MS will increase people's tendency to construe social events as following a just and benevolent order, especially if they are dispositionally inclined to prefer structured knowledge. As one manifestation of this tendency, when people encounter information implying that the world is not just, they often restore justice by convincing themselves that the victims of misfortune deserved what happened to them (Lerner, 1980). Landau et al. (2004) showed that MS increased this victim-blaming tendency, especially among high structure-seeking individuals. For example, in one study, participants who had been reminded of death showed an increased preference for negative over positive information about a victim of a senseless tragedy, presumably in an effort to restore just world beliefs, but this effect held only for high-PNS participants.

In a follow-up study, Landau et al. (2004) tested whether presenting participants with information suggesting that victims of tragedy are actually good people would weaken participants' secure conception of events and therefore unleash mortality concerns. This hypothesis was based on the large body of research, noted earlier, showing that threatening meaning structures increases death-thought accessibility. As predicted, high-PNS participants who read positive (but not negative) information about the victim of a tragedy exhibited heightened death-thought accessibility, whereas low-PNS participants did not (see also Hirschberger, 2006).

PERCEPTUAL SHIFTS AND THE EXTRACTION OF MEANING

Seeing events as connected to a just and benevolent order is one example of a process that involves perceiving events not as isolated acts but rather as connected to the broader scheme of how the world operates. This suggests that mortality reminders will motivate people to adjust their view of even mundane actions and objects because the opportunity for death-transcending value rests on the ability to view these objects and events in terms of how they fit into the bigger picture.

Emerging research has begun to demonstrate how mortality awareness can lead people to shift from viewing the world in local, detail-oriented ways to viewing it in more global or abstract ways (e.g., Landau, Kosloff, & Schmeichel, 2011; Vail, Vess, & Arndt, 2011). To preface an example of this work, keep in mind that extensive research shows that conscious thoughts of death instigate efforts to remove those thoughts from focal awareness and that terror management motives to seek meaning and self-esteem occur when death thought is cognitively accessible but outside of conscious awareness (see, e.g., Goldenberg & Arndt, 2008). Indeed, in all the previously noted effects, death reminders affected meaning-seeking strategies after a distracting exercise designed to remove death thought from focal awareness. As such, Vail, Vess, and Arndt (2011) also reasoned that the shift in perceptual construal from local to global would occur when death-related thought is active but outside of focal awareness.

Thus, Vail, Vess, and Arndt (2011) reminded participants of death or a control topic and then, either immediately or after a delay, presented them with a series of everyday behaviors that were taken from Vallacher and Wegner's (1989) measure of action identification. Participants were asked to decide whether a detail-oriented or an abstract description best fit each behavior (e.g., do they view "locking a door" as inserting a key in a lock [detail oriented] or as securing one's house [abstract]?). The results indicated that, immediately after MS, there was no difference in participants' preferred level of construal. After a delay, however, MS led participants to make more abstract (vs. detail-oriented) descriptions of the behaviors. This research helps demonstrate the role of cognitive construals in the perception of one's actions as meaningful. Even mundane behaviors, such as caring for one's houseplants, would be existentially meaningless if merely viewed as the physical act of pouring water in some soil. But when such actions are identified as an opportunity to make one's home look nice and inviting to others, the individual becomes perceptually ready to pursue a death-denying sense of value according to his or her broader, more abstract system of meaning.

In addition to abstract construals of actions, the perception of our surroundings as composed of purpose-oriented items reinforces micro-level meaning by perceptually organizing otherwise unrelated aspects of one's environment. Consider, for example, teleological reasoning—the belief that things exist for an ultimate purpose. The present analysis predicts that reminders of mortality should intensify such beliefs, and indeed, Davis, Juhl, and Routledge (2011) showed that MS increased belief in teleological statements, even when those teleological statements were scientifically unfounded (e.g., that the earth developed an ozone layer *in order to* protect life from harmful ultraviolet radiation).

Similar efforts to maintain abstract and purposeful construals appear to drive people to seek out more integrative conceptions of how their past experiences relate to their current self as a means of clarifying what they have become in time. In one recent study exploring this idea (Landau et al., 2011), when participants contemplated ways that their own important past experiences (vs. those of others) could have turned out differently, MS increased the perception that they would be very different people, suggesting that they perceived their past experiences as significantly shaping who they are. By a similar token, people who are more prone to nostalgic reflection tend to view the past as more significant rather than pointless, which helps them stave off death-related cognition and anxiety, and preserves their sense of meaning in life (Juhl, Routledge, Arndt, Sedikides, & Wildschut, 2010; Routledge, Arndt, Sedikides, & Wildschut, 2008).

This analysis extends to inform people's perceptions of their futures as well. Clearly, people's ability to perceive themselves, and their way of life, as progressing toward collective ambitions and personal goals bears a significant consequence for their opportunity to maintain a satisfactory sense of worth. If they are *not* able to see a meaningful way to progress toward these aspirations, then they would essentially be left to wallow in a sea of meaningless action with little hope to achieve future success. Consistent with this reasoning, MS makes people more likely to perceive that their daily activities are substantively performed in the service of their long-term life goals (Landau et al., 2011). Related findings show that, at least among Westerners (though possibly others), heightened faith in the continued trajectory of human progress and improvement into the indefinite future—a view that fundamentally rests upon the expectation that people are capable of meaningfully impacting their futures—helped buffer mortality concerns (Rutjens, van der Pligt, & van Harreveld, 2009).

Together, this research suggests that existential concerns motivate people to construe the world in meaningful ways, from reorienting themselves toward more abstract or purposeful construals of basic actions, objects, and phenomena, to enhancing the perception that one's personal past, present, and future experiences are substantively connected across time. But more broadly, this suggests that people maintain a basic perception of meaning to help manage the awareness of death.

IMPLICATIONS FOR THE INTERPLAY BETWEEN THE STRIVINGS FOR MEANING AND SELF-ESTEEM

This analysis allows for a nuanced and generative consideration of the dynamics that exist between people's strivings for meaning and self-esteem. Again, we argue that security in the face of awareness of mortality is based on the perception that one is satisfying the prescriptions of value which are designated by the worldview. This suggests that for self-esteem to effectively serve an anxiety-buffering function, the standards from which it is derived must be perceived as legitimate and important.

Arndt and Greenberg (1999) directly assessed this possibility. They reasoned that if the power of a self-esteem boost to buffer mortality concerns rests on the perception that the relevant standards are legitimate, then a self-esteem boost based on dubious standards will be less effective at buffering mortality concerns and therefore will not reduce MS-induced worldview defense. Supporting this reasoning, after MS, American participants who received neutral feedback about their personality derogated a target who criticized the United States, but not if they had received positive feedback about either their relationship skills or their academic performance within their academic major (thus conceptually replicating Harmon-Jones et al., 1997). However, if the target criticized the academic major itself, participants who received positive feedback about their academic performance continued to derogate the anti-major target. This suggests that even positive feedback on one's performance in a domain loses its capacity to buffer against mortality concerns if the standards on which that feedback is based are discredited.

The current analysis is also relevant for understanding how people react when their strivings for meaning and self-esteem pull them in opposing directions. While meaning and self-esteem normally act in concert to assuage mortality concerns, there are interesting situations in which enhancing self-esteem threatens to undermine faith in the worldview. We can imagine, for example, a scientist on the verge of a breakthrough discovery, or a young adult who makes an apple pie that rivals the one her extended family has made for generations. These individuals might feel ambivalent about, on the one hand, gaining validation for their talent and creativity and, on the other, discrediting the very belief systems that formally kept their world intact. Will they choose to self-enhance regardless of its consequences for the worldview, or will they put the brakes on their self-enhancement?

Our analysis suggests that the worldview is generally the more fundamental basis of security because self-esteem is predicated on meeting the worldview's standards of personal value. A threat to the worldview necessarily entails a threat to the standards of value upon which people stake their self-esteem (Arndt & Greenberg, 1999). However, discounting self-esteem-bolstering accomplishments does not reciprocally entail a worldview threat. This suggests that when faced with a conflict, people will typically opt to preserve faith in the worldview and temper their self-esteem strivings.

Supporting this reasoning, Landau, Greenberg, and Sullivan (2008) showed that MS led people to forego opportunities to bolster or defend self-esteem when doing so would threaten the status or credibility of revered, worldview-representative authorities. Specifically, mortality salient participants discounted the validity of self-esteem bolstering feedback when they were led to believe that institutional authorities dismissed the feedback as bogus, while, conversely, they were reluctant to discount the validity of self-esteem threatening feedback that was ostensibly sanctioned by institutional experts. MS also led participants to rate themselves higher on a valued dimension after rating a close friend who excels on that dimension, but not if people first rated a parent who excels on that dimension. Similarly, MS led participants to judge feedback that they surpassed a current political figure as more valid but feedback that they surpassed a canonical cultural figure as less valid. These findings suggest that heightening mortality concerns generally increases self-enhancement but also increases reluctance to self-enhance when doing so would challenge important aspects of the individual's meaning-providing worldview.

MANAGING TERROR AND FINDING MEANING IN A LESS RIGID FASHION

As the foregoing review has shown, the need to quell existentially distressing concerns about mortality can ultimately give rise to an intensely rigid reliance on existing knowledge about the world. This reliance can manifest itself in a variety of ways, unfortunately often implicating socially maladaptive outcomes ranging from intergroup prejudice (Rosenblatt et al., 1989) to victim derogation (Landau et al., 2004). At the same time, affirming the integrity of macrolevel sources of meaning (i.e., cultural worldview) and possessing coherently structured microlevel foundations of meaning (i.e., basic structure) both contribute to elevated meaning perceptions in the face of mortality concerns (e.g., Vess, Arndt, et al., 2009). This brings us to a crossroad, both in terms of this chapter and the current state of terror management research. Is it the case that all terror management efforts to maintain a sense of meaning require rigidity and must foster socially and individually adverse consequences? We propose this need not be the case. Although sustaining identification with less rigid beliefs may be quite challenging in light of the tolerance for ambiguity they require, embracing cultural diversity, novelty, and growth-oriented engagements with the world has the potential to contribute to perceptions of meaning and help alleviate existential distress. An exciting direction for the next generation of terror management research is to examine the factors that make it possible for people to manage mortality concerns in a less rigid and dogmatic fashion.

Initial insights in this vein come from examining links between mortality concerns, need for simple structure, and reliance on clear interpretations of the world. Given the openness to novelty and tolerance for ambiguity that is characteristic of low-PNS individuals (e.g., Neuberg & Newsom, 1993), Vess, Routledge, et al. (2009) hypothesized that these individuals will show a marked willingness to engage in novel exploration as a way of dealing with mortality concerns. Accordingly, low-PNS participants scored higher on an exploration scale and expressed more interest in countercultural information following reminders of death (see also, Routledge, Juhl, & Vess, 2010). Critically, Vess, Routledge, et al. (2009) also found that these explorative responses did in fact restore meaning for low-PNS individuals when death was salient. Thus, while considerable work has revealed many dogmatic responses to death-related thought, there is optimistic evidence that low levels of dispositional structure-seeking predict more growth-oriented ways of maintaining a buffer of meaning against the threat of death.

Open-mindedness or exploration might also stem, in part, from one's degree of faith in salient sets of beliefs. In this respect, the religious domain offers an occasion to examine how death awareness might influence dogmatic responses when the opportunity for worldview-consistent terror management is available (e.g., among the religious) but also how it might encourage the exploration or contemplation of other meaning structures when such available beliefs are not applicable for terror management purposes (e.g., among atheists). For many, belief in supernatural agents and afterlife can be quite a handy, and potent, defense against existential concerns (Norenzayan & Hansen, 2006). For the religious, then, MS should inspire greater faith and ideological rigidity. For atheists, however, the inapplicability of such beliefs may result in the need to seek out and explore other potential avenues for extracting meaning after death reminders. Indeed, in a recent series of studies, Vail, Arndt, and Abdollahi (in press) found that after being reminded of death, Christians and Muslims each boosted faith in their worldview-consistent deity (i.e., God and Allah, respectively) and reduced faith in their respective worldview-inconsistent deities, but atheists showed a floor effect on all supernatural beliefs. Importantly, in another series of studies, death reminders increased Christians' faith in religion, which in turn led to an increase in dogmatic belief style and decrease in need for cognition (Vail, Arndt, Sheldon, & Ferguson, 2011). In contrast, death reminders reduced atheists' faith in religion, leading to a decrease in their dogmatic belief style and an increase in their need for cognition.

These studies suggest that although firm adherence to a particular ideology can protect against mortality concerns, a willingness to explore ideas may serve a similar function when that particular ideology is less applicable to the individual's worldview. The capacity of a given belief to provide a sense of existential meaning may be what renders that belief more appealing when faced with awareness of death. This may help to explain why Tracy, Hart, and

Martens (2011) recently found that although reminders of death generally increased people's acceptance of intelligent design theory and decreased their acceptance of evolutionary theory, these effects were reversed when naturalism was portrayed as a source of existential meaning.

More broadly, it is critical for future research to continue to explore strategies that facilitate a more open-minded and less defensive orientation to viewing life as meaningful in light of the human existential predicament. Said differently, how can meaning be achieved while, as Becker (1971) questioned, imposing the least harm on those outside the culture and future generations? Although this is an important research agenda to occupy the next generation of inquiry, there already exist some promising lines of work.

One possibility stems from the capacity for creative integration of new information and experiences with existing psychological structures and, in so doing, fashioning a more self-determined sense of meaning. Although often eschewed for dogmatic reliance on what is expected, the possibility of departing from the known makes it possible to create a relatively autonomous constellation of meaning structures that would share many of the features so well articulated in self-determination theory research (e.g., Ryan & Deci, 2000). Perhaps such a constitution could provide expectations and standards that control anxiety and provide for a more open-minded approach to extracting meaning from life. There are a few encouraging findings in this vein. When the cultural value of creativity was primed, participants reminded of mortality expressed more interest in novel social, cultural, and environmental experiences (Routledge & Arndt, 2009). Further, as noted, Vess, Routledge, et al. (2009) demonstrated that giving low-PNS individuals the opportunity to explore alternative cultural perspectives boosted their perceived meaning in life after MS. And finally, Vail, Arndt, and Pope (2011) demonstrated that people can use the basic nutrients of self-determination (needs for autonomy, competence, and relatedness) as a resource for managing the awareness of mortality and facilitating less defensive responses (see also Niemiec et al., 2010).

This possibility of using open-minded thinking to maintain meaning and thus alleviate existential fear is further bolstered by findings concerning the flexibility of the terror management system to rely on situationally salient values and norms (e.g., Jonas et al., 2008). Many belief systems contain prescriptions that encourage tolerance of deviant others, for example, as values to enrich a meaningful life. It may be useful to bring these tenets to the fore as a way of fostering less dogmatic and harmful responses to those outside the conventional belief system. The promise of such an approach can be seen in studies where people encouraged to reconceptualize the nature of ingroup identifications to emphasize their common humanity with different others respond to reminders of mortality with less outgroup derogation (see Pyszczynski, Rothschild, & Abdollah, 2008). Yet another potential direction stems from work suggesting that deeper conscious recognition of mortality can foster greater attention to intrinsic values, which have been found to be a potent contributor to eudemonic well-being. Drawing from the posttraumatic growth literature, studies indicate that a more open and in-depth confrontation with the idea of life's finality can inspire greater attention to self-transcendent values and goals (e.g., Cozzolino, Staples, Meyers, & Samboceti, 2004; Lykins, Segerstrom, Averill, Evans, & Kemeny, 2007). Of course, it is probably difficult to maintain this perspective. Maintaining focus on thoughts of death—particularly in the depth required to foster this orientation—would likely interfere with other endeavors, the business of living as it were, that allows us to experience the routine events and momentous occasions that help to produce a sense of meaning and purpose. And what happens when such ideation fades from conscious attention? Research shows that whereas conscious thoughts of death engender immediate derogation of extrinsic goals, the delayed effect of nonconscious thoughts of death is an inflation of the importance of extrinsic goals (Kosloff & Greenberg, 2009). Still, the possible benefits of a more honest acknowledgement of life's transience are worth exploring.

CONCLUSION: DEATH AS A CATALYST TOWARD MEANING

The available research on manipulating thoughts of death relative to other threats, and the research measuring patterns of death-thought accessibility, as well as the historical record, suggest that death awareness plays a unique role in the development and maintenance of meaning structures. Of course, a number of other threats can, and obviously do, lead to a greater need for meaning as well. The issue, therefore, is not to examine which threat underlies all defensive meaning preferences, but rather to explore and understand the differential influences of these various threats—when and how might they alter individuals' efforts to bolster and defend meaning—and what the influence of those threats ultimately tells us about what people really need. To the extent that meaning reflects, in part, the perception of a network of expected relations that guide one's value-seeking efforts, TMT is able to offer unique and coherent insights into the need for meaning as ultimately reflecting the perception of a clear path toward securing personal value and, thus, symbolically transcending death. This explanation can help us understand why some meanings are more central to guiding one's efforts to accrue value than others, and when.

In this light, it makes sense that departures toward the absurd motivate efforts to reinstate one's sense of meaning (e.g., Proulx & Heine, 2009). A person with an apple as a face, or a red card that was expected to have appeared black, clearly signals a violation of one's broad rule-based system of meaning, but demonstrating such tells us little about why, at a deeper level, people need to see meaning in their lives. Even a child playing a board game knows that without at least some basic rules, there is no way to earn the glory of victory; and by the same token, she also knows that when she is not playing the game, the rules of the game are completely irrelevant. That is, meaning structures are not important for their own sake. Rather, life's basic rules help map out the consequences of our thoughts and behaviors in predictable ways, allowing us to *meaningfully* direct our attitudes and actions in ways that will help us transcend death (i.e., "beat the game"). Transcending death means being good, and ways of being good cannot even be imagined without a stable, structured system of meaning.

REFERENCES

Arndt, J., & Greenberg, J. (1999). The effects of a self-esteem boost and mortality salience on responses to boost relevant and irrelevant worldview threats. *Personality and Social Psychology Bulletin, 25*, 1331–1341. doi:10.1177/0146167299259001

Becker, E. (1971). *The birth and death of meaning: An interdisciplinary perspective on the problem of man* (2nd ed.). New York, NY: Free Press.

Becker, E. (1973). *The denial of death*. New York, NY: Free Press.

Berger, P., & Luckmann, T. (1967). *The social construction of reality*. New York, NY: Anchor Books.

Bowlby, J. (1969). *Attachment and loss (Vol. 1: Attachment)*. London, England: Hogarth Press.

Brewer, M. B. (1988). A dual-process model of impression formation. In T. K. Srull and R. S. Wyer, Jr. (Eds.), *Advances in social cognition* (Vol. 1, pp. 1–36). Hillsdale, NJ: Erlbaum.

Burke, B. L., Martens, A., & Faucher, E. H. (2010). Two decades of terror management theory: A meta-analysis of mortality salience research. *Personality and Social Psychology Review, 14*, 155–195. doi:10.1177/1088868309352321

Cozzolino, P. J., Staples, A. D., Meyers, L. S., & Samboceti, J. (2004). Greed, death, and values: From terror management to transcendence management theory. *Personality and Social Psychology Bulletin, 30*, 278–292. doi:10.1177/0146167203260716

Davis, W., Juhl, J., & Routledge, C. (2011). Death and design: The terror management function of teleological beliefs. *Motivation and Emotion*, 35, 98–104.

Festinger, L. (1957). *A theory of cognitive dissonance*. Stanford, CA: Stanford University Press.

Friedman, R. S., & Arndt, J. (2005). Reexploring the connection between terror management theory and dissonance theory. *Personality and Social Psychology Bulletin, 31*, 1217–1225. doi:10.1177/0146167204274077

Goffman, E. (1959). *The presentation of self in everyday life*. Garden City, NY: Doubleday.

Goldenberg, J. L., & Arndt, J. (2008). The implications of death for health: A terror management health model for behavioral health promotion. *Psychological Review, 115*, 1032–1053. doi:10.1037/a0013326

Greenberg, J., Landau, M. J., & Arndt, J. (in press). Mortal cognition: Viewing self and the world form the precipice. In D. Carlston (Ed.), *Handbook of social cognition*. Oxford, England: Oxford University Press.

Greenberg, J., Pyszczynski, T., & Solomon, S. (1986). The causes and consequences of a need for self-esteem: a terror management theory. In R. F. Baumeister (Ed.), *Public self and private self* (pp. 189–212). New York, NY: Springer-Verlag. doi:10.1007/978-1-4613-9564-5_10

Greenberg, J., Solomon, S., & Arndt, J. (2008). A uniquely human motivation: Terror management. In J. Shah & W. Gardner (Eds.), *Handbook of motivation science* (pp. 114–134). New York, NY: Guilford Press.

Harmon-Jones, E., Simon, L., Greenberg, J., Pyszczynski, T., Solomon, S., & McGregor, H. (1997). Terror management theory and self-esteem: Evidence that increased self-esteem reduces mortality salience effects. *Journal of Personality and Social Psychology, 72*, 24–36. doi:10.1037/0022-3514.72.1.24

Hayes, J., Schimel, J., Arndt, J., & Faucher, E. H. (2010). A theoretical and empirical review of the death-thought accessibility concept in terror management research. *Psychological Bulletin, 136*, 699–739. doi:10.1037/a0020524

Heider, F. (1958). *The psychology of interpersonal relations*. New York, NY: Wiley. doi:10.1037/10628-000

Hirschberger, G. (2006). Terror management and attributions of blame to innocent victims: Reconciling compassionate and defensive responses. *Journal of Personality and Social Psychology, 91*, 832–844. doi:10.1037/0022-3514.91.5.832

Jonas, E., Greenberg, J., & Frey, D. (2003). Connecting terror management and dissonance theories: Evidence that mortality salience increases the preference for supportive information after decisions. *Personality and Social Psychology Bulletin, 29*, 1181–1189. doi:10.1177/0146167203254599

Jonas, E., Martens, A., Kayser, D. N., Fritsche, I., Sullivan, D., & Greenberg, J. (2008). Focus theory of normative conduct and terror-management theory: The interactive impact of mortality salience and norm salience on social judgment. *Journal of Personality and Social Psychology*, 95, 1239–1251. doi:10.1037/a0013593

Jones, E. E., & Davis, K. E. (1965). From acts to dispositions: The attribution process in person perception. In L. Berkowitz (Ed.), *Advances in experimental social psychology* (Vol. 2, pp. 219–266). New York, NY: Academic Press.

Juhl, J., Routledge, C., Arndt, J., Sedikides, C., & Wildschut, T. (2010). Fighting the future with the past: Nostalgia buffers existential threat. *Journal of Research in Personality, 44*, 309–314. doi:10.1016/j.jrp.2010.02.006

Kosloff, S., & Greenberg, J. (2009). Pearls in the desert: The proximal and distal effects of mortality salience on the appeal of extrinsic goals. *Journal of Experimental Social Psychology, 45*, 197–203. doi:10.1016/j.jesp.2008.08.022

Kruglanski, A. W., Webster, D. M., & Klem, A. (1993). Motivated resistance and openness to persuasion in the presence or absence of prior information. *Journal of Personality and Social Psychology, 65*, 861–876. doi:10.1037/0022-3514.65.5.861

Landau, M. J., Greenberg, J., Solomon, S., Pyszczynski, T., & Martens, A. (2006). Windows into nothingness: Terror management, meaninglessness, and negative reactions to modern art. *Journal of Personality and Social Psychology, 90*, 879–892. doi:10.1037/0022-3514.90.6.879

Landau, M. J., Greenberg, J., & Sullivan, D. (2008). Managing terror when worldviews and self-worth collide: Evidence that mortality salience increases reluctance to self-enhance beyond authorities. *Journal of Experimental Social Psychology, 45*, 68–79. doi:10.1016/j.jesp.2008.08.007

Landau, M. J., Greenberg, J., Sullivan, D., Routledge, C., & Arndt, J. (2009). The protective identity: Evidence that mortality salience heightens the clarity and coherence of the self-concept. *Journal of Experimental Social Psychology, 45*, 796–807. doi:10.1016/j.jesp.2009.05.013

Landau, M. J., Johns, M., Greenberg, J., Pyszczynski, T., Martens, A., Goldenberg, J. L., & Solomon, S. (2004). A function of form: Terror management and structuring the social world. *Journal of Personality and Social Psychology, 87*, 190–210. doi:10.1037/0022-3514.87.2.190

Landau, M. J., Kosloff, S., & Schmeichel, B. (2011). Imbuing everyday actions with meaning in response to existential threat. *Self and Identity, 10*, 64–76. doi:10.1080/15298860903557243

Lerner, M. (1980). *The belief in a just world*. New York, NY: Plenum Press.

Lykins, E. L. B., Segerstrom, S. C., Averill, A. J., Evans, D. R., & Kemeny, M. E. (2007). Goal shifts following reminders of mortality: Reconciling posttraumatic growth and terror management theory. *Personality and Social Psychology Bulletin, 33*, 1088–1099. doi:10.1177/0146167207303015

Mead, G. H. (1934). *Mind, self, and society*. Chicago, IL: University of Chicago Press.

Neuberg, S. L., & Newsom, J. (1993). Personal need for structure: Individual differences in the desire for simple structure. *Journal of Personality and Social Psychology, 65*, 113–131. doi:10.1037/0022-3514.65.1.113

Niemiec, C. P., Brown, K. W., Kashdan, T. B., Cozzolino, P. J., Breen, W. E., Levesque-Bristol, C., & Ryan, R. M. (2010). Being present in the face of existential threat: The role of trait mindfulness in reducing defensive responses to mortality salience. *Journal of Personality and Social Psychology, 99*, 344–365. doi:10.1037/a0019388

Norenzayan, A., & Hansen, I. G. (2006). Belief in supernatural agents in the face of death. *Personality and Social Psychology Bulletin, 32*, 174–187. doi:10.1177/0146167205280251

Proulx, T., & Heine, S. J. (2009). Connections from Kafka: Exposure to meaning threats improves implicit learning of an artificial grammar. *Psychological Science*, *20*, 1125–1131. doi:10.1111/j.1467-9280.2009.02414.x

Pyszczynski, T., Greenberg, J., Solomon, S., Arndt, J., & Schimel, J. (2004). Why do people need self-esteem?: A theoretical and empirical review. *Psychological Bulletin*, *130*, 435–468. doi:10.1037/0033-2909.130.3.435

Pyszczynski, T., Rothschild, Z., & Abdollahi, A. (2008). Terrorism, violence, and hope for peace: A terror management perspective. *Current Directions in Psychological Science*, *17*, 318–322. doi:10.1111/j.1467-8721.2008.00598.x

Rosenblatt, A., Greenberg, J., Solomon, S., Pyszczynski, T., & Lyon, D. (1989). Evidence for terror management theory I: The effects of mortality salience on reactions to those who violate or uphold cultural values. *Journal of Personality and Social Psychology*, *57*, 681–690. doi:10.1037/0022-3514.57.4.681

Routledge, C., & Arndt, J. (2009). Creative terror management: Creativity as a facilitator of cultural exploration after mortality salience. *Personality and Social Psychology Bulletin*, *35*, 493–505. doi:10.1177/0146167208329629

Routledge, C., Arndt, J., Sedikides, C., & Wildschut, T. (2008). A blast from the past: The terror management function of nostalgia. *Journal of Experimental Social Psychology*, *44*, 132–140. doi:10.1016/j.jesp.2006.11.001

Routledge, C., Juhl, J., & Vess, M. (2010). Divergent reactions to the terror of terrorism: Personal need for structure moderates the effects of terrorism salience on worldview-related attitudinal rigidity. *Basic and Applied Social Psychology*, *32*, 243–249. doi:10.1080/01973533.2010.495667

Routledge, C., Ostafin, B., Juhl, J., Sedikides, C., Cathey, C., & Liao, J. (2010). Adjusting to death: The effects of self-esteem and mortality salience on well-being, growth motivation, and maladaptive behavior. *Journal of Personality and Social Psychology*, 99, 897–916. doi:10.1037/a0021431

Rutjens, B. T., van der Pligt, J., & van Harreveld, F. (2009). Things will get better: The anxiety-buffering qualities of progressive hope. *Personality and Social Psychology Bulletin*, *35*, 535–543. doi:10.1177/0146167208331252

Ryan, R. M., & Deci, E. L. (2000). Self-determination theory and the facilitation of intrinsic motivation, social development, and well-being. *American Psychologist*, *55*, 68–78. doi:10.1037/0003-066X.55.1.68

Simon, L., Arndt, J., Greenberg, J., Solomon, S., & Pyszczynski, T. (1998). Terror management and meaning: Evidence that the opportunity to defend the worldview in response to mortality salience increases the meaningfulness of life in the mildly depressed. *Journal of Personality*, 66, 359–382. doi:10.1111/1467-6494.00016

Solomon, S., Greenberg, J., & Pyszczynski, T. (1991). Terror management theory of self-esteem. In C. R. Snyder & D. R. Forsyth (Eds.), *Handbook of social and clinical psychology: The health perspective* (pp. 21–40). Elmsford, NY: Pergamon Press.

Taubman-Ben-Ari, O. (2011). Is the meaning of life also the meaning of death? A terror management theory reply. *Journal of Happiness Studies, 12*, 385–399. doi:10.1007/s10902-010-9201-2

Thompson, M. M., Naccarato, M. E., Parker, K. C. H., & Moskowitz, G. B. (2001). The personal need for structure and personal fear of invalidity measures: Historical perspectives, current applications, and future directions. In G. B. Moscowitz (Ed.), *Cognitive social psychology: Princeton Symposium on the Legacy and Future of Social Cognition* (pp. 19–39). Mahwah, NJ: Erlbaum.

Tracy, J. L., Hart, J., & Martens, J. P. (2011). Death and science: The existential underpinnings of belief in intelligent design and discomfort with evolution. *PLoS ONE*, 6, e17349. doi:10.1371/journal.pone.0017349

Vail, K. E. Arndt., J., & Abdollahi, A. (in press). Exploring the existential function of religion and supernatural agent beliefs among Christians, Muslims, atheists and agnostics. *Personality and Social Psychology Bulletin*.

Vail, K. E., Arndt, J., & Pope, B. (2011). *Exploring the connection between terror management and basic need satisfaction*. Unpublished manuscript, University of Missouri, Columbia.

Vail, K. E., Arndt, J., Sheldon, K., & Ferguson, Y. (2011). *Religious identification, atheism, and dogmatic responses to mortality salience*. Unpublished manuscript, University of Missouri, Columbia.

Vail, K. E., Vess, M., & Arndt, J. (2011). *The effect of mortality salience on abstract thought*. Unpublished manuscript, University of Missouri, Columbia.

Vallacher, R. R., & Wegner, D. M. (1989). Levels of personal agency: Individual variation in action identification. *Journal of Personality and Social Psychology, 57*, 660–671. doi:10.1037/0022-3514.57.4.660

Vess, M., Arndt, J., Cox, C. R., Routledge, C., & Goldenberg, J. L. (2009). The terror management of medical decisions: The effect of mortality salience and religious fundamentalism on support for faith-based medical intervention. *Journal of Personality and Social Psychology*, 97, 334–350. doi:10.1037/a0015545

Vess, M., Routledge, C., Landau, M. J., & Arndt, J. (2009). The dynamics of death and meaning: The effects of death-relevant cognitions and personal need for structure on perceptions of meaning in life. *Journal of Personality and Social Psychology*, 97, 728–744. doi:10.1037/a0016417

4

BEYOND MORTALITY AND THE SELF: MEANING MAKES A COMEBACK

TRAVIS PROULX

According to Kierkegaard (1843/1997a), people really don't understand the story of Abraham and Isaac. If you've had any sort of Judeo–Christian upbringing, you're probably familiar with this story, but if you're not, it goes something like this: Abraham is the "father" of the ancient Israelites, and for their lineage to continue, he really needs to have a son. But he doesn't have a son, and after a few decades, he and his wife Sarah are old, and the notion of having a child becomes (literally) laughable (Genesis 18:12). But then they have a son, Isaac, and he is the living embodiment of the continued existence of the Jewish people. And then one day, God tells Abraham to take Isaac to the top of Mount Moriah and kill him. Ever obedient, Abraham sneaks Isaac out of their home, deflects Isaac's suspicious questioning, ties him up, places a knife at his throat, and at the last moment an angel of the Lord appears and tells Abraham to forget about it and take Isaac home. And if you've had any sort of Judeo–Christian upbringing, you're probably also familiar with the

DOI: 10.1037/14040-004
The Psychology of Meaning, Keith D. Markman, Travis Proulx, and Matthew J. Lindberg (Editors)

moral we're told the story was meant to convey: If God tells you to do something really awful, you should do it without question. It's a test of your faith. Because God would obviously never make you actually go through with such an awful thing because he never has in the past, for you or anyone else. You already know this. So in that sense, it can't really be a test of faith at all. And so this moral . . . doesn't actually make a lot of sense.

THE BIRTH OF MEANING

It Begins With the Absurd

Exactly! says Kierkegaard. Unless you assume the following: When Abraham took Isaac to the top of that mountain, he was absolutely convinced that God would prevent him from killing Isaac. But he was *also* absolutely convinced that God would let him go through with it and kill his son. Abraham was fully convinced of *both* the "either" and the "or" of the situation. It wasn't merely that one or the other outcome could plausibly take place—a 50/50 gamble. Abraham was equally and fully convinced of both potential outcomes—100/100. This is, of course, absurd. But according to Kierkegaard, this absurdity isn't merely what true faith is about—it's the only scenario in which we can sensibly use the word *faith*. To act on true faith, we must be fully convinced that we'll be spared the negative outcome—but we must also fully believe that the negative outcome will prevail. Otherwise "faith" is just a matter of playing probabilities—rationally acting on the most likely outcome of a gamble. For true faith to exist, it must be truly *irrational*—obedience in the face of absurd commitments.

Framed in this way, it would seem that making a "leap of faith"—over a chasm of absurdity—would be impossible, or at the very least, an extremely rare event. Which brings Kierkegaard to his ultimate point about the true moral of the story: Abraham isn't just the "father" of the Israelites—he's the "father of us all," insofar as we *all* maintain these absurd commitments—and act on these absurd commitments—every day of every year over the course of our lives. For Kierkegaard, the story of Abraham and Isaac is really about putting a fine point on how people understand themselves and their reality—as frequently contradictory meaning frameworks to which we may be completely committed. Even if there is some grand consistency in an external, objective reality—to the extent that such a reality can be imagined to exist—we don't have access to this reality. What we have is our subjective experience of existence—the ad hoc jumble of associated commitments that we assemble from our experiences and subsequently apply to other experiences. Often, these *meaning frameworks* are consistent with one another, and the experiences they are intended to render comprehensible. All too often, however, Kierkegaard noted the *gaps and fissures* where these commitments should be consistent. We find ourselves staring into absurdities, like a frog lounging at the bottom of an empty beer mug (Kierkegaard, 1848/1997d). In our everyday lives, we may be insensitive to the importance of these frameworks, only aware of their ongoing function when they are pierced by absurdities. We then get that unique sense that something is *wrong*.

As the 19th century wore on, Kierkegaard wrote more and more essays about meaning frameworks and how we deal with the feeling that follows from absurdity. Long after Kierkegaard's death, German manic depressives (Nietzsche) and Russian alcoholics (Dostoevsky) would obsessively develop this notion of the absurd, often reaching the same conclusions—often without any direct familiarity with Kierkegaard or his writings. It was only much later, into the early 20th century, that scholars would draw a circle around a loosely arrayed cluster of texts and label it *existentialism*. And while the style and disposition of those authors varied widely, they found themselves included in this cohort to the extent that they addressed some common questions and generated some similar conclusions:

Q. How is it that we experience reality?

A. As a series of expected relationships between other expected relationships.

Q. How do we feel when these meaning frameworks are violated?

A. In a word: "angsty."

Q. How do we respond to this feeling?

A. We either (a) ignore the absurdity, (b) recognize the absurdity and alter our meaning frameworks, or (c) turn our attention to other meaning frameworks that remain intact and secure. At the risk of sounding glib—this is the gist of a good deal of existentialist theory (and much of the psychological literature of the past century).

Of course, there's much more that can (and should) be said about how this all plays out, but for the purposes of a brief chapter, I focus on the central series of questions that existentialist theorists raised and strove to resolve. It turn, I point out how these somewhat radical notions informed 20th century psychology, especially those developmental, cognitive, and social psychological theorists who situated some notion of cognitive consistency as a psychodynamic prime mover. I suggest that, as the century progressed, interest in meaning became subjugated to the study of one particular meaning framework—the self—and one particular meaning violation—the destruction of the self. Finally, I'll summarize some of the recent research that suggests that meaning—at last—is making a comeback.

The Will to Meaning

For Camus (1955), it all began with what he elegantly termed "the nostalgia for unity"—a fundamental sense that we were once related to a larger whole, which was itself a series of consistent relationships. He positioned this sense of lost connection as the "fundamental impulse of the human drama" (p. 5)—the unequivocal core of human motivation. He justified this stance with two central observations. At the outset he noted the pan-culturally pervasive efforts of individuals to connect things up with other things, whether it's in terms of causal relations, functional importance, conceptual similarity, or logical following. For Camus, human culture, in its totality, represents efforts to achieve a relational unity by one means or another. These efforts may manifest as artistic paradigms, scientific theories, religious dogmas, or philosophical systems, along with the relation between these frameworks and the realities they are meant to represent. However, like Frankl (1946), Camus believed that the fundamental nature of this impulse is best exemplified by its capacity to override all others. While we are all motivated to eat and drink to maintain our survival—and we are all motivated to survive—we are the only animal motivated to forgo survival if our meaning impulse isn't satisfied. More to the point, we'll deliberately end our life if we believe that our life has no meaning. There are, apparently, fates worse than death, such as feeling alienated from a world that makes no sense.

Camus (1955) outlined a wide array of experiences that might undermine our sense of interconnectedness, from simple violations of expectation to experiences that undermine our self-understanding. Camus reaffirmed and reiterated the radicalized, existentialist understanding of meaning, insofar as any experience that violates meaning is understood to arouse the same uncomfortable sensation—a "feeling of absurdity." Kierkegaard understood this same feeling as a specific kind of anxiety, and Heidegger (1956/1996) would go further than other existentialists in trying to pin down the unique qualities of this peculiar feeling. Like Kierkegaard and Camus, Heidegger was interested in people's subjective representation of reality—their conscious experience of existence. Heidegger also understood this representational experience in terms of expected relationships, regardless of what we might be relating to each other or how we might be connecting things together.

According to Heidegger (1956/1996), any experience that violated these relationships constituted an (aptly labeled) *nonrelation* and produced a special feeling that was associated with breakdowns in meaning—whether the meaning framework represented a narrative for one's life or an understanding of physical objects. Heidegger understood this feeling as acute, though often subtle. He hesitated to call it an emotion, for it could sometimes hover outside of conscious awareness: We are often aware of its effect on our behaviors before we are aware of the feeling itself. It also seemed to Heidegger that this feeling was more prolonged than a discrete emotional experience, more like a *mood* than a burst of joy or anger. He called it *angst* and understood it as the central motivating force behind individual and cultural efforts to understand the self as a being *entangled* in its environment (*dasein*).

Following an apparent absurdity, a sense of angst may motivate us to recognize and accept the anomalous nature of the experience. We may contemplate the absurdity and engage in efforts to revise our meaning frameworks to account for this anomaly. More often than not, however, we respond to absurdities in ways that are *inauthentic*, such that the absurdity is willfully unrecognized and the relevant meaning frameworks are not sensibly adjusted. On the one hand, we can engage in a kind of willful blindness, choosing to reinterpret the absurdity in such a way that it actually seems to make sense. Nevertheless, a glimmer of angst may remain, motivating us to restore a sense of meaning by the easiest possible means—by simply affirming another meaning framework. In existentialist literature, this "inauthentic" effort is the most common response to even the most glaring absurdity. For Kierkegaard (1843/1997b) it might simply involve the simple *repetition* of a familiar behavior or activity, like seeing the same play at the same theatre again and again and again. Camus (1955) described efforts towards "returning to the chain" (p. 5)—reengaging in familiar *habits*, even if they share no direct—or indirect—relation to the meaning framework that was violated.

One Particular Meaning Framework and One Particular Meaning Threat

In the face of some meaning violations, the inauthentic affirmation of unrelated commitments is more likely than not. This is especially true of absurdities that threaten our most committed meaning framework, and one particular absurdity that threatens all of our meaning frameworks, all at once. Kierkegaard (1848/1997d) referred to our most committed framework as the "relation that relates itself to its own self, and in relating itself to its own self, relates itself to another" (p. 351). Heidegger (1956/1996) referred to the most acute meaning threat as "one's own most nonrelational potentiality of being, not to be bypassed" (p. 232; nonexistentialist translation: the self and death). For existential theorists, more generally, one's self-understanding is the central orienting meaning framework that allows us to navigate our environment. The expected relationships we hold for our general competencies and sense of what others think of us have been elaborated and reinforced more than any other meaning framework. There is simply no other meaning framework to which we have a stronger commitment. And when this meaning framework collides with experiences that don't match our expectations, we're more likely to *cover over* the anomaly than address its implications and alter our self-concept accordingly. Avoiding direct contemplation of the anomaly, while affirming some other commitment, is the safest and easiest way to deal with any lingering angst that is aroused by experiences that run counter to what we thought about ourselves. Performing conceptual microsurgery on such an elaborated meaning framework can be tricky—changing one aspect of our self-understanding can have catastrophic implications for other self-relevant commitments. In a worst-case scenario, we start to pull at the loose threads of our self-understanding, and the whole thing unravels, revealing "the nothingness that pervades being" (Kierkegaard, 1846/1997c, p. 190).

And nothing exposes the vulnerability of our self-conception more than our own, ultimate, utterly unavoidable demise. While the ashes and dust of our bodies will persist, our self will one day evaporate. Nothing will remain but the representational relations maintained by other selves (i.e., memories), which will themselves meet the same fate. And this isn't the full extent of death's absurdity—it savages the narratives we set out for ourselves, to the extent that all paths lead to the grave. It represents our ultimate epistemic blind spot—no one has died and told us what it's like to be dead. It absolutely alienates us from the rest of existence. In a grim irony, death is the only absurdity shared by all humans, of every culture and every period of human history. We can all relate to angst in the face of death, but ultimately, "only you can die your death." (Heidegger, 1956/1996, p. 284) Given its uniquely catastrophic nature, and the degree to which it's a ubiquitous feature of the human condition, it's of little surprise that existentialist theorists discussed the absurdity of mortality more than any other meaning threat. But existential theorists were unanimous in understanding the threat of mortality as a threat to meaning, and the self as meaning framework; the importance of the self and its ultimate demise are construed as a matter of degree, rather than kind. This central point underlines the radical nature of existential theory—ultimately, all violations of expected relationships bottleneck at the same feeling of angst and originate from the same impulse towards meaning. And this understanding of human meaning making would have a profound impact on the psychologists who would employ the scientific method to understand how humans make sense of their reality.

THE PSYCHOLOGY OF MEANING

Psychology Recapitulates Philosophy

Existentialist theorists often described themselves as *psychologists*, though they made no claims to being experimentalists. Using the term *psychology* was a way for existentialists to disassociate themselves from those systematic philosophical thinkers who aimed to sum reality with a series of equations or logical propositions. Kierkegaard was pushing off from Hegel, and Nietzsche was pushing off from Kant. Heidegger studied under the father of phenomenology, Albrecht Husserl, and was so antagonistic toward established philosophies that he chafed at even being called an existentialist. While Nietzsche (1887/1996), in particular, would suggest that a scientific approach to the study of meaning was a dead end, existentialists who argued in this way were flatly wrong (they couldn't be right about everything). Over the course of the 20th century, psychologists from a variety of fields and disciplines did just this—empirically exploring the network of expected relationship that we abstract from and apply to our environment, along with the efforts we make to keep these meaning frameworks internally consistent and consistently corresponding to our experiences.

To a remarkable extent, the varying perspectives of psychological scientists have been consistent with existentialist theory, and with one another—often without having read existentialist theory or one another—which may speak to the veracity of these notions and the relevant data. For example, Jerome Bruner initiated "new look" psychology by demonstrating the extent to which our expected associations—*paradigms*—impact our subjective experience of reality (Bruner & Postman, 1949). In one study—made famous by the philosopher Thomas Kuhn (1962/1996)—Bruner exemplified the power of paradigms, along with the basic manner in which we deal with violations of relevant expectations. The experiment was simple: show people playing cards that contain features that violate our common understanding of playing cards—like a black four of hearts. As it turns out, people will predominantly engage in one of two responses: They'll *reinterpret* their experience of the card so that it agrees with their playing card paradigm (they "see" a black four of hearts as a spade), or they'll recognize the anomaly and *revise* their playing card paradigm accordingly (assume it was an altered deck of cards and expect that more anomalous cards were on the way). Often, the experience of anomalous cards was accompanied by "acute personal distress" (Kuhn, 1962/1996, p. 63), which Bruner and his colleagues thought was rather odd, given the relatively inconsequential nature of the paradigm in question.

If we skip over a few decades and across a few disciplines, Ronnie Janoff-Bulman (1992) summarized the "shattered assumptions" that lie at the heart of the coping literature (see also Chapter 10, this volume). Janoff-Bulman wasn't interested in the paradigms that govern sense perception but rather the *worldviews* that govern our expectation for traumatic events. Building on Lerner's (1980) belief in a just world, Janoff-Bulman summarized our responses to events that violate a core assumption: Tragedies only befall those who deserve them, either because they brought misfortune on themselves or did not effectively act to avoid it. In the face of instances in which "bad things happen to good people," we can generally engage in one of two responses: We can choose to *reinterpret* the event such that it agrees with our "just world" worldview (those car crash victims must have been speeding or drunk), or we can acknowledge the anomaly and *revise* our worldview accordingly (sometimes bad things do happen to people who don't deserve them). Often, the experience of anomalous tragedies is accompanied by a "double dose of anxiety"—the first of these doses is the negative feeling that follows from negative events. The second dose is unique to situations that violate our committed worldview—and this second dose is what clinicians primarily address.

Skipping back a few decades and across a few more disciplines, Jean Piaget (1960) formulated a systematic theory of how children's systematic theories are formulated and altered in the face of incongruous events. Piaget wasn't interested in distinguishing between children's theories of morality or their theories of causality—for Piaget, these lay theories were all represented as *schemata*—associated propositions representing one corner of reality or another. Understanding a child's understanding of object categorization or naive physics follows from the same general understanding of schemata violation: We begin with a theoretical representation abstracted from our environment, which is continually bombarded by anomalies, especially in childhood, when our nascent intellectual capacities limit the sophistication of our schematic frameworks. When an anomalous experience presents itself, we engage in one of two responses: We *assimilate* the experience so that it appears to agree with the schema that was called up to account for it, or we acknowledge the anomalous nature of the experience and *accommodate* a relevant schema accordingly. Either way, we're likely to experience a unique, uncomfortable sensation that warns us of a mismatch between our schemata and our experiences, a *disequilibrium* that Piaget understood as a driving force behind cognitive development.

Skipping over a few disciplines, we find Piaget's social psychological contemporary, Leon Festinger (1957), formulating a theory of how people feel and act when their theories are violated by dissonant experiences (see also Chapter 5, this volume). In particular, Festinger examined situations where our behaviors don't appear to match up with our attitudes. In these situations we generally feel *cognitive dissonance*, an unpleasant sensation that tells us of a mismatch between our understandings and the realities they should be accounting for. What generally follows are efforts to alter these understandings in such a way that reality no longer appears to be anomalous: More often than not, we accommodate our attitudes to account for the dissonant behaviors. And of course, we could just as easily have drawn relevant examples from Heider's (1958) balance theory or the wide array of coping theories that involve some understanding of a reality that is violated, with negative affective responses and analogous efforts to reinterpret the violations or revise the understandings (e.g., Park & Folkman, 1997; Thompson & Janigan, 1988).

If these theories all sound somewhat the same, and all seem to cohere with existentialist theory, well, I'm not being subtle about drawing these parallels. And I don't think it's an accident that different theorists of different eras and different schools of thought exploring differing contents of cognition should arrive at the same general description of these (this) phenomena (phenomenon): People maintain mental representations of expected associations that they employ to understand themselves, their world, and their relation to the world. When these mental representations are threatened by experiences that they don't adequately represent, we experience a unique arousal state that cues us to the mismatch. We then engage in a series of cognitive compensation behaviors, primarily to deal with this negative arousal state. These few propositions, I would suggest, constitute a core, pan-disciplinary, pan-era, pan-content, and pan-context psychological mechanism that underlies a good deal of what we get up to in everyday life—and the behaviors that psychologists describe and experimentally manipulate. Given the relatively ubiquitous nature of a hypothesized relational framework across eras and disciplines, it would have seemed likely that these different perspectives would have themselves coalesced into a unified relational framework—one that would have become a dominant paradigm of our scientific enterprise, much like any other mature, normal science (Kuhn, 1962/1996).

The Psychology of One Particular Meaning Framework and One Particular Meaning Violation

But this is one of the many ways in which psychology may differ from mature, normal sciences. Rather than applying these core assumptions to any given meaning framework, and any given meaning violation, we instead began to focus our attention on one particular meaning framework and one particular meaning violation. More to the point, many social psychologists have suggested that all meaning violations—whatever they appear to violate—are ultimately violations of one particular meaning framework: the self (e.g., Van den Bos, 2009). And many other social psychologists have argued that any given meaning violation—whatever the experience—ultimately evokes one particular meaning violation: death (Schimel, Hayes, Williams, & Jahrig, 2007). And while it is understandable that social psychologists have mainly focused on the most reliable violation of the most important meaning framework, this may have come at a cost: namely, a more thorough understanding of this general *violation–compensation* phenomenon—in particular, a thorough understanding of the true boundary conditions of this phenomenon, a phenomenon that appears to span research disciplines and the various values, beliefs, and perceptions they aim to account for.

This focus originated, ironically enough, with the first theoretical framework in social psychology to approach this general phenomenon from a broad, relational perspective: cognitive dissonance theory. At its intended core, dissonance theory is about mismatches between understanding and experience—and the attendant violation of expectation. Whether it was a mismatch of one's behaviors and attitudes or walking into the rain and not getting wet (Festinger, 1957), the same cognitive dissonance was imagined to follow: a psychological mechanism so fundamental that even rats were understood to engage in dissonance reduction efforts (Lawrence & Festinger, 1962). Nevertheless, it's much easier to generate dissonance reduction efforts if one's self-concept is the meaning framework under assault. And depending on how one constructed an experiment, in could appear that one's self-concept must be implicated to arouse the most common mode of dissonance reduction effort—the *revision* of relevant attitudes (Nel, Helmreich, & Aronson, 1969). Over the course of the 1970s, cognitive dissonance theory became less about cognitive dissonance and all about "ego-defense" effects to restore some element of self-understanding after some or other self-relevant violation. Some theorists argued for the primacy of self-perception (Bem, 1967). Others argued that it was about the self-concept, more generally (Aronson, 1969). The more ecumenical of these perspectives have argued that it's about subjective uncertainty, more generally, that is, uncertainty about self or goals (e.g., McGregor, Zanna, Holmes, & Spencer, 2001).

And perhaps the most direct way to shatter the self and goals is to remind people that they're going to die. In fact, the most reliable manipulation in social psychology—perhaps in the whole field of psychology—is to ask people the following two questions: (a) Describe what happens to your body when you physically die; and (b) describe the thoughts and emotions that your own death arouses in you. And as part of the most reliable experimental recipe, more generally, you can wait a few minutes, then put one or another meaning framework under the person's nose, stand back, and watch that person affirm it more strongly than another person who wasn't reminded of his or her inevitable demise. In hundreds of studies, with many thousands of participants conducted in dozens of countries, mortality salience primes will evoke efforts to defend whatever cultural worldview one happens to be committed to, more often than not by punishing people who deviate from accepted moral or cultural standards (e.g., McGregor et al., 1998). The explanation offered for these very reliable effects goes something like this: being reminded of death evokes the potential for existential terror—which in turn activates distal efforts to affirm cultural worldviews that allow for a sense of symbolic immortality, insofar as one is associated with a cultural system that will exist after people, as individuals, have ceased to exist. And to the extent that people aim to preserve the self—especially in terms of maintaining self-esteem—this is also construed as a proxy for symbolic immortality: a gauge of how well people conform to the cultural worldview that provides symbolic immortality (Pyszczynski, Greenberg, Solomon, Arndt, & Schimel, 2004; see also Chapter 3, this volume). In fact, by this reckoning, all meaning frameworks serve a single purpose—to defend against the potential terror of mortality by attaching oneself to a broader network of (relatively) enduring meaning.

Now, if you're someone who imagines that ultimately it's all about the self, or ultimately it's all about death, these are pretty easy perspectives to verify: Just threaten people's sense of self, or remind them of their own mortality, and see if they engage in some sort of compensation efforts. And yes, they do. But if your perspective is to really lay claim to having it right, you should be attempting something else: conducting experiments with conditions that could *falsify* your perspective. And in this case, it would mean answering the following questions: Does threatening meaning frameworks *unrelated* to the self evoke the same kinds of compensations behaviors? Do meaning threats that *don't* involve mortality evoke these same compensation behaviors?

To a very large extent, this question may have already been answered. In the decades that preceded the "It's all about the self" and "It's all about death" perspectives, social psychologists and developmental psychologists and cognitive psychologists were exploring violation-compensation behaviors that had nothing whatsoever to do with the self or death. If we think back to Bruner and his peculiar playing cards, it seems a long way to go if we're to imagine that either perspective could account his findings: Could it be that a black four of hearts arouses anxiety insofar as it shatters your self-understanding? Or that accommodating your understanding of playing cards is a means of affirming a sense of symbolic immortality after a red spade reminded you of your unavoidable demise? And if we think back to Piaget's (1960) account of cognitive development, it seems implausible (to say the least) that the self and death underlie the assimilation and accommodation processes he described. For example, if you pour liquid from a tall, skinny container into a short, squat container, then back again, a child is likely to experience a sense of *disequilibrium*. Does this arise from a violated self-understanding? Or perhaps this *conservation task* reminds the child of their ultimate death, and efforts to accommodate their understanding of conserved mass are proxy attempts to nestle themselves within a cultural worldview that provides a sense of symbolic persistence long after their physical body has perished form the earth?

Or perhaps it's easier to say that all of these experiences violate mental representations of expected associations, all of these experiences make you feel a special kind of bad, and all of these experiences prompt you to engage in compensatory efforts to stifle this feeling or make it go away.

Meaning Makes a Comeback

In the past few years, psychologists have been conducting experimental research that offers direct support for this original understanding of meaning compensation and that directly falsifies perspectives that reduce these phenomena to one meaning threat, or one meaning framework. This is to say that you can get identical cognitive compensation behaviors following threats that have nothing to with death or with the self. Given the relatively concrete nature of death-relevant thoughts, pointing to studies that elicit meaning compensation while unambiguously avoiding mortality salience is relatively easy to do. You can elicit the affirmation of cultural worldviews by reminding people they are going to die but also by threatening their sense of belongingness (Baumeister & Leary, 1995), personal control (Kay, Gaucher, Napier, Callan, & Laurin, 2008), or even by having them imagine dust mites on their pillow while they sleep (Burris & Rempel, 2004). None of these manipulations seem manifestly related to mortality, and manipulation checks confirm that they don't prime death-related thoughts. And if all of these manipulations are producing the same sorts of compensatory efforts, it would seem likely that these experiences are tapping into a more general mechanism than what would follow from the specific commitments that are being violated, for example, the self, belongingness, control. Whatever specific commitments these experiences violate, they may fundamentally operate as *violations of commitment*—whatever their content or content. Specifically, these experiences violate meaning frameworks more generally.

Nevertheless, it's much easier to come up with an account in which many of these experiences are construed as violating the self—either as threats to self-esteem (Tesser, 2000) or self-concept (Swann, Stein-Seroussi, & Giesler, 1992), arousing some general uncertainty about self or goals (Hogg, Adelman, & Blagg, 2010). And it doesn't seem implausible to imagine that threatening personal control or belongingness operate primarily by making people feel bad about themselves or by violating aspects of their personal identity to which they were firmly committed (Steele & Liu, 1983). To leave all manifest trace of the self behind, contemporary researchers have turned to manipulations that are at once more exotic and more fundamental in terms of the very basic expectations they aim to violate—expectations that aren't merely unrelated to the self, but are seemingly *pre-self* insofar as they organize core elements of sense perception. For example, in one study, we (Proulx & Heine, 2008) had participants fill out a series of questionnaires that culminated in a "social judgment survey" that involved setting bond for a recently arrested prostitute as if the respondent were the judge assigned to the case. This task is the same dependent measure used in the first study that directly tested the threatening impact of a mortality salience prime; following a reminder of one's death, people set a higher bond for the prostitute than those in a control condition set, and in so doing, acted to affirm their cultural worldview (i.e., prostitution is immoral and should be punished). In our own study, we included a mortality reminder before people judged the prostitute and readily replicated these effects. However, we also included another condition, with an experimental manipulation that had nothing do with mortality and that had no bearing on the self.

In this condition, expected relationships were violated, but for an element of our external reality—namely, an expectation that people's physical appearances don't change dramatically from one moment to the next. Borrowing from some very clever experiments in the change-blindness literature (Simons & Rensink, 2005), we included a "transmogrifying experimenter" condition, in which we switched our experimenter, "Megan," with a different, albeit identically dressed "Megan" who was several inches taller, had a voice an octave lower, and was a brunette instead of a blonde. As it turned out, 97% of our participants did not consciously notice this switch. As it also turned out, these same people seemed to unconsciously note this meaning violation because they set a higher bond for the prostitute relative to those in a control condition and of the same magnitude as by those who had been reminded of their own mortality. Subsequent to this initial study, we've obtained the same results with the same dependent measure, by using subliminal nonsense word pairs (e.g., *quickly blueberry*; Randles, Proulx, & Heine, 2011) and even by having people play blackjack with Bruner's anomalous playing cards (Proulx & Major, 2010).

Now it could be that the transmogrifying experimenter subtly reminded participants of the shifting nature of human existence, which operated as a proxy for human mortality and prompted a heightened commitment to a moral worldview that provides a sense of symbolic immortality. And it could be the case that flashing *quickly blueberry* to participants at 16 ms unconsciously savages their self-esteem insofar as they feel diminished by their inability to implicitly make sense of the word pairs, and by punishing the prostitute, they are affirming moral values closely associated with their identity and thereby acting to restore their violated sense of selfhood.

Or all of these experiences violate mental representations of expected associations, all of these experiences make you feel a special kind of bad, and all of these experiences prompt you to engage in compensatory efforts to stifle that feeling or make it go away.

Calling for a Leap of Faith

Let's imagine that there's a social psychologist, and like many other social psychologists, they are interested in violation-compensation phenomena.

They're likely familiar with studies that threaten beliefs that are highly self-relevant and with the extent to which people respond by affirming moral beliefs that are closely associated with their personal identity (e.g., Steele & Liu, 1983). They're also familiar with theoretical perspectives that understand these "self-threat/self-affirmation" studies as ego-defense efforts of one kind or other—let's imagine that they're 100% convinced by reasonable arguments suggesting that these phenomena can be understood as manifestations of subjective uncertainty (e.g., Van den Bos, 2009).

And this social psychologist is also likely familiar with studies that demonstrate heightened moral affirmation following reminders of one's mortality. They're familiar with the theoretical perspective that frames this research, as it follows from psychodynamic anthropologist Ernst Becker (1973; see also Chapter 23, this volume). Specifically, they've come to understand these "mortality-threat/worldview-affirmation" studies as "cultural worldview defense" efforts to affirm a sense of symbolic immortality after one is confronted with one's own literal mortality (Pyszczynski et al., 2004). Let's even say that our psychologist is 100% convinced by this compelling account.

And let's say that, more recently, they've come across studies that demonstrate heightened moral affirmation following perceptual anomalies and syntax violations (Randles et al., 2011). In these studies, the content of what is violated is entirely unrelated to the beliefs that are recruited in the compensation efforts—so much so that theoretical perspectives that frame these findings speak of *meaning* (Proulx & Heine, 2010; Proulx & Inzlicht, in press) rather than of any particular domain of content. And given the radically "content-general" nature of these "expectation-threat/commitment-affirmation" effects, our psychologist may feel 100% certain that whatever is going on here involves some kind of "relational consistency" phenomena—something more general and fundamental than ego or mortality defense per se.

So let's imagine that our social psychologist surveys these violation-compensation phenomena and is fully, 100% certain that they each represent an entirely distinct violation-compensation phenomenon—even as they are essentially the same phenomena, that is, violation-compensation. To maintain this inconsistent position, it could be suggested, is to maintain an absurdity. And just like Abraham, who was fully convinced that God would both spare Isaac and demand his sacrifice, our psychologist would have to make a leap of faith. This individual would have to select one of these options and operate from its assumptions and argue its merits. And in reality, this leap that all social psychologists make, often more than once, over the course of their career. It's my hope that more psychologists begin "leaping" to a perspective that understands these phenomena from a general, relational perspective—just as Kierkegaard did when he became the first existentialist to call himself a psychologist.

REFERENCES

Aronson, E. (1969). The theory of cognitive dissonance: A current perspective. In L. Berkowitz (Ed.), *Advances in experimental social psychology* (Vol. 4, pp. 1–34). New York, NY: Academic Press.

Baumeister, R. F., & Leary, M. R. (1995). The need to belong: Desire for interpersonal attachments as a fundamental human motivation. *Psychological Bulletin, 117*, 497–529. doi:10.1037/0033-2909.117.3.497

Becker, E. (1973). *The denial of death*. New York, NY: Simon & Schuster.

Bem, D. J. (1967). Self-perception: An alternative interpretation of cognitive dissonance phenomena. *Psychological Review, 74*, 183–200. doi:10.1037/h0024835

Bruner, J. S., & Postman, L. (1949). On the perception of incongruity: A paradigm. *Journal of Personality, 18*, 206–223. doi:10.1111/j.1467-6494.1949.tb01241.x

Burris, C. T., & Rempel, J. K. (2004). "It's the end of the world as we know it": Threat and the spatial-symbolic self. *Journal of Personality and Social Psychology, 86*, 19–42. doi:10.1037/0022-3514.86.1.19

Camus, A. (1955). *An absurd reasoning: The Myth of Sisyphus and other essays*. New York, NY: Vintage Books.

Festinger, L. (1957). *A theory of cognitive dissonance*. Stanford, CA: Stanford University Press.

Frankl, V. E. (1946). *Man's search for meaning*. New York, NY: Washington Square Press.

Heidegger, M. (1996). *Being and time*. New York, NY: State University of New York Press. (Original work published 1956)

Heider, F. (1958). *The psychology of interpersonal relations*. New York, NY: Wiley. doi:10.1037/10628-000

Hogg, M. A., Adelman, J. R., & Blagg, R. D. (2010). Religion in the face of uncertainty: An uncertainty-identity theory account of religiousness. *Personality and Social Psychology Review, 14*, 72–83. doi:10.1177/1088868309349692

Janoff-Bulman, R. (1992). *Shattered assumptions*. New York, NY: The Free Press.

Kay, A. C., Gaucher, D., Napier, L., Callan, M., & Laurin, K. (2008). God and the government: testing a compensatory control mechanism for the support of external systems. *Journal of Personality and Social Psychology, 95*, 18–35. doi:10.1037/0022-3514.95.1.18

Kierkegaard, S. (1997a). Fear and trembling. In H. Hong & E. Hong (Eds.), *The essential Kierkegaard* (pp. 93–101). Princeton, NJ: Princeton University Press. (Original work published 1843)

Kierkegaard, S. (1997b). Repetition. In H. Hong & E. Hong (Eds.), *The essential Kierkegaard* (pp. 102–115). Princeton, NJ: Princeton University Press. (Original work published 1843)

Kierkegaard, S. (1997c). Concluding unscientific postscript to philosophical fragments. In H. Hong & E. Hong (Eds.), *The essential Kierkegaard* (pp. 187–246). Princeton, NJ: Princeton University Press. (Original work published 1846)

Kierkegaard, S. (1997d). The sickness unto death. In H. Hong & E. Hong (Eds.), *The essential Kierkegaard* (pp. 350–372). Princeton, NJ: Princeton University Press. (Original work published 1848)

Kuhn, T. (1962/1996). *The structure of scientific revolutions*. Chicago, IL: University of Chicago Press.

Lawrence, D. H., & Festinger, L. (1962). *Deterrents and reinforcement: The psychology of insufficient reward*. Oxford, England: Stanford University Press.

Lerner, M. J. (1980). *The belief in a just world: A fundamental delusion*. New York, NY: Plenum Press.

Nel, E., Helmreich, R., & Aronson, E. (1969). Opinion change in the advocate as a function of the persuasibility of his audience: A clarification of the meaning of dissonance. *Journal of Personality and Social Psychology, 12*, 117–124. doi:10.1037/h0027566

McGregor, H. A., Lieberman, J. D., Greenberg, J., Solomon, S., Arndt, J., Simon, L., & Pyszczynski, T. (1998). Terror management and aggression: Evidence that mortality salience motivates aggression against worldview-threatening others. *Journal of Personality and Social Psychology, 74*, 590–605. doi:10.1037/0022-3514.74.3.590

McGregor, I., Zanna, M. P., Holmes, J. G., & Spencer, S. J. (2001). Compensatory conviction in the face of personal uncertainty: Going to extremes and being oneself. *Journal of Personality and Social Psychology*, 80, 472–488. doi:10.1037/0022-3514.80.3.472

Nietzsche, F. (1996). *On the genealogy of morals*. Oxford, England: Oxford World's Classics. (Original work published 1887)

Park, L. C., & Folkman, S. (1997). Meaning in the context of stress and coping. *Review of General Psychology, 1*, 115–144. doi:10.1037/1089-2680.1.2.115

Piaget, J. (1960). *The child's conception of the world*. London, England: Routledge.

Proulx, T., & Heine, S. J. (2008). The case of the transmogrifying experimenter: Reaffirmation of moral schema following implicit change detection. *Psychological Science, 19*, 1294–1300. doi:10.1111/j.1467-9280.2008.02238.x

Proulx, T., & Heine, S. J. (2010). The frog in Kierkegaard's beer: Finding meaning in the violation-compensation literature. *Social and Personality Psychology Compass, 4*, 889–905.

Proulx, T., & Inzlicht, M. (in press). The five "A"s of meaning maintenance: Making sense of the theories of sense-making. *Psychological Inquiry*.

Proulx, T., & Major, B. (January, 2010). *A raw deal: Affirmation of liberal beliefs following anomalous playing cards*. Paper presented at the Society for Personality and Social Psychology, Las Vegas, NV.

Pyszczynski, T., Greenberg, J., Solomon, S., Arndt, J., & Schimel, J. (2004). Why do people need self-esteem? A theoretical and empirical review. *Psychological Bulletin, 130*, 435–468. doi:10.1037/0033-2909.130.3.435

Randles, D., Proulx, T., & Heine, S. J. (2011). Turn-frogs and careful-sweaters: Non-conscious perception of incongruous word pairings provokes fluid compensation. *Journal of Experimental Social Psychology, 47*, 246–249. doi:10.1016/j.jesp.2010.07.020

Schimel, J., Hayes, J., Williams, T., & Jahrig, J. (2007). Is death really the worm at the core? Converging evidence that worldview threat increases death-thought accessibility. *Journal of Personality and Social Psychology, 92*, 789–803. doi:10.1037/0022-3514.92.5.789

Simons, D. J., & Rensink, R. A. (2005). Change blindness: Past, present, and future. *Trends in Cognitive Sciences*, 9(1), 16–20. doi:10.1016/j.tics.2004.11.006

Steele, C. M., & Liu, T. J. (1983). Dissonance processes as self-affirmation. *Journal of Personality and Social Psychology, 45*, 5–19. doi:10.1037/0022-3514.45.1.5

Swann, W. B., Jr., Stein-Seroussi, A., & Giesler, R. B. (1992). Why people self-verify. *Journal of Personality and Social Psychology, 62*, 392–401. doi:10.1037/0022-3514.62.3.392

Tesser, A. (2000). On the confluence of self-esteem maintenance mechanisms. *Personality and Social Psychology Review, 4*, 290–299. doi:10.1207/S15327957PSPR0404_1

Thompson, S., & Janigan, A. (1988). Life schemes: A framework for understanding the search for meaning. *Journal of Social and Clinical Psychology, 7*, 260–280. doi:10.1521/jscp.1988.7.2-3.260

Van den Bos, K. (2009). Making sense of life: The existential self trying to deal with personal uncertainty. *Psychological Inquiry, 20*, 197–217. doi:10.1080/10478400903333411

II

EPISTEMIC UNDERSTANDING

5

TRUTH MOTIVATION

E. TORY HIGGINS

I believe that the Bible's Genesis story of Adam and Eve in the Garden of Eden is about motivation. Adam and Eve were blessed by God by being allowed to live in the Garden of Eden. The Garden of Eden was a place of all pleasure and no pain. Moreover, in the midst of the garden was the *tree of life*, and Adam and Eve could eat the fruit from this tree. This meant that they could have pleasure and no pain *forever*. Instead, they chose to eat the fruit from the one tree that God had forbidden them to eat fruit from—knowing that by so doing, they would "surely die." (Instead, they were cast out of paradise.) Given the widespread assumption that humans, and animals more generally, are motivated to approach pleasure and avoid pain (i.e., the hedonic principle), how can we account for their choice to eat the forbidden fruit? I believe the answer lies in the nature of the forbidden fruit. The fruit was from *the tree of knowledge of good and evil*. Only by eating the fruit could Adam and Eve attain the truth about what was right

DOI: 10.1037/14040-005
The Psychology of Meaning, Keith D. Markman, Travis Proulx, and Matthew J. Lindberg (Editors)

and wrong. Their motivation to have truth was stronger than their motivation to have everlasting pleasure.[1]

Humans' strong motivation to have truth is something we have always recognized. Indeed, it is a popular theme in movies. My two favorites are *The Truman Show* and *The Matrix*. Truman, the central character in the former movie, is living the perfect hedonic life. Unknown to him, his entire life is a reality TV show that began airing at his birth. Everyone he knows are actors playing their roles. Close to his 30th birthday, he finally discovers that his life is a fake. Despite his perfect hedonic life, Truman willingly takes on pain and hardship to seek the truth. What he wants is not pleasure but the truth. When he finds a door, he chooses to leave the constructed reality of perfect hedonism for an uncertain, real world. In making this choice, he leaves as the hero of the movie.

Neo is the central character in *The Matrix*. In this movie set in the future, the reality perceived by humans is actually a simulated one—the Matrix—that provides people with a hedonically positive life to pacify them. Morpheus is the leader of the rebels against this constructed world. He gives Neo a choice between a blue pill that will keep him in this comfortable simulated reality and a red pill that offers only the truth. He tells Neo, "All I'm offering is the truth, nothing more." Neo chooses the red pill—truth over hedonic pleasure—and again is the hero of the movie.

These examples demonstrate that there is at least an implicit recognition that people are motivated to establish what's real—that is, people have *truth motivation*. But the kinds of motivation that have received the most attention in psychological theories are the motivation to manage what happens (control) and the motivation to have desired results or outcomes (value). The purpose of this chapter is to distinguish people's motivation for truth from their motivation for control and for value, to highlight how important truth motivation is to humans, and, especially, to examine the different ways that people establish truth. The central question of this chapter is, how do people find and assign meaning to the events in their lives?

Scientists and laypersons alike would typically say that motivation is about being energized and directing that energy in ways that approach pleasure and avoid pain.[2] The central role of hedonic motivation in people's thinking about motivation is reflected in the pervasive idea that the way to motivate people is through incentives. The incentives need not always be "carrots and sticks," but it is all about incentives nonetheless. Where is truth motivation in all this? Nowhere to be seen.

[1]For a fuller discussion of the implications for motivation of the Genesis story, see Higgins (2011).
[2]For a fuller discussion of the major perspectives on what motivation is and what people want, see Higgins (2011).

So why is truth motivation not central to our understanding of what motivation is and how motivation works? I believe that the answer lies in the general tendency—perhaps a natural tendency—for people to emphasize outcomes or final end-states, rather than process, when they think about motivation. From this viewpoint, people are motivated to end up with positive outcomes (and not end up with negative outcomes). Truth would be just another positive outcome, like ending up with food or water. By treating truth like any other positive outcome, it can be subsumed within the notion that people are motivated to approach desired end-states, that they direct their energy to achieve desired results. But finding truth is not just another outcome because there are different ways to find the truth even for the same outcome. There are different expectancies regarding whether some outcome is likely to happen. And even when an outcome does happen, truth motives remain, such as wanting to know whether that outcome is real or imaginary.

This chapter is concerned with the process of establishing what's real. Truth motivation is about assigning meaning to objects and events in the world. It is about making sense of the world. It is about sharing with others the meanings we have found. The objective of this chapter is to discuss the various ways that people find and assign meaning to the events in their lives. To appreciate how this happens, the unique and distinctive role in motivation of establishing what's real needs to be highlighted. Thus, this chapter begins by reviewing the fuller picture of what motivates people.

Elsewhere (Higgins, 2011), in a book called *Beyond Pleasure and Pain: How Motivation Works*, I presented this story in detail. Here, I simply place the story of truth motivation in its proper theoretical context. Then I discuss truth motivation in particular and describe the motivational mechanisms that support people's search for the truth and underlie their assigning meaning to their lives.

WHAT DO PEOPLE REALLY WANT?

What motivates people? What do people really want? There is more than one reasonable answer to what it is that people want, but I believe that some answers are better than others. Here, I briefly review some of the strongest alternative answers and then present my preferred answer.

People Want to Survive

The notion that individuals moment-to-moment want to survive, that they prefer "to stay alive" rather than "to die," is powerful. Indeed, it is so compelling that in the early 20th century it dominated theories of what humans and other animals wanted, and it continues to be a dominant perspective. In psychology, "survival" was often translated into satisfying basic biological needs, basic because they were deemed necessary for the preservation of an individual and species. Satisfying biological needs was considered so central to motivation that even the value of something, such as food or water or social interaction, was thought to depend on the extent to which it satisfied a biological need. Theoretical perspectives ranging from behavioristic to Gestalt to psychodynamic proposed that how much one wants something depends on the extent to which it satisfies some need.

There is little question that some sense of wanting to survive, such as satisfying basic biological needs, is part of what people really want. After all, humans (and other animals as well) want water when they are thirsty and food when they are hungry. They are willing to fight to live rather than die. However, as much as I appreciate the notion that people want to survive, it is not a sufficient answer by itself. It is not sufficient because it gives insufficient attention to people's life experiences. "Survival" as an answer to what a motivated person really wants refers to life versus death, to satisfying biological needs or not. This answer does not tell us how people's life experiences impact what they want. Indeed, the "survival" answer predicts that motivation to do something would be a direct function of the extent to which that something satisfies biological needs or contributes to survival. But this is not the case. For example, people choose to eat junk food snacks, not because they have nutritional value or are healthy for them—indeed, they know the opposite to be true—but because they like the flavor of these snacks. It is about their experience when eating the snack and not about need satisfaction or survival. Emphasizing functions associated with survival will not help us to understand our everyday motivational choices.

People Want to Maximize Pleasure and Minimize Pain

As discussed earlier, the most common answer to what people want is to maximize pleasure and minimize pain. This answer has a long history going back (at least) to Greek discussions of the hedonic principle. Jeremy Bentham (1781/1988), the highly influential 18th-century English philosopher, argued that pleasure and pain dictate what people do. For Bentham, even the value or utility of something was based on its relation to maximizing pleasure. For example, he defined utility as "that principle which approves or disapproves of every action whatsoever, according to the tendency which it appears to have to augment or diminish the happiness of the party whose interest is in question" (p. 2). In the first half of the 20th century, Freud (1950/1920) described motivation as a "hedonism of the future." As another example, Orval Hobart Mowrer (1960) proposed that the fundamental principle underlying motivated learning was approaching hoped for end-states and avoiding feared end-states (see also Atkinson, 1964). Closing out the century, a book edited by Daniel Kahneman, Ed Diener, and Norbert Schwarz (1999), contained over two dozen papers by world-renowned psychologists and economists whose purpose was to set *The Foundations of Hedonic Psychology*.

There is little question that pleasant experiences, such as enjoying sweet drinks or warm baths, are motivating. Indeed, they can be so motivating that they even trump the motivation to satisfy basic biological needs, as when animals make choices on the basis of hedonic experiences independent of any biological need being satisfied (e.g., Eisenberger, 1972). There are early studies, for example, showing that animals not only prefer sweet water with saccharin to regular water, but they also prefer sweet food to a physiologically better food, such as a food that is more beneficial for an animal given its vitamin deficiency (see Woodworth & Schlosberg, 1954).

So did the Greeks have it right? I believe that there is a problem with hedonism being anointed for centuries as *the* answer because it has taken attention away from other basic motivational principles that are independent of pleasure and pain per se. These other principles need to be included in the story of motivation in order to understand phenomena that otherwise would make no sense (see Higgins, 1997).

Consider, for example, the phenomenon of addiction. It is commonly believed that addictive behaviors, such as smoking opium or tobacco, gambling, drinking alcohol, and so on, are fundamentally motivated by a search for pleasure, by the pleasant high or kick that the activity provides. But many experts in the area of addiction call this belief a myth. For example, Lance Dodes (2002), an addiction treatment expert, stated: "No addiction is fundamentally motivated by a search for pleasure. On the contrary, addictions are compulsively driven whether they lead to pleasure or not" (p. 206). Moreover, there are phases of addiction in which the motivation to engage in the addictive activity increases even though the pleasure experienced from engagement in the activity decreases. Kent Berridge and Terry Robinson, experts in the neuroscience of addiction, provided critical insight into these phenomena by distinguishing psychologically between brain systems related to *liking* and those related to *wanting*. Specifically, they distinguished between pleasure/pain (hedonic) feelings related to liking something, and incentive motivations related to wanting something (see Berridge & Robinson, 2003; Robinson & Berridge, 2003).

Phenomena like people engaging in addictive activities, as well as people participating in extreme sports that are both dangerous and grueling, suggest that there is more to what people really want than "survival" and "pleasure." In addiction, the intensity of wanting to engage in an addictive activity need not correspond with the intensity of liking for the activity.

In extreme sports, both survival and pleasure can be risked for the sake of an activity that is extremely difficult and challenging. What, then, is the motivation underlying these activities? What is it that people really want? I believe that the best answer is this: People want to be effective.

People Want to Be Effective in Life Pursuits

This answer to what people really want did not originate with me. There is a long history of great scholars within and outside of psychology who have proposed this answer. In the first half of the 20th century, both John Maynard Keynes, the renowned British economist, and Robert Woodworth, the psychologist who coined the term *drive*, independently recognized the importance of the motivation to be effective. Other major contributors in the 20th century to the notion that people want to be effective include Donald Hebb (e.g., 1955), Jean Piaget (e.g., 1952), Robert White (e.g., 1959), Albert Bandura (e.g., 1982), and Edward Deci and Richard Ryan (e.g., 1985).[3]

My version of the proposal that what people want is to be effective uses the term *effective* rather than *efficacy* (Bandura, 1982) or *effectance* (White, 1959) or other terms because it is a more common term in everyday language and its formal dictionary definitions capture best what I have in mind, and what others have said, about this motivation (see Pearsall, 1998): (a) *having the power of acting upon something;* (b) *that part of a force that is instrumental in producing a result;* (c) *executing or accomplishing a notable effect;* (d) *fit for work or service*. Apart from my use of the term *effective*, the main difference between my approach and the earlier approaches that inspired it is my emphasis on the need to distinguish among three distinct ways of being motivated to be effective. Indeed, it is precisely because of this aspect of my approach that truth motivation can be highlighted as a critical and distinct part of the story of motivation. It is time then to distinguish among the three ways of being effective in life pursuits: value effectiveness, control effectiveness, and truth effectiveness.

Three Ways of Being Effective in Life Pursuits

Value Effectiveness

By *value effectiveness*, I mean actors being successful in ending with the outcomes they desire. Value effectiveness is about success with respect to outcomes, about the consequences of goal pursuit—success in ending with benefits

[3]For descriptions of the contributions of these scholars to the notion that what people want is to be effective, see Higgins (2011).

versus costs, pleasure versus pain, biological needs satisfied versus unsatisfied. Simply put, *value effectiveness is being successful in having what's desired*. It should be emphasized that what matters for value effectiveness is ending with the desired outcomes and not the way this ending came about, whether through a proxy, through collaboration with others, or through our own actions.

Value effectiveness was emphasized by drive theories (e.g., Hull, 1943, 1952) and the hedonic principle. For drive theories, it was the value derived from the benefits of satisfying primary biological needs, such as reducing hunger (e.g., finding food) or reducing fear (e.g., escaping danger). For the hedonic principle, it was the value derived from the benefits of making something pleasant happen or something painful not happen. Goal theories have also emphasized value effectiveness, with motivation constituting forces within us that are goal-directed or purposive (see A. J. Elliot & Fryer, 2008; E. S. Elliott & Dweck, 1988; Kruglanski et al., 2002; McDougall, 1914; Pervin, 1989). In social psychology at least, a major influence on this conceptualization of motivation was Kurt Lewin's work on goal-directed action and goal striving within a field of forces where positive value relates to a force of attraction and negative valence relates to a force of repulsion (Lewin, 1935, 1951). Woodworth (1921), once again, said it clearly: "What persists, in purposive behavior, is the tendency towards some end or goal. The purposeful person wants something he has not yet got, and is striving towards some future result" (p. 70).

Control Effectiveness

By *control effectiveness*, I mean actors experiencing success at managing what is required (procedures, competencies, resources) to make something happen (or not happen). Having control relates to exercising direction or restraint upon action; to having power or authority to guide or manage; to having influence over something (Pearsall, 1998). *Control effectiveness is being successful in managing what happens*. Whereas value effectiveness relates to outcomes (benefits vs. costs) and truth effectiveness relates to reality (real vs. illusion), control effectiveness relates to *strength* (strong vs. weak influence over something). It is very general. People can have strong versus weak muscles, eyesight, intellect, character, arguments, willpower, teamwork, and so on. Managers, leaders, and administrators can be strong or weak.

While high control effectiveness increases the likelihood of beneficial outcomes, it is separate from outcomes, as reflected in maxims such as "It's not whether you win or lose, it is how you play the game." In victory or defeat, you play with skill and courage—with strength. Indeed, control effectiveness can trump value effectiveness. Consider, for example, a study with rats that learned that by pressing a lever they could make a food pellet fall into a food tray where they could eat it. In one experimental condition, a food dish was placed in the cage, which meant that the rats could obtain the same food pellets for free (i.e., without having to work for them). On occasion a rat would accidentally push the free food dish in front of the food tray. Despite the fact that they could effortlessly attain the food from the free food dish in front of them, the rats actually pushed the food dish *out of the way* (not eating from it), and then pressed the lever to make a food pellet fall into the food tray where they ate it (see Carder & Berkowitz, 1970). Such behavior is about control effectiveness and not just about value effectiveness. If it were just about value effectiveness, the rats would eat from the free food dish, thereby maximizing the benefits/costs ratio, given that it would be the same beneficial food for less cost in effort (see also Chapter 7, this volume).

Truth Effectiveness

By *truth effectiveness*, I mean actors being successful in knowing what is real. The root meaning of *truth* (as well as *trust*) relates to *true*; *truth* is the quality of being *true*. Something being *true* means being in accordance with an actual state of affairs, being consistent with the facts; conforming to or agreeing with an essential reality; being that which is the case, representing things as they are—in brief, knowing what is real or what is reality (Pearsall, 1998). *True* also relates to accuracy; to being correct, right, and legitimate; to being genuine, honest, and faithful. It is contrasted with being imaginary, spurious, and counterfeit. Thus, *truth effectiveness is being successful in establishing what's real*.

Value effectiveness—having desired results—is critical for humans and other animals. But so is truth effectiveness—knowing what's real in the world, representing things as they are. Without truth effectiveness we would bump into walls, we would live in a world that William James (1948/1890) referred to as "one great blooming, buzzing confusion" (p. 462).

Young children, and sometimes adults as well, find it difficult to distinguish reality from fantasy. Children may fear what is hiding in their closet, and some adults have paranoid delusions. What is reality to one religious group is mere illusion or delusion to another. But what is clear is that each individual and each group is strongly motivated to know what is real—to attain truth effectiveness. This plays out in various ways, including wanting to know what is accuracy, or what is correct or incorrect, right or wrong, legitimate or illegitimate, honest or deceitful, genuine or fraudulent. The different ways that people establish reality, find and assign meaning to the events in their lives, is the focus of this chapter.

Given the dominant position of the hedonic principle within motivation, the difference between truth effectiveness and the hedonic principle needs to be emphasized. It is common knowledge that learning the truth about ourselves or those we care about can be painful, and yet we often seek the truth even when we know it will be painful. When something pleasant but unexpected happens to people, they often want to know why it happened. Others will tell them to just enjoy it and not be concerned about why it happened. Yet, they still want to know why.

Once again the movie *The Truman Show* illustrates this characteristic clearly. As I mentioned earlier, Truman's life on the reality TV show is designed to be all pleasure and no pain. But there is one exception. He is anxious about being on the water because he believes his father drowned in a boating accident. But unknown to him, this event, like his entire life, was manufactured as part of the TV show. The actor who played his father never actually drowned in a boating accident but, instead, was a victim of his character being written out of the show. When Truman discovers the truth about his "father" when he accidentally sees him again (along with some other accidents), he finally realizes that his life has been manufactured by the TV show. Everyone tries to reassure him, including the executive producer, Christof, who argues that there is no more truth in the real world than there is in his own, artificial world. Despite everyone reassuring him and despite his having a life of pleasure and no pain, Truman risks actual death by sailing across the water he fears because he needs to follow up his discovery and seek the truth. Like Adam and Eve, he leaves a hedonic paradise for an uncertain future, but a future where he can establish what's real.

In sum, truth effectiveness, that is, wanting to be successful in establishing what's real, is one way that people want to be effective in their life pursuits. It is distinct from value effectiveness, that is, wanting to be successful in having desired results, and control effectiveness, wanting to be successful in managing what happens. Historically, truth effectiveness has received the least attention within the major psychological models of motivation. It is value effectiveness that has been given the starring role in most psychological models. But even control effectiveness on occasion has received top billing, as in self-regulation theory (e.g., Carver & Scheier, 1981, 1998), self-determination theory (e.g., Deci & Ryan, 1985, 2000), and action set theory (e.g., Gollwitzer, Fujita, & Oettingen, 2004; Heckhausen & Gollwitzer, 1987). As will be seen in the next section, the importance of truth effectiveness is revealed in several important psychological mechanisms—mechanisms that underlie the different ways that the motive for truth is fulfilled. But these mechanisms have not previously been grouped together as reflecting the general role of truth effectiveness in motivation. In fact, some members of the group, such as categorization processes, have not even been considered part of motivation. But when the mechanisms *are* grouped together, as in the next section, it becomes clear that truth effectiveness is a major player in motivation.

HOW THE MOTIVE FOR TRUTH IS FULFILLED

Is it real? This is a question that everyone asks at one point or another (see Brickman, 1978), and the answer is not always obvious. All of us can find it difficult to distinguish between what is real and what is illusion or imagination, both for present events and past events. If we decide that something is not real, it can become less meaningful to us or even become meaningless, as when we decide that something is "impossible" or "ridiculous." When we fail to establish truth, we feel confused and bewildered. William James (1948/1890) described beliefs as resulting from a *reality check* on thoughts. He described believing as being an emotional experience of consent; that is, we decide that what had been just a thought before is now taken as truth.

Generally speaking, people prefer the stability and solidity of truth over the agitation and contradictions of doubt. This means that when less accurate knowledge of something provides a stronger experience of success at establishing what's real than more accurate knowledge (i.e., more supported by facts or evidence), people will sacrifice the more accurate knowledge in order to experience truth effectiveness. This is the power behind political and religious ideologies, or pet theories, and it is what makes the striving for truth so tricky. We are not only motivated to be accurate but we also want to experience ourselves as accurate. We want to experience ourselves as being successful in having the understandings, beliefs, and knowledge which are the truth, which represent what is real. This additional motive of wanting to experience our inner state representations of the world as being the truth is uniquely human.

Thus, deciding whether something is or is not real is a critical part of assigning meaningfulness to things, which in turn determines our motivational priorities. In this way, seeking truth, trying to establish what's real, is a critical part of motivation. How then do we establish what's real? How do we go about fulfilling our motive for truth?

When answering these questions in this section, my emphasis is on motivational mechanisms rather than cognitive mechanisms, while recognizing that the motivational versus cognitive distinction can itself be problematic (see, e.g., Sorrentino & Higgins, 1986, and, more recently, Eitam & Higgins, 2010). An example of a motivational factor would be deciding something is real because other people with whom one wants a shared reality treat it as real (e.g., Hardin & Higgins, 1996). An example of a cognitive mechanism would be to treat the memory as real (rather than imagined) to the extent that detailed perceptual information, as well as time and place information, was recollected (Johnson & Raye, 1981). Sometimes both motivational and cognitive mechanisms are involved when people seek the truth, as when they question *what* happened and *why* it happened, such as "Did I pass or fail the test?" and, if I failed, "Why did I fail?" People are motivated to find answers to *what* happened and *why* it happened, and cognitive processes are involved in finding such answers. My interest is in people's motivation to find answers to these questions.

This section begins with these *What?* and *Why?* questions as the first mechanisms for fulfilling our motive for truth because of their long-term centrality in the literature on truth seeking. After reviewing these mechanisms, I discuss how reality is established from cognitive consistency. Then I consider the contributions of social reality and shared reality to establishing what's real.[4]

Establishing Reality From Judging "What?"

A mother is awakened by a crying-like sound in the middle of the night. She asks herself a series of questions: "Is that something crying or am I still dreaming?" "Are my ears playing tricks on me?" "Is it a cry that I am hearing or just the wind?" "Is that cry from my cat or from my child?" and "Why is my child crying?" Each step of the way the mother is trying to find the truth, to determine what is real and not real. This is not idle curiosity. It is deadly serious. The mother wants to know the truth, needs to know what is *really* happening. Only then can she know what to do next (recall Chapter 1, this volume).

The mother is not questioning whether an event occurred. Something definitely did happen, but exactly *what* kind of something is it? The something could just be her dreaming. Or she might be certain that there was really a crying-like sound. She might even have initially recognized the crying-like sound as being a cry from some living thing—either her cat or her child. What she is now questioning is whether this initial recognition was real. Was it really a cry from some living thing? For the mother it really matters whether the crying-like sound was made by the wind or was made by her cat or her child. Similarly, when we see what is clearly a friendly appearing behavior, we don't question this appearance. Rather, we question whether the person who produced the behavior is being genuinely friendly or is just faking.

For people generally, it matters *what* someone's behavior really means, and what it really means depends on the inner state of the person that led to its production. Did the person intend to produce the behavior and its consequences, or were they just accidental (see Heider, 1958; Jones & Davis, 1965; Malle, 2004)? There are descriptions of attributional processes in the social psychological literature that begin with a behavior being categorized as "X," such as "aggressive," and then discuss how people decide whether to

[4]In Higgins (2011), I discuss more fully the different mechanisms for establishing what's real.

attribute the cause of the behavior to the actor's character, that is, the actor is "X" (e.g., "aggressive"), or to attribute the cause of the behavior to situational circumstances (e.g., Jones & Davis, 1965). But if the behavior was actually caused by the situational circumstances, then the person was not in full control of the behavior, and thus the behavior and its consequences were *not* intended. And for many behaviors, such as "aggressive" behavior, this means that the conditions for categorizing the behavior as "X" were *not met* to begin with. That is, the fact that the behavior was "aggressive" cannot be treated as a given, as something that's real. This is because for many behavioral categories (e.g., aggressive, kind, helpful, rude, competitive), the *intentions* of the actor are *essential* to the definition of the category.

Once intentionality is inferred (consciously or unconsciously), what comes next? Several person perception models describe the judgmental process as involving a sequence of processing stages that begin with initial low-level steps that are largely automatic or unconscious and proceed to higher level steps that are more controlled or conscious (e.g., Brewer, 1988; Gilbert, 1990; Trope, 1986). For example, there can be two steps in getting from seeing someone's change in mouth expression to categorizing the expression as "friendly." The first step involves treating the expression as a real "smile" (i.e., where the expression and its consequences on the viewer were intended), and the second step involves treating the "smile" as a "friendly" behavior. Yaacov Trope (1986) described how the situation surrounding the production of a behavior, such as observing someone "smiling" when he or she greets another person at an airport versus after receiving a flattering compliment, can be essential for identification, such as identifying the first smile as "friendly" versus the second smile as "embarrassed." But people need not be aware, and often are not aware, of the influence of the situation on this early identification process.

It can be difficult to establish "what" something is, to find the truth about something. But the motivation to do so is strong because "what" something is has implications for what to do next. In this way, establishing what's real can support managing what happens (control) and having desired results (value). But knowing "what" the world is like or will be like does not have to support value or control effectiveness in order for people to want it. More generally, being effective in truth is worthwhile independent of any contribution to value or control effectiveness. This becomes even clearer as we move from wanting to know "what?" to wanting to know "why?"

Establishing Reality From Answering "Why?"

A remarkable fact about humans is that they are time travelers (Tulving, 2005). They think about the future. This includes daydreaming and fantasizing about the future. But what people do most often is plan for the future, and they want the future they are planning for to become real. They want their *predictions* about it to become real. And the psychological literature has shown that predictability is motivating independent of controllability or having desired results (see, e.g., D'Amato & Safarjan, 1979; Miller, Greco, Vigorito, & Marlin, 1983; Mineka, 1985). This occurred to me several years ago when I learned that my downstairs neighbor was suffering from my dog's piercing whining whenever it was left alone in my apartment. I could not stop my dog from whining whenever I left home, and I could not stay home forever. What I could do was leave a message for my neighbor each time I left home that told her (approximately) when I would be leaving and when I would return. In less than a week after instituting this plan, I heard back from my neighbor that she was no longer suffering from my dog's whining. The whining still happened each time I left, and my neighbor had no control over its happening. But she could now predict its beginning and its end, and this predictability made matters much better.

Predictability is important to people (and other animals as well). It is especially important when the predictions concern the actions of self and others. Accurate prediction requires knowing in the present what will remain stable about themselves or others over time. In their search for what is real, people often do not stop at deciding "what" something is. They often want to proceed with additional questions whose answers tell them more about inner states, such as why another person behaved a particular way. This next step of going from "what" people do to "why" they do it is the kind of truth seeking that has received the most attention in the social psychological literature (recall, again, Chapter 1). It concerns the process of drawing inferences about other individuals' abilities, beliefs, attitudes, or personality, including trying to understand our own actions and feelings (for recent reviews of this extensive literature, see Hilton, 2007; Kruglanski & Sleeth-Keppler, 2007; Malle, 2004; Uleman, Saribay, & Gonzalez, 2008). People want especially to know the truth about those inner states of someone that are stable over time, such as that person's abilities, attitudes, goals, and so on, because this knowledge will allow them to make more accurate predictions about what that person is likely to do in the future—seeking in the present to know what will be real about that person in the future (see Heider, 1958; Jones & Davis, 1965; Trope & Higgins, 1993; Weiner et al., 1971).

In addition to learning how individuals' inner states affect what they do, people learn how different kinds of situations press for different kinds of behaviors from people generally. And they use this knowledge to predict future reality, such as learning about the social norms of behavior for a party versus a funeral. They learn as well that there are ethnic, cultural, and personality type differences in determining which kinds of behaviors are likely in which kinds of situations, such as learning that someone with an authoritarian personality will be dominant when interacting with a status inferior but will be submissive when interacting with a status superior. They also learn that different categories of people like different kinds of things, so that when a member of that category chooses to do something, such as a young child choosing to play with a toy, it establishes a reality about the toy being fun for children to play with (the situation) rather than a reality about what the child is like as an individual (the person). People want to know what's real for all of these different kinds of situational information and not just information about individuals' stable traits.

Establishing Reality From Cognitive Consistency

In his introductory chapter to the landmark book *Theories of Cognitive Consistency: A Sourcebook* (Abelson et al., 1968), Theodore Newcomb (1968, p. xv) described the remarkable simultaneous emergence of cognitive consistency theories: "They were proposed under different names, such as balance, congruity, symmetry, dissonance, but all had in common the notion that the person behaves in a way that maximizes the internal consistency of his cognitive system." It is not possible in this chapter to review the conceptual and empirical contributions of the various different theories of cognitive consistency (for overviews, see Abelson et al., 1968; Kruglanski, 1989; Zajonc, 1968). Instead, I briefly illustrate how cognitive consistency motives can establish reality by considering the two cognitive consistency theories that have been the most influential—Fritz Heider's (1958) balance theory and, especially, Leon Festinger's (1957) cognitive dissonance theory.

The classic condition in balance theory involves the relations among three cognitive elements, such as *me*, *my friend*, and *my enemy:* the relation between *me* and *my friend*, the relation between *me* and *my enemy*, and the relation between *my friend* and *my enemy*. What if I were to learn that *my friend* and *my enemy* have become friends? Then there would be an imbalance among the three cognitive elements. People are motivated to resolve the imbalance. It should be emphasized that the motive to resolve an imbalanced reality is not a hedonic motive to reduce a painful condition. Heider (1958) explicitly noted that the tension produced by imbalance can have a pleasing effect and that balance can be unpleasantly boring. Thus, it is not the hedonic nature of imbalance (vs. balance) that is critical to the experience. Rather, imbalance is the feeling that things "do not add up" (p. 180); that is, they are so difficult to understand as to be confusing.

In a thoughtful analysis of Heider's (1958) balance theory, Robert Abelson (1983) gave the following insightful comment:

> Heider wrote as though with two minds on whether imbalanced triads produce intrinsic discomfort, or rather serve as a warning of potential situational trouble or a signal of possible existing trouble. . . . Since certain perceptual structures, such as circles and straight lines, are good figures with imperative properties, by analogy there must be so-called conceptual good figures. . . . The alternative theoretical grounding for the balance principle is motivational rather than perceptual. (p. 40).

I prefer a motivational rather than perceptual grounding for the balance principle.

An imbalance signals that some part of our understanding of a pattern of relations does not accurately represent reality, which is a problem for truth effectiveness. Either my friend does not really like my enemy, or my enemy could become my friend if given a chance, or my friend is really my enemy or soon will become so. The imbalance gives me pause to re-think what I really know about each part of the pattern. What insight or new information could help me to establish a new reality that makes sense? Perhaps my friend is only pretending to like my enemy for some ulterior motive, such as to function like a spy for me. Soon my friend will reveal the pretense and dissolve that relationship. Now that makes sense; my friend does not really like my enemy and that relationship will not last.[5] As illustrated in this example, searching for cognitive balance can establish a new reality—a new present reality or a new future reality.

Resolving cognitive dissonance can also create a new present or future reality. According to Festinger (1957), "the human organism tries to establish internal harmony, consistency, or congruity among his opinions, attitudes, knowledge, and values" (p. 260). When people fail to do so, they experience dissonance, which gives rise to pressures to reduce that dissonance. Importantly, Festinger (1957) stated, "In short, I am proposing that dissonance, that is, the existence of nonfitting relations among cognitions, is a motivating factor in its own right" (p. 3).

A well-known source of dissonance is expectancy disconfirmation, as classically illustrated in *When Prophecy Fails* (Festinger, Riecken, & Schachter, 1956). A group of people believed that alien beings from planet Clarion would arrive on earth on a specific date and take them away on a flying saucer, thereby saving them from the great flood that would then end the world. In preparation for leaving the earth, the group members had made sacrifices, including quitting jobs and giving away money and possessions. The date came and went without any flying saucer, and this created dissonance in the group members

[5]I should note that my motivational account and Abelson's account are not precisely the same. My account emphasizes truth effectiveness more than control effectiveness, whereas the opposite was true for Abelson.

because the belief for which they had sacrificed was disconfirmed by what actually happened. How could the dissonance be resolved?

One possible way that the group members could resolve their dissonance and make sense of what happened would be to establish some new reality. This solution would involve creating new truths that are consistent with their previous beliefs and actions. In fact, the group members did make new judgments about the present and new predictions about the future that were consistent with their original belief, with the disconfirming event being treated like a bump in the road. After disconfirmation, for example, there was a sharp increase in the frequency with which group members decided that other people who telephoned them or visited their group were *actually spacemen*. They tried to get orders and messages from the "spacemen" for a future reality that would be consistent with their original beliefs. One of the leaders of the group even suggested that it was their true beliefs—*the light of truth*—that had spared their area while cataclysms *were* happening elsewhere. Although the case described in *When Prophecy Fails* is unusual, people do often experience discomfort when their expectancies are disconfirmed, and they try to make sense of what happened by changing beliefs and adding new beliefs in order to make the whole set of beliefs consistent.

Establishing Reality From Social and Shared Reality

In his social comparison theory, Festinger (1950, 1954) discussed how physical reality can often be ambiguous and difficult to grasp, and when it is, people initiate social comparison processes in which they depend on others' judgments to construct a *social reality*. Festinger also proposed that physical reality takes precedence over social reality, but that is not always the case. The motivation to establish a shared reality with others can trump physical reality. This is illustrated in Asch's (1952) classic study in which each participant was faced with a unanimous, and incorrect, group decision about which line matched the length of a standard line. When the discrimination was easy and participants were fully confident in their knowing the correct answer, they rarely chose the group's (incorrect) answer. But when the discrimination was more difficult—but still clear enough that they initially all chose the correct answer—then they were more likely to reconsider and change their answer to the group's (incorrect) answer. This shows that individuals can be motivated to treat something as real, to accept something as the truth, even though the physical evidence contradicts their decision.

Another classic study, this one by Sherif (1936), also illustrates how a social reality, a shared reality, can trump people's initial perceptual experience of a physical reality—in this case, a vague physical reality. Sherif had participants in a completely dark room estimate the movement of a point of light that, although actually stationary, perceptually appeared to move (the *autokinetic effect*). When individuals were brought together in a group and each gave independent estimates of the direction and amount of the light's movement, their initial judgments were typically quite disparate. However, over several trials the group members slowly abandoned their initially disparate judgments and converged on a mutually shared estimate of the light's direction and amount of movement—a *social norm* for that group regarding the light's movement.

What is striking about Sherif's (1936) findings is that a norm about what's real can be socially constructed without a basis in physical reality, and this norm will still have real consequences—*it will be treated as real*. Upon reflection, however, we should not be surprised because treating as real our shared realities with others is a necessary condition of human culture. And the medium in which this most often occurs is interpersonal communication.

Communication through language plays a critically important role in human societies. It requires, among other things, that members of a linguistic community agree on what words to use to name different things. One linguistic community agrees to assign the name *dog* to the furry animal that barks and fetches things whereas another linguistic community agrees to call it *chien*. There is no reality that dictates which of these sounds is the right name for this animal. But each linguistic community agrees to use a particular name—a social norm that is maintained across generations and is used by individual members when they are alone by themselves.

But the motive to create a shared reality about things in the world goes beyond social norms about the names of things. The motive to share reality is one of the most important goals of communication more generally (see Echterhoff, Higgins, & Groll, 2005; Echterhoff, Higgins, Kopietz, & Groll, 2008; Higgins, 1981, 1992). And when people have this goal, they are motivated to describe something in a manner that matches their audience's beliefs or attitudes about it.

In an early study on this phenomenon (Higgins & Rholes, 1978), college student participants were asked to describe a target person, Donald, based on a short essay that described his behaviors. The behaviors were evaluatively ambiguous in that they could be labeled either positively or negatively, such as behaviors that could be labeled either as *stubborn* or as *persistent:*

> Once Donald makes up his mind to do something it is as good as done, no matter how long it might take or how difficult the going might be. Only rarely does he change his mind even when it might well be better if he did. (Higgins & Rholes, 1978, p. 366)

The participants were told to describe the target person (without mentioning his name) to an audience who knew him and who would try, based on their message, to identify him from among a set of other possible persons (a referential communication task). After being told in an offhand manner that their audience either likes or dislikes Donald, the participants produced their message for their audience.

What this and dozens of other studies found is that communicators tune their message to suit the attitude of their audience, a phenomenon called *audience tuning;* they produce an evaluatively positive message for an audience they believe likes Donald and a negative message for an audience they believe dislikes Donald. These messages are *not* accurate descriptions of the information the communicators were given about the target because the ambiguous tone of the information is not retained. Instead, the information is changed in an evaluative direction that matches the audience's attitude toward the target. The communicators create *a new truth* about the target that allows them to share reality with their audience.

But this is not all that happened in this and other studies. Later, the participants were asked to recall as accurately as they could, that is, word for word, the information about Donald's behaviors that was contained in the original essay they had received. The study found that the evaluative tone of the communicators' own memory for the original essay information matched the evaluative tone of their previous message; the behaviors were recalled as being more positive when they had tuned positively toward their audience and were recalled as being more negative when they had tuned negatively. And this memory bias was even greater when the recall took place weeks after message production than when it took place in the same session as the message production. In sum, participants ended up believing and remembering what they *said* rather than what they originally learned about the target—the *saying-is-believing* effect (Higgins & Rholes, 1978).

The findings of this study, which have been replicated in many other studies (see Echterhoff, Higgins, & Levine, 2009), show that communicating with a shared reality goal can lead people to treat an audience-tuned message as being the truth about the topic of the message, even though the message is a biased account of the actual facts. But how do we know that this behavior occurs because the communication had a shared reality goal? Might communication with any goal have the same effect because the information contained in the message influences reconstructive memory? If so, then the same memory effect should occur when the communication goal is something other than a shared reality goal, as long as the message tuning to the audience's attitude remains as strong. This is not the case, however. When the communication goal, for example, is entertainment (e.g., it would be fun to exaggerate or caricaturize the target to suit the audience's attitude) or instrumental (e.g., tune toward the audience in order to make the audience like and later reward the communicator), the amount of message tuning to the audience's attitude is just as strong, but the saying-is-believing effect disappears (see Echterhoff et al., 2008).

What about the other shared reality assumption that the message was tuned to agree with the audience's attitude? Does it matter whether or not the communicator regards the audience as being an appropriate partner with whom to share reality? Research on both social comparison processes and group-anchored knowledge indicates that individuals who are sufficiently similar or trustworthy would be regarded as more appropriate partners with whom to share reality than partners lacking such qualities (e.g., Festinger, 1950; Kruglanski, Pierro, Mannetti, & De Grada, 2006; Suls, Martin, & Wheeler, 2002). An audience that is or is not in the communicator's ingroup would be particularly important in this regard. In fact, there is clear evidence from communication studies that the audience's group membership does matter. In contrast to the original studies where the audience belonged to the communicators' ingroup, in studies where the audience belonged to an outgroup, as when communicators were German students and their audience was German-speaking but Turkish, the audience-tuning still occurred, but the saying-is-believing effect disappeared (Echterhoff et al., 2005, 2008).

The fact that people treat audience-tuned messages as saying something real about the world around us, even when the messages are distorted to suit the audience, has important implications for the construction of cultural knowledge. Communicating to others with a shared reality goal is ubiquitous in human interactions. Given this fact, it could play an important role in the construction of culturally-shared memories and evaluations of the world around us—a basic mechanism for constructing social, cultural, and political beliefs (see Echterhoff et al., 2009; Hausmann, Levine, & Higgins, 2008; Jost, Ledgerwood, & Hardin, 2008; Lau, Chiu, & Lee, 2001).

Rather than remembering information as originally given, communicators will remember whichever version of the information was contained in their messages—messages that were tuned to take the viewpoint of their audience into account. Constant social tuning toward audiences creates communities where the members share a biased perspective on the world. And because this process occurs not only for individuals as the topic of the message but also for groups as the topic of the message (e.g., Hausmann et al., 2008; Lyons & Kashima, 2003), it can contribute to the development of community-shared stereotypic beliefs about other groups. This is the downside of our truth motivation, and it contributes to intergroup conflict from different groups having different truths about the world and our place within it. Truth motivation has severe potential costs when it contributes to intergroup conflict—potentially deadly ideological wars. However, truth motivation also has essential benefits for humans because by establishing what's real, why things happen, what makes sense, and then sharing our truth with others, we can acquire the kind of shared knowledge that is the cornerstone of civilizations.

REFERENCES

Abelson, R. P. (1983). Whatever became of consistency theory? *Personality and Social Psychology Bulletin*, 9, 37–64. doi:10.1177/0146167283091006

Abelson, R. P., Aronson, E., McGuire, W. J., Newcomb, T. M., Rosenberg, M. J., & Tannenbaum, P. H. (Eds.). (1968). *Theories of cognitive consistency: A sourcebook*. Chicago: Rand McNally.

Asch, S. E. (1952). *Social psychology*. Englewood Cliffs, NJ: Prentice-Hall. doi:10.1037/10025-000

Atkinson, J. W. (1964). *An introduction to motivation*. Princeton, NJ: Van Nostrand.

Bandura, A. (1982). Self-efficacy mechanism in human agency. *American Psychologist*, *37*, 122–147. doi:10.1037/0003-066X.37.2.122

Bentham, J. (1988). *The principles of morals and legislation*. Amherst, NY: Prometheus Books. (Original work published 1781)

Berridge, K. C., & Robinson, T. E. (2003). Parsing reward. *Trends in Neurosciences*, 26, 507–513. doi:10.1016/S0166-2236(03)00233-9

Brewer, M. B. (1988). A dual-process model of impression formation. In T. K. Srull and R. S. Wyer, Jr. (Eds.), *Advances in social cognition* (Vol. 1, pp. 1–36). Hillsdale, NJ: Erlbaum.

Brickman, P. (1978). Is it real? In J. H. Harvey, W. Ickes, & R. F. Kidd (Eds.), *New directions in attribution research* (Vol. 2, pp. 5–34). Hillsdale, NJ: Erlbaum.

Carder, B., & Berkowitz, K. (1970, February 27). Rats' preference for earned in comparison with free food. *Science*, *167*, 1273–1274. doi:10.1126/science.167.3922.1273

Carver, C. S., & Scheier, M. F. (1981). *Attention and self-regulation: A control-theory approach to human behavior*. New York, NY: Springer-Verlag.

Carver, C. S., & Scheier, M. F. (1998). *On the self-regulation of behavior*. New York, NY: Cambridge University Press.

D'Amato, M. R., & Safarjan, W. R. (1979). Preference for information about shock duration. *Animal Learning & Behavior*, *7*, 89–94. doi:10.3758/BF03209663

Deci, E. L., & Ryan, R. M. (1985). *Intrinsic motivation and self-determination in human behavior*. New York, NY: Plenum Press.

Deci, E. L., & Ryan, R. M. (2000). The "what" and the "why" of goal pursuits: Human needs and the self-determination of behavior. *Psychological Inquiry*, *11*, 227–268. doi:10.1207/S15327965PLI1104_01

Dodes, L. M. (2002). *The heart of addiction*. New York, NY: HarperCollins.

Echterhoff, G., Higgins, E. T., & Groll, S. (2005). Audience-tuning effects on memory: The role of shared reality. *Journal of Personality and Social Psychology, 89*, 257–276. doi:10.1037/0022-3514.89.3.257

Echterhoff, G., Higgins, E. T., Kopietz, R., & Groll, S. (2008). How communication goals determine when audience tuning biases memory. *Journal of Experimental Psychology: General, 137*, 3–21. doi:10.1037/0096-3445.137.1.3

Echterhoff, G., Higgins, E. T., & Levine, J. M. (2009). Shared reality: Experiencing commonality with others' inner states about the world. *Perspectives on Psychological Science, 4*, 496–521. doi:10.1111/j.1745-6924.2009.01161.x

Eisenberger, R. (1972). Explanation of rewards that do not reduce tissue needs. *Psychological Bulletin, 77*, 319–339. doi:10.1037/h0032483

Eitam, B., & Higgins, E. T. (2010). Motivation in mental accessibility: Relevance of a Representation (ROAR) as a new framework. *Social and Personality Psychology Compass, 4*, 951–967. doi:10.1111/j.1751-9004.2010.00309.x

Elliot, A. J., & Fryer, J. W. (2008). The goal construct in psychology. In J. Y. Shah & W. L. Gardner (Eds.), *Handbook of motivation science* (pp. 235–250). New York, NY: Guilford Press.

Elliott, E. S., & Dweck, C. S. (1988). Goals: An approach to motivation and achievement. *Journal of Personality and Social Psychology, 54*, 5–12. doi:10.1037/0022-3514.54.1.5

Feldman, E. S., Niccol, A., Rudin, S., Schroeder, A. (Producers), & Weir, P. (Director). (1998). *The Truman show*. Universal City, CA: Universal.

Festinger, L. (1950). Informal social communication. *Psychological Review, 57*, 271–282. doi:10.1037/h0056932

Festinger, L. (1954). A theory of social comparison processes. *Human Relations, 7*, 117–140. doi:10.1177/001872675400700202

Festinger, L. (1957). *A theory of cognitive dissonance*. Evanston, IL: Row, Peterson.

Festinger, L., Riecken, H. W., & Schachter, S. (1956). *When prophecy fails: A social and psychological study of a modern group that predicted the destruction of the world*. New York, NY: Harper & Row.

Freud, S. (1950). *Beyond the pleasure principle*. New York, NY: Liveright. (Original work published 1920)

Gilbert, D. T. (1990). How mental systems believe. *American Psychologist, 46*, 107–119.

Gollwitzer, P. M., Fujita, K., & Oettingen, G. (2004). Planning and the implementation of goals. In R. F. Baumeister & K. D. Vohs (Eds.), *Handbook of self-regulation: Research, theory, and applications* (pp. 211–228). New York, NY: Guilford Press.

Hardin, C., & Higgins, E. T. (1996). "Shared reality": How social verification makes the subjective objective. In R. M. Sorrentino & E. T. Higgins (Eds.), *Handbook of motivation and cognition: The interpersonal context* (pp. 28–84). New York, NY: Guilford Press.

Hausmann, L. R. M., Levine, J. M., & Higgins, E. T. (2008). Communication and group perception: Extending the "saying is believing" effect. *Group Processes & Intergroup Relations, 11*, 539–554. doi:10.1177/1368430208095405

Hebb, D. O. (1955). Drives and the C. N. S. (conceptual nervous system). *Psychological Review, 62*, 243–254. doi:10.1037/h0041823

Heckhausen, H., & Gollwitzer, P. M. (1987). Thought contents and cognitive functioning in motivational versus volitional states of mind. *Motivation and Emotion, 11*, 101–120. doi:10.1007/BF00992338

Heider, F. (1958). *The psychology of interpersonal relations*. New York, NY: Wiley. doi:10.1037/10628-000

Higgins, E. T. (1981). The "communication game": Implications for social cognition and persuasion. In E. T. Higgins, C. P. Herman, & M. P. Zanna (Eds.), *Social cognition: The Ontario Symposium* (pp. 343–392). Hillsdale, NJ: Erlbaum.

Higgins, E. T. (1992). Achieving "shared reality" in the communication game: A social action that creates meaning. *Journal of Language and Social Psychology, 11*, 107–131. doi:10.1177/0261927X92113001

Higgins, E. T. (1997). Beyond pleasure and pain. *American Psychologist, 52*, 1280–1300. doi:10.1037/0003-066X.52.12.1280

Higgins, E. T. (2011). *Beyond pleasure and pain: How motivation works*. New York, NY: Oxford University Press. doi:10.1093/acprof:oso/9780199765829.001.0001

Higgins, E. T., & Rholes, W. S. (1978). "Saying is believing": Effects of message modification on memory and liking for the person described. *Journal of Experimental Social Psychology, 14*, 363–378. doi:10.1016/0022-1031(78)90032-X

Hilton, D. (2007). Causal explanation: From social perception to knowledge-based attribution. In I. A. W. Kruglanski & E. T. Higgins (Eds.), *Social psychology: Handbook of basic principles* (2nd ed., pp. 232–253). New York, NY: Guilford Press.

Hull, C. L. (1943). *Principles of behavior*. New York, NY: Appleton-Century-Crofts.

Hull, C. L. (1952). *A behavior system: An introduction to behavior theory concerning the individual organism*. New Haven, CT: Yale University Press.

James, W. (1948). *Psychology*. New York, NY: World. (Original work published 1890)

Johnson, M. K., & Raye, C. L. (1981). Reality monitoring. *Psychological Review, 88*, 67–85. doi:10.1037/0033-295X.88.1.67

Jones, E. E., & Davis, K. E. (1965). From acts to dispositions: The attribution process in person perception. In L. Berkowitz (Ed.), *Advances in experimental social psychology* (Vol. 2, pp. 219–266). New York, NY: Academic Press.

Jost, J. T., Ledgerwood, A., & Hardin, C. D. (2008). Shared reality, system justification, and the relational basis of ideological beliefs. *Social and Personality Psychology Compass, 2*, 171–186. doi:10.1111/j.1751-9004.2007.00056.x

Kahneman, D., Diener, E., & Schwarz, N. (1999). *Well-being: The foundations of hedonic psychology*. New York, NY: Russell Sage.

Kruglanski, A. W. (1989). *Lay epistemics and human knowledge: Cognitive and motivational bases*. New York, NY: Plenum.

Kruglanski, A. W., Pierro, A., Mannetti, L., & De Grada, E. (2006). Groups as epistemic providers: Need for closure and the unfolding of group-centrism. *Psychological Review, 113*, 84–100. doi:10.1037/0033-295X.113.1.84

Kruglanski, A. W., Shah, J. Y., Fishbach, A., Friedman, R., Chun, W. Y., & Sleeth-Keppler, D. (2002). A theory of goal systems. In M. P. Zanna (Ed.), *Advances in experimental social psychology* (Vol. 34, pp. 331–378). San Diego, CA: Academic Press.

Kruglanski, A. W., & Sleeth-Keppler, D. (2007). The principle of social judgment. In A. W. Kruglanski & E. T. Higgins (Eds.), *Social psychology: Handbook of basic principles* (2nd ed., pp. 116–137). New York, NY: Guilford Press.

Lau, I. Y.-M., Chiu, C.-Y., & Lee, S.-L. (2001). Communication and shared reality: Implications for the psychological foundations of culture. *Social Cognition, 19*, 350–371. doi:10.1521/soco.19.3.350.21467

Lewin, K. (1935). *A dynamic theory of personality*. New York, NY: McGraw-Hill.

Lewin, K. (1951). *Field theory in social science*. New York, NY: Harper.

Lyons, A., & Kashima, Y. (2003). How are stereotypes maintained through communication? The influence of stereotype sharedness. *Journal of Personality and Social Psychology, 85*, 989–1005. doi:10.1037/0022-3514.85.6.989

Malle, B. F. (2004). *How the mind explains behavior: Folk explanations, meaning, and social interaction*. Cambridge, MA: MIT Press.

McDougall, W. (1914). *An introduction to social psychology* (8th ed.). Boston, MA: Luce.

Miller, R. R., Greco, C., Vigorito, M., & Marlin, N. A. (1983). Signaled tailshock is perceived as similar to a stronger unsignaled tailshock: Implications for a functional analysis of classical conditioning. *Journal of Experimental Psychology. Animal Behavior Processes, 9*, 105–131. doi:10.1037/0097-7403.9.2.105

Mineka, S. (1985). Controllability and predictability in acquired motivation. *Annual Review of Psychology, 36*, 495–529.

Mowrer, O. H. (1960). *Learning theory and behavior*. New York, NY: Wiley. doi:10.1037/10802-000

Newcomb, T. M. (1968). Introduction. In R. P. Abelson, E. Aronson, W. J. McGuire, T. M. Newcomb, M. J. Rosenberg, & P. H. Tannenbaum (Eds.), *Theories of cognitive consistency: A sourcebook* (pp. 28–51). Chicago, IL: Rand McNally.

Osborne, B. M. (Producer), Wachowski, A., & Wachowski, D. (Directors). (1999). *The matrix*. Burbank, CA: Warner Brothers.

Pearsall, J. E. (Ed.). (1998). *The new Oxford dictionary of English*. Oxford, England: Oxford University Press.

Piaget, J. (1952). *The origins of intelligence in children*. New York, NJ: International University Press. doi:10.1037/11494-000

Pervin, L. A. (Ed.). (1989). *Goal concepts in personality and social psychology*. Hillsdale, NJ: Erlbaum.

Robinson, T. E., & Berridge, K. C. (2003). Addiction. *Annual Review of Psychology, 54*, 25–53. doi:10.1146/annurev.psych.54.101601.145237

Sherif, M. (1936). *The psychology of social norms*. New York, NY: Harper & Brothers.

Sorrentino, R. M., & Higgins, E. T. (1986). Motivation and cognition: Warming up to synergism. In R. M. Sorrentino & E. T. Higgins (Eds.), *Handbook of motivation and cognition: Foundations of social behavior* (pp. 3–19). New York, NY: Guilford.

Suls, J., Martin, R., & Wheeler, L. (2002). Social comparison: Why, with whom, and with what effect. *Current Directions in Psychological Science, 11*, 159–163. doi:10.1111/1467-8721.00191

Trope, Y. (1986). Identification and inferential processes in dispositional attribution. *Psychological Review, 93*, 239–257.

Trope, Y., & Higgins, E. T. (1993). The what, when, and how of dispositional inference: New answers and new questions. *Personality and Social Psychology Bulletin*, 19, 493–500.

Tulving, E. (2005). Episodic memory and autonoesis. Uniquely human? In H. S. Terrace & J. Metcalfe (Eds.), *The missing link in cognition: Origins of self-reflective consciousness* (pp. 3–56). Oxford, England: Oxford University Press. doi:10.1093/acprof:oso/9780195161564.003.0001

Uleman, J. S., Saribay, S. A., & Gonzalez, C. M. (2008). Spontaneous inferences, implicit impressions, and implicit theories. *Annual Review of Psychology*, 59, 329–360. doi:10.1146/annurev.psych.59.103006.093707

Weiner, B., Frieze, I., Kukla, A., Reed, L., Rest, S., & Rosenbaum, R. M. (1971). Perceiving the causes of success and failure. In E. E. Jones, D. E. Kanouse, H. H. Kelley, R. E. Nisbett, S. Valins, & B. Weiner (Eds.), *Attribution: Perceiving the causes of behavior* (pp. 95–120). Morristown, NJ: General Learning Press.

White, R. W. (1959). Motivation reconsidered: The concept of competence. *Psychological Review*, 66, 297–333. doi:10.1037/h0040934

Woodworth, R. S. (1921). *Psychology: A study of mental life*. New York, NY: Holt.

Woodworth, R. S., & Schlosberg, H. (1954). *Experimental psychology* (Rev. ed.). New York, NY: Holt, Rinehart, & Winston.

Zajonc, R. B. (1968). Cognitive theories in social psychology. In G. Lindzey & E. Aronson (Eds.), *The handbook of social psychology* (Vol. 1, pp. 320–411). Reading, MA: Addison-Wesley.

6

LAY THEORIES OF PERSONALITY AS CORNERSTONES OF MEANING

CAITLIN M. BURTON AND JASON E. PLAKS

Eleanor and Irene had been friends since childhood and had many things in common. One thing the women disagreed on, however, was whether people's personalities could change. Eleanor had an *entity theory* of personality: She believed that people never really change, for better or for worse. Irene had an *incremental theory* of personality: She believed that people's characteristics can change over time. One thing that the women shared in their adult lives was having troublesome boyfriends. Eleanor's partner, Eric, had a self-diagnosed commitment phobia. Irene's partner, Isaac, did not "believe in marriage." Both women wanted to be in a fully committed relationship and, as a result, decided to dump their respective boyfriends and move on. Six months later, however, Eric and Isaac came back into their lives, begging for a second chance. Eleanor and Irene took them back, wondering whether they were doing the right thing. Within the next month, Eric and Isaac both surprised the women with beautiful rings and proposals of marriage. Irene was

DOI: 10.1037/14040-006
The Psychology of Meaning, Keith D. Markman, Travis Proulx, and Matthew J. Lindberg (Editors)

completely overjoyed; she got her dream outcome, and Isaac had lived up to her expectation that people can change. Eleanor, on the other hand, experienced a mix of emotions. While she was overjoyed to be on the road to the altar, this joy was tinged with anxiety about Eric's apparent change in nature; in Eleanor's mind, such changes were supposed to be impossible.

Eleanor's experience of simultaneous joy and anxiety comes from Eric's improvement having dual implications. On the one hand, she felt overjoyed because she got what she desired (a committed partner). On the other hand, Eric's actions called into question the validity of Eleanor's belief that people's personalities are fixed and stable. And as we demonstrate in this chapter, the verification or violation of people's theories about the fixedness versus malleability of personality is no trivial matter. Rather, we suggest that because these (and related) theories are key sources of social expectancies, they represent cornerstones of meaning in social cognition.

Lay theories are stored assumptions about human dispositions and tendencies (Dweck, 1999; Dweck, Chiu, & Hong, 1995; Dweck & Leggett, 1988; Levy, Plaks, Hong, Chiu, & Dweck, 2001). As such, they help people to derive order and meaning from the complex and often ambiguous web of human behavior in which each individual is embedded. Two such lay theories are the entity theory and the incremental theory. These two theories generate different kinds of behavioral predictions. The entity theory's assumption of trait fixedness predicts stasis and consistency of behavior over time and across situations, whereas the incremental theory's assumption of dynamism predicts greater behavioral variability and greater input from each situation.

Endorsement of the entity and incremental theories may be measured as an individual difference variable, using the Implicit Theories Questionnaire (Dweck, 1999). Each theory may also be primed in the lab via several different methods (e.g., Chiu, Dweck, Tong, & Fu, 1997; Levy, Stroessner, & Dweck, 1998; McConnell, 2001; Molden, Plaks, & Dweck, 2006; Plaks, Grant, & Dweck, 2005; Plaks, Stroessner, Dweck, & Sherman, 2001; Poon & Koehler, 2006). It is important to distinguish the entity and incremental theories from such constructs as attitudes or values; unlike attitudes, theories are not necessarily evaluative or prescriptive (Plaks, Levy, & Dweck, 2009). In other words, they are not necessarily beliefs about how things *should* be—they are ideas about the way that things *are*. As subjective representations of the social landscape, lay theories are a primary source of one's felt ability to understand and navigate the social world successfully.

As we demonstrate in this chapter, lay theories are not mere fleeting ideas in which we have little investment. Rather, because lay theories serve as fundamental starting points for everyday social perception, they are central to one's sense of epistemic confidence (Plaks & Stecher, 2007). Thus, it is generally unsettling to be faced with counterexamples to one's working theory (Plaks et al., 2005). We suggest that this feeling of discomfort is not so much an egocentric response to being wrong (i.e., "I hate that I'm not always right"). Instead, evidence suggests that the experience of lay theory violation induces a sense of uncertainty and low competence in a domain that is important to everyone: understanding human behavior. Put differently, in the face of unexpected behavior, people ask not only, "Does this behavior follow predictably from the person's trait(s)?" but also, "Does this behavior violate my theory of personality?" We describe data suggesting that there are dissociable emotional consequences that come with the answers to these independent questions. We go on to provide demonstrations of the cognitive, emotional, and behavioral consequences of having one's working model violated.

EVIDENCE OF DISTINCT MODES OF SOCIAL THOUGHT

In this section, we describe a sampling of scores of studies done over the past 15 years or so that demonstrate that individuals with different working theories have different interpretations of and reactions to the same behaviors and events. Entity theorists tend to see overt behaviors as more diagnostic of the actor's underlying personality or characteristics than do incremental theorists, who tend to place more emphasis on a person's goals, beliefs, and emotions (Plaks et al., 2009). As a result, entity theorists are more ready and confident to draw conclusions about others' personalities than incremental theorists are. For example, entity theorists tend to assume that individuals' past behaviors are strong predictors of future behaviors, whereas incremental theorists do not necessarily assume that individuals will act consistently with their past behaviors (Chiu, Hong, & Dweck, 1997). Moreover, entity theorists rate specific examples of moral/immoral behavior as more indicative of one's overall morality than do incremental theorists (Chiu, Hong, & Dweck, 1997, Studies 3 and 4). Finally, in several studies, Molden et al. (2006) demonstrated that entity theorists' greater use of trait information and incremental theorists' greater use of situational information both occur even under conditions of high cognitive load. In other words, the use of trait descriptors appears more automatized for entity theorists, whereas the accessing of situational information is more automatized for incremental theorists.

How Do Lay Theories Influence the Perceived Utility of "Try, Try Again?"

These studies suggest that, compared with incremental theorists, entity theorists place less stock in the idea that situational variables will cause significant variation one's behavior or abilities. One would therefore suspect that entity and incremental theorists would have different ideas about whether people (including themselves) can improve in a given domain with time or effort. Numerous studies have investigated how lay theories influence people's ideas about the usefulness of effort, learning, and "trying, trying again."

Butler (2000) investigated how entity and incremental theorists use performance information to judge the underlying skills of others by having students and teachers estimate the underlying mathematical ability of two hypothetical students who had each written 10 math tests on 10 different days. One student's scores improved over the 10 tests (ascending pattern), whereas the other student's scores declined (descending pattern.) Whereas entity theorists attributed more mathematical ability to the student with the descending pattern, incremental theorists attributed more ability to the student with the ascending pattern of scores. In other words, incremental theorists found the final score more diagnostic of the student's overall mathematical ability, whereas entity theorists found the first of 10 scores more informative. Entity theorists were more likely to explain the changing test scores on the later days as the result of good or bad luck, whereas incremental theorists showed no such tendency. Hence, entity theorists anchored on initial performance and, predicting intrapersonal stability, found initial scores most meaningful. Incremental theorists, predicting malleability in ability, found the final scores (after one has had the opportunity to learn and practice) most meaningful.

Likely because of this emphasis on initial performance reflecting stable underlying abilities, entity theorists are less inclined to seek out highly challenging tasks or events than incremental theorists are. That is, to the extent that one believes a given trait (e.g., intelligence) is fixed, one may be more reluctant to challenge oneself in that domain. This is because if a challenge proves too difficult and leads to failure, that person may feel doomed to incompetence in that domain. On the other hand, challenging situations may be more appealing to those who believe a task-relevant trait is malleable, as it gives them an opportunity to learn and grow. Accordingly, individuals who believe that ability in a given domain is fixed (entity theorists) are more prone to having performance goals (the goal to demonstrate one's ability) and therefore react to challenging scenarios with helplessness (Blackwell, Trzesniewski, & Dweck, 2007; Dweck & Leggett, 1988). Incremental theorists are more inclined to have learning goals (the goal to increase one's ability) and are therefore more mastery-oriented in the face of challenges (e.g., Dweck & Leggett, 1988). For instance, when asked about what sort of tasks they would like to take on, children with different lay theories of intelligence expressed very different preferences: Sixty-one percent of incremental theorists expressed interest in taking on problems or tasks that are hard and different from what they are used to, whereas 18% of entity theorists (who believe intelligence is fixed) were interested in new, challenging problems (Dweck & Leggett, 1988). Lay theories about the malleability of intelligence are also related to reactions to upward social comparisons; whether we see a superstar role model as a target to shoot for or as a discouraging manifestation of what we never have been and never will be (Lockwood & Kunda, 1997, Study 3). Nussbaum and Dweck (2008) further demonstrated that incremental theorists are more likely to engage negative feedback and seek opportunities to improve "next time" than are entity theorists, who tend to disengage from negative feedback or opportunities for remediation. Finally, Beer (2002) found that dispositionally shy individuals were more likely to express willingness to engage in social interactions if they were incremental, as opposed to entity, theorists because their beliefs about whether shyness can be changed influenced their perceptions of what opportunities social interaction afforded them. (For conceptually similar findings in the workplace, relationships, and interracial contact, see Carr, Dweck, & Pauker, 2012; Heslin, VandeWalle, & Latham, 2005; Kammrath & Dweck, 2006.)

To summarize, people's lay theories about the fixedness or malleability of traits and abilities influence their ideas about the utility of pursuing new challenges versus sticking to their known strengths. These ideas, in turn, can substantially influence how people judge the abilities of others, as well as how they make choices in their own lives. These findings suggest that lay theories serve a fundamental meaning-making function in people's lives. To the extent that lay theories provide crucial guidance for extracting meaning from the social world, one would expect that people would be motivated to protect the integrity of their lay theories. What evidence is there that the integrity of their lay theories is something that people are concerned about?

How Do We Know That People Prefer Their Lay Theories to Remain Intact?

In a sense, lay theories are self-preserving. Just as professional scientists tend to be biased toward hypothesis-confirmation (Kuhn, 1962), the same holds for "lay social scientists." This makes sense: To the extent that individuals' lay theories provide a framework of expectations for the social world, people are unlikely to welcome threats to these frameworks (Heine, Proulx, & Vohs, 2006). While individuals may be motivated to search for meaning in a domain unrelated to the threatened one (Heine et al., 2006; see also Chapter 4, this volume), another effective way to maintain a sense of meaning is to, wherever possible, insulate one's meaning systems from assailants. In support of these ideas, we turn to several lines of evidence, starting with a series of studies conducted by Plaks et al. (2001).

Prior to the Plaks et al. (2001) studies, the person memory literature sent mixed messages. Some studies suggested that, in general, people pay more attention to stereotype-confirming information (e.g., Macrae, Hewstone, & Griffiths, 1993), while others suggested that people attend more to stereotype-disconfirming information (e.g., Sherman, Lee, Bessenoff, & Frost, 1998). To reconcile these findings, Plaks and colleagues (2001) suggested that individuals' lay theories predict whether one will preferentially attend to stereotype-confirming or stereotype-disconfirming information about a stranger. They predicted that because entity theorists place greater importance on labels and assume that people's personalities are stable across situations and time, they consider stereotype-confirming information more meaningful and thus should attend more to such information. This is indeed what was found: Participants were asked to read about the behaviors of a priest or a neo-Nazi skinhead. The listed behaviors were an even mix of stereotype-consistent, stereotype-inconsistent, or stereotype-irrelevant acts. As participants read sentences, they heard tones at random intervals and were instructed to press a key in response to the tones. The delay to the key press was the variable of interest: longer response times before pressing the button suggest that participants were paying more attention to the sentence they were reading when the tone was sounded. According to this measure, entity theorists paid the most attention to stereotype-consistent behaviors and actually paid less attention to stereotype-inconsistent behaviors than they did to stereotype-irrelevant behaviors. Incremental theorists, on the other hand, paid the most attention to stereotype-disconfirming behaviors and paid roughly equal attention to stereotype-irrelevant and stereotype-inconsistent behaviors.

In another study, Plaks et al. (2001, Study 4) used a dichotic listening paradigm as an alternative means of measuring attention. Participants simultaneously listened via headphones to two different children answering questions about geography, one child in each ear. Participants were told that the child they would hear in their right ear was expected to perform poorly. While the performance of the child in the left ear remained constant, the performance of the child in the right ear was either poor, average, or excellent (i.e., highly consistent, weakly consistent, or highly inconsistent with the expectancy). Plaks et al. (2001) found that the better the right ear child did, the less attention entity theorists paid to him. Incremental theorists' pattern of attention allocation was unaffected by either child's performance. The authors suggested that this pattern may reflect entity theorists' motivated filtering of theory-violating information (see also Skowronski, 2002).

Hence, the work of Plaks et al. (2001) provided evidence that the question of whether people generally attend more to stereotype-consistent or stereotype-inconsistent information is perhaps best reframed as, "Do people pay more attention to *theory*-consistent information?" The answer seems to be yes. Because the entity and incremental theories imply different expectations about the predictive power of stereotypes, people attend to and remember the information that is most meaningful and congruent with their particular theory. As such, it seems that—beyond the motivation to either confirm or disconfirm stereotypes—people strive to perceive the social world in ways that are congruent with their lay theories. This means that they may recruit cognitive and perceptual processes that subtly work to preserve the integrity of their working theory.

Plaks et al. (2005, Study 1) took these conclusions a step further, noting that for entity theorists, virtually all previous studies had confounded stereotype-violation and lay theory-violation. Hence, it was worth probing whether it is truly the violation of the entity theory that entity theorists prefer to avoid or whether it is simply that entity theorists prefer to avoid expectation-inconsistent information in general. The experimenters reasoned that there are behaviors that can violate an expectation derived from a stereotype but not necessarily invalidate one's lay theory of personality. Plaks et al. (2005) called such behaviors *associate-relevant* (not reflective of underlying abilities) as opposed to trait-relevant behaviors. By way of example, in Study 1, participants read about Brad, who was described to participants as either a stereotypical math geek or a humanities geek. These stereotypes were chosen because they are generally seen to have dual implications: A math geek is strong in math/sciences *and* weak in humanities, while a humanities geek is strong in arts/humanities and weak in math. Through a series of pilot tests, it appeared that inconsistent-associate behaviors (e.g., "Brad [the math geek] eagerly renewed his subscription to the New Yorker") were distinguishable from inconsistent-trait behaviors (e.g., "Brad [the math geek] scored 760 on the verbal portion of the GRE and 480 on math"). In other words, trait-relevant behavior speaks to the actor's underlying, defining qualities. Associate-relevant behavior speaks more to the actor's stereotypic interests or hobbies.

In the experimental session, participants completed a measure of incremental versus entity theories and read a description of Brad (either as a "math/sciences person" or an "arts/humanities person"). After firmly connecting Brad with one stereotype or the other, the text indicated that Brad underwent a rigorous remedial program intended to shore up his academic weaknesses (i.e., reading and writing for the "math geek," math for the "artsy type"). Next, participants performed an attentional probe task, in which they were presented with 25 behaviors Brad had performed, representative of five categories: five behaviors were inconsistent-trait, five inconsistent-associate, five consistent-trait, five inconsistent-trait, and five neutral. Tones were sounded during a fraction of the trials (evenly distributed across the five categories), whereas participants were reading Brad's behaviors, and participants were told to press the space bar as quickly as possible in response to the tone. Reaction times provided an index of how much attention participants were paying to the behavior being displayed at the time; the slower the reaction to the tone, the more attention they were presumably paying to the displayed behavior.

Results supported the hypothesis that participants were primarily motivated to protect the integrity of their lay theories, rather than their stereotype-derived expectations for Brad's behavior: Entity theorists seemed to avoid trait-inconsistent behaviors (which are reflective of Brad's underlying abilities) but did not avoid associate-inconsistent behaviors (which are inconsistent with the math/arts geek stereotype but not necessarily inconsistent with the entity theory). Incremental theorists, in contrast, selectively avoided trait-consistent behaviors (evidence of Brad showing an inability to improve his weaknesses), compared with trait-associate behaviors. Hence, this study further demonstrated that it is the violation of lay theories per se, rather than the violation of general expectations, which individuals are motivated to avoid. Moreover, it demonstrated that such selective attention effects are not restricted to entity theorists but apply to incremental theorists as well.

What happens, though, when people do not have the option to screen out theory-violating information and thus are forced to question their working theory? Plaks et al. (2005, Study 3) reasoned that because intact lay theories are crucial to maintaining a sense that one understands human behavior, evidence to the contrary should arouse anxiety and motivate people to compensate with extra thorough information processing, as people tend to do when their ability to predict outcomes is threatened (e.g., Pittman & D'Agostino, 1989; Weary & Jacobson, 1997). To test these ideas, the authors exposed participants to blatant theory-threatening information in stories about Brad. Brad was depicted as an "artsy type" (stereotypically gifted in arts and unskilled at math). The stories described Brad taking a calculus course in school and showing subsequent behaviors which either constituted a substantial change in Brad's artsy nature (acing the math section of the GRE and foundering on the verbal portion) or an outcome that was consistent with Brad's artsy nature (acing the verbal GRE and foundering on the math portion).

Participants also reported their current emotions, including anxiety, and performed a control estimation task (D'Agostino & Pittman, 1982). In this task, on each trial, the computer displayed a row of A's on the screen. After each trial, participants could choose to press the space bar or do nothing. Then the row of A's either changed into a row of B's or did nothing. Based on repeated trial-and-error, participants were asked to estimate on what percentage of trials their action caused the letters to change. The actual proportion of trials over which participants had any control was fixed at 35%, and the dependent variable of interest was how many trials participants chose to undergo before making their estimate of their degree of control. (The assumption was that more trials would indicate more effort to thoroughly process information.)

Entity theorists who read about Brad changing from an artsy type to a math ace reported significantly more state anxiety and performed significantly more trials before rendering a control estimate than either incremental theorists or entity theorists who read about Brad remaining an artsy type (as entity theorists would expect him to). Conversely, incremental theorists reported more anxiety and performed more trials before estimating their degree of control when they read about Brad's abilities remaining static despite his best efforts. Moreover, for both entity and incremental theorists, degree of anxiety mediated the number of trials they took.

In other words, both entity and incremental theorists were made anxious and were motivated to regain a sense of prediction competence, when their respective lay theories were threatened by Brad's behavior. Both exhibited compensatory processes in response to a threat to cognitive structures or expectations, akin to those reported in previous studies (e.g., Kay, Gaucher, Napier, Callan, & Laurin, 2008; McGregor, Zanna, Holmes, & Spencer, 2001; Proulx & Heine, 2008). In this case, it appeared that the destabilizing effect of having one's theory violated caused participants—regardless of their theory—to attempt to restore the sense of confidence in the self as a competent navigator through the social world.

Plaks and Stecher (2007) extended this idea to cases when participants' lay theories about intelligence were supported or violated by their *own* performance on a given task. Participants' lay theories of intelligence were measured at least one week before the experimental session. In the lab participants first completed a challenging cognitive task (identifying the word that unites three very different words, such as *book*, *hook*, and *apple*, which can be unified by *worm*). After their first run through this task, participants were all told that they had performed at the 61st percentile (a score that was shown in pretest to leave room for potential improvement or decline). Then participants underwent a short tutorial designed to improve their performance on this cognitive task. Next, participants completed the same cognitive task of identifying the uniting concept among three words. Upon completion, they were told that their results were, this time, in either the 29th percentile (a decline in performance), the 62nd percentile (static performance), or the 91st percentile (an increase in performance). Then participants completed a measure of various mood states, including happiness, disappointment, and anxiety. Finally, participants took part in the control estimation task that was described in the Plaks et al. (2005) study. Again, the number of trials that each participant chose to perform before estimating the percentage of trials he or she had control over was the dependent variable of interest.

The authors had two primary predictions. First, both decline and improvement in performance would violate the entity theory of intelligence, as individuals with this theory would expect that performance on the task would probably be stable, even despite a tutorial. On the other hand, the incremental theory would be violated by one's scores remaining stable around the 60th percentile (especially despite a tutorial), as these individuals believe that performance is malleable and subject to the effects of practice and learning. Second, participants whose lay theories of intelligence were violated should express higher anxiety and perform more trials of the control estimation task before giving a control estimate, in order to compensate for their diminished sense of competence at predicting outcomes. Results supported these predictions. Both incremental and entity theorists expressed, on the state emotions scale, that they were pleased with improvement feedback and displeased (e.g., "unhappy," "disappointed") with decline-in-performance feedback. What differentiated entity and incremental theorists, though, was the kind of feedback that aroused anxiety in particular. Entity theorists expressed more anxiety than incremental theorists in the decline and improvement conditions, whereas incremental theorists expressed more anxiety than entity theorists in the stasis condition. The number of trials that participants underwent in order to estimate the amount of control they had over the numbers' transformation to letters mirrored this pattern of results: Entity theorists performed significantly more trials than did incremental theorists in the decline and improvement conditions, whereas incremental theorists underwent more trials than did entity theorists only in the stasis condition. These results were replicated in a second study, in which participants were primed with either incremental or entity theories. In a final study (Plaks & Stecher, 2007, Study 3), participants whose theories had been violated showed impairment in their subsequent performance on the task.

These results suggest that when individuals' lay theories are threatened, they are motivated to regain a sense of prediction confidence. This would be predicted from a meaning maintenance standpoint: When individuals' sense of meaning is threatened, they are motivated to seek meaning in an unrelated domain. Finally, it is worth noting that *both* incremental and entity theorists were upset by their theories being threatened. The data suggest that incremental theorists are not expectation-free, all-accepting figures. Indeed, they can be just as close-minded as entity theorists toward information that violates their assumption of personal change (Plaks et al., 2005; Plaks & Stecher, 2007). In their case, evidence of someone who is "stuck" (i.e., incapable of change despite opportunity and effort) directly contradicts the very core of their theory. Thus, regardless of one's lay theory, people react anxiously to evidence that counters the theory's basic tenets.

In summary, these studies suggest that lay theories guide our expectations about the dynamics of our own and others' abilities in a given domain. Feedback we receive about our performance speaks both to the "goodness" or "badness" of our performance but also to the correctness of the implicit predictions that we had for our performance. Hence, when we do unexpectedly well, it is pleasing, but it can also be unsettling. We wish to be skilled and experience positive outcomes, but consistent with classic concepts in social psychology (Festinger, 1954; Trope & Brickman, 1975), we are also highly motivated to know ourselves and accurately predict our own behavior. When we do not feel confident in our ability to predict our own and/or others' behavior, we are willing to redouble our efforts to regain this comfortable sense of prediction confidence, control, and meaning.

DISCUSSION

The studies described in the previous section suggest that lay theories act as organizing frameworks for the smaller scale predictions and expectations that we hold for particular people. They influence how we perceive social categories, where we focus our attention, how we react to incoming information, and what we do when incoming information surprises us. Given that anxiety is aroused and compensatory effort is exerted when lay theories are violated, it seems that we *prefer* our lay theories to seem intact and, whenever possible, remain unchallenged.

These studies also provide evidence for the proposition that lay theories are fundamental to one's sense of prediction ability and social competence. For instance, in many of these studies, participants' lay theories were validated or violated by stimuli that are, on the surface, rather far removed from the content of lay theories. Reading about a stranger's GRE scores, or even learning about one's own performance on a cognitive domain does not necessarily prime the idea of "Is this what I would have thought? No? Well that is problematic." Furthermore, many of these studies did not even measure lay theories in the experimental session; as noted, Plaks and Stecher (2007) and Plaks et al. (2005) measured participants' relevant lay theories weeks before participants were brought into the lab. There were no reminders for participants that they believe certain things about human characteristics and therefore have certain expectations for outcomes. Rather, people seem to generate these expectations so fluently and automatically that they neither need to be reminded that they have expectations for outcomes, nor do they need reminders to compare social "data" to their lay theory-based "hypotheses." That people's expectations for situational outcomes are so sensitive to subtle forms of evidence for or against their theories suggests that lay theories play a central role in fostering the sense that "I am a good predictor of human behavior."

Also suggestive of the fundamental role of lay theories is that people seem to, above anything, want to avoid being left "theory-less." Plaks et al.

(2009) noted that it seems, at first, remarkable that both theories can be so successfully primed in the lab (e.g., by having participants read an article reporting evidence in favor of one or the other). Given that people appear to be quite distressed by their lay theories being called into question, one might expect that attempts to instill a different lay theory would arouse anxiety and/or be met with resistance. Plaks et al. (2009) argued, however, that there is a distinction between theory *violation* and theory *replacement*. Consider the analogy of travelling in another country with an inaccurate map: If someone can give you a better one, you are quite relieved; it is only if you see your map not working but have no replacement that you might become quite anxious. The articles used to prime lay theories are presented as reports of "scientific evidence" validating a given lay theory, and the espoused lay theory therefore constitutes a legitimate replacement for the domain-relevant theory that participants may bring into the lab with them (at least for a while). It therefore seems that people's upset reactions to evidence that clashes with their lay theory(s) is not particularly due to a "hurt ego" reaction, from which the anxiety might come from feeling like one was not "right." Instead, it seems that—rather than being concerned with always being correct—people are primarily concerned with having *some* viable theory (or theories) that can help to predict and account for human behavior. This concern for feeling that one has a reasonable ability to predict social outcomes further supports the fundamental role of lay theories in extracting meaning from human behavior.

In light of this discussion, one might wonder: How closely are lay theories tied to some aspect of one's stable personal constitution? A scattering of studies investigating the properties of lay theories have suggested that lay theories are held independently from trait self-esteem and the Big Five personality traits (e.g., Dweck et al., 1995; Spinath, Spinath, Riemann, & Angleitner, 2003). One might then wonder what, if any, enduring personal characteristics are lay theories tied to? By corollary, are people's chronic lay theories themselves stable across the life span? Is each respective entity/incremental theorist going to live his or her entire life as an entity/incremental theorist? To what degree might someone be an entity theorist in some domains and an incremental theorist in others (e.g., someone who believes that personality traits are stable but also believes that intelligence is malleable)? Perhaps longitudinal studies of how or whether individuals' favored lay theories change over the life span could shed light on these questions.

Another arena in which lay theories beget a host of questions is that of individual differences. Clearly the desire to hold intact lay beliefs and protect them from assault, or compensate when faced with undeniable theory threats, is a generally pervasive phenomenon. One step at which there may be individual differences, though, is the perceptual processes involved in detecting a threat to one's lay theories. We discussed earlier how people seem very sensitive to counterevidence (e.g., Brad's GRE scores) and seem to very readily compare incoming information with what their theories would seem to predict. This may indeed be the case for most people, yet there are likely individual differences in how generally sensitive people are to perceiving threats to their lay theories. For instance, neuroticism, anxious attachment, and political conservatism have all been linked with greater sensitivity to various forms of threat or uncertainty (e.g., DeZavala, Cislak, & Wesolowska, 2010; Fraley, Niedenthal, Marks, Brumbaugh, & Vicary, 2006; Hirsh & Inzlicht, 2008). First, some individuals may be better than others at filtering out threatening stimuli or reinterpreting events such that their lay theories rarely bump up against incongruent outcomes. Second, some individuals may be less inclined to make the connection between more removed or abstract counterexamples and their implicit expectations for that event. Perhaps even if an entity theorist sees that Brad's behavior indicates a drastic change in his nature, that person may discount that particular outcome as the result of some other extenuating circumstance and not become concerned about the well-being of his or her theory at all. In other words, some people may be more sensitive than others to the implications of behavioral outcomes to the validity of their lay theories.

Another step at which there are likely individual differences occurs after people *do* notice counterevidence to their theory. The studies reviewed so far suggest that people, in general, become anxious and motivated to regain a sense of prediction and control mastery. More plainly, people get upset when they feel their lay theories are not working properly. However, there are individual differences in the degree to which people get upset about almost everything. Witness the variety of reactions in travelers who are stuck on the tarmac on a delayed flight, or of people on the receiving end of a personal insult; some people become flustered, ruminate, become anxious, and so on, while others seem to let such things roll off their backs. One might ask, then, whether there are differences in the degree to which individuals are upset by threats to their lay theories. While the holding of an entity versus incremental theory itself is unrelated to the Big Five traits, one might expect that the degree of *upset* and motivated compensatory effort in the face of a threatened theory might be related to trait neuroticism. Higher neuroticism is related to a proneness to experiencing negative emotion, emotional volatility, and anxious reactions to uncertainty (e.g., DeYoung, Quilty, & Peterson, 2007; Hirsh & Inzlicht, 2008), and uncertainty is almost certainly aroused by evidence suggesting that one cannot predict human behavior.

It is also possible that other beliefs and theories might moderate the amount of anxiety people experience in the face of threatened lay theories. In particular, a belief that life maintains a steady course despite transient ups and downs might reduce the felt need to be able to predict focal situational outcomes. Burton and Plaks have begun to investigate this possibility, calling such beliefs *homeostasis beliefs* (HBs; Burton, Kim, & Plaks, 2011; Burton & Plaks, 2010). Note that the homeostasis idea contains elements of both the entity theory and the incremental theory; there is an acknowledgement of significant "local" change but an assumption of "global" stasis.

HBs appear to be measurable. An HB scale with items such as "Whatever good or bad fortune comes my way, I will end up where I'm supposed to be in life" and "Even though the future probably holds negative and positive events, I'm sure I will be fine in the end" has good psychometric properties (Burton & Plaks, 2010). HBs are related to, but distinguishable from, satisfaction with life, optimism, religiosity, and the Big Five traits. We hypothesize that HBs may moderate individuals' reactions to threatened lay theories or other uncertainty-inducing or meaning-threatening events. If one believes that one will be just fine in the long term, then the consequences of a given focal event are less important, as is the felt ability to predict particular outcomes. So far, inducing high belief in homeostasis has been shown to reduce the magnitude of affective forecasting errors (Burton et al., 2011). Specifically, students primed with high HBs were accurate at predicting how happy they would be after achieving a goal mark on a test, whereas students primed with low HBs made the expected overestimation of how happy they would be following this positive event (see Gilbert, Pinel, Wilson, Blumberg, & Wheatley, 1998). We are continuing to test the effects of homeostasis beliefs on individuals' reactions to certainty- or meaning-threatening events, such as violations of lay theories.

The question of who gets more or less anxious in the face of threatened lay theories relates to another question of how most people compensate and regain a sense of prediction control and mastery in their natural habitat (as opposed to the lab). Presumably, most of these compensatory processes are benign and internal, but it raises the question of what sort of beliefs or traits, in combination with the tendency to be reactive to lay theory threats, might lead one to the "dark side" of anxiety reduction. Might someone limit his or her social perceptual processes so strictly that he or she never encounters threats to his or her lay theories but also scarcely perceives the "real world" anymore? Might someone prone to extremity in beliefs turn to derogating or hating those who present threats to their meaning systems? This is arguably the case for some individuals (Peterson & Flanders, 2002), and it would be valuable to know what sort of individual difference variables predispose individuals to react to threatened lay theories (or other meaning threats) in limiting or destructive ways.

Another question that is often raised in light of discussing entity and incremental lay theories is whether one is "better" than the other. Implicitly in studies' results and conclusions, it does seem that incremental theory is, perhaps by liberal standards, the more "appropriate" worldview, but this is not the whole story. It does seem that individuals with an incremental theory of their abilities are more open to challenging themselves, exposing themselves to new things, and allowing for themselves and others to change. Change is a process that we all undergo naturally over the course of our lifetimes, and it may be adaptive to be cognitively equipped to deal with the process of change. However, there are situations in which entity theorists would be more "on the right page." For instance, Polivy and Herman (2002) described how overestimating the ease with which one can change can increase the likelihood of failure to achieve a goal, such as losing weight or quitting smoking. Similarly, setting a goal that is overly ambitious can increase the chance of failure. The authors called the cycle of failure and renewed effort *false hope syndrome*. It is quite likely that the majority of individuals who end up mired in the cycle of false hope are incremental theorists, who may be overestimating the likelihood and magnitude of self-change efforts succeeding. Entity theorists, on the other hand, are unlikely to fall prey to the effects of false hope.

Summary

There is considerable evidence for the influence of individuals' personal theories about human characteristics on basic cognitive, emotional, and motivational processes. Lay theories are part of the foundation of people's meaning systems; these theories provide a framework for expected relations between social variables. As such, they function as the wellsprings of predictions that we make for social outcomes. People prefer to feel that they are travelling the social realm with a good map to guide them and are understandably anxious when that sense of security and competence is threatened by incoming information. Let us consider, once again, Eleanor, who doubts that her fiancé, Eric, has truly outgrown his commitment phobia, even as he presented her with a diamond ring. Guided by her entity theory of personality, then, Eleanor may continue be a little unsettled by her new and improved fiancé. But perhaps if her theory were somehow able to evolve into an incremental one like her friend Irene's, Eleanor might finally be able to trust her current state of happiness and look to the future with optimism.

REFERENCES

Beer, J. S. (2002). Implicit self-theories of shyness. *Journal of Personality and Social Psychology, 83*, 1009–1024. doi:10.1037/0022-3514.83.4.1009

Blackwell, L. S., Trzesniewski, K., & Dweck, C. S. (2007). Implicit theories of intelligence predict achievement across an adolescent transition: A longitudinal study and an intervention. *Child Development, 78*(1), 246–263. doi:10.1111/j.1467-8624.2007.00995.x

Burton, C., Kim, H., & Plaks, J. E. (2011, January). *Homeostasis beliefs increase the accuracy of positive affective forecasts*. Poster presented at the 12th annual convention of the Society of Personality and Social Psychology, San Antonio, TX.

Burton, C., & Plaks, J. E. (2010, January). *Validating a measure of homeostasis beliefs*. Poster presented at the 11th annual convention of the Society of Personality & Social Psychology, Las Vegas, NV.

Butler, R. (2000). Making judgments about ability: The role of implicit theories of ability in moderating inferences from temporal and social comparison information. *Journal of Personality and Social Psychology, 78*, 965–978. doi:10.1037/0022-3514.78.5.965

Carr, P. B., Dweck, C. S., & Pauker, K. (2012). *Prejudice without prejudice? Beliefs about the malleability of prejudice affect interracial interactions*. Manuscript submitted for publication.

Chiu, C.-Y., Dweck, C. S., Tong, J. Y., & Fu, J. H. (1997). Implicit theories and conceptions of morality. *Journal of Personality and Social Psychology, 73*, 923–940. doi:10.1037/0022-3514.73.5.923

Chiu, C.-Y., Hong, Y., & Dweck, C. S. (1997). Lay dispositionism and implicit theories of personality. *Journal of Personality and Social Psychology, 73*, 19–30. doi:10.1037/0022-3514.73.1.19

D'Agostino, P. R., & Pittman, T. S. (1982). Effort expenditure following control deprivation. *Bulletin of the Psychonomic Society, 19*, 282–283.

DeYoung, C. G., Quilty, L. C., & Peterson, J. B. (2007). Between facets and domains: 10 aspects of the Big Five. *Journal of Personality and Social Psychology, 93*, 880–896. doi:10.1037/0022-3514.93.5.880

De Zavala, A. G., Cislak, A., & Wesolowska, E. (2010). Political conservatism, need for cognitive closure, and intergroup hostility. *Political Psychology, 31*, 521–541. doi:10.1111/j.1467-9221.2010.00767.x

Dweck, C. S. (1999). *Self-theories: Their role in motivation, personality, and development*. Philadelphia, PA: Psychology Press.

Dweck, C. S., Chiu, C., & Hong, Y. (1995). Implicit theories and their role in judgments and reactions: A world from two perspectives. *Psychological Inquiry, 6*, 267–285. doi:10.1207/s15327965pli0604_1

Dweck, C. S., & Leggett, E. L. (1988). A social-cognitive approach to motivation and personality. *Psychological Review, 95*, 256–273. doi:10.1037/0033-295X.95.2.256

Festinger, L. (1954). A theory of social comparison processes. *Human Relations, 7*, 117–140. doi:10.1177/001872675400700202

Fraley, R. C., Niedenthal, P. M., Marks, M., Brumbaugh, C., & Vicary, A. (2006). Adult attachment and the perceptions of emotional expressions: Probing the hyperactivating strategies underlying anxious attachment. *Journal of Personality, 74*, 1163–1190. doi:10.1111/j.1467-6494.2006.00406.x

Gilbert, D. T., Pinel, E. C., Wilson, T. D., Blumberg, S. J., & Wheatley, T. P. (1998). Immune neglect: A source of durability bias in affective forecasting.

Journal of Personality and Social Psychology, 75, 617–638. doi:10.1037/0022-3514.75.3.617

Heine, S. J., Proulx, T., & Vohs, K. D. (2006). The meaning maintenance model: On the coherence of social motivations. *Personality and Social Psychology Review, 10*, 88–110. doi:10.1207/s15327957pspr1002_1

Heslin, P. A., VandeWalle, D., & Latham, G. P. (2006). Keen to help? Manager's implicit person theories and their subsequent employee coaching. *Personnel Psychology*, 59, 871–902. doi:10.1111/j.1744-6570.2006.00057.x

Hirsh, J. B., & Inzlicht, M. (2008). The devil you know: Neuroticism predicts neural response to uncertainty. *Psychological Science, 19*, 962–967. doi:10.1111/j.1467-9280.2008.02183.x

Inzlicht, M., & Ben-Zeev, T. (2000). A threatening intellectual environment: Why females are susceptible to experiencing problem-solving deficits in the presence of males. *Psychological Science, 11*, 365–371. doi:10.1111/1467-9280.00272

Kammrath, L. K., & Dweck, C. (2006). Voicing conflict: Preferred conflict strategies among entity and incremental theorists. *Personality and Social Psychology Bulletin, 32*, 1497–1508. doi:10.1177/0146167206291476

Kay, A. C., Gaucher, D., Napier, J. L., Callan, M. J., & Laurin, K. (2008). God and the government: Testing a compensatory control mechanism for the support of external systems. *Journal of Personality and Social Psychology*, 95, 18–35. doi:10.1037/0022-3514.95.1.18

Kuhn, T. (1962). *The structure of scientific revolutions*. Chicago, IL: University of Chicago Press.

Levy, S. R., Plaks, J. E., Hong, Y., Chiu, C., & Dweck, C. S. (2001). Static versus dynamic theories and the perception of groups: Different routes to different destinations. *Personality and Social Psychology Review, 5*, 156–168. doi:10.1207/S15327957PSPR0502_6

Levy, S. R., Stroessner, S. J., & Dweck, C. S. (1998). Stereotype formation and endorsement: The role of implicit theories. *Journal of Personality and Social Psychology, 74*, 1421–1436. doi:10.1037/0022-3514.74.6.1421

Lockwood, P., & Kunda, Z. (1997). Superstars and me: Predicting the impact of role models on the self. *Journal of Personality and Social Psychology, 73*, 91–103. doi:10.1037/0022-3514.73.1.91

Macrae, C. N., Hewstone, M., & Griffiths, R. J. (1993). Processing load and memory for stereotype-based information. *European Journal of Social Psychology, 23*(1), 77–87. doi:10.1002/ejsp.2420230107

McConnell, A. R. (2001). Implicit theories: Consequences for social judgment of individuals. *Journal of Experimental Social Psychology, 37*, 215–227.

McGregor, I., Zanna, M. P., Holmes, J. G., & Spencer, S. J. (2001). Compensatory conviction in the face of personal uncertainty: Going to extremes and being oneself. *Journal of Personality and Social Psychology, 80*, 472–488. doi:10.1037/0022-3514.80.3.472

Molden, D. C., Plaks, J. E., & Dweck, C. S. (2006). "Meaningful" social inferences: Effects of implicit theories on inferential processes. *Journal of Experimental Social Psychology, 42*, 738–752. doi:10.1016/j.jesp.2005.11.005

Nussbaum, D. A., & Dweck, C. S. (2008). Defensiveness versus remediation: Self-theories and modes of self-esteem maintenance. *Personality and Social Psychology Bulletin, 34*, 599–612. doi:10.1177/0146167207312960

Peterson, J. B., & Flanders, J. L. (2002). Complexity management theory: Motivation for ideological rigidity and conflict. *Cortex: A Journal Devoted to the Study of the Nervous System and Behavior*, 38, 429–458. doi:10.1016/S0010-9452(08)70680-4

Pittman, T. S., & D'Agostino, P. R. (1989). Motivation and cognition: Control deprivation and the nature of subsequent information processing. *Journal of Experimental Social Psychology, 25*, 465–480. doi:10.1016/0022-1031(89)90001-2

Plaks, J. E., Grant, H., & Dweck, C. S. (2005). Violations of implicit theories and the sense of prediction and control: Implications for motivated person perception. *Journal of Personality and Social Psychology*, 88, 245–262. doi:10.1037/0022-3514.88.2.245

Plaks, J. E., Levy, S. R., & Dweck, C. S. (2009). Lay theories of personality: Cornerstones of meaning in social cognition. *Social and Personality Psychology Compass*, 3, 1069–1081. doi:10.1111/j.1751-9004.2009.00222.x

Plaks, J. E., & Stecher, K. (2007). Unexpected improvement, decline, and stasis: A prediction confidence perspective on achievement success and failure. *Journal of Personality and Social Psychology*, 93, 667–684. doi:10.1037/0022-3514.93.4.667

Plaks, J. E., Stroessner, S. J., Dweck, C. S., & Sherman, J. W. (2001). Person theories and attention allocation: Preferences for stereotypic vs. counterstereotypic information. *Journal of Personality and Social Psychology*, 80, 876–893. doi:10.1037/0022-3514.80.6.876

Plaks, J. E. & Xu. X. (2011). [Varieties of social expectancy violations: Insights from event-related potentials.] Unpublished raw data. University of Toronto, Toronto, Ontario, Canada.

Polivy, J., & Herman, C. P. (2002). If at first you don't succeed: False hopes of self-change. *American Psychologist, 57*, 677–689. doi:10.1037/0003-066X.57.9.677

Poon, C. S. K., & Koehler, D. J. (2006). Lay personality knowledge and dispositionist thinking: A knowledge activation framework. *Journal of Experimental Social Psychology, 42*, 177–191. doi:10.1016/j.jesp.2005.04.001

Proulx, T., & Heine, S. J. (2008). The case of the transmogrifying experimenter: Affirmation of a moral schema following implicit change detection. *Psychological Science, 19*, 1294–1300. doi:10.1111/j.1467-9280.2008.02238.x

Sherman, J. W., Lee, A. Y., Bessenoff, G. R., & Frost, L. A. (1998). Stereotype efficiency reconsidered: Encoding flexibility under cognitive load. *Journal of Personality and Social Psychology, 75*, 589–606. doi:10.1037/0022-3514.75.3.589

Skowronski, J. J. (2002). Honesty and intelligence judgments of individuals and groups: The effects of entity-related behavior diagnosticity and implicit theories. *Social Cognition, 20,* 136–169. doi:10.1521/soco.20.2.136.20993

Spinath, B., Spinath, F. M., Riemann, R., & Angleitner, A. (2003). Implicit theories about personality and intelligence and their relationship to actual personality and intelligence. *Personality and Individual Differences, 35,* 939–951. doi:10.1016/S0191-8869(02)00310-0

Trope, Y., & Brickman, P. (1975). Difficulty and diagnosticity as determinants of choice among tasks. *Journal of Personality and Social Psychology, 31,* 918–925.

Weary, G., & Jacobson, J. A. (1997). Causal uncertainty beliefs and diagnostic information seeking. *Journal of Personality and Social Psychology, 73,* 839–848. doi:10.1037/0022-3514.73.4.839

7

MAKING MEANING BY SEEING HUMAN

ADAM WAYTZ

On October 3, 2003, entertainers Siegfried and Roy took the stage to perform in their legendary show—a combination of magic, illusions, and stunts performed with live tigers—at The Mirage in Las Vegas. Although the duo had been performing on the Vegas strip for almost 30 years, that night they experienced something they never had before. One of the trained tigers attacked Roy, biting him in the neck and causing him massive blood loss. Following the uproar that the event generated, comedian Chris Rock expressed his surprise at the public response to the incident and disdain for the public's view that "the tiger went crazy." Rock stated, "That tiger didn't go crazy—that tiger went *tiger*!" This incident, and Rock's response, illustrate people's tendency to turn to anthropomorphic descriptions to explain the actions of nonhumans when things do not go according to plan. Given such an unexpected event as this tiger attack, many people sought to explain the tiger's actions in more mentalistic, human terms. However, as Rock suggested, the actions of the tiger were not psychotic, they were merely the

DOI: 10.1037/14040-007
The Psychology of Meaning, Keith D. Markman, Travis Proulx, and Matthew J. Lindberg (Editors)

characteristic action of a tiger taken from its natural habitat and forced to perform on a Vegas stage.

Many years earlier, in attempting to explain the origins of religion, the philosopher David Hume (1757/1957) came to a similar conclusion about people's proclivity for anthropomorphism as a means of sense making:

> There is a universal tendency among mankind to conceive all beings like themselves, and to transfer to every object, those qualities, with which they are familiarly acquainted, and of which they are intimately conscious . . . No wonder, then, that mankind, being placed in such an absolute ignorance of causes, and being at the same time so anxious concerning their future fortune, should immediately acknowledge a dependence on invisible powers, possessed of sentiment and intelligence. The unknown causes, which continually employ their thought, appearing always in the same aspect, are all apprehended to be of the same kind or species. Nor is it long before we ascribe to them thought and reason and passion, and sometimes even the limbs and figures of men, in order to bring them nearer to a resemblance with ourselves.

This statement reveals Hume to have had insights about humans' attributional tendencies that psychologists would not test until a quarter millennium later. In particular, Hume described the conditions under which people tend to attribute human characteristics to nonhuman entities. This insightful account, however, also overstated humans' proclivity toward anthropomorphism, which he described as a process in which humans engage promiscuously rather than as a process activated by specific psychological factors and circumstances.

Anthropomorphism, at its essence, is the attribution of higher order mental states (e.g., beliefs, desires, thoughts, feelings, intentions) to nonhuman entities (Epley, Waytz, & Cacioppo, 2007). Although the *capacity* to perceive mental states is nearly universal, the tendency to apply these mental states to other entities and to treat nonhumans as humanlike mental agents is not as inevitable as Hume suggested (Waytz, Klein, & Epley, in press). Rather than a *universal* tendency that people apply to *all* beings and *every* object, the attribution of minds to nonhumans in anthropomorphism is a process in which people engage only when they are triggered to do so. Hume's major insight from his description of anthropomorphism is his identification of the triggers that play a major role in turning this tendency on or off. "Being placed in an ignorance of causes, and being at the same time so anxious concerning [one's] future fortune" describes both the experience of causal uncertainty and unpredictability that commonly motivates a desire for predictability, understanding, and sense making (Berlyne, 1962; Kelley, 1967; Weary & Edwards, 1996; Weiner, 1985; White, 1959). This motivation is a major determinant of anthropomorphism as well.

THE DESIRE FOR MEANING AND ANTHROPOMORPHISM

White (1959) termed the all-encompassing desire to have effective interaction in one's environment through establishing control, predictability, and understanding as *effectance motivation*. In 2007, my colleagues and I (Epley et al., 2007; see also Chapter 5, this volume) identified effectance motivation as one of three primary psychological determinants of anthropomorphism, in addition to sociality motivation (i.e., the motivation for affiliation and belonging) and the elicitation of anthropocentric knowledge (i.e., the extent to which the concept "human" is accessible and activated). Scholars from a variety of disciplines linked effectance with anthropomorphism, yet a formal and comprehensive theory of anthropomorphism's determinants had not yet been developed. For example, linguists described how people use anthropomorphic metaphors (e.g., "inflation has attacked the foundation of our economy") to explain complex concepts such as financial markets (Lakoff & Johnson, 1980). Anthropologists described how anthropomorphism facilitated the evolution of agriculture and hunting by providing a useful way of making sense of complex artifacts and tools (Humphrey, 1983; Mithen, 1996). Religious scholars described religious traditions function as fundamentally explanatory systems that elucidate the workings of universe through anthropomorphism of the physical world (Guthrie, 1993). Computer scientists and artificial intelligence researchers described how the anthropomorphism of technology can be used to facilitate effective user interaction with intelligent systems (Kiesler & Goetz, 2002).

Philosophers such as Daniel Dennett (1987) have similarly described how considering an entity's behavior in terms of mental properties can provide explanation. Dennett (1987) wrote the following in his landmark work on the topic, *The Intentional Stance:*

> Here is how it works: first you decide to treat the object whose behavior is to be predicted as a rational agent; then you figure out what beliefs that agent ought to have, given its place in the world and its purpose. Then you figure out what desires it ought to have, on the same considerations, and finally you predict that this rational agent will act to further its goals in the light of its beliefs. A little practical reasoning from the chosen set of beliefs and desires will in most instances yield a decision about what the agent ought to do; that is what you predict the agent will do. (p. 17)

Here, Dennett described how treating an entity as though it has intentions and reason can provide a framework for making predictions about its behavior.

The first mention of the relationship between effectance and anthropomorphism in psychology comes from discussion of the first study of anthropomorphism in psychology. In 1944, Heider and Simmel presented

30 participants with animations of shapes moving around a screen. When asked to describe what was occurring in the scene, all participants except one described the scene as a human drama, with each shape an actor that possessed its own intentions, motives, and feelings. Heider (1958/1964) described these findings:

> As long as the pattern of events shown in the film is perceived in terms of movements as such, it presents a chaos of juxtaposed items. When, however, the geometrical figures assume personal characteristics so that their movements are perceived in terms of motives and sentiments, a unified structure appears. . . . But motives and sentiments are psychological entities. . . . They are "mentalistic concepts," so-called intervening variables that bring order into the array of behavior mediating them. (pp. 31–32)

Heider's interpretation of his subjects' attributions suggests that without mentalistic terminology, it would be difficult for them to create a coherent story about the shapes' movement. Ascribing mental states to these shapes, on the other hand, creates a sense of meaning within the scene. Hume, Heider, and Dennett all converge on the same idea that the desire to see meaning in the world—manifested in needs for explanation, order, and prediction—serves as a major cause of anthropomorphism.

POSSIBLE MECHANISMS

Although there appears to be agreement across various disciplines that people anthropomorphize to attain a sense of meaning and order, it is not completely clear why humanizing a nonhuman entity should provide this sense of meaning. Three possible nonexclusive mechanisms exist for why people employ anthropomorphism as a means of sense making: (a) pattern completion, (b) information seeking, and (c) inductive reasoning.

Pattern completion refers to the identification of a meaningful and coherent relationship between stimuli that may or may not in fact be related. A recent set of studies demonstrated the relationship between pattern perception and the desire for meaning by showing that participants induced to experience a loss of control were more likely to seek out patterns than participants who did not experience a loss of control (Whitson & Galinsky, 2008). In these studies, some participants experienced a lack of control either through receiving random feedback in response to performance on a concept formation task or through writing about a time when they lacked control; other participants did not experience a lack of control. Participants induced to experience a loss of control were subsequently more likely to perceive stable patterns in the stock market and to perceive concrete objects in images of fuzzy dots. These participants were also more likely to develop belief in superstitions and conspiracies as a means of making sense of events. Just as these studies demonstrate that being deprived of control increases pattern perception, in the case of anthropomorphism, attributing intentions and desires to a nonhuman entity's actions can similarly generate a meaningful pattern of behavior rather than—in Heider's (1958/1964) terms—"a chaos of juxtaposed items."

The second reason why the motivation for mastery might increase anthropomorphism is because mental states are informative to understanding another agent's behavior. Knowing what an entity is thinking, intending, wanting, or feeling provides insight into its actions, and successful communication requires understanding what others are thinking (Barr & Keysar, 2007). Even the egocentric use of one's own mental states to make inferences about others can be useful and accurate (Dawes & Mulford, 1996; Hoch, 1987; Neyer, Banse, & Asendorpf, 1999). Anthropomorphism as mental state inference, therefore, may be a reasonable strategy because it provides additional information about an entity's behavior.

A third reason that anthropomorphism serves as a reasonable strategy for sense making is through inductive reasoning. Anthropomorphism can be thought of as a form of induction whereby we reason about some lesser known entity (e.g., a nonhuman animal, a technological gadget, a supernatural agent) by applying the features of a very well-known concept, human. There is perhaps no concept with which humans are more familiar than the self, the prototypical human. Furthermore, the concept of the self is highly accessible and therefore is an immediately available source of knowledge for reasoning about others (Epley, Keysar, Van Boven, & Gilovich, 2004; Nickerson, 1999). Just as humans use the self to reason about other people, so too do they use this rich knowledge base for reasoning about nonpeople as well. Young children from industrialized, urban cultures, for example, tend to reason anthropocentrically about nonhuman animals—attributing human capacities to living things—before they have developed a more sophisticated biological understanding (Carey, 1985; Inagaki & Hatano, 1987). When knowledge about a particular entity is lacking, using a familiar concept can provide a guide for making inferences about that entity's behavior.

EVIDENCE FOR ANTHROPOMORPHISM AS AN ATTEMPT AT MEANING MAKING

In recent years, psychologists have begun directly testing the hypothesis that the motivation for mastery leads people to anthropomorphize. Support for this hypothesis comes from multiple lines of work and shows how people anthropomorphize stimuli of all types—animals, technological gadgets, and supernatural beings—when the need for mastery is heightened.

One set of studies examines people's proclivity for teleological explanations of natural events. *Teleology* refers to the tendency to explain events (e.g., why the sun radiates) in terms of intentional design (e.g., to nurture life). Individuals who lack well-developed causal reasoning abilities, such as young children (DiYanni & Kelemen, 2005) and Alzheimer's patients (Lombrozo, Kelemen, & Zaitchik, 2007), show a teleological bias in their reasoning about nature. These populations tend to state that rocks, trees, and the sun exist for some purposeful function. In addition, normal adults, when placed under cognitive load, demonstrate this same teleological bias, endorsing descriptions of natural events as intentionally caused (Kelemen & Rosset, 2009). Cognitive load diminishes the ability for more elaborate causal reasoning, and when causal uncertainty decreases, the tendency to attribute intentions to the workings of nature increases.

Endorsing teleological explanations often implies a belief in the presence of some divine creator, and in line with the research on teleology, people often endorse belief in an anthropomorphic God when they seek meaning. For example, when people are reminded of their death—a situation that evokes existential meaninglessness—they are more likely to report belief in God as well as other supernatural agents (Norenzayan & Hansen, 2006). When they encounter the death of a loved one, they are also likely to turn to God (e.g., McIntosh, Silver, & Wortman, 1993; Spilka, Hood, & Gorsuch, 1985; Wuthnow, Christiano, & Kuzloski, 1980). Similarly, individuals who encounter suffering or are asked to explain a situation in which people suffered are more likely to do so in terms of invoking a God with plans and purpose (Gray & Wegner, 2010). In addition, threats to one's sense of certainty increase religious belief (McGregor et al., 2008; McGregor, Nash, & Prentice, 2010) and experiencing a loss of control or encountering randomness increases people's belief in an agentic God with plans and intentions (Kay et al., 2008; Kay, Moscovitch, & Laurin, 2010). These findings suggest that a desire for meaning increases the tendency to seek God, an agent often depicted in a humanlike form.

In addition to studies on religious belief, a recent number of studies demonstrate that factors that directly increase the motivation for mastery and meaning increase the attribution of mind to nonhumans. In one study, experimenters either did or did not provide participants the opportunity to control a set of animate marbles and then asked them to describe the marbles (and coded their description for anthropomorphic language). Participants who controlled an electromagnet that moved the marbles rarely attributed intentions to the marbles, but those who did not control the magnet were significantly more likely to use intentional language (Barrett & Johnson, 2003).

Having control in this case enabled people to predict the marbles' movements and therefore required no attribution of intentional agency, whereas a lack of control required an appeal to some other causal force, in this case intentionality in the marbles themselves. In a separate set of studies, participants played a series of monetary exchange games with an unknown agent. When the games resulted in negative outcomes (losses or unfair distributions of money to the participant), participants were more likely to infer that they were playing with an intentional agent rather than with a mindless computer (Morewedge, 2009). Negative outcomes tend to be outcomes that require more explanation than positive outcomes (Taylor, 1991; Weiner, 1985), and thus, participants attributed greater intentionality to the agent when motivated to explain their circumstances.

Other studies point to the tendency for people to anthropomorphize when they encounter unpredictability. In one, participants who expected interaction with an unpredictable robot (compared to participants expecting interaction with a predictable robot, or participants not expecting interaction) anthropomorphized the robot more (Eyssel, Kuchenbrandt, & Bobinger, 2011). In another study, participants completed a measure of dispositional desire for control and viewed a video of two dogs—one moving in a relatively predictable manner and one moving in a relatively unpredictable manner. After viewing the video, participants rated both dogs on anthropomorphic characteristics. Results from this study showed that participants were more likely to anthropomorphize the unpredictable dog (versus the predictable dog) likely because of a greater need to explain this dog's behavior. In addition, participants high in desire for control were more likely to anthropomorphize both dogs (Epley et al., 2008). These studies suggest that when people are deprived of control or encounter stimuli that require explanation, they are more likely to anthropomorphize nonhuman entities.

In the most comprehensive test of the hypothesis that the motivation for mastery and meaning increases anthropomorphism, my colleagues and I conducted five studies in which participants evaluated technological or robotic entities (Waytz et al., 2010). In a first study, participants reported how often their personal computers malfunctioned and how much they considered these computers to have minds. The more people's computers malfunctioned, the more they attributed mental states to these gadgets probably because computer malfunction heightens the need for explanation and understanding. In three separate studies, participants evaluated gadgets and robots that operated in a predictable manner as well as gadgets and robots that operated in an unpredictable manner. Across all three studies, participants attributed more mental states to entities that operated unpredictably and evoked a greater desire for mastery. These results manifested not only in self-reported anthropomorphism but also in increased activation in brain regions associated with mentalizing when participants evaluated unpredictable entities. In one additional study, participants watched videos of a robot and were randomly assigned either to a condition in which they received money to predict the robot's behavior or to a condition in which they did not receive money for predicting the robot's behavior. After viewing the videos, participants rated the robot on anthropomorphic and nonanthropomorphic characteristics. Participants who were incentivized to predict the robot's behavior reported greater anthropomorphism of the robot. Taken together, these studies provide considerable evidence for mastery motivation as a primary determinant of anthropomorphism.

OUTSTANDING QUESTIONS

The relationship between mastery motivation and anthropomorphism presents three questions for future research: (a) What are the consequences of anthropomorphism for perceptions of a particular entity's behavior? (b) Does anthropomorphism, in fact, satiate this desire for meaning and provide a real sense of mastery? (c) If the desire for mastery increases humanization, does the converse hold true—that satisfying this desire increases dehumanization? The remainder of this chapter addresses these questions.

Anthropomorphizing an entity to understand its behavior entails seeing its behavior as driven by intentions. This perception of intentionality can make its behavior seem patterned and purposeful. For example, research demonstrates that describing the stock market in anthropomorphic terms can make people feel that trends in the market are more likely to continue (Caruso, Waytz, & Epley, 2010; Morris, Sheldon, Ames, & Young, 2007). Intentional behavior often implies the presence of skill (Malle & Knobe, 1997), and when people perceive behavior as skillfully driven, they often intuit that the pattern of behavior will continue (Gilovich, Vallone, & Tversky, 1985). Additional research is necessary to test the full extent to which anthropomorphism leads people to see an entity's behavior as more routine and patterned.

Another open question is whether anthropomorphizing actually satiates the desire for mastery. One study my colleagues and I conducted speaks to this question (Waytz et al., 2010). In this study, participants viewed short movies of four different stimuli—a set of animate shapes, a puppy, a mobile alarm clock, and a humanoid robot. Participants were instructed to write anthropomorphically about two of the stimuli and to write objectively about the other two. After each writing exercise, participants rated how much they understood and felt they could predict the behavior of the stimulus, as a measure of perceived mastery. Participants reported greater mastery over stimuli that they anthropomorphized, compared with those they treated objectively. Although this study provides preliminary evidence that anthropomorphism can provide perceived mastery, future studies must address whether anthropomorphism can provide *real* mastery. For example, is one more likely to win a chess match against a computer if one anthropomorphizes the computer? Is one more likely to beat cancer if one anthropomorphizes the disease? Can one master the stock market by treating it like an intentional agent? As of now, it is unclear whether anthropomorphism can provide actual mastery or simply illusions of control.

Finally, future research can test the inverse prediction that satisfying the desire for mastery enables dehumanization by lessening the extent to which one must see others as having minds. Some evidence already exists in support of this hypothesis, demonstrating that people induced to experience power—that is, to have control and mastery over their social environments—are more likely to dehumanize others. One set of studies showed that putting people in high-power roles increased their tendency to objectify others and to treat them as means to an end rather than as mindful agents (Gruenfeld, Inesi, Magee, & Galinsky, 2008). Another set of studies showed that powerful people or people induced to experience high power were less likely to describe out-group members using traits that are distinctively human (Lammers & Stapel, 2011). These findings suggest that people who have attained a sense of mastery have a reduced need to explain and understand the actions of others and therefore are more likely to treat others as mindless entities rather than as the humans they really are.

CONCLUSION

Seeing human is one method by which people make sense of the world around them. Imbuing trees, animals, gadgets, and gods with humanlike feelings and intentions may not be as automatic as Hume suggested, but it is a widespread tendency. By seeing things as human, people attempt to create the familiar in relatively unfamiliar entities. It is for future research to determine the consequences of this process, for both perceivers of nonhumans and the entities perceived, and to determine whether satisfying the motivation for mastery and meaning may, in fact, diminish the desire and tendency to see others as fundamentally human.

REFERENCES

Barr, D. J., & Keysar, B. (2007). Perspective taking and the coordination of meaning in language use. In M. J. Traxler & M. A. Gernsbacher (Eds.), *Handbook of psycholinguistics* (2nd ed., pp. 901–938). New York, NY: Academic Press.

Barrett, J. L., & Johnson, A. H. (2003). The role of control in attributing intentional agency to inanimate objects. *Journal of Cognition and Culture, 3*, 208–217. doi:10.1163/156853703322336634

Berlyne, D. E. (1962). Uncertainty and epistemic curiosity. *British Journal of Psychology, 53*, 27–34. doi:10.1111/j.2044-8295.1962.tb00811.x

Carey, S. (1985). *Conceptual change in childhood.* Cambridge, MA: Bradford Books, MIT Press.

Caruso, E. M., Waytz, A., & Epley, N. (2010). The intentional mind and the hot hand: Perceiving intentions makes streaks seem likely to continue. *Cognition, 116*, 149–153. doi:10.1016/j.cognition.2010.04.006

Dawes, R. M., & Mulford, M. (1996). The false consensus effect and overconfidence: Flaws in judgment, or flaws in how we study judgment? *Organizational Behavior and Human Decision Processes*, 65, 201–211. doi:10.1006/obhd.1996.0020

DiYanni, C., & Kelemen, D. (2005). Time to get a new mountain? The role of function in children's conceptions of natural kinds. *Cognition, 97*, 327–335. doi:10.1016/j.cognition.2004.10.002

Dennett, D. C. (1987). *The intentional stance*. Cambridge, MA: MIT Press.

Epley, N., Keysar, B., Van Boven, L., & Gilovich, T. (2004). Perspective taking as egocentric anchoring and adjustment. *Journal of Personality and Social Psychology, 87*, 327–339. doi:10.1037/0022-3514.87.3.327

Epley, N., Waytz, A., Akalis, S., & Cacioppo, J. T. (2008). When I need a human: Motivational determinants of anthropomorphism. *Social Cognition, 26*, 143–155. doi:10.1521/soco.2008.26.2.143

Epley, N., Waytz, A., & Cacioppo, J. T. (2007). On seeing human: A three–factor theory of anthropomorphism. *Psychological Review, 114*, 864–886. doi:10.1037/0033-295X.114.4.864

Eyssel, F., Kuchenbrandt, D., & Bobinger, S. (2011). Effects of anticipated human-robot interaction and predictability of robot behavior on perceptions of anthropomorphism. *Proceedings of the 6th HRI International Conference on Human-Robot Interaction*, 61–67.

Gilovich, T., Vallone, R., & Tversky, A. (1985). The hot hand in basketball: On the misperception of random sequences. *Cognitive Psychology, 17*, 295–314. doi:10.1016/0010-0285(85)90010-6

Gray, K., & Wegner, D. M. (2010). Blaming God for our pain: Human suffering and the divine mind. *Personality and Social Psychology Review, 14*, 7–16. doi:10.1177/1088868309350299

Gruenfeld, D. H., Inesi, M. E., Magee, J. C., & Galinsky, A. D. (2008). Power and the objectification of social targets. *Journal of Personality and Social Psychology*, 95, 111–127. doi:10.1037/0022-3514.95.1.111

Guthrie, S. (1993). *Faces in the clouds*. Oxford, England: Oxford University Press.

Heider, F. (1964). *The psychology of interpersonal relations*. New York, NY: Wiley. (Original work published 1958)

Heider, F., & Simmel, M. (1944). An experimental study of apparent behavior. *The American Journal of Psychology, 57*, 243–259. doi:10.2307/1416950

Hoch, S. J. (1987). Perceived consensus and predictive accuracy: The pros and cons of projection. *Journal of Personality and Social Psychology, 53*, 221–234. doi:10.1037/0022-3514.53.2.221

Hume, D. (1957). *The natural history of religion*. Stanford, CA: Stanford University Press. (Original work published 1757)

Humphrey, N. (1983). *Consciousness regained*. Oxford, England: Oxford University Press.

Inagaki, K., & Hatano, G. (1987). Young children's spontaneous personification as analogy. *Child Development, 58*, 1013–1020. doi:10.2307/1130542

Kay, A. C., Gaucher, D., Napier, J. L., Callan, M. J., & Laurin, K. (2008). God and the Government: Testing a compensatory control mechanism for the support of external systems. *Journal of Personality and Social Psychology, 95*, 18–35. doi:10.1037/0022-3514.95.1.18

Kay, A. C., Moscovitch, D. M., & Laurin, K. (2010). Randomness, attributions of arousal, and belief in God. *Psychological Science, 21*, 216–218. doi:10.1177/0956797609357750

Kelemen, D., & Rosset, E. (2009). The human function compunction: Teleological explanation in adults. *Cognition, 111*, 138–143. doi:10.1016/j.cognition.2009.01.001

Kelley, H. H. (1967). Attribution theory in social psychology. In D. Levine (Ed.), *Nebraska Symposium on Motivation* (Vol. 15, pp. 192–240). Lincoln: University of Nebraska Press.

Kiesler, S., & Goetz, J. (2002). Mental models and cooperation with robotic assistants. *Proceedings of CHI'02 on Human Factors in Computing Systems* (pp. 576–577). Minneapolis, MN.

Lakoff, G., & Johnson, M. (1980). *Metaphors we live by*. Chicago, IL: University of Chicago Press.

Lammers, J., & Stapel, D. A. (2011). Power increases dehumanization. *Group Processes & Intergroup Relations, 14*, 113–126. doi:10.1177/1368430210370042

Lombrozo, T., Kelemen, D., & Zaitchik, D. (2007). Inferring design: Evidence of a preference for teleological explanations in patients with Alzheimer's disease. *Psychological Science, 18*, 999–1006. doi:10.1111/j.1467-9280.2007.02015.x

McGregor, I., Haji, R., Nash, K., & Teper, R. (2008). Religious zeal and the uncertain self. *Basic and Applied Social Psychology, 30*, 183–188. doi:10.1080/01973530802209251

McGregor, I., Nash, K., & Prentice, M. (2010). Reactive approach motivation (RAM) for religion. *Journal of Personality and Social Psychology, 99*, 148–161. doi:10.1037/a0019702

McIntosh, D. N., Silver, R. C., & Wortman, C. B. (1993). Religion's role in adjustment to a negative life event: Coping with the loss of a child. *Journal of Personality and Social Psychology, 65*, 812–821. doi:10.1037/0022-3514.65.4.812

Malle, B. F., & Knobe, J. (1997). The folk concept of intentionality. *Journal of Experimental Social Psychology, 33*, 101–121. doi:10.1006/jesp.1996.1314

Mithen, S. (1996). *The prehistory of the mind*. London, England: Thames & Hudson.

Morewedge, C. K. (2009). Negativity bias in attribution of external agency. *Journal of Experimental Psychology: General, 138*, 535–545. doi:10.1037/a0016796

Morris, M. W., Sheldon, O. J., Ames, D. R., & Young, M. J. (2007). Metaphor and the market: Consequences and preconditions of agent and object metaphors in stock market commentary. *Organizational Behavior and Human Decision Processes, 102*, 174–192. doi:10.1016/j.obhdp.2006.03.001

Neyer, F. J., Banse, R., & Asendorpf, J. B. (1999). The role of projection and empathic accuracy in dyadic perception between older twins. *Journal of Social and Personal Relationships, 16*, 419–442. doi:10.1177/0265407599164001

Nickerson, R. S. (1999). How we know—and sometimes misjudge—what others know: Imputing one's own knowledge to others. *Psychological Bulletin, 125*, 737–759. doi:10.1037/0033-2909.125.6.737

Norenzayan, A., & Hansen, I. G. (2006). Belief in supernatural agents in the face of death. *Personality and Social Psychology Bulletin, 32*, 174–187. doi:10.1177/0146167205280251

Spilka, B., Hood, R., & Gorsuch, R. (1985). *The psychology of religion: An empirical approach*. Englewood Cliffs, NJ: Prentice-Hall.

Taylor, S. E. (1991). Asymmetric effects of positive and negative events: The mobilization-minimization hypothesis. *Psychological Bulletin, 110*, 67–85. doi:10.1037/0033-2909.110.1.67

Waytz, A., Klein, N., & Epley, N. (In press). Imagining other minds: Hair triggered but not hare brained. In M. Taylor (Ed.), *The development of imagination*. New York, NY: Oxford University Press.

Waytz, A., Morewedge, C., Epley, N., Monteleone, G., Gao, J., & Cacioppo, J. T. (2010). Making sense by making sentient: Effectance motivation increases anthropomorphism. *Journal of Personality and Social Psychology, 99*, 410–435. doi:10.1037/a0020240

Weary, G., & Edwards, J. E. (1996). Causal uncertainty and related goal structures. In R. Sorrentino & E. T. Higgins (Eds.), *The handbook of motivation and cognition: The interpersonal context* (Vol. 3, pp. 148–181). New York, NY: Guilford Press.

Weiner, B. (1985). "Spontaneous" causal thinking. *Psychological Bulletin, 97*, 74–84. doi:10.1037/0033-2909.97.1.74

White, R. W. (1959). Motivation reconsidered: The concept of competence. *Psychological Review, 66*, 297–333. doi:10.1037/h0040934

Whitson, J. A., & Galinsky, A. D. (2008, October 3). Lacking control increases illusory pattern perception. *Science, 322*, 115–117. doi:10.1126/science.1159845

Wuthnow, R., Christiano, K., & Kuzloski, J. (1980). Religion and bereavement: A conceptual framework. *Journal for the Scientific Study of Religion, 19*, 408–430. doi:10.2307/1386134

III

TELEOLOGICAL UNDERSTANDING: A GUIDE FOR LIVING

8

AUTOBIOGRAPHICAL MEMORY AND THE CREATION OF MEANING FROM PERSONALLY EXPERIENCED EVENTS

W. RICHARD WALKER AND JOHN J. SKOWRONSKI

Experiences are transient. Memory allows experiences to be recalled, examined, and used for many purposes. These might include solving mundane problems of everyday existence (Where can I find food?) or coping with complicated issues of self-evaluation (How have I changed since I turned 18?). Although the functional importance of personal memories to daily existence should be easily intuited, that functionality is driven home by the problems that arise in those whose ability to remember their personal pasts is severely impaired (for additional insight, see Klein, German, Cosmides, & Gabriel, 2004).

THE SLOW EMERGENCE OF AUTOBIOGRAPHICAL MEMORY IN SCIENTIFIC PSYCHOLOGY

The ancients almost certainly respected the functionality of personal memories. In fact, they regarded memory so highly that they wrote treatises about memory (for various discussions, see Burnham, 1888; Fuller, 1898;

DOI: 10.1037/14040-008
The Psychology of Meaning, Keith D. Markman, Travis Proulx, and Matthew J. Lindberg (Editors)

Herrmann & Chaffin, 1988; Middleton, 1888; Yates, 1966) and created gods or goddesses to handle the memory problems of mere mortals. Examples are Thoth in ancient Egypt, Mnemosyne in ancient Greece, and Minerva in ancient Rome (she kept an owl as a familiar, which is the likely reason that owls became associated with wisdom). Buddhism offers the god Kokuzo Bosatsu, a deity of memory and wisdom and a protector of artisans. Such activities suggest that the ancients recognized the importance and complexity of memory processes and that they understood that memory was inherently linked to the ability of humans to give meaning to their experiences.

However, in this historical context, it is curious that the study of autobiographical memory was a relative latecomer to mainstream psychology. True, there were exceptions, most notably in the domain of childhood amnesia (Hall, 1904; Miles, 1895). Research in this area prompted an early review of the literature (Dudycha & Dudycha, 1941) and was co-opted into theories of psychological functioning (e.g., see Adler, 1937; Freud, 1920/1952). However, despite such developments, perhaps because of concern with establishing scientific credentials, many early memory researchers were children of Ebbinghaus (1885/1964): They pursued memory research in laboratory contexts using carefully constructed stimuli devoid of personal meaning.

To be clear, although we criticize this approach, we respect its aims and rigor. We simply point out that one consequence of this emphasis is that it inhibited work exploring autobiographical memories, in part because the methods needed to explore such memories were sometimes perceived as less "scientific" than the precise but relatively (by necessity) sterile laboratory methods (e.g., see Banaji & Crowder, 1989).

A number of factors converged to break this bias. One was the recognition that the use of multiple methods could minimize the error and bias associated with each individual method used to study autobiographical memory, thus allowing researchers to triangulate in on effects of interest. Another was the spread of sophisticated data analysis techniques and the software to implement those techniques. Such techniques were often necessary to analyses of messy and multilayered autobiographical memory data derived from the real world. Yet a third factor was the emergence of theories such as Tulving's notions of episodic memory and autonoetic consciousness (e.g., Tulving, 1985, 2002) that virtually demanded investigation of the autobiographical memory domain.

Even so, early autobiographical memory studies tended to adhere to ideas derived from the laboratory, especially ideas about the importance of processes occurring when first encountering an event to subsequent event memory. For example, in one program that paralleled laboratory approaches (e.g., reflected in Thompson, Skowronski, Larsen, & Betz, 1996), research focused on how stimulus characteristics of events (e.g., extremity, positivity) influenced both event recall and a person's ability to place events in time. A second example comes from studies whose results showed that identification of the perpetrator of a crime was impaired when the perpetrator used a weapon, presumably because attention to the weapon distracted attention from the perpetrator's appearance (e.g., Cutler, Penrod, O'Rourke, & Martens, 1986).

MEANING MAKING AND AUTOBIOGRAPHICAL MEMORY: ON THE IMPORTANCE OF BOTH THE SELF AND THE SOCIAL

However, as research in the area progressed, researchers began to realize that there was at least one feature of autobiographical memory that prompted some degree of decoupling of such research from the study of memory as practiced in laboratory contexts: *postevent processing*. One famous element of such postevent processing has been highlighted by the research program of Loftus, which shows that people's memories can easily be influenced by postevent information that is obtained from other individuals (for a recent update of scholarship in this area, see Laney & Loftus, 2010).

Certainly, it is a truism that laboratory research has often focused on one form of such processing, the relation between rehearsal and memory, and it has done so for a long time (see Herrmann & Chaffin, 1988). What is unique about autobiographical memory is that autobiographical events are often not rehearsed in isolation. Instead, they are often woven into parables, stories, and narratives. Moreover, when people relate autobiographical memories, they are often doing so because the memories can be made to "mean something," either to the self or to others (for related ideas, see Alea & Bluck, 2003; Nelson, 2003; Pasupathi, 2006; Pillemer, 1992; Webster, 2003). For example, some of the time such stories are constructed and related for the purpose *of conveying events to others* (e.g., with the goal of conveying history). However, these parables can be produced for numerous other reasons. Examples are to promote *self-understanding;* to *make a point or convey a lesson to others; and to present oneself,* regardless of whether conveying the actual self or an idealized sense of self.

We can easily see times when this has occurred in our own lives. For example, Jessie, the mother of John J. Skowronski, was a native of Poland who was ripped from her home and parents by the Russian Army in World War II. Many children of Poland (one estimate places the number at 380,000) experienced such an event. Collectively, they were sent on a long sojourn across Asia before being scattered across the globe. After departing from India, some ended up in the United States by way of Mexico (the fate of Jessie and three of her siblings); some ended up in England (the fate of some of Jessie's sisters); and some ended up in Africa (such events are chronicled by Adamczyk, 2004; Krolikowski, 1983/2001).

These recalled events often served as the context for points that Jessie wanted to convey to others. Some of these points concerned personal qualities. For example, when Jessie wanted to convey her tenacity to others, she would tell the story of how she battled starvation by sneaking out to catch turtles to make turtle soup, providing protein to an impoverished diet. When Jessie wanted to make a point about her worldliness, she would cite the numerous countries through which she traveled as the Russians moved the Polish exiles from place to place on their sojourn through Asia. However, these stories were often put to uses other than to illustrate personal qualities. For example, to illustrate the capriciousness of life, Jessie would tell the story of how she and a sister were rattling along in a transport vehicle in Afghanistan when, at a crossroads, they happened to see another transport vehicle at an intersection. The vehicle was heading in another direction, but Jessie spied two of her brothers on the second transport and managed to grab them before the transports separated. When Jessie wanted to convey the point to her young son that the problems that he was experiencing in his comfortable American life were minor, she would talk about the experienced of being ripped from her parents and being starved while being shuttled across Asia. When her children felt deprived, the turtle soup story served to make a point about what "real" deprivation was and how it was combated.

As research into autobiographical memory progressed, it became clear that to understand autobiographical memory one needed to understand the ways in which people like Jessie thought about and conveyed information about their personal pasts and the motives that drove such efforts. Researchers recognized the importance of such efforts in that they can influence autobiographical memory in a number of ways. For example, storytelling motives can affect those events that are selected for inclusion in narratives, how those events are woven together, how often such narratives are conveyed, and how such narratives change as one matures and as life circumstances change.

As an example, consider how a person might reply to the prompt "Tell me about Becky, your first love" at different times of the person's life. While in high school, recall of the fifth-grade romance with Becky might prompt her denigration: She might be described as terribly prudish in comparison with the adventurous new high school paramour. While away at college, one might describe Becky with fondness because of the memories of home cued by recall of Becky. Later, after one's marriage breaks down, one might talk about Becky with malice because it was she who first caused the pain of a breakup. As one moves into old age, one might talk about Becky fondly as one recalls one's own developing ability to love others and the role that Becky played in the emergence of that capability.

As one might suspect, the pursuit of research in this area requires acquisition and use of a diverse set of research skills and perspectives. One must be aware of the self, how the mental structures and processes that are linked to the self function, and how these are guided by self-motives and self-goals. One must be aware of groups and societies: The kinds of disclosures that might be seen as appropriate may vary across groups and cultures, as might the contexts that are appropriate for such disclosures as well as the points that are attempted to be made in such disclosures. For example, a self-focused Westerner might tell stories to others that illustrate his or her personal qualities; a group-focused Asian might convey stories illustrating his or her relation to his or her family. One must be aware of issues in development: As people's lives change, their needs and concerns may change, and these may shape the ways in which people think about their life events. For example, being dumped by a romantic partner may be seen as a crushing event 4 months after it happened, but it may be seen as a blessing 6 years later after one has met one's soul mate. Moreover, these personal and social perspectives are not independent. The self-context, the social context, and the developmental context are all affected by each other.

EXTRACTION OF SELF-RELEVANT MEANING FROM AUTOBIOGRAPHICAL EVENT SEQUENCES

Extremely powerful data concerning how the self fits in with the development of autobiographical life stories come from those researchers who have been interested in narrative approaches to the study of individual lives (for an overview, see McAdams, 2008; see also Chapter 9, this volume). A key concept in this work is the idea of a *narrative identity:* An individual's integrated, internalized, and evolving idea of the self. Research now suggests that these narratives are conveyed frequently (e.g., Rimé, Mesquita, Philippot, & Boca, 1991), begin to be constructed in adolescence and young adulthood (e.g., Blagov & Singer, 2004; Habermas & Bluck, 2000; McLean, 2005; Thorne, 2000), and develop and change across the life span. That such stories should have implications for how people think about themselves seems fairly clear. For example, consider this memory narrative produced by an adolescent in McLean's (2005) study:

> I was at my friend's house one night with my main group of friends. They were all smoking marijuana and drinking. I did not feel comfortable with trying marijuana. They tried hard to get me to try it, but I chose not to. One of my friends (my best) supported my choice. I learned who my real friends were. But more importantly, I learned that I can be strong with my decisions if I choose to, regardless of the outside influence. (p. 687)

We hasten to note that not all stories may have implications for the self. For example, sometimes people sometimes construct narratives for the purpose of entertaining others. The McLean (2005) study also contained nice examples of such narratives:

> We had this one planned out for weeks before. It is not that we did not like the girls, but they were just our opposites, the female version of us. So we decided to use my house as a home base and proceeded at 1 a.m. to do as much damage as humanly possible to all six houses. This was probably one of the more fun moments of my life as we raced around the San Fernando Valley toilet papering their houses till they looked like white waterfalls. And the best part, the following Monday at school, five of the six girls ended up blaming the sixth one and her house got toilet papered the following week too. Truly a great couple of weeks. (pp. 687–688)

Nonetheless, many recounted events do have implications for the self. Indeed, one of the ideas that underlies research in this area is that people think about major events and major changes in their lives and that one function of such thought is the incorporation of such events into a life story that projects a theme of *productive growth* (e.g., Bauer & McAdams, 2004). Events incorporated into such narratives often involve conflicts and negative life changes, such as the loss of loved ones and the loss of personal resources. Indeed, losses, conflicts, and negative life changes often threaten an individual's sense of personal continuity and are thought to mobilize the individual's cognitive, motivational, and biological systems (e.g., Taylor, 1991). The key goal of mobilization is to minimize the impact of such events.

One way in which this can be done is to explain negative events in ways that discount the events (e.g., Freeman, 1993), for example, by suggesting that the event has no relevance to one's life. However, from a practical perspective, discounting can be difficult. As an alternative, one can attempt to integrate the negative events into the self in positive ways. One option is to reflect on negative events in such a way as to inform the self about potential to change and progress. For example, after a reviewing missteps made when interacting with a valued colleague, a one might draw a life lesson that can be applied to one's future behavior. Indeed, research now suggests that the capacity to make sense of losses occurs frequently in response to such negative events and can lead to personal resilience in the face of those events (Bauer & Bonanno, 2001; McAdams, 2008; Pasupathi, Weeks, & Rice, 2006).

Moreover, Pals (2006) suggested that there is consistency in how people approach such a process. An individual first explores the event in depth, thinking long and hard about the experience: how the event came to be, how it felt, the directions in which the event might lead, and the implications that the event might have for the self. The second step involves a resolution of the event that supports the theme of a positive self. Such themes can involve seeing personal growth as a consequence of negative events and seeing eventual good as coming out of past bad ("It was good thing that Bob dumped me; otherwise I would not have found my soul mate, Jim"). Such meaning-making activity can obviously buffer the self from the consequences of the negative events.

SOME IMPLICATIONS OF MEANING MAKING FOR AUTOBIOGRAPHICAL MEMORY

It makes sense that the mental activities (rehearsal, narrative construction) required for meaning making should produce measurable aftereffects on memory. Certainly, given that active processing is thought to be important to remembering, one would expect that the active processing of meaning making should affect memory for events included in the meaning making. Such effects may be discernible in both the memory for event content as well as memory for the temporal qualities of an event, such as memory for when an event occurred or an event's age. However, meaning-making activity may also affect how recalling events makes people feel when events are recalled. These ideas are treated in the next three sections.

Emotional Responses to Memories

One consequence of the cognitive activity that follows negative events might be to reduce the emotional sting associated with the recall of negative events. For example, Crawley (2010) examined *psychological closure:* a subjective assessment of how well a remembered experience feels resolved. Crawley found that the recall of open memories was accompanied by more intense, more negative, and less positive emotion than the recall of closed memories. Hence, when postevent processing is unable to lead people to a satisfactory psychological resolution of events, one consequence may be continued high negative affect associated with events (also see Beike & Wirth-Beaumont, 2005; Ritchie et al., 2006).

The retention of such high negative affect may be fairly unusual. Research into the *fading affect bias* suggests that the negative affect associated with events typically fades faster than the positive affect associated with events (Walker & Skowronski, 2009). To exemplify this effect, imagine that the intense anger that might have accompanied a betrayal by a friend when the event occurred might provoke a mild anger response when the sequence of events leading to the betrayal is recalled at a later point in time. In comparison, the intense joy that might have accompanied striking a goal that won the city football championship might provoke a substantial sense of happiness when later examining photos of the event in old newspaper clippings.

Research conducted so far suggests that the fading affect bias is a real characteristic of autobiographical event recall and cannot be accounted for by variables such as differences in the initial extremity of unpleasant events and pleasant events, better recall of pleasant events than unpleasant events, distorted memory for the affect that accompanied the initial event, the arousal of the emotion prompted by the initial event, the mood of the judge at the time of rating, or theories of emotion change (Ritchie & Skowronski, 2008; Ritchie, Skowronski, Hartnett, Wells, & Walker, 2009; Ritchie et al., 2006; Skowronski, Gibbons, Vogl, & Walker, 2004; Walker, Skowronski, Gibbons, Vogl, & Thompson, 2003; Walker, Skowronski, & Thompson, 2003). Instead, the bias seems to be related to storytelling activity. The more that one relates the event to others and the greater the diversity in the audience for the tales, the larger the bias, in part because of rapid fading of negative affect.

More recent research suggests that fading affect is not the whole story. Walker and Skowronski (2009) found that although fading affect holds true for about half of the sampled autobiographical events in their studies, emotions can change in three other ways. First, some events show no changes in affect (*fixed affect*). Second, some events increase in their affective intensity (*flourishing affect*). Third, a few events actually change affective valence, often shifting from negative affect at the time of the event to positive affect at the time of recall (*flexible affect*). At least some of the change in affect that emerges reflects reevaluation of events in light of current life circumstances, a point anticipated by Levine and Bluck (2004). Thus, one variable that must be accounted for when trying to understand the emotions prompted by event recall is the process that people use to construe events. Such construals do not end with the occurrence of the event but instead might persist through life as an individual attempts to make sense of his or her "life story" (see McLean, Pasupathi, & Pals, 2007). To the extent that individuals' activities in this regard will tend to emphasize the positive in the self and to minimize the negative, the emergence of the fading affect bias makes considerable sense.

Aspects of Autobiographical Memory Content

It bears repeating that memory is reconstructive rather than reproductive. For autobiographical memory, this essential truth of memory has many implications. At the level of individual memories, it means that specific details may be misperceived at the time of the event, misremembered at a point after the event, or completely forgotten. As individual event memories are incorporated into clusters of memories representative of particular periods or epochs in peoples' lives, individual event memories are further reinterpreted, edited, combined with other memories, or eliminated altogether. This is a process that is continually in a state of flux. However, it would be incorrect to conclude that the construction of autobiographical memory is random or chaotic.

As Skowronski and Walker (2004) argued, one reason why it is important to understand these attempts at meaning making is because they have implications for the reconstruction of autobiographical memories. They point to the fact that meaning-making activity might alter elements of rehearsal. Some events might be described to others, whereas other events might not be. Some event details might be included in the descriptions but not other details. Some event details might be accurately described to others, but other details might be distorted in the retelling. Some extra-event information (e.g., the statement "He looked just like Harrison Ford") might be included in some descriptions but not in other descriptions. Skowronski and Walker argued that a number of factors, including self-presentational concerns and concerns about the self and self-construal, might affect these kinds of selectivity in autobiographical event rehearsal. Thus, meaning-making efforts can ultimately have an impact on the conveyor's later memory.

These memories might be affected in several ways. For example, in telling stories about self-improvement, temporal recategorizations of events (e.g., "That happened when I was a young and naïve kid") might be facilitated by describing the event to others. These recategorizations might make such events seem older than if such discourse did not occur. Another possible outcome of such storytelling is that one's tendency to retrieve events might be linked to the contexts of the storytelling. That is, as one recounts the events from one's own life, various situational cues and communication goals might become linked to the autobiographical memories that are recounted. Such cues and goals might prompt reinstatement of the events when those goals are activated or those cues are encountered at a later time. As events become linked with a greater number of cues, the probability of retrieving such memories should increase. Hence, diversity in storytelling settings and goals might also play an important role in the extent to which an individual recalls autobiographical events.

Empirical examples of such changes already exist. Consider work done by Wilson, Ross, and their colleagues (for an overview, see Cameron, Wilson, & Ross, 2004; for similar results, see McFarland & Alvaro, 2000; Safer & Keuler, 2002). These authors suggested that self-enhancement and self-protective motives operate to maintain the positivity of the current self. They suggested that one way that this can occur is when people engage in postevent meaning-making activities. In doing so, it is postulated that these motives can sometimes produce enhanced memory for *negative* past events.

For example, one way in which one might glorify one's current ability to play golf is to remember how bad one was at the activity when one started to play the game. The meaning to be derived from the parable that one constructs about oneself is, "Look at how far I've come—I could barely find the course when I started, but now I can actually manage to break bogey occasionally."

For this self-parable to have maximum impact, one must remember just how bad one was at the start of one's attempts at play. The word *remember* should be used with caution here because one possibility is that people in such situations will reconstruct their early performance level so that it is recalled to be worse than the facts might suggest. Indeed, the Wilson and Ross team found evidence for exactly this effect in their research.

Similar results were reported by Dewhurst and Marlborough (2003). These authors asked participants to rate their anxiety levels 48 hours prior to an exam and to later recall these levels after receiving their exam results. The exaggerated recall of preexam anxiety was observed in students who surpassed their target grade. Hence, one possible outcome of the narrative goal of accentuating the positive in the current self is that the goal can actually *maintain or enhance memory for the negative*. Although this enhancement may seem to violate the idea that one goal of self-processing is the minimization of negativity over the long term (e.g., Taylor, 1991), the finding does not actually do so because in the context of the narrative one consequence of recalling the negative event is that one feels more positive about the *current* self.

However, the effects of meaning-making activity clearly extend beyond these valence-based effects. For example, Thompson et al. (1996) made an important distinction between the core details of an event memory and peripheral details of an event memory. They presented evidence from hundreds of diary studies conducted on college students that showed that the core details of an event were much less likely to fade or show distortion than peripheral details of an event. The work of Herlihy, Scragg, and Turner (2002) emphasized this point. They examined the memories of refugees from Kosovo and Bosnia seeking asylum in England in the late 1990s. When refugees are repeatedly interviewed for asylum, the consistency of their interviews weighs heavily in whether they actually receive asylum. The underlying assumption is that discrepancies in recall are an indicator of a person seeking asylum under false pretenses. Many of these refugees were survivors of war atrocities and were subsequently diagnosed with posttraumatic stress disorder. Despite their extreme experiences and their clinical diagnoses, the memories of these refugees showed the same pattern as in the Thompson et al. (1996) studies: Peripheral details showed evidence of fading and distortion, but core details did not.

This emphasis on core details is also exhibited in another reliable finding in the autobiographical memory literature known as the *reminiscence bump*. The reminiscence bump is the tendency for adults to evince a heightened frequency of event recollections for events that occurred during periods in their lives that were important to them, typically (but not limited to) adolescence and early adulthood (e.g., Rubin, Rahhal, & Poon, 1998). The bump has been explicitly linked to the stories that people tell about themselves and has also been shown to have significant cross-cultural variation that fits with the influence of such norms on the nature of self-stories (Wang & Conway, 2004).

Perceptions of Event Age

Meaning making can also impact autobiographical memory through perceptions of the event ages. For example, some events can become temporal landmarks. These are often major life events and often refer to the beginning or the end of a part of life that can be characterized as a *life stage*. Examples might be as follows: when I started graduate school at Kansas State University or when I left the psychology department at The Ohio State University. One of the characteristics of such landmarks is that they are spontaneously used by people to place events in sequence relative to each other (Shum, 1998).

Evidence of temporal landmarking emerged in a study reported by Thompson, Skowronski, and Betz (1993). These authors argued that many events in our lives are part of a sequence of themed events. There are themes with relatively long time frames, such as being a parent or attending college. There are also themes with short time frames, such as preparing for a large party or shopping for a new apartment. Such themes can emerge as one engages in postevent processing that involves sense-making activity. Thus, Thompson et al. (1993) speculated that events that were seen as thematically related might contain one or more events that could reasonably be used as an anchor to date other events. Indeed, this might happen if an event was particularly important or was the "logical" starting point for a series of related events. Indeed, Thompson et al. (1993) found evidence for such a process by finding that some event sequences were all erroneously dated in the same way—as if the first event was both erroneously placed in time and then was used to erroneously place the remainder of the thematically events in time.

This perception is reinforced by results reported by Skowronski et al. (2007; see also Skowronski, Walker, & Betz, 2003). Those authors speculated that people can organize events by life periods, which can often become attached to events in the process of retelling events as a part of a life narrative. Skowronski et al. (2007) speculated that these temporal era tags have implications for judgments of event order (e.g., judgments of which event in a pair was older or younger). They found that regardless of whether the eras were defined in terms of (a) college versus high school, (b) academic quarter within year, or (c) academic year within school, between-eras judgments were faster than within-era judgments. This effect occurred even when controlling for the actual time difference between event pairs.

However, sense-making activity can directly affect perceptions of event age, even in the likely absence of temporal landmarking activity. For example, research has found that events can be made to "feel" older or younger, depending on how they relate to current self-needs (for an overview, see Cameron et al., 2004). For example, if the self-narrative construction emphasizes the extent to which one might have been a fine scholar when one was younger, then one influence of such a narrative might be to make it seem as if that first publication in an American Psychological Association journal feels as if it happened only yesterday. On the other hand, if the current self influences a self-narrative in such a way as to present oneself as a much better scholar now than in one's youth, then the memory of that first rejection letter may feel as if it happened a very long time ago, indeed.

LIMITS ON MEANING FLEXIBILITY: EVENTS SOMETIMES HAVE INTRINSIC MEANING

As reflected in the studies described previously, the theoretical zeitgeist emphasizes that autobiographical memory is a reconstruction of the past. Memory experts and students alike recognize that memory is imprecise, prone to confusion and error, and sometimes completely false (Loftus, 1993). Indeed, psychologists have taken almost perverse delight in documenting reconstruction errors in memory, errors that range from the relatively minor (false recognitions of events that are consistent with the stereotype of an actor) to the amusing (falsely recalling meeting inappropriate cartoon characters at amusement parks) to the profound (falsely recalling evidence of abuse from parents).

Lost in this "one-upsmanship" of describing the faults of memory is the basic observation that human memory does a reasonably good job of creating representations of past experiences. That is, the meaning that is given to the human experience through memory is not capricious. Meaning is inherently tied to reality. Indeed, for memory to be functional, it *must* have some tie to reality. This was recognized by Martianus Cappella, who in his *De septem disciplinis* ("On the seven disciplines") conceptualized memory as a god whose role was to make mankind behave in a more realistic manner by grounding the understanding of experiences in reality. In other words, in this view, memory usually provides a useful representation of reality.

However, this is not to say that memory is perfect—the key idea is that it needs to be useful. Indeed, a completely accurate and bias-free recollection of experience may be laudable, but it is also unwieldy. A perfectly recalled event memory could potentially be laden with many sensory details, a complete record of a person's state of mind at the time of the event, and a precise temporal sequence of the event. Such a detailed memory may be difficult to use in everyday circumstances. Indeed, cases of hyperthymesia indicate that maintaining a perfect set of autobiographical memories creates a number of secondary problems for those with the condition (Parker, Cahill, & McGaugh, 2006).

Clearly, then, a memory system's functionality may benefit from the creation of memory representations that are reasonably faithful (but neither complete nor perfect) representations of reality. In this regard, we find it helpful to draw on Gibson's (1977) notion of *affordances* to explain how memories can represent reality without being 100% accurate. For an event memory to be useful in the Gibsonian sense, it must (a) contain valuable information, (b) be able to help an individual in understanding or problem solving, and (c) be easily accessible. We consider these elements in reverse order.

Sperling (1960) showed that the contents of sensory memory appear to be an almost exact copy of what a person senses. Studies of very-long-term memory (Bahrick, Hall, & Berger, 1996) suggest that although some memories can be accurately recalled after periods of time over 40 years, much information is grossly distorted or lost to time. It would seem reasonable that because sensory information is highly accurate, it should also be highly accessible. In fact, the opposite is true. The search rate in sensory memory is about 100 ms per item, whereas in long-term memory, the search rate is much faster—about 4 or 5 ms per item (Atkinson & Shiffrin, 1968). Sensory memory is also notoriously fragile and short in duration, whereas very-long-term memories have a high degree of permanence and seem invaluable to a person's general world knowledge. Thus, the information that is often judged to be the least accurate (constructed long-term representations) seems to be the most accessible. Why?

These differences in accessibility can be explained, in part, by the ability of information stored in each of these systems to help people understand current situations or solve problems. Laboratory investigations often require recalling information verbatim. Everyday life rarely imposes this requirement.

Sensory memories are richly detailed traces of the energy sources detected by the sensory organs during unique experiences. As this information is continuously updated, very little of that information is attended to in a way conducive to rapid access. Hence, in real-world scenarios these highly accurate memories have little value. In contrast, long-term memories are much more likely to contain *gist* information that includes broad generalizations based on hundreds or thousands of similar (but not identical) experiences. Most everyday uses of memory rely on gist memory. For example, Nickerson and Adams (1979) cleverly pointed out that Americans had difficulty discriminating a real penny from a group of similar frauds in spite of the fact that most people deal with pennies every day. However, though people are seldom given the task of looking for phony pennies, they can perform the task well when the stakes are high. For instance, in Las Vegas in 1995 a ring of counterfeiters were caught passing fake $50 and $100 bills not by high-tech optical readers (which failed to detect the same bills) but by observant casino patrons and staff who quickly spotted them (Schneier, 2003, p. 195).

Time is an important element of event memory that can make that memory helpful in solving problems. The Watergate scandal is frequently associated with the question "What did the President know and when did he know it?" (often asked by Republican Senator Howard Baker). Here again, gist information appears to rule the roost is in establishing the temporal location of events. Remembering exactly when an event occurred is often very difficult, a conclusion drawn from studies showing that people only remember the exact dates of about 10% of events recorded in daily diaries (Thompson et al., 1996). The errors made by such individuals, however, are far from random: When able to use a calendar as a dating aid, errors often occur in intervals of 7 (7 days of error, 14 days of error, 21 days of error, etc.). The reason for such a pattern is obvious to any person looking at a calendar. Participants were remembering or inferring the day of the week the event occurred and were using that information to estimate the date on which the event occurred (Thompson et al., 1993).

After the attributes of accessibility and utility comes the characteristic of value. The literature suggests that select autobiographical episodes can have lasting effects on a person's life or their views on life. For example, Holmes and Rahe (1967) created a social readjustment rating scale that sought to reflect the psychological significance of many life events. Holmes and Rahe found that most psychologically significant events were related to family members and family situations. In addition, highly significant events were typically associated with coping and adapting behaviors, indicating that the events induced stress in participants who experienced them. Other results from studies using different methods led to similar conclusions (Ensel, 1991; Palmer & Braud, 2002; Porter & Birt, 2001; Santiago-Rivera, Gard, & Bernstein, 1999; Sheldon, Elliot, Kim, & Kasser, 2001). Moreover, results from such studies also suggested that important life events seem to include at least one of three common thematic characteristics: autonomy, relatedness/intimacy, and competence/achievement.

Recalling a meaningful memory does not always involve recalling a factually correct memory. An event memory may retain significant meaning despite the loss or distortion of specific event details. Ulric Neisser famously misremembered his "flashbulb memory" of the attack on Pearl Harbor by misremembering that he was listening to a radio broadcast of a baseball game that was interrupted by the news flash detailing the attack. Given that the attack occurred in December, it is unlikely that Neisser was listening to a baseball game; his memory report was likely influenced by modern-day team names (Giants vs. Dodgers; see Thompson & Cowan, 1986). However, this error does not invalidate the memory or strip it of its value to a boy trying to understand an event that would shape world history. As the mind saturates events with organization and emotion, such details are likely lost as the event (and its consequences) are more fully realized by the individual. The "reality" being captured by the mind reflects the *essences of event experiences*, not necessarily the minute details of those experiences.

EVENT MEMORY, EVENT VALENCE, AND MEANING MAKING: A FUNCTIONAL VIEW

Determining whether information in memory has value can be a very difficult task for the mind. After all, situational demands placed on individuals often necessitate that different kinds of information be given different values at different times. Hence, depending on the situation, an item (or in this case a memory) may have an almost limitless number of values, However, it seems that the mind does not spend a great deal of time enumerating the various affordances that are associated with objects or memories. Instead, it relies on a more primitive system for assigning value to the experiences it encounters: The primitive brain assigns value to experiences largely on the basis of the emotional qualities of those experiences (Damasio, 1994). Good experiences lead to a set of approach behaviors (positive valuation), whereas bad experiences lead to a set of avoidance behaviors (negative valuation). Damasio (1994) theorized that experiences are given value through the use of somatic markers, which represent the brain's reactions to experiences. Indeed, when people have damage to the regions of the brain that assign emotional value to experiences (e.g., the ventromedial prefrontal cortex), they often undergo dramatic personality changes and lose the ability to make evidence-based rational choices. Thus, without emotional valuation experiences may lose a good deal of their meaning. In other words, when events lose valuation, people behave in ways that suggest that they are no longer able to give the appropriate meaning to their experiences.

Damasio (1994) is not the only scholar to link emotion and meaning making. Neuroscientists have long suspected this linkage. For example, replicating Babinski's (1914) work, Bear (1983) showed that patients with right-hemisphere damage expressed indifference to their own illnesses as well as difficulty doing tasks involving information weighting and decisions(e.g., tasks related to financial decisions or relationship issues).

Indeed, giving meaning to reality seems to involve imbuing experiences with emotion. This has led to a great deal of speculation as to which set of emotions, positive or negative, is stronger. Evolutionary pressures figure prominently in arguments made on both sides of the debate. Baumeister, Bratslavsky, Finkenauer, and Vohs (2001) made the case that negative emotions demand a greater physiological response and therefore have an especially large impact on the central nervous system and behavioral systems. On the other hand, Fredrickson (2001) suggested that positive emotions create a physiological state that encourages skill development and personal growth.

Studies show that both positive emotional states and negative emotional states can drive attentional resources and the memories formed from those experiences (Öhman, Flykt, & Esteves, 2001). Similarly, when participants record their life experiences, they inherently record events infused with both positive emotions and negative emotions and seldom record memories that are emotionally neutral (Suedfeld & Eich, 1995; Thompson et al., 1996). Walker, Skowronski, and Thompson (2003) reviewed data from 229 participants who had recorded a combined 23,202 event memories and found that only 24% of the events were described as emotionally neutral. This likely grossly underestimates the occurrence of neutral events in a person's life. That is, although it is very likely that in their daily lives people experience many events that lack specific emotions, the fact is that relatively few of those events are deemed worthy of recollection. In comparison, it is the emotion-inducing events that prompt storage of an event memory. In fact, when normal people fail to remember significant positive or negative events, it is often seen as a potential sign of a psychological or biological illness (Freud, 1920/1952).

It makes a great deal of sense that emotion should be critical to the process of meaning making. Humans evolved in a complex world filled with dangers that were not always obvious. With a limited capacity for short-term memory and a long-term memory system prone to creating gist memories, the evolving brain needed to quickly evaluate hundreds or thousands of novel experiences a day. Valuation helped to sort the good from the bad and the important from the irrelevant. This valuation had to occur in a world in which language had yet to develop and civilization was still far off.

CODA

However, this emphasis on emotion and valuation extended to the domain of language. What is it that people talk about? What is it that people try to understand and explain? Clearly, the events that are woven into narratives, that are the focus of attempts at understanding, tend to be those events that are perceived to be highly relevant to an individual's existence. As we have argued in this chapter, these attempts at meaning making are powerful forces that drive autobiographical memory through elements of selective rehearsal. These attempts can affect those events that are selected for inclusion in the narratives, how those events are woven together, and how often such narratives are conveyed, all of which can change as one matures and as life circumstances change. Obviously, such attempts can help to determine which life events are recalled and which are forgotten, which details of recalled events are retained and which are forgotten, the kinds of distortions that creep into one's memories, one's ability to place events in time, and the emotional responses that one experiences at event recall. Although the children of Ebbinghaus have contributed much to researchers' understanding of human memory, clearly that understanding would be incomplete without the contributions of those autobiographical memory researchers who ply their trade in real-world memories and who try to understand how those memories are influenced by people's attempts to understand the events of their lives.

REFERENCES

Adamczyk, W. (2004). *When God looked the other way: A tale of war, exile, and redemption*. Chicago, IL: University of Chicago Press.

Adler, A. (1937). The significance of early recollections. *International Journal of Individual Psychology, 3*, 283–287.

Alea, N., & Bluck, S. (2003). Why are you telling me that? A conceptual model of the social function of autobiographical memory. *Memory, 11*, 165–178. doi:10.1080/741938207

Atkinson, R. C., & Shiffrin, R. M. (1968). Human memory: A proposed system and its control processes. In K. W. Spence & J. R. Spence (Eds.), *The psychology of learning and motivation: Advances in research and theory* (Vol. 2, pp. 89–195). New York, NY: Academic Press.

Babinski, J. (1914). Contribution of cerebral hemispheric organization in the study of mental troubles. *Revista de Neurologia, 27*, 845–848.

Bahrick, H. P., Hall, L. K., & Berger, S. A. (1996). Accuracy and distortion in memory for high school grades. *Psychological Science, 7*, 265–271. doi:10.1111/j.1467-9280.1996.tb00372.x

Banaji, M. R., & Crowder, R. G. (1989). The bankruptcy of everyday memory research. *American Psychologist, 44*, 1185–1193. doi:10.1037/0003-066X.44.9.1185

Bauer, J. J., & Bonanno, G. A. (2001). Continuity amid discontinuity: Bridging one's past and present in stories of conjugal bereavement. *Narrative Inquiry, 11*, 123–158. doi:10.1075/ni.11.1.06bau

Bauer, J. J., & McAdams, D. P. (2004). Personal growth in adults' stories of life transitions. *Journal of Personality, 72*, 573–602. doi:10.1111/j.0022-3506.2004.00273.x

Baumeister, R. F., Bratslavsky, E., Finkenauer, C., & Vohs, K. D. (2001). Bad is stronger than good. *Review of General Psychology, 5*, 323–370. doi:10.1037/1089-2680.5.4.323

Bear, D. M. (1983). Hemispheric specialization and the neurology of emotion. *Archives of Neurology*, *40*, 195–202.

Beike, D. R., & Wirth-Beaumont, E. T. (2005). Psychological closure as a memory phenomenon. *Memory*, *13*, 574–593. doi:10.1080/09658210444000241

Blagov, P. S., & Singer, J. A. (2004). Four dimensions of self-defining memories (specificity, meaning, content, and affect) and their relationships to self-restraint, distress, and repressive defensiveness. *Journal of Personality*, *72*, 481–511. doi:10.1111/j.0022-3506.2004.00270.x

Burnham, W. H. (1888). Memory, historically and experimentally considered. *The American Journal of Psychology*, *2*, 39–90, 225–270, 431–464, 566–622. doi:10.2307/1411406

Cameron, J. J., Wilson, A. E., & Ross, M. (2004) Autobiographical memory and self-assessment. In D. R. Beike, J. M. Lampinen, & D. A. Behrend (Eds.), *The self and memory* (pp. 207–226). New York, NY: Psychology Press.

Crawley, R. A. (2010). Closure of autobiographical memories: The effects of written recounting from first- or third-person visual perspective. *Memory*, *18*, 900–917. doi:10.1080/09658211.2010.524650

Cutler, B. L., Penrod, S. D., O'Rourke, T. E., & Martens, T. K. (1986). Unconfounding the effects of contextual cues on eyewitness identification accuracy. *Social Behaviour*, *1*, 113–134.

Damasio, A. R. (1994). *Descartes' error. Emotion, reason, and the human brain*. New York, NY: Putnam.

Dewhurst, S. A., & Marlborough, M. (2003). Memory bias in the recall of pre-exam anxiety: The influence of self-enhancement. *Applied Cognitive Psychology*, *17*, 695–702. doi:10.1002/acp.903

Dudycha, G. J., & Dudycha, M. M. (1941). Childhood memories: A review of the literature. *Psychological Bulletin*, *38*, 668–682. doi:10.1037/h0055678

Ebbinghaus, H. (1964). *Memory: A contribution to experimental psychology*. New York, NY: Dover. (Original work published 1885)

Ensel, W. M. (1991). Important life events and depression among older adults: The role of psychological and social resources. *Journal of Aging and Health*, *3*, 546–566. doi:10.1177/089826439100300407

Fredrickson, B. L. (2001). The role of positive emotions in positive psychology: The broaden-and-build theory of positive emotions. *American Psychologist*, *56*, 218–226. doi:10.1037/0003-066X.56.3.218

Freeman, M. (1993). *Rewriting the self: History, memory, narrative*. London, England: Routledge.

Freud, S. (1952). *A general introduction to psychoanalysis*. New York, NY: Washington Square Press. (Original work published 1920)

Fuller, H. H. (1898). *The art of memory: Being a comprehensive and practical system of memory culture*. St Paul, MN: National.

Gibson, J. J. (1977). The theory of affordances. In R. Shaw & J. Bransford (Eds.), *Perceiving, acting, and knowing* (pp. 127–135). Hillsdale, NJ: Erlbaum.

Habermas, T., & Bluck, S. (2000). Getting a life: The emergence of the life story in adolescence. *Psychological Bulletin, 126,* 748–769. doi:10.1037/0033-2909.126.5.748

Hall, G. S. (1904). *Adolescence.* New York, NY: D. Appleton.

Herlihy, J., Scragg, P., & Turner, S. (2002). Discrepancies in autobiographical memories—implications for the assessment of asylum seekers: Repeated interviews study. *BMJ, 324,* 324–327. doi:10.1136/bmj.324.7333.324

Herrmann, D. J., & Chaffin, R. (1988). *Memory in historical perspectives: The literature on memory before Ebbinghaus.* New York, NY: Springer-Verlag.

Holmes, T. H., & Rahe, R. H. (1967). The social readjustment rating scale. *Journal of Psychosomatic Research, 11,* 213–218. doi:10.1016/0022-3999(67)90010-4

Klein, S. B., German, T. P., Cosmides, L., & Gabriel, R. (2004). A theory of autobiographical memory: Necessary components and disorders resulting from their loss. *Social Cognition, 22,* 460–490. doi:10.1521/soco.22.5.460.50765

Krolikowski, L. (2001). *Stolen childhood: A saga of Polish war children* (K. J. Rozniatowski, Trans.). San Jose. CA: Authors Choice Press. (Original work published 1983)

Laney, C., & Loftus, E. F. (2010). False memory. In J. Brown & E. Campbell (Eds.), *The Cambridge handbook of forensic psychology* (pp. 187–194). Cambridge, England: Cambridge University Press. doi:10.1017/CBO9780511730290.023

Levine, L. J., & Bluck, S. (2004). Painting with broad strokes: Happiness and the malleability of event memory. *Cognition and Emotion, 18,* 559–574. doi:10.1080/02699930341000446

Loftus, E. F. (1993). The reality of repressed memories. *American Psychologist, 48,* 518–537. doi:10.1037/0003-066X.48.5.518

McAdams, D. P. (2008). Personal narratives and the life story. In O. John, R. Robins, & L. A. Pervin (Eds.), *Handbook of personality: Theory and research* (3rd ed., pp. 242–262). New York, NY: Guilford Press.

McFarland, C., & Alvaro, C. (2000). The impact of motivation on temporal comparison: Coping with traumatic events by perceiving personal growth. *Journal of Personality and Social Psychology, 79,* 327–343. doi:10.1037/0022-3514.79.3.327

McLean, K. C. (2005). Late adolescent identity development: Narrative meaning making and memory telling. *Developmental Psychology, 41,* 683–691. doi:10.1037/0012-1649.41.4.683

McLean, K. C., Pasupathi, M., & Pals, J. L. (2007). Selves creating stories creating selves: A process model of narrative self development in adolescence and adulthood. *Personality and Social Psychology Review, 11,* 262–278. doi:10.1177/1088868307301034

Middleton, A. E. (1888). *Memory systems new and old.* New York, NY: Fellows.

Miles, C. (1895). Minor studies from the psychological laboratory of Clark University. VIII. A study of individual psychology. *The American Journal of Psychology, 6*, 534–558. doi:10.2307/1411191

Nelson, K. (2003). Self and social functions: Individual autobiographical memory and collective narrative. *Memory, 11*, 125–136. doi:10.1080/741938203

Nickerson, R. S., & Adams, M. J. (1979). Long-term memory for a common object. *Cognitive Psychology, 11*, 287–307. doi:10.1016/0010-0285(79)90013-6

Öhman, A., Flykt, A., & Esteves, F. (2001). Emotion drives attention: Detecting the snake in the grass. *Journal of Experimental Psychology: General, 130*, 466–478. doi:10.1037/0096-3445.130.3.466

Palmer, G., & Braud, W. (2002). Exceptional human experiences, disclosure, and a more inclusive view of physical, psychological, and spiritual well-being. *Journal of Transpersonal Psychology, 34*, 29–59.

Pals, J. L. (2006). Narrative identity processing of difficult life events: Pathways of personality development and positive self-transformation in adulthood. *Journal of Personality, 74*, 1079–1110. doi:10.1111/j.1467-6494.2006.00403.x

Parker, E. S., Cahill, L., & McGaugh, J. L. (2006). A case of unusual autobiographical remembering. *Neurocase, 12*, 35–49. doi:10.1080/13554790500473680

Pasupathi, M. (2006). Silk from sows' ears: Collaborative construction of everyday selves in everyday stories. In D. P. McAdams, R. Josselson, & A. Lieblich (Eds.), *Identity and story: Creating self in narrative* (pp. 129–150). Washington, DC: American Psychological Association. doi:10.1037/11414-006

Pasupathi, M., Weeks, T., & Rice, C. (2006). Reflecting on life: Remembering as a major process in adult development. *Journal of Language and Social Psychology, 25*, 244–263. doi:10.1177/0261927X06289425

Pillemer, D. B. (1992). Remembering personal circumstances: A functional analysis. In E. Winograd & U. Neisser (Eds.), *Affect and accuracy in recall: Studies of "flashbulb" memories. Emory Symposia in Cognition* (Vol. 4, pp. 236–264). New York, NY: Cambridge University Press.

Porter, S., & Birt, A. R. (2001). Is traumatic memory special? A comparison of traumatic memory characteristics with memory for other emotional life experiences. *Applied Cognitive Psychology, 15*, 101–116. doi:10.1002/acp.766

Rimé, B., Mesquita, B., Philippot, P., & Boca, S. (1991). Beyond the emotional event: Six studies on the social sharing of emotion. *Cognition and Emotion, 5*, 435–465. doi:10.1080/02699939108411052

Ritchie, T. D., & Skowronski, J. J. (2008). Perceived change in the affect associated with dreams: The fading affect bias and its moderators. *Dreaming, 18*, 27–43. doi:10.1037/1053-0797.18.1.27

Ritchie, T. D., Skowronski, J. J., Hartnett, J. L., Wells, B. M., & Walker, W. R. (2009). The fading affect bias in the context of emotion activation level, mood, and personal theories of emotion change. *Memory, 17*, 428–444. doi:10.1080/09658210902791665

Ritchie, T. D., Skowronski, J. J., Wood, S. E., Walker, W. R., Vogl, R. J., & Gibbons, J. A. (2006). Event self-importance, event rehearsal, and the fading affect bias in autobiographical memory. *Self and Identity, 5*, 172–195. doi:10.1080/15298860600591222

Rubin, D. C., Rahhal, T. A., & Poon, L. W. (1998). Things learned in early adulthood are remembered best. *Memory & Cognition, 26*, 3–19. doi:10.3758/BF03211366

Safer, M. A., & Keuler, D. J. (2002). Individual differences in misremembering prepsychotherapy distress: Personality and memory distortion. *Emotion, 2*, 162–178. doi:10.1037/1528-3542.2.2.162

Santiago-Rivera, A. L., Gard, T., & Bernstein, B. L. (1999). The importance of achievement, intimacy, autonomy, and life events among first year college students. *Journal of College Student Psychotherapy, 13*, 57–73. doi:10.1300/J035v13n03_05

Schneier, B. (2003). *Beyond fear: Thinking sensibly about security in an uncertain world.* New York, NY: Copernicus Books.

Sheldon, K. M., Elliot, A. J., Kim, Y., & Kasser, T. (2001). What's satisfying about satisfying events? Comparing 10 candidate psychological needs. *Journal of Personality and Social Psychology, 80*, 325–339. doi:10.1037/0022-3514.80.2.325

Shum, M. S. (1998). The role of temporal landmarks in autobiographical memory processes. *Psychological Bulletin, 124*, 423–442. doi:10.1037/0033-2909.124.3.423

Skowronski, J. J., Gibbons, J. A., Vogl, R. J., & Walker, W. R. (2004). The effects of social disclosure on the affective intensity provoked by autobiographical memories. *Self and Identity, 3*, 285–309. doi:10.1080/13576500444000065

Skowronski, J. J., Ritchie, T. D., Walker, W. R., Betz, A. L., Sedikides, C., Bethencourt, L. A., & Martin, A. L. (2007). Ordering our world: The quest for traces of temporal organization in autobiographical memory. *Journal of Experimental Social Psychology, 43*, 850–856. doi:10.1016/j.jesp.2006.10.001

Skowronski, J. J., & Walker, W. R. (2004). How describing autobiographical events transforms autobiographical memory. *Social Cognition, 22*, 555–590. doi:10.1521/soco.22.5.555.50764

Skowronski, J. J., Walker, W. R., & Betz, A. L. (2003). Ordering our world: An examination of time in autobiographical memory. *Memory, 11*, 247–260. doi:10.1080/09658210244000009a

Sperling, G. (1960). The information available in brief visual presentations. *Psychological Monographs: General and Applied, 74*(11), 1–29. doi:10.1037/h0093759

Suedfeld, P., & Eich, E. (1995). Autobiographical memory and affect under conditions of reduced environmental stimulation. *Journal of Environmental Psychology, 15*, 321–326. doi:10.1006/jevp.1995.0028

Taylor, S. E. (1991). Asymmetrical effects of positive and negative events: The mobilization-minimization hypothesis. *Psychological Bulletin, 110*, 67–85. doi:10.1037/0033-2909.110.1.67

Thompson, C. P., & Cowan, T. (1986). Flashbulb memories: A nicer interpretation of a Neisser recollection. *Cognition, 22*, 199–200. doi:10.1016/0010-0277(86)90058-2

Thompson, C. P., Skowronski, J. J., & Betz, A. L. (1993). The use of partial temporal information in dating personal events. *Memory & Cognition, 21*, 352–360. doi:10.3758/BF03208267

Thompson, C. P., Skowronski, J. J., Larsen, S. F., & Betz, A. L. (1996). *Autobiographical memory: Remembering what and remembering when*. Mahwah, NJ: Erlbaum.

Thorne, A. (2000). Personal memory telling and personality development. *Personality and Social Psychology Review, 4*, 45–56. doi:10.1207/S15327957PSPR0401_5

Tulving, E. (1985). Memory and consciousness. *Canadian Psychology, 26*, 1–12. doi:10.1037/h0080017

Tulving, E. (2002). Episodic memory: From mind to brain. *Annual Review of Psychology, 53*, 1–25. doi:10.1146/annurev.psych.53.100901.135114

Walker, W. R., & Skowronski, J. J. (2009). The fading affect bias: But what the hell is it for? *Applied Cognitive Psychology, 23*, 1122–1136. doi:10.1002/acp.1614

Walker, W. R., Skowronski, J. J., Gibbons, J. A., Vogl, R. J., & Thompson, C. P. (2003). On the emotions that accompany autobiographical memories: Dysphoria disrupts the fading affect bias. *Cognition and Emotion, 17*, 703–723. doi:10.1080/02699930302287

Walker, W. R., Skowronski, J. J., & Thompson, C. P. (2003). Life is pleasant—and memory helps to keep it that way! *Review of General Psychology, 7*, 203–210. doi:10.1037/1089-2680.7.2.203

Wang, Q., & Conway, M. A. (2004). The stories we keep: autobiographical memory in American and Chinese middle-aged adults. *Journal of Personality, 72*, 911–938. doi:10.1111/j.0022-3506.2004.00285.x

Webster, J. D. (2003). The reminiscence circumplex and autobiographical memory functions. *Memory, 11*, 203–215. doi:10.1080/741938202

Yates, F. A. (1966). *The art of memory*. London, England: Routledge & Kegan Paul.

9

HOW ACTORS, AGENTS, AND AUTHORS FIND MEANING IN LIFE

DAN P. McADAMS

What does *meaning* mean? When we claim that our lives are meaningful, what are we really saying? And what does a person mean when he or she says that life has lost its meaning?

For starters, meaning in life is almost always viewed to be *good*. And losing meaning is *bad*. If a close friend tells you that her life feels especially meaningful these days, you are almost certain to classify her statement as a positive self-attribution. You are happy for her, and you may assume that she is happy about the meaning she has found. By contrast, if a friend tells you that her life has lost all its meaning, you will likely feel concern, even alarm. People who say such things are unhappy, right? Yes, they usually are. Not only is meaning good, and loss of meaning bad, but things that provide meaning are usually seen as good, and those that strip meaning away are bad. Your friend may report that she finds meaning in her family, or in helping others, or in a new career, or in her religious faith. Family, career, faith, helping others—these are all good things, right? Of course they are, at least usually.

DOI: 10.1037/14040-009
The Psychology of Meaning, Keith D. Markman, Travis Proulx, and Matthew J. Lindberg (Editors)

If your friend told you, instead, that she feels her deep meaning stems from a lifelong desire to watch more television or from her latest plan to cheat her sister out of the family inheritance, you would probably be surprised. Watching television does not seem good enough, lofty enough, to support life meaning. And cheating your sister—well, that sounds really bad. In principle, a person should be able to find life meaning in doing something crass, mindless, ignoble, or even evil. But we do not expect it—perhaps even resist it—so positively valenced is the concept of meaning in our minds.

What are the good sources of the good thing we feel when we have meaning? And what good things have we lost when we make the very negative claim that our lives lack meaning? The long list of good sources for meaning includes those that are external to the self—such as good friends, good food, good jobs, family, religion, and cultural traditions—and those that seem to spring from within. On the internal side, Baumeister (1991) asserted that life meanings stem from four basic human needs: purpose, value, efficacy, and self-worth. By comparison, Maddi (1998) contended that meaning comes from challenge, control, and commitment. Other perspectives suggest that *good* meaning is inextricably linked to overcoming or defying *bad* circumstances: Meaning comes from working through suffering or loss (Neimeyer, 2001) or by managing the terror of death (see Chapter 3, this volume).

While there is considerable merit in these views, I submit that no extant list of external sources or taxonomy of psychological motives fully captures what people mean when they say that their lives have meaning. This is not just because people mean so many different things. It is also, and more fundamentally, because people make these different claims about meaning from qualitatively different standpoints as meaning makers. In other words, meaning makers themselves, the very people who make meaning out of their lives, take on the meaning-making task from different ontological positions in life. Following McAdams and Cox (2010), I submit that there are at least three positions: social *actor*, motivated *agent*, and autobiographical *author*. What meaning actually means, then, depends on the particular position or standpoint—whether it be actor, agent, or author—from which the meaning maker (explicitly or implicitly) evaluates his or her life.

We begin life as social *actors*, performing on a social stage. Even as infants, our social performances, driven as they are by basic temperament traits and skills, elicit strong and reinforcing responses from parents, family members, and other audiences. In mid-to-late childhood, we become motivated *agents*, as well, striving to attain the personal goals and fulfill the projects upon which our self-esteem comes to be based. In late adolescence or young adulthood, we typically add the autobiographical *author* to the mix as we work to find or construct a self-defining life story. By the time we are adults, then, all three self-positions—social actor, motivated agent, and autobiographical author—are powerful players in our psychological lives. Each, furthermore, holds out its own criteria for meaning. From the standpoint of the social actor, meaning comes from effective role performance, which itself is strongly shaped by basic traits and skills. From the standpoint of the motivated agent, meaning comes from the goals we pursue, the projects we set forth for our lives, and the values that give these goals and projects their worth and justification. As autobiographical authors, life meaning becomes instantiated in the stories of our lives—internalized and evolving narratives of the self that explain who we were in the past, who we are today, and who we hope to be in the future. Each self-position, therefore, suggests its own corresponding meanings, and each may lose meaning in its own uniquely painful way.

MEANING AND THE SOCIAL ACTOR: THE ROLES WE PLAY

Two years ago, I reluctantly agreed to serve as chair of the psychology department at Northwestern University. This is a new social role for me. Among other things, the role involves running departmental meetings, setting agendas, working with deans and other administrators, evaluating my faculty colleagues, checking in with staff members, developing a vision for the department's future, and solving a wide range of problems, many of them interpersonal, that arise from one day to the next. Surprisingly to me, I do not hate the job. I like hanging out with the staff, for example—talking Chicago politics, hearing the latest gossip, finding out what people did over the weekend. I get a weird kind of satisfaction in meeting with individual faculty members or students to address delicate personal and ethical problems. I really like running meetings—or to put it more accurately, I hate it if somebody else runs them because I do it so much better. I like the fact that when I go to a faculty party or university event, I no longer feel any awkwardness about fitting in. As department chair, I always seem to have a place and function; I never need to explain why I am there. And people laugh at my jokes now, much more than they used to.

I do not think it is a stretch to say that I find meaning in my new role as department chair. In Baumeister's (1991) terms, I "value" the role, and the role provides me with some degree of "self-worth" and "efficacy." But there seems to be more to it than that—and less. For the most part, I *enjoy* performing the role. It *feels* good, feels right. The role seems to call upon tendencies in my personality that get fewer chances to express themselves in other realms of my life. For example, I experience a great deal of social dominance in this role, which feels remarkably comfortable and correct. People in the department seem to like my taking control of certain matters. They seem to like it when I tell them what to do, as long as I impose reasonable demands. They like the way I use humor to defuse difficult situations. People compliment me for the work I do as department chair, and when they criticize me, I take note and try to change. I value effective role performance; I want to do this job well.

At the same time, though, I realize, as do my colleagues, that being department chair is *only a job.* I routinely experience both satisfaction and frustration with this job, but not passion, nor deep angst. Only part of my identity is tied up with this role. I have no vision for transforming the department into a magnificent extension of myself. I am not aiming to leave a legacy. In truth, I am not aiming to achieve anything really important at all by being department chair. I have no long-term aspirations to make Northwestern the top psychology department in the world, and I am not using this position as a stepping-stone for higher administrative posts. I will serve my allotted time as department chair, and then I will go back to doing what I was doing before.

What is the nature of the meaning I experience in my role as department chair? It is the most basic form of human meaning that social actors like ourselves have always felt, I would argue, even in the tribal groups and bands through which human nature was forged thousands of years ago. As cognitively gifted social animals who evolved to live in complex groups, human beings are designed to feel meaning and value in the social roles upon which group life depends. This is especially easy to imagine for generative roles such as parent and leader (McAdams, 2001). Given how difficult it can be to raise children, for example, we are fortunate that human beings are indeed designed to feel that their generative and nurturant roles as parents are inherently meaningful. Otherwise, they might routinely ignore the annoying demands of their offspring, much to the ultimate detriment of their children's (and their own) inclusive fitness (Wilson, 1978).

In a broader and less obvious sense, however, human beings are likely to invest meaning in a wide assortment of roles that open up on the social stage of group life. In our ancestral environment of evolutionary adaptedness, effective role performance was arguably *the* key factor in determining the extent to which an individual human being managed to get along and get ahead in group life, which in turn helped to determine how successful an individual might be in garnering the resources needed for passing copies of his or her genes down to the next generation (Hogan, 1982). There is good reason to believe that those who performed valued social roles effectively—formed strategic alliances and friendships, defended the group against outside threats, gathered or produced food and other resources for the group, effectively nurtured and cared for the young, found some kind of productive function in the social structure of the group, proved to be good team players, as examples—tended on average to increase their chances for survival and reproductive success, relative to group members who failed at their roles (Buss, 2008). It should not be surprising, therefore, to observe that human beings manage to derive substantial meaning from the culturally scripted roles they play in group life, even the relatively trivial role of department chair.

The famous sociologist Erving Goffman (1959) asserted, like Shakespeare before him, that all the world is but a stage, upon which human actors perform their allotted roles. Daily life is punctuated by discrete scenes, which string together over time to compose a never-ending theatrical play. Actors enter and exit the stage, reciting their lines and enacting their roles, as they manage the impressions of other actors and elicit responses from the audiences who look on. For Goffman, human beings never leave the social stage; they simply move from one role performance to the next. According to Goffman, there is often nothing behind the role, no deeper motive or existential intent that explains why the actors do what they do. Critics sometimes dismiss Goffman's dramaturgical perspective as psychologically superficial. There must be more to social life than play-acting, many psychologists maintain. But Goffman's radical focus on the everyday presentation of self through social performance suggests a profound psychological truth, I believe. For most people most of the time, life is about performing social roles, sometimes mindlessly but often, at the same time, conscientiously. We do our jobs. We finish our homework. We raise our children. We pay our bills. We chat with our friends. These activities entail some planning and effort, but they do not typically require transcendent motivational agendas or well-articulated philosophies of life. Because human beings evolved to adapt to their environments through complex group behavior, social role-playing feels meaningful, even if we rarely think about it. When we lose a valued social role, we lose a piece of what gives our lives meaning.

Even though social actors can perform their roles effectively without accessing meaning sources that go beyond the performance itself, psychological factors nonetheless exert a strong impact on how actors act. Of special significance in this regard are the actor's *dispositional traits* and *skills*. Even before they consciously realize that they are actors on the social stage, human infants perform social behavior in accord with the temperament dispositions with which their genotypes have endowed them. A smiley infant tends to elicit positive responses from an adoring audience; fussier babies draw less applause. Through repeated and complex transactions between genes and environments over developmental time, early temperament differences morph into the broad traits of personality that may be observed in adulthood and that are broadly encompassed within the well-known five-factor taxonomy, or Big Five: Extraversion (vs. introversion), Neuroticism (vs. emotional stability), Agreeableness, Conscientiousness, and Openness to Experience (Caspi, Roberts, & Shiner, 2005; McCrae & Costa, 2008). Dispositional traits account for important differences in how social actors find meaning in the world. For example, high levels of conscientiousness are associated with meaningful, prosocial involvements in the community, such as church attendance and volunteerism (Lodi-Smith & Roberts, 2007). By contrast, high levels of neuroticism are a risk factor for a wide range of problems in social life, including those implicated in personal meaning. People high in neuroticism tend to feel vulnerable and insecure and more apt, than those low in neuroticism, to report guilt, shame, anguish, despair, and alienation in life (Ozer & Benet-Martinez, 2006).

Research suggests a strong association between extraversion and meaning. Traditional conceptions of extraversion have suggested that this trait is mainly about being gregarious and sociable. For example, Jung (1936/1971) argued that extraverts tend to draw energy from people and social relationships, whereas introverts tend to draw energy from the inner life of the mind. A substantial body of empirical data now shows, however, that extraversion is just as much about the tendency to pursue rewards and to experience positive emotion as it is about being with people (Smillie, Pickering, & Jackson, 2006). Again and again, studies show that people high in extraversion report more positive emotions in life, even when they are *not* with people (Lucas & Diener, 2001). Furthermore, Laura King and her colleagues have shown that when people experience positive emotion, they tend to report that their lives feel especially meaningful, compared to individuals who experience lower levels of positive emotion (King, Hicks, Krull, & Del Gasio, 2006; see also Chapter 22, this volume). King's findings hold when considering both the short-term effects of situationally induced positive emotion and the long-term effects of trait-based dispositions toward positive emotionality.

Fredrickson (2001) argued that positive emotions "build and broaden" a healthy and meaningful life. In simpler and more prosaic terms, it may also be true that when people *feel good,* they have better access to—can recall and savor—the sources of life meaning that have been present in their lives all along, such as their past successes in role performance, their good friendships and family ties, and the bonds they feel through work, play, and religious or spiritual activities. The dispositional tendency to enjoy life, to find joy and excitement in what social life has to offer, may promote high levels of felt meaning in life—both in the immediate presence of a good mood and over developmental time, as actors continue to experience good feelings as they move from one social performance to the next.

MEANING AND THE MOTIVATED AGENT: THE ENDS WE PURSUE

During the year before I agreed to become chair of the psychology department, I spent nearly every morning working on a book about former U.S. President George W. Bush (McAdams, 2011). My *goal* was to construct a psychological biography of Bush, with special emphasis on exploring the personality factors that may have influenced his decision (put into action in March 2003) to launch a preemptive military invasion of Iraq. I read many books, articles, and websites about the Bush presidency and about Bush's life. I pored over 25 years of notes and writings on personality, developmental, social, cognitive, and political psychology to shape and support my interpretation of Bush's decision. I outlined and reoutlined, and I wrote countless memos to myself about how to develop my arguments in the best possible way. As the chapters gradually took form, I shared my ideas with students and colleagues and used many of their responses to fine-tune what I was writing. During this period, I was nearly obsessed with my Bush project. More than a few times, I woke up in the middle of the night and ran upstairs to the computer to complete a thought or a sentence for the book. Even though I lost sleep over the project, I woke up nearly every morning energized and excited to push the whole thing forward to its inevitable end. The day after I sent the completed manuscript to the publisher, I sank into a (mild) depression. I still feel the loss.

Many psychologists have observed that the goals people choose to pursue often prove to be rich sources of life meaning (e.g., Freund & Riediger, 2006; Little, 1998). Many daily activities are organized around goals, and goals provide direction and a sense of purpose for human action. People invest substantial amounts of energy into goal pursuit. We feel good when we sense that we are making progress toward achieving our most important goals; we experience frustration when progress in goal pursuit is stymied. As William James noted over 100 years ago, our self-esteem is largely a function of how successful we are in realizing our aspirations (James, 1892/1963). In my case, the goal of writing a psychological biography of George W. Bush provided a nearly overwhelming source of meaning, joy, self-esteem, and personal motivation during the period when I was working on the Bush book. In keeping with research on goal disengagement, withdrawing from my cherished goal—even after I experienced the success of achieving it—proved to be a difficult process (Freund & Riediger, 2006; McAdams & Olson, 2010).

Personal goals often follow from social roles. My goal to produce the Bush book fit with my overall role of being a college professor whose activities routinely include teaching, research, and writing. Most social roles entail many goals, sometimes sequenced over time and sometimes organized within complex goal hierarchies. In contemporary middle-class North America, the role of "mother," for example, involves setting and pursuing a wide range of goals, ranging from daily tasks such as "making sure my kid catches the school bus in the morning" to long-term goals such as saving money to pay for a college education. But goals are different from roles, as well, especially when we consider major life goals such as my Bush project. Psychologically speaking, goals stand out from social roles as explicit products of personal volition (Sheldon, 2004). In most cases, we *choose* our goals, or at least it feels as if we choose them. We *decide*. We *aspire*. We *strive* to achieve the ends that we *want* or *desire*. More than social roles, furthermore, goals explicitly orient us to the future, setting up desired ends to which we aspire over time. Relatedly, goals often suggest the metaphor of *progress*. Over time, I desire to get closer and closer to achieving my goal. I move forward or upward over time. If many social roles are like *jobs* that we do in life, a personal goal may be structured more like a *career*, in the sense that it challenges us to advance in some way over time, to progress through stages, to grow or develop, to get closer and closer to the desired end over time.

When it comes to major life goals, then, we operate from the perspective of a motivated agent. To be an agent is to strive for what we want or desire in accord with self-determined plans, rooted in personal decisions and choice (McAdams & Cox, 2010; Ryan & Deci, 2006). Whereas even an infant's behavior shows signs of goal-direction, it is not until children reach the age of 7 or 8 years (and sometimes later) that they begin to organize their daily activities and their understandings of themselves in terms of personal goals (McAdams & Olson, 2010; Walls & Kollat, 2006). The success and failure children experience in pursuit of their most important personal goals come to impact their characteristic levels of self-esteem (Harter, 2006). As we move through childhood and into adolescence, actors continue to perform on the social stage. But the newly emergent perspective of the self as a motivated agent adds complexity to their behaviors and personalities, suggesting goals, plans, desires, and projects that lie behind the performance—ends that agents envision for the future, into which they now invest hope, energy, and meaning.

As my Bush example makes clear, different goals arise, develop, and go away over the course of life. As situations change, as people grow older, as individuals move from one social role to the next, goals and projects change to meet new demands and constraints. Research suggests that goals in early adulthood often focus on expanding the self and gaining new information, whereas goals in later adulthood may focus more on the emotional quality of ongoing relationships (Helson, Soto, & Cate, 2006). At any given point in the life course, the content of people's goals reflect important sources of life meaning. Research in personality psychology has examined those sources at the broad levels of motivational categories (e.g., intrinsic vs. extrinsic motivation; motives for power, achievement, and affiliation/intimacy) and with respect to the particularities of a given person–situation ecology. Studies of the former type, for example, have found that intrinsic, growth-oriented goals and strong needs to care for others and make positive contributions to society are often associated with greater psychological well-being and reports of higher life meaning (Bauer & McAdams, 2004; Emmons, 1999; Kasser & Ryan, 1996). Beyond content, process variables are just as important for life meaning. People tend to feel that their lives are most meaningful when they are making steady progress on their personal goals and when their goals are congruent rather than conflicting (Little, 1998).

In the structure of the self as a motivated agent, goals connect closely to values (McAdams & Cox, 2010). When we claim a particular value, we typically suggest a desired means (instrumental value) or end (terminal value) regarding an idealized vision of reality for the future (Rokeach, 1973; Schwartz & Bilsky, 1990). To value "honesty," for example, is to make a claim regarding how people should behave *in order to* accomplish a positive end of some kind (e.g., a good society, a world of integrity). To value "a world at peace" is to specify what that idealized end state might be. Therefore, goals and values orient explicitly to a vision for the future in ways that social roles and personality traits cannot. If I know that you are an extraverted mother (trait + role), I may be able to predict certain features of your role performance, but I am still relatively clueless about what you hope or envision for the future. By contrast, if I know your personal goals and values, I can begin to understand what kind of person you wish to be in the future and what kind of world you want the future to be. Whereas social actors orient mainly to the present, motivated agents look to the future.

People hold values in many different domains in life, but political and religious values often hold especially powerful life meanings. Research shows that political conservatives and liberals make sense of themselves and the world in very different ways. In the United States, people who hold to strongly conservative political values show higher levels of mortality concerns and greater needs for order and closure than do liberals (Jost, Glaser, Kruglanski, & Sulloway, 2003). Political liberals are more likely to say that a moral person should promote justice and alleviate suffering above all else, whereas conservatives are more likely to affirm the values of authority, loyalty, and purity of the self (Haidt, 2007; McAdams et al., 2008). Religious values shape how people the world over make meaning in life. For many people, religious traditions provide a source of ultimate life meaning and purpose (Emmons, 1999). By specifying how people should live on earth (an idealized society, the Ten Commandments, the Golden Rule) or what may lie in store in the next world (heaven, the afterlife, reincarnation), religious values capture life meanings as they orient to the future. Furthermore, religion also shapes how social actors understand their most important roles in the here-and-now. Take religious faith away, and life would suddenly be bereft of a major source of meaning, many people would say.

MEANING AND THE AUTOBIOGRAPHICAL AUTHOR: THE STORIES WE LIVE BY

Like many readers of this chapter, I began to assume authorship of my own life in the late-adolescent and early-adult years—a period in the life course that is now often labeled *emerging adulthood* (Arnett, 2000). The central psychosocial task of the emerging adulthood years is to construct and commit to an overall identity, described by Erikson (1963) as a broad pattern of living that situates the self in the adult world of work and love while providing life with a sense of inner sameness and temporal continuity. Each person's identity trajectory in emerging adulthood is unique, of course, and contingent upon a host of personal, situational, cultural, and historical factors and upon the vicissitudes of chance. In my case, emerging adulthood featured a sequence of decisions and re-orientations, beginning with leaving home to attend college and moving through big transitions regarding religious belief, career choice, romantic involvements and marriage, and eventually establishing a family and a home. I began the period as an evangelical Christian with conservative leanings, few social obligations or close relationships, and only a vague sense of what the future might hold. I ended the period as a secular humanist with strong inclinations toward social justice, conflicted about but still loosely connected to religion, married and involved in a broad and diverse social network, and struggling to find an intellectual theme to integrate my work as a college teacher, research scientist, and writer.

A central challenge within the identity project in emerging adulthood is the development of an initial story for life. Even as the actor continues to perform on the many social stages of life and the motivated agent continues to pursue self-determined goals and values, an autobiographical author enters the psychological scene in emerging adulthood, for the express purpose of making sense of it all through narrative. In emerging adulthood, the self becomes an autobiographical author who works to construct, refine, revise, and live according to an internalized and evolving life story, or what psychologists now often call a *narrative identity* (McAdams, 1985; McLean, Pasupathi, & Pals, 2007; Singer, 2004). Narrative identity adds a new layer of meaning to life. Through the life story the author is able to explain, for the self and for others, how he or she came to be and where life may be going in the future, integrating the reconstructed past, experienced present, and imagined future into a personal narrative that gives new meaning and purpose to life. Like most readers of this chapter, I am still working on my life story, which itself is deeply intertwined with the stories of significant others in my life and with stories that prevail in my culture.

What brings narrative identity to the psychological fore in the emerging adulthood years? Cognitive factors are surely important. With the advent of what Piaget called *formal operational thought*, adolescents are now able to take their own lives as objects of systematic reflection (McAdams, 1985; recall Chapter 1, this volume). Whereas young children can dream about what they might someday be, adolescents can think through the possibilities in a hypothetico-deductive manner. They can now ask themselves questions like these: What does my life really mean? Who might I be in the future? What if I decide to reject my parent's religion? How might my life develop if I am gay? This newfound philosophical inclination requires a narrative frame for self-construction. The earliest drafts of narrative identity may take the form of what Elkind (1981) called the *personal fable*—fantastical stories of the self's greatness. But later drafts become more realistic as reality testing improves and narrative skills become further refined. Habermas and Bluck (2000) showed how adolescents gradually master the cognitive skills required for constructing a coherent narrative of the self. By the end of the teenaged years, people regularly engage in sophisticated forms of *autobiographical reasoning*. They can link together multiple autobiographical scenes in causal sequences to explain what they believe to be their own development in a given area of life (see Chapter 8, this volume). And they can extract underlying themes that they believe characterize unique aspects of their lives in full.

Social and cultural factors also contribute to the rise of narrative identity in emerging adulthood. Their peers and their parents expect adolescents to begin sorting out what their lives mean, both for the future and the past. Given what I have done up to this point in my life, where do I go now? What kind of life should I make for myself? Paralleling the cognitive and emotional changes taking place within the individual are shifts in society's expectations about what the individual, who was a child but who is now almost an adult, should be doing, thinking, and feeling. Erikson (1959) wrote,

> It is of great relevance to the young individual's identity formation that he be responded to, and be given function and status as a person whose gradual growth and transformation make sense to those who begin to make sense to him. (p. 111)

In general, modern societies expect their adolescents and young adults to examine occupational, ideological, and interpersonal opportunities around them and to begin to make some decisions about what their lives as adults are to be about. This is to say that both society and the emerging adult are ready for the explorations in narrative identity by the time that person has, in fact, become an emerging adult. Erikson (1959) described it in the following way:

> The period can be viewed as a psychosocial moratorium during which the individual through free role experimentation may find a niche in some section of his society, a niche which is firmly defined and yet seems to

> be uniquely made for him. In finding it the young adult gains an assured sense of inner continuity and social sameness, which will bridge what he was as a child and what he is about to become and will reconcile his conception of himself and his community's recognition of him. (p. 111)

Over the past decade personality psychologists and other social scientists have examined the content, the structure, and the functions of the narrative identities that people begin to construct in the emerging adulthood years and continue to construct as they move through the adult life course. Researchers have catalogued common narrative forms and themes, connected features of narrative identity to personality traits and motives, examined developmental change in narrative identity, and explored the interpersonal and cultural contexts within which life stories are constructed and performed (for reviews, see Baddeley & Singer, 2007; McAdams, 2008; McLean, 2008).

A central emphasis in contemporary research on narrative identity is the role of culture in shaping the form and the meaning of life stories (Hammack, 2008). In constructing a life story, people choose from the menu of images, themes, plots, and characters provided by their culture (McAdams, 2006; Rosenwald & Ochberg, 1992). The ways in which personal and cultural meanings come together in life stories are especially apparent in my own research on redemptive life stories in American adults. In a series of nomothetic and idiographic studies conducted over the past 15 years, my colleagues and I have consistently found that midlife American adults who score especially high on self-report measures of generativity—suggesting a strong commitment to promoting the well-being of future generations and improving the world in which they live—tend to see their own lives as tales of redemption (e.g., McAdams, 2006; McAdams et al., 1997, 2001; Walker & Frimer, 2007). In a redemptive story, bad events are repeatedly followed by positive outcomes, as the protagonist is repeatedly enlarged, ennobled, or improved through suffering. Compared with their less generative American counterparts, highly generative adults tend to construct life stories that feature redemption sequences.

Redemption sequences constitute but one of a suite of themes that differentiate the life stories told by highly generative American adults and their less generative peers. In addition, highly generative adults tend to construct life stories in which the protagonist (a) enjoys a special advantage or blessing early in life, (b) expresses sensitivity to the suffering of others or societal injustice as a child, (c) establishes a clear and strong value system in adolescence that remains a source of unwavering conviction through the adult years, (d) experiences significant conflicts between desires for agency/power and desires for communion/love, and (e) looks to achieve goals to benefit society in the future. Taken together, these themes articulate a general script or narrative prototype—what I call *the redemptive self*—that many highly generative American adults employ to make sense of their own lives. For highly productive and caring midlife American adults, the redemptive self is a narrative model of an especially good and meaningful life.

The redemptive self is a life-story prototype that serves to support the generative efforts of midlife men and women. Their redemptive life narratives tell how generative adults seek to give back to society in gratitude for the early advantages and blessings they feel they have received. In every life, generativity is tough and frustrating work, as every parent or community volunteer knows. But if an adult constructs a narrative identity in which the protagonist's suffering in the short run often gives way to reward later on, he or she may be better able to sustain the conviction that seemingly thankless investments today will pay off for future generations. Redemptive life stories support the kind of life strivings that a highly generative man or woman is likely to set forth. The story may continue to provide life with meaning and purpose even in the face of social role disappointments and the frustrations that come from failure in goal pursuit.

For some autobiographical authors, moreover, a redemptive story can support the idea that the protagonist is living out his or her unique *calling* (McAdams, 2006; Weber, 1904/1976) or mission in life. The person may feel that he or she has been "called" (by God, by fate, by the basic circumstances of life) to carry out some task or vocation that fits identity perfectly. For some people in some cultural contexts, the social roles they live out as actors may feel like the jobs they do in life, the goals they pursue as motivated agents may feel like their self-determined careers, and the life stories they construct as autobiographical authors may narrate their most profound life callings. Jobs, careers, and callings: All three of these psychosocial forms provide life with meaning, but the meanings are very different. As a social actor, I experience meaning in the job well done—the satisfaction that follows from effective social performance in meeting the demands of an important social role. As a motivated agent, I experience meaning in the pursuit of the chosen goal—the excitement and anticipation of the chase toward the future, guided by values that I hold dear. As an autobiographical author, I convey life meaning through the integrative story I construct that ties together the reconstructed past, experienced present, and imagined future, a story whose meaning may bring a sense of life coherence, integrity, and the fulfillment of a unique identity.

Even as redemptive stories provide life with personal meaning and identity, the redemptive self may say as much about American culture and tradition as it does about the highly generative American adults who tend to tell this kind of story about their lives. The life-story themes expressed by highly generative American adults recapture and couch in a psychological language especially cherished, as well as hotly contested, ideas in American cultural history—ideas that appear prominently in spiritual accounts of the 17th-century Puritans, Benjamin Franklin's 18th-century autobiography, slave narratives and Horatio Alger stories from the 19th century, and the literature of self-help and American entrepreneurship from more recent times (McAdams, 2006). Evolving from the Puritans to Emerson to Oprah, the redemptive self has morphed into many different storied forms in the past 300 years as Americans have sought to narrate their lives as redemptive tales of atonement, emancipation, recovery, self-fulfillment, and upward social mobility. The stories speak of heroic individual protagonists—the *chosen people*—whose *manifest destiny* is to make a positive difference in a dangerous world, even when the world does not wish to be redeemed. The stories translate a deep and abiding script of American exceptionalism into the many contemporary narratives of success, recovery, development, liberation, and self-actualization that so pervade American talk, talk shows, therapy sessions, sermons, and commencement speeches. It is as if especially generative American adults, whose lives are dedicated to making the world a better place for future generations, are, for better and sometimes for worse, the most ardent narrators of a general life story script as American as apple pie and the Super Bowl.

CONCLUSION

Meaning in life means correspondingly different things for social actors, motivated agents, and autobiographical authors. The most basic forms of meaning are tied to the social roles that actors perform on the behavioral stage of life. Human beings evolved to live in social groups wherein effective role performance was and continues to be a prime determinant of individual adaptation (see Chapter 5, this volume). We are designed to feel that the social roles we perform are inherently meaningful. We value effective performance in our roles as students, fathers, mothers, brothers, sisters, teachers, workers, leaders, citizens, and stakeholders in society. When our performances meet with the audience's approval, we feel pride and the satisfaction of a job well-done. When the reviews are less favorable, we are likely to experience a great deal of negative emotion. Repeated failures and frustrations in the performance of valued social roles may give rise to a troubling sense that the roles are not as meaningful as we once believed them to be. And the sudden loss or prolonged deprivation of valued roles may exact a huge cost in life meaning. The man who prides himself on performing the valued social role of breadwinner for the family may feel that his life no longer has meaning when he loses his job and cannot find another. A devoted mother may feel that her life is now empty when her children leave home for college.

We begin life as social actors, unself-consciously performing our roles, even as infants on a social stage. Early on, temperament traits and skills shape the way we play our roles. As these basic dimensions of psychological individuality develop over the life course, they continue to affect the quality of our role performances. And the quality of role performance partly determines how meaningful we feel our lives to be. Research suggests that people whose personality traits show high levels of positive emotionality and sociability tend to feel that their lives are more meaningful, compared with those of individuals scoring lower on these traits. By contrast, high levels of neuroticism and related traits correlate with negative emotion and low levels of meaning. For social actors, meaning and emotion are intimately tied to one another. When people feel good about their social performances, they typically feel that their lives have meaning.

From the standpoint of the motivated agent, life meaning is captured in the self-determined goals we pursue and the values we hold up as justifying those goals. To be an agent is to make choices and plans for life, to set forth valued ends and develop programs for approaching or achieving those ends. The motivated agent finds meaning in the self's orientation toward the future. Meaning is enhanced by successful goal pursuit. The agent feels that life is meaningful as long as progress is being made toward achieving the valued end.

By the time they enter middle school, children set up personal goals to achieve in life, and they, along with other socializing agents in their environments (e.g., parents, teachers), structure their daily activities around goals. Goals also become important parts of the self-concept at this time and determinants of self-esteem. Goals change markedly over the life course, with changing circumstances and advancing age. Research suggests that young people tend to pursue goals that involve self-expansion and gaining new experiences, whereas older adults aim to maintain valued relationships and manage loss. Studies also show that goals tied to intrinsic motivation, personal growth, intimacy, and prosocial pursuits tend to be especially powerful sources of life meaning for many people. At the same time, frustration and loss in valued goal areas may readily undermine meaning. When valued goals are repeatedly thwarted, people may feel that their lives lack direction and purpose. They may feel that they have lost their way in life. They do not know where their life is headed.

The human quest for meaning reaches its developmental and epistemic apex with the construction of narrative identity, a process that typically begins in the emerging adulthood years. People become autobiographical authors at this time in life, as they move beyond social roles and personal goals to articulate a broad and integrative story of the self. Who am I? How did I come to be who I am? What am I meant to do and to be in life? It takes a story to answer big questions like these, a story that provides a full temporal orientation for the self—encompassing the reconstructed past, experienced present, and imagined future. The life stories that autobiographical authors construct to make meaning in life are contoured by culture. Indeed, culture provides the canonical set of images, themes, plots, and character from which people draw in fashioning their own unique stories—stories that say as much about cultural meanings as they do about the meaning of the author's life itself.

Research suggests that a favored life-narrative form in American society is the *redemptive self:* a story about a gifted and morally steadfast protagonist who journeys forth into a dangerous world, transforms suffering into growth, and aims to leave a positive legacy of the self for future generations. Epitomized in American stories of atonement, liberation, recovery, and upward social mobility, the redemptive self shows how many highly generative American adults make narrative meaning in their own lives. In the minds of many, a life that tracks the redemptive movement from adversity to enhancement is the ideal model for what a meaningful life should look like and sound like. For other people, and in other cultures, different stories may prove just as meaningful.

When adults cannot script their lives into a culturally valued story, they may feel that they have fallen short in the quest to articulate a meaningful identity. Even if they perform their social roles well and successfully achieve self-determined goals, they may still feel that they do not know who they really are and have not truly found their life's calling. At the end of the day, the most meaningful lives are those that project cultural value and self-worth for all three ontological positions in life—for social actors, motivated agents, and autobiographical authors. We find the greatest meaning in life when we find it abundantly in the different roles we play, the different goals we pursue, and the integrative story we tell about it all.

REFERENCES

Arnett, J. J. (2000). Emerging adulthood: A theory of development from the late teens through the twenties. *American Psychologist, 55*, 469–480. doi:10.1037/0003-066X.55.5.469

Baddeley, J., & Singer, J. A. (2007). Charting the life story's path: Narrative identity across the life span. In D. J. Clandinin (Ed.), *Handbook of narrative inquiry: Mapping a methodology* (pp. 177–202). Thousand Oaks, CA: Sage. doi:10.4135/9781452226552.n7

Bauer, J. J., & McAdams, D. P. (2004). Growth goals, maturity, and well-being. *Developmental Psychology, 40*, 114–127. doi:10.1037/0012-1649.40.1.114

Baumeister, R. F. (1991). *Meanings of life*. New York, NY: Guilford Press.

Buss, D. M. (2008). Human nature and individual differences: Evolution of human personality. In O. P. John, R. W. Robins, & L. A. Pervin (Eds.), *Handbook of personality: Theory and research* (3rd ed., pp. 29–60). New York, NY: Guilford Press.

Caspi, A., Roberts, B. W., & Shiner, R. L. (2005). Personality development: Stability and change. *Annual Review of Psychology, 56*, 453–484. doi:10.1146/annurev.psych.55.090902.141913

Elkind, D. (1981). *Children and adolescents* (3rd ed.). New York, NY: Oxford University Press.

Emmons, R. A. (1999). *The psychology of ultimate concerns: Motivation and spirituality in personality*. New York, NY: Guilford Press.

Erikson, E. H. (1959). Identity and the life cycle: Selected papers. *Psychological Issues, 1*, 1–171.

Erikson, E. H. (1963). *Childhood and society* (2nd ed.). New York, NY: Norton.

Fredrickson, B. L. (2001). The role of positive emotions in positive psychology: The broaden-and-build theory of positive emotions. *American Psychologist, 56*, 218–226. doi:10.1037/0003-066X.56.3.218

Freund, A. M., & Riediger, M. (2006). Goals as building blocks of personality and development in adulthood. In D. K. Mroczek & T. D. Little (Eds.), *Handbook of personality development* (pp. 353–372). Mahwah, NJ: Erlbaum.

Goffman, E. (1959). *The presentation of self in everyday life*. Garden City, NY: Doubleday.

Habermas, T., & Bluck, S. (2000). Getting a life: The emergence of the life story in adolescence. *Psychological Bulletin, 126*, 748–769. doi:10.1037/0033-2909.126.5.748

Haidt, J. (2007, May 18). The new synthesis in moral psychology. *Science, 316*, 998–1002. doi:10.1126/science.1137651

Hammack, P. L. (2008). Narrative and the cultural psychology of identity. *Personality and Social Psychology Review, 12*, 222–247. doi:10.1177/1088868308316892

Harter, S. (2006). The self. In N. Eisenberg (Ed.) and W. Damon & R. W. Lerner (Series Eds.), *Handbook of child psychology: Vol. 3. Social, emotional, and personality development* (pp. 505–570). New York, NY: Wiley.

Helson, R., Soto, C. J., & Cate, R. A. (2006). From young adulthood through the middle age. In D. K. Mroczek & T. Little (Eds.), *Handbook of personality development* (pp. 337–352). Mahwah, NJ: Erlbaum.

Hogan, R. (1982). A socioanalytic theory of personality. In M. Paige (Ed.), *Nebraska symposium on motivation* (pp. 55–89). Lincoln: University of Nebraska Press.

James, W. (1963). *Psychology*. Greenwich, CT: Fawcett. (Original work published 1892)

Jost, J. T., Glaser, J., Kruglanski, A. W., & Sulloway, F. J. (2003). Political conservatism as motivated social cognition. *Psychological Bulletin, 129*, 339–375. doi:10.1037/0033-2909.129.3.339

Jung, C. G. (1936/1971). Psychological typology. In H. Read & Associates. (Eds.), *The collected works of* C. G. *Jung* (Vol. 6, pp. 542–555). Princeton, NJ: Princeton University Press.

Kasser, T., & Ryan, R. M. (1996). Further examining the American dream: Well-being correlates of intrinsic and extrinsic goals. *Personality and Social Psychology Bulletin, 22*, 280–287. doi:10.1177/0146167296223006

King, L. A., Hicks, J. A., Krull, J. L., & Del Gaiso, A. K. (2006). Positive affect and the experience of meaning in life. *Journal of Personality and Social Psychology, 90*, 179–196. doi:10.1037/0022-3514.90.1.179

Little, B. R. (1998). Personal project pursuit: Dimensions and dynamics of personal meaning. In P. Wong & P. S. Fry (Eds.), *The human quest for meaning* (pp. 193–212). Mahwah, NJ: Erlbaum.

Lodi-Smith, J., & Roberts, B. W. (2007). Social investment and personality: A meta-analysis of the relationship of personality traits to investment in work, family, religion, and volunteerism. *Personality and Social Psychology Review, 11*, 1–19. doi:10.1177/1088868306294590

Lucas, R. E., & Diener, E. (2001). Understanding extraverts' enjoyment of social situations: The importance of pleasantness. *Journal of Personality and Social Psychology, 81*, 343–356. doi:10.1037/0022-3514.81.2.343

Maddi, S. R. (1998). Creating meaning through making decisions. In P. T. Wong & P. S. Fry (Eds.), *The human quest for meaning* (pp. 3–26). Mahwah, NJ: Erlbaum.

McAdams, D. P. (1985). *Power, intimacy, and the life story: Personological inquiries into identity*. New York, NY: Guilford Press.

McAdams, D. P. (2001). Generativity in midlife. In M. E. Lachman (Ed.), *Handbook of midlife development* (pp. 395–443). New York, NY: Wiley.

McAdams, D. P. (2006). *The redemptive self: Stories Americans live by*. New York, NY: Oxford University Press.

McAdams, D. P. (2008). Personal narratives and the life story. In O. P. John, R. Robins, & L. A. Pervin (Eds.), *Handbook of personality: Theory and research* (3rd ed., pp. 242–262). New York, NY: Guilford Press.

McAdams, D. P. (2011). *George W. Bush and the redemptive dream: A psychological portrait*. New York, NY: Oxford University Press.

McAdams, D. P., Albaugh, M., Farber, E., Daniels, J., Logan, R. L., & Olson, B. D. (2008). Family metaphors and moral intuitions: How conservatives and liberals narrate their lives. *Journal of Personality and Social Psychology, 95*, 978–990. doi:10.1037/a0012650

McAdams, D. P., & Cox, K. S. (2010). Self and identity across the life span. In A. Freund & R. Lerner (Eds.), *Handbook of life-span development* (Vol. 2, pp. 158–207). New York, NY: Wiley. doi:10.1002/9780470880166.hlsd002006

McAdams, D. P., Diamond, A., de St. Aubin, E., & Mansfield, E. D. (1997). Stories of commitment: The psychosocial construction of generative lives. *Journal of Personality and Social Psychology, 72,* 678–694. doi:10.1037/0022-3514.72.3.678

McAdams, D. P., & Olson, B. D. (2010). Personality development: Continuity and change over the life course. *Annual Review of Psychology, 61,* 517–542. doi:10.1146/annurev.psych.093008.100507

McAdams, D. P., Reynolds, J., Lewis, M., Patten, A., & Bowman, P. J. (2001). When bad things turn good and good things turn bad: Sequences of redemption and contamination in life narrative, and their relation to psychosocial adaptation in midlife adults and in students. *Personality and Social Psychology Bulletin, 27,* 474–485. doi:10.1177/0146167201274008

McCrae, R. R., & Costa, P. T., Jr. (2008). The five-factor theory of personality. In O. P. John, R. W. Robins, & L. A. Pervin (Eds.), *Handbook of personality: Theory and research* (3rd ed., pp. 159–181). New York, NY: Guilford Press.

McLean, K. C. (2008). The emergence of narrative identity. *Social and Personality Psychology Compass, 2,* 1685–1702. doi:10.1111/j.1751-9004.2008.00124.x

McLean, K. C., Pasupathi, M., & Pals, J. L. (2007). Selves creating stories creating selves: A process model of self-development. *Personality and Social Psychology Review, 11,* 262–278. doi:10.1177/1088868307301034

Neimeyer, R. A. (Ed.). (2001). *Meaning reconstruction and the experience of loss.* Washington, DC: American Psychological Association Press. doi:10.1037/10397-000

Ozer, D. J., & Benet-Martinez, V. (2006). Personality and the prediction of consequential outcomes. *Annual Review of Psychology, 57,* 401–421. doi:10.1146/annurev.psych.57.102904.190127

Rokeach, M. (1973). *The nature of human values.* New York, NY: The Free Press.

Rosenwald, G. C., & Ochberg, R. L. (Eds.). (1992). *Stories lives: The cultural politics of self-understanding.* New Haven, CT: Yale University Press.

Ryan, R. M., & Deci, E. L. (2006). Self-regulation and the problem of human autonomy: Does psychology need choice, self-determination, and will? *Journal of Personality, 74,* 1557–1586. doi:10.1111/j.1467-6494.2006.00420.x

Schwartz, S. H., & Bilsky, W. (1990). Toward a theory of the universal content and structure of values: Extensions and cross-cultural replications. *Journal of Personality and Social Psychology, 58,* 878–891. doi:10.1037/0022-3514.58.5.878

Sheldon, K. M. (2004). *Optimal human being.* Mahwah, NJ: Erlbaum.

Singer, J. A. (2004). Narrative identity and meaning making across the adult lifespan: An introduction. *Journal of Personality, 72,* 437–460. doi:10.1111/j.0022-3506.2004.00268.x

Smillie, L. D., Pickering, A. D., & Jackson, C. J. (2006). The new reinforcement sensitivity theory: Implications for personality measurement. *Personality and Social Psychology Review, 10*, 320–335. doi:10.1207/s15327957pspr1004_3

Walker, L. J., & Frimer, J. A. (2007). Moral personality of brave and caring exemplars. *Journal of Personality and Social Psychology, 93*, 845–860. doi:10.1037/0022-3514.93.5.845

Walls, T. A., & Kollat, S. H. (2006). Agency to agentic personalities: The early to middle childhood gap. In D. K. Mroczek & T. Little (Eds.), *Handbook of personality development* (pp. 231–244). Mahwah, NJ: Erlbaum.

Weber, M. (1976). *The Protestant ethic and the spirit of capitalism*. New York, NY: Macmillan. (Original work published 1904)

Wilson, E. O. (1978). *On human nature*. Cambridge, MA: Harvard University Press.

10

MEANING AND MORALITY: A NATURAL COUPLING

RONNIE JANOFF-BULMAN

Despite claims that human society was an artificial, voluntary creation by inherently asocial, solitary creatures (see, e.g., Hobbes, 1991/1665), our evolutionary lineage clearly suggests otherwise. As renowned primatologist Frans de Waal (2006) noted, "there never was a point at which we became social; descended from highly social ancestors—a long line of monkeys and apes—we have been group-living forever. . . . Humans started out—if a starting point is discernible at all—as interdependent . . ." (p. 4). Group living helps members avoid predators and locate food, and group-oriented members are likely to leave more offspring; thus, as de Waal (2006) noted, credit for any decision to create societies should really go to Mother Nature rather than ourselves.

Our inherent group-based sociality is the source of morality's fundamental role in human endeavors. Morality functions as the glue that facilitates group living and social coordination by fostering prosocial, cooperative behaviors and restraining individual selfishness. Morality is absolutely central to

DOI: 10.1037/14040-010
The Psychology of Meaning, Keith D. Markman, Travis Proulx, and Matthew J. Lindberg (Editors)

human experience—I believe so central, that it pervades our basic perceptions and interpretations of people and events and our very understanding of the world we inhabit. Morality and meaning are fundamentally interconnected.

My aim in this chapter is to try to convince the reader of this natural coupling. From automatic, effortless attempts to make sense of simple social stimuli to effortful processes to create lives of significance, the imprint of morality is pervasive in human meaning-making; this chapter attempts to illustrate the strong links between meaning and morality with examples from both ends of the meaning-making spectrum.

A CLOSER LOOK AT MEANING AND MORALITY

Both *meaning* and *morality* are grand constructs that are familiar and known, yet difficult to pin down precisely. In earlier work we distinguished between two types of meaning:

> meaning as comprehensibility and meaning as significance. The first involves questions regarding whether something 'makes sense'; in other words, whether it fits with an accepted system of rules or theories. The second involves questions regarding whether something is of value or worth. (Janoff-Bulman & Frantz, 1997, p. 91; see also Davis, Nolen-Hoeksema, & Larson, 1998; Klinger, 1998)

I believe that both types of meaning making are saturated with morality. When we try to make sense of people, actions, and events, we are likely to use moral considerations as the relevant system of rules to interpret the stimuli; and in creating lives of meaning, we turn to morality to establish significance and value.

Morality is a set of rules or standards regarding right and wrong conduct focused on benefiting the group and not over-benefiting the self. Thus, moral rules include proscriptions against harming group members, as well as "other-regarding" prescriptions focused on reciprocity, fairness, and helping (De Waal, 1996; Gert, 1998; Haidt, 2007, 2008; Janoff-Bulman, Sheikh, & Hepp, 2009; Krebs, 2008). Some aspects of morality are universal; across moral systems people have a duty to refrain from unjustified harm to another and a duty to reciprocate, which leads to an expectation that one's deeds, good and bad, will receive in-kind treatment. Further, a number of moral virtues seem to exist in all cultures, including justice, humanity (which includes love and kindness), and temperance (Peterson & Seligman, 2004). Most generally, all moral systems have some form of the Golden Rule (Krebs, 2008), and humans' very strong interest in knowing others' reputations and making their own reputation known, as well as our strong concern for distributive justice and particular sensitivity to cheats, all speak to the powerful role of reciprocation in morality (Joyce, 2006).[1] The "meta rules" for moral conduct, which emphasize harm-avoidance and helping as well as fairness and reciprocity, are similar across societies, but their specific manifestations clearly differ (Shweder, Much, Mahapatra, & Park, 1997).

Much has been written about the evolutionary bases of morality (see, e.g., Sinott-Armstrong, 2008). There is no gene for morality, nor is there a particular anatomical region of the brain solely devoted to moral evaluations and judgments (see Greene, Sommerville, Nystrom, & Cohen, 2001). Nevertheless, many psychologists have argued that there is a biological preparedness to learn moral rules. Researchers have posited a "universal moral grammar" (e.g., Mikhail, 2007) akin to Chomsky's (1988) "universal grammar" with regard to language, in which there are universal underlying principles and a restricted range of parameters that produce differences across cultures (see Chomsky's, 1988, principles and parameters model). Humans' empathic abilities (e.g., Batson & Shaw, 1991; Eisenberg & Miller, 1987) and the discovery of mirror neurons (Rizzolatti, Fadiga, Gallese, & Fogassi, 1996) at the very least suggest a human readiness for moral concern. Further, research has shown that similar areas of the cortex respond to both physical and social harm (Eisenberger, Liberman, & Williams, 2003), although intentional harm is perceived as more painful than the same physical harm that is unintentional (Gray & Wegner, 2008).

Whether based in our biological or cultural heritage, morality developed as an ingroup phenomenon, providing rules for social coordination of ingroup members. That we can find ample evidence of mistreatment and abuse in the world does not belie the expectation of ingroup morality. If the net defining our ingroup were cast over all of humanity, the world would certainly be a better place. Our ingroups can vary based on self-categorization processes (Turner, Hogg, Oakes, Reicher, & Wetherell, 1987), but regardless of its members, the default for our ingroup is trust, an expectation of morality in social exchange. Outgroup members are not accorded this consideration and must earn our trust (see Brewer, 1981; see also Janoff-Bulman & Parker,

[1]Purity concerns (i.e., proscription of some types of "impure" behaviors) have been posited as universal as well (e.g., Haidt, 2007; Haidt & Joseph, 2004; Krebs, 2008). However, with others I believe that the moralization of disgust evident in purity concerns (and typically reflected in rules and taboos around food and sex), though important for building group commitment, probably involved the "co-opting" of a mechanism that evolved for other purposes, such as avoiding rotten food (see Joyce, 2006; Rozin, Haidt, & McCauley, 1993). Haidt and colleagues (Haidt, 2007; Haidt & Joseph, 2004) have also posited Ingroup/Loyalty and Authority/Respect as foundational moral concerns, suggesting universality as well. Although they are represent available intuitive systems, as posited by their moral foundations theory, their own empirical work raises questions about the universality of these concerns, whereas their Harm/Care and Fairness/Reciprocity concerns generally appear to be endorsed by all (e.g., Graham, Haidt, & Nosek, 2009).

in press). And although we expect ingroup morality, we are also not naïve; rather, as Cosmides (1989; Cosmides & Tooby, 1992) has demonstrated, humans seem to have specialized adaptations for detecting cheaters in social exchange.

For our purposes, morality entails right conduct centered on not harming, but rather supporting and helping one's group, and on reciprocal relations and fairness. Moral codes based on these meta-rules not only serve to bind members of a community but contribute to the survival of the community as well. Specific manifestations are presumed to broadly reflect these basic principles.

MEANING AS SIGNIFICANCE: THE PIVOTAL ROLE OF MORALITY

To fully appreciate the role of morality in meaning making, it is important to recognize the extent to which morality and meaning are bound together in our basic understanding of the world. From this perspective, a comprehensible world is a moral world, and the loss of a meaningful world is based in the loss of a "moral universe." The expectation of a moral universe can best be understood by beginning with the primacy of morality in self- and ingroup perception.

Moral Perceptions of One's Group and the Self

Humans' group-based nature renders social inclusion a primary motivation, and thus social psychologists refer to our "need to belong" (Baumeister & Leary, 1995). Perhaps not surprisingly, then, the most important attribute in people's judgments of their own group is morality. Leach, Ellemers, and Barreto (2007) found that morality is more important than competence or sociability, and in their studies morality explained the most variance in positive ingroup traits for both lab-created and preexisting groups. Further, in this research, identification with a group led to ascriptions of morality. Relatedly, in their early cross-cultural studies of ethnocentrism, Brewer and Campbell (1976; see also LeVine & Campbell, 1972) found that only the attribute of morality was consistently attributed by ingroups to themselves more than to outgroups. Thus, ingroups sometimes regarded themselves as less competent, less sociable, less strong, and less prestigious than outgroup neighbors, but definitely not less moral. And morality is universally selected as the most important attribute in judging a person as a worthy group member (Schwartz, 1992).

Given the centrality of morality to ingroup identity, it follows that we also regard ourselves as moral. Moral self-regard provides us with a sense that we are valued group members, and thus our need to belong is reflected in the virtual universality of moral self-perceptions. Although we typically want feedback about our own competence and others' morality, we assume our own morality (Wojciszke, 2005; Wojciszke, Bazinska, & Jaworski, 1998). As Wojciszke (2005) noted, "in judging the self, an inference of immorality seems to be a psychological impossibility, because it would mean a generalized expectancy of (deserved) exclusion. Therefore, judgments of own morality become *a priori* positive (meaning 'I deserve inclusion')" (p. 69).

The downside of this high moral self-regard is blindness to our own transgressions. Although specific behaviors may elicit guilt, our overall self-evaluation is that of a moral person, for the presumed consequence of an immoral self-perception is expected social rejection. We are likely to question the validity of information about our own immorality, and through rationalization and creative justification we are able to interpret "immoral" behaviors as moral (see Tsang, 2002). Studies of moral hypocrisy provide strong evidence that moral self-perceptions are maintained even when one engages in morally proscribed behaviors (see, e.g., Batson, Thompson, Seuferling, Whitney, & Strongman, 1999; Valdesolo & DeSteno, 2008). In situations of moral hypocrisy, individuals do not compare their behavior to internalized moral standards, but instead reinterpret internalized moral standards in terms of the action they just engaged in (Batson et al., 1999). Even in instances involving clearly inhumane treatment, we generally manage to justify our behavior; Bandura (1999) labeled this process *moral disengagement*, for we suspend the moral sanctions we would otherwise apply in such instances. But this label may be somewhat misleading, for although the perpetrators of harm suspend the moral sanctions, they certainly do not disengage from morality; rather, they specifically reinterpret their behavior so as to maintain a self-perception of morality. Through such processes as reinterpreting the behavior, minimizing the harmful consequences, displacing responsibility, and dehumanizing the victim, we avoid self-condemnation (Bandura, 1999).

Occasionally there are instances of inhumane behavior that are sufficiently extreme or powerful to crush our moral self-perceptions, and the psychological impact is devastating. Recently, researchers identified this phenomenon in veterans who have served in Vietnam, Iraq, and Afghanistan, where soldiers have been confronted with extremely difficult moral challenges (Litz et al., 2009). The unconventional aspects of these wars—civilian threats, an unmarked enemy, improvised explosive devices—create tremendous uncertainty and risks of harm among both combatants and noncombatants, which produce moral dilemmas and a greatly increased potential for moral transgressions and atrocities (see Litz et al., 2009). Thus, in a study of Vietnam veterans (Beckham, Feldman, & Kirby, 1998), a majority of participants reported direct involvement in perpetrating or endorsing atrocities. The researchers found that both combat exposure and atrocity exposure were related to posttraumatic stress disorder (PTSD) severity, and when they controlled for combat exposure, atrocity exposure continued to predict PTSD (Beckham et al., 1998). There are numerous studies suggesting a strong association between perpetrating atrocities and PTSD (for a review, see Litz et al., 2009); such acts seriously challenge beliefs about one's own goodness. To see oneself as immoral is to see oneself as unfit for group membership and social inclusion. The crucial role of moral self-perceptions becomes apparent when we acknowledge the destructive impact of their loss.

A Meaningful World Is a Moral World

Morality is vital to our perceptions of the self and our ingroups. These moral perceptions, in turn, have implications for our larger assumptions about the world we inhabit. In considering the nature of "the" world, we are really considering the nature of "our" world. "Generalizations move outward from experience, such that our own experience with people and events form the basis for more general assumptions about the world" (Janoff-Bulman, 1992, p. 7). If we are moral and those around us—close others and members of our ingroup(s)—are perceived as moral, the world we inhabit ("our world") will also be perceived as a moral world. This is a world characterized by communal concern, helping, and an absence of unjustified harm; it is a world characterized by fairness and outcomes based on reciprocity, which suggests that I will receive in-kind treatment. This is a world defined by goodness and deservingness, just desserts rather than unexpected suffering (see also Lerner, 1980).

Religion, which is universal (in the sense of being present in all human societies, rather than embraced by all people) is essentially an extension or further reflection of our moral worldview. Here meaning and morality are again tightly interwoven. Religions attempt to create meaning, and they do so largely through the imposition of a moral universe—typically with a benevolent deity, a caring God that responds to human behavior in a reciprocal fashion, rewarding the good and punishing the bad. To try to ensure the perception of a moral universe in the face of seemingly unjust deserts, religions often propose an afterlife or successive lives. My concern here is not with the validity of such claims but with the natural coupling of meaning and morality in religion. In creating meaning, religions fundamentally rely on morality and reinforce human assumptions regarding a moral universe.

Trauma and the Loss of Meaning in a Morally Inverted Universe

In the aftermath of extreme negative events—a debilitating accident, criminal assault, natural disaster, life-threatening illness, off-time death of a loved one—survivors struggle to make sense of their experience: "Why did this happen?" and in particular, "Why did this happen to me?" (e.g., Bulman

& Wortman, 1977; Davis, Nolen-Hoeksema, & Larson, 1998; Kiecolt-Glaser & Williams, 1987; McIntosh, Silver, & Wortman, 1993; Taylor, Lichtman, & Wood, 1984; see also Chapter 12, this volume). There is a lack of any contingency between the victim and the outcomes. Traumatic events shatter survivors' fundamental assumptions about the world (Janoff-Bulman, 1989, 1992), and the assumption of meaningfulness of the world is particularly challenged. It is as if extreme negative events are distributed at random—not at all based on who we are or what we do. In years of research with trauma survivors, one sentence was voiced time and again: "I never thought it could happen to me." Postvictimization, survivors confront an incomprehensible world that induces extreme anxiety and dread: They recognize human fragility and vulnerability, for it is impossible to protect oneself against arbitrarily distributed tragic outcomes (see Janoff-Bulman, 1992; see also Becker, 1973, and Chapter 4, this volume).

In the loss of meaning posttrauma, the world does not make sense. The very negative, extreme event simply cannot be accounted for by one's actions or character. Yet this sense of meaninglessness seems to rely largely on an underlying belief in a moral universe, where there is an absence of great harm and unjustified suffering, and where goodness is reciprocated. The confrontation with a loss of meaning is also a recognition of "moral inversion" (see Lifton & Mitchell, 1995); the disintegration of meaning is essentially a disintegration of one's moral world as well.

For the trauma victim, the world now appears meaningless and uncaring—at best indifferent, at worst malevolent. Human-induced victimizations involving a perpetrator highlight a perception of immorality and also tend to be more psychologically devastating (see the review by Chavurastra & Cloitre, 2008). However, extreme negative events that do not involve a perpetrator (e.g., natural disasters) are also apt to involve a perception of moral inversion. It is not just that another (the perpetrator) is evil but rather that the victim has experienced unjustified harm, undeserved suffering. Trauma victims confront an unfamiliar, immoral world—a terrifying universe that does not make sense.

Meaning Making Posttrauma

Over time survivors rebuild their assumptive worlds and, in doing so, shift their meaning-related concerns:

> The survivor's confrontation with meaninglessness, in the sense of incomprehensibility, essentially serves as a catalyst for the construction of meaningfulness, in the sense of significance. It is through a terrifying realization of fragility, mortality, and loss as ever-present possibilities that survivors recognize their own power to create lives of value and commitment. (Janoff-Bulman & Yopyk, 2004, p. 131)

Survivors demonstrate this commitment by choosing activities that are deemed valuable and worthwhile and thereby contribute to a meaningful existence.

What is particularly interesting from a meaning-morality perspective is the great extent to which prosocial, altruistic acts become the activities of choice for survivors. Whether volunteering to directly provide help to others or working for a "good cause" with the ultimate aim of improving the world, moral considerations are commonly seen in the meaning-making choices of trauma survivors. Rape victims volunteer at women's centers or serve on crisis hotlines, cancer and AIDS survivors volunteer time at wellness centers, disaster survivors work for the benefit of their recovering community, veterans devote time to various outreach projects, and grieving parents establish living memorials that provide a benefit to others (e.g., Stanford University, MADD). Further, survivors commonly create meaning post-victimization through close relationships; here, too, other-regarding behaviors become paramount, as survivors engage in their own demonstrations of caring and kindness with close friends and family. This is where morality operates most easily and is most evident; the more surprising posttrauma domain for meaning making is that of the altruistic acts on behalf of others who are likely to be strangers. In large and small ways, survivors engage morality in the service of meaning-making.[2] This response may somehow seem natural, but there is no a priori reason to assume that the two should or will go together.

Yet in light of the loss of assumptions regarding meaning based in morality, it is not surprising that in the aftermath of trauma, during the process of coping and recovery, survivors often engage in explicitly altruistic acts and prosocial behaviors. In their attempts to reestablish meaning by creating meaningful lives—lives of value and significance—they are simultaneously acting to reestablish the perception of a moral universe, and the reality of a moral world, through their own choices and commitments. It is also little wonder that in the aftermath of traumatic life events, social support—the presence of caring, concerned others—is strongly associated with recovery (see meta-analyses: Brewin, Andrews, & Valentine, 2000; Ozer, Best, Lipsey, & Weiss, 2000). Here is powerful evidence of morality in the survivor's world.

[2]It is also not uncommon for survivors to interpret their experience in terms of sacrifice—as redemptive act that will benefit others. Parents believe the loss of their child will contribute to medical knowledge that will help others; concentration camp survivors speak of "bearing witness" so similar genocides won't happen again (see Janoff-Bulman, 1992). These also reflect moral considerations, but are interpretations rather than actions.

MORALITY AND MAKING SENSE OF "SIMPLE" STIMULI

Morality pervades meaning; and moral concerns are evident not only in active and weighty efforts to create lives of meaning and *significance*, but also in everyday, effortless attempts to *make sense* of our world. For the latter to occur, moral judgments themselves presumably must be immediate and automatic—implicit evaluations that color the perception and interpretation of subsequent stimuli. The earlier, decades-long domination of moral psychology by psychologists focused on moral reasoning, best represented in the work of Kohlberg (1981, 1984), precluded such a role for morality. However, the recent "revolution" in morality, best reflected in the social intuitionist perspective of Haidt (2001, 2007; Haidt & Joseph, 2004), provides ample support for a view of moral judgment as "quick and automatic" (Haidt & Bjorklund, 2008, p. 181). According to Haidt and colleagues, slow, conscious reasoning may follow, but typically functions as a justification for one's intuitions or as a means to persuade others regarding our moral position. We surely can engage in effortful moral reasoning, and complex moral dilemmas make these processes particularly evident (see Monin, Pizarro, & Beer, 2007; see also neuroscience evidence, as in Greene et al., 2001), but intuitive moral judgments—fast "gut" reactions—seem to be the rule rather than the exception.

This is a perspective consistent with work in psychology on the primacy of implicit processes in human judgment (see, e.g., Bargh, 1989; Bargh & Chartrand, 1999), and in particular the primacy of evaluation (i.e., like/dislike, good/bad). As Zajonc (1980) noted in his classic paper on affective primacy, we can know that we like something even before we know what it is; thus, he presents studies showing affective discrimination in the absence of recognition memory. Zajonc argued for an automatic affective system, different from a newer, slower cognitive system, a perspective that ushered in the vast work on dual processing models in the ensuing years (see, e.g., Chaiken & Trope, 1999). It appears that we automatically engage in evaluating the world around us; evaluations based on morality (e.g., good/bad evaluations of people, right/wrong evaluations of actions) are key elements of these implicit processes.

The Primacy of Morality in Basic Cognition

Recent research on basic cognitive judgments and theory-of-mind is particularly instructive regarding the formative role of morality in relatively "simple" meaning-making tasks. More specifically, Knobe (2005, 2010) has demonstrated an unexpected ordering of impact from morality to meaning rather than vice versa in understanding psychological phenomena. Knobe

(2010) is interested in "the way the human mind ordinarily makes sense of the world" (p. 315). He began by investigating judgments of blame (a moral judgment) and judgments of intention (a theory of mind judgment). There is a widely shared assumption that we first judge a person's mental state (i.e., intentionality) and use this information to yield a moral judgment—that is, that the perceived intention of the agent is input to a moral judgment process. Yet in a series of studies, Knobe (2010) found precisely the opposite—that is, that the process works in reverse; the moral judgment of right and wrong, or morally good or bad, comes first and impacts judgments about the mind, or more specifically the perceived intention of the agent.

Knobe's (2005, 2010) experimental evidence is based on brief vignettes that ask people to judge whether behaviors were performed intentionally; when he leaves the agent's mental state unchanged but systematically varies the moral status of the behavior in the vignettes, Knobe found large differences in perceived intentionality. For example, consider a CEO who is told that the company is thinking of starting a new program that will increase profits but harm the environment. The CEO's response is, "I don't care at all about harming the environment. I just want to make as much profit as I can. Let's start the new program" (Knobe, 2010, p. 317). The company starts the program, and the environment is harmed. Now consider the same situation, but in this case the CEO is told that the new program will help the environment. The CEO responds, "I don't care at all about helping the environment. I just want to make as much profit as I can. Let's start the new program" (Knobe, 2010, p. 317). The company starts the program and helps the environment.

As Knobe (2010) noted, the two cases are the same in terms of the mental state of the agent. Yet fully 85% of subjects reported that the CEO intentionally harmed the environment in the first (harm) case, whereas only 23% attributed intentionality in the helping case. People's judgments about intention were clearly heavily influenced by their beliefs about whether the targeted behavior was morally good or bad, right or wrong.

Knobe (2010) did much to rule out alternative hypotheses (e.g., motivational bias, conversational pragmatics) and provided strong evidence that morality shifts basic defaults, which then affect intention judgments; that is, moral concerns provided the basis from which to make sense of subsequent information. The same effect arises with people's judgments of causation; that is, people's moral judgments affect their interpretations of causality (Alicke, 2000; Cushman, Knobe, Sinnott-Armstrong, 2008; Knobe & Fraser, 2008). Research has also found that morality has an impact on people's intuitions of freedom, knowledge, and valuing (Beebe & Buckwalter, 2010; Knobe & Preston-Roedder, 2009; Phillips & Knobe, 2009). Knobe's initial work on intentions is illustrative of a larger phenomenon—the powerful influence of moral evaluations on a whole range of fundamental concepts.

Knobe argued that the influence of moral considerations that he finds in his studies tells us about the basic competencies we use to understand our world. He noted that in the literature on theory-of-mind and causal cognition, there has clearly been a belief that we ordinarily make sense of the world in ways analogous to the scientific method. Yet Knobe (2010) concluded, "Even the processes that look most 'scientific' actually take moral considerations into account. It seems that we are moralizing creatures through and through" (p. 328). We make sense of our world through the lens of morality.

Judging Faces: Morality and Making Sense of People

The primacy and centrality of moral considerations in human understanding are also evident in our most basic attempts to make sense of other people. This moral lens for "rudimentary" meaning-making is apparent in the work of Todorov and his colleagues (Todorov, Baron, & Oosterhof, 2008; Todorov, Pakrashi, & Oosterhof, 2009; Willis & Todorov, 2006), who have used both behavioral measures and functional neuroimaging to better understand impression formation, or more specifically, how we begin to make sense of people through judgments of their faces. They have found that we rapidly infer socially significant attributes from facial appearance and have studied a number of trait judgments, including likeability, competence, trustworthiness, aggressiveness, and attractiveness. When they analyzed the underlying structure of these judgments, trustworthiness clearly had the highest loading (.94) on the overall evaluation component (Todorov et al., 2008; see also Willis & Todorov, 2006); that is, "trustworthiness judgments best approximate the valence dimension of face evaluation. In other words, a single trustworthiness judgment can serve as a reliable proxy of the valence evaluation of novel faces" (Todorov et al., 2009, p. 814).

These trustworthiness judgments are made extremely rapidly (after only 100 ms), and of all the traits studied, they show the highest correlation between these very early evaluations and judgments made in the absence of time constraints (Willis & Todorov, 2006). Todorov et al. (2009) also presented faces below the threshold of objective awareness and showed the same effects of temporal stability. They concluded that people automatically make these trustworthiness judgments.

It is noteworthy that it is trustworthiness, not aggressiveness or likeability, that is most central to our evaluation of faces. Trustworthiness is a morality-based trait—and judgments of trustworthiness are based in moral considerations. Morality and trust go hand in hand, for it follows that we are likely to trust those who share our moral views and distrust those who do not. As Messick and Kramer (2001) noted, trust entails the belief that the other will abide by "ordinary ethical rules" (p. 91), the most basic of which is avoiding harm. Uslaner (2002), too, noted the strong association between trust and morality by suggesting that trusting others means accepting them into our "moral communities" (p. 1). When we regard a person as trustworthy, we are willing "to accept vulnerability based upon positive expectations of the intentions or behavior of another" (Rousseau, Sitkin, Burt, & Camerer, 1998, p. 395); a trustworthy person is one who can be counted on to "do the right thing." Thus, in our initial efforts to make sense of people, we rely first and foremost on moral considerations, evident in our automatic judgments of trustworthiness.

Other models of person and group perception recognize the importance of morality in our impressions of others. Thus, in the stereotype content model, Fiske, Cuddy, Glick, and Xu (2002) noted that we want to know two things about outgroups: whether their intentions are good or bad toward me and my group, and whether they're able to enact their intentions. They labeled these dimensions *warmth* and *competence*, but the concern about the outgroup's good or bad intentions is really about morality rather than warmth per se, although warmth may operate as a crude gauge of morality. Morality is clearly important in our views of others, but what is of particular interest in the work of Todorov and colleagues (Todorov et al., 2008, 2009; Willis & Todorov, 2006) is how early these moral evaluations arise in the meaning-making process. Assessments of trustworthiness are essentially spontaneous (as well as temporally stable), no doubt reflecting their importance in our understanding of others and their likely impact on subsequent person-related judgments.

MEANING AND MORALITY: IMPLICATIONS FOR WELL-BEING

There seems to be a natural coupling between morality and meaning. The research by Knobe, Todorov, and their colleagues has provided initial evidence for the pervasiveness of morality at one end of the meaning-making continuum; that is, rapid, automatic moral evaluations play a pivotal role in relatively simple judgments of people and their actions. And the responses of trauma survivors in the aftermath of their victimization is suggestive of the interconnection between meaning and morality in more profound instances of meaning making that involve the creation of meaning and, in particular, meaningful lives. In recent years, psychologists have recognized the relationship between meaning in life and psychological well-being, and thus the proposed coupling of morality and meaning is likely to have implications for well-being. However, although the role of meaning has been increasingly recognized as important for well-being, any role for morality has essentially been ignored.

Meaning in Life and Well-Being

In their comprehensive review, Ryan and Deci (2001) distinguished between two views of well-being:

> the hedonic approach, which focuses on happiness and defines well-being in terms of pleasure attainment and pain avoidance; and the eudaimonic approach, which focuses on meaning and self-realization and defines well-being in terms of the degree to which a person is fully functioning. (p. 141)

Increasingly, psychologists have acknowledged the importance of meaning in conceptualizations of well-being (see Ryan & Deci, 2001, for a review) and have recognized happiness and meaning as distinct constructs (e.g., McGregor & Little, 1998). Lay conceptions of the good life also seem to distinguish between happiness and meaning (King & Napa, 1998). Although distinct, happiness and meaning are nevertheless often related; thus, in a series of studies, King, Hicks, Krull, and Del Gaiso (2006) found an association between positive affect and meaning in life (see also Chapter 22, this volume). Not only does the experience of meaning enhance positive feelings, but they also found the reverse to be the case as well: Positive affect enhances people's reports of the experience of meaning in their lives. Ultimately it seems that well-being is not based solely in pleasure but rather is a combination of both pleasure and a sense of meaning in life.

In addressing the nature of meaning in life, psychologists have posited numerous constructs, including a sense of coherence (e.g., Antonovsky, 1993; Reker & Wong, 1988), investment in valued goal attainment (e.g., Ryff & Singer, 1998), and fulfillment of basic needs, such as purpose, self-efficacy, value, and self-worth (Baumeister, 1992). King et al. (2006) concluded,

> In general, then, we can broadly state that a life is meaningful when it is understood by the person living it to matter in some larger sense. Lives may be experienced as meaningful when they are felt to have significance beyond the trivial or momentary, to have purpose, or to have a coherence that transcends chaos. (p. 180)

We seem to know a meaningful life when we experience it (or don't), but nevertheless, psychologically it remains a fairly amorphous construct. In labeling the meaning-based type of well-being the *eudaimonic* approach, Ryan and Deci (2001) intentionally borrowed the term from Aristotle; however, despite the use of the word, the "eudaimonic approach" seems to have lost sight of what Aristotle meant when he discussed "eudaimonia." A return to Aristotle and the origins of eudaimonic well-being may be instructive in an attempt to better understand meaning in life.

Eudaimonia and the Meaningful Life: Returning to Aristotle

In the *Nichomachean Ethics* Aristotle presented (trans. 1998) *eudaimonia* as the greatest good; variously defined as happiness, well-being, flourishing, and optimal functioning, eudaimonia is nevertheless distinct from the "happiness" and "meaning" accounts of well-being typically put forward by psychologists, for central to Aristotle's perspective is an emphasis on virtue. Aristotle wrote that the good life involves acting in conformity with excellence and virtue. For Aristotle, virtue was equivalent to goodness of character and includes intellectual excellence as well. Nussbaum (1998) noted that among the most important of the virtues recognized by Aristotle are generosity, courage, moderation, justice, truthfulness, easy grace (in contrast to rudeness and insensitivity), and proper judgment (in contrast to enviousness and spitefulness). Echoing contemporary perspectives, Aristotle believed we have a natural capacity to acquire moral virtues, which can be fostered by training. For Aristotle, eudaimon is attained through the cultivation of human virtues; it is a life of excellence, based particularly in excellence of character.

Two further aspects of Aristotle's conception of eudaimonia are important in the context of "eudaimonic well-being." First, for Aristotle it is activity that matters: "We can do noble acts without ruling earth and sea; for even with moderate advantages one can act excellently" (Aristotle, *Nichomachean Ethics*, Book 10). Eudaimonia involves cultivating virtues and *acting* on them (also see Brickman, 1987, on the importance of action in establishing meaning). Pleasure arises from engaging in an activity in a virtuous way—in accordance with the best in us; seeking pleasure for its own sake does not lead to eudaimonia. By acting virtuously—and specifically engaging in activity "in accordance with virtue"—we will achieve well-being. This is the good, meaningful life rather than the life of hedonic well-being.

Second, for Aristotle, action based on human virtue is associated with human flourishing, or more accurately, acting on our "true natures." There is something fundamentally human about virtuous, moral acts, and it is through these acts that we best reach our human potential—and operate on the basis of what is best in humanity. In a very real sense, these are the behaviors that we are meant to do; and, of course, Aristotle is correct to the extent that our "true natures" are our inherently group-based social natures. Generosity, truthfulness, and justice, for example, may not only represent what is best in us but may also reflect a morality based in our fundamental interdependence as social animals.

Aristotle's view of eudaimonia is obviously far richer and more complex than the simple view presented above, but an undeniable aspect of his perspective is an emphasis on human excellences, particularly moral virtues. Psychologists have embraced the term *eudaimonia* to describe a type of well-being distinct from hedonic, pleasure-based well-being, but it is noteworthy that this key aspect of Aristotle's own perspective has been lost in descriptions of eudaimonic well-being.[3] Ironically, psychologists have essentially substituted meaning for virtue. The irony here may be that meaning is a requirement for well-being, but that it is by linking meaning to morality, rather than by omitting morality, that meaning in life may be most readily achieved.

I propose that the good life—and, in particular, *meaning* in life—is strongly associated with moral action. This claim draws from three aspects of Aristotelean thought: that eudaimonia is based in virtues and morality, that it derives from activity or action, and that these actions represent something fundamental about humans (the "function" of human beings). The latter echoes our basic communal orientation and natural existence as group-based animals; we are not simply selfish gene carriers. From this perspective, meaning in life can be achieved through activities that reflect this moral, group-based orientation. It involves engagement not only with something larger than oneself but also with something other than oneself (see Wolf, 2010). Interestingly, in people's narratives, it is communal rather than agentic themes that are correlated with well-being (Mansfield & McAdams, 1996; McAdams, 1985; see also Chapter 9, this volume). Further, recent research linking altruistic acts to well-being has found that we derive considerable pleasure from such activities; in other words, apparently Aristotle was correct in claiming that pleasure, or happiness, arises from engaging in virtuous action. Dunn, Aknin, and Norton (2008), for example, found that spending money on others has a more positive impact on happiness than spending it on ourselves, and this was the case whether studied cross-sectionally in a national survey or through random assignment in the laboratory. And recent neuroscience research supports the existence of positive brain receptors for altruistic acts. Donating to charity activates the pleasure centers of the brain; in this research the brain activation occurred even when the contribution was mandatory (Harbaugh, Mayr, & Burghart, 2007).

A recent study by Van Tongeren and Green (2010) found that participants who received (and accepted as valid) feedback indicating low levels of morality reported less meaning in life than those who received high-morality feedback. There seems to be a natural affinity between morality and a meaningful life, as evidenced when asking for names of people who have had particularly meaningful lives; here those devoted to helping others—through altruistic acts (e.g., Mother Teresa) or social causes (e.g., Martin Luther King, Jr.)—seem to come readily to mind (Wolf, 2010). And somehow altruistic acts are spontaneously perceived as meaningful. As a philosopher, Wolf (2010) maintained

[3]Even when relatedness and belongingness needs are mentioned, they are discussed in terms of the person's own needs, not in terms of a moral, prosocial orientation towards others (see Ryan & Deci, 2001).

that an interest in meaning will reinforce moral concerns; I believe an interest in morality will augment a sense of meaning as well. She wrote,

> Meaning involves an appreciation of what is valuable independently of one's own interests and attitudes, and an interest in meaning involves an interest in realizing and affirming what is valuable in this way. Moral concerns are perhaps the most obvious and most typically engaging of such valuable aims. Though few people are likely to get meaning from the abstract project of "being moral"—a passion for morality would be a peculiar and puzzling thing—many if not most people get meaning from more specific projects and relationships that morality should applaud: from being good and doing good in their roles as parent, daughter, lover, friend, and from furthering or trying to further social and political goods. (pp. 114–115)

Connecting to others through activities based in our own morality or "goodness of character" is a route to a life of meaning. It reflects the best and the basic in us.

Following the recent earthquake and nuclear disaster in Japan, there were moving reports of newfound meaning in life and a renewed sense of well-being by young Japanese who were not victims themselves:

> While many of their elders wrote them off as too coddled to live up to traditional Japanese values of self-sacrifice and hard work, many young people are finding meaning in the crisis . . . [Many] have found purpose volunteering to work at nonprofit groups shuttling aid to the newly destitute in the prefectures north of here. Students have taken to the streets to collect donations for those in need. Blogs and social networking sites are flooded with comments from young people asking what they can do to help. (Belson, 2011, p. A1)

In the words of one recent college graduate, "Before the earthquake, I thought about myself and what I can do for my new company, but now I think what I can do for all of society" (Belson, 2011, p. A1). Many of the young felt alienated in modern Japanese society, where a slavish commitment to work was expected in exchange for stable wages and benefits. Now their prosocial, altruistic acts provided young Japanese with a sense of meaning and, more generally, well-being. Although the morality route is unlikely to be the only path to a meaningful life, it nevertheless seems to be a readily available path with a strong likelihood of success.

A FEW FINAL WORDS

From the interpretation of simple social stimuli to the creation of meaningful lives, morality and meaning are tightly interconnected, with morality underpinning meaning making, understood in terms of both comprehensibility and significance. Moral considerations are paramount when trying to make sense of our world, whether in basic cognitive tasks or following traumatic life events that shatter perceptions of meaningfulness. And efforts to successfully craft lives of value are closely tied to morality as well. To suggest that meaning in life is largely based in prosocial, moral actions is neither utopian nor Pollyannish. Rather, it reflects the fact that we are group-based social animals. Morality is a fundamental aspect of our humanity, and thus, moral considerations suffuse our meaning making, from the mundane to the profound.

REFERENCES

Alicke, M. D. (2000). Culpable control and the psychology of blame. *Psychological Bulletin, 126*, 556–574. doi:10.1037/0033-2909.126.4.556

Antonovsky, A. (1993). The structure and properties of the Sense of Coherence scale. *Social Science & Medicine, 36*, 725–733. doi:10.1016/0277-9536(93)90033-Z

Bandura, A. (1999). Moral disengagement in the perpetuation of inhumanities. *Personality and Social Psychology Review, 3*, 193–209. doi:10.1207/s15327957pspr0303_3

Bargh, J. A. (1989). Conditional automaticity: Varieties of automatic influence in social perception and cognition. In J. S. Uleman & J. A. Bargh (Eds.), *Unintended thought* (pp. 5–51). New York, NY: Guilford.

Bargh, J. A., & Chartrand, T. L. (1999). The unbearable automaticity of being. *American Psychologist, 54*, 462–479. doi:10.1037/0003-066X.54.7.462

Batson, C. D., & Shaw, L. L. (1991). Evidence for altruism: Toward a pluralism of prosocial motives. *Psychological Inquiry, 2*, 107–122. doi:10.1207/s15327965pli0202_1

Batson, C. D., Thompson, E., Seuferling, G., Whitney, H., & Strongman, J. (1999). Moral hypocrisy: Appearing moral to oneself without being so. *Journal of Personality and Social Psychology, 77*, 525–537. doi:10.1037/0022-3514.77.3.525

Baumeister, R. F. (1992). *Meanings in life*. Hillsdale, NJ: Erlbaum.

Baumeister, R. F., & Leary, M. R. (1995). The need to belong: Desire for interpersonal attachments as a fundamental human motivation. *Psychological Bulletin, 117*, 497–529. doi:10.1037/0033-2909.117.3.497

Becker, E. (1973). *The denial of death*. New York, NY: Free Press.

Beckham, J. C., Feldman, M. E., & Kirby, A. C. (1998). Atrocities exposure in Vietnam veterans with chronic posttraumatic stress disorder: Relationship to combat exposure, symptom severity, guilt, and interpersonal violence. *Journal of Traumatic Stress, 11*, 777–785. doi:10.1023/A:1024453618638

Beebe, J. R., & Buckwalter, W. (2010). The epistemic side-effect effect. *Mind & Language, 25*, 474–498.

Belson, K. (2011, March 31). Sour economy and multiple new crises test Japan's young. *The New York Times*. p. A1.

Brewer, M. B. (1981). Ethnocentrism and its role in interpersonal trust. In M. B. Brewer & Collins (Eds.), *Scientific inquiry and the social sciences* (pp. 345–360). San Francisco, CA: Jossey-Bass.

Brewer, M. B., & Campbell, D. T. (1976). *Ethnocentrism: East African evidence*. New York, NY: Wiley.

Brewin, C. R., Andrews, B., & Valentine, D. (2000). Meta-analysis of risk factors for posttraumatic stress disorder in trauma-exposed adults. *Journal of Consulting and Clinical Psychology*, 68, 748–766. doi:10.1037/0022-006X.68.5.748

Brickman, P. (1987). *Commitment, conflict, and caring*. Englewood Cliffs, NJ: Prentice Hall.

Bulman, R., & Wortman, C. B. (1977). Attributions of blame and coping in the "real world": Severe accident victims react to their lot. *Journal of Personality and Social Psychology, 35*, 351–363. doi:10.1037/0022-3514.35.5.351

Chaiken, S., & Trope, Y. (Eds.). (1999). *Dual process theories in social psychology*. New York, NY: Guilford Press.

Charuvastra, A., & Cloitre, M. (2008). Social bonds and posttraumatic stress disorder. *Annual Review of Psychology, 59*, 301–328. doi:10.1146/annurev.psych.58.110405.085650

Chomsky, N. (1988). *Language and problems of knowledge*. Cambridge, MA: MIT Press.

Cosmides, L. (1989). The logic of social exchange: Has natural selection shaped how humans reason? Studies with the Wason selection task. *Cognition, 31*, 187–276. doi:10.1016/0010-0277(89)90023-1

Cosmides, L., & Tooby, J. (1992). Cognitive adaptations for social exchange. In J. Barkow, L. Cosmides, & J. Tooby (Eds.), *The adapted mind* (pp. 163–228). New York: Oxford University Press.

Cushman, F., Knobe, J., & Sinnott-Armstrong, W. (2008). Moral appraisals affect doing/allowing judgments. *Cognition, 108*, 353–380. doi:10.1016/j.cognition.2008.03.006

Davis, C. G., Nolen-Hoeksema, S., & Larson, J. (1998). Making sense of loss and benefiting from the experience: two construals of meaning. *Journal of Personality and Social Psychology*, *75*, 561–574. doi:10.1037/0022-3514.75.2.561

De Waal, F. (1996). *Good natured: The origins of right and wrong in humans and other animals*. Cambridge, MA: Harvard University Press.

De Waal, F. (2006). *Primates and philosophers: How morality evolved*. Princeton, NJ: Princeton University Press.

Dunn, E. W., Aknin, L. B., & Norton, M. (2008, March 21). Spending money on others promotes happiness. *Science*, *319*, 1687–1688. doi:10.1126/science.1150952

Eisenberg, N., & Miller, P. A. (1987). The relation of empathy to prosocial and related behaviors. *Psychological Bulletin, 101*(1), 91–119. doi:10.1037/0033-2909.101.1.91

Eisenberger, N. I., Liberman, M. D., & Williams, K. D. (2003, October 10). Does rejection hurt? An fMRI study of social exclusion. *Science, 302*, 290–292. doi:10.1126/science.1089134

Fiske, S. T., Cuddy, A. J., Glick, P., & Xu, J. (2002). A model of (often mixed) stereotype content: Competence and warmth respectively follow from perceived status and competition. *Journal of Personality and Social Psychology, 82*, 878–902. doi:10.1037/0022-3514.82.6.878

Gert, B. (1998). *Morality: Its nature and justification*. New York, NY: Oxford University Press.

Graham, J., Haidt, J., & Nosek, B. A. (2009). Liberals and conservatives rely on different sets of moral foundations. *Journal of Personality and Social Psychology, 96*, 1029–1046. doi:10.1037/a0015141

Gray, K., & Wegner, D. M. (2008). The sting of intentional pain. *Psychological Science, 19*, 1260–1262. doi:10.1111/j.1467-9280.2008.02208.x

Greene, J. D., Sommerville, R. B., Nystrom, L. E., Darley, J. M., & Cohen, J. D. (2001, September 14). An fMRI investigation of emotional engagement in moral judgment. *Science, 293*, 2105–2108. doi:10.1126/science.1062872

Haidt, J. (2001). The emotional dog and its rational tail: A social intuitionist approach to moral judgment. *Psychological Review, 108*, 814–834. doi:10.1037/0033-295X.108.4.814

Haidt, J. (2007, May 18). The new synthesis in moral psychology. *Science, 316*, 998–1002. doi:10.1126/science.1137651

Haidt, J. (2008). Morality. *Perspectives on Psychological Science, 3*, 65–72. doi:10.1111/j.1745-6916.2008.00063.x

Haidt, J., & Bjorklund, F. (2008). Social intuitionists answer six questions about morality. In W. Sinnott-Armstrong (Ed.), *Moral psychology, Vol. 2: The cognitive science of morality* (pp. 181–217). Cambridge, MA: MIT Press.

Haidt, J., & Joseph, C. (2004). Intuitive ethics: How innately prepared intuitions generate culturally variable virtues. *Daedalus* (Fall), 55–66. doi:10.1162/0011526042365555

Harbaugh, W. T., Mayr, U., & Burghart, D. (2007, June 15). Neural responses to taxation and voluntary giving reveal motives for charitable donations. *Science, 316*, 1622. doi:10.1126/science.1140738

Hobbes, T. (1991). *Leviathan*. Cambridge, England: Cambridge University Press. (Original work published 1651)

Janoff-Bulman, R. (1989). Assumptive worlds and the stress of traumatic events: Applications of the schema construct. *Social Cognition, 7*, 113–136. doi:10.1521/soco.1989.7.2.113

Janoff-Bulman, R. (1992). *Shattered assumptions: Towards a new psychology of trauma*. New York, NY: Free Press.

Janoff-Bulman, R., & Frantz, C. M. (1997). The impact of trauma on meaning: From meaningless world to meaningful life. In M. Power & C. Brewin (Eds.),

The transformation of meaning in psychological therapies (pp. 91–106). London, England: Wiley.

Janoff-Bulman, R., & Parker, M. (in press). The moral bases of public distrust: Politics, partisanship, and compromise. In R. Kramer & T. Pittinsky (Eds.), *Restoring trust: Challenges and prospects*. New York, NY: Oxford University Press.

Janoff-Bulman, R., Sheikh, S., & Hepp, S. (2009). Proscriptive versus prescriptive morality: Two faces of moral regulation. *Journal of Personality and Social Psychology*, *96*, 521–537. doi:10.1037/a0013779

Janoff-Bulman, R., & Yopyk, D. (2004). Random outcomes and valued commitments: Existential dilemmas and the paradox of meaning. In J. Grenberg, S. L. Koole, & T. Pyszczynski (Eds.), *Handbook of experimental existential psychology* (pp. 122–138). New York, NY: Guilford Press.

Joyce, R. (2006). *The evolution of morality*. Cambridge, MA: MIT Press.

Kiecolt-Glaser, J. K., & Williams, D. A. (1987). Self-blame, compliance, and distress among burn patients. *Journal of Personality and Social Psychology*, *53*, 187–193. doi:10.1037/0022-3514.53.1.187

King, L. A., Hicks, J., Krull, J. L., & Del Gaiso, A. K. (2006). Positive affect and the experience of meaning in life. *Journal of Personality and Social Psychology*, *90*, 179–196. doi:10.1037/0022-3514.90.1.179

King, L. A., & Napa, C. K. (1998). What makes a life good? *Journal of Personality and Social Psychology*, *75*, 156–165. doi:10.1037/0022-3514.75.1.156

Klinger, E. (1998). The search for meaning in evolutionary perspective and its clinical implications. In P. T. P. Wong & P. S. Fry (Eds.), *The human quest for meaning: A handbook of psychological research and clinical applications* (pp. 27–50). Mahwah, NJ: Erlbaum.

Knobe, J. (2005). Theory of mind and moral cognition: Exploring the connections. *Trends in Cognitive Sciences*, *9*, 357–359. doi:10.1016/j.tics.2005.06.011

Knobe, J. (2010). Person as Scientist, Person as Moralist. *Behavioral and Brain Sciences*, *33*, 315–329. doi:10.1017/S0140525X10000907

Knobe, J., & Fraser, B. (2008) Causal judgment and moral judgment: Two experiments. In W. Sinnott-Armstrong (Ed.), *Moral psychology: Vol. 2. The cognitive science of morality: Intuition and diversity* (pp. 441–448). Cambridge, MA: MIT Press.

Knobe, J., & Preston-Roedder, E. (2009). The ordinary concept of valuing. *Philosophical Issues*, *19*, 131–147.

Kohlberg, L. (1981). *Essays on moral development: Vol. I. The philosophy of moral development*. San Francisco, CA: Harper & Row.

Kohlberg, L. (1984). *Essays on moral development: Vol. II. The psychology of moral development*. San Francisco, CA: Harper & Row.

Krebs, D. L. (2008). Morality: An evolutionary account. *Perspectives on Psychological Science*, *3*, 149–172. doi:10.1111/j.1745-6924.2008.00072.x

Leach, C. W., Ellemers, N., & Barreto, M. (2007). Group virtue: The importance of morality (vs. competence and sociability) in the positive evaluation of in-groups. *Journal of Personality and Social Psychology, 93*, 234–249. doi:10.1037/0022-3514.93.2.234

Lerner, M. J. (1980). *The belief in a just world*. New York, NY: Plenum.

LeVine, R. A., & Campbell, D. T. (1972). *Ethnocentrism*. New York, NY: Wiley.

Lifton, R. J., & Mitchell, G. (1995). *Hiroshima in America: Fifty years of denial*. New York, NY: Putnam.

Litz, B., Stein, N., Delaney, E., Lebowitz, L., Nash, W. P., Silva, C., & Naguen, S. (2009). Moral injury and moral repair in war veterans: A preliminary model and intervention strategy. *Clinical Psychology Review, 29*, 695–706. doi:10.1016/j.cpr.2009.07.003

Mansfield, E. D., & McAdams, D. P. (1996). Generativity and themes of agency and communion in adult autobiography. *Personality and Social Psychology Bulletin, 22*, 721–731. doi:10.1177/0146167296227006

McAdams, D. P. (1985). *Power, intimacy, and the life story: Personological inquiries into identity*. Homewood, IL: Dorsey Press.

McGregor, I., & Little, B. R. (1998). Personal projects, happiness, and meaning: On doing well and being yourself. *Journal of Personality and Social Psychology, 74*, 494–512. doi:10.1037/0022-3514.74.2.494

McIntosh, D. N., Silver, R. C., & Wortman, C. B. (1993). Religion's role in adjustment to a negative life event: Coping with the loss of a child. *Journal of Personality and Social Psychology, 65*, 812–821. doi:10.1037/0022-3514.65.4.812

Messick, D. M., & Kramer, R. M. (2001). Trust as a shallow form of morality. In K. S. Cook (Ed.), *Trust in society* (Vol. 2, pp. 89–118). New York, NY: Russell Sage Foundation.

Mikhail, J. (2007). Universal moral grammar: Theory, evidence, and the future. *Trends in Cognitive Sciences, 11*, 143–152. doi:10.1016/j.tics.2006.12.007

Monin, B., Pizarro, D., & Beer, J. S. (2007). Deciding versus reacting: Conceptions of moral judgment and the reason-affect debate. *Review of General Psychology, 11*, 99–111. doi:10.1037/1089-2680.11.2.99

Nussbaum, M. (1998). Non-relative virtues: An Aristotelian approach. In J. P. Sterba (Ed.), *Ethics: the big questions* (pp. 259–276). Oxford, England: Blackwell.

Ozer, E. J., Best, S. R., Lipsey, T. L., & Weiss, D. S. (2003). Predictors of posttraumatic stress disorder and symptoms in adults: A meta-analysis. *Psychological Bulletin, 129*, 52–73. doi:10.1037/0033-2909.129.1.52

Peterson, C., & Seligman, M. E. P. (2004). *Character strengths and virtues*. Oxford, England: Oxford University Press.

Phillips, J., & Knobe, J. (2009). Moral judgments and intuitions about freedom. *Psychological Inquiry, 20*, 30–36. doi:10.1080/10478400902744279

Reker, G. T., & Wong, P. T. (1988). Aging and the individual process: Toward a theory of personal meaning. In J. E. Birren & V. L. Bengston (Eds.), *Emergent theories of aging* (pp. 214–246). New York, NY: Springer.

Rizzolatti, G., Fadiga, L., Gallese, V., & Fogassi, L. (1996). Promoter cortex and the recognition of motor actions. *Brain Research. Cognitive Brain Research, 3,* 131–141. doi:10.1016/0926-6410(95)00038-0

Rousseau, D. M., Sitkin, S. B., Burt, R. S., & Camerer, C. (1998). Not so different after all: A cross-discipline view of trust. *Academy of Management Review, 23,* 393–404. doi:10.5465/AMR.1998.926617

Rozin, P., Haidt, J., & McCauley, C. R. (1993). Disgust. In M. Lewis & J. Haviland (Eds.), *Handbook of Emotions* (pp. 575–594). New York, NY: Guilford Press.

Ryan, R. M., & Deci, E. L. (2001). On happiness and human potentials: A review of research on hedonic and eudaimonic well-being. *Annual Review of Psychology, 52,* 141–166. doi:10.1146/annurev.psych.52.1.141

Ryff, C. D., & Singer, B. H. (1998). The contours of positive human health. *Psychological Inquiry,* 9, 1–28. doi:10.1207/s15327965pli0901_1

Schwartz, S. H. S. (1992). Universals in the content and structure of values: Theoretical advances and empirical tests in 20 countries. *Advances in Experimental Social Psychology, 25,* 1–65. doi:10.1016/S0065-2601(08)60281-6

Shweder, R. A., Much, N. C., Mahapatra, M., & Park, L. (1997). The "big three" of morality (autonomy, community, divinity) and the "big three" explanations of suffering. In A. Brandt & P. Rozin (Eds.), *Morality and health* (pp. 119–169). New York, NY: Routledge.

Sinott-Armstrong, W. (Ed.). (2008). *Moral psychology—Vol. 1: The evolution of morality: Adaptations and innateness.* Cambridge, MA: MIT Press.

Taylor, S. E., Lichtman, R. R., & Wood, J. V. (1984). Attributions, beliefs about control, and adjustment to breast cancer. *Journal of Personality and Social Psychology,* 46, 489–502. doi:10.1037/0022-3514.46.3.489

Todorov, A., Baron, S., & Oosterhof, N. N. (2008). Evaluating face trustworthiness: A model based approach. *Social Cognitive and Affective Neuroscience, 3,* 119–127. doi:10.1093/scan/nsn009

Todorov, A., Pakrashi, M., & Oosterhof, N. N. (2009). Evaluating faces on trustworthiness after minimal time exposure. *Social Cognition, 27,* 813–833. doi:10.1521/soco.2009.27.6.813

Tsang, J. (2002). Moral rationalization and the integration of situational factors and psychological processes in immoral behavior. *Review of General Psychology,* 6, 25–50. doi:10.1037/1089-2680.6.1.25

Turner, J. C., Hogg, M. A., Oakes, P. J., Reicher, S. D., & Wetherell, M. S. (1987). *Rediscovering the social group: A self-categorization theory.* Oxford, England: Blackwell.

Uslaner, E. M. (2002). *The moral foundations of trust.* New York, NY: Cambridge University Press.

Valdesolo, P., & DeSteno, D. (2008). The duality of virtue: Deconstructing the moral hypocrite. *Journal of Experimental Social Psychology, 44*, 1334–1338. doi:10.1016/j.jesp.2008.03.010

Van Tongeren, D. R., & Green, J. D. (2011, January). *Morality gives us meaning: Perceived moral standing affects subjective meaning in life*. Poster presented at the annual meeting of the Society for Personality and Social Psychology, Austin, TX.

Willis, J., & Todorov, A. (2006). First impressions: making up your mind after a 100-ms exposure to a face. *Psychological Science, 17*, 592–598. doi:10.1111/j.1467-9280.2006.01750.x

Wojciszke, B. (2005). Morality and competence in person and self-perception. *European Review of Social Psychology, 16*, 155–188. doi:10.1080/10463280500229619

Wojciszke, B., Bazinska, R., & Jaworski, M. (1998). On the dominance of moral categories in impression formation. *Personality and Social Psychology Bulletin, 24*, 1251–1263. doi:10.1177/01461672982412001

Wolf, S. (2010). *Meaning in life and why it matters*. Princeton, NJ: Princeton University Press.

Zajonc, R. B. (1980). Feelings and thinking: Preferences need no inferences. *American Psychologist, 35*, 151–175. doi:10.1037/0003-066X.35.2.151

11

WRESTLING WITH OUR BETTER SELVES: THE SEARCH FOR MEANING IN LIFE

MICHAEL F. STEGER

Joshu asked Nansen: "What is the path?"
Nansen said: "Everyday life is the path."
Joshu asked: "Can it be studied?"
Nansen said: "If you try to study, you will be far away from it."
Joshu asked: "If I do not study, how can I know it is the path?"

Mumon (2006, p. 37)

How would you know if you found something if you never have been looking for it? Why would you look for something you already have?

Questions such as these capture the two poles that psychological ideas about meaning in life have been drawn to over the past century or so. One idea about meaning in life blends the effort with the outcome, mingling seeking and finding, pursuing and experiencing. The search for meaning and the presence of meaning whirl around each other in the uniquely human navigation of existential tides. The other idea about meaning in life separates the two, as if seeking meaning was like eating and experiencing meaning was like the rest of life. Most of the time, people are satiated, content, full enough of meaning that it is out of their awareness. On the one hand, the process of seeking meaning is the structure of experiencing meaning. On the other hand, we seek only when we hunger and our previous stores of meaning have been depleted.

DOI: 10.1037/14040-011
The Psychology of Meaning, Keith D. Markman, Travis Proulx, and Matthew J. Lindberg (Editors)

The search for meaning straddles this duality. It is easy to see it as a natural, ongoing mental process. We *make* meaning all of the time. It is also easy to see it as a process that normally slumbers, waiting for when it is needed. We appreciate homeostasis. This chapter explores the dual nature of the search for meaning in life and examines some of the research that supports this perspective.

A BRIEF HISTORY OF THE SEARCH FOR MEANING IN LIFE

For many of you reading this book (and many of us writing it), our awakening to the pursuit and experience of meaning in life came while holding Viktor Frankl's (1963) masterpiece, *Man's Search for Meaning.* Frankl really represents the first fully psychological idea about meaning in life. Prior to that, meaning and meaningful living had made scattered appearances in the philosophical literature, but the importance of meaning seems to have been considered in parenthetical asides. It is somewhat common to see *meaningful* used as a synonym for important parts of other, more carefully considered constructs. For example, Aristotle argued that the vigorous development of our most virtuous selves was the path to the ultimate aim of happiness (*eudaimonia;* see also Chapter 10, this volume). This notion of happiness, or maybe more accurately *fulfillment*, has been referred to as *meaning*, and the development of the virtuous self has also been referred to as *meaningful living* (e.g., Becker, 1992; Kenyon, 2000). Other philosophical accounts targeted the subjective, malleable nature of life to argue that there is no such thing as a given "meaning of life" (e.g., Camus, 1955; Kekes, 1986; Nietzsche, 1882/1974). This focus on meaninglessness allowed the focus to shift to one's individual ability, perhaps even responsibility, to weave one's own meaning into life (e.g., Kekes, 2000). Within an infinitely ductile world, the objective meaninglessness of life led to a variety of possibilities. Some interpretations emphasized the idea that forceful individuals could and should impose their willpower to shape the world around them (Nietzsche, 1909/1961). Others used this meaninglessness to develop the infinitely flexible seeds of postmodernist moral and ontological pluralism (e.g., Foucault, 1970; Wong, 1986). Still, despite the lack of any guarantee regarding some rock-solid meaning in life on which individuals could rely, their lives nonetheless demanded to have meaning. Camus (1955) regarded meaning as a necessity and portrayed meaninglessness as a kind of cold shadow that could choke the value out of life (see Chapter 4, this volume). So, if meaning is a philosophical necessity, yet there is no ready-made meaning waiting for us out there, what are we to do?

One can sense great sympathy from the stark, existentially inspired philosophers, particularly the French ones, Sartre and Camus. Sartre (1938/2007) wrote about the scourge of inescapable freedom. In this view, freedom amounts to the responsibility we each must bear to justify our lives, to find meaning. And yet, we must take up this responsibility and patch together some kind of meaning the best way we can. In some ways, this perspective echoes the first question at the beginning of this chapter—how can we find meaning if we are not looking for it? In this view, meaning does not present itself, and no one can bequeath it to us. We must craft it anew, as our understanding of our stock in life changes with the events of our lives. In essence, at some point in time, we must each search for our meaning in life.

Of course, this is only one narrative. Although the existentialists, moral relativists, and postmodernists appear drawn to the multiplicity of perspectives and the difficulty of establishing irrefutable givens about how and why we are to live, other traditions highlight what they consider to be unimpeachable truths. Prominent among these traditions, religious entities can be seen to provide the answers to what is meaningful about life. Rather than being an inevitable and perhaps endlessly negotiated dialogue, meaning is an answer, a truth, a way. Meaninglessness is less a natural and unavoidable state of existence than what results when people forget, stray away from, or violate eternal truths.

Each tradition tends to offer followers specific guidance about attaining a life of enduring meaning. "I am the way and the truth and the life." This is the message Jesus conveys to his worried followers (John 14:6; New International Version). The Judeo-Christian Old Testament also offers Ten Commandments to guide actions. *Dharma, artha, kama,* and *moksa*—righteousness, prosperity and purpose, pleasure, and spiritual liberation. These are the four goals of life according to the epic Hindu holy book, *The Mahabharata*. The Qur'an provides five pillars of belief and conduct for Muslims. Religions offer certainty of action and belief and often provide certainty about the consequences of action and belief as well, whether that includes ideas about the afterlife or preferred social responses to transgressions.

In a similar vein, moral philosophy seeks to provide best estimates of universal virtues, a tradition at least as old as Aristotle's arguments about the path to eudaimonia. These traditions echo the second question at the beginning of this chapter—the answer to your life's meaning is right here, why look elsewhere? For example, a recent prescription for the good life is to develop wisdom (Tiberius, 2008). Peeling back this idea, Tiberius confides that a life of wisdom means reflecting upon and identifying the things that will sustain us and give us good experiences, having a sense of perspective about our successes and failures, and cultivating some degree of self-awareness and cautious optimism about human nature. Finally, wisdom means knowing when we need to reflect more deeply on life and when to just live it. As with this example, moral philosophy often provides fairly explicit criteria and objectives—even if those objectives seem more daunting and nuanced in practice than they do in theory.

Somewhere between the phenomenological relativism of existential philosophy and the prescribed absolutism of many religions and moral philosophies lies the empirical relativism of psychology. At the lead of psychology's study of meaning in life, Frankl was uniquely suited to argue for the Nietzschean and French existentialist view that each of us needs a meaning, that each of us must find an individually apt meaning, and that possessing this meaning provides a critical resilience in the face of hardship. The loss of his family in Nazi concentration camps and his own survival of Auschwitz solidified insights and arguments Frankl had been working on during the 1930s. Frankl described the evolution of insight into a fundamental human urge—the urge to find purpose for one's life. He argued that Nietzsche was right in saying that people who felt they had a "why" for their lives could better endure challenges, obstacles, and privation. In the concentration camps, Frankl asserted, the primary difference between those who succumbed to the horrors of daily camp life and those who survived was the possession of a purpose. So, even in Frankl's writing, we see the tension at the heart of searching for meaning. Seeking meaning and purpose is a natural, human urge, yet we need meaning to endure life's travails, and this meaning should presumably be stable. It does not seem right to have to rely on a meaning that one is still striving to identify, construct, or understand.

EMPIRICAL EVIDENCE ABOUT SEARCHING FOR MEANING

In previous work, defining the search for meaning in life as "the strength, intensity, and activity of people's desire and efforts to establish and/or augment their understanding of the meaning, significance, and purpose of their lives" (Steger, Kashdan, Sullivan, & Lorentz, 2008, p. 200) held appeal because it captured the dual senses of the construct as it had been portrayed in the psychological literature. Frankl (1963) and Maddi (1970) came down on the side of viewing searching for meaning as "the primary motivational force" (Frankl, 1963, p. 121) among humans. However, Baumeister (1991) and Klinger (1998) both perceived the possibility that searching for meaning might be spurred primarily by perceived deficiencies in meaning. This dual nature of searching for meaning in life—arising from both life-affirming and deficit-correcting roots—was laid out by Steger, Frazier, Oishi, and Kaler (2006, pp. 89–90) in their development of the Meaning in Life Questionnaire (MLQ). This measurement tool allowed the empirical examination of these two possibilities in later studies from the same researchers (Steger, Kashdan, et al., 2008; Steger, Oishi, & Kesebir, 2011). In this research, these distinctions were framed in terms of models in which a lack of meaning led to searching, or an abundance of searching led to found meaning, and the focus was on attempting to identify underlying personality dimensions that might predict which model worked for whom.

Overall, not much research has been conducted on searching for meaning. Until the MLQ was published, there was no psychometrically sound measure of search for meaning. Since that time, research using the MLQ has generally shown that self-reported searching for meaning in life is usually negatively related to well-being and positively related to psychological distress, although it is also unrelated to some of these variables. Steger, Kashdan, et al. (2008) found this pattern for a wide array of personality traits (+neuroticism, +stress reactance), well-being (−self-acceptance), and social cognitive (−relatedness) variables. The pattern of correlations for meaning seeking most often mirrors the pattern of correlations found for experiencing meaning. So, whereas searching for meaning is positively correlated with rumination (i.e., present fatalistic and past negative time perspectives), experiencing the presence of meaning in life is negatively correlated with these variables. However, there were exceptions, and in some cases search for meaning was positively correlated with variables many would consider to be desirable (e.g., openness to experiences, particularly ideas; curiosity; behavioral activation system drive subscale) and negatively correlated with variables many would consider to be less desirable (e.g., dogmatism). In other cases, search for meaning was correlated with neutral, yet fitting, variables (i.e., absorption). And, of course, search for meaning was negatively correlated with experiencing meaning (see also Steger et al., 2006; Steger & Kashdan, 2007). More interesting, a consistent pattern emerged among moderators of that relationship. The slope of the relation between seeking meaning and having meaning was steepest among people low in openness, low in behavioral activation system indicators, and high in behavioral inhibition system indicators (see Chapter 18, this volume). This was interpreted as affirming the idea that for some, more open-minded people, search for meaning might not be so bad; for other, more structure- and certainty-appreciating people, searching for meaning was a sign of problems.

Other research from diverse sources has painted a picture suggesting that people who are searching for meaning are actively, but perhaps not particularly effectively, casting about for answers to their problem in the world around them. For example, people high in search for meaning were more likely to adopt a normative approach to identity development, which is seen as a somewhat reactive and reflexive approach to identity formation (Beaumont, 2009). If identity does not seem to provide a deep or consistent solution for the search for meaning, meaning itself seems fairly important. Correlational research has found that experiencing high levels of meaning, both in life in general (Park, Park, & Peterson, 2010; Steger, Kawabata, Shimai, & Otake, 2008) and in one's career life (Steger & Dik, 2009), seems to ameliorate the usually negative profile of meaning seekers. In probing the consequences of this relationship between seeking and experiencing meaning, a lab experiment showed that people high in search for meaning are particularly likely to focus on information about overall levels of meaning in life on the part of a fictitious character when judging whether that character would feel his life was satisfying (Steger et al., 2011). Finally, some research suggests that taking some of the judgmentalism out of daily life helps ease the search for meaning a bit. A 6-week mindfulness intervention produced marginally significant decreases in searching for meaning (Cohen & Miller, 2009).

IS SEARCHING FOR MEANING GOOD OR BAD? AN ARGUMENT FOR A NEW PERSPECTIVE

The search for meaning has had an implied but rarely tested importance, and it has attracted some divergent perspectives on whether it is a good thing or a bad thing. The most direct empirical evidence says, "Yes. No. Sometimes." Although this is interesting, it is not particularly helpful. When my research on this topic began, empirical data were practically nonexistent. Drawing primarily on the cross-cultural variation we had observed in the search for meaning between American and Japanese college students, Steger, Kawabata, et al. (2008) argued that basic epistemological orientations may undergird the eventual impact of searching for meaning. Among Western cultures, an atomistic, positivistic, dichotomizing epistemology seemed dominant, in which process and outcome were separated. One either sought meaning or had meaning, not both. Among Eastern cultures, a more holistic, dialectical epistemology seemed dominant, in which process and outcome were inseparable. One possessed by seeking.

Relevant research has accelerated in an exciting fashion. Not only has the quantity increased, but the sophistication and diversity of methods have grown dramatically. Based on intriguing new perspectives and data, it seems possible to propose two dimensions that may clarify and unify the ambiguous nature of the search for meaning. These two dimensions are the maintain/restore dimension and the augment/consolidate dimension. Both dimensions have parallels in psychobiological models of motivation and can be informed by existing data to help answer the question "Should people search for meaning?"

Basic Biological Motivations

One point to make here is that there is a pragmatism to not searching if you do not need to. It flies in the face of a general biological preference for homeostasis, depleting resources that could be better spent elsewhere. This preference runs very deep. For example, the various tissues of the human body function in tandem to maintain a consistent balance of fuel; glycogen in the liver (mostly), triacylglycerols in adipose tissue, and protein in skeletal muscle (mostly). Homeostasis at the fundamental level of biological functioning means that constant supplies of several forms of fuel are available in the bloodstream for the diverse needs of different tissues (Garrett & Grisham, 2010). Larger deviations in supplies require more effort by the entire organism to reestablish homeostasis. Nowhere is the risk of homeostasis failure greater than in the brain. Despite its small proportional size, the brain consumes roughly 20% of the oxygen needs of an adult human. However, even though the brain places tremendous metabolic demands on the body, it does not have the ability to store any significant amount of the fuel it needs (glucose, metabolized in the liver). Homeostasis is critical for brain functioning, including cognition, as levels of glucose in the bloodstream bear on the availability of glucose in the brain. At low levels of glucose, brain metabolism is compromised and critical impairments may appear (Meierhans et al., 2010). Very primal regions of the brain are responsive to this kind of homeostatic monitoring. Relevant structures—the hypothalamus, pituitary, midbrain, medulla, reticular formation, and pons—are located in proximity to the spinal cord and are dedicated to noncognitive functions like metabolism, digestion, respiration, circulation, and endocrine functioning.

Frankl (1963) argued that people have a "will to meaning." That is, each of us has an innate drive for meaning in our life. Although Frankl seems to have felt that the search for meaning was normal, healthy, and desirable, his framing of the search for meaning in terms of "will," so evocative of needs and drives, provides one rationale for why the search for meaning might be so miserable for many of us. The early notions of drives relied on a broad understanding of the biological preference for homeostasis I described in the previous paragraph. Hull's (1943) drive model argues that homeostatic imbalances create the psychological impression of a need, which instigates people to seek out whatever matter is required to restore homeostasis. For example, if the body's stores of glucose had been depleted, people should experience not only difficulty thinking clearly but also a craving for sugar-rich foods. If meaning functions along the lines of a need or drive, then as meaning is depleted, people should be driven to seek it out and obtain more of it. Thus, the search for meaning might be stimulated by a homeostatic imbalance or depletion of meaning.

Another venerable model of motivation argues that homeostasis is just one, rather passive, means for directing people's efforts. After all, as long as people had a box of Twinkies, some Slim Jims, and an endless supply of Mr. Pibb, they would have pretty sufficient quantities of fuel and water and would not necessarily need to do anything else. Although an alarming number of Americans do seem to demonstrate the appeal of the Mr. Pibb model of human nature, many more people engage in activities that do not seem to satisfy any biological drives. People fork over hard-earned cash to see movies, hike up windswept mountain peaks for the fleeting thrill of skiing fresh powder, and stand in never-ending lines under the mute harassment of costumed Disney characters in order to scream on a roller coaster. Hebb's (1955) optimal arousal model says that people will make efforts to maintain their preferred level of arousal.

For some, this means occasionally cracking a Dr. Pepper to shake things up. For others, this means novelty seeking and engaging in stimulating but risky activities like substance abuse and sexual acting out (Zuckerman, 2005; Zuckerman & Kuhlman, 2000). High levels of sensation seeking have been linked consistently to greater dopamine receptor availability and concentrations, particularly in pleasure centers of the brain like the striatum (Gjedde, Kumakura, Cumming, Linnet, & Møller, 2010), insula, and posterior medial orbitofrontal cortex (Joseph, Liu, Jiang, Lynam, & Kelly, 2009). Low levels of sensation seeking have been linked to parts of the brain that are associated with emotional regulation, the anterior medial orbitofrontal cortex and the anterior cingulate cortex (Joseph et al., 2009). So, sensation seekers are more responsive to pleasure, and those who eschew sensation seeking appear to do so through emotional regulation.

Sensation and novelty seeking crop up in surprising places. For example, people's intentions to revisit vacation destinations not only are influenced by whether they had a good time there but also are reduced by high levels of sensation seeking (Assaker, Vinzi, & O'Connor, 2011). People's decisions about experiences such as vacations and travel are related to happiness and well-being (Van Boven, 2005; Van Boven & Gilovich, 2003), and, apparently, some people want to go back to a familiar place, and some want to visit the next spot down the road. If the search for meaning resembles optimal arousal models, people will vary in how appealing seeking meaning seems to be. For dispositional or experiential reasons, some people may be restless in their meaning seeking, always looking to the next meaning down the road. Others may prefer to revisit the same meanings over and over again, directing their emotional resources toward consolidating meaning rather than continually exploring it.

Maintain or Restore

If these basic motivational models have any parallel to searching for meaning, it should be possible to identify some patterns in how and when people seek meaning. Homeostasis models would push for a "maintain or restore" type of searching for meaning. Heine, Proulx, and Vohs (2006; see also Chapter 4, this volume) proposed the meaning maintenance model, arguing that humans are powerfully motivated to establish and maintain the network of mental representations they have formed about the world around them. The coherence of these representations provides a sense of meaning in life. When meaning systems are disrupted, people strive to restore their meaning systems. People also may switch their focus from threatened components of the greater meaning system to unthreatened and intact components. Thus, the meaning maintenance model emphasizes that people dedicate resources to maintaining a subjective sense of meaning and restoring the integrity of broader meaning systems of mental representations (Proulx & Heine, 2006). The research supporting this model is diverse and encouraging. People affirm intact meaning systems when they are exposed to nonsensical or expectation-violating stimuli ranging from absurdist literature, comedy sketches, and art (Proulx, Heine, & Vohs, 2010) to inexplicable—though subliminal—switching of key personnel in experimental paradigms (Proulx & Heine, 2008). A key proposition, that people would "switch" from a challenged meaning structure to an intact meaning structure, has been supported by research showing that people appear to rely on stable attitudes and dispositions that provide positive information regarding meaning in life judgments (e.g., positive affect, religious conviction) when other potential sources of meaning are threatened (Hicks & King, 2008; King, Hicks, Krull, & Del Gaiso, 2006; see also Chapter 22, this volume). This theoretical and empirical work would support the notion that searching for meaning functions similarly to a need or drive; people are motivated to maintain homeostasis generally and to restore homeostasis by reallocating resources. The fact that these efforts appear to obtain even when threats to meaning occur out of consciousness (e.g., Proulx & Heine, 2008; Randles, Proulx, & Heine, 2011) provides another interesting parallel between meaning maintenance model research, related work, and the "maintain/restore" aspects of homeostatic processes. The brain structures that monitor and regulate homeostatic functioning are not associated with conscious experience.

Consolidate or Augment

Optimal arousal models would push for a "consolidate or augment" type of searching for meaning. Some people would naturally prefer to search for meaning out of a desire to add to their résumé, broaden their exposure to the world, and continually augment their experience of life. Some people would naturally prefer to find one meaning and—if even necessary at all—devote any time they must spend on the matter to buttressing their beliefs, protecting their perspective, and consolidating their life experience within their existing meaning system. Individual differences in levels in the activity and reactivity of the brain's pleasure centers could connect to searching for meaning.

People certainly have the capacity to find or create new meaning, but is there evidence that people might prefer to layer new meaning atop old? In a number of studies, people have been seen to exhibit creative, adaptive efforts either to create new meaning or to adopt novel ways of generating meaning. When exposed to meaning threats, like inscrutable passages of Kafka, participants showed the predicted increase in motivation to find meaning in strings of letters (Proulx & Heine, 2009). This fits well with a maintain or restore kind of meaning seeking. However, participants went beyond simply wishing their meaning could be restored; participants whose meaning had been threatened showed increased aptitude for detecting the artificial grammar that existed in those strings of letters. Randles et al. (2011) also found that threats to meaning led to enhanced detection of patterns. This is a subtle shift from the kind of compensatory mechanism proposed in the meaning maintenance model and suggested by King, Hicks, and colleagues in their work on positive affect and meaning in life (e.g., Hicks & King, 2008; King et al., 2006). Neither of these models requires there actually to be any additional meaning available in the environment or any improvement in people's abilities to detect it. They just stipulate that people should be motivated to shift attention and emphasis to intact meanings and should feel better when they do so.

An increase in pattern-detection abilities seems like an awfully strong response to reading something that doesn't make any sense. Do I really see more patterns around me every time I grade papers? A strong, resource-intensive response helps underscore the potentially significant importance of meaning to human functioning, but it also suggests that we have these capabilities, which go unused in many of us until sparked into action. Perhaps the mind's tolerable range of homeostatic fluctuation is small. Small insults are met with a robust response. Or perhaps people can be motivated to seek meaning even when threats to meaning are not significant enough to truly upset their meaning systems. Expectations appear to have something to do with it. When people were led to expect that something they were about to read was going to be a typical adventure story for boys, their encounter with an absurd Monty Python sketch resulted in a more harshly conforming moral response to a vignette (Proulx et al., 2010). So, maybe all it takes is a sharp bend in an otherwise unimportant road to catch our attention.

It is also possible to argue that these small meaning threats tap into both a fundamental human need and differences in people's desire for arousal, stimulation, and novelty. Proulx et al. (2010; Study 3) found that hard-to-understand, ambiguous art stimulated people's need for structure to a similar—and even slightly greater—extent as being reminded of their own death. So, at least in terms of unsettling people's desire for order and consistency in their world, Magritte and death trump Constable's landscapes. Although this study showed that personal need for structure could be influenced by exposure to meaning threats, other research has examined how dispositional levels of personal need for structure affect people's responses to threats—in this case, the threat posed by reminders of death. In a vast number of studies conducted under terror management theory, people typically respond to being reminded of death by supporting dominant cultural narratives, which is presumed to help them restore their familiar structure in life (e.g., Landau et al., 2004; see also Chapter 3, this volume). When reminded of their own death, people with a high personal need for structure were thought to have reaffirmed their valued structures in life, because they showed signs of having restored a sense of meaning in life, at least compared to people with a low personal need for structure (Vess, Routledge, Landau, & Arndt, 2009). Thus, threats to meaning and mortality appear to stimulate a need for structure, and we assume that people who already have a high need for structure are moved to reaffirm their cherished structures to restore their sense of meaning. In contrast, people low in personal need for structure were much more fired up about exploring new things than were those high in personal need for structure (Vess et al., 2009; Studies 2–5). In essence, people who had little need for structure responded to mortality threats with increased novelty seeking. This is the group of people who may prefer to constantly seek meaning, satisfying their higher need for novelty and stimulation and their higher preference for arousal.

These studies might be interpreted as giving some credence to the possibility of a "consolidate or augment" type of searching for meaning. Novelty seeking would be compatible with a preference for greater arousal. Higher levels of activity in the striatum and insula could provide a push toward seeking meaning. Personal need for structure would be compatible with a preference for lesser arousal. Individual differences in activity and reactivity in the emotional regulation centers of the brain could also feed into the augment or consolidate type of searching for meaning. Higher levels of activity in the anterior cingulate and anterior medial orbitofrontal cortex could put the brakes on searching for meaning.

FURTHER EXPLORING THE MODEL—REVISITING STEGER, OISHI, AND KASHDAN (2009)

Can we make predictions based on these two models? The principal focus of this chapter is on whether searching for meaning is good, and, in particular, whether it is good for finding meaning. As a starting place for considering whether the homeostasis/arousal model adds anything, I focus on predictions that can be made about the relation between seeking and experiencing meaning in life.

Previous correlational research typically has found a negative relation between the two variables (e.g., Steger, Kashdan, et al., 2008), and experimental research has shown momentary responses that also fit with the maintain/restore model (e.g., Proulx et al., 2010). The maintain/restore model suggests that people who have a deficit of meaning will seek it, and people who are experiencing few deficits in meaning will be disinclined to search for it. This idea has most often been tested in simple, linear terms. However, there may be nonlinear relations depending on people's levels of meaning. Figure 11.1 contrasts a linear model (light gray line) with a curvilinear model (in this case cubic) representing a rethinking of the maintain/restore model, with the two subscales of the MLQ used to anchor seeking meaning (Search for Meaning) and experiencing meaning (Presence of Meaning). The bold line shows a steep negative slope at low levels of meaning, signifying significant distress, driven by meaning deficits. At medium levels of meaning, this slope flattens somewhat—homeostatic pressures should be fairly minimal in this normal range of functioning. At maximal levels of meaning, the slope steepens again, where searching should yield few, if any, benefits.

The consolidate/augment model presumes an acceptable level of meaning in life . . . otherwise what is there to consolidate? As such, the consolidate/augment framing of the search for meaning would be most relevant at

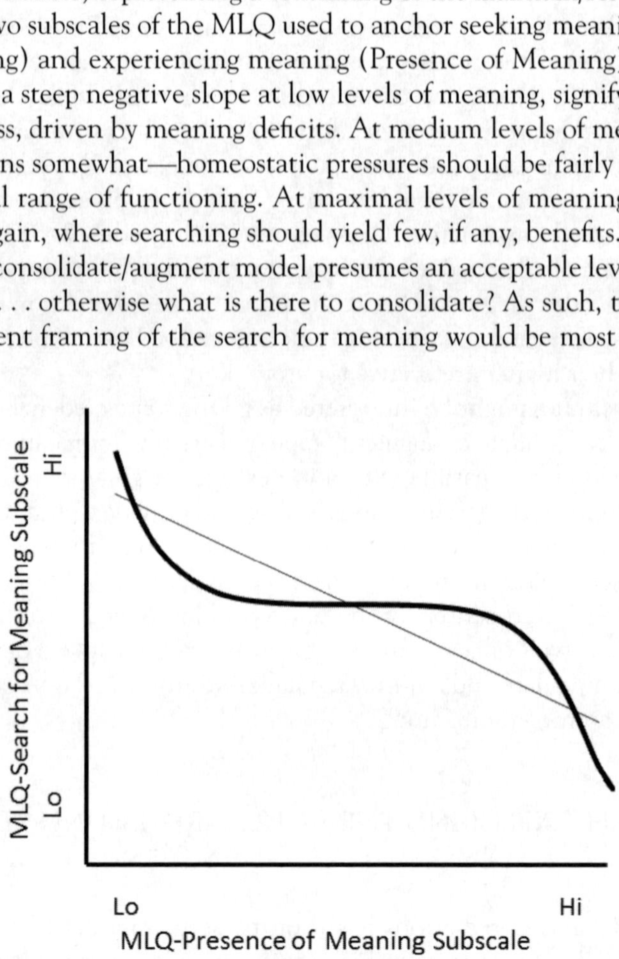

Figure 11.1. Simple linear (lighter line) and curvilinear (bold line) depiction of the maintain/restore model of seeking meaning. The curvilinear model suggests that the relation between presence of meaning and searching for meaning is strongest at the extremes, furthest away from comfortable homeostatic ranges. MLQ = Meaning in Life Questionnaire.

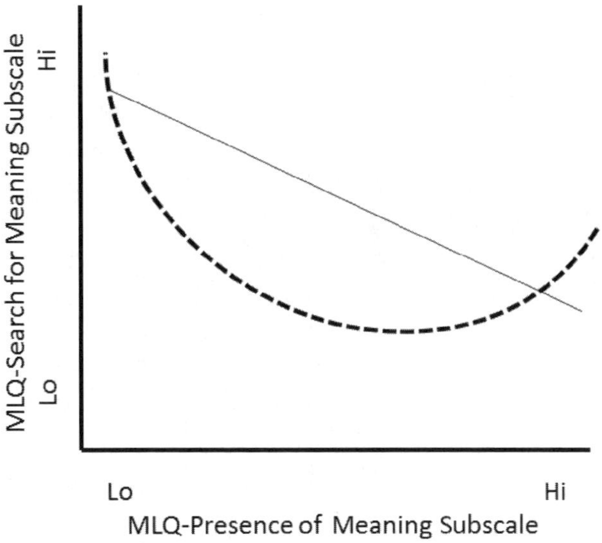

Figure 11.2. Simple linear (lighter line) and curvilinear (dashed line) depiction of the consolidate/augment model of seeking meaning. The curvilinear model suggests that the relation between presence of meaning and searching for meaning may be driven by meaning deficits at low levels of meaning in life but reverses at high levels of meaning in life, as people are motivated to augment solid meaning systems. MLQ = Meaning in Life Questionnaire.

high levels of experiencing meaning in life. This would lead to the prediction that the inverse relation between searching for meaning and the presence of meaning would be weakest and, optimally, reverse at high levels of presence of meaning. A regression line such as this would resemble a crooked smile or smirk, with one side of the mouth elevated above the other. This curvilinear model (in this case quadratic) is contrasted with the linear regression line in Figure 11.2.

To test these predictions, I subjected the data from Steger et al. (2009) to the curve estimation function of SPSS 18. Curve estimation tests the fit of a variety of nonlinear regression lines in the scatterplot of two variables. In the original study, we were interested in levels and correlates of seeking and experiencing meaning across different age groups. It was clear that there were some important differences at the extremes of the age range. Therefore, as a preliminary test of the competing models I discuss here, analyses focused on the four largest groups of participants, with the oldest and youngest removed from the sample. The sample being analyzed here consists of 6,764 adults, ages 25 to 64, who volunteered to complete the MLQ as part of a positive psychology website (http://www.authentichappiness.org).

A cubic model provided a slightly better fit to the data than the quadratic curve, explaining a significant amount of variance in the American

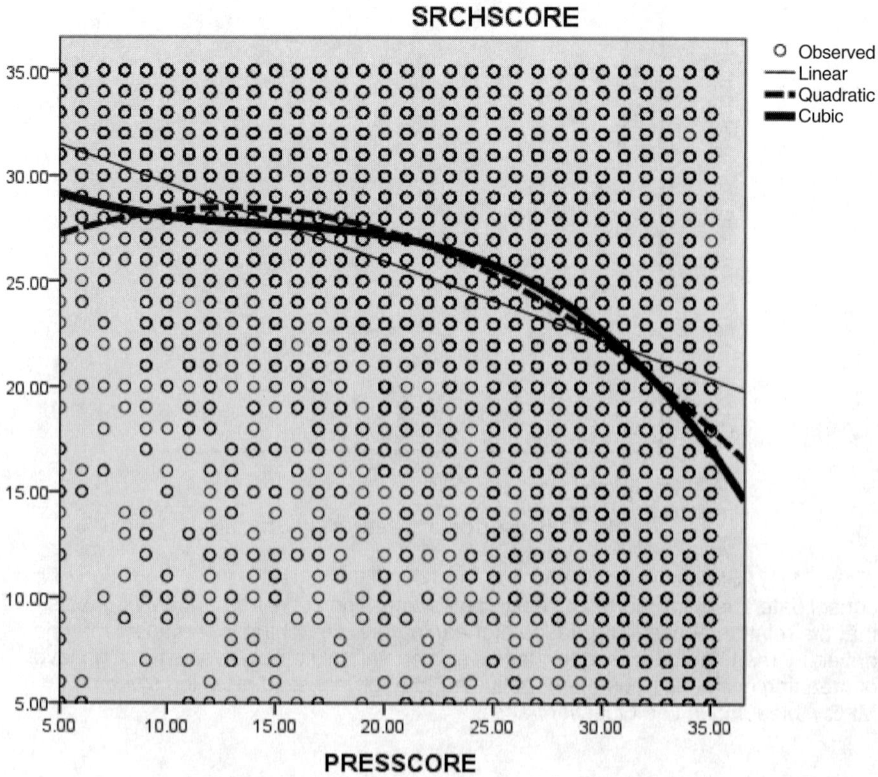

Figure 11.3. Relationship between searching for meaning (SRCHSCORE) and the presence of meaning (PRESSCORE).

sample ($R^2 = .160$, $p < .001$; compared with $R^2 = .156$, $p < .001$ for quadratic). Both curves explained more variance than the linear regression line ($R^2 = .122$, $p < .001$). Figure 11.3 shows the cubic curve plotted in the data (a constant was included to avoid forcing the curve through the origin). The cubic curve is the thickest, bold line. Circles indicate observations, with darker circles depicting multiple observations at that point in the scatterplot. The linear and quadratic curves are also plotted for the sake of comparison. The linear relationship between searching for meaning (SRCHSCORE) and the presence of meaning (PRESSCORE) is negative. Steger et al. (2009) reported that the magnitude of this negative relation was –.36 among 26- to 44-year-olds and –.34 among 46- to 64-year-olds.

The shape of the cubic curve resembles an attenuated version of the proposed curve for the maintain/restore model. Thus, at least this analysis in this sample provides additional support for what could be termed the maintain/restore model of searching for meaning. It does appear that, in the middle of the distribution of presence of meaning scores, among these adults, there was a weaker relation between seeking and experiencing meaning. This relation also appeared to steepen at high levels of meaning, where the maintain/restore model would predict there would be little benefit to further meaning seeking. The observed curve differs from the proposed curve in one notable way: The "falloff" in the slope of the curve above the midpoint of the MLQ–Presence scale is steeper and begins earlier than expected. This suggests that—in terms of searching for meaning—people become satiated above a fairly moderate homeostasis point. As a personal note, this result is a bit of a bummer. When I began this line of research, I fully expected to learn that the search for meaning in life was a pleasant, captivating pastime, not what data seem to consistently suggest . . . that it is a chore best left alone unless necessary.

Although the usual limitations about using cross-sectional, correlational methods are relevant here, there are two other limitations that warrant additional attention. First, both the maintain/restore model and the consolidate/augment model may be most relevant to within-person dynamics. If an individual experiences a decline in meaning, she or he may be propelled to seek meaning, or if an individual has a satisfactory amount of meaning, she or he may be satisfied with that homeostasis according to the maintain/restore model or want to add to that meaning according to the consolidate/augment model. Although different dynamics were ascribed to people at different levels of experienced meaning, it may be that the specific dynamics vary depending on other personality traits (see Steger, Kashdan, et al., 2008). The curve estimations presented here focus on the aggregate level and miss any potential within-person dynamics. Second, this sample consists of adult Americans. The sole cross-cultural investigation of the search for meaning found that although there was an inverse relation among American college students, there was a positive relation among Japanese college students (Steger, Kawabata, et al., 2008). When combined with the finding that the inverse relation between search for meaning and presence of meaning was progressively stronger among older age groups (Steger, Kashdan, et al., 2008), there is a distinct possibility that some model other than the maintain/restore model would obtain in other cultures. Consider the completion of the Zen koan that opened this chapter:

Joshu asked Nansen: "What is the path?"

Nansen said: "Everyday life is the path."

Joshu asked: "Can it be studied?"

Nansen said: "If you try to study, you will be far away from it."

Joshu asked: "If I do not study, how can I know it is the path?"

Nansen said: "The path does not belong to the perception world, neither does it belong to the nonperception world. Cognition is a delusion and noncognition is senseless. If you want to reach the true path beyond doubt, place yourself in the same freedom as sky. You name it neither good nor not-good."

At these words Joshu was enlightened. (Mumon, 2006, p. 37)

CONCLUSION

The search for meaning has been part of the conversation about the ultimate aims of human life for decades. Until very recently, however, there has been a paucity of data to help us evaluate the often-conflicting claims made about searching for meaning. In the new millennium, views emerged that fused the dual possibilities that searching for meaning could be a natural part of the rich complexity of humanness, or it could be a sign of psychological vulnerabilities demanding remediation (Steger et al., 2006). In this chapter, I have tried to build off of biological models of homeostasis and optimal arousal to propose modest reformulations of the dual poles of meaning seeking: maintain/restore and consolidate/augment. In a preliminary test of these models, findings converged with the maintain/restore model, which itself is compatible with models presented by Baumeister (1991), Klinger (1998), and Heine et al. (2006). It remains to be seen, however, whether other ways of navigating the challenge and promise of seeking meaning wait to be found in other cultures, perspectives, and intrapersonal dynamics.

REFERENCES

Assaker, G., Vinzi, V. E., & O'Connor, P. (2011). Examining the effect of novelty seeking, satisfaction, and destination image on tourists' return pattern: A two factor, non-linear latent growth model. *Tourism Management, 32*, 890–901. doi:10.1016/j.tourman.2010.08.004

Baumeister, R. F. (1991). *Meanings of life*. New York, NY: Guilford Press.

Beaumont, S. L. (2009). Identity processing and personal wisdom: An information-oriented identity style predicts self-actualization and self-transcendence. *Identity: An International Journal of Theory and Research, 9*, 95–115. doi:10.1080/15283480802669101

Becker, L. C. (1992). Good lives: Prolegomena. *Social Philosophy and Policy, 9*, 15–37. doi:10.1017/S0265052500001382

Camus, A. (1955). *The myth of Sisyphus and other essays*. New York, NY: Knopf.

Cohen, J. S., & Miller, L. J. (2009). Interpersonal mindfulness training for well-being: A pilot study with psychology graduate students. *Teachers College Record, 111*, 2760–2774.

Foucault, M. (1970). *The order of things*. New York, NY: Pantheon Books.

Frankl, V. E. (1963). *Man's search for meaning: An introduction to logotherapy*. New York, NY: Washington Square Press.

Garrett, R. H., & Grisham, C. H. (2010). *Biochemistry*. Stamford, CT: Cengage Learning.

Gjedde, A., Kumakura, Y., Cumming, P., Linnet, J., & Møller, A. (2010). Inverted-U-shaped correlation between dopamine receptor availability in striatum and sensation seeking. *Proceedings of the National Academy of Sciences, USA, 107*, 3870–3875. doi:10.1073/pnas.0912319107

Hebb, D. O. (1953). On human thought. *Canadian Journal of Psychology, 7*, 99–110.

Heine, S. J., Proulx, T., & Vohs, K. D. (2006). The meaning maintenance model: On the coherence of social motivations. *Personality and Social Psychology Review, 10*, 88–110. doi:10.1207/s15327957pspr1002_1

Hicks, J. A., & King, L. A. (2008). Religious commitment and positive mood as information about meaning in life. *Journal of Research in Personality, 42*, 43–57. doi:10.1016/j.jrp.2007.04.003

Hull, C. (1943). *Principles of behavior*. New York, NY: Appleton-Century-Crofts.

Joseph, J. E., Liu, X., Jiang, Y., Lynam, D., & Kelly, T. H. (2009). Neural correlates of emotional reactivity in sensation seeking. *Psychological Science, 20*, 215–223. doi:10.1111/j.1467-9280.2009.02283.x

Kekes, J. (1986). The informed will and the meaning of life. *Philosophy and Phenomenological Research, 47*, 75–90. doi:10.2307/2107725

Kekes, J. (2000). The meaning of life. *Midwest Studies in Philosophy, 24*, 17–34. doi:10.1111/1475-4975.00018

Kenyon, G. M. (2000). Philosophical foundations of existential meaning. In G. T. Reker & K. Chamberlain (Eds.), *Exploring existential meaning: Optimizing human development across the life span* (pp. 7–22). Thousand Oaks, CA: Sage. doi:10.4135/9781452233703.n2

King, L. A., Hicks, J. A., Krull, J. L., & Del Gaiso, A. K. (2006). Positive affect and the experience of meaning in life. *Journal of Personality and Social Psychology, 90*, 179–196. doi:10.1037/0022-3514.90.1.179

Klinger, E. (1998). The search for meaning in evolutionary perspective and its clinical implications. In P. T. P. Wong & P. S. Fry (Eds.), *The human quest for meaning: A handbook of psychological research and clinical application* (pp. 27–50). Mahwah, NJ: Erlbaum.

Landau, M. J., Johns, M., Greenberg, J., Pyszczynski, T., Solomon, S., & Martens, A. (2004). A function of form: Terror management and structuring of the social world. *Journal of Personality and Social Psychology, 87*, 190–210. doi:10.1037/0022-3514.87.2.190

Maddi, S. R. (1970). The search for meaning. In W. J. Arnold & M. Page (Eds.), *Nebraska Symposium on Motivation* (pp. 137–186). Lincoln: University of Nebraska Press.

Meierhans, R., Béchir, M., Ludwig, S., Sommerfeld, J., Brandi, G., Haberthür, G., . . . Stover, J. F. (2010). Brain metabolism is significantly impaired at blood glucose below 6 mM and brain glucose below 1 mM in patients with severe traumatic brain injury. *Critical Care, 14*, R13. doi:10.1186/cc8869

Mumon. (2006). *The gateless fate: All 48 koans, with commentary by Ekai, called Mumon*. West Valley City, UT: Waking Lion Press.

Nietzsche, F. (1961). *Thus spoke Zarathustra* (R. J. Hollindale, Trans.). New York, NY: Penguin Books. (Original work published 1909)

Nietzsche, F. (1974). *The gay science* (W. Kaufmann, Trans.). New York, NY: Vintage Books. (Original work published 1882)

Park, N., Park, M., & Peterson, C. (2010). When is the search for meaning related to life satisfaction? *Applied Psychology: Health and Well-Being, 2*, 1–13. doi:10.1111/j.1758-0854.2009.01024.x

Proulx, T., & Heine, S. (2006). Death and black diamonds: Meaning, mortality, and the meaning maintenance model. *Psychological Inquiry, 17*, 309–318. doi:10.1080/10478400701366985

Proulx, T., & Heine, S. J. (2008). The case of the transmogrifying experimenter: Reaffirmation of moral schemas following implicit change detection. *Psychological Science, 19*, 1294–1300. doi:10.1111/j.1467-9280.2008.02238.x

Proulx, T., & Heine, S. J. (2009). Connections from Kafka: Exposure to meaning threats improves implicit learning of an artificial grammar. *Psychological Science, 20*, 1125–1131. doi:10.1111/j.1467-9280.2009.02414.x

Proulx, T., Heine, S. J., & Vohs, K. D. (2010). When is the unfamiliar the uncanny? Meaning affirmation after exposure to absurdist literature, humor, and art. *Personality and Social Psychology Bulletin, 36*, 817–829. doi:10.1177/0146167210369896

Randles, D., Proulx, T., & Heine, S. J. (2011). Turn-frogs and careful sweaters: Subliminal presentations of incongruous word pairings invoke meaninglessness. *Journal of Experimental Social Psychology, 47*, 246–249. doi:10.1016/j.jesp.2010.07.020

Sartre, J. P. (2007). *Nausea* (L. Alexander, Trans.). New York, NY: New Directions. (Original work published 1938)

Steger, M. F., & Dik, B. J. (2009). If one is searching for meaning in life, does meaning in work help? *Applied Psychology: Health and Well-Being, 1*, 303–320. doi:10.1111/j.1758-0854.2009.01018.x

Steger, M. F., Frazier, P., Oishi, S., & Kaler, M. (2006). The Meaning in Life Questionnaire: Assessing the presence of and search for meaning in life. *Journal of Counseling Psychology, 53*, 80–93. doi:10.1037/0022-0167.53.1.80

Steger, M. F., & Kashdan, T. B. (2007). Stability and specificity of meaning in life and life satisfaction over one year. *Journal of Happiness Studies, 8*, 161–179. doi:10.1007/s10902-006-9011-8

Steger, M. F., Kashdan, T. B., Sullivan, B. A., & Lorentz, D. (2008). Understanding the search for meaning in life: Personality, cognitive style, and the dynamic between seeking and experiencing meaning. *Journal of Personality*, *76*, 199–228. doi:10.1111/j.1467-6494.2007.00484.x

Steger, M. F., Kawabata, Y., Shimai, S., & Otake, K. (2008). The meaningful life in Japan and the United States: Levels and correlates of meaning in life. *Journal of Research in Personality*, *42*, 660–678. doi:10.1016/j.jrp.2007.09.003

Steger, M. F., Oishi, S., & Kashdan, T. B. (2009). Meaning in life across the life span: Levels and correlates of meaning in life from emerging adulthood to older adulthood. *Journal of Positive Psychology*, *4*, 43–52. doi:10.1080/17439760802303127

Steger, M. F., Oishi, S., & Kesebir, S. (2011). Is a life without meaning satisfying? The moderating role of the search for meaning in satisfaction with life judgments. *Journal of Positive Psychology*, *6*, 173–180. doi:10.1080/17439760.2011.569171

Tiberius, V. (2008). *The reflective life: Living wisely within our limits*. Oxford, England: Oxford University Press.

Van Boven, L. (2005). Experientialism, materialism, and the pursuit of happiness. *Review of General Psychology*, *9*, 132–142. doi:10.1037/1089-2680.9.2.132

Van Boven, L., & Gilovich, T. (2003). To do or to have? That is the question. *Journal of Personality and Social Psychology*, *85*, 1193–1202. doi:10.1037/0022-3514.85.6.1193

Vess, M., Routledge, C., Landau, M. J., & Arndt, J. (2009). The dynamics of death and meaning: The effects of death-relevant cognitions and personal need for structure on perceptions of meaning in life. *Journal of Personality and Social Psychology*, *97*, 728–744. doi:10.1037/a0016417

Wong, D. B. (1986). *Moral relativity*. Berkeley: University of California Press.

Zuckerman, M. (2005). *Psychobiology of personality*. Cambridge, England: Cambridge University Press.

Zuckerman, M., & Kuhlman, D. M. (2000). Personality and risk-taking; Common biosocial factors. *Journal of Personality*, *68*, 999–1029. doi:10.1111/1467-6494.00124

IV

TELEOLOGICAL UNDERSTANDING: EXPLANATIONS FOR EVENTS

12

SEARCHING FOR AND FINDING MEANING FOLLOWING PERSONAL AND COLLECTIVE TRAUMAS

ROXANE COHEN SILVER AND JOHN A. UPDEGRAFF

Adversity is common. Most individuals will experience a personal tragedy in their lifetimes, whether it is a sudden unexpected loss, traumatic injury, or life-threatening illness (Seery, Holman, & Silver, 2010). Many will experience an undesirable life event in any given year (Norris, 1992). Sometimes an entire community will be exposed to a natural or technological disaster, school shooting, or terrorist attack, although those directly affected often seem to be selected at random, and others appear to be spared at random (cf. Wayment, Silver, & Kemeny, 1995). These collective traumatic events become a shared experience among many victims.

Both personally experienced and collective traumas are often sudden, unexpected, and unpredictable. Because of these features, they have the potential to challenge people's expectations about living in an orderly, understandable, meaningful world (Janoff-Bulman, 1992; Park & Folkman, 1997). Indeed, some have argued that what makes traumatic events so distressing is that they violate many of the basic assumptions people have about

DOI: 10.1037/14040-012
The Psychology of Meaning, Keith D. Markman, Travis Proulx, and Matthew J. Lindberg (Editors)

themselves and the world (Janoff-Bulman, 1992; Silver & Wortman, 1980; Taylor, 1983; see also Chapter 10, this volume).

Over the years, many theorists and researchers have examined the processes through which individuals confront these events, think about or process them, and either try to integrate the events into their preexisting views of the world or develop new views to accommodate the new reality. Sometimes the individual is unable to make sense of the event, and this process is unsuccessful. In this chapter, we review a 3-decade program of research conducted by ourselves and our colleagues that has examined how individuals and community members seek to cope with and come to terms with traumatic experiences, as well as the psychological consequences when they are unable to make sense of these experiences.

MEANING MAKING IN THE CONTEXT OF PERSONAL TRAUMA

A number of influential theories exist on how people cognitively and emotionally adapt to life stressors, as well as the influence that stress and trauma can have on people's understandings of themselves and their world (Janoff-Bulman, 1992; Neimeyer, 2001; Taylor, 1983; Thompson & Janigan, 1988). As noted by Park (2010; see also Chapter 13, this volume), these theories share tenets that postulate a central role for meaning making in how people adjust to stress and trauma. These tenets include (a) people possess global belief systems that motivate behavior and allow interpretation of ongoing experiences; (b) some life experiences have the capability to challenge these belief systems, and people assign meaning to these experiences; (c) people experience distress to the extent that the meaning they assign to a life experience is discrepant from their more global belief systems; and (d) this distress prompts a process by which people seek reduce the discrepancy between their appraised meaning of a life experience and their global belief systems. When people are able to adjust their global beliefs and/or their appraised meaning of the life experience so this discrepancy is reduced, distress should be alleviated and a sense of order and coherence may be maintained.

Janoff-Bulman (1992) eloquently argued that the global belief systems that are challenged by trauma include fundamental assumptions that the world is benevolent, the world is meaningful, and the self is worthy. These assumptions often manifest themselves in beliefs that the world is a good and safe place, that good things happen to good people, and that people hold substantial control over their situations. When people experience a sudden and severe misfortune, these fundamental beliefs are often "shattered" (Janoff-Bulman, 1992). The world is no longer a safe and predictable place, and a person may come to believe that bad things can befall good people or instead that people are deserving of their lot.

People also construct *situational meanings* (Park, 2010), which are understandings of a particular situation or life experience. The form of these situational meanings can be rather varied and complex, ranging from appraisals of the situation's predictability and controllability, attributions regarding the cause the situation, or assignments of blame to the self or others to understandings of what the event means in terms of current goals and one's future (Aldwin, 2007). When the person's initial situational meaning of an event clashes with his or her global belief system, it can initiate a search for *meaning as comprehensibility* (Janoff-Bulman & Frantz, 1997), or attempts to make the event make sense and fit with existing belief structures.

Because the specific meanings that people can assign to situations are likely to be tied to the specific nature of the stressor, it is often most fruitful to examine people's meaning making with broad questions that get at how people in general make sense of or understand the situations with which they are coping. Indeed, most studies of meaning making in the context of trauma have assessed meaning with simple questions such as "How often have you found yourself trying to make sense of your experiences?" "Have you ever asked yourself, 'Why me?'" and "How have you been able to make sense of your experiences?" From simple questions such as these, it is possible to get a rich understanding of how people make sense of misfortunes.

Early Studies of Meaning in the Context of Personal Trauma

One of the first systematic investigations of the issue of meaning in personal trauma was a cross-sectional study of 29 patients with paralyzing spinal cord injuries (Bulman & Wortman, 1977). The injuries were sustained up to 1 year prior to the study. All the patients reported a search for meaning by asking themselves the question "Why me?" All but one of the patients had come to some answer. However, the particular forms of meaning that they found varied widely. Although one of the most common explanations was that their accident was merely a result of chance, many of the patients viewed their accident as something that could be explained based on preexisting worldviews or conceptions of justice. For example, the most commonly reported form of meaning was viewing the accident as something that was part of God's plan for them. Another common response was viewing the accident as something that was fated and predetermined, potentially as a consequence of past misdeeds. Others sought a way of viewing their experience in a positive light by reevaluating the accident as something that was positive. What influence, if any, might these explanations have on people's ability to adapt to misfortune? Perhaps because the sample was small and the categories were derived post hoc from open-ended questions, there was no evidence that the particular form of meaning ascribed for the accident was associated with adjustment in these data. Nonetheless, this landmark study yielded provocative findings and suggested that these complex issues might be fruitfully examined in methodologically rigorous studies in the "real world."

Silver (1982) attempted to replicate Bulman and Wortman's (1977) findings with a larger sample of individuals who were interviewed starting 1 week after a serious injury that left many of them permanently paralyzed. These individuals were injured in variety of ways, including auto accidents, falls, sporting accidents, and violent crimes. In all, 102 patients with spinal cord injuries were interviewed within the first 8 weeks after their accident. In trying to understand how people made sense of their accidents and resulting disability, Silver found a curious result. In contrast to the findings of Bulman and Wortman, 54% of the sample had never asked the question at 3 weeks after their accidents; 46% had not done so by 8 weeks ("I've really never given it a thought" or "I haven't tried to make sense of it"; see Silver, 1982). Even those who asked the question seemed to vary in terms of how much it concerned them (e.g., "It's a question I haven't, um, dwelled on"). Searching for meaning in this study was not associated with the severity of the injury and its consequences. That is, individuals who were left paraplegic were no less likely to search for meaning than those who were left quadriplegic.

In fact, individuals who were injured but remained neurologically intact (e.g., broke their back but were not left with permanent spinal cord injury) were no less likely to search for meaning (or more likely to find it) than individuals who were permanently paralyzed. Instead, searching for meaning was intricately tied to attributions of blame. That is, searching for an explanation was more common among respondents who blamed another for their accidents. In fact, independent coders saw those respondents who were blaming others to be innocent victims in the accident (e.g., pedestrians hit by a car, victims of sniper fire; see Davis, Lehman, Silver, Wortman, & Ellard, 1996).

The variability in these victims' search for meaning allowed for an examination of how the search for meaning relates to coping and adjustment. Compared with individuals who were not asking the question "Why me?" individuals engaged in the search for meaning were more likely to blame, have increased ruminations about the accident, and report increased perceptions of unfairness surrounding the accident, and they reported significantly more depression, anger, and anxiety within the first several weeks after their injury.

Although this search for meaning might seem to be maladaptive, it did appear to facilitate adjustment when the search resulted in an answer to the question. Indeed, those patients who could generate an answer to the question (with answers ranging from the simple "that's life" to complicated explanations about "God's will") reported significantly less depression, less anger, and fewer ongoing ruminations about the accident than patients for whom no answer to the question was available. In addition, those who blamed others for their accidents had the most difficulty finding an answer to the question. The specific answer to "Why me?"—that is, how a person found meaning—did not appear to matter for adjustment. Regardless of the specific form of meaning found, those who were able to find meaning reported less distress than those who were not able to do so.

These findings are striking, as they provided the first evidence that the search for meaning could be a maladaptive response to personal trauma, at least to the extent that it does not yield an answer. Yet, it may often be the case that victims of personal trauma are unable to find meaning in their experience, despite being preoccupied with the search. Silver, Boon, and Stones (1983) surveyed 77 adult women who were survivors of childhood sexual abuse at the hands of their father or other male guardian. In this study, the sexual abuse occurred, on average, 2 decades earlier. Despite the time that had passed since the trauma, over 80% of the women in this study still searched to find some reason, meaning, or way to make sense of their experiences. A similar proportion of women also reported that this search for meaning was still important to them. Yet, over half of the women who were searching for meaning were still unable to make any sense of their experience, despite the passing of time. Furthermore, the women who reported an ongoing search for meaning had greater levels of distress and more frequent ruminations about the abuse. Of course, Silver et al. (1983) noted, because these data were cross-sectional, it is impossible to tease apart whether searching drives distress, whether distress drives the search to understand the distress, or whether the two go hand in hand.

As had been seen in the study of physically disabled individuals described earlier (Silver, 1982), the frequency of the search for meaning among the adult survivors of childhood sexual abuse was not associated with "objective" circumstances of their abuse. That is, relationships between the frequency of the search for meaning and the "severity" of the outcome, such as the frequency of the incestuous encounters, whether the sex had been accompanied by physical violence, and whether the contact progressed to intercourse, failed to reveal any significant effects.

The forms of meaning found were unique to the trauma of childhood sexual abuse. Over 50% saw the incest as an explainable consequence of dynamics in the household; 40% sympathized with the perpetrator's need for love or sexual satisfaction. Almost one third of the sample saw the perpetrator as being mentally ill or having a characterological disorder. Over 20%, however, made sense of their incest experience by focusing on positive outcomes of the situation. In contrast to explanations generated for spinal cord injury, very few women made sense of the incest with religious or philosophical explanations. As was seen in the search, finding meaning was also not associated with "objective" circumstances of the abuse. There were no differences in the number of years since the incest had terminated among those who were successful in their search for meaning and those who were not; nor were there differences in age at onset or termination of the abuse, in the duration or frequency of the encounters, whether violence had accompanied the sex, or whether the abuse had continued to intercourse. Moreover, it was not simply true that the longer these women searched, the more likely they were to find meaning. Unfortunately, time did not assist the women in making sense of their experiences.

Silver et al. (1983) also noted that attempts to cognitively process or make sense of the event could take the form of repeated ruminations about the "unfinished business." Indeed, as they noted, repeated reviewing of an experience could be interpreted as a means of "working through" the event so as to gain mastery over it. Struggles to reconcile the experience of the event with beliefs about the world could be manifest through recurrent, involuntary, intrusive thoughts of the trauma. Although the direction of causality was unanswerable with these correlational data, Silver et al. (1983) suggested that there likely was an interplay between ruminations about the abuse and a search for meaning in it. As they discussed,

> mentally reviewing disturbing memories of the past may be the mechanism by which our respondents attempted to make sense of their experience. . . . However, intrusive ruminations may also prompt a need to understand the experience and its persistent effects. (Silver et al., 1983, p. 88).

This issue was subsequently examined in some detail by Tait and Silver (1989), who interviewed 45 senior citizens about the worst event of their lives (which had occurred on average almost 23 years previously). Almost 40% of those sampled reported still searching at least sometimes for a meaningful perspective from which to view their most negative event. Searching for meaning was also associated with an ongoing desire to talk about the event as well as attempts to cognitively "undo" the experience (cf. Davis, Lehman, Wortman, Silver, & Thompson, 1995). This ongoing cognitive and emotional involvement was associated with frequent intrusive ruminations, as well as ongoing distress surrounding the negative event. Tait and Silver maintained that ongoing intrusions suggested that the individual had not been able to integrate the event successfully and thus may signal and cause continued distress (cf. Silver et al., 1983). It is interesting that none of these measures of ongoing impact were related to the amount of time that had passed since the event.

Longitudinal Studies of Meaning in Personal Trauma

These fundamental questions in the study of meaning making have been more closely examined in a number of longitudinal studies, many of which focused on bereavement (Davis, Nolen-Hoeksema, & Larson, 1998; Davis, Wortman, Lehman, & Silver, 2000). The first of these was a study of 124 parents who had suffered the loss of a child to sudden infant death syndrome (SIDS; Davis et al., 2000; Downey, Silver, & Wortman, 1990). SIDS is a unique trauma because it represents a devastating loss and is unexpected. There is typically no known cause for SIDS. Thus, it may represent a trauma for which issues of explanation and meaning are paramount.

Parents were first interviewed within a month of the death of their infant and were asked if they had ever searched for meaning in their loss. Only 14% said that it was "not at all" important to make sense of their baby's death. In contrast, an overwhelming majority of the parents (86%) reported no longer searching by the time of the interview. Of these, most reported having been unable to find any meaning in their loss.

The parents who reported that they were actively searching for meaning at the first interview were no more likely than those who reported that they were not doing so to report finding meaning, either at the first interview or during the following interviews (Davis et al., 2000). Furthermore, rates of finding meaning were strikingly similar across the three interviews. At 1 month, 65% were unable to find meaning. At both 3 months and 18 months, approximately 75% were unable to find meaning. Thus, this longitudinal study provides more compelling evidence that ability to find meaning appears either early on in the coping process or not at all. When meaning was found, it largely came in three forms: attributing the loss to God's will, attributing it to fate, or finding something positive in the loss.

How did this search for meaning relate to long-term adjustment? Across three measures of adjustment (depression, well-being, and negative emotions), the results were consistent. Parents who were not searching for meaning in the first month postloss were doing better across the entire 18-month period than those who were searching for meaning. Thus, the search for meaning was associated with long-term adjustment problems.

Was finding meaning in the loss associated with adjustment? To address this question, Downey et al. (1990) divided parents into three groups based on their search for meaning in the first month: (a) those who were not searching for meaning and had never found meaning, (b) those who were searching for meaning but were unable to find any, and (c) those who had searched and found meaning. As expected, the parents who searched for meaning but were unable to find any did worse on all outcomes than the two other groups. However, those parents who reported never searching at all and never finding meaning fared the best. Thus, these analyses suggest that finding meaning may facilitate adjustment for those who are actively searching for meaning. However, being concerned with a search for meaning in the first place may be indicative of coping difficulties.

One limitation of this study of parents coping with SIDS is that preloss measures of distress were not available, given the unexpected nature of SIDS. Thus, there is the potential that the parents' search for meaning and their long-term adjustment may have been driven, in part, by their adjustment prior to their loss. However, we note that these findings are consistent with those found in a longitudinal study of 205 adults coping with the death of a hospice-residing family member (Davis et al., 1998). These researchers were able to interview their participants prior to the loss of their loved one and observed adjustment from preloss through 13 months postloss. At 6 months postloss, 68% of their participants reported that they had been able to make sense of the death, and 19% reported that they were completely unable to make sense of it. Furthermore, these proportions were strikingly similar to the proportions of individuals who were able to make sense of the death at 13 months postloss.

However, this study also noted that making sense was not necessarily consistent over time. Despite the consistent rates over time, Davis et al. (1998) noted that people switched categories from 6 to 13 months. That is, although over half of the respondents reported no change in their ability to make sense over time, 32% had changed from the 6-month to 13-month interview. Almost one third of these respondents (32%) "gained sense," and a smaller percentage (7%) "lost sense" over time.

What is noteworthy about these findings, however, is how they related to adjustment over time. When preloss levels of distress were controlled for, respondents who were able to make sense of their loss at the 6-month interview experienced less distress at the 13-month follow-up. More important, it was only the ability to make sense at the earlier interview that predicted longer term adjustment. In fact, Davis et al. (1998) observed that those people who had "gained sense" from 6 months to 13 months were still experiencing more distress than those who had made sense all along, suggesting that the meanings that respondents found later may not have been "particularly comforting" (p. 569). Indeed, the types of explanations found by the "sense gainers" at 13 months tended to lack an ability to make sense, for example by concluding that these kinds of events "just happen" (Davis et al., 1998, p. 569).

Summary of Meaning in the Context of Personal Trauma

Across diverse types of personal trauma—bereavement, sexual abuse, and spinal cord injury—there is clear evidence that the search for meaning is a common response to trauma and one that may likely influence longer term adjustment to trauma. These early empirical studies of meaning following personal trauma brought to light several important findings in the study of meaning. First, the search for meaning is a common response to personal traumas, but it is also not a universal response. Second, searching for meaning may not necessarily be adaptive, particularly when the search persists without any resolution. Third, the passage of time does not appear to assist in finding meaning. When people are able to find meaning, they may be likely to do so early in the process. Last, finding meaning may be more difficult for events that are perceived as particularly unfair, as the people may be most likely to search for meaning—and least likely to find it—following particularly severe, directly experienced traumas.

MEANING MAKING IN COLLECTIVE TRAUMA

Traumatic events impact both individuals and collectives. Community-wide disasters, such as natural-, technological-, or human-caused traumatic events (e.g., mass shootings), can cause death and physical damage, but they also disrupt life, alter or interrupt the rhythm of routine patterns, and tear the social fabric of the community (e.g., Erikson, 1976). Even if one is not directly affected by the incident, such community-wide events often strip individuals of a sense of security in their surroundings, highlight the fragility of life, and shatter perceptions of individual vulnerability.

With few exceptions (Pennebaker & Banasik, 1997; Wayment, 2004), limited research has examined the process of meaning making following collective traumas. Yet, it is clear that communities are deeply concerned about how their story is told (Pennebaker & Banasik, 1997). Given the work that has been conducted following personally experienced events, we suspected that individuals exposed to collective traumas would also try to make sense of these shared events. Moreover, we hypothesized that one would not need to have been directly exposed to a collective trauma to search for meaning in it.

These themes were evident in a small qualitative study of almost a dozen parents and children who were interviewed within the first 2 weeks after the shootings at Columbine High School in Littleton, Colorado, where two male students murdered 13 students and teachers and subsequently took their own lives (Hawkins, McIntosh, Silver, & Holman, 2007). All respondents reported having tried to make some sense of the tragic events, although the importance of finding meaning in the events was highly variable. The extent to which the topic consumed thought processes in the early aftermath of the shooting was also highly variable, with some admitting thinking about the issue only rarely and others reporting thinking about it all the time. For some, meaning was facilitated via identifying with the perpetrators: understanding their motivations and acknowledging the pain they felt as a result of social exclusion. Others had been unable to find any answers.

Meaning Making in a Community Natural Disaster

In October 1993, a firestorm ravaged two small coastal communities in Southern California a week apart. Almost 600 homes were destroyed, and hundreds more sustained significant fire damage. Both communities were evacuated in a matter of hours, and residents were left to wonder about the state of their homes and possessions while they sought refuge and watched the extensive media coverage of the disaster. In the end, it was unclear what started the fires, although initial reports suggested it could have been the result of arson.

Within 36 hours after residents' return from the forced evacuation, our research team was able to interview 85 residents about the firestorm (see Holman & Silver, 1998). Some of the interviewees suffered a loss of their home. Others suffered the threat of losing their home, suffered financial damage, or witnessed neighbors and friends suffer the loss of their homes. Thus, some respondents experienced a direct loss, whereas others were indirectly affected. In the first interview, over 50% of the respondents reported searching for meaning in the firestorm and its aftermath. Over 75% of these individuals reported that they were able to find meaning in the firestorm and its aftermath "at least sometimes." Despite the initial suggestions that arson may have been the cause, very few participants (5%) made sense of the firestorm by blaming others for the disaster. Instead, the most common response (30%) was to interpret the events in terms of some larger philosophical or religious perspective (fate, chance, God's plan). Perhaps due to the nature of the situation, another common response (19%) was to focus on actions taken to repair the situation, by fixing damage, helping neighbors, or contacting insurance companies (Updegraff, Silver, & Holman, 1996).

At several times over the 2 years following the firestorm, respondents were again asked whether they had searched for meaning and, if so, how they had found it. Across the years, the prevalence of the search for meaning remained stable. Half of the respondents reported an active search for meaning, and half of them did not. Moreover, most reported being able to make sense of the fires (almost 90% answered affirmatively at 1 year and almost 85% did so at 2 years). However, there was some change in the content of people's statements. In particular, there was a marked increase in the number of people who make sense by making use of cognitive restructuring, for example, by focusing on positive aspects of the situation. In contrast, respondents were less likely to make sense by interpreting within a philosophical or religious perspective over time. Thus, there was some evidence to suggest that time might have changed the particular explanations with which respondents explained the disaster.

Although it was difficult to assess whether the severity of the trauma influenced the particular forms of meaning that respondents found, we were able to examine whether the severity influenced the intensity of the search for meaning. Across the first 2 weeks of this collective trauma, there was no difference in the intensity of the search among those respondents who lost their house and those who did not. This is arguably due to the fact that all respondents were threatened by the fire and witnessed the damage to their community in the first weeks of the disaster. It was only at the 6-month interview that a difference emerged: Those who had lost their home were significantly more likely still to be searching for meaning in the experience than those who had not lost their home. Nonetheless, this difference did not maintain at one and two years after the fires. In general, it appears that the degree to which community residents searched for and found meaning in the firestorm was not associated with severity of fire damage. As has been seen with very different sorts of adversity (physical disability, childhood sexual abuse), individuals who had lost their home were not more likely to search for meaning than those who had not lost it, and those who had not lost their home were no more likely to make sense of the firestorm than those who had lost it.

However, across time, the degree to which individuals searched for meaning in this collective trauma and whether or not they reported finding it were associated with distress. In particular, those who were searching for meaning in the first several hours after the forced evacuation reported higher distress over time; those who reported searching for meaning at 2 weeks after the firestorm reported more distress up to 2 years later. Finally, those who had found meaning by 2 weeks after the fires reported significantly less distress over the next several years; the ability to find meaning also predicted a more rapid decrease in distress over the 6 months following the firestorm (Updegraff et al., 1996).

Thus, it appears from the local collective traumas we studied (Columbine High School shooting and Southern California firestorm) that such events appear to initiate the same psychological processes in the search for meaning as seen following personally traumatic events. Even without direct loss from these collective traumas, residents are nonetheless confronted with challenges to basic assumptions about living in a predictable, understandable world and their role in it. In confronting these challenges, individuals exhibit remarkably similar responses to both indirectly and directly experienced traumatic events.

Meaning Making in the September 11, 2001, Terrorist Attacks

The terrorist attacks of September 11, 2001, represented a collective trauma for the entire United States. Although residents of New York City and Washington, DC, were largely the people who experienced direct personal trauma as a result of the attacks, the entire country was shaken by vivid television images and extensive media coverage. Indeed, nearly half of Americans reported symptoms of posttraumatic stress in the days following the attacks, with symptoms remaining elevated in the months following 9/11 (Schuster et al., 2001; Silver, Holman, McIntosh, Poulin, & Gil-Rivas, 2002). These symptoms were accompanied by substantial fears of additional terrorist attacks, as more than half of Americans expressed concerns for the safety of themselves and their loved ones (Silver et al., 2002). Although only a small proportion of Americans was directly traumatized by the attacks (by witnessing them or losing a loved one), the attacks represented a widespread collective trauma for the country.

These attacks provided an unusual opportunity to examine meaning making among individuals coping with a collective trauma. Updegraff, Silver, and Holman (2008) examined the predictors and long-term consequences both of searching for meaning and of finding meaning in a large, nationally representative longitudinal study of American's responses to 9/11. This study was unique to meaning studies in a number of important respects. First, it was a longitudinal study that included preattack measures of mental health and followed respondents for 2 years. The baseline measures are particularly noteworthy, as the attacks represented an unanticipated event, unlike prior studies that have included pre-event measures of adjustment (e.g., Davis et al., 1998). Second, this study had measures of early stress and coping responses at 2 weeks postattack, which enabled an examination of the early predictors of long-term adjustment. Last, the study assessed beliefs that have been theorized to explain the link between finding meaning and adjustment.

Respondents in this study also had varying levels of exposure to the attacks. Over half (60%) viewed the attacks on live TV, and a smaller proportion lived within 100 miles of the attacks (8%) or had direct exposure to them (3%). Thus, this study was able to assess the role of direct exposure in the search for meaning.

The first interview that asked Americans about their search for meaning was administered in November 2001. Over two thirds (69%) of those sampled reported searching for meaning in the terrorist attacks and their aftermath at the 2-month interview. This proportion was similar at the 1-year interview (71%), so the search for meaning did not appear to abate over time. At 2 months, the intensity of people's search for meaning was not predicted at all by direct experience with the attacks. Rather, the intensity of the search for meaning was predicted by respondents' level of acute stress symptoms in the weeks following the attacks, after controlling for preattack indices of mental health. Early coping strategies did little to predict the extent of people's search for meaning. Thus, direct exposure to the trauma was not required for a search for meaning to occur. All that mattered was that a person experience subjective distress resulting from exposure to the collective trauma.

Despite the high proportion of Americans searching for a way to make sense of the attacks, only 40% of those sampled reported being able to find meaning. Furthermore, this percentage remained stable at the 1-year follow-up. Again, direct exposure to the attacks was not related to the ability to find meaning, but acute stress symptoms were: Those who experienced more early acute stress symptoms were less likely to report finding meaning. However, early coping strategies played a greater role in predicting the ability to find meaning. People who sought instrumental support from others—as by seeking advice—were more likely to find meaning in the terrorist attacks than were people who engaged in positive reframing. People who sought emotional support from others or who engaged in denial coping were less likely to find meaning. These findings suggest an important role for the social environment in meaning making, particularly in the context of a collective trauma.

Of greatest importance, this study provided perhaps the most compelling evidence to date that searching for and finding meaning in a traumatic experience facilitate long-term adjustment. After controlling for pre-event mental health, exposure to the attacks, as well as early acute stress response, we found that both searching for and finding meaning predicted posttraumatic stress symptoms over the following 2 years. The more people searched for meaning in the early months, the more posttraumatic stress symptoms they experienced over time. In contrast, the more people were able to find meaning, the fewer posttraumatic stress symptoms they experienced over time.

This study also identified a link that could explain why finding meaning facilitated long-term adjustment. That is, we found that finding meaning facilitated adjustment by reducing fears of future terrorism. These findings can be taken to suggest that something in the explanations that Americans found for the attacks enabled them to be less preoccupied with the potential that future attacks were likely. In short, finding meaning may have served to restore some order or coherence in an event that was—at its core—unanticipated, threatening to national security, and devastating.

What kinds of meanings did Americans find? The most common way of explaining the terrorist attacks was either to derogate the terrorists or to assert American's moral superiority over the terrorists (30%). Another common response was to find meaning by seeking to understand the motivations behind the terrorists' actions (24%). Smaller proportions of Americans found meaning by looking to religious explanations (15%) or interpreting the events within a political or historical perspective (12%). The least common ways of finding meaning in the early aftermath were by blaming the U.S. government (8%) or by looking for positive consequences resulting from the attacks (5%). A striking pattern to these explanations is how they map onto some of the fundamental assumptions that have been argued to provide a sense of coherence in people's lives (Janoff-Bulman, 1992)—world as just place, world as benevolent, self as worthy. Nonetheless, of these, only finding meaning by seeking to understand the motives of the terrorists was related to better adjustment. Otherwise, the particular form of meaning found was inconsequential.

SUMMARY AND FUTURE DIRECTIONS

For decades, psychologists have maintained that the need to make sense of the events in one's social world is a fundamental part of everyday social cognition, as well as a central part of theories of adaptation to trauma (Janoff-Bulman, 1992; Park, 2010; Taylor, 1983). Empirical research conducted over the past several decades makes it clear that individuals frequently seek to make sense of traumatic life events—both personally experienced and socially shared events. In fact, in the case of collective traumas, one does not need to have been directly exposed to an event to search for meaning in it. Across several populations it is also clear that searching for meaning tends to be associated with distress. Of course, the causal direction of this relationship is impossible to clarify definitively. Rather than distress driving the search for meaning or the search for meaning driving distress, it is likely that there is a constant interplay between the two. In addition, some individuals appear to avoid the search for meaning in adversity altogether, and they appear to have better psychological outcomes over time.

Many but not all individuals are able to reconcile an individually or collectively experienced traumatic event with their preexisting worldviews by finding some kind of meaning in the event (Silver & Wortman, 1980; Taylor, 1983). This may take the form of blaming oneself or others for the event (Bulman & Wortman, 1977), interpreting the experience through one's philosophical or religious beliefs (McIntosh, Silver, & Wortman, 1993), or believing that the event has had some positive consequences or social benefits (Poulin, Silver, Gil-Rivas, Holman, & McIntosh, 2009; Torabi & Seo, 2004). Nonetheless, across a variety of studies it has become clear that the type of answer generated following the search for meaning appears less important than whether an answer is generated at all. That is, regardless of the particular form of the explanation, it is thought that making some kind of sense out of a trauma or loss facilitates long-term adaptation (Janoff-Bulman, 1992; Silver & Wortman, 1980; Taylor, 1983). This process appears to take the form of restoring people's sense of invulnerability and shutting down continued ruminations about the traumatic experience (Silver et al., 1983; Updegraff et al., 2008).

Our review also highlights the substantial variability in the frequency of the search and ability to find meaning depending on characteristics of the traumatic event. For example, the proportion of people who have been able to find meaning in adversity ranges from 8% among spouses who lost a loved one in a motor vehicle accident (Lehman, Wortman, & Williams, 1987), to roughly half among victims of childhood sexual abuse (Silver et al., 1983), women diagnosed with breast cancer (Kernan & Lepore, 2009), and parents of children who died of SIDS (Davis et al., 2000) or died violently (Murphy, Johnson, & Lohan, 2003), to almost 70% among older adults suffering the loss of a loved one residing in a hospice (Davis et al., 1998). Only by examining a wide variety of stressful experiences could this variability be seen. Events that are particularly unfair or are perpetrated by others appear to be associated with a greater search for and more difficulty in finding meaning.

Research also demonstrates that time does not appear to assist in finding meaning—if individuals are able to find meaning, they appear to do so early in the process. Although it has been suggested that time can facilitate finding meaning (Murphy et al., 2003), many studies have relied on cross-sectional designs that cannot assess longitudinal patterns. However, in our longitudinal study of parents coping with the sudden death of an infant (Davis et al., 2000), meaning was found early, if it was found at all. At this stage, further development of the construct requires longitudinal research to examine how the processes of searching and finding meaning remain stable versus change over time.

Future research should also continue to explore what factors (both individual and contextual) trigger the search for meaning and facilitate finding meaning. For example, surprisingly little research has explored the link between the social environment's response to victims and the process by which these individuals come to terms with their experiences. The social environment often reacts in widely divergent ways toward victims of negative life events, ranging from understanding and empathy to indifference and rejection (Silver & Wortman, 1980). A thorough consideration of how these reactions impact individuals' attempts to understand their experiences may prove useful in explaining variability as well as assist in the design of professional or social interventions for individuals who are stuck in an unproductive cycle of "searching for meaning" (e.g., Davis et al., 2000).

As Janoff-Bulman (1992) argued, the social environment can give victims invaluable posttrauma feedback regarding themselves, their coping attempts, and the world in general. Supportive and empathic responses can help the individual retain a belief in a benevolent world by facilitating the recognition that he or she is loved, is cared for, and belongs to a network of mutual help and obligation. Individuals whose social networks remain supportive may be able to retain previously held assumptions about themselves and the world, and they may be less likely to engage in an extended search for meaning in their misfortune. Further, individuals who receive effective support from others may be more likely to recognize benefits resulting from the experience. For example, in Thompson's (1985) study of community fire victims, the most frequent benefit that individuals reported was "finding out about the helpfulness of others" (see Poulin et al., 2009, for a comparable finding post 9/11).

Positive social relations may also influence the ability to find meaning by allowing the victim to discuss trauma-related thoughts and feelings with others. Talking with others about the experience may help to structure it by emphasizing cause–effect relationships, clarifying feelings, and increasing one's insight (Pennebaker, 1993). Although having individuals available with whom one can share the trauma does not guarantee that discussions will be responded to favorably (Silver & Wortman, 1980) or will allow the in-depth and feeling-focused discussion that appears to facilitate these benefits, a supportive social environment will be much more likely to provide the opportunities necessary to discuss and explore one's thoughts and feelings surrounding the experience.

Recently, studies have identified some promising individual-level factors that may be associated with the meaning process. For example, spirituality may provide schemata that help individuals more easily assimilate events into their worldviews, which may facilitate a more effective processing of traumatic events (McIntosh, Poulin, Silver, & Holman, 2011). Religiosity may facilitate interpretation and assimilation of traumatic events because social interactions, especially in religious contexts, can offer collaborative opportunities to interpret traumatic events (Lepore, Silver, Wortman, & Wayment, 1996; Pennebaker & Harber, 1993; Tait & Silver, 1989). These and other factors have great potential in advancing conceptual and empirical work on how individuals process and come to terms with the inevitable adversities encountered over the life course.

REFERENCES

Aldwin, C. M. (2007). *Stress, coping, and development: An integrative approach*. New York, NY: Guilford Press.

Bulman, R. J., & Wortman, C. B. (1977). Attributions of blame and coping in the "real world": Severe accident victims react to their lot. *Journal of Personality and Social Psychology, 35*, 351–363. doi:10.1037/0022-3514.35.5.351

Davis, C. G., Lehman, D. R., Silver, R. C., Wortman, C. B., & Ellard, J. H. (1996). Self-blame following a traumatic event: The role of perceived avoidability. *Personality and Social Psychology Bulletin, 22*, 557–567. doi:10.1177/0146167296226002

Davis, C. G., Lehman, D. R., Wortman, C. B., Silver, R. C., & Thompson, S. C. (1995). The undoing of traumatic life events. *Personality and Social Psychology Bulletin*, *21*, 109–124. doi:10.1177/0146167295212002

Davis, C. G., Nolen-Hoeksema, S., & Larson, J. (1998). Making sense of loss and benefiting from the experience: Two construals of meaning. *Journal of Personality and Social Psychology*, *75*, 561–574. doi:10.1037/0022-3514.75.2.561

Davis, C. G., Wortman, C. B., Lehman, D. R., & Silver, R. C. (2000). Searching for meaning in loss: Are clinical assumptions correct? *Death Studies*, *24*, 497–540. doi:10.1080/07481180050121471

Downey, G., Silver, R. C., & Wortman, C. B. (1990). Reconsidering the attribution–adjustment relation following a major negative event: Coping with the loss of a child. *Journal of Personality and Social Psychology*, *59*, 925–940. doi:10.1037/0022-3514.59.5.925

Erikson, K. T. (1976). Loss of communality at Buffalo Creek. *American Journal of Psychiatry*, *133*, 302–305.

Hawkins, N. A., McIntosh, D. N., Silver, R. C., & Holman, E. A. (2007). Early responses to school violence: A qualitative analysis of students' and parents' immediate reactions to the shootings at Columbine High School. *Journal of Emotional Abuse*, *4*, 197–223. doi:10.1300/J135v04n03_12

Holman, E. A., & Silver, R. C. (1998). Getting "stuck" in the past: Temporal orientation and coping with trauma. *Journal of Personality and Social Psychology*, *74*, 1146–1163. doi:10.1037/0022-3514.74.5.1146

Janoff-Bulman, R. (1992). *Shattered assumptions: Towards a new psychology of trauma*. New York, NY: Free Press.

Janoff-Bulman, R., & Frantz, C. M. (1997). The impact of trauma on meaning: From meaningless world to meaningful life. In M. J. Power & C. Brewin (Eds.), *The transformation of meaning in psychological therapies: Integrating theory and practice* (pp. 91–106). Hoboken, NJ: Wiley.

Kernan, W. D., & Lepore, S. J. (2009). Searching for and making meaning after breast cancer: Prevalence, patterns, and negative affect. *Social Science & Medicine*, *68*, 1176–1182. doi:10.1016/j.socscimed.2008.12.038

Lehman, D. R., Wortman, C. B., & Williams, A. F. (1987). Long-term effects of losing a spouse or child in a motor vehicle crash. *Journal of Personality and Social Psychology*, *52*, 218–231. doi:10.1037/0022-3514.52.1.218

Lepore, S. J., Silver, R. C., Wortman, C. B., & Wayment, H. A. (1996). Social constraints, intrusive thoughts, and depressive symptoms among bereaved mothers. *Journal of Personality and Social Psychology*, *70*, 271–282. doi:10.1037/0022-3514.70.2.271

McIntosh, D. N., Poulin, M. J., Silver, R. C., & Holman, E. A. (2011). The distinct roles of spirituality and religiosity in physical and mental health after collective trauma: A national longitudinal study of responses to the 9/11 attacks. *Journal of Behavioral Medicine*. Advance online publication. doi:10.1007/s10865-011-9331-y

McIntosh, D. N., Silver, R. C., & Wortman, C. B. (1993). Religion's role in adjustment to a negative life event: Coping with the loss of a child. *Journal of Personality and Social Psychology*, *65*, 812–821. doi:10.1037/0022-3514.65.4.812

Murphy, S. A., Johnson, L. C., & Lohan, J. (2003). Finding meaning in a child's violent death: A five-year prospective analysis of parents' personal narratives and empirical data. *Death Studies*, *27*, 381–404. doi:10.1080/07481180302879

Neimeyer, R. A. (Ed.). (2001). *Meaning reconstruction and the experience of loss*. Washington, DC: American Psychological Association. doi:10.1037/10397-000

Norris, F. H. (1992). Epidemiology of trauma: Frequency and impact of different potentially traumatic events on different demographic groups. *Journal of Consulting and Clinical Psychology*, *60*, 409–418. doi:10.1037/0022-006X.60.3.409

Park, C. L. (2010). Making sense of the meaning literature: An integrative review of meaning making and its effects of adjustment to stressful life events. *Psychological Bulletin*, *136*, 257–301. doi:10.1037/a0018301

Park, C. L., & Folkman, S. (1997). Meaning in the context of stress and coping. *Review of General Psychology*, *1*, 115–144. doi:10.1037/1089-2680.1.2.115

Pennebaker, J. W. (1993). Putting stress into words: Health, linguistic, and therapeutic implications. *Behaviour Research and Therapy*, *31*, 539–548. doi:10.1016/0005-7967(93)90105-4

Pennebaker, J. W., & Banasik, B. L. (1997). On the creation and maintenance of collective memories: History as social psychology. In J. W. Pennebaker, D. Paez, & B. Rime (Eds.), *Collective memories of political events* (pp. 3–19). Hillsdale, NJ: Erlbaum.

Pennebaker, J. W., & Harber, K. D. (1993). A social stage model of collective coping: The Loma Prieta earthquake and the Persian Gulf war. *Journal of Social Issues*, *49*(4), 125–145. doi:10.1111/j.1540-4560.1993.tb01184.x

Poulin, M. J., Silver, R. C., Gil-Rivas, V., Holman, A. E., & McIntosh, D. (2009). Finding social benefits after a collective trauma: Perceiving societal changes and well-being following 9/11. *Journal of Traumatic Stress*, *22*, 81–90. doi:10.1002/jts.20391

Schuster, M. A., Stein, B. D., Jaycox, L. H., Collins, R. L., Marshall, G. N., Elliott, M. N., . . . Berry, S. H. (2001). A national survey of stress reactions after the September 11, 2001, terrorist attacks. *New England Journal of Medicine*, *345*, 1507–1512. doi:10.1056/NEJM200111153452024

Seery, M. D., Holman, E. A., & Silver, R. C. (2010). Whatever does not kill us: Cumulative lifetime adversity, vulnerability, and resilience. *Journal of Personality and Social Psychology*, *99*, 1025–1041. doi:10.1037/a0021344

Silver, R. C., Holman, E. A., McIntosh, D. N., Poulin, M., & Gil-Rivas, V. (2002). Nationwide longitudinal study of psychological responses to September 11. *JAMA*, *288*, 1235–1244. doi:10.1001/jama.288.10.1235

Silver, R. L. (1982). *Coping with an undesirable life event: A study of early reactions to physical disability* (Unpublished doctoral dissertation). Northwestern University, Evanston, IL.

Silver, R. L., Boon, C., & Stones, M. H. (1983). Searching for meaning in misfortune: Making sense of incest. *Journal of Social Issues*, *39*(2), 81–101. doi:10.1111/j.1540-4560.1983.tb00142.x

Silver, R. L., & Wortman, C. B. (1980). Coping with undesirable life events. In J. Garber & M. E. P. Seligman (Eds.), *Human helplessness: Theory and applications* (pp. 279–340). New York, NY: Academic Press.

Tait, R., & Silver, R. C. (1989). Coming to terms with major negative life events. In J. S. Uleman & J. A. Bargh (Eds.), *Unintended thought* (pp. 351–382). New York, NY: Guilford Press.

Taylor, S. E. (1983). Adjustment to threatening events: A theory of cognitive adaptation. *American Psychologist*, *38*, 1161–1173. doi:10.1037/0003-066X.38.11.1161

Thompson, S. C. (1985). Finding positive meaning in a stressful event and coping. *Basic and Applied Social Psychology*, *6*, 279–295. doi:10.1207/s15324834basp0604_1

Thompson, S. C., & Janigan, A. S. (1988). Life schemes: A framework for understanding the search for meaning. *Journal of Social and Clinical Psychology*, *7*, 260–280. doi:10.1521/jscp.1988.7.2-3.260

Torabi, M. R., & Seo, D.-C. (2004). National study of behavioral and life changes since September 11. *Health Education & Behavior*, *31*, 179–192. doi:10.1177/1090198103259183

Updegraff, J. A., Silver, R. C., & Holman, E. A. (1996). *Making sense of trauma: A longitudinal approach* (Unpublished honors thesis). University of California at Irvine.

Wayment, H. A. (2004). It could have been me: Vicarious victims and disaster-focused distress. *Personality and Social Psychology Bulletin*, *30*, 515–528. doi:10.1177/0146167203261892

Wayment, H. A., Silver, R. C., & Kemeny, M. (1995). Spared at random: Survivor reactions in the gay community. *Journal of Applied Social Psychology*, *25*, 187–209. doi:10.1111/j.1559-1816.1995.tb01590.x

13

SPIRITUALITY AND MEANING MAKING IN CANCER SURVIVORSHIP

CRYSTAL L. PARK

Spirituality and meaning are important aspects of the experiences of many cancer survivors (Stefanek, McDonald, & Hess, 2005). Spirituality is centrally involved in the global meaning systems of many people and is particularly salient in meaning-making efforts in times of high stress (Pargament, 1997). A large and growing literature documents the myriad ways that spirituality is involved in the cancer experience (e.g., Lavery & O'Hea, 2010).

The present chapter describes the ways in which spirituality is involved in the meaning-making processes of cancer survivors. The material is framed within an integrated model of meaning making in the context of stress (Park, 2010; Park & Folkman, 1997) that distinguishes between global and situational levels of meaning. Both levels of meaning are involved in coping with stressful experiences such as cancer. Using this framework, I review research on spirituality and meaning in the context of cancer survivorship. Suggestions for future research on the many remaining questions regarding spirituality and meaning in cancer survivorship conclude the chapter.

DOI: 10.1037/14040-013
The Psychology of Meaning, Keith D. Markman, Travis Proulx, and Matthew J. Lindberg (Editors)

THE MEANING-MAKING MODEL OF COPING WITH LIFE STRESS

The meaning-making model of coping addresses both global and situational aspects of meaning (Park & Folkman, 1997). *Global meaning* refers to individuals' general orienting systems. *Situational meaning* consists of initial appraisals of a particular situation as well as the processes by which global and appraised situational meanings are revised and the outcomes of these processes. The meaning-making model is illustrated in Figure 13.1.

Global meaning consists of the structures through which people perceive and understand themselves and the world, encompassing beliefs, goals, and subjective feelings of purpose or meaning in life (Dittmann-Kohli & Westerhof, 2000; Park & Folkman, 1997). Global meaning consists of cognitive, motivational, and affective components, termed, respectively, global beliefs, global goals, and a sense of meaning or purpose (Park, 2010; Reker & Wong, 1988).

Global beliefs concerning fairness, justice, luck, control, predictability, coherence, benevolence, personal vulnerability, and identity constitute the core schemas through which people interpret their experiences of the world (Janoff-Bulman & Frantz, 1997; Koltko-Rivera, 2004). *Global goals* are individuals' ideals, states, or objects toward which they work to be, obtain, accomplish, or maintain (Karoly, 1999). Common global goals include relationships, work, health, wealth, knowledge, and achievement (Emmons, 2003). *Subjective feelings of meaning* refers to a sense of "meaningfulness" or purpose in life (Klinger, 1977; Reker & Wong, 1988). This sense of meaningfulness comes from seeing one's life as containing those goals that one values as well as feeling one is making adequate progress toward important future goals (Steger, 2009; Wrosch, Scheier, Miller, Schulz, & Carver, 2003; cf. King, Hicks, Krull, & Del Gaiso, 2006; see also Chapter 11, this volume). Together, global beliefs and goals and the resultant sense of life meaning form individuals' meaning systems, forming the lens through which individuals interpret, evaluate, and respond to their experiences.

Situational Meaning: The Meaning of Potentially Stressful Encounters

People assign meanings to, or appraise, potentially stressful situations (Lazarus & Folkman, 1984). These appraised meanings are to some extent determined by the specifics of the particular situation but are also largely informed by individuals' global meaning. For example, the appraised meaning of receiving a diagnosis of cancer is based on individuals' understanding of that disease (e.g., time course, severity; Leventhal, Weinman, Leventhal, & Phillips, 2008) as well as their beliefs in their ability to manage the cancer, its perceived impact on their future life and lifestyle, and their general sense of control over their life (Peacock & Wong, 1996; Weinstein & Quigley, 2006).

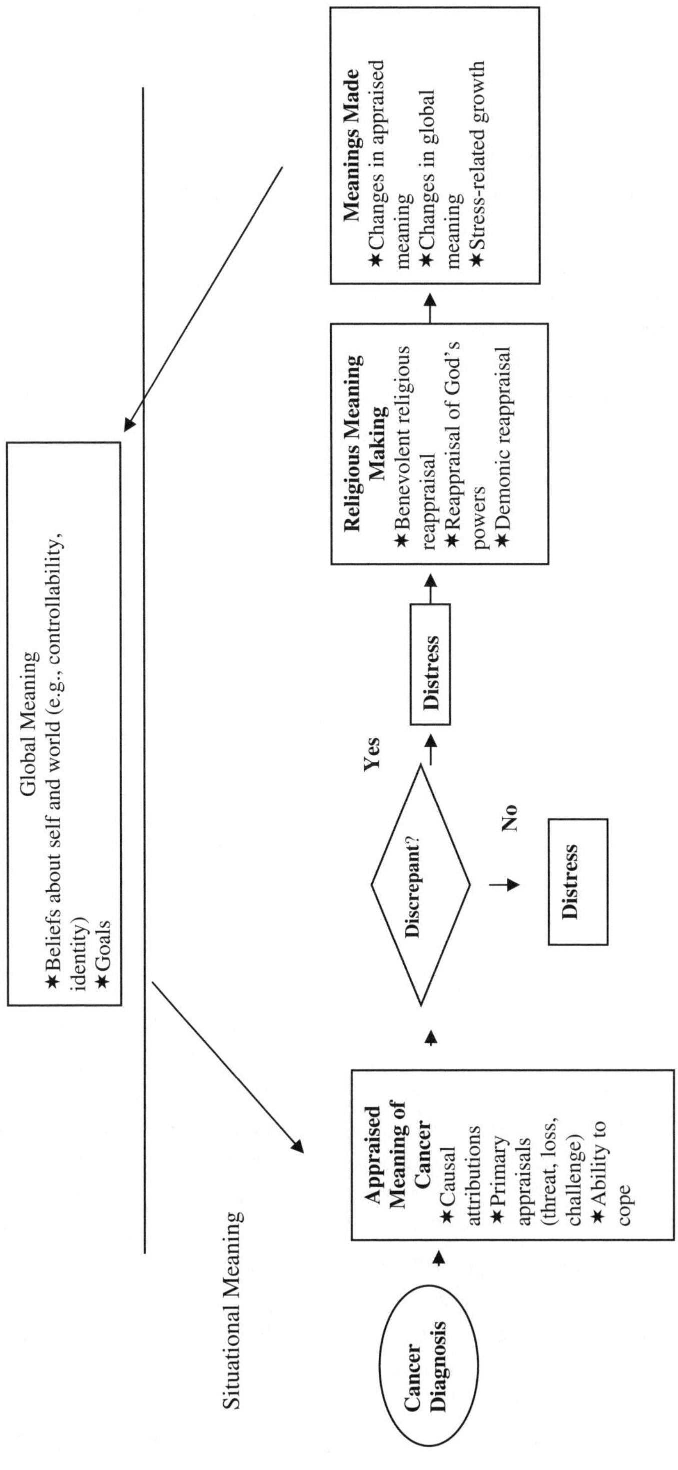

Figure 13.1. The meaning-making model.

Stress as Discrepancy Between Global and Situational Meaning

The meaning-making model is based on the notion that stress occurs when people perceive discrepancies between their global meaning (i.e., what they believe and desire) and their appraised meaning of a particular situation (Park, 2010). This discrepancy-related distress motivates individuals to resolve their problems and dissipate the resultant negative emotions (Park, Zlateva, & Blank, 2009). Confrontation with a severe stressor is thought to have the potential to violate or even shatter global meaning systems (i.e., individuals' global beliefs about the world and themselves and their overarching goals). Such violations or discrepancies are thought to initiate individuals' cognitive and emotional processing—meaning-making efforts—to rebuild their meaning systems. Meaning making involves individuals' efforts to understand and conceptualize a stressor in a way more consistent with their global meaning and to incorporate that understanding into their larger system of global meaning through assimilation and accommodation processes (Park & Folkman, 1997).

Resolving stressful events entails reducing discrepancies between appraised meanings and global meanings (Greenberg, 1995; Janoff-Bulman, 1992; Joseph & Linley, 2005). Discrepancies can be reduced in many ways, and, to this end, people engage in many types of coping (e.g., Manne, Ostroff, Fox, Grana, & Winkel, 2009; Park, Edmondson, Fenster, & Blank, 2008). People may engage in problem-focused coping, taking direct actions to reduce the discrepancy by changing the conditions that create or maintain the problem. When encountering stress, individuals can also engage in emotion-focused coping, much of which is targeted at directly alleviating distress, albeit temporarily, by disengaging mentally or behaviorally (e.g., focusing on some distraction). Emotion-focused coping, by definition, does not reduce discrepancies, which may be why it is generally associated with distress (Aldwin, 2007).

Stressful situations vary in the extent to which they are amenable to problem-focused coping (e.g., Moos & Holahan, 2007; Park, Armeli, & Tennen, 2004), which is the type of coping typically considered most adaptive (Aldwin, 2007). In low control situations such as trauma, loss, and serious illness, meaning-making coping is particularly relevant and potentially more adaptive because these situations are not amenable to direct repair or problem solving (Park, Folkman, & Bostrom, 2001). In contrast to problem-focused coping, which seeks to directly change the situation, or emotion-focused coping, which aims to alleviate emotional distress, meaning making refers to approach-oriented, intrapsychic efforts to reduce discrepancies between appraised and global meaning. Meaning-focused coping aims to reduce discrepancy by changing either the very meaning of the stressor itself (appraised meaning) or one's global beliefs and goals; either way, meaning-focused coping aims to improve the fit between the appraised meaning of the stressor and global meaning.

Following highly stressful events, individuals' meaning-making processes typically involve searching for some more favorable or consistent understanding of the event and its implications for their beliefs about themselves and their lives. Meaning making may also entail reconsidering global beliefs and revising goals (see Wrosch et al., 2003) and questioning or revising their sense of meaning in life (Steger, 2009).

This rebuilding process is assumed to lead to better adjustment, particularly if adequate meaning is found or created (for reviews, see Collie & Long, 2005; Lee, Cohen, Edgar, Laizner, & Gagnon, 2004; Skaggs & Barron, 2006). However, protracted attempts to assimilate or accommodate may devolve into maladaptive rumination over time if satisfactory meanings cannot be constructed (Segerstrom, Stanton, Alden, & Shortridge, 2003). That is, meaning making is helpful to the extent that it produces a satisfactory product (i.e., meaning made; Park, 2010).

Meanings Made

The products that result from meaning making, termed *meanings made*, involve changes in global or situational meaning, such as revised identity, growth, or reappraised situational or global meaning. The outcomes of the meaning-making process involve changes in global or situational meaning. As illustrated in Figure 13.1, individuals may make many different types of meaning through their meaning-making processes. Among the most commonly discussed meanings made are a sense of having "made sense" or found resolution, a sense of acceptance (e.g., Pakenham, 2007), causal understanding (e.g., Janoff-Bulman & Frantz, 1997), reconstructed or transformed identity that integrates the stressful experience into one's identity (Gillies & Neimeyer, 2006), reappraised or transformed meaning of the stressor (e.g., Manne et al., 2009), changed global beliefs (e.g., Park, 2005), changed global goals (e.g., Thompson & Janigian, 1988), restoration or changed sense of meaning in life (e.g., Janoff-Bulman & Frantz, 1997), and perceptions of growth or positive life changes, the latter of which is the most commonly assessed meaning made (e.g., Calhoun & Tedeschi, 2006).

Meaning making is an important part of everyday life (Park & Edmondson, 2012), but it becomes particularly critical when people confront highly stressful experiences, such as serious illness (Moadel et al., 1999). Such highly stressful encounters often bring meaning to the fore (Lee, Cohen, Edgar, Laizner, & Gagnon, 2006). The following section reviews how spirituality and meaning making are involved in the psychological adjustment of cancer survivors, people who have been forced by circumstance to face the possibilities of great uncertainty, prolonged suffering, and a foreshortened future (Little & Sayers, 2004). Cancer survivors encounter many challenges as they make their way through primary treatment, hoping to return to their "normal" lives that will be forever altered by their experiences of cancer diagnosis and treatment. Recent research suggests that even long-term survivors commonly report lingering fears and physical fragility (Bower et al., 2005; Demark-Wahnefried, Aziz, Rowland, & Pinto, 2005). However, survivorship also presents opportunities for individuals to transform their experiences and create a more meaningful life (Jim, Richardson, Golden-Kreutz, & Andersen, 2006).

Spirituality

Efforts to define the constructs of religion and spirituality and to distinguish between them have proliferated in recent years (e.g., WHOQOL SRPB Group, 2006; Zinnbauer & Pargament, 2005). Although consensus appears unlikely, one reasonable solution was advanced by Zinnbauer and Pargament (2005) in which *spirituality*, proposed to be the superordinate construct, is defined as "a personal or group search for the sacred" (p. 35). *Religiousness* is defined as a search for the sacred "that unfolds within a traditional sacred context" (p. 35); thus, spirituality is often but not always expressed through religiousness. In this chapter, the term *spirituality* is used to denote this broader search, although *religiousness* is used to describe constructs explicitly derived from traditional sacred contexts.

Although not all individuals are religious or spiritual, religion and spirituality appear to form a central part of the meaning systems of many individuals (Park, 2005; Silberman, 2005), influencing their global beliefs (McIntosh, 1995; Ozorak, 2005), goals (Emmons, 2005), and sense of meaning in life (Steger & Frazier, 2005). Surveys of large-scale, nationally representative samples reflect the high prevalence of religious beliefs and behaviors in the United States. For example, a recent poll found that 92% of Americans believe in God or a universal spirit, 90% pray, 85% say religion is very or fairly important to them, and 41% attend religious services weekly or more often (Gallup, 2007; cited in Slattery & Park, in press). Although studies conducted in other countries have reported lower levels of religion and spirituality than those found in the United States, they are still fairly high (e.g., Hank & Schaan, 2008; WHOQOL SRPB Group, 2006; Williams & Sternthal, 2007). Religion and spirituality have been documented as important to cancer survivors all over the world. For example, see studies from Israel (Baider et al., 1999), India (Thombre, Sherman, & Simonton, 2010), and Australia (Boscaglia, Clarke, Jobling, & Quinn, 2005).

CANCER SURVIVORSHIP

In recent years, the term *survivor* has become widely used to refer to individuals who have experienced cancer. This term was chosen with great care by the National Coalition for Cancer Survivorship to explicitly promote empowerment of those with cancer. Through both public health and public relations efforts, survivorship has come to denote the state or process of living after a diagnosis of cancer, regardless of how long a person lives (National Cancer Institute [NCI], 2011a). By this definition, a person is considered to be a cancer survivor at the point of diagnosis and remains a survivor throughout treatment and through the rest of his or her life (NCI, 2011a). There are an estimated 12 million cancer survivors in the United States, representing approximately 4% of the U.S. population (NCI, 2011b), and an estimated 25 million survivors worldwide (Stull, Snyder, & Demark-Wahnefried, 2007). Many survivors are in longer term survivorship; approximately 14% of cancer survivors in the United States were diagnosed over 20 years ago (NCI, 2011b).

The different phases of the cancer experience have been described as living with cancer, living through cancer, and living beyond cancer (Anderson, 2011; Mullan, 1985); in each phase, the cancer survivor faces different stresses and may experience different emotional responses. The first phase, *living with cancer*, refers to the time of diagnosis and active treatment. Fear, anxiety, and pain resulting from both illness and treatment are common. While individuals are in primary treatment, the cancer experience often becomes life's central focus, involving intensive and immediate coping with medical issues, decision making, and the many chaotic emotions that ensue, including fear, hope, pain, and grief (Ganz et al., 2004).

The second phase, *living through cancer*, refers to the time following remission or treatment completion. Transitioning from primary treatment, although a relief in many ways, is often highly stressful in its own right, due in part to reduced frequency of visits with and access to medical providers, change in daily routines, adjustment to cancer- and treatment-related physical limitations, and uneasiness about being on one's own (Ganz et al., 2004; Hewitt, Greenfield, & Stovall, 2005; Holland & Reznik, 2005). In terms of their psychology, survivors are often in a state of watchful waiting, with high fears of recurrence (Lethborg, Kissane, Burns, & Snyder, 2000; Tross & Holland, 1989).

The third phase, *living beyond cancer*, refers to a time when the "activity of the disease or likelihood of its return is sufficiently small that the cancer can now be considered permanently arrested" (Mullan, 1985, p. 272). Even when survivors reach this phase, they may continue to experience a sense of vulnerability, fears of recurrence, and psychosocial problems related to their cancer experience (Bower et al., 2005).

Spirituality, Meaning Making, and Cancer

The literature on cancer survivors and spirituality has proliferated in recent years (for reviews, see Lavery & O'Hea, 2010; Sherman & Simonton, 2007; Stefanek et al., 2005; Thuné-Boyle, Stygall, Keshtgar, & Newman, 2006), and it is clear that spirituality often plays a pervasive role in the lives of those with cancer. To date, however, little of this research has been conducted explicitly from a meaning-making perspective. The following review highlights what is known about spirituality and meaning making in the context of cancer survivorship; as the review makes clear, this is an area with more questions than answers.

Religion and Global Meaning in Cancer Survivors

Prediagnosis, the global meanings of people who go on to develop cancer would not be expected to differ from those of the general population. However, at diagnosis, individuals' precancer religiousness and spirituality will likely influence the situational meaning the individuals assign to their cancer, including its appraised meaning and the extent to which global meaning is violated by that meaning. Some studies have found that global religious beliefs are related to the ways that cancer patients approach their illness. For example, one study of patients in treatment for a variety of cancers that focused on the role of religious beliefs (e.g., "I believe that God will not give me a burden I cannot carry") found that although beliefs were not directly related to psychological adjustment, those with higher religious beliefs had a higher sense of efficacy in coping with their cancer, which was related to higher levels of well-being (Howsepian & Merluzzi, 2009). Similarly, a study of breast cancer survivors found that women who viewed God as benevolent and involved in their lives appraised their cancer as more of a challenge and an opportunity to grow (Gall, 2000).

Religious beliefs about God's role in suffering, also known as *theodicies*, may also play an important role in how patients deal with their cancer. One study identified five types of theodicy beliefs: that their suffering is God's punishment for sinful behavior, that they will become a better person as a consequence of their suffering, that a reward for suffering will come in Heaven, that God has a reason for suffering that cannot be explained, and that by suffering with illness, one shares in the suffering of Christ (Moschella, Pressman, Pressman, & Weissman, 1997). To date, no research has examined how these different theodicies influence coping with and adjustment to cancer, but recently developed theodicy measurement tools should facilitate this effort.

Research examining global religious or spiritual goals and reactions to cancer is virtually nonexistent. In research on people living with other serious chronic and life-limiting illnesses, sanctified goals were related to higher levels of well-being (Emmons, 2005); similar relations may be observed for those living with cancer, although this link remains to be empirically established.

Religion and Appraised Meaning in Cancer Survivorship

People appraise the meaning of their cancer diagnosis based on the information they receive from their health care providers, their understanding of the disease of "cancer," and their appraisals of their ability to manage the illness and its perceived impact on their future life and lifestyle (Leventhal et al., 2008). Research indicates that the meanings that survivors assign to their cancer experience predict not only their coping and subsequent adjustment but also their treatment-related decisions and ultimate physical well-being (e.g., Bickell, Weidmann, Fei, Lin, & Leventhal, 2009; Bjorck, Hopp, & Jones, 1999). However, the roles of religiousness and spirituality in the appraised meaning of cancer have been minimally examined.

Studies assessing the associations of religious causal attributions and control appraisals with well-being in cancer survivors have produced mixed results. In a sample of recently diagnosed cancer patients receiving chemotherapy, appraisals that God was in control of the cancer and that the cancer was due to chance were related to higher self-esteem and lower distress regarding the cancer, and control attributions to self, natural causes, and other people were unrelated (Jenkins & Pargament, 1988). A study focusing more specifically on different types of religious attributions in a sample of young to middle-aged adult survivors of various cancers found that attributing the cancer to an angry or punishing God was related to more anger at God and poorer psychological adjustment (Exline, Park, Smyth, & Carey, 2011). However, in a sample of prostate cancer survivors, causal attributions to God, regardless of their negative (God's anger) or positive (God's love) nature, were related to poorer quality of life. In addition, prostate cancer survivors who had a more benevolent relationship with God reported experiencing lower perceived control over their health.

Different types of cancer may elicit different types of causal attributions. Costanzo, Lutgendorf, Bradley, Rose, and Anderson (2005) proposed that women with gynecological cancers were less likely to attribute their cancer to specific causes and more likely to attribute their cancer to chance or God's will, perhaps because of the lack of information on environmental or behavioral causes of gynecological cancer. In that study of gynecological cancer survivors, God's will was mentioned as a factor contributing to the development of cancer by 39% of the sample, ranking third behind genetics/heredity and stress. Further, in the factors perceived to prevent a cancer recurrence, prayer was mentioned by 90% of the sample, ranking third behind medical checkups and a positive attitude. God's will, assessed as a separate factor, was mentioned by 69% of the sample. These appraisals were related the survivors' later health behaviors, illustrating the importance of the appraised meaning of the cancer (Costanzo et al., 2005).

Although very little quantitative research has examined religious aspects of coping efficacy, qualitative research suggests that patients facing cancer who appraise their situation as aligned with their spiritual life perceive a stronger ability to cope with their cancer as well as a powerful sense of relief and comfort (e.g., Gall & Cornblat, 2002). Howsepian and Merluzzi (2009) assessed cancer patients' appraisal of their cancer as part of their spiritual life with the item "I believe because God is with me in very difficult times; these difficult times will contribute to my well-being either in this life or the afterlife"; results suggested that although not directly related to psychological adjustment, this appraisal was related to patients' sense of efficacy in coping with their cancer, which was related to well-being.

Religion and Discrepancy Between Global and Situational Meaning in Cancer Survivors

The meaning-making model proposes not only that appraised meaning is related to adjustment but, further, that the *discrepancy* between appraised and global meaning is the cause of distress. That is, the more that individuals' assigned meanings of their cancer diagnosis violate their beliefs and goals, the more resultant distress they will experience. Receiving a diagnosis of cancer can violate important global beliefs, such as in the fairness, benevolence, and controllability of the world, as well as one's own sense of invulnerability and personal control (Holland & Reznik, 2005; Lepore, 2001). Further, having cancer almost invariably violates individuals' goals for their current lives and their plans for the future (Carver, 2005). Aspects of religious global meaning, such as beliefs in a loving God, may be violated (Gall, 2004). Different types of cancer and the specifics of an individual's illness (e.g., prognosis) likely influence the situational meaning given and the extent of discrepancy with global meaning (e.g., McBride, Clipp, Peterson, Lipkus, & Demark-Wahnefried, 2000), although very little research has yet examined these issues.

The extent to which having cancer is perceived as inconsistent with global beliefs about identity (e.g., I live a healthy lifestyle) and health (e.g., living a healthy lifestyle protects people from illness) and with global goals (e.g., desire to live a long time with robust health and without disability) determines the extent to which the diagnosis is distressing (e.g., Nordin, Wasteson, Hoffman, Glimelius, & Sjödén, 2001). This link between discrepancy of appraised and global meaning with adjustment in cancer survivorship has rarely been directly examined, and the ways that religiousness or spirituality may be implicated in the appraisal of discrepancy are unknown at this point. The role of existential belief violation was explored in a longitudinal study of survivors of various cancers, which found that the extent to which survivors appraised cancer as violating their beliefs in a just world was negatively related to their psychological well-being across the year of the study (Park et al., 2008). However, spirituality was not included in those analyses; research that more directly addresses discrepancy as a central component of the meaning-making model and the roles played by religion and spirituality is needed.

Religion and Meaning-Making Processes in Cancer Survivorship

Researchers have posited that meaning-making efforts are essential to adjustment by helping survivors either to assimilate the cancer experience into their preexisting global meaning or to change their global meaning to accommodate it (Lepore, 2001). Indeed, it is hard to imagine that survivors could get through a cancer experience without some reconsideration of their lives vis-à-vis cancer (Moadel et al., 1999; Schroevers, Ranchor, & Sanderman, 2004; Taylor, 1983; Tomich & Helgeson, 2002). Meaning making can be attempted in many different ways, and it often involves religious and spiritual methods. For example, people can redefine their cancer experience as an opportunity for spiritual growth or as a punishment from God, or they may reappraise whether God has control in their lives or even whether God exists (Exline & Rose, in press). Researchers typically assess religious meaning making with subscales from Pargament's RCOPE measure (Pargament, Koenig, & Perez, 2000), which includes a benevolent religious reappraisal subscale (sample item: "Saw my situation as part of God's plan") as a component of positive religious coping and a punishing God reappraisal subscale (sample item: "Decided that God was punishing me for my sins") as a component of negative religious coping.

Studies of people dealing with cancer have generally indicated that positive religious coping is weakly and inconsistently related to adjustment and well-being in cancer survivorship (Lavery & O'Hea, 2010; Thuné-Boyle et al., 2006). In contrast, negative religious coping, although less frequently used, tends to be strongly and consistently associated with poorer adjustment and quality of life (e.g., Sherman, Plante, Simonton, Latif, & Anaissie, 2009; Zwingmann, Wirtz, Muller, Korber, & Murken, 2006). However, very few studies of coping with cancer have separated out the religious meaning-focused coping subscales from other types of positive or negative religious coping or examined the resultant meanings made through meaning making. Further, different types of spiritual and religious coping efforts may be differentially related to well-being depending on the particular phase under study, although very few studies have examined spirituality and meaning making across phases. An important exception, a prospective study of breast cancer patients from prediagnosis to 2 years postsurgery (Gall, Guirguis-Younger, Charbonneau, & Florack, 2009), found that religious coping strategies changed significantly over time. During particularly high stress points, such as presurgery, religious coping strategies that provided comfort, such as active surrender of control to God, were highest; religious coping processes reflecting meaning making remained elevated or increased over time (Gall et al., 2009).

Religious Meanings Made From the Cancer Experience

Through the meaning-making process, survivors often make changes in how they understand their situation vis-à-vis their cancer (changed appraised meaning). They may also make changes in their global beliefs and goals. Not all of these changes have a religious aspect, but many do. For example, through meaning making, survivors may revise their initial understanding of their cancer; these reappraised meanings may be of a religious nature. Summarizing findings from a qualitative study of breast cancer survivors, Gall and Cornblat (2002) noted,

> When used in the creation of meaning, relationship with God allowed some women to reframe the cancer from a disruptive, crisis event to a "blessing" and a "gift." These women believed that the cancer served some Divine purpose in their lives and so they were better able to accept it. (p. 531)

At this point, little quantitative research on reappraised religious meanings has been conducted.

People are thought to make meaning of stressful experiences primarily by changing the meaning of those experiences (i.e., their situational meaning); however, violations of global meaning are sometimes too great to be assimilated, and accommodation processes, which produce changes in global meaning, are relied upon (Janoff-Bulman & Frantz, 1997). The global meaning change most studied among cancer survivors is that of stress-related growth, positive changes people report experiencing as the result of stressful encounters (Park, 2009). Some survivors have reported profound growth, reorienting their lives and rededicating themselves to their reconsidered priorities. For others, the growth involves smaller changes, such as being more intimate with loved ones, handling stress more effectively, taking better care of themselves, seeing their own identities more clearly, feeling closer to God, being more appreciative of the aspects of everyday life, and having the courage to try new things (Park, 2009).

Many religious traditions contend that suffering is an important aspect of human life that is essential for developing character, compassion, a base of life experience, and deeper spirituality (Aldwin, 2007). One of the most consistent findings regarding predictors of positive life change following cancer is that religiousness, assessed by many different dimensions such as intrinsic religious motivation and religious coping, strongly predicts reports of growth (e.g., Park, Edmondson, & Blank, 2009; Thombre et al., 2010).

Further, this stress-related growth is often religious in nature. For example, research has demonstrated that following a stressful encounter, many people report feeling closer to God, more certain of their faith, and more religious; they often report using more religious coping and increasing their commitment to their religion and their involvement in their religious community as well as behaving more compassionately and having more spiritual meaning in their relationships with others and themselves (e.g., Cole, Hopkins, Tisak, Steel, & Carr, 2008). It should be noted that although this is less common, cancer survivors report spiritual decrements as well. For example, in a sample of survivors of various types of cancer, some reported having a diminished spiritual life and a loss of spiritual meaning as a result of their cancer experience (Cole et al., 2008).

SUMMARY AND DIRECTIONS FOR FUTURE RESEARCH

The meaning-making model is a useful framework for considering the ways in which spirituality influences survivors' responses and adjustment to their cancer experience, and this brief literature review reveals myriad linkages between survivors' spirituality and their meaning making. However, this review also makes clear that a great deal of further research is needed to better understand these linkages. There are many gaps in the literature, areas that are completely unexamined at this point. For example, no studies to date have tracked the spiritual and secular meanings of cancer over time and phases of survivorship, let alone the coping process and other determinants of the changes in those meanings. In addition, most researchers focused on spiritual aspects of meaning making in cancer survivorship have relied on cross-sectional, correlational designs, which has created severe limitations in their ability to make causal inferences. Although many of their findings are consistent with the meaning-making model, the influences among these variables are likely to be multidirectional; further, many links may be due to underlying (and unmeasured) third variables. For example, people higher in optimism may report both more benevolent views of God or spiritual growth and higher levels of psychological well-being.

Future research examining links between spirituality and meaning making in cancer survivors must use more sophisticated approaches, including longitudinal designs and thoughtful assessment of all of the components of meaning making, including global meaning, appraisals of the cancer, perceptions of violations of global meaning, meaning-making processes, and meanings made (Park, 2010). Such prescriptions may seem like a tall order, but without such careful and comprehensive study, an incomplete and distorted view of spirituality and meaning making in cancer survivorship will prevail.

In addition, researchers should attend to the differences among cancer survivors, including their personal characteristics, their disease, and their context. For example, spirituality may have very different influences on meaning making based on the specific aspects of that spirituality, such as religious traditions and affiliation and perceived closeness to God. The centrality of spirituality relative to other influences on an individual's meaning system may also have important influences on meaning making. For example, religious and secular social support may undermine or reinforce a survivor's spiritual meaning-making pathways. Cancer comprises not a single disease but many (NCI, 2011c), and every cancer patient has a very specific diagnosis and prognosis. Different types of cancer and different severity levels may influence the meanings assigned to the cancer and the types of reappraisals people make of their cancer. Studies tend to focus on survivors at a particular phase of survivorship (e.g., at diagnosis, during treatment, in long-term survivorship); spiritual influences on meaning making during these phases are likely quite different (Lavery & O'Hea, 2010). Research would ideally follow people through the course of diagnosis and treatment through long-term survivorship, but such studies are very rare (cf. Gall et al., 2009).

Spirituality is clearly an important aspect of the meaning making of many cancer survivors around the world. Although much remains to be learned, the research to date is strong enough to demonstrate that researchers and clinicians must attend to the spiritual aspects of cancer patients' and survivors' experiences. Such an understanding will likely lead to clinical interventions for cancer patients and survivors (e.g., Cole & Pargament, 1999). More important, it may lead to increased awareness of, sensitivity to, and understanding of the experience of making meaning in the context of a frightening, life-threatening disease.

REFERENCES

Aldwin, C. M. (2007). *Stress, coping, and development: An integrative approach* (2nd ed.). New York, NY: Guilford Press.

Anderson, M. D. (2011). Stages of cancer survivorship. Retrieved from http://www.mdanderson.org/patient-and-cancer-information/cancer-information/cancer-topics/survivorship/stages-of-cancer-survivorship/index.html

Baider, L., Russak, S. M., Perry, S., Kash, K., Gronert, M., Fox, B., . . . Kaplan-Denour, A. (1999). The role of religious and spiritual beliefs in coping with malignant melanoma: An Israeli sample. *Psycho-Oncology, 8,* 27–35. doi:10.1002/(SICI)1099-1611(199901/02)8:1<27::AID-PON334>3.0.CO;2-V

Bickell, N. A., Weidmann, J., Fei, K., Lin, J. J., & Leventhal, H. (2009). Underuse of breast cancer adjuvant treatment: Patient knowledge, beliefs, and medical mistrust. *Journal of Clinical Oncology, 27,* 5160–5167. doi:10.1200/JCO.2009.22.9773

Bjorck, J. P., Hopp, D., & Jones, L. W. (1999). Prostate cancer and emotional functioning: Effects of mental adjustment, optimism, and appraisal. *Journal of Psychosocial Oncology, 17,* 71–85. doi:10.1300/J077v17n01_05

Boscaglia, N., Clarke, D. M., Jobling, T. W., & Quinn, M. A. (2005). The contribution of spirituality and spiritual coping to anxiety and depression in women with a recent diagnosis of gynecological cancer. *International Journal of Gynecological Cancer, 15,* 755–761. doi:10.1111/j.1525-1438.2005.00248.x

Bower, J. E., Meyerowitz, B. E., Desmond, K. A., Bernaards, C. A., Rowland, J. H., & Ganz, P. A. (2005). Perceptions of positive meaning and vulnerability following breast cancer: Predictors and outcomes among long-term breast cancer survivors. *Annals of Behavioral Medicine, 29,* 236–245. doi:10.1207/s15324796abm2903_10

Calhoun, L. G., & Tedeschi, R. G. (2006). *Handbook of posttraumatic growth: Research and practice.* Mahwah, NJ: Erlbaum.

Carver, C. S. (2005). Enhancing adaptation during treatment and the role of individual differences. *Cancer, 104,* 2602–2607. doi:10.1002/cncr.21247

Cole, B. S., Hopkins, C. M., Tisak, J., Steel, J. L., & Carr, B. I. (2008). Assessing spiritual growth and spiritual decline following a diagnosis of cancer: Reliability and validity of the Spiritual Transformation Scale. *Psycho-Oncology, 17,* 112–121. doi:10.1002/pon.1207

Cole, B., & Pargament, K. (1999). Re-creating your life: A spiritual/psychotherapeutic intervention for people diagnosed with cancer. *Psycho-Oncology, 8,* 395–407. doi:10.1002/(SICI)1099-1611(199909/10)8:5<395::AID-PON408>3.0.CO;2-B

Collie, K., & Long, B. C. (2005). Considering "meaning" in the context of breast cancer. *Journal of Health Psychology, 10,* 843–853. doi:10.1177/1359105305057318

Costanzo, E. S., Lutgendorf, S. K., Bradley, S. L., Rose, S. L., & Anderson, B. (2005). Cancer attributions, distress, and health practices among gynecologic cancer survivors. *Psychosomatic Medicine, 67,* 972–980. doi:10.1097/01.psy.0000188402.95398.c0

Demark-Wahnefried, W., Aziz, N. M., Rowland, J. H., & Pinto, B. M. (2005). Riding the crest of the teachable moment: Promoting long-term health after the diagnosis of cancer. *Journal of Clinical Oncology, 23,* 5814–5830. doi:10.1200/JCO.2005.01.230

Dittmann-Kohli, F., & Westerhof, G. J. (2000). The personal meaning system in a life-span perspective. In G. T. Reker & K. Chamberlain (Eds.), *Exploring existential meaning: Optimizing human development across the lifespan* (pp. 107–122). Thousand Oaks, CA: Sage. doi:10.4135/9781452233703.n8

Emmons, R. A. (2003). *The psychology of ultimate concerns: Motivation and spirituality in personality*. New York, NY: Guilford Press.

Emmons, R. A. (2005). Striving for the sacred: Personal goals, life meaning, and religion. *Journal of Social Issues, 61*, 731–745. doi:10.1111/j.1540-4560.2005.00429.x

Exline, J. J., Park, C. L., Smyth, J. M., & Carey, M. P. (2011). Anger toward God: Social-cognitive predictors, prevalence, and links with adjustment to bereavement and cancer. *Journal of Personality and Social Psychology, 100*, 129–148. doi:10.1037/a0021716

Exline, J. J., & Rose, E. D. (in press). Religious and spiritual struggles. In R. F. Paloutzian & C. Park (Eds.), *Handbook of the psychology of religion and spirituality* (2nd ed.). New York, NY: Guilford Press.

Gall, T. (2000). Integrating religious resources within a general model of stress and coping: Long-term adjustment to breast cancer. *Journal of Religion and Health, 39*, 167–182. doi:10.1023/A:1004670717144

Gall, T. L. (2004). Relationship with God and the quality of life of prostate cancer survivors. *Quality of Life Research, 13*, 1357–1368. doi:10.1023/B:QURE.0000040789.49691.59

Gall, T. L., & Cornblat, M. W. (2002). Breast cancer survivors give voice: A qualitative analysis of spiritual factors in long-term adjustment. *Psycho-Oncology, 11*, 524–535. doi:10.1002/pon.613

Gall, T. L., Guirguis-Younger, M., Charbonneau, C., & Florack, P. (2009). The trajectory of religious coping across time in response to the diagnosis of breast cancer. *Psycho-Oncology, 18*, 1165–1178. doi:10.1002/pon.1495

Gallup. (2007). *Questions and answers about Americans' religion*. Retrieved from http://www.gallup.com/poll/103459/Questions-Answers-About-Americans-Religion.aspx

Ganz, P. A., Kwan, L., Stanton, A. L., Krupnick, J. L., Rowland, J. H., Meyerowitz, B. E., . . . Belin, T. R. (2004). Quality of life at the end of primary treatment of breast cancer: First results from the moving beyond cancer randomized trial. *Journal of the National Cancer Institute, 96*, 376–387. doi:10.1093/jnci/djh060

Gillies, J., & Neimeyer, R. A. (2006). Loss, grief, and the search for significance: Toward a model of meaning reconstruction in bereavement. *Journal of Constructivist Psychology, 19*, 31–65. doi:10.1080/10720530500311182

Greenberg, M. A. (1995). Cognitive processing of traumas: The role of intrusive thoughts and reappraisals. *Journal of Applied Social Psychology, 25*, 1262–1296. doi:10.1111/j.1559-1816.1995.tb02618.x

Hank, K., & Schaan, B. (2008). Cross-national variations in the correlation between frequency of prayer and health among older Europeans. *Research on Aging, 30*, 36–54. doi:10.1177/0164027507307923

Hewitt, M., Greenfield, S., & Stovall, E. (Eds.). (2005). *From cancer patient to cancer survivor: Lost in transition*. Washington, DC: Institute of Medicine.

Holland, J. C., & Reznik, I. (2005). Pathways for psychosocial care of cancer survivors. *Cancer, 104*, 2624–2637. doi:10.1002/cncr.21252

Howsepian, B. A., & Merluzzi, T. V. (2009). Religious beliefs, social support, self-efficacy and adjustment to cancer. *Psycho-Oncology, 18*, 1069–1079. doi:10.1002/pon.1442

Janoff-Bulman, R. (1992). *Shattered assumptions: Towards a new psychology of trauma*. New York, NY: Free Press.

Janoff-Bulman, R., & Frantz, C. M. (1997). The impact of trauma on meaning: From meaningless world to meaningful life. In M. Power & C. Brewin (Eds.), *The transformation of meaning in psychological therapies: Integrating theory and practice* (pp. 91–106). Hoboken, NJ: Wiley.

Jenkins, R. A., & Pargament, K. I. (1988). Cognitive appraisals in cancer patients. *Social Science & Medicine, 26*, 625–633. doi:10.1016/0277-9536(88)90027-5

Jim, H. S., Richardson, S. A., Golden-Kreutz, D. M., & Andersen, B. L. (2006). Strategies used in coping with a cancer diagnosis predict meaning in life for survivors. *Health Psychology, 25*, 753–761. doi:10.1037/0278-6133.25.6.753

Joseph, S., & Linley, P. A. (2005). Positive adjustment to threatening events: An organismic valuing theory of growth through adversity. *Review of General Psychology, 9*, 262–280. doi:10.1037/1089-2680.9.3.262

Karoly, P. (1999). A goal systems-self-regulatory perspective on personality, psychopathology, and change. *Review of General Psychology, 3*, 264–291. doi:10.1037/1089-2680.3.4.264

King, L. A., Hicks, J. A., Krull, J. L., & Del Gaiso, A. K. (2006). Positive affect and the experience of meaning in life. *Journal of Personality and Social Psychology, 90*, 179–196. doi:10.1037/0022-3514.90.1.179

Klinger, E. (1977). *Meaning and void: Inner experience and the incentives in people's lives*. Minneapolis: University of Minnesota Press.

Koltko-Rivera, M. E. (2004). The psychology of worldviews. *Review of General Psychology, 8*, 3–58. doi:10.1037/1089-2680.8.1.3

Lavery, M. E., & O'Hea, E. L. (2010). Religious/spiritual coping and adjustment in individuals with cancer: Unanswered questions, important trends, and future directions. *Mental Health, Religion & Culture, 13*, 55–65. doi:10.1080/13674670903131850

Lazarus, R. S., & Folkman, S. (1984). *Stress, appraisal, and coping*. New York, NY: Springer.

Lee, V., Cohen, S. R., Edgar, L., Laizner, A. M., & Gagnon, A. J. (2004). Clarifying "meaning" in the context of cancer research: A systematic literature review. *Palliative & Supportive Care, 2*, 291–303. doi:10.1017/S1478951504040386

Lee, V., Cohen, S. R., Edgar, L., Laizner, A. M., & Gagnon, A. J. (2006). Meaning-making intervention during breast or colorectal cancer treatment improves self-esteem, optimism, and self-efficacy. *Social Science & Medicine, 62*, 3133–3145. doi:10.1016/j.socscimed.2005.11.041

Lepore, S. J. (2001). A social–cognitive processing model of emotional adjustment to cancer. In A. Baum & B. L. Anderson (Eds.), *Psychosocial interventions for cancer* (pp. 99–116). Washington, DC: American Psychological Association. doi:10.1037/10402-006

Lethborg, C. E., Kissane, D., Burns, W. I., & Snyder, R. (2000). "Cast adrift": The experience of completing treatment among women with early stage breast cancer. *Journal of Psychosocial Oncology, 18*, 73–90. doi:10.1300/J077v18n04_05

Leventhal, H., Weinman, J., Leventhal, E. A., & Phillips, L. A. (2008). Health psychology: The search for pathways between behavior and health. *Annual Review of Psychology, 59*, 477–505. doi:10.1146/annurev.psych.59.103006.093643

Little, M., & Sayers, E. (2004). The skull beneath the skin: Cancer survival and awareness of death. *Psycho-Oncology, 13*, 190–198. doi:10.1002/pon.720

Manne, S., Ostroff, J., Fox, K., Grana, G., & Winkel, G. (2009). Cognitive and social processes predicting partner psychological adaptation to early stage breast cancer. *British Journal of Health Psychology, 14*, 49–68. doi:10.1348/135910708X298458

McBride, C. M., Clipp, E., Peterson, B. L., Lipkus, I. M., & Demark-Wahnefried, W. (2000). Psychological impact of diagnosis and risk reduction among cancer survivors. *Psycho-Oncology, 9*, 418–427. doi:10.1002/1099-1611(200009/10)9:5<418::AID-PON474>3.0.CO;2-E

McIntosh, D. N. (1995). Religion-as-schema, with implications for the relation between religion and coping. *International Journal for the Psychology of Religion, 5*, 1–16. doi:10.1207/s15327582ijpr0501_1

Moadel, A., Morgan, C., Fatone, A., Grennan, J., Carter, J., Laruffa, G., . . . Dutcher, J. (1999). Seeking meaning and hope: Self-reported spiritual and existential needs among an ethnically-diverse cancer patient population. *Psycho-Oncology, 8*, 378–385. doi:10.1002/(SICI)1099-1611(199909/10)8:5<378::AID-PON406>3.0.CO;2-A

Moos, R. H., & Holahan, C. J. (2007). Adaptive tasks and methods of coping with illness and disability. In E. Martz & H. Livneh (Eds.), *Coping with chronic illness and disability: Theoretical, empirical, and clinical aspects* (pp. 107–126). New York, NY: Springer. doi: 10.1007/978-0-387-48670-3_6

Moschella, V. D., Pressman, K. R., Pressman, P., & Weissman, D. E. (1997). The problem of theodicy and religious response to cancer. *Journal of Religion and Health, 36*, 17–20. doi:10.1023/A:1027432730591

Mullan, F. (1985). Seasons of survival: Reflections of a physician with cancer. *New England Journal of Medicine, 313*, 270–273. doi:10.1056/NEJM198507253130421

National Cancer Institute. (2011a). *Cancer survivorship research*. Retrieved from http://dccps.nci.nih.gov/ocs/definitions.html

National Cancer Institute. (2011b). *Prevalence*. Retrieved from http://dccps.nci.nih.gov/ocs/prevalence/prevalence.html#time

National Cancer Institute. (2011c). *What is cancer?* Retrieved from http://www.cancer.gov/cancertopics/cancerlibrary/what-is-cancer

Nordin, K., Wasteson, E., Hoffman, K., Glimelius, B., & Sjödén, P. O. (2001). Discrepancies between attainment and importance of life values and anxiety and depression in gastrointestinal cancer patients and their spouses. *Psycho-Oncology, 10,* 479–489. doi:10.1002/pon.536

Ozorak, E. W. (2005). Cognitive approaches to religion. In R. F. Paloutzian & C. L. Park (Eds.), *Handbook of the psychology of religion and spirituality* (pp. 216–234). New York, NY: Guilford Press.

Pakenham, K. I. (2007). Making sense of multiple sclerosis. *Rehabilitation Psychology, 52,* 380–389. doi:10.1037/0090-5550.52.4.380

Pargament, K. I. (1997). *The psychology of religion and coping: Theory, research, practice.* New York, NY: Guilford Press.

Pargament, K. I., Koenig, H. G., & Perez, L. M. (2000). The many methods of religious coping: Development and initial validation of the RCOPE. *Journal of Clinical Psychology, 56,* 519–543. doi:10.1002/(SICI)1097-4679(200004)56:4<519::AID-JCLP6>3.0.CO;2-1

Park, C. L. (2005). Religion and meaning. In R. F. Paloutzian & C. L. Park (Eds.), *Handbook of the psychology of religion and spirituality* (pp. 295–314). New York, NY: Guilford Press.

Park, C. L. (2009). Overview of theoretical perspectives. In C. L. Park, S. Lechner, M. H. Antoni, & A. Stanton (Eds.), *Medical illness and positive life change: Can crisis lead to personal transformation?* (pp. 11–30). Washington, DC: American Psychological Association.

Park, C. L. (2010). Making sense of the meaning literature: An integrative review of meaning making and its effects on adjustment to stressful life events. *Psychological Bulletin, 136,* 257–301. doi:10.1037/a0018301

Park, C. L., Armeli, S., & Tennen, H. (2004). Appraisal-coping goodness of fit: A daily Internet study. *Personality and Social Psychology Bulletin, 30,* 558–569. doi:10.1177/0146167203262855

Park, C. L., & Edmondson, D. (2012). Religion as a source of meaning. In P. Shaver & M. Mikulincer (Eds.), *Meaning, mortality, and choice: The social psychology of existential concerns* (pp. 145–162). Washington, DC: American Psychological Association. doi:10.1037/13748-008

Park, C. L., Edmondson, D., & Blank, T. O. (2009). Religious and non-religious pathways to stress-related growth in cancer survivors. *Applied Psychology: Health and Well-Being, 1,* 321–335. doi:10.1111/j.1758-0854.2009.01009.x

Park, C. L., Edmondson, D., Fenster, J. R., & Blank, T. O. (2008). Meaning making and psychological adjustment following cancer: The mediating roles of growth, life meaning, and restored just world beliefs. *Journal of Consulting and Clinical Psychology, 76,* 863–875. doi:10.1037/a0013348

Park, C. L., & Folkman, S. (1997). Meaning in the context of stress and coping. *Review of General Psychology, 1,* 115–144. doi:10.1037/1089-2680.1.2.115

Park, C. L., Folkman, S., & Bostrom, A. (2001). Appraisals of controllability and coping in caregivers and HIV+ men: Testing the goodness-of-fit hypothesis.

Journal of Consulting and Clinical Psychology, 69, 481–488. doi:10.1037/0022-006X.69.3.481

Park, C. L., Zlateva, I., & Blank, T. O. (2009). Self-identity after cancer: "Survivor," "victim," "patient," and "person with cancer." *Journal of General Internal Medicine, 24*(Suppl. 2), S430–S435. doi: 10.1007/s11606-009-0993-x

Peacock, E. J., & Wong, P. T. P. (1996). Anticipatory stress: The relation of locus of control, optimism, and control appraisals to coping. *Journal of Research in Personality, 30*, 204–222. doi:10.1006/jrpe.1996.0014

Reker, G. T., & Wong, P. T. P. (1988). Aging as an individual process: Toward a theory of personal meaning. In J. E. Birren & V. L. Bengston (Eds.), *Emergent theories of aging* (pp. 214–246). New York, NY: Springer.

Schroevers, M. J., Ranchor, A. V., & Sanderman, R. (2004). The role of age at the onset of cancer in relation to survivors' long-term adjustment: A controlled comparison over an eight-year period. *Psycho-Oncology, 13*, 740–752. doi:10.1002/pon.780

Segerstrom, S. C., Stanton, A. L., Alden, L. E., & Shortridge, B. E. (2003). A multidimensional structure for repetitive thought: What's on your mind, and how, and how much? *Journal of Personality and Social Psychology, 85*, 909–921. doi:10.1037/0022-3514.85.5.909

Sherman, A. C., Plante, T. G., Simonton, S., Latif, U., & Anaissie, E. J. (2009). Prospective study of religious coping among patients undergoing autologous stem cell transplantation. *Journal of Behavioral Medicine, 32*, 118–128. doi:10.1007/s10865-008-9179-y

Sherman, A. C., & Simonton, S. (2007). Spirituality and cancer. In T. G. Plante & C. E. Thoresen (Eds.), *Spirit, science, and health: How the spiritual mind fuels physical wellness* (pp. 157–175). Westport, CT: Praeger.

Silberman, I. (2005). Religion as a meaning system: Implications for the new millennium. *Journal of Social Issues, 61*, 641–663. doi:10.1111/j.1540-4560.2005.00425.x

Skaggs, B. G., & Barron, C. R. (2006). Searching for meaning in negative events: Concept analysis. *Journal of Advanced Nursing, 53*, 559–570. doi:10.1111/j.1365-2648.2006.03761.x

Slattery, J. M., & Park, C. L. (in press). Religious and spiritual beliefs in psychotherapy: A meaning perspective. In J. Aten, K. O'Grady, & E. V. Worthington (Eds.), *The psychology of religion and spirituality for clinicians: Using research in your practice*. New York, NY: Routledge.

Stefanek, M., McDonald, P. G., & Hess, S. A. (2005). Religion, spirituality and cancer: Current status and methodological challenges. *Psycho-Oncology, 14*, 450–463. doi:10.1002/pon.861

Steger, M. F. (2009). Meaning in life. In S. J. Lopez (Ed.), *Encyclopedia of positive psychology* (pp. 605–610). Oxford, England: Wiley-Blackwell.

Steger, M. F., & Frazier, P. (2005). Meaning in life: One link in the chain from religiousness to well-being. *Journal of Counseling Psychology, 52*, 574–582. doi:10.1037/0022-0167.52.4.574

Stull, V. B., Snyder, D. C., & Demark-Wahnefried, W. (2007). Lifestyle interventions in cancer survivors: Designing programs that meet the needs of this vulnerable and growing population. *Journal of Nutrition, 137,* 243S–248S. Retrieved from http://jn.nutrition.org/content/137/1/243S.short

Taylor, S. E. (1983). Adjustment to threatening events: A theory of cognitive adaptation. *American Psychologist, 38,* 1161–1173. doi:10.1037/0003-066X.38.11.1161

Thombre, A., Sherman, A. C., & Simonton, S. (2010). Religious coping and posttraumatic growth among family caregivers of cancer patients in India. *Journal of Psychosocial Oncology, 28,* 173–188. doi:10.1080/07347330903570537

Thompson, S. C., & Janigian, A. S. (1988). Life schemes: A framework for understanding the search for meaning. *Journal of Social and Clinical Psychology, 7,* 260–280. doi:10.1521/jscp.1988.7.2-3.260

Thuné-Boyle, I. C., Stygall, J. A., Keshtgar, M. R., & Newman, S. (2006). Do religious/spiritual coping strategies affect illness adjustment in patients with cancer? A systematic review of the literature. *Social Science & Medicine, 63,* 151–164. doi:10.1016/j.socscimed.2005.11.055

Tomich, P. L., & Helgeson, V. S. (2002). Five years later: A cross-sectional comparison of breast cancer survivors with healthy women. *Psycho-Oncology, 11,* 154–169. doi:10.1002/pon.570

Tross, S., & Holland, J. C. (1989). Psychological sequelae in cancer survivors. In J. C. Holland & J. H. Rowland (Eds.), *Handbook of psychooncology: Psychological care for the patient with cancer* (pp. 101–116). New York, NY: Oxford University Press. doi:10.1037/0278-6133.20.3.176

Weinstein, S. E., & Quigley, K. S. (2006). Locus of control predicts appraisals and cardiovascular reactivity to a novel active coping task. *Journal of Personality, 74,* 911–932. doi:10.1111/j.1467-6494.2006.00396.x

WHOQOL SRPB Group. (2006). A cross-cultural study of spirituality, religion, and personal beliefs as components of quality of life. *Social Science & Medicine, 62,* 1486–1497. doi:10.1016/j.socscimed.2005.08.001

Williams, D. R., & Sternthal, M. J. (2007). Spirituality, religion, and health: Evidence and research directions. *Medical Journal of Australia, 186,* S47–S50. Retrieved from https://www.mja.com.au/public/issues/186_10_210507/wil11060_fm.pdf

Wrosch, C., Scheier, M. F., Miller, G. E., Schulz, R., & Carver, C. S. (2003). Adaptive self-regulation of unattainable goals: Goal disengagement, goal reengagement, and subjective well-being. *Personality and Social Psychology Bulletin, 29,* 1494–1508. doi:10.1177/0146167203256921

Zinnbauer, B. J., & Pargament, K. I. (2005). Religiousness and spirituality. In R. F. Paloutzian & C. L. Park (Eds.), *Handbook of the psychology of religion and spirituality* (pp. 21–42). New York, NY: Guilford Press.

Zwingmann, C., Wirtz, M., Muller, C., Korber, J., & Murken, S. (2006). Positive and negative religious coping in German breast cancer patients. *Journal of Behavioral Medicine, 29,* 533–547. doi:10.1007/s10865-006-9074-3

14

FINDING SILVER LININGS: MEANING MAKING AS A COMPENSATORY RESPONSE TO NEGATIVE EXPERIENCES

JOANNA E. ANDERSON, AARON C. KAY, AND GRÁINNE M. FITZSIMONS

People do not proceed through their lives in a state of naive acceptance of everything they perceive and experience. Instead, their reality is shaped by a set of core beliefs about the self and the world. Over the years, researchers have described these important, fundamental beliefs in a variety of ways. They have been called "assumptive worlds," "general orienting systems," and "global meaning," among other things, but regardless of the terminology used, it is clear that researchers agree on the existence of a set of beliefs that guide an individual's life (Pargament, 1997; Park, 2010; Parkes, 1971; see also Chapter 13, this volume). Some aspects of these beliefs may be idiosyncratic—for instance, attachment theory's "working models" of self and other, which depend on the circumstances of one's childhood care (Bowlby, 1969)—whereas others, though held to varying degrees, appear to be relatively universal. Several of these universal beliefs involve ideas of fairness or justice; people seem to prefer to see themselves as existing within a system

DOI: 10.1037/14040-014
The Psychology of Meaning, Keith D. Markman, Travis Proulx, and Matthew J. Lindberg (Editors)

that operates fairly (Janoff-Bulman, 1992; Jost & Banaji, 1994; Lerner, 1980; see also Chapter 10, this volume). For example, system justification theory describes how, when people feel the current status quo cannot be changed, or would rather it did not, they will find ways to justify its unjust aspects. This generally entails believing the advantaged of society deserve what they have, and the underprivileged deserve their disadvantaged status and the bad things that happen to them (Jost & Banaji, 1994; Kay, Banfield, & Laurin, 2010). Doing so allows the individual to maintain beliefs in the fairness and justice of the system.

In this chapter, we review research investigating another method of dealing with evidence that bad things happen to decent people—evidence that contradicts one's fundamental beliefs. Specifically, we describe research demonstrating compensatory strategies that allow one to perceive negative outcomes as "balanced out" by other benefits to the victim. These strategies allow the perceiver to maintain his or her beliefs.

We begin with a review of the content of beliefs in the world as meaningful and just, and research on the psychological consequences of negative experiences for meaning making, then turn to research on the use of compensatory strategies specifically.

JUSTICE BELIEFS

Janoff-Bulman (1992) provided evidence that people possess three core beliefs or *fundamental assumptions* about reality. First, people tend to assume the world is a good place: They rate the benevolence of people and events quite positively (Janoff-Bulman, 1989). Second, they believe in the meaningfulness of the world. This is essentially a justice belief: People expect individuals' outcomes to be distributed according to what kind of people they are. In other words, people believe in a just world, one in which "people get what they deserve and deserve what they get" (Lerner, 1980). Finally, the third core belief is in one's own self-worth, as a good, capable, and moral person. This last point is perhaps the most contentious, given the universality of the need to maintain a positive self-view (see Boucher, 2010, for a review). At least in the Western world, however, self-esteem is typically high, and people assume they are better than average on numerous dimensions (e.g., Lerner, Somers, Reid, Chiriboga, & Tierney, 1991; Lovett, 1997; Svenson, 1981).

Together, these fundamental assumptions cohere around the notion that only good things happen to good people, and the self is good. These beliefs appear to provide a sense of the world as safe and controllable. Evidence from research on cognitive biases supports this conclusion. For example, people operate under an illusion of invulnerability to negative events and unrealistic optimism about positive events (Janoff-Bulman & Frieze, 1983; Janoff-Bulman, Madden, & Timko, 1983; Weinstein, 1980, 1982; Weinstein & Lachendro, 1982).

In the assumptive world created by Janoff-Bulman's core beliefs, the self is invincible. Thus, it is little surprise that when those beliefs are shaken, the focus turns to restoring them.

NEGATIVE EXPERIENCES THREATEN THE MEANINGFUL WORLD

Negative experiences typically contradict one or more of a person's fundamental assumptions. How can one continue to believe in the benevolence of the world when an infant dies of SIDS? How can one believe the world is meaningful and the self is worthy when that infant is one's own child?

In a model describing how people cope with trauma, Park (2010) labeled the psychological result of a discrepancy between the appraisal of a situation (e.g., as unjust) and global meaning systems (e.g., a belief in the world as benevolent) *distress*. This model bears some similarity to the theory of cognitive dissonance (Festinger, 1957), albeit grounded in a more specific psychological situation. Both models tell us that to reduce their psychological discomfort, people must resolve the conflict between their appraisal of the situation and their global beliefs, by changing one or the other. In the language of Park's model, this effort is an attempt at "meaning making," bringing meaning back to a world in which it was temporarily lost because of this psychological conflict. In cases where the discomfort-inducing situation is beyond one's personal control—for instance, when an innocent person is assaulted—changing the situation is not a plausible dissonance-reduction strategy. Given the fundamental nature of one's core beliefs, changing them is—arguably—not a plausible strategy either (for an opposing viewpoint, see Brandtstädter, 2002). Thus, reappraisal of the situation is likely to be the most tenable solution to reduce psychological discomfort.

Reappraising a victim's troubles as self-caused is one means of reappraising the situation. According to Hafer and Bègue (2005), researchers who study belief in a just world (Lerner, 1980) have focused their empirical efforts quite narrowly in this direction. The majority of studies have assigned their participants the role of observer, not experiencer, of an unjust, negative event, and have examined only one route for reducing discomfort: Most research has focused on the assignment of blame to victims. For instance, people who learn about innocent victims of layoff, sexual assault, or HIV tend to derogate the victims or blame them for their circumstances (V. N. Anderson, 1992; Karuza & Carey, 1984; Skarlicki, Ellard, & Kelln, 1998). By doing so, they are able to restore their belief that people deserve what they get. Thus, the world may be seen as benevolent and meaningful again.

The consequences of assigning blame to innocent victims are obvious. Not only does it have negative effects for the victim himself, it might also sway jury decision-making when deciding how to sentence an offender, or influence police behavior. For these reasons, victim derogation and blame have received a lot of empirical attention.

When the self is the victim, derogation would violate another of the fundamental assumptions, that the self is a good person. As a result, reappraisal of the situation may be more difficult and time consuming. Indeed, there is a wealth of evidence showing that traumatic life events cause distress and cause people to engage in efforts to reappraise (make meaning from) the situation (for a review, see Park, 2010). Although research on this topic has not been especially systematic nor experimentally rigorous, Park (2010) noted in her review of the literature documenting reactions to stressful events that meaning-making attempts were reported by most individuals facing highly stressful events (p. 290). Among those reported were a tendency for victims to ask "Why?" or "Why me?" and attempts at "making sense" of what happened (e.g., Eton, Lepore, & Helgeson, 2005; Silver, Boon, & Stones, 1983; Updegraff, Silver, & Holman, 2008; Uren & Wastell, 2002; see also Chapter 12, this volume).

Attempts at meaning making, when successful in providing an explanation for one's suffering, could be adaptive if they help one avoid a recurrence of *preventable* negative experiences. For instance, realizing that a car accident was one's own fault might serve as a painful lesson in the importance of driving safely or of not taking unnecessary risks. However, when an explanation is not forthcoming because the negative experience was not under personal control, an inability to find a meaningful explanation for one's suffering may become a source of further distress. If the car accident that left one with chronic pain was the fault of a drunk driver, there may be no satisfactory answer to the question "Why me?" Indeed, an unresolved search for meaning has been shown to lead to a host of unpleasant consequences, including alcohol abuse, symptoms of posttraumatic stress, and suicidal ideation (Heisel & Flett, 2004; Lecci, MacLean, & Croteau, 2002; Updegraff et al., 2008).

FINDING THE SILVER LINING: MOTIVATED PERCEPTION OF INCREASED POSITIVE OUTCOMES AS AN ALTERNATIVE TO VICTIM BLAMING

Although finding an explanation for a victim's suffering is one way to reduce discomfort, there are certainly others. For instance, although system justification theory has typically focused on the tendency to derogate the underprivileged of society, the system justification motive can also motivate people to restore their sense of meaning by finding a "silver lining" in the plight of the underprivileged (Kay, Banfield, & Laurin, 2010).

Groups that are disadvantaged relative to the majority group in society are often negatively stereotyped (e.g., older people as incompetent, working women as cold). For years, it was thought that derogating society's disadvantaged was the main way to maintain a view of the system as just in the face of obvious suffering and inequality. However, attributing offsetting positive traits to those individuals may serve the same goal. It may be for that reason that stereotypes are often bivalent, including a mix of positive and negative components (Glick & Fiske, 2001). People may be able to alleviate their discomfort at societal injustice by stereotyping older people as not only incompetent but also warm, and working women as not only cold but also competent.

As more direct evidence in support of this possibility, other research has found that people exposed to an exemplar of a poor person with a positive trait (e.g., happiness) felt the status quo was fairer, the system more justified, than did those exposed to a poor but unhappy exemplar (Kay & Jost, 2003; Kay, Jost, & Young, 2005). This finding seems to indicate that observers' belief in a meaningful world was satisfied by the mere presence of a positive trait, despite the fact that victims' poverty was not causally related to their level of happiness.

This work on system justification has focused on trait attributions. However, in recent research, we found support for the existence of other means to the same end. Specifically, this research suggests that observers may see victims as possessing more *meaningful* lives. In the first of two studies, people whose motivation to see the world as fair and meaningful was temporarily heightened perceived offsetting positive outcomes in the later life of a victim (J. E. Anderson, Kay, & Fitzsimons, 2010). Participants read a story about a target who either had or had not suffered a traumatic injury in high school, then wrote a paragraph about the target's later life. When their motivation to see the world as meaningful was heightened (by an article claiming success is based on connections, not merit), participants wrote life stories imbued with greater meaning and enjoyment for a target who had suffered than one who had not suffered, as rated by participants themselves and independent observers. Thus, when a core belief is sufficiently threatened, people will perceive a victim's later life to be more meaningful and enjoyable. This positive belief helps to balance the overall impact of the negative experience on the target and thus to mitigate its implications for the self.

In a second study, we examined whether a dispositional need to see the world as just would moderate these effects (J. E. Anderson et al., 2010). Although the fundamental assumptions proposed by Janoff-Bulman (1992) are presumed to be common to most people, they are held to varying degrees by different people. Participants reported the extent of their belief in the fairness and meaningfulness of the world using an abbreviated version of the Belief in Ultimate Justice Scale (BUJ; Schumann & Ross, 2010), a scale that measures belief in the tendency for goodness to be rewarded and badness to be punished. They then read one of the two stories from the previous study, about a target who did or did not suffer early in life, but for the purpose of this study, instead of leaving the ending open for participants to conclude, we concluded the story in a moderately positive way, and then asked participants to rate the amount of meaning and enjoyment they thought the target would get out of life. Participants high in BUJ reported perceiving more positive outcomes in the life of a target who had suffered than one who had not, despite the fact that the description of the target's life was held constant across conditions. Participants low in BUJ reported perceiving the target's outcomes no more positively than did participants high in BUJ, who believed the target had not suffered.

Together, these two studies provide evidence for a new response to threats to fundamental beliefs about the world. They suggest that perceiving positive outcomes—including meaning and enjoyment—in a victim's life can offset the threatening effects of perceiving the victim to have suffered for no reason. This perception, we posit, allows the perceiver to restore meaning to his or her own assumptive world.

THE SELF AS VICTIM: CAN MEANING EVER BE MADE IN THE ABSENCE OF PERSONAL CONTROL OVER THE EXPERIENCE?

Thus, observers can find meaning in the suffering of others. When the self is the victim, however, how do people react to a negative experience? As we posited earlier, finding an explanation or lesson learned is likely to be simpler if one had personal control over the experience—for instance, if one smoked and ate fatty foods and then had a heart attack. But what about common situations over which one has no control—for instance, the death of a loved one? Is it more difficult to make meaning out of such a situation as the victim or as an observer? On the one hand, it should be easier to interpret another person's life (relative to one's own) in whichever light one chooses, given the amount of additional information one possesses about oneself. On the other hand, a person should be particularly motivated to rationalize one's own suffering, as it is highly salient and threatening. We propose that it is possible, and perhaps even preferable, to engage compensatory rationalizations when coping with injustices to the self.

Indeed, research on system justification suggests that it may be possible. Jost and Kay (2005) showed that drawing attention to women's positive communal traits led other women to justify gender inequality in society, as though being reminded of their other positive qualities made female participants think that (often discriminatory) gender policies and roles in the United States were fairer. Similarly, research has shown that both men and women will self-stereotype in complementary ways when presented with information that threatens their perceptions of the fairness of their social system, and that those complementary self-stereotypes function to increase their perceptions of the system's legitimacy (Laurin, Kay, & Shepherd, 2011).

The literature on coping with trauma also suggests that victims of major negative experiences will sometimes attempt to *reappraise* their difficulties in a positive way. For instance, they may reinterpret them as challenges to be overcome, or in positive spiritual terms (Ano & Vasconcelles, 2005; Park & Fenster, 2004). Recently, more research has begun to examine questions of religious beliefs and beliefs in fate (e.g., Burrus & Roese, 2006; Norenzayan & Lee, 2010; see also Chapters 16 and 17, this volume). To the extent that God or Fate is seen as a benevolent force, belief may allow for the hope that one's suffering will be balanced out by rewards later in life, or in the afterlife. In addition, attributing one's suffering to a higher power protects one from the specter of randomness, the antithesis of meaning. Although doing so means acknowledging one's lack of direct control over the situation, it establishes *vicarious control*—that is, the feeling that one is associated with a powerful other who does exert control over the situation (Rothbaum, Weisz, & Snyder, 1982).

Evidence about the success of reappraisal coping as a general strategy is mixed, but some studies suggest it may lead to more positive outcomes (Park, 2010). Other studies have shown that a majority of people who have experienced adversity report finding at least some benefit in their experiences (Tennen & Affleck, 2002). For instance, bereaved individuals reported benefits such as strengthened family bonds and personal growth; similarly, men who suffered a first heart attack reported increased enjoyment of life and positive changes in their values (Affleck, Tennen, Croog, & Levine, 1987; Davis, Nolen-Hoeksema, & Larson, 1998).

Indeed, we contend that when the self is the victim, even minor, everyday negative experiences may activate a desire for rationalization or explanation. Negativity strongly impacts people's lives and drives attempts at explanation to a much greater extent than positive experiences (Baumeister, Bratslavsky, Finkenauer, & Vohs, 2001; Bohner, Bless, Schwarz, & Strack, 1988; Rozin & Royzman, 2001; Weiner, 1985; Wong & Weiner, 1981). It seems that people possess a basic need to find the cause of the bad things that happen to them—a need that may extend to even minor occurrences. After all, if one's core beliefs are correct, the self is good, and according to the principle of the world as benevolent and meaningful, bad things are not supposed to happen to good people.

Relatively little research has examined the day-to-day maintenance of a meaningful life in the face of negative experiences. Existing research has tended to focus on responses to major traumatic events, but such events are (thankfully) relatively rare. What about the more mundane day-to-day "tragedies" we all experience, such as losing a wallet or spilling food on a favorite pair of jeans? Although such events are not likely to cause much more than a ripple in one's faith that the world is a fair and meaningful place, we believe that even such minor threats to this fundamental belief can have important consequences, activating a motivation to rationalize one's suffering. Importantly, we further suggest that if that motivation produces a rationalization stronger than the opposing threat, a person's sense of meaning in life may actually increase from a presuffering baseline. In other words, people may possess an *if–then* contingency that looks something like this: "If suffering, then perceive increased meaning in life as a result." If the amount of meaning to be perceived is not precisely calibrated to the amount lost, one may overshoot the mark, resulting in a greater sense of meaning than was experienced before the threat.

Research on the theory of compensatory control provides support for the possibility of motivated compensation. Compensatory control theory states that people prefer to think of the world as nonrandom and controlled, and has shown that psychological systems exist to compensate for threats to personal control (Kay, Gaucher, Napier, Callan, & Laurin, 2008; Kay, Whitson, Gaucher, & Galinsky, 2009). For instance, when personal control is lacking, people may increase their support for external systems of control, using them as substitutes for internal control (Kay, Gaucher, McGregor, & Nash, 2010; Laurin, Kay, & Moscovitch, 2008). In this chapter, we have demonstrated that people prefer to think of the world as benevolent and meaningful; the existence of a parallel psychological system to compensate in the face of threats is very plausible. Such a system would demonstrate a similar flexibility: A perception of increased meaning in life after a negative experience might be perceived as substituting for the reduced positive affect that came of encountering the negative experience.

Why meaning? If the goal is to rationalize a negative experience, theoretically, any perceived benefit should do. However, the problem with many potentially compensatory perceptions is that negative experiences are almost synonymous with negative affect. Thus, perceiving benefits in one's own negative experiences is a challenge. In contrast, meaning is both more independent of negative affect and more esoteric: It is more difficult to "objectively" assess the meaningfulness of one's existence than it is one's happiness. As a side effect of this vagueness and of the difficulty of assessing meaning, we suggest that meaning in life may be especially susceptible to the influence of motivated perception. Its abstract nature makes it easier to interpret it in line with one's preferences. Given the remarkable flexibility people demonstrate in interpreting the events of their own lives in line with their goals and motivations (e.g., Dunning, Meyerowitz, & Holzberg, 1989; Murray & Holmes, 1993), we suggest that increasing perceptions of meaning in life after a negative experience may be a plausible rationalization strategy.

A wealth of previous research has demonstrated that traumatic experiences can shatter one's belief in the world as a meaningful place (see Park, 2010). In one's day-to-day life, however, minor catastrophes are commonplace. How do people maintain meaning in the face of these mundane negative experiences? We contend that although any negative experience may threaten meaning, the strength of the motivation to maintain their fundamental beliefs is more than sufficient to compensate for a minor threat. Indeed, in an ongoing line of research, we have collected data that support this assertion.

In this study (J. E. Anderson, Fitzsimons, & Kay, 2011), participants completed a baseline measure of meaning in life, the Life Regard Index (Battista & Almond, 1973), then participated in a series of activities, one of which involved eating several pieces of chocolate. For participants randomly assigned to the negative experience, the chocolate was extremely bitter baking chocolate; for those assigned to the positive experience, the chocolate was sweet milk chocolate. At the conclusion of the activities, participants indicated their enjoyment of the study as a whole, and again their feelings of meaning in life. The results indicated that experiencing something negative led participants to report less enjoyment in the experiment but more meaning in their lives, compared with participants who had a positive experience. Relative to baseline, meaning in the positive condition was unchanged, whereas meaning in the negative condition had increased. Thus, this study provides evidence that people perceived meaning in their lives to have increased following a negative experience.

MECHANISM: DISCOMFORT WITH INCONGRUENCE BETWEEN BELIEFS

Thus far, we have speculated but not shown that negative experiences can lead to an increase in meaning in one's own life because of a need to resolve the discomfort produced by the incongruence between beliefs that (a) the world is a fair and meaningful place, (b) the self is worthy of positive outcomes, and the knowledge that (c) the self experienced a negative outcome.

Two recent studies support the more specific claim that negative experiences produce discomfort as a result of the incongruence between cognitions, which can be resolved by perceiving increased meaning in life (J. E. Anderson et al., 2011). In short, we hypothesized that the increase in meaning is driven by a need to rationalize unexplained negative experiences (recall Chapter 1, this volume). In the first test of this hypothesis, we examined a chronic trait variable, Personal Need for Structure (PNS; Neuberg & Newsom, 1993). People high in PNS prefer a mode of existence low in ambiguity. Thus, if a negative experience casts doubt on the certainty of one's core beliefs, the resultant discomfort should be especially strong for people high in PNS. They should therefore be the people most likely to report increased meaning as compensation.

Participants completed the PNS scale (Neuberg & Newsom, 1993) and a single-item baseline measure of meaning in life ("I have a lot of meaning in my life"). They were then randomly assigned to describe a positive or negative memory from any time in their past. After reporting the memory, participants completed a package of questionnaires that included the Search subscale of the Meaning in Life Questionnaire (Steger, Frazier, Oishi, & Kaler, 2006; see also Chapter 11, this volume), a measure that examines the extent to which people are interested in finding meaning in their existence. An interaction between PNS and valence of memory was observed, such that participants who indicated a high PNS reported increased interest in meaning following the negative experience task (relative to the positive experience task). Participants low in PNS did not experience the same increase. These results held when controlling for baseline meaning scores, as well as the amount of control people felt they had over the events they reported.

These results suggest that having a high need for structure makes people especially likely to look for meaning in negative experiences, which in turn suggests that the increase in meaning is driven by a need to rationalize unexplained negative experiences. However, a second study more convincingly rules out alternative explanations.

If the propensity to perceive increased meaning in life after a negative experience is the result of a desire to justify one's suffering, providing participants with an external justification should eliminate the drive to rationalize. Under such circumstances, no increase in meaning should occur. In a paradigm similar to that used by Festinger (1957), we gave some participants monetary compensation for the negative experience we put them through in the laboratory. We expected these participants to see their experience as justified, insofar as they had a readily available reason for why they engaged in this negative experience, and thus not report increased meaning in life. We had participants look at negative photographs from the International Affective Picture System, such as a disabled toddler (Lang, Bradley, & Cuthbert, 2005). Half the participants were told beforehand that they would receive $5 for looking at them, and half were not. Participants in each condition examined 20 photographs, then assigned a monetary value to some of the meaningful aspects of their life (e.g., their own name). To the extent that these aspects were assigned high values, it suggests the participant considered the meaningful aspects of life important.

Results supported our proposed mechanism: Although they looked at the same negative photos, participants who received a compensatory payment reported less meaning in their lives—in this case, measured as assigning higher monetary values to their meaningful possessions—relative to participants who did not receive compensation.

In Festinger's (1957) seminal study, participants who were paid $20 to lie experienced no dissonance between their behavior and their knowledge, because the payment justified it. Participants who were paid only $1 did not see their actions as justified, so their feelings of dissonance changed their perceptions of the study to align with their behavior. In the study described here, participants who received $5 would have experienced no dissonance between their negative experience and their belief in the benevolence of the world because the payment balanced out the negative experience. Participants who did not receive money were forced to resolve the dissonance resulting from the conflict between their negative experience and their belief that the world is benevolent. Like Festinger's participants, they changed their perceptions of the negative experience to align with their beliefs—in this case, by perceiving a silver lining to the experience, in the form of increased meaning.

SUMMARY AND CONCLUDING REMARKS

Our goal in this chapter has been to demonstrate that negative experiences can sometimes have a positive effect on perceptions of meaning in one's own life—or the life of a victim—and that this happens because of a need to explain or justify those experiences. Doing so reduces the conflict between the experiences and one's beliefs about the benevolent and meaningful nature of the world.

The evidence presented in this chapter shows that perceiving benefits arising from negative experiences is not uncommon (Tennen & Affleck, 2002). Indeed, there may be another means of perceiving a silver lining that we have not yet discussed. Research on counterfactual thinking (i.e., thinking about hypothetical alternatives to one's current reality) has shown that downward counterfactuals are most common following uncontrollable and nonrepeating experiences, suggesting people use them to improve affect about their outcome (Markman, Gavanski, Sherman, & McMullen, 1993; Roese & Olson, 1995). In the case of negative experiences, this tendency may also serve as a kind of silver lining: "It may not have been fun, but it could easily have been worse." In related research, Kray et al. (2010; see also

Chapter 16, this volume) showed that counterfactual thinking increases the meaning associated with major life experiences. In combination, these two findings suggest counterfactual thinking as another route to increases in meaning following a negative experience.

The recent research by J. E. Anderson et al. (2010, 2011) suggests that the perception of benefits is motivated by needs proposed by Janoff-Bulman (1992): to see the world as benevolent and meaningful, and the self as worthy. When those needs are strong, people report that negative experiences increase meaning in their own lives as well as the lives of victims.

Previous research on the experiences of trauma victims has shown decreased meaning as a result of their suffering (e.g., Updegraff et al., 2008). Research on the reactions of observers to trauma victims has typically focused on a propensity to blame the victim (Hafer & Bègue, 2005). These new results represent a departure from both sets of findings. Thus, it is important to consider the specific circumstances under which one might expect to see those reactions, versus perceiving increased meaning in one's own or a target's life.

The stronger the threat (e.g., with more negative experiences, or self-experienced events rather than observed events), we propose, the less meaning one will experience as a result. If the defensive resources recruited in the face of threat are not calibrated to its degree, they are most likely to result in increased meaning (relative to baseline) when the threat is small and decreased meaning when the threat is large. This account allows for the finding that even victims of trauma often report benefits—sometimes including meaning benefits—as a result of their experiences, but on average feel less meaningful. A distinction can also be made between studies demonstrating victim derogation and our results showing increased perceptions of meaning and enjoyment, in terms of psychological proximity to the victim's difficulty. Previous research has examined immediate reactions to a victim of trauma whose plight is present and severe (e.g., Karuza & Carey, 1984). In the work we discuss here, by contrast, we examined reactions to a victim of trauma whose suffering was in the past, thereby rendering it less psychologically threatening to an observer. Victim derogation may be more likely when the threat is strong, but perceiving a compensatory meaning boost may be more likely when it is less strong.

Overall, the findings presented in this chapter point to the importance of compensatory benefit-finding as a strategy for dealing with threats to fundamental assumptions about the world (Janoff-Bulman, 1992). In particular, recent experimental findings demonstrate that meaning in life sometimes functions to compensate psychologically for an undeserved negative experience and preserve fundamental assumptions about the benevolence of the world.

REFERENCES

Affleck, G., Tennen, H., Croog, S., & Levine, S. (1987). Causal attribution, perceived benefits, and morbidity after a heart attack: An 8-year study. *Journal of Consulting and Clinical Psychology, 55*, 29–35. doi:10.1037/0022-006X.55.1.29

Anderson, J. E., Fitzsimons, G. M., & Kay, A. C. (2011). *Rationalizing your way to a meaningful life: The motivated increase in meaning after a negative experience*. Manuscript in preparation.

Anderson, J. E., Kay, A. C., & Fitzsimons, G. M. (2010). In search of the silver lining: The justice motive fosters perceptions of benefits in the later lives of tragedy victims. *Psychological Science, 21*, 1599–1604. doi:10.1177/0956797610386620

Anderson, V. N. (1992). For whom is this world just? Sexual orientation and AIDS. *Journal of Applied Social Psychology, 22*, 248–259. doi:10.1111/j.1559-1816.1992.tb01538.x

Ano, G. G., & Vasconcelles, E. (2005). Religious coping and psychological adjustment to stress: A meta-analysis. *Journal of Clinical Psychology, 61*, 461–480. doi:10.1002/jclp.20049

Battista, J., & Almond, R. (1973). The development of meaning in life. *Psychiatry: Journal for the Study of Interpersonal Processes, 36*, 409–427.

Baumeister, R. F., Bratslavsky, E., Finkenauer, C., & Vohs, K. D. (2001). Bad is stronger than good. *Review of General Psychology, 5*, 323–370. doi:10.1037/1089-2680.5.4.323

Bohner, G., Bless, H., Schwarz, N., & Strack, F. (1988). What triggers causal attributions? The impact of valence and subjective probability. *European Journal of Social Psychology, 18*, 335–345. doi:10.1002/ejsp.2420180404

Boucher, H. C. (2010). Understanding Western–East Asian differences and similarities in self-enhancement. *Social and Personality Psychology Compass, 4*, 304–317. doi:10.1111/j.1751-9004.2010.00266.x

Bowlby, J. (1969). *Attachment and loss: Vol. 1. Attachment*. New York, NY: Basic Books.

Brandtstädter, J. (2002). Searching for paths to successful development and aging: Integrating developmental and action-theoretical perspectives. In L. Pulkinnen & A. Caspi (Eds.), *Paths to successful development: Personality in the life course* (pp. 380–408). New York, NY: Cambridge University Press. doi:10.1017/CBO9780511489761.016

Burrus, J., & Roese, N. J. (2006). Long ago it was meant to be: The interplay between time, construal, and fate beliefs. *Personality and Social Psychology Bulletin, 32*, 1050–1058. doi:10.1177/0146167206288282

Davis, C. G., Nolen-Hoeksema, S., & Larson, J. (1998). Making sense of loss and benefiting from the experience: Two construals of meaning. *Journal of Personality and Social Psychology, 75*, 561–574. doi:10.1037/0022-3514.75.2.561

Dunning, D., Meyerowitz, J. A., & Holzberg, A. (1989). Ambiguity and self-evaluation: The role of idiosyncratic trait definitions in self-serving assessments of ability. *Journal of Personality and Social Psychology, 57*, 1082–1090. doi:10.1037/0022-3514.57.6.1082

Eton, D. T., Lepore, S. J., & Helgeson, V. S. (2005). Psychological distress in spouses of men treated for early-stage prostate carcinoma. *Cancer, 103*, 2412–2418. doi:10.1002/cncr.21092

Festinger, L. (1957). *A theory of cognitive dissonance*. Stanford, CA: Stanford University Press.

Glick, P., & Fiske, S. T. (2001). An ambivalent alliance: Hostile and benevolent sexism as complementary justifications of gender inequality. *American Psychologist, 56*, 109–118. doi:10.1037/0003-066X.56.2.109

Hafer, C. L., & Bègue, L. (2005). Experimental research on just-world theory: Problems, developments, and future challenges. *Psychological Bulletin, 131*, 128–167. doi:10.1037/0033-2909.131.1.128

Heisel, M. J., & Flett, G. L. (2004). Purpose in life, satisfaction with life, and suicide ideation in a clinical sample. *Journal of Psychopathology and Behavioral Assessment, 26*, 127–135. doi:10.1023/B:JOBA.0000013660.22413.e0

Janoff-Bulman, R. (1989). Assumptive worlds and the stress of traumatic events: Applications of the schema construct. *Social Cognition, 7*, 113–136. doi:10.1521/soco.1989.7.2.113

Janoff-Bulman, R. (1992). *Shattered assumptions: Towards a new psychology of trauma*. New York, NY: Free Press.

Janoff-Bulman, R., & Frieze, I. H. (1983). A theoretical perspective for understanding reactions to victimization. *Journal of Social Issues, 39*, 1–17. doi:10.1111/j.1540-4560.1983.tb00138.x

Janoff-Bulman, R., Madden, M., & Timko, C. (1983). Victims' reactions to aid: The role of perceived vulnerability. In A. Nadler, J. D. Fisher, & B. M. DePaulo (Eds.), *New directions in helping* (Vol. 3, pp. 21–42). New York, NY: Academic Press.

Jost, J. T., & Banaji, M. R. (1994). The role of stereotyping in system-justification and the production of false consciousness. *British Journal of Social Psychology, 33*, 1–27. doi:10.1111/j.2044-8309.1994.tb01008.x

Jost, J. T., & Kay, A. C. (2005). Exposure to benevolent sexism and complementary gender stereotypes: Consequences for specific and diffuse forms of system justification. *Journal of Personality and Social Psychology, 88*, 498–509. doi:10.1037/0022-3514.88.3.498

Karuza, J., Jr., & Carey, T. O. (1984). Relative preference and adaptiveness of behavioral blame for observers of rape victims. *Journal of Personality, 52*, 249–260. doi:10.1111/j.1467-6494.1984.tb00880.x

Kay, A. C., Banfield, J. C., & Laurin, K. (2010). The system justification motive and the maintenance of social power. In A. Guinote & T. Vescio (Eds.), *The social psychology of power* (pp. 313–340). New York, NY: Guilford Press.

Kay, A. C., Gaucher, D., McGregor, I., & Nash, K. (2010). Religious belief as compensatory control. *Personality and Social Psychology Review, 14*, 37–48. doi:10.1177/1088868309353750

Kay, A. C., Gaucher, D., Napier, J. L., Callan, M. J., & Laurin, K. (2008). God and the government: Testing a compensatory control mechanism for the support of external systems. *Journal of Personality and Social Psychology, 95*, 18–35. doi:10.1037/0022-3514.95.1.18

Kay, A. C., & Jost, J. T. (2003). Complementary justice: Effects of "poor but happy" and "poor but honest" stereotype exemplars on system justification and implicit activation of the justice motive. *Journal of Personality and Social Psychology, 85*, 823–837. doi:10.1037/0022-3514.85.5.823

Kay, A. C., Jost, J. T., & Young, S. (2005). Victim derogation and victim enhancement as alternate routes to system justification. *Psychological Science, 16*, 240–246. doi:10.1111/j.0956-7976.2005.00810.x

Kay, A. C., Whitson, J. A., Gaucher, D., & Galinsky, A. D. (2009). Compensatory control: Achieving order through the mind, our institutions, and the heavens. *Current Directions in Psychological Science, 18*, 264–268. doi:10.1111/j.1467-8721.2009.01649.x

Kray, L. J., George, L. G., Liljenquist, K. A., Galinsky, A. D., Tetlock, P. E., & Roese, N. J. (2010). From what *might* have been to what *must* have been: Counterfactual thinking creates meaning. *Journal of Personality and Social Psychology, 98*, 106–118. doi:10.1037/a0017905

Lang, P. J., Bradley, M. M., & Cuthbert, B. N. (2005). *International Affective Picture System (IAPS): Affective ratings of pictures and instruction manual* (Tech. Rep. A-6). Gainesville: University of Florida.

Laurin, K., Kay, A. C., & Moscovitch, D. A. (2008). On the belief in God: Towards an understanding of the emotional substrates of compensatory control. *Journal of Experimental Social Psychology, 44*, 1559–1562. doi:10.1016/j.jesp.2008.07.007

Laurin, K., Kay, A. C., & Shepherd, S. (2011). Self-stereotyping as a route to system justification. *Social Cognition, 29*, 360–375. doi:10.1521/soco.2011.29.3.360

Lecci, L., MacLean, M. G., & Croteau, N. (2002). Personal goals as predictors of college student drinking motives, alcohol use and related problems. *Journal of Studies on Alcohol, 63*, 620–630.

Lerner, M. J. (1980). *The belief in a just world: A fundamental delusion*. New York, NY: Plenum Press.

Lerner, M. J., Somers, D. G., Reid, D., Chiriboga, D., & Tierney, M. (1991). Adult children as caregivers: Egocentric biases in judgments of sibling contributions. *The Gerontologist, 31*, 746–755. doi:10.1093/geront/31.6.746

Lovett, F. (1997, Spring). Thinking about values [Report of December 13, 1996, *Wall Street Journal* national survey]. *The Responsive Community, 7*(2), 87.

Markman, K. D., Gavanski, I., Sherman, S. J., & McMullen, M. N. (1993). The mental simulation of better and worse possible worlds. *Journal of Experimental Social Psychology, 29*, 87–109. doi:10.1006/jesp.1993.1005

Murray, S. L., & Holmes, J. G. (1993). Seeing virtues in faults: Negativity and the transformation of interpersonal narratives in close relationships. *Journal of Personality and Social Psychology, 65,* 707–722. doi:10.1037/0022-3514.65.4.707

Neuberg, S. L., & Newsom, J. T. (1993). Personal need for structure: Individual differences in the desire for simple structure. *Journal of Personality and Social Psychology, 65,* 113–131. doi:10.1037/0022-3514.65.1.113

Norenzayan, A., & Lee, A. (2010). It was meant to happen: Explaining cultural variations in fate attributions. *Journal of Personality and Social Psychology, 98,* 702–720. doi:10.1037/a0019141

Pargament, K. I. (1997). *The psychology of religion and coping: Theory, research, practice*. New York, NY: Guilford Press.

Park, C. L. (2010). Making sense of the meaning literature: An integrative review of meaning making and its effects on adjustment to stressful life events. *Psychological Bulletin, 136,* 257–301. doi:10.1037/a0018301

Park, C. L., & Fenster, J. R. (2004). Stress-related growth: Predictors of occurrence and correlates with psychological adjustment. *Journal of Social and Clinical Psychology, 23,* 195–215. doi:10.1521/jscp.23.2.195.31019

Parkes, C. M. (1971). Psycho-social transitions: A field of study. *Social Science & Medicine, 5,* 101–115. doi:10.1016/0037-7856(71)90091-6

Roese, N. J., & Olson, J. M. (1995). Outcome controllability and counterfactual thinking. *Personality and Social Psychology Bulletin, 21,* 620–628. doi:10.1177/0146167295216008

Rothbaum, F., Weisz, J. R., & Snyder, S. S. (1982). Changing the world and changing the self: A two-process model of perceived control. *Journal of Personality and Social Psychology, 42,* 5–37. doi:10.1037/0022-3514.42.1.5

Rozin, P., & Royzman, E. (2001). Negativity bias, negativity dominance, and contagion. *Personality and Social Psychology Review, 5,* 296–320. doi:10.1207/S15327957PSPR0504_2

Schumann, K., & Ross, M. (2010). *Belief in Ultimate Justice Scale*. Unpublished manuscript.

Silver, R. L., Boon, C., & Stones, M. H. (1983). Searching for meaning in misfortune: Making sense of incest. *Journal of Social Issues, 39,* 81–101. doi:10.1111/j.1540-4560.1983.tb00142.x

Skarlicki, D. P., Ellard, J. H., & Kelln, B. R. C. (1998). Third-party perceptions of a layoff: Procedural, derogation, and retributive aspects of justice. *Journal of Applied Psychology, 83,* 119–127. doi:10.1037/0021-9010.83.1.119

Steger, M. F., Frazier, P., Oishi, S., & Kaler, M. (2006). The meaning in life questionnaire: Assessing the presence of and search for meaning in life. *Journal of Counseling Psychology, 53,* 80–93. doi:10.1037/0022-0167.53.1.80

Svenson, O. (1981). Are we all less risky and more skillful than our fellow drivers? *Acta Psychologica, 47,* 143–148. doi:10.1016/0001-6918(81)90005-6

Tennen, H., & Affleck, G. (2002). The challenge of capturing daily processes at the interface of social and clinical psychology. *Journal of Social and Clinical Psychology, 21*, 610–627. doi:10.1521/jscp.21.6.610.22796

Updegraff, J. A., Silver, R. C., & Holman, E. A. (2008). Searching for and finding meaning in collective trauma: Results from a national longitudinal study of the 9/11 terrorist attacks. *Journal of Personality and Social Psychology, 95*, 709–722. doi:10.1037/0022-3514.95.3.709

Uren, T. H., & Wastell, C. A. (2002). Attachment and meaning-making in perinatal bereavement. *Death Studies, 26*, 279–308. doi:10.1080/074811802753594682

Weiner, B. (1985). "Spontaneous" causal thinking. *Psychological Bulletin, 97*, 74–84. doi:10.1037/0033-2909.97.1.74

Weinstein, N. D. (1980). Unrealistic optimism about future life events. *Journal of Personality and Social Psychology, 39*, 806–820. doi:10.1037/0022-3514.39.5.806

Weinstein, N. D. (1982). Unrealistic optimism about susceptibility to health problems. *Journal of Behavioral Medicine, 5*, 441–460. doi:10.1007/BF00845372

Weinstein, N. D., & Lachendro, E. (1982). Egocentrism as a source of unrealistic optimism. *Personality and Social Psychology Bulletin, 8*, 195–200. doi:10.1177/0146167282082002

Wong, P. T., & Weiner, B. (1981). When people ask "why" questions, and the heuristics of attributional search. *Journal of Personality and Social Psychology, 40*, 650–663. doi:10.1037/0022-3514.40.4.650

15

FINDING MEANING IN ONE'S PAST: NOSTALGIA AS AN EXISTENTIAL RESOURCE

CLAY ROUTLEDGE, CONSTANTINE SEDIKIDES, TIM WILDSCHUT, AND JACOB JUHL

Imagine being asked the following question: What gives your life a sense of meaning? Perhaps you would respond, as many people would, by talking about family, friends, personal accomplishments, your religious faith, or other personally valued traditions. These would be good answers that are echoed empirically in the literature on existential meaning.

Another question, then, would be: How do you use these sources to derive meaning? This question is more complex. It concerns psychological processes that are difficult to access and identify. You might thus respond by simply stating that you do not know how precisely you use these sources, but you know that they make your life feel meaningful. In the current analysis, we seek to answer this question of how people are able to attain and maintain a sense of meaning in life. Specifically, we propose that reflecting nostalgically on the past is an important method people use to meet their existential needs. Family and friends, as well as beliefs, accomplishments, and experiences, may

DOI: 10.1037/14040-015
The Psychology of Meaning, Keith D. Markman, Travis Proulx, and Matthew J. Lindberg (Editors)

provide the ingredients to a life full of meaning, but nostalgia is how people actually make meaning.

On the pages that follow, we offer an analysis of nostalgia as a meaning-making tool. We begin our consideration of nostalgia by providing a brief historical overview of the fascinating and occasionally amusing theoretical perspectives on what nostalgia is and what it does. We then review the current scientific literature that elucidates the content, triggers, and functions of nostalgia. We brush up against other topics of psychological science such as mental health and well-being, intergroup conflict, consumer behavior, and positive psychology. Critically, however, we explore a diverse body of recent work that provides, in our opinion, a strong case for nostalgia as a meaning-making resource. We conclude by discussing future research possibilities as well as the potential for developing nostalgia-based interventions to promote psychological health.

THE HISTORY OF NOSTALGIA

Nostalgia is defined by *The New Oxford Dictionary* (Pearsall, 1998) as a "sentimental longing for the past," and contemporary theory and research cast this emotion in a psychologically positive light (Sedikides, Wildschut, Arndt, & Routledge, 2008). However, nostalgia has not always enjoyed this treatment (Sedikides, Wildschut, & Baden, 2004). The concept of an emotion representing a longing for the past has been featured in literary works dating back thousands of years (e.g., the Bible, Homer's *The Odyssey*). The term *nostalgia,* however, was not actually introduced until the 17th century. The word was coined by Swiss physician Johannes Hofer (1688/1934) to describe physical and psychological symptoms suffered by Swiss mercenaries. Symptoms of this pathology included bouts of weeping, anorexia, irregular heartbeat, and insomnia (McCann, 1941). However, the causes of this supposed disease were debated. Hofer believed that nostalgia was caused by "continuous vibration of animal spirits through those fibers of the middle brain in which impressed traces of ideas of the Fatherland still cling" (p. 384). Another physician, J. J. Scheuchzer (1732, cited in Davis, 1979) believed that nostalgia was linked to altitude, as it was supposedly Swiss mercenaries who left their Alpine homes to fight in wars on the plains of Europe that were most vulnerable to this ailment. Scheuchzer thus proposed that nostalgia was caused by "a sharp differential in atmospheric pressure causing excessive body pressurization, which in turn drove blood from the heart to the brain, thereby producing the observed affliction of sentiment" (cited in Davis, 1979, p. 2). Unsatisfied with these explanations, other physicians speculated that the true trigger of nostalgia could be damage to the eardrum and brain caused by the unremitting clanging of cowbells in the Alps (Davis, 1979). Clearly, the study of nostalgia started off with some tentative, yet extravagant and amusing, theoretical treatments.

In the early 19th century, nostalgia became viewed less as a neurological condition confined to the Swiss and more as a psychological illness akin to depression that could affect anyone separated from one's homeland or longing to return to a desired past state (McCann, 1941; Rosen, 1975). Though perspectives on the causes of nostalgia varied, it was, for the most part, viewed as a mental illness well into the 20th century.

Later in the 20th century, a more discerning analysis of the psychologically aversive outcomes associated with a longing for aspects of the past revealed that it was specifically homesickness (i.e., longing to return to one's home after a period of absence), and not nostalgia, that led to psychological problems. Whereas homesickness was better characterized as psychologically unpleasant, nostalgia was found to be related to fond memories and warm feelings toward the past (Davis, 1979). It was then that nostalgia began to be regarded as conceptually distinct from homesickness. This shift away from perceiving nostalgia as a sickness paved the way for a fresh theoretical and empirical consideration of nostalgia as a psychological resource.

This new perspective did not immediately materialize, however. Though the topic of homesickness received a good deal of empirical attention (Fisher, 1989; Van Tilburg, Vingerhoets, & van Heck, 1996), the same cannot be said about nostalgia. In fact, until about five years ago, most of the empirical work on nostalgia was largely confined to the disciplines of marketing and consumer psychology, and was primarily focused on predicting consumption based on prevalent trends from an individual's youth (Holak & Havlena, 1998; Schindler & Holbrook, 2003). This dearth of research on nostalgia in the psychological sciences sparked us, along with some of our colleagues, to launch a program of research investigating the construct (Routledge & Arndt, 2005; Sedikides, Wildschut, Arndt, & Routledge, 2006; Sedikides et al., 2008). We initiated this program of research by asking questions such as: How prevalent or commonplace is the experience of nostalgia? What is the emotional landscape of nostalgia? What are people nostalgic about? What prompts nostalgic reflection? And, more important, what does nostalgia do for people? That is, is nostalgia beneficial for psychological health and well-being? We summarized these types of questions in the categories of content, triggers, and functions of nostalgia. And with these general categories in mind, we began our scientific journey into the realm of nostalgia.

AN EMOTION REDEEMED: CONTEMPORARY RESEARCH ON THE CONTENT, TRIGGERS, AND FUNCTIONS OF NOSTALGIA

Our consideration of nostalgia started with the proposition that nostalgia would be both commonplace and, unlike homesickness, a largely positively valenced emotion (Sedikides et al., 2004). First, is nostalgia a common emotional experience, or is it a rare sentiment largely observed in specific populations? Despite assertions that nostalgia is an emotion for the elderly, our research suggests that nostalgia is frequently experienced by people of all ages. For example, we asked British undergraduate students to indicate how often they bring to mind nostalgic experiences by checking one of the following options: *at least once a day*, *three to four times a week*, *approximately twice a week*, *approximately once a week*, *once or twice a month*, *once every couple of months*, or *once or twice a year*. Around 80% of British undergraduate students reported experiencing nostalgia approximately once a week (Wildschut et al., 2006). Our research, taken as a whole, indicates that nostalgia is common among young and older adults alike. In fact, rarely do participants state that nostalgia is absent from their lives.

Second, is nostalgia a positive emotional experience? It is this question that launched our empirical study of the content of nostalgia. For example, in one study, we asked participants to bring to mind a past event that they think about in a nostalgic way. We instructed them to take a few minutes to think about the nostalgic experience and then to write about it in vivid detail. We content analyzed these nostalgia narratives and found that though these narratives often featured both positively and negatively valenced emotions, positive emotions were roughly three times more frequent than negative emotions (Wildschut et al., 2006). In addition, the majority of narratives had a redemptive quality, in which negative incidences (e.g., a socially awkward start to a family reunion) progressed into positive ones (e.g., eating, drinking, singing together). In other words, nostalgia narratives were commonly tinged with negative affect but were largely positive and usually had happy endings. Similarly, music-evoked nostalgia is associated strongly with feelings of joy but is not devoid of some sadness (Barrett et al., 2010).

This examination of the content of nostalgia allowed us to ask a related question: What are the objects about which people become nostalgic? We found that nostalgia narratives are typically focused on the self but are also highly social in nature (Wildschut et al., 2006). During nostalgic reverie, people write about momentous life events and, in particular, social interactions in which the self is featured prominently. In sum, nostalgia is commonplace, ambivalent but largely positively toned, self-relevant, and focused on important life events and close relationships.

Armed with evidence that nostalgia is a predominantly positive emotional experience, we began to examine its triggers. When are people likely to engage in nostalgic reflection? We initially addressed this question by asking participants to report the circumstances under which they wax nostalgic. Specifically, we instructed participants to give a detailed written description of the circumstances that trigger nostalgia and then we developed coding categories for these descriptions. We found that bad mood was the most frequently reported trigger (Wildschut et al., 2006). Further, loneliness was the most frequently reported discrete negative affect. On the basis of these findings, we conducted experiments to further test the role of bad mood and loneliness as triggers of nostalgia (Wildschut et al., 2006).

In one experiment, we manipulated mood by having participants read a sad, happy, or neutral news story. Manipulation checks confirmed that these stories produced the desired moods. We then had participants complete two measures of state nostalgia. In one measure, participants endorsed level of agreement with statements such as "Right now, I am feeling quite nostalgic," and in the other measure they were provided a list of 18 aspects of their past and reported the extent to which they currently miss or long for them (e.g., "having someone to depend on," "the way people were," "my family house"; Batcho, 1995). As predicted, the sad news story increased state nostalgia (on both measures) relative to the happy and neutral news stories, which did not differentially impact state nostalgia.

In a second experiment, we manipulated loneliness by giving participants false feedback on a "loneliness" test. Participants who were led to believe that they suffered from loneliness evidenced higher levels of state nostalgia than participants in a control condition. We have since replicated this pattern of findings among Chinese children, Chinese undergraduate students, and Chinese factory workers (Zhou, Sedikides, Wildschut, & Gao, 2008). In a conceptual replication, we found that dispositional levels of sad mood (Barrett et al., 2010) or loneliness (Zhou et al., 2008) predict dispositional levels of nostalgia. In sum, negative affective states (e.g., bad mood, loneliness) activate, or predict, elevated levels of nostalgia (Wildschut, Sedikides, & Cordaro, 2011).

We then shifted our attention to the functions question. What psychological functions might nostalgia serve? Considering that our findings depict nostalgia as largely positive, self-relevant, and socially oriented, as well as triggered by negative affect, we proposed that nostalgia serves at least three psychological functions. First, we hypothesized that nostalgia serves to increase positive mood. To test this hypothesis, we experimentally manipulated nostalgia by instructing participants to "bring to mind a nostalgic event in your life. Specifically, try to think of a past event that makes you feel most nostalgic." Participants in the control condition were given similar instructions but were instead asked to bring to mind an ordinary life event. We found that nostalgia, relative to the control condition, increased positive affect but had no impact on negative affect (Wildschut et al., 2006). Thus, although the content of nostalgic narratives featured some negatively valenced elements, the predominantly positive and redemptive nature of these narratives contributes to an exclusively positive affective outcome.

Second, we hypothesized that nostalgia enhances or protects the self. We also found support for this hypothesis in several experiments. Nostalgia, compared with a control condition, increased state self-esteem (Wildschut et al., 2006). In addition, nostalgia, compared to a control condition, increased the accessibility of positive self-attributes and reduced the self-serving attribution bias (Vess, Arndt, Routledge, Sedikides, & Wildschut, 2010). Specifically, in the first study from Vess et al. (2010), participants who reflected and wrote about a nostalgic event, relative to those who reflected and wrote about a positive future event, were significantly faster at categorizing positive self-attributes. In the second study, participants received success or failure performance feedback on a laboratory task and subsequently thought about a nostalgic or ordinary event from their past. Next, participants were asked to what extent they attributed their performance to ability (an internal attribution). As one might predict from past research on the self-serving bias (Campbell & Sedikides, 1999), participants were less likely to attribute failure to one's own ability than success. However, nostalgia moderated this effect. Nostalgic participants were more willing to attribute failure to one's own ability than participants in the control condition. In other words, bolstering the self with nostalgia reduced the need to protect the self through the self-serving bias. In sum, nostalgia promotes and protects a positive view of self.

Third, we hypothesized that nostalgia strengthens social connectedness. In support of this hypothesis, we found (Wildschut et al., 2006; Zhou et al., 2008) that nostalgic, relative to control, participants reported feeling (a) more interpersonal competence (in the domains of relationship initiation, self-disclosure, and emotional support), (b) more socially supported, and (c) more loved and protected. In addition, nostalgic participants reported feeling less attachment-anxiety (reduced relationship worry) and attachment-avoidance (reduced concern with relationship closeness). A more recent empirical interface between nostalgia and attachment theory further elucidated the social function of nostalgia (Wildschut, Sedikides, Routledge, Arndt, & Cordaro, 2010). In particular, individuals low (compared with high) in attachment-related avoidance derived a stronger sense of social connectedness from nostalgia. In another recent series of studies, we observed a similar pattern when examining coupled individuals' satisfaction with their romantic relationships and single individuals' desire to pursue romantic relationships (Sand, Juhl, & Routledge, 2011). For individuals low, but not high, in attachment-related avoidance, nostalgia greased the wheels of romance by increasing relationship satisfaction among coupled participants and the desire to seek out a romantic relationship among single participants. In sum, nostalgia heightens belongingness and social competence, and promotes positive relationship outcomes.

Taken together, this recent body of research demonstrates that nostalgia elevates positive mood, enhances and protects the self, and strengthens social connectedness. Importantly, nostalgia may also serve a fourth critical psychological function. Specifically, nostalgia may imbue life with a sense of meaning (Routledge & Arndt, 2005; Sedikides et al., 2004). This existential function of nostalgia is the primary focus of the current analysis, and thus we now turn our attention to the relevant program of research.

THE PAST AS AN EXISTENTIAL RESOURCE: NOSTALGIA MAKES MEANING

At the beginning of this chapter we posed the question of what makes life meaningful. We highlighted domains such as family, friends, cultural traditions, and personal triumphs as ingredients of a meaningful life. We then turned our attention to the question driving the current analysis: How do people use these sources to find meaning? We suggest that nostalgia is one method of acquiring and preserving a sense of meaning in life. Specifically, we propose that when people are pressed to find meaning, they reflect nostalgically on treasured past experiences (e.g., family functions, personal accomplishments). We have conducted a number of diverse studies to test this position.

Our consideration of nostalgia as a source of meaning begins with a return to the content question. When waxing nostalgic, people focus on the self and close relationships; however, these narratives also revolve around momentous life events (Wildschut et al., 2006). Nostalgic episodes could thus be characterized as snapshots of the personally treasured life experiences that infuse life with a sense of meaning. Since such precious life experiences cannot occur every day, we reasoned that people are able to regularly tap into these meaning-providing experiences via nostalgic reflection. However, once we observed narrative data consistent with the notion that nostalgia involves meaning-providing life experience, it became crucial to test the idea that nostalgia augments meaning. We did so in two ways. First, we relied on terror management theory (TMT; Solomon, Greenberg, & Pyszczynski, 1991) to test hypotheses consistent with the proposition that nostalgia is a meaning-making resource. Second, we tested directly whether nostalgia provides meaning.

Is Nostalgia a Meaning-Making Resource?

We started our examination of nostalgia as an existential tool by consulting the literature in experimental existential social psychology. The most prominent and empirically substantiated theory relevant to the human need for meaning is TMT (Solomon et al., 1991; see also Chapter 3, this volume). According to TMT, one reason why people strive to perceive their lives as meaningful is their awareness of their own mortality. Like all animals, humans strive for self-preservation. However, humans uniquely possess the requisite cognitive capabilities to understand that despite all efforts to thrive, death is certain and can come without warning. This realization, according to the theory, has the potential to generate a great deal of psychological distress. The theory proposes that people are able, at least for the most part, to avoid distress associated with the awareness of their inevitable demise by believing that their lives are meaningful. Physical death cannot be defeated, but the sting of mortality can be softened by the belief that existence is about more than living, it is about living a life of purpose and meaning.

In support of TMT, extensive experimental research has demonstrated that heightened awareness of mortality leads to heightened investment in socially and culturally derived meaning-providing structures (e.g., family, religion, social identities) and that such investment reduces the accessibility of death-related thoughts (Greenberg, Solomon, & Arndt, 2008) as well as psychological distress (e.g., anxiety; Routledge & Juhl, 2010; Routledge et al., 2010).

Drawing upon research derived from TMT, we hypothesized that if nostalgia is a meaning-providing resource, then, like other meaning-providing resources, it will mitigate the effects of death-related cognition. We first tested this hypothesis in three experiments (Routledge, Arndt, Sedikides, & Wildschut, 2008). In the first study, we measured individual differences in nostalgia proneness (e.g., "How often do you engage in nostalgia?") and manipulated death-related cognition with a mortality salience induction (Rosenblatt, Greenberg, Solomon, Pyszczynski, & Lyon, 1989). In the experimental condition, participants pondered their mortality (e.g., "Briefly describe the emotions that the thought of your own death arouses in you"), whereas in the control condition they pondered an aversive experience not related to death (e.g., "Briefly describe the emotions that the thought of your dental pain arouses in you"). Subsequently, we administered a measure of meaning in life (e.g., "All strivings in life are futile and absurd"; Kunzendorf & Maguire, 1995). We proposed that mortality salience would undermine a sense of meaning in life, but only among individuals not disposed to reflect on meaning-providing life experiences—that is, among those low in nostalgia proneness. This pattern is precisely what we found. Individuals prone to nostalgia did not show a reduction in meaning in response to the existential threat of mortality salience, but those not prone to nostalgia did.

We examined nostalgia as an existential resource in follow-up research that focused on the accessibility of death thoughts (Routledge et al., 2008). As noted, previous research demonstrates that when mortality is made salient, investment in meaning-proving structures (e.g., religion) reduces the accessibility of death thoughts. We thus hypothesized that nostalgia would reduce the accessibility of death thoughts after such thoughts are activated via a mortality salience induction. In one experiment, we measured nostalgia proneness and then rendered mortality salient. In another experiment, we manipulated nostalgia as before (i.e., Wildschut et al., 2006), that is, by asking participants to conjure up a nostalgic versus ordinary autobiographical event from their lives. In both experiments, the dependent variable was death-thought accessibility, which we assessed with a stem completion task. Specifically, participants received a list of incomplete words, some of which could be completed with death or non-death-related words (e.g., *COFF__* could be *COFFIN* or *COFFEE*; Greenberg, Pyszczynski, Solomon, Simon, & Breus, 1994). The more words that are completed to be death related, the more death thoughts are accessible. Both experiments yielded results consistent with our hypothesis. Mortality salience increased the accessibility of death-related thoughts, but only at low levels of nostalgia (when nostalgia proneness was measured) and in the "ordinary" condition (when nostalgia was manipulated). In all, nostalgia buffered the effects of mortality salience on increased death thoughts.

In a subsequent investigation, we further considered nostalgia as a means through which people protect against the negative psychological consequences of mortality salience (Juhl, Routledge, Arndt, Sedikides, & Wildschut, 2010). Previous research has implicated death-related cognition as a facilitator of intergroup conflict, as people respond to mortality salience with ingroup bias and outgroup derogation (Greenberg et al., 2008). Group identities are a source of meaning, and thus, when meaning is needed because death is salient, one way in which people find and preserve meaning is by defending their own group identities, often at the expense of other groups. We have maintained that nostalgia is another way through which people are able to attain and preserve meaning. In fact, we believe it to be a particularly powerful way. Thus, we hypothesized that people who regularly engage in nostalgia (high-proneness individuals) would not respond to mortality salience with the typically observed ingroup identity defense. To test this prediction, we measured nostalgia proneness, manipulated mortality salience, and then asked participants to evaluate an essay critical of their university (an identity threat). As hypothesized, mortality salience increased negative evaluations of the critical essay, but only among individuals low on nostalgia proneness. People who frequently used nostalgia did not need to defend other sources of meaning when death was salient. Another experiment further highlighted the relevance of nostalgia as a source of meaning (Juhl et al., 2010). Specifically, mortality salience increased death anxiety, but only among individuals low on nostalgia proneness. Thus, nostalgia keeps death thoughts from turning into death fears.

In a final experiment (Juhl et al., 2010), we sought to provide a more rigorous test of the hypothesis that people high on nostalgia proneness in fact implement nostalgia as a meaning-providing resource when mortality is salient. We measured nostalgia proneness, manipulated mortality salience, and assessed state nostalgia (by asking participants how much they miss various aspects of their past; Wildschut et al., 2006). The findings provided unequivocal support for nostalgia as the means by which nostalgia-prone individuals resolve mortality concerns. For people high, but not low, in nostalgia proneness, mortality salience increased state nostalgia. People who regularly wax nostalgic employ nostalgia when grappling with the existential threat of death awareness.

In sum, across six experiments, we obtained consistent evidence for the notion that nostalgia provides meaning in life. Mortality salience compromised a sense of meaning, increased death thought accessibility, motivated ingroup identity defense, and heightened death anxiety. However, none of these effects emerged among individuals who are frequently nostalgic or when nostalgia was experimentally induced. In addition, people high on nostalgia proneness used nostalgia in response to mortality salience. Yet, one drawback of these experiments is that they were all focused on nostalgia as an existential resource in response to a specific existential threat (i.e., death awareness). These experiments did not consider broadly nostalgia in meaning-making endeavors that were unrelated to mortality concerns. Further, in none of the experiments did we directly test the hypothesis that nostalgia increases meaning. Instead, we used TMT and research derived from the theory to evaluate hypotheses aligned with the possibility that nostalgia contributes to feelings of meaning in life. Therefore, we determined that it was crucial both to take a broader approach, not limited to one particular existential threat, and to test more explicitly whether nostalgia provides meaning.

Does Nostalgia Provide Meaning?

We began our empirical efforts by examining the covariation between nostalgia and meaning (Routledge et al., 2011). We hypothesized that if nostalgia is one prevalent way through which people derive and maintain meaning, then people who frequently, rather than infrequently, wax nostalgic would evidence higher levels of perceived meaning in life. We obtained support for this hypothesis in two studies. The first study used an American undergraduate sample. Participants completed a measure of nostalgia proneness (Routledge et al., 2008) and two measures of the perceived presence of meaning in life (e.g., "My personal existence is purposeful and meaningful", "I have a good sense of what makes my life meaningful"; McGregor & Little, 1998; Steger, Frazier, Oishi, & Kaler, 2006; see also Chapter 11, this volume). Nostalgia proneness was positively and significantly correlated with both meaning measures. In the second study, Dutch nationals ranging in age from 10 to 71 took part in an online study examining music-evoked nostalgia. Participants listed their favorite songs and also listened to popular songs. Then, they rated how nostalgic each song made them feel and to what extent each song made them feel that life is worth living (an indicator of meaning). We obtained evidence for nostalgia as meaning-making across all age ranges. The more people reported that music made them feel nostalgic, the more they reported deriving meaning from that music.

Our first direct assessment of nostalgia as a meaning provider yielded supportive evidence. Our next task was to find experimental confirmation for this proposition. To this end, we conducted three laboratory experiments testing the hypothesis that nostalgia bolsters meaning (Routledge et al., 2011; Routledge, Wildschut, Sedikides, Juhl, & Arndt, 2012). In the first experiment, we used song lyrics to manipulate nostalgia. Specifically, in a preliminary session we asked participants to list the titles and artists of three songs that made them feel nostalgic. Prior to the experimental session, we randomly allocated participants to the nostalgia or control condition. For participants in the nostalgia condition, we retrieved the lyrics of a song they listed as personally nostalgic. Participants in the control condition were yoked to a participant in the nostalgia condition and were designated to receive the same lyrics as this person, after we ascertained that the relevant song was not one that the control participant had also identified as nostalgic.

One week after the preliminary session, participants were brought back to the laboratory for the experimental session and given the song lyrics to read as just described. Then, they completed a manipulation check to ensure that the lyrics appropriately induced nostalgia. Finally, they completed a measure of meaning in life (Steger et al., 2006). As hypothesized, participants who read the lyrics that they had identified as nostalgia inducing, compared to those in the control condition, were more nostalgic (as measured by the manipulation check) and, critically, perceived life as more meaningful.

In two additional experiments (Routledge et al., 2012), we used our previously validated nostalgia manipulations in which participants wrote about nostalgic versus autobiographical control experiences (e.g., recent positive past experience, ordinary past experience, future anticipated experience; Vess et al., 2010; Wildschut et al., 2006). We assessed meaning with a presence of meaning scale as well as a search for meaning scale (Steger et al., 2006). Nostalgia, compared with controls, raised meaning. Specifically, induced nostalgia elevated the presence of meaning and decreased the active search for meaning (these two measures were inversely correlated). Thus, not only did nostalgia bolster meaning, it did so sufficiently to decrease the need to search for meaning elsewhere. In all, survey and experimental data provided compelling evidence that nostalgia strengthens a sense of meaning in life.

We returned, in this research, to our analysis of nostalgia triggers. We previously presented findings demonstrating that bad mood and loneliness trigger nostalgia. On the basis of the growing body of evidence that nostalgia provides meaning, we sought to consider meaninglessness as another nostalgia trigger. To this end, we conducted an experiment in which we threatened meaning and then measured state nostalgia (Routledge et al., 2011). To threaten meaning, we had participants read a philosophical essay arguing that life has no real meaning or purpose. Participants in the control condition read a philosophical essay regarding the limitations of computers. A pilot study confirmed that the meaning threat essay undermined perceptions of meaning. Next, participants completed a state measure of nostalgia (Wildschut et al., 2006). As hypothesized, participants who read the meaning threat essay were more nostalgic compared to those who read the control essay. Meaning threat emerged as a potent trigger of nostalgia.

Building upon our findings indicating that nostalgia reduces defensiveness in response to the threat of mortality salience, we then sought to determine whether nostalgia would reduce defensiveness to a more direct threat to meaning (Routledge et al., 2011). We proceeded to manipulate nostalgia (Wildschut et al., 2006) and then have participants read the meaning threat or no-meaning threat philosophical essays that we described above. Next, we had participants evaluate these essays and the essay authors. We assumed that negative evaluations of the threatening essay would reflect defensiveness against the claim that life is meaningless. Participants evaluated the meaning threat essay and author more negatively than the no-meaning threat essay and author. However, this effect was only significant in the control condition; it was nullified in the nostalgia condition. Nostalgia bolsters meaning and by doing so lowers people's sensitivity to existentially threatening information, thus reducing defensiveness.

Finally, in elucidating nostalgia as a meaning-making tool, we sought to examine the extent to which nostalgia protects psychological well-being when meaning is under threat. Meaning in life is a hallmark of healthy psychological functioning and is associated with quality of life (King & Napa, 1998; Krause, 2007), psychological well-being (Steger & Frazier, 2005; Updegraff, Silver, & Holman, 2008), and successful coping with stress or illness (Janoff-Bulman, 1992; Jim & Andersen, 2007; Park, 2010; see also Chapters 10, 12, and 13, this volume). Therefore, people with meaning deficits are at risk of poor psychological and physical health. Having established that nostalgia bolsters meaning, we proposed that nostalgia could be used as a meaning intervention in efforts to counteract the ill psychological effects that result from a lack of perceived meaning in life. We started this consideration of nostalgia as an intervention with two laboratory studies (Routledge et al., 2011).

In the first study, we measured individual differences in perceptions of meaning and then manipulated nostalgia with the narrative task (Wildschut et al., 2006). We then measured state vitality as an indicator of psychological well-being (Ryan & Frederick, 1997). Vitality is considered a reflection of eudaemonic well-being (i.e., feeling alive and vital) and correlates with other measures of well-being (e.g., satisfaction with life; Ryan & Frederick, 1997). The results were consisted with the idea that nostalgia has intervention potential. There was a significant negative relation between perceived meaning and vitality, but nostalgia mitigated this effect. In particular, nostalgia increased vitality among individuals who lacked a sense of meaning. Nostalgia, then, elevates well-being among those with existing meaning deficits (see Chapter 23, this volume).

We followed up with a similar intervention study to find out whether nostalgia mitigates the effects of stress experienced by people with meaning deficits. We measured perceptions of meaning, manipulated nostalgia with the narrative task, and then implemented the Trier Social Stress Test, an established laboratory stress paradigm in which participants engage in a mock job interview and perform challenging mental arithmetic before an audience (Kudielka, Hellhammer, & Kirschbaum, 2007). We subsequently assessed subjective stress. Meaning was a significant predictor of subjective stress after the stressor task. People with meaning deficits reported high levels of stress after the task compared to those without meaning deficits. Critically, nostalgia mitigated this effect. In particular, nostalgia significantly attenuated feelings of stress among individuals who had low levels of meaning at the start of the study. Nostalgia thus appears to improve well-being and assist in coping with stressful experiences among individuals vulnerable to poor well-being and elevated stress (i.e., individuals low in meaning in life). These two intervention studies provide encouragement for future research seeking to develop and test nostalgia-related therapies for mental health treatment. We return to this topic shortly.

In sum, building upon previous findings that nostalgia serves several psychological functions, we conducted a range of studies showcasing an existential function of nostalgia. Nostalgia not only increases positive mood, self-positivity, and social connectedness, but it also contributes to meaning making. Specifically, nostalgia mitigates the effects of existential threats (i.e., mortality salience, undermining meaning), increases perceptions of meaning, decreases the need to further search for meaning, and promotes psychological health for those with low levels of perceived meaning. Further, threats to meaning increase nostalgia. In all, the evidence strongly demonstrates that nostalgia aids people in finding and preserving a sense of life meaning.

THE FUTURE OF NOSTALGIA: CURRENT PLANS AND PROPOSALS

Though research provides compelling evidence that nostalgia helps people perceive their lives as meaningful, key questions remain unanswered. For example, how precisely does nostalgia provide meaning? In other words, is the effect of nostalgia on meaning mediated by any other function of nostalgia? As previously discussed, nostalgia serves functions related to affect, the self, and relationships. In addition, theory and research suggest that each of these functions is associated with meaning. For example, positive affect is a prominent predictor of judgments of meaning (King, Hicks, Krull, & Del Gaiso, 2006; see also Chapter 22, this volume). In addition, research derived from TMT suggests that both self-esteem (Greenberg et al., 2008) and close relationships (Mikulincer, Florian, & Hirschberger, 2003) contribute to a sense of meaning. Finally, belongingness facilitates meaning (Hicks, Schlegel, & King, 2010; Lambert et al., in press). Therefore, there is reason to believe that nostalgia may offer meaning via one or more of these routes.

We recently began to explore this question. In particular, we considered the question of mediation, in two studies, when examining the link between nostalgia and meaning (Routledge et al., 2011). As a starting point, we focused on social connectedness as the mediator because close relationships played a prominent role in most of the nostalgic narratives about momentous life events. In other words, events that people identified as being of great personal value were interpersonal in nature (e.g., family gatherings, weddings, holidays, graduations). In both studies, in addition to measuring or manipulating nostalgia and then measuring meaning, we assessed social connectedness as a mediator. Social connectedness mediated the effects of nostalgia on meaning in both studies. Therefore, preliminary research suggests that a sense of social connectedness that emanates from nostalgic engagement accounts, in part, for the way in which nostalgia contributes to perceptions of meaning in life.

The issue of mediation deserves prioritization in future research plans. What are other critical mediators, besides social connectedness? Moreover, are different mediators more impactful for different people? This latter question returns us to the beginning of this chapter, when we discussed what makes life seem meaningful. People may vary in the extent to which specific domains offer meaning, and thus people may vary in the extent to which tapping into these domains via nostalgia elevates meaning. For example, people low in attachment-related avoidance may garner meaning from reflecting nostalgically on past social experiences. Likewise, cultural differences may emerge. For example, individuals from individualistic cultures may derive more meaning for agentic experiences (e.g., personal accomplishments), whereas individuals from collectivistic cultures may derive more meaning from communal experiences (e.g., harmonious relationships). In sum, more research is needed to examine the nuanced ways in which people use nostalgia to find meaning.

How about the relation between nostalgia and psychological health? We discussed the results from two studies supporting the idea that nostalgia has intervention potential. However, neither of these studies tested a clinical population or examined longer term effects of a nostalgia induction. Therefore, much work is needed to advance nostalgia as a potential therapeutic tool. Given that nostalgia fosters a sense of meaning, we believe that the potential for nostalgia to be used as a form of treatment by mental health practitioners is strong. Preliminary findings indeed point to a relation between meaning and positive mental health outcomes. For example, a sense of meaning in life predicted improvement during psychotherapy (Debats, 1996). In addition, a lack of meaning is associated with psychological dysfunction and maladaptive health behavior. For example, a lack of meaning is a predictor of depression (Wong, 1998) and even a precursor to suicide (Harlow, Newcomb, & Bentler, 1986). Frankl (1997) proposed that the existential pain of meaninglessness and an inability to find meaning could result in the development of negative health-related behaviors such as excessive drinking, drug abuse, and gambling. Consistent with this assertion, excessive drinking has been related to poor purpose in life (Marsh, Smith, Piek, & Saunders, 2003; Waisberg & Porter, 1994), as has drug abuse (Padelford, 1974). Therefore, future research examining nostalgia as a mental health intervention may offer therapists and counselors another weapon in their arsenal to combat psychopathology and problem behaviors (see Chapter 23, this volume).

The utility of nostalgia as a mental health treatment depends, of course, on the extent to which nostalgia is a predominantly positive experience. Our research suggests that it is; however, all of our studies thus far have focused on "normal" populations, and thus another critical direction for research is to consider the possibility that nostalgia may not be a net positive experience for everyone. Perhaps there are certain groups of people (e.g., people high in neuroticism, people with negative attitudes toward their past) for whom increased nostalgia might contribute to undesirable psychological consequences (e.g., anxiety, unhappiness).

IN CLOSING

As a collective, society emphasizes the present and the future, and de-emphasizes the past, when making judgments about our lives. People admonish one another to live in moment, plan for the future, and not to dwell on the past. Certainly, there is value to this advice. Appreciating the present can be rewarding, and goal-related behavior that paves the way for a better future is advantageous. However, turning to the past may be beneficial as well. Historians like to remind us that there is much to learn from the past. We, as psychologists, also propose that the past should not be underrated. Reflecting nostalgically on the past betters one's affective state, bolsters and protects the positivity of the self, strengthens a sense of social connectedness, and as this chapter highlighted, imbues life with purpose and meaning.

REFERENCES

Barrett, F. S., Grimm, K. J., Robins, R. W., Wildschut, T., Sedikides, C., & Janata, P. (2010). Music-evoked nostalgia: Affect, memory, and personality. *Emotion, 10*, 390–403. doi:10.1037/a0019006

Batcho, K. I. (1995). Nostalgia: A psychological perspective. *Perceptual and Motor Skills, 80*, 131–143. doi:10.2466/pms.1995.80.1.131

Campbell, K. W., & Sedikides, C. (1999). Self-threat magnifies the self-serving bias: A meta-analytic integration. *Review of General Psychology, 3*, 23–43. doi:10.1037/1089-2680.3.1.23

Davis, F. (1979). *Yearning for yesterday: A sociology of nostalgia.* New York, NY: Free Press.

Debats, D. L. (1996). Meaning in life: Clinical relevance and predictive power. *British Journal of Clinical Psychology, 35*, 503–516. doi:10.1111/j.2044-8260.1996.tb01207.x

Fisher, S. (1989). *Homesickness, cognition and health.* Hove, England: Erlbaum.

Frankl, V. E. (1997). *Man's search for ultimate meaning.* New York, NY: Plenum.

Greenberg, J., Pyszczynski, T., Solomon, S., Simon, L., & Breus, M. (1994). Role of consciousness and accessibility of death-related thoughts in mortality salience effects. *Journal of Personality and Social Psychology, 67*, 627–637. doi:10.1037/0022-3514.67.4.627

Greenberg, J., Solomon, S., & Arndt, J. (2008). A basic but uniquely human motivation: Terror management. In J. Y. Shah & W. L. Gardner (Eds.), *Handbook of motivation science* (pp. 114–134). New York, NY: Guilford Press.

Harlow, L. L., Newcomb, M. D., & Bentler, P. M.(1986). Depression, self-derogation, substance abuse, and suicide ideation: Lack of purpose in life as a mediational factor. *Journal of Clinical Psychology, 42*, 5–21. doi:10.1002/1097-4679(198601)42:1<5::AID-JCLP2270420102>3.0.CO;2-9

Hicks, J. A., Schlegel, R. J., & King, L. A. (2010). Social threats, happiness, and the dynamics of meaning in life judgments. *Personality and Social Psychology Bulletin*, *36*, 1305–1317. doi:10.1177/0146167210381650

Hofer, J. (1934). Medical dissertation on nostalgia (C. K. Anspach, Trans.). *Bulletin of the History of Medicine*, *2*, 376–391. (Original work published 1688)

Holak, S. L., & Havlena, W. J. (1998). Feelings, fantasies, and memories: An examination of the emotional components of nostalgia. *Journal of Business Research*, *42*, 217–226. doi:10.1016/S0148-2963(97)00119-7

Janoff-Bulman, R. (1992). *Shattered assumptions: Towards a new psychology of trauma*. New York, NY: Free Press.

Jim, H. S., & Andersen, B. L. (2007). Meaning in life mediates the relationship between social and physical functioning and distress in cancer survivors. *British Journal of Health Psychology*, *12*, 363–381. doi:10.1348/135910706X128278

Juhl, J., Routledge, C., Arndt, J., Sedikides, C., & Wildschut, T. (2010). Fighting the future with the past: Nostalgia buffers existential threat. *Journal of Research in Personality*, *44*, 309–314. doi:10.1016/j.jrp.2010.02.006

King, L. A., Hicks, J. A., Krull, J. L., & Del Gaiso, A. K. (2006). Positive affect and the experience of meaning in life. *Journal of Personality and Social Psychology*, *90*, 179–196. doi:10.1037/0022-3514.90.1.179

King, L. A., & Napa, C. K. (1998). What makes a good life? *Journal of Personality and Social Psychology*, *75*, 156–165. doi:10.1037/0022-3514.75.1.156

Krause, N. (2007). Evaluating the stress-buffering function of meaning in life among older people. *Journal of Aging and Health*, *19*, 792–812. doi:10.1177/0898264307304390

Kudielka, B. M., Hellhammer, D. H., & Kirschbaum, C. (2007). Ten years of research with the Trier Social Stress Test—Revisited. In E. Harmon-Jones & P. Winkielman (Eds.), *Social neuroscience: Integrating biological and psychological explanations of social behavior* (pp. 56–83). New York, NY: Guilford Press.

Kunzendorf, R. G., & Maguire, D. (1995). *Depression: The reality of "no meaning" versus the delusion of negative meaning*. Unpublished manuscript, University of Massachusetts, Lowell.

Lambert, N. M., Stillman, T. F., Baumeister, R. F., Fincham, F. D., Hicks, J. A., & Graham, S. M. (in press). Family begets meaning: The unique contribution of family relationships to purpose in life. *The Journal of Positive Psychology*.

Marsh, A., Smith, L., Piek, J., & Saunders, B. (2003). The Purpose in Life Scale: Psychometric properties for social drinkers and drinkers in alcohol treatment. *Educational and Psychological Measurement*, *63*, 859–871. doi:10.1177/0013164403251040

McCann, W. H. (1941). Nostalgia: A review of the literature. *Psychological Bulletin*, *38*, 165–182. doi:10.1037/h0057354

McGregor, I., & Little, B. R. (1998). Personal projects, happiness, and meaning: On doing well and being yourself. *Journal of Personality and Social Psychology*, *74*, 494–512. doi:10.1037/0022-3514.74.2.494

Mikulincer, M., Florian, V., & Hirschberger, G. (2003). The existential function of close relationships: Introducing death into the science of love. *Personality and Social Psychology Review, 7*, 20–40. doi:10.1207/S15327957PSPR0701_2

Padelford, B. L. (1974). Relationship between drug involvement and purpose in life. *Journal of Clinical Psychology, 30*, 303–305. doi:10.1002/1097-4679(197407)30:3<303::AID-JCLP2270300323>3.0.CO;2-2

Park, C. L. (2010). Making sense of the meaning literature: An integrative review of meaning making and its effects on adjustment to stressful life events. *Psychological Bulletin, 136*, 257–301. doi:10.1037/a0018301

Pearsall, J. E. (Ed.). (1998). *The new Oxford dictionary of English*. Oxford, England: Oxford University Press.

Rosen, G. (1975). Nostalgia: A "forgotten" psychological disorder. *Psychological Medicine, 5*, 340–354. doi:10.1017/S003329170005697X

Rosenblatt, A., Greenberg, J., Solomon, S., Pyszczynski, T., & Lyon, D. (1989). Evidence for terror management theory I: The effects of mortality salience on reactions to those who violate or uphold cultural values. *Journal of Personality and Social Psychology, 57*, 681–690. doi:10.1037/0022-3514.57.4.681

Routledge, C., & Arndt, J. (2005). Time and terror: Managing temporal consciousness and the awareness of mortality. In A. Strathman & J. Joireman (Eds.), *Understanding behavior in the context of time: Theory, research, and application* (pp. 59–84). Mahwah, NJ: Erlbaum.

Routledge, C., Arndt, J., Sedikides, C., & Wildschut, T. (2008). A blast from the past: The terror management function of nostalgia. *Journal of Experimental Social Psychology, 44*, 132–140. doi:10.1016/j.jesp.2006.11.001

Routledge, C., Arndt, J., Wildschut, T., Sedikides, C., Hart, C., Juhl, J., . . . Schlotz, W. (2011). The past makes the present meaningful: Nostalgia as an existential resource. *Journal of Personality and Social Psychology, 101*, 638–652. doi:10.1037/a0024292

Routledge, C., & Juhl, J. (2010). When death thoughts lead to death fears: Mortality salience increases death anxiety for individuals who lack meaning in life. *Cognition & Emotion, 24*, 848–854. doi:10.1080/02699930902847144

Routledge, C., Ostafin, B., Juhl, J., Sedikides, C., Cathey, C., & Liao, J. (2010). Adjusting to death: The effects of mortality salience and self-esteem on psychological well-being, growth motivation, and maladaptive behavior. *Journal of Personality and Social Psychology, 99*, 897–916. doi:10.1037/a0021431

Routledge, C., Wildschut, T., Sedikides, C., Juhl, J., & Arndt, J. (2012). The power of the past: Nostalgia as a meaning-making resource. *Memory*. Advance online publication. doi:10.1080/09658211.2012.677452

Ryan, R. M., & Frederick, C. (1997). On energy, personality, and health: Subjective vitality as a dynamic reflection of well-being. *Journal of Personality, 65*, 529–565. doi:10.1111/j.1467-6494.1997.tb00326.x

Sand, E., Juhl, J., & Routledge, C. (2011). *When the past plays Cupid: Nostalgia bolsters relationship satisfaction and desire*. Unpublished manuscript, North Dakota State University, Fargo.

Schindler, R. M., & Holbrook, M. B. (2003). Nostalgia for early experience as a determinant of consumer preferences. *Psychology & Marketing, 20,* 275–302. doi:10.1002/mar.10074

Sedikides, C., Wildschut, T., Arndt, J., & Routledge, C. D. (2006). Affect and the self. In J. P. Forgas (Ed.), *Affect in social thinking and behavior: Frontiers in social psychology* (pp. 197–215). New York, NY: Psychology Press.

Sedikides, C., Wildschut, T., Arndt, J., & Routledge, C. (2008). Nostalgia: Past, present, and future. *Current Directions in Psychological Science, 17,* 304–307. doi:10.1111/j.1467-8721.2008.00595.x

Sedikides, C., Wildschut, T., & Baden, D. (2004). Nostalgia: Conceptual issues and existential functions. In J. Greenberg, S. L. Koole, & T. Pyszczynski (Eds.), *Handbook of experimental existential psychology* (pp. 200–214). New York, NY: Guilford Press.

Solomon, S., Greenberg, J., & Pyszczynski, T. (1991). Terror management theory of self-esteem. In C. R. Snyder & D. R. Forsyth (Eds.), *Handbook of social and clinical psychology: The health perspective* (pp. 21–40). New York, NY: Pergamon Press.

Steger, M. F., & Frazier, P. (2005). Meaning in life: One link in the chain from religiousness to well-being. *Journal of Counseling Psychology, 52,* 574–582. doi:10.1037/0022-0167.52.4.574

Steger, M. F., Frazier, P., Oishi, S., & Kaler, M. (2006). The Meaning in Life Questionnaire: Assessing the presence of and search for meaning in life. *Journal of Counseling Psychology, 53,* 80–93. doi:10.1037/0022-0167.53.1.80

Updegraff, J. A., Silver, R. C., & Holman, E. A. (2008). Searching for and finding meaning in collective trauma: Results from a national longitudinal study of the 9/11 terrorist attacks. *Journal of Personality and Social Psychology, 95,* 709–722. doi:10.1037/0022-3514.95.3.709

Van Tilburg, M. A. L., Vingerhoets, A. J. J. M., & van Heck, G. L. (1996). Homesickness: A review of the literature. *Psychological Medicine, 26,* 899–912. doi:10.1017/S0033291700035248

Vess, M., Arndt, J., Routledge, C., Sedikides, C., & Wildschut, T. (2010). Nostalgia as a resource of the self. *Self and Identity*. Advance online publication. doi:10.1080/15298868.2010.521452

Waisberg, J. L., & Porter, J. E. (1994). Purpose in life and outcome of treatment for alcohol dependence. *British Journal of Clinical Psychology, 33,* 49–63. doi:10.1111/j.2044-8260.1994.tb01093.x

Wildschut, T., Sedikides, C., Arndt, J., & Routledge, C. (2006). Nostalgia: Content, triggers, functions. *Journal of Personality and Social Psychology, 91,* 975–993. doi:10.1037/0022-3514.91.5.975

Wildschut, T., Sedikides, C., & Cordaro, F. (2011). Self-regulatory interplay between negative and positive emotions: The case of loneliness and nostalgia.

In I. Nyklíček, A. Vingerhoets, & M. Zeelenberg (Eds.), *Emotion regulation and well-being* (pp. 67–83). New York, NY: Springer. doi:10.1007/978-1-4419-6953-8_5

Wildschut, T., Sedikides, C., Routledge, C., Arndt, J., & Cordaro, F. (2010). Nostalgia as a repository of social connectedness: The role of attachment-related avoidance. *Journal of Personality and Social Psychology*, 98, 573–586. doi:10.1037/a0017597

Wong, P. T. P. (1998). Implicit theories of meaningful life and the development of the personal meaning profile. In P. T. P. Wong & P. S. Fry (Eds.), *The human quest for meaning. A handbook of psychological research and clinical applications* (pp. 111–140). Mahwah, NJ: Erlbaum.

Zhou, X., Sedikides, C., Wildschut, C., & Gao, D.-G. (2008). Counteracting loneliness: On the restorative function of nostalgia. *Psychological Science, 19*, 1023–1029. doi:10.1111/j.1467-9280.2008.02194.x

16

TWISTS OF FATE: MOMENTS IN TIME AND WHAT MIGHT HAVE BEEN IN THE EMERGENCE OF MEANING

LAURA J. KRAY, HAL E. HERSHFIELD, LINDA G. GEORGE, AND ADAM D. GALINSKY

What we call the beginning is often the end
And to make an end is to make a beginning.
The end is where we start from.
—T. S. Eliot, Little Gidding (No. 4 of "Four Quartets")

Life is full of beginnings and endings. And it is often a seemingly insignificant chance event that dramatically alters one's current path to produce a new beginning, a new trajectory. Consider the 2011 keynote address at the Society of Personality and Social Psychology's annual meeting by bestselling author Malcolm Gladwell. Reflecting on the beginning of his career as a disseminator of social psychological research, he recalled his first day on the job as a science reporter for *The Washington Post*. Upon inheriting the academic journal subscriptions of his predecessor, he grabbed the journal at the top of the stack and began perusing it for interesting research. Looking back now, he noted how different his career might have been if the *Journal of Personality and Social Psychology* had been buried at the bottom of the stack rather than positioned prominently at the top. By identifying this precise moment when his career path might easily have been diverted, Gladwell psychologically pinpointed the origin of his destiny. Given his mind-boggling success, it is

DOI: 10.1037/14040-016
The Psychology of Meaning, Keith D. Markman, Travis Proulx, and Matthew J. Lindberg (Editors)

difficult to imagine a world in which his introduction to social psychology had not occurred. In the current chapter, we propose that how people think about past events—whether and how they consider those seemingly chance events and the alternative realties in which they had not occurred—fosters an appreciation for the pivotal moments in time when the past gives way to the present.

Counterfactual thinking is the pondering of "what might have been." This cognitive process often plays a crucial role in the construction of life stories. Starting in adolescence, individuals develop personal identities on the basis of their experiences, both positive and negative. The passage of a lifetime is marked by defining moments, including new beginnings, endings, and unforeseen twists of fate when life suddenly changes direction. A personal conceptualization of the significance of these key experiences gives individuals a sense of who they are, fortifies their most cherished relationships, and clarifies their most deeply felt values. In addition to providing raw material for dramatic storytelling, as in Gladwell's speech, "what iffing" also plays a central role in the construction of personal meaning by highlighting the significance of these pivotal moments in time. Overall, personal narratives consist of these critical moments in time that seem to shape and reveal individuals' destiny.

In this chapter, we explore the relationship between counterfactuals and meaning (see also Chapter 17, this volume). To do so, we have organized our thoughts into three sections. First, we review previous research on the role of counterfactual mind-sets, or cognitive orientations, in establishing causal relationships. Second, we explore the implications of the deliberate construction of counterfactuals for the emergence of personal meaning. We claim that the psychosocial construction of autobiographical life stories are inexorably linked with counterfactual thought. Third, we identify unanswered questions regarding the relationship between counterfactual thought and meaning.

COUNTERFACTUAL MIND-SETS: UNDERSTANDING RELATIONSHIPS AND PROBLEM SOLVING

Imagine you are at a concert of one of your favorite bands. Seating is on a first-come, first-served basis. At the concert, the announcer reveals that a trip to Hawaii will be given to a lucky fan whose seat number is drawn from a lottery. Now imagine you see a person move seats because her view of the stage is partially obstructed. Shortly after she changes seats, the winning seat number is announced. It turns out that the winning seat was the seat that person *had just moved from*. If you are like the hundreds of participants who have participated in our experiments using the previous scenario, you would instantly and spontaneously conjure up thoughts such as, "If only she had not moved, she would have won" (Kahneman & Miller, 1986).

Counterfactual thought is activated by near misses and unusual paths—what researchers call almost and abnormal counterfactuals. For example, missing a plane flight by 5 minutes generates more counterfactual what ifs than missing the flight by 45 minutes (Kahneman & Miller, 1986). Unusual or abnormal components within a sequence of events, such as taking a new route to the airport (and subsequently missing the flight), can also produce counterfactual thinking.

Constructing a counterfactual thought implicitly involves laying out a causal chain of events in a sequence of actions and mutating one step in the process to construct an alternate reality. For example, while standing at the gate looking at one's barely missed departing flight, one might well consider the sequences of actions leading up to this point: running into friends and grabbing a cup of coffee with them, then encountering traffic en route to the airport and having a long wait at the security checkpoint. Reviewing the sequence, an alternate, unrealized outcome emerges by changing a single step of the process: if only I had skipped the coffee. When a mutation undoes the outcome, that mutated event is seen as the causal force behind what happened later (Wells, Taylor, & Turtle, 1987). Thus, running a counterfactual simulation in one's head is the mental equivalent of conducting an experiment (Einhorn & Hogarth, 1986; Mandel & Lehman, 1996; Wells & Gavanski, 1989).

As it turns out, simply engaging in counterfactual thought is critical for proper mental functioning. For example, both patients with schizophrenia (Hooker, Roese, & Park, 2000) and patients with Parkinson's disease (McNamara, Durso, Brown, & Lynch, 2003) have difficulty in articulating counterfactual thoughts. Considering counterfactuals helps people prepare more effectively for tomorrow; engaging in counterfactual thinking helps people both capitalize on their successes and avoid their past failures (Galinsky, Seiden, Kim, & Medvec, 2002; Roese, 1994).

Not only does generating counterfactual thoughts in one domain affect subsequent behavior in that exact same domain but also considering counterfactual possibilities directs subsequent information processing and problem solving in completely unrelated domains. Thinking counterfactually activates a particular mind-set that carries through to affect later decision making, group interaction, and creative output.

Just having people read the scenario we provided at the beginning of this section affects how they approach subsequent unrelated tasks. The sum total of work on the counterfactual mind-set is that it appears to activate a particular processing style, what Kray, Galinsky, and Wong (2006) termed a *relational processing style*. Because counterfactuals involve a consideration of both reality and what might have been, they are inherently relational in nature: Constructing counterfactual thoughts in one context produces a counterfactual mind-set characterized by a tendency to process information relationally in subsequent contexts. Thus, counterfactual mind-sets facilitate performance on tasks by capitalizing on linkages among known information (Galinsky & Kray, 2004; Galinsky & Moskowitz, 2000; Kray & Galinsky, 2003; Kray, Galinsky, & Markman, 2009), but counterfactual mind-sets hinder performance on novel tasks that reach beyond existing knowledge structures (Kray et al., 2006).

PERSONAL MEANING: COUNTERFACTUALS REVEAL LIFE STORIES

Building on the notion that counterfactual thinking enables an understanding of the relationships between variables, one can see that generating counterfactuals about key elements of personal histories helps to sharpen and define one's autobiography. In this section, we explore a framework for understanding narrative identity by interweaving counterfactual reflection into this constructive process. To do so, we review recent empirical work demonstrating an intimate link between two uniquely human processes, counterfactual reflection and the search for meaning (Bruner, 1990; Frankl, 1985).

People tell stories to make sense of their lives. An influential framework for understanding the process of constructing a life story can be found in the work of Dan McAdams (e.g., McAdams, 1996; see also Chapter 9, this volume). According to McAdams (1996), the life story is "an internalized and evolving narrative of the self that incorporates the reconstructed past, perceived present, and anticipated future" (p. 307).

In his qualitative approach, narrative accounts of personally meaningful events from the past are analyzed for themes of redemption wherein a negative state is transformed into a positive one. By means of a lengthy structured interview, successive episodes and personal epochs from the past are subjectively defined, and specific "nuclear episodes" that stand out from the past are elicited, including low points, high points, turning points, and beginning points. Though descriptively interesting on its own, how individuals tell the story of their lives is important because it predicts generativity, or psychosocial adaptation in the midlife years (Erikson, 1963). Highly generative individuals invest more in future generations as a way of giving back to their communities.

We contend that examining these markers of the passage of time through a counterfactual lens enhances their significance. Just as the use of counterfactuals helps establish causal relationships in abstract problem-

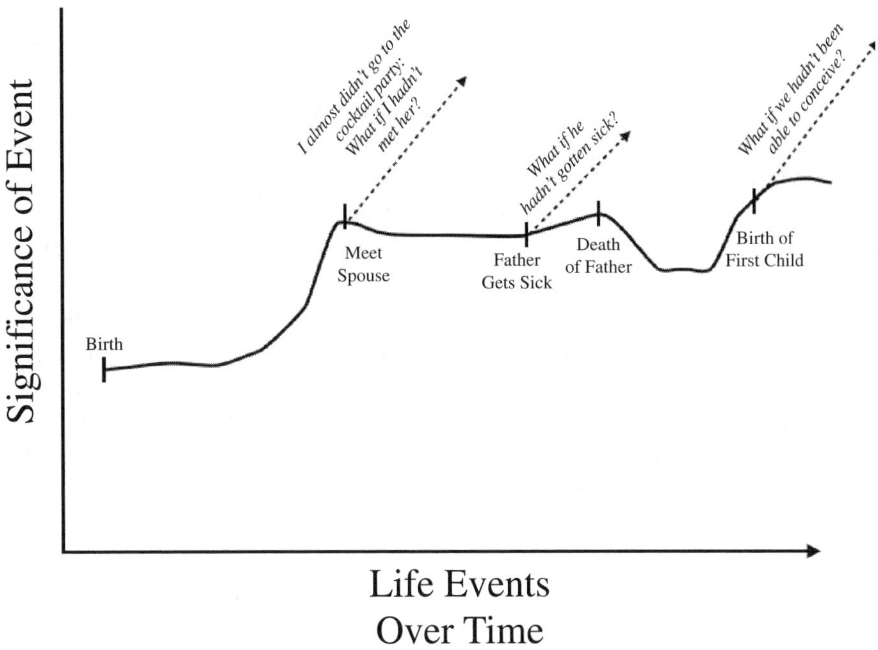

Figure 16.1. Hypothetical example of nuclear episodes along the life course.

solving domains, thinking counterfactually about one's own life facilitates causal connections that enable meaning to emerge. Figure 16.1 illustrates the chronology of nuclear episodes in a hypothetical life story over a slice of time. Beginning with the birth of a protagonist and ending with his or her death, the life course is marked by transitions separating the various chapters of the person's life. In the next section, we consider the chronology of events comprising narrative identities and how their significance is likely to be influenced by counterfactual reflection. Our example in Figure 16.1 is a middle-aged man who has already experienced marriage, the death of a parent, and the birth of his first child. With each of these major life events, it is not difficult to imagine the counterfactuals that might arise. What if, for instance, instead of going to a routine cocktail party at a friend's house, our protagonist stayed home and did not subsequently meet his future wife?

Turning Points

Change often happens suddenly and completely. *Turning points* are nonlinear moments in time in which clear and rapid change occurs (McAdams, 1985; McAdams & Bowman, 2001). They are quintessential forks in the road when initiated internally; when driven by forces beyond an individual's control, they are often akin to being blindsided, arising without warning and shifting the direction of life in an instant. The events themselves can be positive, such as first encounters and pregnancies, or negative, such as sudden deaths and imprisonments. From a narrative identity perspective, understanding how turning points are processed sheds substantial light on an individual's ability to make sense of the twists and turns of fate that invariably occur in life. Because turning points most closely capture the notion of counterfactual existences—without the turning point's occurrence, life would have proceeded on its earlier course—they are prime candidates for exploring the relationship between counterfactual thinking and meaning.

How does counterfactual reflection affect the meaning derived from turning points? On one hand, mentally exploring a world in which a particular turning point had not occurred may simply reinforce an existential angst, or a sense that life is absurd and therefore devoid of any meaningful essence (Camus, 1955/1991). The more vividly and plausibly an alternate universe can be imagined, the less significant reality may seem. On the other hand, rather than promoting a sense of randomness, counterfactual musings may enhance a sense that life is full of meaning, as revealed by the path that life actually took. In fact, the latter is what our research found.

Kray et al. (2010) identified several reasons why counterfactual reflection creates rather than destroys the meaning of turning points. First, counterfactuals help to connect the dots between life events. By their very nature, counterfactuals establish causal relationships, illuminating how one event led to another. If a given turning point had not occurred, life as experienced today would not exist. This realization can lead to an appreciation of destiny unfolding: To be here now, the turning point was necessary. This realization can foster a sense that the turning point *had* to happen. In a sense, it was a product of fate.

A second practical reason why counterfactuals aid in identifying the meaning underlying turning points is that they bring to light the ensuing benefits. By imagining a world in which a turning point had not occurred, the downstream positive consequences of life's plot twists come into focus more sharply. By subtracting the turning point from the past, more often than not, worse possible worlds are conjured.

Beginnings

Beginnings play a prominent role in developing a narrative identity. McAdams (2006) contended that individuals who recall early blessings and advantages are more likely to be highly generative adults. By recognizing their personal destiny early on, along with the misfortunes of others, these individuals are morally challenged to repay society. In our research, we have explored the stories that people tell about the origins of a collective's existence and how counterfactual thought bolsters their commitment to the collective. For example, one night in 1973, Fred Smith, the founder of FedEx, flew to a Las Vegas casino in a desperate attempt to help his then-floundering company meet payroll. He won $27,000 at the blackjack table and was able to keep his company afloat. This origin story, which is a significant part of FedEx culture (Foust, 2004), easily breeds counterfactual thought (e.g., What if Smith had not flown to Vegas?) and subsequent commitment to the company: FedEx is regularly listed in *Fortune* magazine's list of top companies to work for (Levering & Moskowitz, 2009).

Counterfactual reflection about origins affects subsequent commitment behavior (Ersner-Hershfield, Galinsky, Kray, & King, 2010). In one study, for example, participants in a counterfactual condition were asked to think about what the world would be like if their country of origin and all the relevant people and events that led to its creation had never existed. In a control condition (i.e., the factual condition), participants simply reflected on what the world is like now *because* their country of origin existed. Those participants who had reflected counterfactually about their country's origins expressed higher levels of patriotism (a measure of commitment) on a subsequent task. Similar results were obtained in a different study wherein counterfactual reflection enhanced commitment to an employer.

Such effects, however, are not just confined to attitudes and intentions; they also affect relationships. In one study, participants either thought counterfactually or factually about the origins of a significant business relationship. Approximately two weeks later, we surveyed these participants and asked them to report how often they had contacted a host of different people in their lives. Strikingly, participants in our experimental condition were significantly more likely to have demonstrated behavioral commitment by reaching out to the targets of their reflection (i.e., the important business contact) than participants in the control condition.

Endings

Though counterfactuals are by definition about the past (counter to the facts of what actually happened), and the stories people tell about their own lives are by definition works in progress, how people feel about future anticipated endings is also influenced by counterfactual thought. Previous work has found that when individuals face meaningful endings in their lives, a mixed emotional experience known as *poignancy* occurs (Ersner-Hershfield, Mikels, Sullivan, & Carstensen, 2008). Graduation day, for example, is marked by poignancy because although it is a happy occasion due to the progress and accomplishments that it marks, it is also sad: Graduating seniors realize that many cherished aspects of their life will not be with them anymore. Similarly, thinking counterfactually about important people or entities evokes this same *near-loss* mind-set. In other words, when thinking about what might have been, implicit thoughts arise about what it would have been like to live in a world without the targets of our counterfactual reflection. Given these similarities, how does counterfactual thinking relate to poignancy? In previous empirical work on organizational commitment (Ersner-Hershfield et al., 2010), we hypothesized that the poignant feelings that arise from counterfactual reflection would make people more attached to the target in question. Thinking about losing something cherished makes individuals want to hold on to that thing more and more (King, Hicks, & Abdelkhalik, 2009; Kurtz, 2008). Behaviorally and attitudinally, these feelings are expressed as commitment. Indeed, we found that feelings of poignancy mediated the relationship between counterfactual reflection about one's company or firm and commitment to that entity.

High Points and Low Points

In addition to turning points, beginnings, and endings, life narratives comprise both high points and low points. Though our research has not explicitly elicited reflections on these precise episodes, many of the experiences considered by participants in Kray et al.'s (2010) research were likely to correspond with high versus low points in their lives. For example, the subject who identified a father's suicide as a turning point probably regarded this tragedy as a low point. Conversely, the subject who identified the use of psychedelic mushrooms as a turning point may have regarded this hallucinogenic experience as a high point (no pun intended). Regardless of the valence of these pivotal moments, counterfactual reflection serves a meaning-making function.

Past research on the functional basis of counterfactuals has identified the direction of the counterfactual as a key determinant of the response it elicits. *Upward* counterfactuals consider better possible worlds and tend to elicit negative emotions such as regret; *downward* counterfactuals consider worse possible worlds and tend to elicit positive emotions such as relief (Roese, 1994). Upward counterfactuals typically result from negative realities, whereas downward counterfactuals typically result from positive realities. In terms of life stories, the logical implication of this work is that high points would elicit downward counterfactuals whereas low points would elicit upward counterfactuals.

Are people as likely to envision better possible lives as they are worse possible lives? Upon undoing pivotal events, are people as likely to believe their lives are characterized by sour grapes as they are silver linings? In our research, we find the answer to both of these questions is a resounding no. Instead, people manifest a strong gravitational pull in the downward counterfactual direction. In Kray et al. (2010), participants who were guided through a counterfactual reflection process generated four times as many downward counterfactuals as upward counterfactuals, and this pattern occurred regardless of the valence of the event being undone. In other words, counterfactually recalling a negative event in one's life produced not sour grapes but rather an appreciation for silver linings. A vivid illustration of the selective generation of worse possible worlds, even in the face of objectively negative events, concerns a research participant who had been an Olympics-bound athlete but who had a career-ending injury. She wrote: "Maybe I would be a professional athlete. But I think that I would discover that something is missing because that would never fulfill me. From my point of view today, I can't imagine being a professional athlete." Though undoubtedly a devastating experience at the time, she had come to see it in a decidedly positive light: By becoming injured, she was able to avoid a career that would have left her wanting more.

The literature on coping with adversity demonstrates that focusing on the benefits accrued through the avoidance of worse possible worlds offers adaptive advantages. Consider the psychological cousin of downward counterfactuals, downward social comparisons. *Downward social comparisons* involve identifying others who are worse off. Their generation increases the ability to withstand both psychological and physical adversity (Taylor, 1989). Focusing on individuals who are worse off lightens one's load by promoting an optimistic view of stressful events (Taylor, 1983). Just as downward social comparisons predict coping with adversity, the tendency to generate downward counterfactuals for turning points for positive and negative events alike enhances meaning. Indeed, Teigen and Jensen (2011) found that, overwhelmingly, survivors of the 2004 Asian tsunami that claimed over 200,000 lives described themselves as lucky survivors rather than unlucky victims. By imagining how they could have been worse off, they experienced gratitude for how life actually unfolded (cf. Koo, Algoe, Wilson, & Gilbert, 2008).

Consistent with McAdams's work documenting a beneficial pattern of negative emotional states to more positive ones, the groundbreaking work by Taylor and Brown (1988) illustrated the adaptive benefits of positive illusions for mental health. Healthy adults exhibit a pronounced tendency to be positively biased in their self-perceptions, believing they are better, more in control, and more likely to experience a bright future than possible. This pattern does not reflect a defensive and maladaptive response to threats. Instead, it is constructive and adaptive, predicting psychological well-being. As Taylor and Brown (1994) articulated, "positive illusions are directly responsive to threatening circumstances, whereas defenses are conceptualized as inversely responsive to threatening information" (p. 25). Our work suggests that psychological health is also characterized by a tendency to imagine counterfactual worlds as inferior to the world actually occupied.

Life Trajectories and Redemption Themes

Counterfactual reflection may not only provide an understanding of discrete life events but also affect considerations of overall life trajectories. The abstract themes and affective tones evident in descriptions of the past, present, and future comprise life trajectories. Though idiosyncrasies surely distinguish each individual's life story, common themes emerge that predict positive (or negative) psychological states. In the work of McAdams, highly generative adults are characterized by a tendency to see future growth and progress even when future obstacles are expected. Through their contributions to others, they expect to leave a positive legacy.

The almost universal tendency for people to construct life narratives raises the question about the origins of this need to narrate one's life. To answer this question, it is helpful to consider the influential work of Joseph Campbell on human mythology. In his classic text, *The Hero With a Thousand Faces*, Campbell (1949) argued that across cultures and time, human mythology is rife with an archetypal pattern of self-discovery (a "monomyth") known as *the hero's journey*. One's story describes the transformative process by which one comes to know one's life purpose. First, the protagonist is separated from the past with a "call to adventure" that leads him or her to cross a threshold into the unknown, or unconscious. Second, the protagonist must face his or her darkest fears ("entering the abyss to slay the dragon") to achieve atonement from the past. Finally, the protagonist returns to society with a new gift of maturity, better positioned to contribute to society as a hero. This shared structure for organizing human experiences is evident on the silver screen. For example, the struggle of Luke Skywalker, the protagonist of *Star Wars*, to harness the Force to vanquish the dark side epitomizes the hero's journey.

McAdams (2006) examined personal narrative themes consistent with the hero's journey. When people see their lives in terms consistent with the hero's journey, themes of redemption are prevalent. Life progresses from an affectively negative episode to a positive affective state, rather than the other way around (termed a contamination sequence). Examples of this adaptive sequencing include moving from sickness to health, from poverty to wealth, or from ignorance to enlightenment. As in the positive conclusion of the mythic hero's journey, individuals who recognize a negative-to-positive transformation in their life journey are poised to give back to the society that helped cultivate their good fortune.

Counterfactual thinking not only helps people to recognize the arrival of blessings in the past but also creates an optimistic outlook of the future. In the work of Ersner-Hershfield et al. (2010), participants were asked to select a drawing that most closely captured their expectations of the future of an organization to which they belonged. Participants who had just engaged in counterfactual reflection about the origins of the chosen organization were more likely to select an upward sloping trajectory compared with baseline conditions. Taken together, counterfactual reflection's impact on how the past and future are understood in relation to each other is consistent with the upward-moving redemption sequence.

LINGERING QUESTIONS ABOUT COUNTERFACTUALS AND MEANING

In the previous section, we detailed the myriad ways in which counterfactuals weave a tapestry of meaning into personal life stories. In this section, we articulate important and unanswered questions about the relationship between counterfactual reflection and meaning in an effort to stimulate future research. First, we compare and contrast deliberate versus spontaneous counterfactual reflection. Second, we explore fate attributions, an important mediator of the relationship between counterfactual reflection and meaning. Third, we consider individual difference variables likely to be important for understanding the relationship between counterfactual reflection and meaning. Finally, we juxtapose our conceptualization of counterfactuals as a tool for constructing meaning with the body of literature documenting the psychological processes that give rise to defensive meaning making.

Spontaneous Counterfactuals and Personal Meaning

Counterfactuals can be both spontaneously generated and deliberately elicited. Though earlier work on counterfactual mind-sets examined the impact of counterfactuals that effortlessly jumped out as the result of an event *almost* occurring, our research examining personal meaning has involved a deliberate and effortful reflection exercise. This raises two questions. First, do spontaneous and deliberate counterfactuals operate similarly? Second, if they do not, what effect might spontaneous counterfactuals have on meaning?

To begin, we consider how spontaneous counterfactuals operate. In his Nobel Prize lecture, Kahneman (2003) identified both effortless intuition and deliberate reasoning as fundamental decision-making approaches. We contend that spontaneous counterfactual generation, like what pops out when reading a scenario about the woman who won the trip to Hawaii by switching seats at a rock concert, is most akin to an intuitive process. Whereas the intuitive system tends to be emotional, fast, effortless, and associative, the deliberate system is serial, slow, effortful, and controllable.

Recent advances in cognitive neuroscience suggest that deliberate versus spontaneous counterfactual generation are distinct processes. Specifically, Beldarrain, Garcia-Monco, Astigarraga, Gonzalez, and Grafman (2005) showed that lesions in the prefrontal cortex have differential effects on spontaneous versus deliberate counterfactual generation. Whereas patients with this impairment were unable to generate spontaneous counterfactuals compared with control participants, the difference between these two groups in the generation of cued counterfactuals was not statistically significant. These results suggest that different brain regions may be at work when counterfactuals are generated spontaneously versus deliberately.

We propose that the spontaneous and implicit generation of counterfactuals may be experienced as synchronicities, or meaningful coincidences (Richo, 2007). Synchronicities are characterized by the sentiment "you can't make this stuff up" and may arise when an event's occurrence seems too improbable to be due to chance alone. The experience of synchronistic grace in life may occur through unusual and unlikely pathways, two signposts for counterfactual thought. The more easily an event's nonoccurrence can be simulated (in other words the more easily counterfactual possibilities can be conjured), the more infused with significance it seems to be. Important for understanding synchronicities as spontaneous counterfactuals is the realization that their origin is outside the bounds of conscious will and deliberation. They just appear.

A classic example of synchronicity can be found in M. Scott Peck's (1977) *The Road Less Traveled: A New Psychology of Love, Traditional Values and Spiritual Growth,* wherein he recounts Jung's story of seeing a particular rare beetle appear on a ledge of a window in a room where at that exact moment a patient was recounting a dream in which this very same beetle appeared to deliver a message. These apparent synchronicities help people spontaneously attach meaning to that precise moment in time, tapping into an apparent cosmic consciousness in which everything makes sense. Exploring how and when people perceive synchronicities is important for understanding descriptively the ways that people intuit meaning in their own lives. Indeed, belief in synchronicity appears to be on the rise in American society. The 2009 religion and public life survey of the Pew Research Center for the People and the Press found that 49% of Americans reported having experienced a "moment of sudden religious insight or awakening," up from 33% just 15 years prior and only 22% in 1962. Though this statistic likely reflects a general increase in the role of religion in American society, it is notable that the question refers to a precise moment in time in which this faith emerged.

Meaning emerges in an instant; when it does, it is often not through an effortful process.

Exploring synchronicities on a societal level may also prove to be fruitful. Consider the recent attempted assassination of Congresswoman Gabrielle Giffords in Tucson, Arizona. Though the tragedy took the lives of nine victims, none was more poignant than the 9-year-old girl Christina Taylor Green. Aside from the fact that she was the youngest victim, the most remarkable aspect of her loss of life concerns when her life began. She was born on September 11, 2001, which will forever be remembered as a day of national tragedy of an unparalleled magnitude. She even appeared in a book titled *Face of Hope: Babies Born on 9/11* (Naman, 2002). The irony that a girl born on a day of national tragedy would die in the spotlight on a day of national tragedy is lost on few. We contend that part of the sense that this coincidence is meaningful is its sheer improbability. The endless counterfactual alternatives loom large: She might have been born on any of the 364 other days of the year or in a different year altogether. It will be interesting to see if this synchronistic event lessens the grief of 9/11 survivors by invoking a sense of higher meaning or infuses the Tucson tragedy with a special purpose by moving the national conversation forward in a way that would not have happened if the Giffords assassination attempt did not involve this innocent victim.

What Is Fate?

> Though I cannot tell why it was exactly that those stage managers, the Fates, put me down for this shabby part of a whaling voyage, when others were set down for magnificent parts in high tragedies, and short and easy parts in genteel comedies, and jolly parts in farces—though I cannot tell why this was exactly; yet, now that I recall all the circumstances, I think I can see a little into the springs and motives which being cunningly presented to me under various disguises, induced me to set about performing the part I did, besides cajoling me into the delusion that it was a choice resulting from my own unbiased free will and discriminating judgment. (Melville, 1851/2002)

The concept of fate has played an important role in the understanding of counterfactual thought. First, in both Kray et al.'s (2010) and Ersner-Hershfield et al.'s (2010) research, reflecting counterfactually led to a sense that how life actually unfolded was meant to be, a product of fate. A belief in fate should, therefore, facilitate reconciliation of an unexpected or surprising event, deepening a sense of meaning and coherence. Indeed, Kray et al. (2010) found that the relationship between counterfactual thought and the meaning imparted to a turning point was mediated by perceptions of fate, suggesting that counterfactual reflection produced meaning by influencing the degree to which pivotal life events were judged to be fated. Essentially, if fate was involved the event *had* to happen the way it did.

Fate has been conceptualized as an impersonal force or power immutably predestining events. Even people who disavow a belief in fate are reluctant to tempt it (Risen & Gilovich, 2008). Pepitone and Saffiotti (1997) investigated types of life events associated with beliefs in fate. Across a series of scenarios, nonmaterial beliefs such as fate, luck, chance, and belief in God were invoked to help understand life events that were difficult to explain in more concrete, material ways. Fate was most strongly associated with a scenario in which a man improbably finds his long-lost brother.

Recently, we have explored the motivational basis of fate attributions (Kray, George, Tetlock, & Roese, 2012). Fate attributions were hypothesized to satisfy a fundamental need for meaning (Heine, Proulx, & Vohs, 2006). Heine et al. (2006) argued that certainty, which is experienced as subjectively knowing how the world works, contributes to meaning. If a life event is attributed to fate, and therefore meant to be, then it implies there is no other way the event could have turned out. By manipulating whether a life event is described in close-call counterfactual terms (which necessarily introduce uncertainty), Kray et al. (2012) showed that uncertainty causes fate attributions to strengthen. In describing the initial encounter of two young lovers on a subway train, the sequence of events immediately preceding it were described as either consistent with the protagonist's daily routine or as almost not occurring (because the protagonist overslept and almost missed the train). Rather than seeing the encounter as more random when its uncertainty was emphasized, participants saw the meeting that almost did not occur as more fated. Presumably, the situational uncertainty inherent in the close-call counterfactual stimulated a search for meaning that ended in an attribution to fate.

As the quote from Melville's (1851/2002) *Moby Dick* suggests, fate seems to imply that life is directed by an external "stage manager" operating outside the bounds of an individual's personal control. Given the negative relationship between an external locus of control and psychological well-being (Ryff, 1989), how does one reconcile the positive function that fate attributions appear to be serving? Rather than being an overly simplistic interpretation of the causal forces directing one's life, fate appears to be positively related to causal complexity (Norenzayan & Lee, 2010). Consistent with this observation is Burrus and Roese's (2006) finding that a belief in fate often coexists with a belief that personal action could have altered a given course of events. Understanding the precise role that beliefs in fate or that an event was meant to be plays in psychological well-being is certainly fodder for more research.

Individual Differences in Counterfactual Thought

We have described how counterfactual reasoning can relate to constructions of life stories that are unique to each individual. Life stories have been formulated as one component of a multilevel framework for personality (McAdams, 1996), complementing the study of broad personality dimensions such as Big Five Conscientiousness and more narrowly defined traits such as self-control or need for closure. We know little, however, about relationships between counterfactual thought and personality traits or dimensions, although we expect that certain forms of individual differences would predict the use of counterfactual reasoning. And, given the range of implications related to counterfactual thought, it is important to consider whether additional individual differences predict this fundamental cognitive process. Here we consider two individual difference variables likely to influence the counterfactual reflection process.

Need for closure is a motivational construct that has been related to an unwillingness to consider counterfactuals as plausible (Hirt, Kardes, & Markman, 2004; Tetlock, 1998; Tetlock & Lebow, 2001). Individuals higher in need for closure seek definite knowledge about issues or other life occurrences and should be particularly inclined to invoke fate as a causal explanation, closing the door to the consideration of realities that might have happened.

In their research linking fate attributions to certainty, Kray et al. (2012) provided evidence that need for closure predicts fate attributions. First, individuals high in dispositional need for closure were particularly likely to attribute fate to a variety of life events. Second, by manipulating time pressure in a task involving reviewing the underlying cause of various life events, individuals high in situational need for certainty were shown to make stronger fate attributions than those not burdened by such pressures. Consistent with Kruglanski and Webster's (1996) description of the "freezing" function of need for closure, fate attributions appear to be used by those individuals seeking certainty about the underlying causes of life events. Given that sensing the hands of fate contributes to personal meaning (Kray et al., 2010), this research suggests a benefit to being high in need for closure. Individuals particularly motivated to find answers may be most attuned to spontaneous counterfactuals arising from close calls.

Another individual difference that is likely to influence how counterfactuals are experienced is Openness to Experience, one of the Big Five personality dimensions that has gained prominence for its ability to predict important life outcomes. (The other four dimensions are Conscientiousness, Extraversion, Agreeableness, and Emotional Stability.) Openness to Experience indicates a willingness to embrace new ideas, thoughts, feelings, and experiences; intellectual adventurousness; and comfort with complexity. High

Openness to Experience is related to traits such as curiosity and unconventionality (McCrae, 1996; McCrae & John, 1992) and has been associated with divergent thinking (McCrae, 1987). Examining the opposite end of the Openness to Experience scale, McCrae (1996) noted that need for closure can be viewed as "a particular form of Closedness" (p. 328). Though Openness to Experience has been conceptualized in terms of actual life experiences, we contend that it may also impact openness to counterfactual life experiences.

We contend that openness (or closedness) to what ifs has important implications for how individuals experience life. An example that captures this hypothesis can be found in McAdams's (2010) case study of George W. Bush's decision to invade Iraq. Because the 43rd president was extremely low in Openness to Experience, which predicts a simplistic view of situations, he may have been unwilling to consider alternative views before making major decisions. However, a subtler, identity-based counterfactual might have driven his actions. McAdams proposed that President Bush had constructed a redemptive story for his own life in which a hero emerged through adversity to gain unforeseen rewards. The contrast between his turning point and subsequent personal triumphs in middle adulthood versus how his life might have gone may have strengthened his conviction that his redemption was fated and that an invasion of Iraq would have a similarly positive outcome, restoring freedom and perhaps saving the world. Though this interpretation may have ultimately been misguided from the outsider's perspective, it allowed "the decider" to sleep well at night. From a purely descriptive standpoint, it also allows outsiders to understand his fateful decision.

Constructive Versus Defensive Meaning Making

A recurring question that arises in this area of research is whether counterfactual thinking about one's life is inherently threatening. If so, the resulting boost in meaning may simply be a defensive reaction to the existential threat that has arisen. We contend that this view may derive in part from an overly narrow interpretation of existential philosophy. Social psychology has been influenced mainly by the writings of Ernest Becker concerning the fear of death as a driver of defensive meaning making. Yet existentialists from Sartre to Camus regarded finding meaning amidst the absurdity of life as the ultimate challenge of mankind in a positive sense. Despair may arise from the breaking down of pillars of one's identity, a process perhaps magnified through counterfactual reflection about possible selves. When this happens, who one thought one was has crumbled and a new sense of self must be rebuilt to restore hope. Meaning derived through counterfactuals may affirm and help reconstruct the self in new ways that result in growth, authenticity, and acceptance of what is.

The formulation of a coherent autobiography buffers against fear arising from the awareness that everyone one knows will one day die, including oneself. By enhancing a sense of significance over the past and predictability over the future, mortality concerns are soothed (Landau, Greenberg, & Sullivan, 2009). This of course raises the question of whether meaning derived from counterfactual musings is simply a defensive reaction against the awareness that life could have just as easily gone a different way. Although turning points can produce negative or positive consequences, people appear far more inclined to focus on what was found rather than lost (e.g., King & Raspin, 2004). This lopsided tendency to focus on the positive rather than dwell on the negative has adaptive benefits (Taylor & Brown, 1988). Rather than becoming heartless cynics through adversity, the human condition thrives when hardship turns people into hopeful dreamers. Counterfactual reflection fosters this appreciation for one's actual life path and enhances one's sense of meaning about life's sometimes-incomprehensible events.

One way to identify compensatory or defensive mechanisms underlying psychological phenomena is to invoke self-affirmations to neutralize the ego threat (Steele & Liu, 1983). In recent work, Kray, Hershfield, and Galinsky (2011) found that participants who affirmed their most important value before thinking counterfactually about their professional identity were more likely to see the pursuit of their chosen career path as fated than those who thought factually about this identity. If counterfactual reflection were simply a defensive process, then researchers would not expect to see this difference following self-affirmations. Future research is desired to continue teasing apart the threatening versus affirming aspects of counterfactual reflection and to determine how counterfactual reflection affects identity.

CONCLUSION

In this chapter, we have reviewed the literature connecting counterfactual reflection to personal meaning in life. In so doing, we have solidified the importance of the relationship between two uniquely human characteristics—the ability to reflect about "what might have been" and the quest for meaning (Bruner, 1990). Consistent with the beneficial role that counterfactual reflection plays in understanding relationships between variables when applied to personal life stories, counterfactual reflection facilitates the construction of the story of one's life. By seeing the twists and turns of life as fated and by recognizing the benefits that they brought about, counterfactual reflection serves an important autobiographical function.

REFERENCES

Beldarrain, M. G., Garcia-Monco, J. C., Astigarraga, E., Gonzalez, A., & Grafman, J. (2005). Only spontaneous counterfactual thinking is impaired in patients with prefrontal cortex lesions. *Cognitive Brain Research, 24*, 723–726. doi:10.1016/j.cogbrainres.2005.03.013

Bruner, J. S. (1990). *Acts of meaning*. Cambridge, MA: Harvard University Press.

Burrus, J., & Roese, N. J. (2006). Long ago it was meant to be: The interplay between time, construal, and fate beliefs. *Personality and Social Psychology Bulletin, 32*, 1050–1058. doi:10.1177/0146167206288282

Campbell, J. (1949). *The hero with a thousand faces*. Princeton, NJ: Princeton University Press.

Camus, A. (1991). *The myth of Sisyphus and other essays*. New York, NY: Vintage International. (Original work published 1955)

Einhorn, H. J., & Hogarth, R. M. (1986). Judging probable cause. *Psychological Bulletin, 99*, 3–19. doi:10.1037/0033-2909.99.1.3

Erikson, E. (1963). *Childhood and society*. New York, NY: Norton.

Ersner-Hershfield, H., Galinsky, A. D., Kray, L. J., & King, B. G. (2010). Company, country, connections: Counterfactual origins increase organizational commitment, patriotism, and social investment. *Psychological Science, 21*, 1479–1486. doi:10.1177/0956797610382123

Ersner-Hershfield, H., Mikels, J. A., Sullivan, S. J., & Carstensen, L. L. (2008). Poignancy: Mixed emotional experience in the face of meaningful endings. *Journal of Personality and Social Psychology, 94*, 158–167. doi:10.1037/0022-3514.94.1.158

Foust, D. (2004, September 20). Frederick W. Smith: No overnight success. *Business Week*, p. 18.

Frankl, V. E. (1985). *Man's search for meaning*. New York, NY: Simon & Schuster.

Galinsky, A. D., & Kray, L. J. (2004). From thinking about what might have been to sharing what we know: The effects of counterfactual mind-sets on information sharing in groups. *Journal of Experimental Social Psychology, 40*, 606–618. doi:10.1016/j.jesp.2003.11.005

Galinsky, A. D., & Moskowitz, G. B. (2000). Counterfactuals as behavioral primes: Priming the simulation heuristic and consideration of alternatives. *Journal of Experimental Social Psychology, 36*, 257–383.

Galinsky, A. D., Seiden, V., Kim, P. H., & Medvec, V. H. (2002). The dissatisfaction of having your first offer accepted: The role of counterfactual thinking in negotiations. *Personality and Social Psychology Bulletin, 28*, 271–283. doi:10.1177/0146167202282012

Heine, S. J., Proulx, T., & Vohs, K. D. (2006). The meaning maintenance model: On the coherence of social motivations. *Personality and Social Psychology Review, 10*, 88–110. doi:10.1207/s15327957pspr1002_1

Hirt, E. R., Kardes, F. R., & Markman, K. D. (2004). Activating a mental simulation mind-set through generation of alternatives: Implications for debiasing in related and unrelated domains. *Journal of Experimental Social Psychology, 40,* 374–383. doi:10.1016/j.jesp.2003.07.009

Hooker, C., Roese, N. J., & Park, S. (2000). Impoverished counterfactual thinking is associated with schizophrenia. *Psychiatry: Interpersonal and Biological Processes, 63,* 326–335.

Kahneman, D. (2003). A perspective on judgment and choice: Mapping bounded rationality. *American Psychologist, 58,* 697–720. doi:10.1037/0003-066X.58.9.697

Kahneman, D., & Miller, D. T. (1986). Norm theory: Comparing reality to its alternatives. *Psychological Review, 93,* 136–153. doi:10.1037/0033-295X.93.2.136

King, L. A., Hicks, J. A., & Abdelkhalik, J. (2009). Death, life, scarcity, and value: An alternative perspective on the meaning of death. *Psychological Science, 20,* 1459–1462. doi:10.1111/j.1467-9280.2009.02466.x

King, L. A., & Raspin, C. (2004). Lost and found possible selves, subjective well-being, and ego development in divorced women. *Journal of Personality, 72,* 603–632. doi:10.1111/j.0022-3506.2004.00274.x

Koo, M., Algoe, S. B., Wilson, T. D., & Gilbert, D. T. (2008). It's a wonderful life: Mentally subtracting positive events improves people's affective states, contrary to their affective forecasts. *Journal of Personality and Social Psychology, 95,* 1217–1224. doi:10.1037/a0013316

Kray, L. J., & Galinsky, A. D. (2003). The debiasing effect of counterfactual mind-sets: Increasing the search for disconfirmatory information in group decisions. *Organizational Behavior and Human Decision Processes, 91,* 69–81. doi:10.1016/S0749-5978(02)00534-4

Kray, L. J., Galinsky, A. D., & Markman, K. (2009). Counterfactual structure and learning from experience in negotiations. *Journal of Experimental Social Psychology, 45,* 979–982. doi:10.1016/j.jesp.2009.03.008

Kray, L. J., Galinsky, A. D., & Wong, E. M. (2006). Thinking within the box: The relational processing style elicited by counterfactual mind-sets. *Journal of Personality and Social Psychology, 91,* 33–48. doi:10.1037/0022-3514.91.1.33

Kray, L. J., George, L. G., Liljenquist, K. A., Galinsky, A. D., Tetlock, P. E., & Roese, N. J. (2010). From what might have been to what must have been: Counterfactual thinking creates meaning. *Journal of Personality and Social Psychology, 98,* 106–118. doi:10.1037/a0017905

Kray, L. J., George, L. G., Tetlock, P. E., & Roese, N. J. (2012). *The motivational basis of fate attributions: Navigating uncertainty for the faithless.* Unpublished manuscript, University of California, Berkeley, Haas School of Business.

Kray, L. J., Hershfield, H. E., & Galinsky, A. D. (2011). *Fate attributions and self-affirmation.* Unpublished manuscript, University of California, Berkeley, Haas School of Business.

Kruglanski, A. W., & Webster, D. M. (1996). Motivated closing of the mind: "Seizing" and "freezing." *Psychological Review, 103*, 263–283. doi:10.1037/0033-295X.103.2.263

Kurtz, J. L. (2008). Looking to the future to appreciate the present: The benefits of perceived temporal scarcity. *Psychological Science, 19*, 1238–1241. doi:10.1111/j.1467-9280.2008.02231.x

Landau, M. J., Greenberg, J., & Sullivan, D. (2009). Defending a coherent autobiography: When past events appear incoherent, mortality salience prompts compensatory bolstering of the past's significance and the future's orderliness. *Personality and Social Psychology Bulletin, 35*, 1012–1020. doi:10.1177/0146167209336608

Levering, R., & Moskowitz, M. (2009, February 2). And the winners are . . . *Fortune, 159*, 67–78.

Mandel, D. R., & Lehman, D. R. (1996). Counterfactual thinking and ascriptions of cause and preventability. *Journal of Personality and Social Psychology, 71*, 450–463. doi:10.1037/0022-3514.71.3.450

McAdams, D. P. (1985). *Power, intimacy and the life story: Personological inquiries into identity*. Homewood, IL: Dorsey Press.

McAdams, D. P. (1996). Personality, modernity, and the storied self: A contemporary framework for studying persons. *Psychological Inquiry, 7*, 295–321. doi:10.1207/s15327965pli0704_1

McAdams, D. P. (2006). The redemptive self: Generativity and the stories Americans live by. *Research in Human Development, 3*, 81–100.

McAdams, D. P. (2010). *George W. Bush and the redemptive dream: A psychological portrait*. New York, NY: Oxford University Press.

McAdams, D. P., & Bowman, P. J. (2001). Narrating life's turning points: Redemption and contamination. In D. P. McAdams, R. Josselson, & A. Lieblich (Eds.), *Turns in the road: Narrative studies of lives in transition* (pp. 3–34). Washington, DC: American Psychological Association. doi:10.1037/10410-001

McCrae, R. R. (1987). Creativity, divergent thinking, and openness to experience. *Journal of Personality and Social Psychology, 52*, 1258–1265. doi:10.1037/0022-3514.52.6.1258

McCrae, R. R. (1996). Social consequences of experiential openness. *Psychological Bulletin, 120*, 323–337. doi:10.1037/0033-2909.120.3.323

McCrae, R. R., & John, O. P. (1992). An introduction to the five-factor model and its applications. [Special issue]. *Journal of Personality, 60*, 175–215.

McNamara, P., Durso, R., Brown, A., & Lynch, A. (2003). Counterfactual cognitive deficit in persons with Parkinson's disease. *Journal of Neurology, Neurosurgery & Psychiatry, 74*, 1065–1070. doi:10.1136/jnnp.74.8.1065

Melville, H. (2002). *Moby Dick or, the whale*. New York, NY: Penguin Classics. (Original work published 1851)

Naman, C. P. (2002). *Face of hope: Babies born on 9/11*. Deerfield Beach, FL: Health Communications.

Norenzayan, A., & Lee, A. (2010). It was meant to happen: Explaining cultural variations in fate attributions. *Journal of Personality and Social Psychology, 98,* 702–720. doi:10.1037/a0019141

Peck, M. S. (1977). *The road less traveled: A new psychology of love, traditional values and spiritual growth*. New York, NY: Simon & Schuster.

Pepitone, A., & Saffiotti, L. (1997). The selectivity of nonmaterial beliefs in interpreting life events. *European Journal of Social Psychology, 27,* 23–35. doi:10.1002/(SICI)1099-0992(199701)27:1<23::AID-EJSP805>3.0.CO;2-B

Richo, D. (2007). *The power of coincidence: How life shows us what we need to know.* Boston, MA: Shambhala.

Risen, J. L., & Gilovich, T. (2008). Why people are reluctant to tempt fate. *Journal of Personality and Social Psychology, 95,* 293–307. doi:10.1037/0022-3514.95.2.293

Roese, N. J. (1994). The functional basis of counterfactual thinking. *Journal of Personality and Social Psychology, 66,* 805–818. doi:10.1037/0022-3514.66.5.805

Ryff, C. D. (1989). Happiness is everything, or is it? Explorations on the meaning of psychological well-being. *Journal of Personality and Social Psychology, 57,* 1069–1081. doi:10.1037/0022-3514.57.6.1069

Steele, C. M., & Liu, T. J. (1983). Dissonance processes as self-affirmation. *Journal of Personality and Social Psychology, 45,* 5–19. doi:10.1037/0022-3514.45.1.5

Taylor, S. E. (1983). Adjustment to threatening events. *American Psychologist, 38,* 1161–1173. doi:10.1037/0003-066X.38.11.1161

Taylor, S. E. (1989). *Positive illusions: Creative self-deception and the healthy mind.* New York, NY: Basic Books.

Taylor, S. E., & Brown, J. D. (1988). Illusion and well-being: A social psychological perspective on mental health. *Psychological Bulletin, 103,* 193–210. doi:10.1037/0033-2909.103.2.193

Taylor, S. E., & Brown, J. D. (1994). Positive illusions and well-being revisited: Separating fact from fiction. *Psychological Bulletin, 116,* 21–27. doi:10.1037/0033-2909.116.1.21

Teigen, K. H., & Jensen, T. K. (2011). Unlucky victims or lucky survivors: Spontaneous counterfactual thinking by families exposed to the tsunami disaster. *European Psychologist, 16,* 48–57. doi:10.1027/1016-9040/a000033

Tetlock, P. E. (1998). Close-call counterfactuals and belief-system defenses: I was not almost wrong but I was almost right. *Journal of Personality and Social Psychology, 75,* 639–652. doi:10.1037/0022-3514.75.3.639

Tetlock, P. E., & Lebow, R. N. (2001). Poking counterfactual holes in covering laws: Cognitive styles and historical reasoning. *The American Political Science Review,* 95, 829–843.

Wells, G. L., & Gavanski, I. (1989). Mental simulation of causality. *Journal of Personality and Social Psychology, 56,* 161–169. doi:10.1037/0022-3514.56.2.161

Wells, G. L., Taylor, B. R., & Turtle, J. W. (1987). The undoing of scenarios. *Journal of Personality and Social Psychology, 53,* 421–430. doi:10.1037/0022-3514.53.3.421

17

"IT WAS MEANT TO BE": RETROSPECTIVE MEANING CONSTRUCTION THROUGH MENTAL SIMULATION

MATTHEW J. LINDBERG, KEITH D. MARKMAN, AND HYEMAN CHOI

Shortly before 9 a.m. on September 11, 2001, Greer Epstein, an executive director at Morgan Stanley, received a phone call from a friend asking if she was interested in taking a cigarette break. On the elevator ride down from the 67th floor, Epstein noticed a jolt but chalked it up to typical problems with the elevators. When she stepped out of the South Tower, she noticed the damage done to the North Tower by the first plane right about the time the second plane struck less than a dozen floors above her office (Park, 2011). Reflecting on the events of that day, Epstein said,

> I never took a break before noon, it was something that happened that day. And thank God for it. I was safely out of the building when the plane hit. A fireball went through my office. Had I been sitting there, who knows what would've been? (Park, 2011)

Epstein and many other individuals that day would have lost their lives had it not been for the occurrence of coincidental events such as scheduling errors, traffic jams, and illness.

DOI: 10.1037/14040-017
The Psychology of Meaning, Keith D. Markman, Travis Proulx, and Matthew J. Lindberg (Editors)

When individuals attempt to make sense of unexpected events, they are often struck by the feeling that larger forces were at work—fate, perhaps, or the intervention of some deity. Moreover, the perceived meaning and purpose of life events can seemingly be clarified by the occurrence of later events. For some, the events that altered the course of the day—the decision to stay and have breakfast, take one's child to the first day of school, swing by the post office on the way to work, and even step out for a cigarette break—take on a sense of meaning when they consider what might have happened if they had made it to work on time or had still been in their office that day in September.

For much of America and the world, the factual events of 9/11 were traumatic enough. But for many, the events that did not happen, but could have or would have happened had a single preceding event transpired differently, can be equally traumatic. The mental simulation of outcomes and events that did not happen, that are contrary to the factual events, has been labeled *counterfactual thinking*. These thoughts of "what might have been" invoke counterfactual simulations of alternative realities, a process that has been shown to impact numerous domains of social and psychological life, including causal reasoning (e.g., Hilton & Slugoski, 1986; Mandel & Lehman, 1996; Wells & Gavanski, 1989), emotion (e.g., Connolly & Zeelenberg, 2002; Mellers, Schwartz, Ho, & Ritov, 1997), blame (Alicke, Buckingham, Zell, & Davis, 2008; Miller & Gunasegaram, 1990), and behavior (Markman & McMullen, 2003; Roese, 1994; Sanna, 1996).

To date, researchers in this area have primarily explored two functions of counterfactual thinking: an affective function and a preparative function. Research on the affective function suggests that the comparison of reality with a simulated better or worse alternative evokes affective contrast (e.g., Markman, Gavanski, Sherman, & McMullen, 1993; Roese, 1994; Taylor & Schneider, 1989; but for exceptions, note Markman & McMullen, 2003). Reflecting on how an outcome could have been worse—*downward* counterfactual thinking—often ameliorates affect and may thereby aid in coping and psychological adjustment. With regard to the preparative function, on the other hand, reflecting on how an outcome could have been better—*upward* counterfactual thinking—may serve to identify behaviors or actions that will elicit more desirable outcomes in the future (e.g., Epstude & Roese, 2008; Kray, Galinsky, & Markman, 2009; Nasco & Marsh, 1999). The goal of the current chapter is to discuss how counterfactual thinking serves a more general sense-making function and to delineate the mechanisms by which this may occur (see also Chapter 16, this volume).

TWO TYPES OF MEANING

Although many researchers study meaning, there remain a multitude of ways to approach and define meaning. At perhaps the broadest level, *meaning* has been defined as "mental representations of expected relationships" (Proulx & Heine, 2006, p. 310; see also Chapter 4, this volume). When considering what makes one's life meaningful, King, Hicks, Krull, and Del Gaiso (2006; see also Chapter 22, this volume) proposed that "lives may be experienced as meaningful when they are felt to have significance beyond the trivial or momentary, to have purpose, or to have a coherence that transcends chaos" (p. 180). Steger and colleagues distinguished between the presence of meaning in one's life and the search for meaning, defining the search for meaning as "the strength, intensity, and activity of people's desire and effort to establish and/or augment their understanding of the meaning, significance, and purpose of their lives" (Steger, Kashdan, Sullivan, & Lorentz, 2008, p. 200; see also Chapter 11, this volume). In an attempt to better understand the psychological processes of finding meaning in the aftermath of loss and trauma, Davis, Nolen-Hoeksema, and Larson (1998) proposed that the various definitions of meaning could be conceptualized as two separate construals of meaning—benefit finding and sense making (see also Janoff-Bulman & Frantz, 1997; Chapter 10, this volume).

Construing meaning as benefit finding involves assigning value and personal significance to the experience of the event or trauma. The focus is not on understanding the event but rather on understanding the self in the context of experiencing the event. In contrast, Davis et al. (1998) argued that when a traumatic event is perceived as a threat to one's assumptive worldview that the world is meaningful, just, and controllable, one must make sense of the event by reconciling it with one's worldview. Davis et al. found evidence that these two construals of meaning independently fostered psychological adjustment to the loss of a loved one, leading them to conclude that the two construals of meaning are the result of different psychological mechanisms. Using this framework, we hope to delineate the distinct processes by which counterfactual thinking provides personally significant meaning and enhances the coherence and comprehensibility of unusual or unexpected events.

Benefit Finding

Although much of the research on benefit finding has focused on personal benefits (e.g., growth in character, change in life perspective, strengthened relationships), work investigating the affective function of counterfactual thinking has demonstrated that individuals can also find comfort in simulating how events could have turned out worse (Markman et al., 1993; McMullen & Markman, 2000; White & Lehman, 2005). Downward counterfactual thinking, the mental simulation of worse possible outcomes, has been found to be a robust reaction to negative events. Burgess and Holmstrom (1979) reported that rape victims frequently consider how they could have suffered more violently or been killed, and Taylor, Wood, and Lichtman (1983) found that cancer patients frequently considered how their bout with cancer could have lasted longer or resulted in death. Comparison of one's situation with a worse alternative is a commonly reported experience across clinical populations. Often, downward counterfactual thinking serves to make one feel better by identifying the "silver lining" or helping to find "the good in the bad" (Gilovich & Medvec, 1995).

Koo, Algoe, Wilson, and Gilbert (2008) found that mentally undoing positive life events—by considering how they might not have occurred—led to more surprise and positive affect than simply reflecting on the occurrence. Additionally, the surprise generated from considering how one might *not* have met their romantic partner led participants to feel more satisfied with the relationship than when they simply thought about how they met their romantic partner. Kray et al. (2010) provided an even more direct demonstration of how mentally undoing major life moments enhances personal meaning. After having participants reflect on their decision to attend a particular college, Kray and colleagues had some of them engage in counterfactual thinking by describing how events could have turned out differently following an alternative college decision. After simulating how their lives might have changed had they chosen to attend a different college, the actual college decision they made attained more personal meaning and significance.

In addition to creating personal meaning, Kray et al. (2010) proposed an ironic effect of considering counterfactual alternatives, specifically, that counterfactual thinking could enhance meaning perceptions through its effects on heightening fate-based explanations. By revealing all the possible alternative ways that a life event could have turned out differently, counterfactual thinking highlights the *improbability* of the way events *did* unfold. The sense of defying the odds, that the event was the product of fate, "amounts to rejecting that counterfactual world as somehow not 'fitting' one's evolving life narrative, and instead embracing life as it is" (Kray et al., 2010, p. 110). Consistent with the defying the odds account, the increase in positive affect reported by Koo et al. (2008) was mediated by feelings of surprise, suggesting that counterfactual thinking reduces the perceived probability of a focal event. In support, Kray et al. (2010) found that having participants reflect on a turning point in their life and how their life would have been different had the event not occurred made the event personally meaningful by influencing the perception that the event was the product of fate. From this perspective, then, considering counterfactual alternatives serves to highlight the improbability of factual life events, thereby highlighting the benefits to be found in the way events actually did turn out.

Sense Making

In addition to enhancing benefit finding within the domain of the self, there is good reason to believe that counterfactual thinking serves a more general epistemic function. The consideration of counterfactual alternatives can serve to elucidate an underlying order to events and facilitate the creation of a comprehensible account of how event outcomes are consistent with fundamental assumptions about the world. Rather than serving as a standard against which to assess the probability of an event, a counterfactual in this case would serve to highlight what would have happened had some external force, fate or destiny, not intervened to change the course of events. We propose that counterfactuals provide a sense of causal coherence to chains of events that elicit the conclusion that "things happen for a reason." Furthermore, we suggest that when individuals perceive that an outcome was "meant to be," they are acknowledging the existence of external forces that help ensure that life events unfold in meaningful and coherent ways, thereby assimilating the outcome to their worldview.

Hindsight Bias

A common finding regarding reactions to unexpected events is that after having learned the outcome, the event seems in hindsight to have been more predictable and inevitable than it would have been without the benefit of outcome knowledge. This phenomenon, known as the *hindsight bias*, has been described as a projection of new knowledge into the past paired with a denial of the influence of outcome information (Hawkins & Hastie, 1990). In a landmark study exploring the hindsight bias (Fischhoff, 1975), participants read about an obscure historical event, the 19th century wars between the British and the Ghurka of Nepal. Some participants read of a battle that ended with a British victory, others with a Ghurka victory, and some were provided with no outcome information. Those participants who received outcome information reported a higher a priori likelihood of that outcome occurring than did those who did not receive outcome information. The result is what Fischhoff (1975) aptly described as "creeping determinism": a post hoc perception of outcome inevitability. Attempts to makes sense of the outcome and create a coherent causal narrative lead one to selectively recall outcome-consistent antecedent information and assimilate it with outcome knowledge.

It seems intuitive that the consideration of counterfactuals would diminish the hindsight bias. Indeed, counterfactual thinking was originally thought to reduce inevitability perceptions by illustrating how alternative outcomes were in fact possible. Sherman (1991) succinctly argued that "to the extent that counterfactuals are easily and spontaneously generated, the past seems less inevitable: other outcomes were clearly possible" (p. 182). Fischhoff and colleagues were able to reduce the strength of the hindsight bias by instructing participants to consider alternative outcomes (Fischhoff, 1976; Slovic & Fischhoff, 1977). Considering opposing or alternative outcomes aids in shifting the focus from the focal hypothesis—that the focal outcome had to occur—to an alternative hypothesis that a different outcome could have occurred (Hirt & Markman, 1995; Koehler, 1991). Thus, the consideration of how the same antecedent events could lead to a different outcome has been found to reduce the hindsight bias.

However, others have argued that counterfactual thinking could lead individuals to perceive events as *more* rather than less determined. Roese and colleagues proposed that counterfactual thinking would actually enhance the hindsight bias to the extent that counterfactual thinking could aid in the identification and creation of a coherent causal narrative (Roese & Maniar, 1997; Roese & Olson, 1996). These researchers suggested that counterfactual thinking does not necessitate the consideration of an alternative outcome but rather can be used to make sense of the outcome.

Roese (2004) argued that a single counterfactual inference identifying a causal connection between antecedent and consequent events may provide a satisfying feeling of coherence and comprehension that leads to greater post hoc certainty. To illustrate, Roese and Maniar (1997) described how a sports fan could make sense of a team's loss by suggesting a counterfactual that the team would have won had it not been for an injury that occurred earlier in the game. In the absence of the injury the team would have won, but given the injury, the loss is construed as inevitable. Using both laboratory studies and field research, Roese and colleagues found that counterfactual thinking directed toward an explanation led to increases in the hindsight bias (Roese & Maniar, 1997; Roese & Olson, 1996). Similarly, Nestler and von Collani (2008) found that both priming counterfactual thinking and activating a counterfactual mind-set led to an increase in the hindsight bias.

Fatalistic Determinism

Thus, it appears that counterfactual thinking directed at undoing a focal outcome reduces the hindsight bias, whereas counterfactual thinking directed at understanding *why* a specific outcome occurred enhances the perception that the event was meant to be. The specific type of determinism to which Roese and his colleagues (e.g., Roese, 2004; Roese & Maniar, 1997) referred is *scientific determinism*: To the extent that a counterfactual alternative helps explain the occurrence of a factual event, then the factual event is perceived as more certain. However, when the event that needs to be explained is a counterfactual event, deterministic perceptions may take on a more fatalistic nature. In this way, a previously inexplicable factual event may be perceived as "happening for a reason" when that event is used to explain why a counterfactual event did *not* occur. Downward counterfactual thinking of this sort not only renders a negative outcome as "not so bad" in comparison with a worse alternative but also may suggest that greater, perhaps external, forces are at work.

The counterfactual fallacy as proposed by Miller and Turnbull (1990) refers to "the confusion of what *might have been* the case and what *ought to have been* the case" (p. 2; italics in original). This phenomenon is particularly relevant to downward counterfactual thinking because it suggests that the easier it is to imagine a worse alternative, the more likely it will seem that the alternative *ought* to have happened and, further, that the alternative was more likely to *have* happened. For example, Teigen (1998) found that in hindsight, participants perceived that a car hit by a boulder in a rockslide had a lower probability of being hit then the car parked next to it. In other words, the car that *almost* got hit, but did not, was perceived to have had a higher a priori chance of getting hit than the car that *actually* got hit by the boulder. Making use of autobiographical accounts of traffic accidents and near accidents, Teigen (2005) found that participants believed the probability of death was three times higher when they were *nearly* in an accident than when an accident *actually* occurred. Moreover, "close-call" accidents in industrial settings are considered to be even more predictive of future disaster than actual accidents. Taken together, these studies demonstrate that the easier it is to imagine a worse outcome occurring, the higher the perceived a priori probability that it would have occurred.

When one imagines a worse alternative that *ought* to have happened but did not, one is more likely to believe that extrapersonal forces played a role in preventing the worse outcome from happening. For example, after surviving a horrific car crash in which their vehicle flipped over a guardrail and plummeted 60 feet, survivors later reflected, "We both believe there is a higher power out there who said, 'It's not their time,'" suggesting that the accident would have been worse had someone or something not intervened. Moreover, the state police sergeant who was at the scene of the accident commented, "These people are extremely lucky they were able to come through the way that they did" (Ellis, 2010, p. 1). The salient counterfactual—they could have died in the accident—is potent enough to imply that they *should* have died. Rather than rejecting the counterfactual, the perception of extrapersonal forces at work amounts to an *embracing* of the counterfactual. This sort of reaction is not unusual; newspapers frequently describe situations in which luck, fate, and higher powers are assumed to have served as causal agents intervening on the behalf of individuals (Teigen, 1988).

HOLY CROSS VERSUS BOSTON COLLEGE, 1942

To demonstrate the meaning as sense-making function of counterfactual thinking, we (Lindberg & Markman, 2012) selected a historical event that was likely to be compelling to most student participants, yet not one with which most students would be familiar. This allowed for the manipulation of event details for the purpose of examining underlying cognitive mechanisms believed to influence the sense-making process. A real-life event borrowed from the headlines of Boston newspapers afforded us such an opportunity. In 1942, football rivals Boston College (BC) and Holy Cross (HC) met for the final game of the season. A heavily favored BC (9–0), seeking to finish the season undefeated, experienced a surprising upset at the hands of HC (4–4–1), losing by a score of 55–12. After losing the game, the dejected BC players chose not to attend a celebration planned for the evening at the Cocoanut Grove nightclub. That night, a fire broke out at the Grove, killing more than 500 patrons. Newspaper accounts of this event over the years have run with headlines such as "Hands of Destiny—Football Upset Spared BC Players from Tragedy 50 Years Ago" (Tye, 1992). The most salient counterfactuals evoked by this event are that the BC players "almost" died in the fire and that "if BC had won the game, they would have died in the fire."

Study Set 1

We first examined whether present-day students would have a similar reaction to reading about the football game as did Bostonians back in 1942. Participants read a condensed version of a *Boston Globe* article from 1992 that marked the 50-year anniversary of the BC defeat and subsequent tragedy at the Cocoanut Grove nightclub. Participants were prompted to write their reactions to the article, after which they responded to questions assessing their perceptions of fate and meaning about the outcome of the football game. Roughly half of the participants did spontaneously generate counterfactual thoughts in their written reactions, and these thoughts were positively related to their fate and meaning judgments.

The next step was to demonstrate that counterfactual thinking elicited by the sequence of events, rather than simply the unexpected outcome of the football game, was responsible for heightening fate and meaning judgments. In a second study, some participants read the counterfactual eliciting article, whereas others read a control version that omitted any information about the subsequent fire. After reading the article, participants provided written reactions. These written protocols were then submitted to the Linguistic Inquiry and Word Count text analysis program (Pennebaker, Francis, & Booth, 2001). A dictionary was created to determine the number of words related to sense making that were spontaneously evoked (e.g., *fate, meaning, luck, reason, purpose*). As predicted, the counterfactual version elicited more words related to sense making than did the control version.

Study 3 was then designed to directly demonstrate that thinking counterfactually about the fire enhanced judgments of fate and meaning with regard to the outcome of the HC–BC football game. Participants read about the rivalry and game and were either provided with information about the subsequent fire at the Cocoanut Grove (counterfactual version) or received no information about the fire (control version). As predicted, participants who read the counterfactual version exhibited stronger fate and meaning judgments about the outcome of the game than did participants who read the control version. Thus, considering BC's surprising loss within the context of the subsequent counterfactual appears to have imbued their loss with greater meaning.

We then shifted our attention toward demonstrating that counterfactual thinking serves a mediating role in enhancing ascriptions of fate and predetermination. Rather than using the same open-ended format for assessing counterfactual thinking, in Study 4 we used questions that were created to provide continuous measures of counterfactual thinking (cf. Miller, Visser, & Staub, 2005). The first question focused on an *antecedent–consequent* relationship: "To what extent are you thinking about ways in which the outcome of the football game could have turned out differently?" The second question, by contrast, focused on a *consequent–subsequent* relationship: "To what extent are you thinking about what would have happened if Boston College won the game against Holy Cross?" The last pair of questions then assessed agreement with two counterfactual statements that focused on the relationship between the outcome of the game and events that occurred later that evening: "Boston College lost the game [Holy Cross won the game], which prevented the Boston College players from going to the Cocoanut Grove."

For this study, it was predicted that there would be no difference between the counterfactual and control conditions on the antecedent–consequent question—in both conditions, participants read about the surprising outcome of the football game and thus should have engaged in similar levels of counterfactual thinking regarding how the game could have turned out differently. However, because the two conditions differed with regard to the subsequent information provided, it was predicted that participants who read about the fire would engage in more consequent–subsequent thinking than would those who did not read about the fire. In turn, it was predicted that an increase in consequent–subsequent thinking would yield enhanced ascriptions of fate and predetermination.

Consistent with the previous studies, participants in the counterfactual condition did in fact endorse more fate and meaning ascriptions for BC's surprising loss than did those in the control condition. As predicted, there was no difference in counterfactual thinking on the antecedent–consequent question (i.e., the extent to which participants indicated that they were considering how the game could have turned out differently). On the other hand, participants in the counterfactual condition did report engaging in significantly more consequent–subsequent counterfactual thinking (i.e., what would have happened if BC had won). Additionally, and importantly, the measure of consequent–subsequent counterfactual thinking was found to statistically mediate the positive relationship between scenario type (counterfactual vs. control) and the strength of the fate and meaning ascriptions.

Study Set 2

The first set of studies established that counterfactual thinking lends explanatory coherence to surprising events, imbuing the unexpected with perceived meaning and purpose. These studies also established that the consideration of counterfactuals that arise *after* a focal event can still impact one's construal of that focal event. The second set of studies then sought to identify contextual factors that render factual outcomes particularly amenable to such a retrospective sense-making process.

Part of what makes a traumatic event so psychologically devastating is that it can call into question many of our assumptions regarding the nature of the world around us (Janoff-Bulman, 1992). At a more basic level, research on causal attribution has found that individuals are particularly prone to engage in causal reasoning in the face of disconfirmed expectancies (e.g., Clary & Tesser, 1983; Hastie, 1984; Newtson, 1973; Pyszczynski & Greenberg, 1981; Stern, Marrs, Millar, & Cole, 1984). In such cases, individuals focus more attention on unexpected than expected events (Newtson, 1973), engage in more cognitive activity (Stern et al., 1984), and spontaneously generate explanations (Clary & Tesser, 1983).

Consistent with these attributional findings, the search for meaning that typically occurs following events that challenge assumptive worldviews focuses on assimilating the event with preexisting worldviews. Individuals spontaneously engage in sense making with the goal of construing the outcome as congruent with their worldview. If an event outcome is already consistent with individuals' worldview, on the other hand, then there is no need to initiate a search for meaning.

Thus, in Study 5 we manipulated expectations regarding the outcome of the focal (i.e., factual) event. To do so, two versions of the *Boston Globe* article were created. Both versions described BC losing the game, electing to go to another club, and thereby avoiding the fire at the Grove. However, different expectations were created regarding who should most likely be expected to win the game. On the basis of past attributional findings, it was predicted that an unexpected loss (when BC is 9–0 and Holy Cross is 4–4–1) would be more likely to initiate a search for meaning than would an expected loss (when BC is 4–4–1 and HC is 9–0). Although there is still benefit to be gained from finding meaning in BC's expected loss, there should be substantially less motivation to engage in sense making than when BC's loss is unexpected. To this end, we assessed the effect of expectations on motivations by asking participants to indicate the extent to which they were trying to make sense of BC's loss to HC while they were reading the article.

The hypothesized relationship was supported. Participants in the *unexpected loss* condition reported engaging in more sense making than did participants in the *expected loss* condition, and those in the former condition also reported enhanced ascriptions of fate and meaning. Despite receiving the same subsequent counterfactual information in both conditions, participants were less likely to use counterfactual thinking to provide meaning when the focal event did not violate expectations. These results demonstrate that counterfactual thinking is more likely to serve a sense-making function when expectancies are violated than when they are not.

The next study was designed to examine whether sense making was more likely to occur when the subsequent counterfactual provided a satisfactory explanation for the factual outcome. Roese (2004) noted that counterfactuals enhance the hindsight bias when they provide a *satisfying* causal explanation. If counterfactual thinking is activated to provide a sense-making function, then it should only influence ascriptions of fate and predetermination to the extent that it assimilates the event into one's assumptive worldview. In kind, Janoff-Bulman (1992) argued that one of these primary assumptions is the meaningfulness of the world—that events are not random or unpredictable and that they follow notions of justice and equity.

Study 6, then, was designed to examine the moderating role of assumptive worldviews in determining the relationship between counterfactual thinking and sense making. The previous five studies used a scenario that strongly implied a downward counterfactual ("If BC had won the game, they would have died in the fire"). In turn, thinking about the fire was shown to lead participants to ascribe fate and meaning to the outcome of the game. However, we theorized that the same contingency of events would not provide as satisfying a causal explanation if they instead led to tragedy and disaster. Thus, in this study we manipulated the scenario ending so that the change in plans led the BC players to either avoid the fire (downward counterfactual condition) or perish in the fire (upward counterfactual condition). Although the counterfactual "If BC had won the players would *not* have died in the fire" could be used to make sense of the loss, the perspective that the team was *meant* to lose the game so that they could *die* in the fire is incongruent with typical assumptive worldviews. Indeed, the results supported such an interpretation. Participants in the downward counterfactual condition (the players changed plans, avoided the fire, and lived) ascribed more fate and meaning to the outcome of the game than did participants in the upward counterfactual condition (the players changed plans and perished in the fire). Despite having the same event structure—the outcome of the game led the BC players to change their plans in both conditions—the upward counterfactual apparently did not provide as satisfying an explanation as did the downward counterfactual (see Chapter 16, this volume).

Moreover, to assess for the first time the fatalistic belief that extrapersonal forces were at least in part responsible for BC's surprising loss, participants were asked to indicate how much control they perceived the teams to have had over the eventual outcome of the game. To the extent that participants viewed the game as being influenced by fate, the less control BC should have been perceived as having had over the eventual outcome. Intriguingly, and as hypothesized, participants who read that the BC players avoided dying in the fire after changing their plans believed that BC had less control over the outcome of the game than did participants who read that the BC players perished in the fire after changing their plans.

Most importantly, differential levels of perceived control over the game were found to mediate the relationship between counterfactual direction and ascriptions of fate and meaning. These results provide further evidence of the explanatory coherence that counterfactual thinking can lend to unexpected events. The surprising loss by BC explains why the players avoided the fire at the nightclub, but a subsequent explanation is also needed to account for why BC lost when they "should have" won. Apparently, by using knowledge of the fire, participants came to believe that some external force—with knowledge, perhaps, of the future event—facilitated BC's loss. More generally, then, individuals may be motivated to consider divine intervention when it would protect life but seem reluctant to do so when such intervention would claim life.

MAKING MEANING THE COUNTERFACTUAL WAY

Together with the research of Kray and her colleagues (2010), the current work lends further support for the sense-making function of counterfactual thinking. Against the backdrop of a well-established distinction developed in the trauma literature between construals of meaning as benefit finding versus sense making (e.g., Davis et al., 1998; Janoff-Bulman & Frantz, 1997), we described the role of counterfactual thinking in contributing to each of these types of meaning. Consistent with Davis et al.'s (1998) suggestion that benefit finding and sense making are the result of different psychological mechanisms, we also posit that the mechanism by which counterfactual thinking impacts sense making is different for each meaning type. Kray et al. (2010) proposed a *defying-the-odds* account by which counterfactual thinking serves to highlight the improbability of life events having happened otherwise. According to this account, finding personal meaning in the life event amounts to an ironic *rejection* of counterfactual alternatives. In other words, the defying-the-odds account requires the individual to override the implications of counterfactual alternatives and conclude that the factual event is more personally significant because it occurred despite the plausibility of other possibilities.

In contrast, the present *explanatory coherence* account is congruent with the meaning as sense-making construal, and arguably, this account suggests a more direct relationship between counterfactual thinking and meaning. As opposed to the more commonly explored antecedent–consequent type of causal analysis, the explanatory coherence account is relevant for event chains in which a counterfactual is used to make sense, retrospectively, of a *prior* and surprising factual outcome. Thus, whereas the defying-the-odds account applies to conditions under which individuals question *how* a given outcome occurred, the explanatory coherence account applies to conditions under which individuals concern themselves with the perhaps deeper existential question of *why* an outcome occurred (recall Chapter 1, this volume). To test and establish the boundary conditions of both accounts, future research might be profitably directed toward delineating those factors that make individuals more or less likely to ask *how* as opposed to *why*.

REFERENCES

Alicke, M. D., Buckingham, J., Zell, E., & Davis, T. (2008). Culpable control and counterfactual reasoning in the psychology of blame. *Personality and Social Psychology Bulletin, 34*, 1371–1381. doi:10.1177/0146167208321594

Burgess, A. W., & Holmstrom, L. (1979). Adaptive strategies and recovery from rape. *The American Journal of Psychiatry, 136*, 1278–1282.

Clary, E. G., & Tesser, A. (1983). Reactions to unexpected events: The naive scientist and interpretive activity. *Personality and Social Psychology Bulletin, 9*, 609–620. doi:10.1177/0146167283094010

Connolly, T., & Zeelenberg, M. (2002). Regret in decision making. *Current Directions in Psychological Science, 11*, 212–216. doi:10.1111/1467-8721.00203

Davis, C. G., Nolen-Hoeksema, S., & Larson, J. (1998). Making sense of loss and benefiting from the experience: Two construals of meaning. *Journal of Personality and Social Psychology, 75*, 561–574. doi:10.1037/0022-3514.75.2.561

Ellis, S. (2010, January 20). It wasn't their time: Surviving crash changed duo's view on miracles. *Idaho State Journal*, pp. 1, 7.

Epstude, K., & Roese, J. (2008). The functional theory of counterfactual thinking. *Personality and Social Psychology Review, 12*, 168–192. doi:10.1177/1088868308316091

Fischhoff, B. (1975). Hindsight is not equal to foresight: The effect of outcome knowledge on judgment under uncertainty. *Journal of Experimental Psychology: Human Perception and Performance, 1*, 288–299. doi:10.1037/0096-1523.1.3.288

Fischhoff, B. (1976) The effect of temporal setting on likelihood estimates. *Organizational Behavior and Human Performance, 15*, 180–194. doi:10.1016/0030-5073(76)90036-2

Gilovich, T., & Medvec, H. (1995). The experience of regret: What, when, and why. *Psychological Review, 102*, 379–395. doi:10.1037/0033-295X.102.2.379

Hastie, R. (1984). Causes and effects of causal attribution. *Journal of Personality and Social Psychology, 46*, 44–56. doi:10.1037/0022-3514.46.1.44

Hawkins, S. A., & Hastie, R. (1990). Hindsight: Biased judgments of past events after the outcomes are known. *Psychological Bulletin, 107*, 311–327. doi:10.1037/0033-2909.107.3.311

Hilton, D. J., & Slugoski, R. (1986). Knowledge-based causal attribution: The abnormal conditions focus model. *Psychological Review, 93*, 75–88. doi:10.1037/0033-295X.93.1.75

Hirt, E. R., & Markman, K. D. (1995). Multiple explanation: A consider-an-alternative strategy for debiasing judgments. *Journal of Personality and Social Psychology, 69*, 1069–1086. doi:10.1037/0022-3514.69.6.1069

Janoff-Bulman, R. (1992). *Shattered assumptions: Towards a new psychology of trauma*. New York, NY: Free Press.

Janoff-Bulman, R., & Frantz, C. M. (1997). The impact of trauma on meaning: From meaningless world to meaningful life. In M. Power & C. Brewin (Eds.), *The transformation of meaning in psychological therapies* (pp. 91–106). London, England: Wiley.

King, L. A., Hicks, J. A., Krull, J. L., & Del Gaiso, A. K. (2006). Positive affect and the experience of meaning in life. *Journal of Personality and Social Psychology, 90*, 179–196. doi:10.1037/0022-3514.90.1.179

Koehler, D. J. (1991). Explanation, imagination, and confidence in judgment. *Psychological Bulletin, 110*, 499–519. doi:10.1037/0033-2909.110.3.499

Koo, M., Algoe, S. B., Wilson, T. D., & Gilbert, D. T. (2008). It's a wonderful life: Mentally subtracting positive events improves people's affective states, contrary to their affective forecasts. *Journal of Personality and Social Psychology, 95*, 1217–1224. doi:10.1037/a0013316

Kray, L. J., Galinsky, A. D., & Markman, K. D. (2009). Counterfactual structure and learning from experience in negotiations. *Journal of Experimental Social Psychology, 45*, 979–982. doi:10.1016/j.jesp.2009.03.008

Kray, L. J., George, L. G., Liljenquist, K. A., Galinsky, A. D., Tetlock, P. E., & Roese, N. J. (2010). From what might have been to what must have been: Counterfactual thinking creates meaning. *Journal of Personality and Social Psychology, 98*, 106–118. doi:10.1037/a0017905

Lindberg, M. J., & Markman, K. D. (2012). *When tomorrow explains yesterday: The retrospective meaning function of counterfactual thinking*. Unpublished manuscript, Department of Psychology, Ohio University.

Mandel, D. R., & Lehman, R. (1996). Counterfactual thinking and ascriptions of cause and preventability. *Journal of Personality and Social Psychology, 71*, 450–463. doi:10.1037/0022-3514.71.3.450

Markman, K. D., Gavanski, I., Sherman, S. J., & McMullen, M. N. (1993). The mental simulation of better and worse possible worlds. *Journal of Experimental Social Psychology, 29*, 87–109. doi:10.1006/jesp.1993.1005

Markman, K. D., & McMullen, N. (2003). A reflection and evaluation model of comparative thinking. *Personality and Social Psychology Review, 7*, 244–267. doi:10.1207/S15327957PSPR0703_04

McMullen, M. N., & Markman, K. D. (2000). Downward counterfactuals and motivation: The wake-up call and the Pangloss effect. *Personality and Social Psychology Bulletin, 26*, 575–584. doi:10.1177/0146167200267005

Mellers, B. A., Schwartz, A., Ho, K., & Ritov, I. (1997). Decision affect theory: Emotional reactions to the outcomes of risky options. *Psychological Science, 8*, 423–429. doi:10.1111/j.1467-9280.1997.tb00455.x

Miller, D. T., & Gunasegaram, S. (1990). Temporal order and the perceived mutability of events: Implications for blame assignment. *Journal of Personality and Social Psychology, 59*, 1111–1118. doi:10.1037/0022-3514.59.6.1111

Miller, D. T., & Turnbull, W. (1990). The counterfactual fallacy: Confusing what might have been with what ought to have been. *Social Justice Research, 4*, 1–19. doi:10.1007/BF01048532

Miller, D. T., Visser, P. S., & Staub, B. D. (2005). How surveillance begets perceptions of dishonesty: The case of the counterfactual sinner. *Journal of Personality and Social Psychology, 89*, 117–128. doi:10.1037/0022-3514.89.2.117

Nasco, S. A., & Marsh, L. (1999). Gaining control through counterfactual thinking. *Personality and Social Psychology Bulletin, 25*, 557–569. doi:10.1177/0146167299025005002

Nestler, S., & von Collani, G. (2008). Hindsight bias and the activation of counterfactual mind-sets. *Experimental Psychology, 55*, 342–349. doi:10.1027/1618-3169.55.5.342

Newtson, D. (1973). Attribution and the unit of perception of ongoing behavior. *Journal of Personality and Social Psychology, 28*, 28–38. doi:10.1037/h0035584

Park, M. (2011). *Small choices, saved lives: Near misses of 9/11*. Retrieved from http://www.cnn.com/2011/US/09/03/near.death.decisions/

Pennebaker, J. W., Francis, M. E., & Booth, R. J. (2001). Linguistic Inquiry and Word Count (LIWC) [Computer software]. Mahwah, NJ: Erlbaum.

Proulx, T., & Heine, S. J. (2006). Death and black diamonds: Meaning, mortality, and the Meaning maintenance model. *Psychological Inquiry, 17*, 309–318. doi:10.1080/10478400701366985

Pyszczynski, T. A., & Greenberg, J. (1981). Role of disconfirmed expectancies in the instigation of attributional processing. *Journal of Personality and Social Psychology, 40*, 31–38. doi:10.1037/0022-3514.40.1.31

Roese, N. J. (1994). The functional basis of counterfactual thinking. *Journal of Personality and Social Psychology, 66*, 805–818. doi:10.1037/0022-3514.66.5.805

Roese, N. J. (2004). Twisted pair: Counterfactual thinking and the hindsight bias. In D. J. Koehler & N. Harvey (Eds.), *Blackwell handbook of judgment and decision making* (pp. 258–273). Malden, MA: Blackwell. doi:10.1002/9780470752937.ch13

Roese, N. J., & Maniar, D. (1997). Perceptions of purple: Counterfactual and hindsight judgments at Northwestern Wildcats football games. *Personality and Social Psychology Bulletin, 23*, 1245–1253. doi:10.1177/01461672972312002

Roese, N. J., & Olson, J. M. (1996). Counterfactuals, causal attributions, and the hindsight bias: A conceptual integration. *Journal of Experimental Social Psychology, 32*, 197–227. doi:10.1006/jesp.1996.0010

Sanna, L. J. (1996). Defensive pessimism, optimism, and stimulating alternatives: Some ups and downs of prefactual and counterfactual thinking. *Journal of Personality and Social Psychology, 71*, 1020–1036. doi:10.1037/0022-3514.71.5.1020

Sherman, S. J. (1991). Thought systems for the past as well as for the future. In R. S. Wyer, Jr., & T. K. Srull (Eds.), *Advances in social cognition* (Vol. 4, pp. 173–195). Hillsdale, NJ: Erlbaum.

Slovic, P., & Fischhoff, B. (1977). On the psychology of experimental surprises. *Journal of Experimental Psychology: Human Perception and Performance, 3*, 544–551. doi:10.1037/0096-1523.3.4.544

Steger, M. F., Kashdan, T. B., Sullivan, B. A., & Lorentz, D. (2008). Understanding the search for meaning in life: Personality, cognitive style, and the dynamic between seeking and experiencing meaning. *Journal of Personality, 76*, 199–228. doi:10.1111/j.1467-6494.2007.00484.x

Stern, L. D., Marrs, S., Millar, M. G., & Cole, E. (1984). Processing time and the recall of inconsistent and consistent behaviors of individuals and groups. *Journal of Personality and Social Psychology, 47*, 253–262. doi:10.1037/0022-3514.47.2.253

Taylor, S. E., & Schneider, K. (1989). Coping and the simulation of events. *Social Cognition, 7*, 174–194. doi:10.1521/soco.1989.7.2.174

Taylor, S. E., Wood, J. V., & Lichtman, R. R. (1983). It could be worse: Selective evaluation as a response to victimization. *Journal of Social Issues, 39*(2), 19–40. doi:10.1111/j.1540-4560.1983.tb00139.x

Teigen, K. H. (1988). Reddet av flaks [Saved by luck]. *Tidsskrift for Norsk Psykologforening, 25*, 439–446.

Teigen, K. H. (1998). When the unreal is more likely than the real: Post hoc probability judgments and counterfactual closeness. *Thinking & Reasoning, 4*, 147–177. doi:10.1080/135467898394193

Teigen, K. H. (2005). The proximity heuristic in judgments of accident probabilities. *British Journal of Psychology, 96*, 423–440. doi:10.1348/000712605X47431

Tye, L. (1992, November 27). Hands of destiny: Football upset spared BC players from tragedy 50 years ago. *Boston Globe*, p. 63.

Wells, G. L., & Gavanski, I. (1989). Mental simulation of causality. *Journal of Personality and Social Psychology, 56*, 161–169. doi:10.1037/0022-3514.56.2.161

White, K., & Lehman, D. R. (2005). Looking on the bright side: Downward counterfactual thinking in response to negative life events. *Personality and Social Psychology Bulletin, 31*, 1413–1424. doi:10.1177/0146167205276064

V

RESTORING MEANING

18

MEANING MAKING FOLLOWING ACTIVATION OF THE BEHAVIORAL INHIBITION SYSTEM: HOW CARING LESS ABOUT WHAT OTHERS THINK MAY HELP US TO MAKE SENSE OF WHAT IS GOING ON

KEES VAN DEN BOS

In this chapter, I focus on what I think may be a common denominator of many processes involved in meaning making and sense making. That is, I explore how people make sense of situations in which they are surprised, conflicted, or flabbergasted by what is happening and do not know how to respond to the situation at hand. I argue that in these situations the behavioral inhibition system (BIS) may be activated because now is the time to find out what is going on and to determine what is the appropriate behavior. It is after people have made sense of the situation that the inhibition system is deactivated and the behavioral activation system (BAS) is turned on so that people can perform the behavior that they think is appropriate.

I further argue that in this process of sense making people may think too much and may weigh in too much information. That is, because people tend to be social beings, quite often they become concerned about what others will think of their future actions. I propose that this may lead the BIS to be

I thank Michèlle Bal, Chantal den Daas, and Keith Markman for their comments and suggestions on earlier drafts of this chapter and Leonie Venhoeven for her assistance during the writing of this chapter.
DOI: 10.1037/14040-018
The Psychology of Meaning, Keith D. Markman, Travis Proulx, and Matthew J. Lindberg (Editors)

activated longer than needed and, in fact, may impair people's ability to take appropriate action (Van den Bos, Müller, & Van Bussel, 2009; Van den Bos, Van Lange, et al., 2011). Thus, I put forward here that caring less about what others think may help to deactivate the BIS and that this may be conducive to people doing the right thing.

In what follows, I first give a brief overview of the types of situations I am focusing on here. I then discuss what role the BIS may have in the process of making sense of these situations. This is followed by a discussion of how reminders of behavioral disinhibition may moderate this process and affect people's subsequent behaviors.

THE FLABBERGASTED INDIVIDUAL

One important issue on which I focus here is that in social psychology researchers often study the flabbergasted individual who is trying to make sense of what is going on. The existing literature on meaning making and sense making has revealed many important insights on how people make sense (see, e.g., Chapters 4, 5, 6, 12, 16, 17, and 21, this volume). One of these insights is that meaning making often occurs in response to expectancy violations (see, e.g., Förster, Liberman, & Shapira, 2009; Heine, Proulx, & Vohs, 2006; Major, Kaiser, O'Brien, & McCoy, 2007; McGregor, Nash, & Inzlicht, 2009; McGregor, Nash, Mann, & Phills, 2010; McGregor, Prentice, & Nash, 2009; McGregor, Zanna, Holmes, & Spencer, 2001; Plaks, Grant, & Dweck, 2005; Proulx, 2009; Proulx & Heine, 2008, 2009; Proulx, Heine, & Vohs, 2010; Van den Bos, 2009a; Van den Bos, Vermunt, & Wilke, 1996).

Building on and extending these insights, my colleagues and I mentioned in a recent research article (Van den Bos, Van Lange, et al., 2011) that a recurring theme in social psychology is the notion that the social situation in which people find themselves can overwhelm their individual inclinations. This has been a core message of classic studies in this field, such as Asch's research on public conformity (e.g., Asch, 1956), Milgram's work on obedience to authority (e.g., Milgram, 1963), and Latané and Darley's research on bystander nonintervention (e.g., Latané & Darley, 1968). A central outcome of these studies has been that people ultimately comply with the situational pressures put on them. A somewhat less noticed result is that in these situations people are generally surprised, conflicted, or even flabbergasted (i.e., "extremely surprised;" Flabbergasted, 2011) by what is happening and often do not know how to respond to the situation at hand.

For example, Asch (1956) reported that research participants in his studies could hardly believe what was happening and that they experienced difficulty making an appropriate response to the wrong answers given by the confederate participants. Milgram (1963) observed that his participants often showed signs of nervous tension and emotional distress and disturbance. In postexperimental interviews, Milgram's participants pointed out that this was not because they are sadistic types but rather because they were having trouble figuring out what was going on in the situation they had encountered. Latané and Nida (1981) noted that an important determinant of nonintervention when bystanders are around is behavioral inhibition: In the presence of a nonintervening audience people may feel inhibited about intervening in the situation (see also Van den Bos et al., 2009).

Other situations less central in the history of social psychology can have similar effects on people, leaving them in a whirl about how to make sense of the situation at hand. For example, Van den Bos, Van Lange, et al. (2011) showed comparable effects when people received better outcomes than they deserved. Consider, for example, Adams's observations concerning workers at General Electric in the early 1960s, which stimulated him to begin his impressive research program on equity theory (see, e.g., Adams, 1965). Adams (1965) noted that employees seek to maintain equity between the inputs that they bring to a job and the outcomes that they receive from it in comparison to the perceived inputs and outcomes of others. When individuals find themselves participating in inequitable relationships, they become distressed. As a result, the person who gets too much may feel guilt or shame (Adams, 1965) and often reports "feelings of unease" about getting too much (Jacques, 1961; S. L. Peters, 2005).

Of course, those who get too little may feel angry or humiliated. It is noteworthy, though, that being underpaid is much easier to interpret than being overpaid (Adams, 1965; Jacques, 1961; S. L. Peters, 2005) and hence is not very likely to lead to confusion or inhibition. After all, being underpaid often energizes immediate action or action tendencies (e.g., anger, reactance, protest). Yet being overpaid is an interesting situation in which immediate action is strongly tempered by inhibition; because guilt, shame, and feelings of unease do not directly imply action, the conflict between advantageous outcomes and personal values triggers feelings of "what's going on here" and behavioral inhibition.

Adams's (1965) research program studied many aspects of the social psychology of equity, but his true fascination with the topic focused on people's reactions to getting too much. Part of this fascination came from people's reactions to equity restoration. For example, the employees at General Electric who got too much tried to restore the inequity by working harder, thus raising the inputs they brought to the working relationship and making their situation more equitable (Adams, 1965). Reactions to overpayment are interesting not only in their own right but also because they carry built-in social-cognitive conflicts (Van den Bos, Peters, Bobocel, & Ybema, 2006) that make it difficult for the overpaid person to know how to respond to the outcome. After all, when a person experiences advantageous inequity, there is a conflict between the tendency to accept a desirable outcome (and in doing so avoiding a challenge to the authority who has given the outcome) and doing what is fair. Furthermore, in advantageous inequity there is a source of positive affect and a source of negative affect: (a) The positive source is the egoism-based pleasure of receiving a relatively good outcome, whereas (b) the negative source is the fairness-based feeling of being unfairly advantaged (Van den Bos, Lind, Vermunt, & Wilke, 1997; Van den Bos, Wilke, Lind, & Vermunt, 1998).

Because of this mixed-motive quality of advantageous inequity arrangements (Jacques, 1961; S. L. Peters, Van den Bos, & Karremans, 2008), studying these situations may shed light on the relationship between people's egoism-oriented tendencies and their inclinations to do the right thing (Van den Bos et al., 2006). Furthermore, Van den Bos, Van Lange, et al. (2011) recently showed that when people receive better outcomes than are deserved (Adams, 1965), the actions of an authority or a coworker push in the direction of accepting and enjoying the unfair outcome, whereas personal values for most people push in the direction of rejecting or being displeased with the outcome. This conflict may inhibit people's ability to respond to advantageous but unfair outcomes.

THE INHIBITED INDIVIDUAL

Thus, I note that various situations may lead people to be surprised, conflicted, or flabbergasted by what is happening. To find out how to respond to the situation at hand, people engage in appraisal processes. Appraisal is probably easier when the BAS shuts down temporarily and the BIS is activated. Therefore, I argue in this chapter that an important area of focus in the psychology of sense making and meaning making should center on the inhibited individual who tries to interpret how to behave in the situation at hand. What do I mean when I talk about behavioral inhibition (and the associated concept of behavioral disinhibition)?

The concepts of inhibition and disinhibition have been used to refer to different processes in disparate research literatures (see, e.g., Amodio, Master, Yee, & Taylor, 2008; Carver, 2005; Carver & White, 1994; Gable, Reis, & Elliot, 2000; Gray, 1987; Gray & McNaughton, 2000; Knyazev, Schutter, & Van Honk, 2006; Latané & Nida, 1981; Monteith, 1993; Nigg, 2000; Sawyer & Behnke, 2002). Many important (and sometimes not so important) distinctions between various associated concepts have been made. Different conceptualizations of the BIS have been formulated, and different literatures focus on different components of the BIS, for example, examining neurological substrates, cognitive processes, and/or behavioral responses.

Furthermore, the antecedents of BIS activation are assumed to differ from highly anxiety-triggering stimuli (e.g., Carver & White, 1994; Gray & McNaughton, 2000) to less anxiety-related issues such as novelty (e.g., Gable et al., 2000). Carver and White (1994) argued that the BIS regulates people's responses to anxiety-related cues and inhibits behavior that can lead to negative or painful consequences. The BIS has also been used to explain self-regulation and inhibition of prejudiced responses (Monteith, 1993). In addition, most authors contrast the BIS with a BAS, but some focus on a behavioral approach system. Many social psychologists have good reasons to consider the BIS and BAS as constituting independent systems (e.g., Carver & White, 1994; Gable et al., 2000; see also Gray & McNaughton, 2000), but current cognitive psychologists also tend to focus on the interaction between the BIS and BAS (e.g., Knyazev et al., 2006).

My take on the BIS and its relationship with the psychology of sense making is that its main function is to inhibit ongoing behavioral action and action tendencies to make interpretation and appraisal processes of what is going on possible. Thus, the chief role of the BIS, as I see it, is to enable processes of psychological sense making. The BIS is thus important for people because they are meaning makers, trying to provide meaning to the lives they are living and trying to make sense of the situations in which they find themselves.

Furthermore, in my view the human organism may activate the BIS in response to subtle or not so subtle stimuli in its environment that signal to the organism that something potentially alarming may be going on in the environment that may warrant the attention of the individual. These stimuli may involve things such as punishment that the individual finds aversive, as initially assumed by Carver and White (1994), Gray and McNaughton (2000), and others. More generally, in my perspective these stimuli may also involve all phenomena reported in social cognition and social neuroscience that can activate the "human alarm system."

The human alarm system is a psychological system that people use to detect and handle alarming situations and that prompts people to process more alertly (Eisenberger & Lieberman, 2004; Eisenberger, Lieberman, & Williams, 2003; Lieberman & Eisenberger, 2004). The working of such an alarm system is assumed to be adaptive (see Eisenberger & Lieberman, 2004), and the system can be activated quite quickly by somewhat subtle stimuli, such as the presentation of exclamation marks on computer screens (Van den Bos et al., 2008; Van den Bos & Rijpkema, 2008). The human alarm system may also be activated in response to unexpected events (cf. Förster et al.,

2009; Major et al., 2007; McGregor et al., 2001; Plaks et al., 2005; Proulx & Heine, 2009; Van den Bos et al., 1996) or events that may make people feel uncertain about themselves (Van den Bos, 2009a, 2009b, 2010). For example, Murray, Holmes, and Collins (2006) suggested that personal uncertainty and felt insecurity in close relationships activate the human alarm system so that, among other things, people process more alertly what is happening in their relationships.

Related to this, Eisenberger et al. (2003) argued that being ostracized or experiencing other self-threatening events activates parts of the human brain that Eisenberger et al. labeled the *human alarm system*. Furthermore, Eisenberger and Lieberman (2004; Lieberman & Eisenberger, 2004) proposed that the alarm system is responsible for detecting cues that might be harmful to survival and, after activation, for recruiting attention and coping responses to minimize threat. For example, Eisenberger et al. noted that experiencing social exclusion or other self-threatening events may be an experience of social pain. Like physical pain, the experience of social pain may trigger the human alarm system, hence "alerting us when we have sustained injury to our social connections" (Eisenberger et al., 2003, p. 292).

As noted, in my view the BIS and the associated alarm system may be activated not only in response to anxious or threatening stimuli (Carver & White, 1994; Eisenberger et al., 2003; Gray & McNaughton, 2000) but also in reaction to stimuli that the human organism has learned to associate with alarming situations (Van den Bos et al., 2008) or more generally to events or situations that are hard to interpret (Van den Bos et al. 2009). Thus, these situations involve circumstances in which unexpected things happen (Gable et al., 2000) or in which people are confused, dumbfounded, or perhaps flabbergasted about what is happening and how to respond (Van den Bos, Van Lange, et al., 2011).

In developing our ideas about inhibition, my colleagues and I built our theorizing not only on the BIS, as developed by Gray (e.g., 1972, 1990; Gray & McNaughton, 2000) and Carver and White (1994), but also on the work on public inhibition, as defined by Latané and Nida (1981). Latané and Nida noted that in public settings, such as bystander situations, the presence of others constrains people from showing their personal inclinations. For example, in a bystander dilemma a person may want to engage in helping behavior but may be restrained from doing so because of the presence of others (bystanders) who are not helping. Thus, I believe that important elements in the psychology of inhibition and sense making involve issues of *public* and *behavioral* inhibition—public because the inhibition of primary importance may often be instigated by thoughts of what others will think of one's actions and behavioral because the main consequences of interest in this line of work are the effects on behaviors that people subsequently demonstrate.

Furthermore, building and extending on Monteith (1993) and Gray and McNaughton (2000), I argue that the BIS is initially activated when a signal for sense making occurs, such as an aversive or alarming stimulus or a confusing or hard-to-interpret event. This is followed by increased arousal and an automatic, momentary pausing or interruption of ongoing behavior (i.e., behavioral inhibition) that is similar to an orienting response (see Gray & McNaughton, 2000). The stimulus that is occurring when the sense-making signal was detected is then tagged with a "faulty, needs checking" indicator and is allotted enhanced attention. In addition, the organism engages in exploratory-investigative behavior, searching for indications of what is going on and what should be appropriate behavioral responses. The enhanced attention and exploratory-investigative processes probably work in concert (Gray & McNaughton, 2000), enabling the organism to identify stimuli and appropriate behavioral responses. In other words, through appraisal and reflection, an association is built between cues present when the sense-making signal occurred and the appropriate behavioral response to be shown in the future.

I note explicitly here that my perspective on the working of the BIS and its central role in processes of sense making is grounded in part on the work by Carver and Gray (e.g., Carver, 2005; Carver & White, 1994; Gray, 1972, 1987, 1990; Gray & McNaughton, 2000) and at the same time diverges from this work in important aspects, especially in my emphasis on less anxiety-provoking and more general sense-making triggering stimuli that are assumed to instigate activation of the BIS.

Carver (2005; Carver & White, 1994) and Gray (e.g., 1972, 1987, 1990; Gray & McNaughton, 2000) have referred to the BIS as the *aversive motivational system*. The system comprises the septohippocampal system, its monoaminergic afferents from the brainstem, and its neocortical projection in the frontal lobe. Gray (1972, 1987, 1990; Gray & McNaughton, 2000) has argued that this physiological mechanism controls the experience of anxiety in response to anxiety-relevant cues. The BIS, according to Gray, is sensitive to signals of punishment, nonreward, and novelty. It inhibits behavior that may lead to negative or painful outcomes. Thus, BIS activation causes inhibition of movement toward goals. Gray (1987, 1990) has also held that BIS functioning is responsible for the experience of negative feelings such as fear, anxiety, frustration, and sadness in response to these cues. In terms of individual differences in personality, greater BIS sensitivity is reflected in greater proneness to anxiety, provided the person is exposed to the proper situational cues. The Carver and Gray theory also attributes sensitivity to signals of punishment—resulting in inhibition and the creation of negative affect—to the activity of the BIS. People with high BIS sensitivity are assumed to be especially responsive behaviorally to punishment cues and to experience great anxiety in situations with cues of impending punishment (compared with people with lower BIS sensitivity). At the extreme, heightened BIS sensitivity may render the person susceptible to anxiety or depressive disorders (Fowles, 1993).

As noted, my own work on inhibition and disinhibition focuses on sense-making signals that may trigger the activation of the BIS. Furthermore, in my research I try to examine the public behavioral consequences this assumed process may have. More specifically, I study whether behavioral disinhibition—defined as a state in which people do not or only weakly care about what others think of their actions (Van den Bos, Müller, & Damen, 2011; Van den Bos et al., 2009; Van den Bos, Van Lange, et al. 2011)—may make it easier for people to follow their own personal inclinations (which in the majority of people may be a prosocial orientation; Van den Bos, Van Lange, et al., 2011; Van Lange, Otten, De Bruin, & Joireman, 1997). It is to a discussion of this work that I now turn.

THE DISINHIBITED INDIVIDUAL

The BIS and BAS have been put forward in the literature as a framework for understanding how mechanisms for behavioral regulation relate to human motivation, personality, and, by extension, psychological dysfunction (Gray & McNaughton, 2000). With respect to this latter aspect, very strong BIS is compatible with anxiety-related disorders (Fowles, 1993), whereas very weak BIS relates to primary psychopathy (Newman, MacCoon, Vaughn, & Sadeh, 2005). Low levels of BIS correspond to having no or very weak behavioral inhibitions. These levels of BIS are usually called *behavioral disinhibition*, and in the current chapter I use this label as well. Psychological research has shown that behavioral disinhibition may lead to antisocial acts (Lilienfeld, 1992) and psychopathological behaviors (Nigg, 2000). As a result, F. Peters et al. (2006) referred to behavioral disinhibition as the *production of unwanted acts*.

Related to this, there have been several pleas for humans to refrain from disinhibited behavior. For example, Kant (1785/1959) proposed that if people would think more carefully about what is going on in the situation at hand before they start acting, this might lead them to do what is better for society at large. Thus, Kant was arguing that it would be conducive for the greater good if people acted with somewhat more inhibition than they normally do. Although this may indeed often be the case, in our research program my colleagues and I argued that at least some levels of behavioral disinhibition may have positive, benign effects on what people do.

In a first set of studies examining this benign disinhibition hypothesis, my colleagues and I explored whether reminders of behavioral disinhibition may help to overcome the bystander effect (Van den Bos et al., 2009). The *bystander effect* refers to how helping behavior is inhibited in situations in which people are confronted with someone in need of help but in which many bystanders are present who also might provide help (Darley & Latané, 1968). In their review of the literature, Latané and Nida (1981) identified three important determinants of the bystander effect: (a) diffusion of responsibility (the presence of bystanders creates confusion about who is responsible for intervening), (b) social influence (other nonintervening bystanders communicate that not acting is the norm and people tend to adhere to that norm), and (c) public inhibition (in the presence of a nonintervening audience people may feel inhibited about intervening in the situation at hand). It is on this last determinant that my colleagues and I focused our research efforts.

Although many publications on the bystander effect suggest that to understand the effect it is important to focus on the fact that people may feel inhibited about whether to help in bystander situations (Karakashian, Walter, Christopher, & Lucas, 2006; Latané & Darley, 1970; Latané & Nida, 1981; Schwartz & Gottlieb, 1976, 1980). Strikingly, however, there have been no studies reported that directly examine the role of behavioral inhibition on helping in bystander situations. For instance, previous studies that focused on the inhibition account of the bystander effect have measured fear of negative evaluations as an individual difference variable (Karakashian et al., 2006) or manipulated whether the bystanders would be aware of participants' actions and found mixed results of this manipulation on helping behavior (Schwartz & Gottlieb, 1976, 1980). In the Van den Bos et al. (2009) article, my colleagues and I focused more directly on the role of behavioral inhibition in understanding the bystander effect.

More specifically, we examined an as of yet unexamined conceptual implication of the role of behavioral inhibition in understanding helping behavior in bystander situations. That is, we proposed that if a nonintervening audience indeed inhibits intervention, then it should be the case that weakening more general behavioral inhibitions (as defined by Carver & White, 1994) should positively affect helping behavior in bystander situations. Thus, we developed a disinhibition manipulation that was successful in doing precisely this. Specifically, we asked our participants to complete only three open-ended questions that reminded them of having acted with no behavioral inhibitions in the past. We argued that this should weaken behavioral inhibition among our participants in a way that fits our behavioral inhibition analysis, and we showed that this manipulation successfully lowered behavioral inhibition as assessed by a state version of the most popular and well-validated measure of BIS sensitivity, the Carver and White (1994) BIS scale.

Furthermore, the benign disinhibition hypothesis we proposed states that people may feel inhibited to intervene in situations in which nonintervening bystanders are present and that, therefore, behavioral disinhibition may help to overcome the bystander effect. Findings presented in the Van den Bos et al. (2009) article provided evidence supporting this prediction both inside and outside the psychology laboratory: In both real-life and controlled bystander situations, people were more likely and faster to provide help when (unrelated to the bystander situations) they had (vs. had not) been reminded about having acted in the past with no inhibitions. These findings suggest that in contrast with what various theories and worldviews dictate, behavioral disinhibition may have positive effects on helping behavior and hence may be conducive for the greater good.

Extending these insights, Van den Bos, Van Lange, et al. (2011) recently argued that feelings of surprise and inhibition often arise from a deep-seated conflict between social pressures and personal values. Because people are social beings (Aronson, 1999; De Waal, 1996), they want to act in concert with their fellows and the authorities present in the situation. Furthermore, because most people (but not all) adhere to prosocial values (e.g., Van Lange et al., 1997), many want to do what is normatively appropriate and good and correct. In situations that pose a conflict between responding in accordance with what seems to be accepted by others versus reacting in terms of what seems to be the right thing to do, these two important determinants of social behavior are pushing in different directions. The net result is that people in such situations are flabbergasted: confused about what to do (Asch, 1956), emotionally distressed (Milgram, 1974), and inhibited regarding how to respond (Latané & Nida, 1981).

But suppose it were possible to "turn off" the social inhibitions that limit actions in line with personal preferences. Certainly most people are able to throw off social pressure at times, and given this capacity for disinhibition, there must be a mechanism for putting aside the social demands involved in the confusion experiences my colleagues and I address here. Van den Bos, Van Lange, et al. (2011) suggested that the activation of a disinhibition process—by recalling instances of relatively independent and unfettered action in the past or even by simply attending to statements about not caring or only weakly caring about what others think of one's actions—will allow people to overcome the pressures of conformity or social authority and follow their personal preferences to enact behaviors that fit with their personal values.

My colleagues and I studied the possible implications of this analysis by examining reactions to a classic situation-based conflict of social and normative pressures, namely, people's reactions to receiving better outcomes than they deserve (see, e.g., Adams, 1965; Blau, 1964; Jacques, 1961). This situation contains the same essential elements as the studies by Asch (1956), Milgram (1974), and Latané and Darley (1968)—the actions of an authority (in our studies, the experimenter, a coworker who knows more than the person, or the person's boss) push in the direction of accepting and enjoying the unfair outcome, whereas personal values for most people push in the direction of rejecting or at least discounting the outcome (Lind & Tyler, 1988).

In social contexts, consequences such as rejection or disapproval by an authority or coworker can be negative or painful and may well inhibit people from showing displeasure with an advantageous but unfair outcome. If this is the case, then an important issue becomes how one can disengage people's inhibitory responses, with the result that they can respond more in line with their personal values when reacting to inequitably advantageous outcomes. In our studies, my colleagues and I attempted to produce this disengagement of the BIS by simply reminding people that it is possible to behave without great concern about the reactions of others.

On the basis of the reasoning laid out in the previous sections, my colleagues and I hypothesized that behavioral disinhibition can weaken a person's pleasure with receiving advantageous but unfair outcomes. In our first four studies, we reminded participants about times at which they acted without inhibitions (disinhibition conditions) or we reminded them about their normal actions on a regular day (no-disinhibition conditions). After this, in ostensibly unrelated parts of the studies, we confronted participants with advantageous but undeserved outcomes and we observed their reactions to these outcomes. The first four studies provided evidence that reminders of behavioral disinhibition can weaken (not strengthen) pleasure with advantageously unfair outcomes. Findings also revealed that following reminders of behavioral disinhibition people are more likely to actually reject unfair overpayment (Van den Bos, Van Lange, et al., 2011, Study 3). This suggests that the disinhibited individual can be driven to do the right thing (Van den Bos et al., 2006), in this case reject outcomes that would yield them a profit but that are unfair.

In the Van den Bos, Van Lange, et al. (2011) article, we further argued that people are somewhat flabbergasted and inhibited regarding how to respond to advantageous but unfair outcomes because many people are social (e.g., Aronson, 1999; De Waal, 1996), indeed prosocial beings (e.g., Van Lange et al., 1997), and, as a result, care too much about what others think of their reactions. If this line of reasoning has merit, then it should be the case that lowering public inhibition by reminding people of having behaved in disinhibited ways will weaken pleasure with unfairly obtained goods particularly for people who adhere to a prosocial orientation or who have adopted a prosocial mind-set, but not among those with a proself orientation or mind-set. The last four studies in the Van den Bos, Van Lange, et al. (2011) article indeed showed that the benign effects of reminders of behavioral disinhibition are moderated in this way by social value orientations and associated mind-sets.

CONCLUSIONS

By discussing the psychology of the flabbergasted individual, the inhibited individual, and the disinhibited individual, I tried to shed light on processes of sense making and meaning making. Specifically, I argued that an important issue in social psychology is the study of how people make sense of situations in which they are surprised, conflicted, or flabbergasted by what is happening and do not know how to respond to the situation at hand. I proposed that in these situations the BIS is activated in such a way that the human organism inhibits ongoing behavioral action. The organism does this, I assumed, to facilitate processes of sense making: What is going on here, and what is the appropriate behavior that I should perform now? I also argued that in this process of sense making, people are likely to incorporate the issue of what others will think of their future actions. In fact, I discussed research findings that suggest that people may overdo this such that their prosocial thoughts may impair their ability to do what they think is the right thing. Thus, an ironic implication of the line of reasoning put forward here is that priming people to care a bit less about what others think may help to deactivate the BIS and that this may be conducive to people doing what is good and appropriate. In what follows I briefly discuss some issues that may contribute to the understanding of the BIS, the regulation of the genuine self, and (some) processes pertaining to making sense and providing meaning to the world.

Behavioral Inhibition System

Many different perspectives on the BIS and the psychological functions it serves have been distinguished in the literature (see, e.g., Amodio et al., 2008; Carver, 2005; Carver & White, 1994; Gable et al., 2000; Gray, 1987; Gray & McNaughton, 2000; Knyazev et al., 2006; Latané & Nida, 1981; Monteith, 1993; Nigg, 2000; Sawyer & Behnke, 2002). It was my explicit purpose to focus on some components of the system mentioned in the literature, including some components mentioned by Carver and White (1994) and Gray and McNaughton (2000). These included the appraisal process that in my view seems to be a pivotal psychological function of the system. This also included the public component of the system, as can be derived from the work by Latané and Nida (1981). I also highlighted some components of the system that may be derived from other literatures, such as the literature on the human alarm system (Eisenberger & Lieberman, 2004; Eisenberger et al., 2003; Lieberman & Eisenberger, 2004; Van den Bos et al., 2008). Furthermore, I proposed that in my perspective the BIS and the associated alarm system may be activated not only in response to anxious or threatening stimuli (Carver & White, 1994; Eisenberger et al., 2003; Gray & McNaughton, 2000; Van den Bos et al., 2008) but also in reaction to events or situations that are hard to interpret. Following this perspective, I related the BIS to the appraisal and interpretation of circumstances in which unexpected things happen (Gable et al., 2000) or in which people are slightly confused, in a whirl, or even flabbergasted about what is going on (Van den Bos et al., 2009; Van den Bos, Van Lange, et al., 2011).

I hasten to note here that obviously I did not examine the BIS in as much detail as researchers like Amodio et al. (2008), Carver (e.g., 2005; Carver & White, 1994), Gray (e.g., 1972, 1987, 1990; Gray & McNaughton, 2000), and Knyazev et al. (2006) did. Thus, many of the propositions put forward here should be taken for what they are: hypotheses, explicitly proposed to stimulate future research and thinking about the BIS and its psychological functions.

I also note that in my research I focused on the lowering of public inhibition such that people care less about what others think of their actions (Van den Bos, Müller, & Damen, 2011; Van den Bos et al., 2009; Van den Bos, Van Lange, et al., 2011). Specifically, in my research studies with colleagues, we used a "behavioral disinhibition manipulation," which asked participants to complete three simple open-ended questions that reminded them about their thoughts and feelings about having behaved without inhibitions (see Van den Bos, Müller, & Damen, 2011; Van den Bos et al., 2009; Van den Bos, Van Lange, et al., 2011). A scrambled sentence version of this manipulation yields the same results (Van den Bos, Van Lange, et al., 2011, Study 8). Similarly, low levels of trait behavioral inhibition (as assessed by the Carver & White, 1994, scale) have been shown to have similar effects on reactions to moral dilemmas (Van den Bos, Müller, & Damen, 2011).

Van den Bos et al. (2009) showed that using the three open-ended questions as reminders of having acted without behavioral inhibitions successfully lowered behavioral inhibition (assessed by a state version of the most popular and well-validated measure of BIS sensitivity by Carver & White, 1994). Furthermore, this manipulation did not trigger behavioral activation (no effects were found on state versions of the Carver and White, 1994, scales measuring behavioral activation) nor did it influence positive or negative affective states. In addition, our recent findings showed that the manipulation neither affected self-monitoring nor experienced accountability or self-awareness. Thus, the reminders of behavioral disinhibition that my colleagues and I used in the majority of our studies weakened behavioral inhibition, did not influence behavioral activation, and did not influence affective states, self-monitoring, or accountability. The reminders also did not trigger strong experimenter demands and were robust with respect to gender differences (Van den Bos, Müller, & Damen, 2011; Van den Bos et al., 2009; Van den Bos, Van Lange, et al. 2011). Furthermore, the reminders did seem to trigger "benign" responses (Suler, 2004).

The Genuine Self

The line of reasoning that I propose here holds that reminding people of how they acted without inhibitions should lead them to care less of what others think of their reactions and hence show their more genuine reactions to, for example, bystander situations (Van den Bos et al., 2009) and outcomes that are advantageous to them but are achieved by unfair means (Van den Bos, Van Lange, et al., 2011). In the Van den Bos, Van Lange, et al. (2011) article we indeed found that those participants who adhered to prosocial values were less pleased with receiving their advantageous but unfair outcome following reminders of behavioral disinhibition than following reminders of how they normally act on regular days.

We also found that those participants who adhered to proself values did not show the benign disinhibition effect. This also supports our line of reasoning. In fact, we found that those who held proself values were more pleased with the advantageous outcomes following the reminders of behavioral disinhibition than following the reminders of how they normally react. One implication of these findings seems to be that reminders of behavioral disinhibition lead both prosocials and proselfs to react to advantageous unfair outcomes in ways that are more true to their genuine (prosocial or proself) selves. That is, following disinhibition reminders those with prosocial orientations react to advantageous unfair outcomes in ways that are more true to their genuine (i.e., prosocial) selves such that prosocial participants are less pleased with receiving advantageous unfair outcomes. Furthermore, reminders of behavioral disinhibition lead those with proself orientations to show reactions that are more true to their genuine (i.e., proself) selves such that these proself participants are more pleased with receiving advantageous unfair outcomes.

It is important to note here that in the majority of people the genuine self may in fact be a prosocial self. Van Lange et al. (1997) developed a nine-item decomposed game measure of social value orientation and classified participants as either prosocial, individualistic, or competitive if the majority of their choices were consistent with one of these three social value orientations. Using this measure, researchers have found that the largest group of participants tends to be prosocial as opposed to individualistic or competitive. For example, Van Lange et al. (1997, Study 4) observed that in a representative sample of the Dutch adult population ($N = 1{,}728$) 71% of the respondents could be identified as prosocials. Van Lange (1999) concluded that it is common to find in student samples that more than 50% of the participants can be identified as prosocial. Prosocial participants assign a positive weight to the outcomes of others (i.e., other things being equal, seek to enhance others' welfare) and assign a positive weight to equality in outcomes (i.e., other things being equal, seek to minimize absolute differences in outcomes for self and others; Van Lange, 1999). Moreover, the prevalence of prosocials tends to be even more pronounced in the adult population than in student samples in the psychology laboratory (Van Lange et al., 1997).

I hasten to point out that clearly more research in different cultures and with different populations of participants is needed before researchers can completely understand the psychology of the true and genuine self. I also encourage future research studies to examine in more detail the psychological processes that behavioral disinhibition instigates. Future research should focus also on examining the benign and the less benign or even malignant effects of behavioral disinhibition on people's reactions to advantageous unfair outcomes as well as the effects of behavioral disinhibition on responses to other situations (see, e.g., Lilienfeld, 1992; Nigg, 2000; F. Peters et al., 2006).

For example, in his study of human behavior on the Internet, Suler (2004) noted that people often say and do things in cyberspace that they would not ordinarily say and do in the face-to-face world. Suler called this the *online disinhibition effect*. Particularly relevant to the current chapter is Suler's (2004) observation that people "loosen up, feel less restrained, and express themselves more openly" (p. 321). In our opinion, these liberating effects of disinhibition seem to be related to the effects my colleagues and I have revealed here. In correspondence with our findings, the online disinhibition effect can work in two opposing directions. "Sometimes people share very personal things about themselves on the Internet. They reveal secret emotions, fears, wishes. They show unusual acts of kindness and generosity, sometimes going out of their way to help others" (Suler, 2004,

p. 321). Suler called this *benign disinhibition*, and I have followed his lead in using this terminology.

But Suler (2004) also observed that disinhibition on the Internet does not always have salutary consequences. For instance, people sometimes engage in rude language on the Internet, and they vent harsh criticisms, anger, hatred, and even threats via e-mail. "Or people visit the dark underworld of the Internet—places of pornography, crime, and violence—territory they would never explore in the real world" (Suler, 2004, p. 321). Suler called this *toxic disinhibition*. Our research raises the possibility that what tips the scale between benign effects of disinhibition and more toxic effects can be the social value orientations the person in question adheres to, in ways similar to the weakening versus strengthening of people's pleasure with advantageous outcomes depending on the person's social orientation (Van den Bos, Van Lange, et al., 2011).

CODA

What I attempted to do in this chapter was to convey my current thoughts on the relationship between sense and meaning making and behavioral inhibition and disinhibition. I explicitly note here that in formulating my ideas I tried to propose them as hypotheses that by intention are speculative, have been tested in recent research, and can be tested in more detail in the future. I also note that in this chapter I focused on processes of how people make sense of what is going on in situations. I realize that the psychology of meaning making involves more than the sensemaking processes I focused on here. Future theorizing is needed to examine relations between the various theories in the meaning- and sense-making literatures in more detail.

I believe that inhibition and disinhibition are both critical aspects of making meaning and sense more generally. Speculating a bit about this issue, perhaps the activation of the BIS represents a more *reactive* or *epistemic* type of sense making (e.g., What is going on here?), whereas disinhibition represents a more *proactive* or *problem-solving-oriented* type of sense making (e.g., What can I do to make sense of this situation or to improve this situation?). If this distinction were to have merit, then it perhaps implies that expectancy violation activates the BIS, whereas factors that encourage disinhibition lead individuals to activate the true or authentic self (see, e.g., Kernis & Goldman, 2005, 2006; Schlegel, Hicks, Arndt, & King, 2009). Furthermore, the activation of the true self elicits proactive attempts to behave in a manner consistent with the true self and thereby imbues one's construal of the situation and/or behavior within the situation with greater meaning.

Self-regulation and activation of the BIS can certainly serve important functions. For example, self-regulation of prejudiced responses can be achieved by means of activation of the BIS (Monteith, 1993). This noted, I also think that people sometimes overdo it and may activate the BIS too long or too strongly. Thus, deactivating the system a bit may loosen people up so that they can react in a more genuine (often prosocial) manner. This may yield benign behavioral responses and hence may be conducive for the greater good. Thus, sometimes caring a bit less about what others think may, ironically, lead to a better world.

REFERENCES

Adams, J. S. (1965). Inequity in social exchange. In L. Berkowitz (Ed.), *Advances in experimental social psychology* (Vol. 2, pp. 267–299). New York, NY: Academic Press.

Amodio, D. M., Master, S. L., Yee, C. M., & Taylor, S. E. (2008). Neurocognitive components of the behavioral inhibition and activation systems: Implications for theories of self-regulation. *Psychophysiology*, *45*, 11–19.

Aronson, E. (1999). *The social animal* (8th ed.). New York, NY: Worth.

Asch, S. E. (1956). Studies of independence and conformity: A minority of one against a unanimous majority. *Psychological Monographs*, *70* (9, Whole No. 416).

Blau, P. M. (1964). *Exchange and power in social life*. New York, NY: Wiley.

Carver, C. S. (2005). Impulse and constraint: Perspectives from personality psychology, convergence with theory in other areas, and potential for integration. *Personality and Social Psychology Review*, *9*, 312–333. doi:10.1207/s15327957pspr0904_2

Carver, C. S., & White, T. L. (1994). Behavioral inhibition, behavioral activation, and affective responses to impending reward and punishment: The BIS/BAS scales. *Journal of Personality and Social Psychology*, *67*, 319–333. doi:10.1037/0022-3514.67.2.319

Darley, J. M., & Latané, B. (1968). Bystander intervention in emergencies: Diffusion of responsibility. *Journal of Personality and Social Psychology*, *8*, 377–383. doi:10.1037/h0025589

De Waal, F. (1996). *Good natured: The origins of right and wrong in humans and other animals*. Cambridge, MA: Harvard University Press.

Eisenberger, N. I., & Lieberman, M. D. (2004). Why rejection hurts: A common neural alarm system for physical and social pain. *Trends in Cognitive Sciences*, *8*, 294–300. doi:10.1016/j.tics.2004.05.010

Eisenberger, N. I., Lieberman, M. D., & Williams, K. D. (2003, October 10). Does rejection hurt? An fMRI study of social exclusion. *Science, 302*, 290–292. doi:10.1126/science.1089134

Flabbergasted. (2011). In *Collins Dictionary*. Retrieved from http://www.collinsdictionary.com/dictionary/english

Förster, J., Liberman, N., & Shapira, O. (2009). Preparing for novel versus familiar events: Shifts in global and local processings. *Journal of Experimental Social Psychology, 138*, 389–399.

Fowles, D. C. (1993). Biological variables in psychopathology: A psychobiological perspective. In P. B. Sutker & H. E. Adams (Eds.), *Comprehensive handbook of psychopathology* (2nd ed., pp. 57–82). New York, NY: Plenum Press. doi:10.1007/978-1-4615-3008-4_4

Gable, S. L., Reis, H. T., & Elliot, A. J. (2000). Behavioral activation and inhibition in everyday life. *Journal of Personality and Social Psychology, 78*, 1135–1149. doi:10.1037/0022-3514.78.6.1135

Gray, J. A. (1972). The psychophysiological basis of introversion–extraversion: A modification of Eysenck's theory. In V. D. Nebylitsyn & J. A. Gray (Eds.), *The biological bases of individual behaviour* (pp. 182–205). New York, NY: Academic Press.

Gray, J. A. (1987). *The psychology of fear and stress*. Cambridge, England: Cambridge University Press.

Gray, J. A. (1990). Brain systems that mediate both emotion and cognition. *Cognition and Emotion, 4*, 269–288. doi:10.1080/02699939008410799

Gray, J. A., & McNaughton, N. (2000). *The neuropsychology of anxiety: An enquiry into the functions of the septo-hippocampal system*. Oxford, England: Oxford University Press.

Heine, S. J., Proulx, T., & Vohs, K. D. (2006). The meaning maintenance model: On the coherence of social motivations. *Personality and Social Psychology Review, 10*, 88–110. doi:10.1207/s15327957pspr1002_1

Jacques, E. (1961). *Equitable payment*. London, England: Heinemann Educational Books.

Kant, I. (1959). *Foundation of the metaphysics of morals*. Indianapolis, IN: Bobbs-Merrill. (Original work published 1785)

Karakashian, L. M., Walter, M. I., Christopher, A. N., & Lucas, T. (2006). Fear of negative evaluation affects helping behavior: The bystander effect revisited. *North American Journal of Psychology, 8*, 13–32.

Kernis, M. H., & Goldman, B. M. (2005). Authenticity, social motivation, and psychological adjustment. In J. P. Forgas, K. D. Williams, & S. M. Laham (Eds.), *Social motivation: Conscious and unconscious processes* (pp. 210–227). Cambridge, England: Cambridge University Press.

Kernis, M. H., & Goldman, B. M. (2006). A multicomponent conceptualization of authenticity: Theory and research. In M. P. Zanna (Ed.), *Advances in experimental social psychology* (Vol. 38, pp. 283–357). San Diego, CA: Academic Press.

Knyazev, G. G., Schutter, D. J. L. G., & Van Honk, J. (2006). Anxious apprehension increases coupling of delta and beta oscillations. *International Journal of Psychophysiology, 61*, 283–287. doi:10.1016/j.ijpsycho.2005.12.003

Latané, B., & Darley, J. M. (1968). Group inhibition of bystander intervention in emergencies. *Journal of Personality and Social Psychology, 10*, 215–221. doi:10.1037/h0026570

Latané, B., & Darley, J. M. (1970). *The unresponsive bystander: Why doesn't he help?* New York, NY: Appleton-Century-Crofts.

Latané, B., & Nida, S. (1981). Ten years of research on group size and helping. *Psychological Bulletin, 89*, 308–324. doi:10.1037/0033-2909.89.2.308

Lieberman, M. D., & Eisenberger, N. I. (2004). The neural alarm system: Behavior and beyond. Reply to Ullsperger et al. *Trends in Cognitive Sciences, 8*, 446–447. doi:10.1016/j.tics.2004.08.014

Lilienfeld, S. O. (1992). The association between antisocial personality and somatization disorders: A review and integration of theoretical models. *Clinical Psychology Review, 12*, 641–662. doi:10.1016/0272-7358(92)90136-V

Lind, E. A., & Tyler, T. R. (1988). *The social psychology of procedural justice*. New York, NY: Plenum Press.

Major, B., Kaiser, C. R., O'Brien, L. T., & McCoy, S. K. (2007). Perceived discrimination as worldview threat or worldview confirmation: Implications for self-esteem. *Journal of Personality and Social Psychology, 92*, 1068–1086. doi:10.1037/0022-3514.92.6.1068

McGregor, I., Nash, K. A., & Inzlicht, M. (2009). Threat, high self-esteem, and reactive-approach motivation: Electroencephalographic evidence. *Journal of Experimental Social Psychology, 45*, 1003–1007. doi:10.1016/j.jesp.2009.04.011

McGregor, I., Nash, K. A., Mann, N., & Phills, C. E. (2010). Anxious uncertainty and reactive approach motivation (RAM). *Journal of Personality and Social Psychology, 99*, 133–147. doi:10.1037/a0019701

McGregor, I., Prentice, M., & Nash, K. (2009). Personal uncertainty management by reactive approach motivation. *Psychological Inquiry, 20*, 225–229. doi:10.1080/10478400903333460

McGregor, I., Zanna, M. P., Holmes, J. G., & Spencer, S. J. (2001). Compensatory conviction in the face of personal uncertainty: Going to extremes and being oneself. *Journal of Personality and Social Psychology, 80*, 472–488. doi:10.1037/0022-3514.80.3.472

Milgram, S. (1963). Behavioral study of obedience. *Journal of Abnormal and Social Psychology, 67*, 371–378. doi:10.1037/h0040525

Milgram, S. (1974). *Obedience to authority: An experimental view*. New York, NY: Harper & Row.

Monteith, M. J. (1993). Self-regulation of prejudiced responses: Implications for progress in prejudice-reduction efforts. *Journal of Personality and Social Psychology, 65*, 469–485. doi:10.1037/0022-3514.65.3.469

Murray, S. L., Holmes, J. G., & Collins, N. L. (2006). Optimizing assurance: The risk regulation system in relationships. *Psychological Bulletin, 132*, 641–666. doi:10.1037/0033-2909.132.5.641

Newman, J. P., MacCoon, D. G., Vaughn, L. J., & Sadeh, N. (2005). Validating a distinction between primary and secondary psychopathy with measures of Gray's BIS and BAS constructs. *Journal of Abnormal Psychology, 114*, 319–323. doi:10.1037/0021-843X.114.2.319

Nigg, J. T. (2000). On inhibition/disinhibition in developmental psychopathology: Views from cognitive and personality psychology and a working inhibition taxonomy. *Psychological Bulletin, 126*, 220–246. doi:10.1037/0033-2909.126.2.220

Peters, F., Perani, D., Herholz, K., Holthoff, V., Beuthien-Baumann, B., Sorbi, S., . . . Salmon, E. (2006). Orbitofrontal dysfunction related to both apathy and disinhibition in frontotemporal dementia. *Dementia and Geriatric Cognitive Disorders, 21*, 373–379. doi:10.1159/000091898

Peters, S. L. (2005). *The social psychology of being better off than others* (Doctoral thesis, Utrecht University, Utrecht, the Netherlands). Retrieved from http://igitur-archive.library.uu.nl/dissertations/2005-0530-200022/UUindex.html

Peters, S. L., Van den Bos, K., & Karremans, J. C. (2008). On the psychology of the advantaged: How people react to being overpaid. *Social Justice Research, 21*, 179–191. doi:10.1007/s11211-008-0063-2

Plaks, J. E., Grant, H., & Dweck, C. S. (2005). Violations of implicit theories and the sense of prediction and control: Implications for motivated person perception. *Journal of Personality and Social Psychology*, 88, 245–262. doi:10.1037/0022-3514.88.2.245

Proulx, T. (2009). The feeling of the absurd: Towards an integrative theory of sense-making. *Psychological Inquiry, 20*, 230–234. doi:10.1080/10478400903333494

Proulx, T., & Heine, S. J. (2008). The case of the transmogrifying experimenter: Affirmation of a moral schema following implicit change detection. *Psychological Science, 19*, 1294–1300. doi:10.1111/j.1467-9280.2008.02238.x

Proulx, T., & Heine, S. J. (2009). Connections from Kafka: Exposure to meaning threats improves implicit learning of an artificial grammar. *Psychological Science, 20*, 1125–1131. doi:10.1111/j.1467-9280.2009.02414.x

Proulx, T., Heine, S. J., & Vohs, K. D. (2010). When is the unfamiliar the uncanny? Meaning affirmation after exposure to absurdist literature, humor, and art. *Personality and Social Psychology Bulletin, 36*, 817–829. doi:10.1177/0146167210369896

Sawyer, C. R., & Behnke, R. R. (2002). Behavioral inhibition and the communication of public speaking state anxiety. *Western Journal of Communication*, 66, 412–422. doi:10.1080/10570310209374747

Schlegel, R. J., Hicks, J. A., Arndt, J., & King, L. A. (2009). Thine own self: True self-concept accessibility and meaning of life. *Journal of Personality and Social Psychology, 96*, 473–490. doi:10.1037/a0014060

Schwartz, S. H., & Gottlieb, A. (1976). Bystander reactions to a violent theft: Crime in Jerusalem. *Journal of Personality and Social Psychology, 34*, 1188–1199. doi:10.1037/0022-3514.34.6.1188

Schwartz, S. H., & Gottlieb, A. (1980). Bystander anonymity and reactions to emergencies. *Journal of Personality and Social Psychology, 39*, 418–430. doi:10.1037/0022-3514.39.3.418

Suler, J. (2004). The online disinhibition effect. *CyberPsychology & Behavior, 7*, 321–326. doi:10.1089/1094931041291295

Van den Bos, K. (2009a). Making sense of life: The existential self trying to deal with personal uncertainty. *Psychological Inquiry, 20*, 197–217. doi:10.1080/10478400903333411

Van den Bos, K. (2009b). On the psychology of the uncertain self and the integration of the worldview defense zoo. *Psychological Inquiry, 20*, 252–261. doi:10.1080/10478400903448532

Van den Bos, K. (2010). Self-regulation, homeostasis, and behavioral disinhibition in normative judgments. In D. R. Bobocel, A. C. Kay, M. P. Zanna, & J. M. Olson (Eds.), *The psychology of justice and legitimacy: The Ontario Symposium* (Vol. 11, pp. 205–228). New York, NY: Psychology Press.

Van den Bos, K., Ham, J., Lind, E. A., Simonis, M., Van Essen, W. J., & Rijpkema, M. (2008). Justice and the human alarm system: The impact of exclamation points and flashing lights on the justice judgment process. *Journal of Experimental Social Psychology, 44*, 201–219. doi:10.1016/j.jesp.2007.03.001

Van den Bos, K., Lind, E. A., Vermunt, R., & Wilke, H. A. M. (1997). How do I judge my outcome when I do not know the outcome of others? The psychology of the fair process effect. *Journal of Personality and Social Psychology, 72*, 1034–1046. doi:10.1037/0022-3514.72.5.1034

Van den Bos, K., Müller, P. A., & Damen, T. (2011). A behavioral disinhibition hypothesis of interventions in moral dilemmas. *Emotion Review, 3*, 281–283. doi:10.1177/1754073911402369

Van den Bos, K., Müller, P. A., & Van Bussel, A. A. L. (2009). Helping to overcome intervention inertia in bystander's dilemmas: Behavioral disinhibition can improve the greater good. *Journal of Experimental Social Psychology, 45*, 873–878. doi:10.1016/j.jesp.2009.03.014

Van den Bos, K., Peters, S. L., Bobocel, D. R., & Ybema, J. F. (2006). On preferences and doing the right thing: Satisfaction with advantageous inequity when cognitive processing is limited. *Journal of Experimental Social Psychology, 42*, 273–289. doi:10.1016/j.jesp.2005.04.003

Van den Bos, K., & Rijpkema, M. (2008). *Studying effects of exclamation point primes using functional neuroimaging*. Unpublished manuscript, Department of Social Psychology, Utrecht University, Utrecht, Netherlands.

Van den Bos, K., Van Lange, P. A. M., Lind, E. A., Venhoeven, L. A., Beudeker, D. A., Cramwinckel, F. M., . . . Van der Laan, J. (2011). On the benign qualities of behavioral disinhibition: Because of the prosocial nature of people behavioral disinhibition can weaken pleasure with getting more than you deserve. *Journal of Personality and Social Psychology, 101*, 791–811. doi: 10.1037/a0023556

Van den Bos, K., Vermunt, R., & Wilke, H. A. M. (1996). The consistency rule and the voice effect: The influence of expectations on procedural fairness judgements and performance. *European Journal of Social Psychology, 26*, 411–428. doi:10.1002/(SICI)1099-0992(199605)26:3<411::AID-EJSP766>3.0.CO;2-2

Van den Bos, K., Wilke, H. A. M., Lind, E. A., & Vermunt, R. (1998). Evaluating outcomes by means of the fair process effect: Evidence for different processes in fairness and satisfaction judgments. *Journal of Personality and Social Psychology, 74*, 1493–1503. doi:10.1037/0022-3514.74.6.1493

Van Lange, P. A. M. (1999). The pursuit of joint outcomes and equality in outcomes: An integrative model of social value orientation. *Journal of Personality and Social Psychology, 77*, 337–349. doi:10.1037/0022-3514.77.2.337

Van Lange, P. A. M., Otten, W., De Bruin, E. M. N., & Joireman, J. A. (1997). Development of prosocial, individualistic, and competitive orientations: Theory and preliminary evidence. *Journal of Personality and Social Psychology, 73*, 733–746. doi:10.1037/0022-3514.73.4.733

19

THE EMBODIMENT OF MEANING VIOLATIONS

SARAH S. M. TOWNSEND, DINA ELIEZER, AND BRENDA MAJOR

In the United States, millions of students enroll in college every year. They believe, as most Americans do, that education is the key to getting ahead and that hard work in school will lead to success after graduation. On the basis of this belief or worldview, they invest the time and money required to complete their college degrees. They expect that when they graduate they will find lucrative and/or rewarding jobs. However, in the spring of 2009, at the height of the economic crisis, a cohort of students graduated from college facing very limited job prospects. Contrary to their expectations, hard work in college did not bring them success. For many, it did not even bring them a job.

These graduates experienced a *meaning violation*—their expectations, assumptions, or predictions were disconfirmed. Numerous theoretical perspectives suggest that when people's meaning systems are violated, regardless of the particular belief or expectation that is violated, they experience a state of *aversive arousal*. This state, in turn, is assumed to motivate people to engage

DOI: 10.1037/14040-019
The Psychology of Meaning, Keith D. Markman, Travis Proulx, and Matthew J. Lindberg (Editors)

in actions to restore their sense of meaning. For example, some graduates may have tried to restore meaning by focusing on graduation itself as the achievement that they expected to attain through their hard work (i.e., assimilation). Others may have modified their belief system to include the idea that factors other than hard work will influence who is successful (i.e., accommodation). Yet, other students may have affirmed an unrelated source of meaning in their lives, such as their belief in God (i.e., compensation; e.g., Heine, Proulx, & Vohs, 2006; see also Chapter 4, this volume). Engaging in these meaning-restoring actions, in turn, is assumed to alleviate the state of aversive arousal (Festinger, 1957; Heine et al., 2006). Thus, this state plays a central and causal role in the chain of events from meaning violation to meaning restoration and is a common thread among theories positing a motivation to maintain one's sense of meaning.

Despite the important role aversive arousal may play in meaning maintenance, this state remains relatively unspecified and difficult to measure. We define aversive arousal as the psychological experience of anxiety or threat and its embodiment, that is, the accompanying physiological responses. In this chapter, we describe measures of peripheral physiological responses that provide means of indexing this state, and we review research that has used these measures to demonstrate links in the causal chain from meaning violation to threat to meaning restoration and reduced threat. Using this definition and measurement of aversive arousal allows us to take into account findings from work on several forms of meaning violations and helps to reveal areas in which additional research is needed to establish the entire causal chain.

This chapter consists of three sections. In the first section, we briefly review the meaning violation literature and then elaborate on our definition of aversive arousal as threat and explain the specific physiological responses that can be measured to index the psychological experience of threat. In the second section, we review research using peripheral physiological measures that has demonstrated each link in the causal chain from meaning violations to threat to meaning restoration and decreased threat. Specifically, we review evidence that (a) meaning violations trigger threat, (b) threat leads to meaning restoration attempts, and (c) threat is dampened when meaning restoration takes place. Whereas extensive research has shown that meaning violations of various forms are followed by attempts to restore meaning, relatively little work has directly examined the experience of aversive arousal as a response to meaning violations and/or as a cause or motivator of meaning restoration. Finally, we summarize and conclude with a discussion of the gaps that exist in the current literature and suggest how peripheral physiological measures can be used in future work to establish the entire causal chain.

MEANING VIOLATIONS

We adopt a broad definition of *meaning* as a set of mental representations of the expected relationships or associations connecting people, places, objects, and beliefs to each other (e.g., Baumeister, 1991; Heine et al., 2006; McGregor & Little, 1998). This conceptualization of meaning includes both explicit and implicit expected associations and encompasses many related concepts, such as worldviews (e.g., Major, Kaiser, O'Brien, & McCoy, 2007), folk psychologies (Bruner, 1990), system-relevant ideologies (Jost & Banaji, 1994), cultural models (e.g., Fiske, Kitayama, Markus, & Nisbett, 1998), and self-schemas (e.g., Markus, 1977). Meaning serves as a lens through which people view and interpret the world, provides guidelines for how people should behave in various situations, helps people cope with traumatic life and events, and even buffers people from existential terror. Thus, meaning provides individuals with expectations for themselves, others, and the world around them, and maintaining a sense of meaning has been argued to possibly be a "fundamental human need" (see, e.g., Chapter 11, this volume).

The meaning frameworks that people hold, however, are imperfect reflections of reality. Interactions, information, or events, whether they are consciously perceived or outside of people's awareness, can violate people's sense of meaning. For example, witnessing an innocent victim suffer violates just world expectations (Lerner, 1980), or encountering an Asian American who speaks with a Southern accent violates category-based expectations (stereotypes; e.g., Mendes, Blascovich, Hunter, Lickel, & Jost, 2007). Violations can intimately involve the self, such as when an individual's expectations about his or her own abilities are disconfirmed by inconsistent feedback (e.g., Ayduk, Gyurak, Akinola, & Mendes, 2011), or they can be relatively unrelated to the self, such as when an individual's expectations about the colors of playing card suits are disconfirmed by a doctored deck of cards (Proulx & Major, 2011). Meaning violations do not only occur when people encounter unexpected negative information; people can also have their sense of meaning violated by positive information (e.g., Plaks, Grant, & Dweck, 2005; see also Chapter 6, this volume).

Given individuals' need for meaning, many theories propose that violations of meaning systems lead to a state of aversive arousal, which then prompts individuals to restore their sense of meaning as a way to reduce the aversive state (e.g., Festinger, 1957; Proulx, Heine, & Vohs, 2010; Sherman & Cohen, 2006; see also Chapter 20, this volume). For instance, cognitive dissonance leads to psychological discomfort, which motivates people to restore meaning (e.g., Elliot & Devine, 1994; Galinsky, Stone, & Cooper, 2000). Similarly, personal uncertainty is experienced as an aversive or uncomfortable feeling, which motivates people to restore their sense of meaning and certainty (e.g., Van den Bos, 2009). In integrating across these various theories, Proulx and Heine (2010) argued that violations of one's sense of meaning lead to a unique arousal state, which motivates attempts to restore meaning. However, this unique, aversive arousal state is relatively unspecified and difficult to assess with self-report measures. For example, asking participants who are experiencing cognitive dissonance to report their degree of psychological discomfort can have the unintended effect of providing them with a way to reduce dissonance or restore meaning (e.g., Galinsky et al., 2000). In the section that follows, we explain our definition of this unique arousal state as threat and discuss how this experience may be embodied and therefore measured by several physiological indexes.

AVERSIVE AROUSAL AS THREAT: PHYSIOLOGICAL INDEXES

The psychological experience of threat occurs when individuals appraise the demands of their current situation as exceeding their resources to cope with those demands (e.g., Blascovich, 2008; Lazarus, 1966). Meaning violations heighten situational demands by increasing unpredictability and perceptions of uncertainty. For instance, during an interpersonal interaction, being unsure of how to behave or what to expect of one's interaction partner will make that interaction more difficult. As a result, when individuals encounter information, events, or people who violate their sense of meaning, they should experience threat.

Attempts to index threat with self-report measures have often been unsuccessful. Self-reports are vulnerable to self-presentational concerns and depend on individuals' conscious awareness (e.g., Matheson & Cole, 2004). However, the psychological experience of threat is embodied and can be indexed by measuring physiological responses. These measures offer a way to directly index the threat that is triggered by meaning violations and offer several advantages over self-report data. Indexing threat with physiological responses circumvents potential distortions or omissions that might be present in self-reports and has the advantages of being covert, continuous, and on-line (Blascovich & Mendes, 2010).

Broadly speaking, physiological responses can be divided into (a) central neurophysiological processes that are assessed by measuring activity in the brain and (b) peripheral neurophysiological processes that are assessed by measuring activity in the visceral, somatic, and endocrine systems. Of course, both central and peripheral measures offer unique advantages and present unique challenges (for a review, see Blascovich, Vanman, Mendes, & Dickerson, 2011). We focus on measures of peripheral physiological responses that are associated with the psychological experience of threat. These measures have the practical advantage of being less costly to collect and the methodological advantage of being less intrusive and allowing for data collection while participants are in more ecologically valid situations, including field settings.

Peripheral physiological responses can index activation of the two primary biological systems that are active during affective and cognitive processes—the sympathetic adrenal medullary (SAM) and hypothalamic–pituitary–adrenal cortical (HPA) axes (Blascovich & Mendes, 2010). Of particular relevance here, both the SAM and HPA axes are activated by the experience of stress or threat. The SAM system responds quickly during fight-or-flight situations, whereas the HPA system activates after longer experiences of threat or stress. SAM activation triggers the release of epinephrine from the adrenal medulla, which has the effect of increasing heart rate, blood pressure, and skin conductance; decreasing the preejection period (i.e., the time between the initiation of the cardiac cycle and the opening of the aortic valve); dilating pupils; and inhibiting the gastrointestinal tract. These responses have the downstream effects of increasing energy, alertness, and blood flow to the muscles. HPA activation sets off a chain of reactions beginning with the release of corticotropin-releasing hormone by the hypothalamus, which triggers the anterior pituitary to release adrenocorticotropin hormone, which stimulates an area of the adrenal cortex to release cortisol. Cortisol is important for coping with prolonged experiences of stress because it helps to increase energy or fuel that is available by elevating the level of glucose in the blood. Although both SAM and HPA activation help individuals respond to and cope with physical stressors, they are often triggered by the experience of psychological stress or threat, such as public speaking or thinking about one's mortality (Sapolsky, 2004).

Common peripheral physiological measures of SAM activation include changes in heart rate, blood pressure, and skin conductance. Increases in these individual physiological responses indicate heightened arousal, and measuring these responses provides a way to roughly index the psychological experience of threat. However, because these measures only indicate a general state of heightened arousal, they do not have a one-to-one correspondence with the specific psychological state of threat (Blascovich & Kelsey, 1990; Cacioppo, Tassinary, & Berntson, 2007). Measuring these responses may indicate an experience of threat, but it may also indicate more affectively neutral or even positive arousal. Nonetheless, these measures may serve as a useful approximation of threat because they are relatively easy to administer and because they can measure arousal in passive and active situations.

HPA activation is often assessed by measuring increases in cortisol and can be used as an index of prolonged threat (Dickerson & Kemeny, 2004).

In particular, Dickerson and Kemeny (2004) argued that cortisol is released when people's central goals are threatened as part of an adaptive response to increase available energy to deal with, and it is hoped reduce, the threat. These central goals include the preservation of individuals' physical and social selves and, we argue, the preservation of individuals' sense of meaning. Although cortisol may offer more precision in indexing the psychological state of threat, this measure is not without its limitations. Specifically, increases in cortisol are most reliably found when individuals are in situations, such as cognitive tasks or verbal interaction tasks, that are goal relevant and engender some degree of evaluation, that is, motivated performance situations. Thus, cortisol responses may not provide a reliable index of threat when participants are engaged in more passive tasks.

The biopsychosocial (BPS) model of challenge and threat has identified and validated specific patterns of cardiovascular responses, indicating SAM and HPA activation, which index the psychological states of threat versus challenge (see Blascovich, 2008, for a review). Threat occurs when individuals appraise situational demands as outweighing their appraisal of their personal resources, the definition we mentioned previously. Conversely, challenge occurs when individuals appraise their resources as exceeding demands.

Both challenge and threat states are associated with activation of the SAM axis; however, activation of the HPA axis is greater during threat than challenge. Specifically, challenge states are characterized by greater cardiac responses and lower vascular responses. In contrast, threat states are characterized by greater vascular responses relative to cardiac responses. Thus, threat, relative to challenge, is indexed by lower cardiac output and greater systemic vascular resistance, which is measured as total peripheral resistance. The threat response results in a constriction of arteries, whereas the challenge response functions to increase blood flow to skeletal muscles and dilate arteries to accommodate this blood. As with indexing threat by measuring changes in cortisol, these physiological indexes of the psychological states of threat and challenge have only been validated for situations in which individuals are in motivated performance situations.

The physiological measures described represent promising ways to index the threat that accompanies meaning violations. Measures of cortisol or the pattern of cardiovascular responses outlined in the BPS model provide more specific indexes of threat but are limited to situations in which people are engaged in active coping tasks, which may not cover the range of experiences of meaning violations. Single measures of SAM activation such as blood pressure and skin conductance can serve as rough indexes of threat. Although these measures lack specificity, they may be useful in common meaning violation paradigms, which use more passive coping situations (i.e., participants are exposed to an unexpected event or asked to write about uncertainty or mortality). Overall, we believe that under the right conditions, peripheral physiological measures can be successfully adapted to meaning threat paradigms.

In the next three sections, we discuss how physiological measures have been or could be integrated with meaning violation research to explore the full causal chain from meaning violations to threat to meaning restoration.

THE FIRST LINK: MEANING VIOLATIONS TRIGGER THREAT

Next, we review evidence for the first link in the chain, that meaning violations trigger threat. These studies are important for both theoretical and methodological reasons. Theoretically, these studies demonstrate that different types of meaning violations, including uncertainty (e.g., Van den Bos, 2009), dissonance (e.g., Croyle & Cooper, 1983; Elkin & Leippe, 1986), and expectancy (e.g., Major et al., 2007; Mendes et al., 2007), lead to a common set of physiological responses. Methodologically, these studies provide examples of how meaning violation paradigms can be integrated with physiological measurement techniques.

Uncertainty Triggers Threat

The experience of uncertainty, particularly uncertainty about one's understanding of the self, the world, or the relationship between the two (Van den Bos, 2009) is one type of meaning violation. Being unable to predict one's surroundings, such as when certain stimuli will occur or how another person will behave, may make individuals feel uncertain in that situation. As with other meaning violations, personal uncertainty is experienced as an aversive or uncomfortable feeling (e.g., Hogg, 2007; Van den Bos, 2009). Through the examination of these types of situations, the following research makes the important direct link between uncertainty and threat as measured by several different physiological indicators.

First, the experience of uncertainty due to unpredictability is associated with greater SAM activation (Jennings, Averill, Opton, & Lazarus, 1970; Monat, Averill, & Lazarus, 1972). For example, Jennings and colleagues (1970) gave participants a signal that indicated, with varying degrees of certainty, that they would receive a shock. When the signal was played, participants who were uncertain about whether they would receive a shock showed the greatest increase in heart rate—even greater than those who were certain that they would receive a shock. Monat and colleagues (1972) replicated these findings, showing a similar pattern for threat in response to uncertainty as indicated by greater galvanic skin response.

Individual differences in the extent to which people perceive uncertainty as stressful also contribute to the threat-related arousal people experience in unpredictable situations. Specifically, Greco and Roger (2003) measured the extent to which participants reported that being uncertain was stressful and then exposed them to distressing stimuli at times that they were either able or unable to predict. Participants who reported that they experienced stress from uncertainty and those who were unable to predict when they would be exposed to the distressing stimulus had the highest blood pressure responses.

Work on intergroup interactions also provides evidence that uncertainty is threatening (e.g., Blascovich, Mendes, Hunter, Lickel, & Kowai-Bell, 2001; Mendes, Blascovich, Lickel, & Hunter, 2002). Compared with interactions between individuals who are members of the same social group (e.g., two White Americans), interactions between individuals who are members of different social groups are characterized by greater uncertainty (e.g., Vorauer, 2006). Given this greater uncertainty, intergroup interactions should lead to greater aversive arousal or threat than intragroup interactions. Indeed, Blascovich et al. (2001) found that nonstigmatized people (e.g., people without facial birthmarks, White Americans) showed cardiovascular reactivity patterns consistent with threat when they interacted with members of a stigmatized outgroup (e.g., people with facial birthmarks, Black Americans). In addition, people who reported having had more contact with Black Americans were less threatened during these intergroup interactions presumably because the additional experience led them to feel more certain about how the interaction would proceed.

Uncertainty, in the form of uncontrollability, has also been associated with increased threat as indexed by heightened cortisol levels (e.g., Dickerson & Kemeny, 2004). In their meta-analysis, Dickerson and Kemeny (2004) found that people who are engaged in uncontrollable tasks show larger cortisol responses than those who are engaged in controllable tasks. In particular, it seems to be the knowledge or perception that a desired outcome is not contingent on one's behavior that leads to increases in cortisol. This experience is largely consistent with meaning violations. One key function of meaning is to provide people with a sense of predictability and control over outcomes. Thus, meaning violations may lead people to feel that they are unable to predict or control their outcomes. The findings reported by Dickerson and Kemeny provide suggestive evidence that meaning violations trigger threat as indexed by cortisol.

Dissonance Triggers Threat

Another type of meaning violation is cognitive dissonance, which is experienced when individuals perceive a logical inconsistency between their thoughts and/or their behavior (Festinger, 1957). For example, a college student who believes that tuition should remain stable and also believes he or she has freely chosen to write an essay in support of a tuition increase will experience dissonance. The following research demonstrates the direct link between dissonance and threat as measured by several different physiological indicators.

In one of the first studies to assess physiological responses to dissonance, Gerard (1967) examined participants' finger pulse amplitude in response to a spreading of alternatives paradigm. In this study, participants were asked to select between two paintings. In one condition, one of the paintings was strongly preferred over the other; however, in the second condition, the two paintings were equally liked. Dissonance was presumed to arise in the latter condition because there was an inconsistency between individuals' choice of the selected painting and their liking for the unselected painting. Of participants who were forced to choose between two similar alternatives, those experiencing greater dissonance showed greater decreases in finger pulse amplitude, which indicates greater vasoconstriction.

Subsequent studies replicated this finding using skin conductance responses as a measure of threat (Croyle & Cooper, 1983; Elkin & Leippe, 1986; Losch & Cacioppo, 1990). For example, Robinson and Demaree (2007) examined responses to expressive dissonance, when an individual's emotional expression is inconsistent with his or her actual emotional state. While watching sad film clips, participants in one condition were allowed to express their emotions naturally; however, those in a second condition were asked to express the opposite of their true feelings, inducing expressive dissonance. Participants in the expressive dissonance condition showed greater skin conductance responses, indicating greater threat.

Violation of Expectancies Triggers Threat

Expectancy violations are another type of meaning violation and have been linked to the experience of threat. This research, reviewed in the section that follows, also makes the important contribution of demonstrating that a range of expectancy violations trigger threat.

Violation of Self-Image-Based Expectancies

Self-verification theory proposes that people are motivated to maintain a consistent self-concept and want others to see them in ways that are consistent with their views of themselves (e.g., Swann, Rentfrow, & Guinn, 2002). Even when people have negative self-conceptions, they often desire to interact with people who confirm their negative self-image (for a review, see Swann, 2012). However, people are not always able to obtain verifying feedback from others. Instead, they often receive feedback that is inconsistent with their self-view, which may violate their sense of meaning. A recent study by Ayduk et al. (2011) provided the most direct evidence that violations of one's self-views elicit threat as indexed by blood pressure reactivity. Participants with high and low self-esteem were given feedback that was either positive or negative and, therefore, consistent or inconsistent with their self-views. Among people with low self-esteem, positive (i.e., inconsistent) feedback led to marginally higher blood pressure reactivity than negative (i.e., consistent) feedback. The same pattern was found for people with high self-esteem; negative (i.e., inconsistent) feedback led to greater blood pressure reactivity than positive (i.e., consistent) feedback.

Violation of Worldview-Based Expectancies

Meaning violations can also occur when people's worldviews are disconfirmed (Major et al., 2007). A *worldview* is a set of implicit and explicit assumptions about oneself, the world, and one's place in the world. Worldviews provide people with expectations for themselves and others. In worldview verification theory, Major and colleagues (2007) argued that people are motivated to maintain consistency between their worldview and their experiences and that experiences that are inconsistent with an individual's worldview constitute a meaning violation.

Research on worldview verification has examined one central component of people's worldviews: their beliefs about and explanations for status inequality in society, that is, their status ideology. In the United States the dominant status ideology is meritocracy, which holds that hard work and ability lead to success and that the status system is fair (O'Brien & Major, 2005). Like other components of a person's worldview, meritocracy beliefs guide perceptions and expectations, including people's implicit expectations for how intergroup interactions will unfold. For example, members of low-status groups who believe in meritocracy believe that the status system is fair and implicitly expect that they will be treated fairly by members of high-status groups. Conversely, members of low-status groups who reject meritocracy believe the status system is unfair and implicitly expect that they will be treated unfairly by members of high-status groups. Information or experiences that are inconsistent with these expectations will disconfirm people's worldviews, violating their sense of meaning and triggering the experience of threat.

A series of studies examining cardiovascular responses during face-to-face intergroup interactions found support for these predictions (Townsend, Major, Sawyer, & Mendes, 2010). With the use of the BPS model, threat was indexed as relatively greater total peripheral resistance and lower cardiac output. In one study, Latinas interacted with a White female partner who expressed prejudiced or unprejudiced attitudes toward ethnic minorities. In a second study, White American women interacted with a White American man who had previously evaluated them negatively for either unfair, prejudicial reasons or ostensibly fair, merit-based reasons. As predicted, participants' beliefs about the fairness of the status system moderated their experience of threat during these interactions. Among participants who believed the status system is fair, interacting with a prejudiced partner compared with an unprejudiced partner disconfirmed their worldview and resulted in greater threat. Conversely, among those who rejected meritocracy and believed that the status system is unfair, interacting with an unprejudiced compared with a prejudiced partner disconfirmed their worldview and resulted in greater threat.

Eliezer, Townsend, Sawyer, Major, and Mendes (2011) found a similar pattern in White women's levels of threat as indexed with resting blood pressure. Specifically, women reported the degree to which they endorsed meritocracy and the amount of discrimination they experienced as a result of being a woman. Given that women who endorse meritocracy implicitly expect that intergroup interactions will be fair, perceiving high levels of discrimination should be a meaning threat and, therefore, associated with higher blood pressure. As confirmation of this, among women who endorsed meritocracy, perceived discrimination was positively related to threat.

Violation of Category-Based Expectancies

Mendes and colleagues (2007) examined responses to the violation of category-based expectancies during interpersonal interactions. Participants interacted with confederate interaction partners, some of whom violated participants' expectations given the confederate's membership in a particular social group. For example, one confederate was an Asian American who spoke with a Southern U.S. accent. She violated participants' stereotypical expectation that Asian Americans are not from the Southern United States. Interactions with these expectancy-violating partners should be experienced as meaning violations and should, therefore, lead to increased threat relative to interactions with partners who match their expectations. Threat was indexed according to the BPS model. Consistent with this reasoning, participants interacting with expectancy-violating partners exhibited cardiovascular responses consistent with threat, whereas participants interacting with partners who confirmed their category-based expectancies showed the challenge pattern.

Together this work shows that different forms of meaning violation, including uncertainty, dissonance, self-view inconsistencies, worldview violations, and disconfirmed stereotypes, all lead to a similar set of physiological responses characteristic of a psychological state of threat. Sometimes participants' also reported consciously feeling threatened, but self-reported results were inconsistent. Thus, by using peripheral physiological measures that avoid the necessity for conscious self-report, researchers have been able to more directly assess the aversive arousal that characterizes threat.

THE SECOND LINK: THREAT MOTIVATES MEANING RESTORATION

Given that meaning violations induce threat, the subsequent link in the causal chain holds that this threat should motivate people to restore their sense of meaning as a way to reduce the threat. However, few studies have directly demonstrated that threat leads to sense making, and the studies that have done so used self-reported measures of affect to index threat. For example, Plaks et al. (2005) gave participants information that violated or confirmed their theories of personality (i.e., that human attributes are fixed or malleable), measured their self-reported anxiety, and then examined their subsequent efforts to reestablish control. Not only were participants whose theories were violated more anxious but also those who reported being more anxious exerted more effort to reestablish control. This is consistent with the idea that the threat triggered by meaning violations induces attempts to restore meaning.

Additional supporting evidence comes from research showing that people make fewer attempts to restore meaning when they misattribute the arousal they are experiencing to sources unrelated to the meaning threat (Kay, Moscovitch, & Laurin, 2010; Losch & Cacioppo, 1990; Proulx & Heine, 2008; Zanna & Cooper, 1974). For example, Kay et al. (2010) primed participants with either randomness-related words to dampen their sense of meaning or with negative words and then measured their belief in supernatural sources of control such God or karma as an index of meaning restoration. They found that participants who were primed with randomness attempted to restore their sense of meaning more than those who were primed with negative words. However, this difference was not present among participants who could misattribute any arousal they were feeling to a placebo pill they received at the beginning of the study; even those primed with randomness were presumably not motivated to restore their sense of meaning. This research highlights the role of physiological arousal in prompting people to engage in meaning restoration in the face of a meaning violation.

Additionally, Cooper, Zanna, and Taves (1978) manipulated the actual arousal participants experienced. All participants believed they were given a placebo pill, but some were given a pill that actually contained a sedative (i.e., phenobarbital) or amphetamine. Among participants who were experiencing dissonance as a result of writing a counterattitudinal essay under conditions of high choice, those who were given the sedative showed less subsequent attitude change, and those who were given the amphetamine showed increased attitude change. In addition, even among participants not experiencing dissonance, those who took the amphetamine also showed some attitude change. These results also support the second link in the chain, that arousal motivates efforts to restore meaning even if the arousal is from a source other than the dissonance.

Additional support for the second link in the chain from threat to meaning restoration is provided by evidence that threat may increase the effectiveness of meaning-making attempts by triggering an orienting response and vigilance. The orienting response entails an individual focusing on a stimulus, physically turning toward it, and mentally attending to it. Similarly, vigilance is the process of excessive monitoring of one's environment. These responses may accompany the threat caused by meaning violations and may help to prepare people to restore their sense of meaning. The peripheral physiological responses of cardiac deceleration and increases in electrodermal activity provide an excellent means of measuring orienting and vigilance (Blascovich & Mendes, 2010).

Some work suggests that vigilance and orienting responses do indeed accompany meaning violations (e.g., Richards & Casey, 1991). For example, when people are processing feedback that violates their expectations compared with feedback that confirms their expectations, they show greater heart rate deceleration (e.g., Gunther Moor, Crone, & van der Molen, 2010), and people who are in heightened states of uncertainty show greater electrodermal responses (i.e., increased galvanic skin response; Monat et al., 1972). Le Poire and Burgoon (1996), in their work on interpersonal communication, provided evidence of a link between orienting and threat. Specifically, during an interaction, participants' partners changed their behavior in a way that violated participants' expectations. This change led to an initial orienting response shown by decreases in heart rate, which was followed by a threat response, shown by increases in heart rate and skin temperature. Overall, these findings suggest that vigilance and an orienting response may accompany the experience of threat when an individual's sense of meaning is violated. Importantly, these responses may indicate increased attention and focus on meaning, which may prime people to perceive meaning in their environments.

THE THIRD LINK: RESTORED MEANING REDUCES THREAT

The final link in the chain specifies that when individuals successfully restore their sense of meaning, their experience of threat should be dampened or eliminated. Elliot and Devine (1994) provided evidence of this using a self-report measure of threat, specifically, psychological discomfort. Using the experience of dissonance as the meaning violation, they found that making a counterattitudinal argument caused psychological discomfort, which was alleviated when meaning was restored through attitude change. To our knowledge, only one study has examined this link in the chain using peripheral physiological measures of threat. Using skin conductance as a measure of threat, Elkin and Leippe (1986) found that meaning violations, in this case dissonance, lead to threat. Then, they offered some participants the opportunity to restore their sense of meaning through attitude change. Contrary to predictions, attitude change did not reduce skin conductance. However, given the relatively nonspecific measure of threat used as well as significant advances in physiological recording equipment and methodology that have occurred since their article was published, additional research is needed before claiming a lack of support for this link in the chain.

SUMMARY AND SUGGESTIONS FOR FUTURE RESEARCH

People need meaning in their lives; they need a framework of ideas that delineates the relationships that exist between themselves, others, and their environments. However, such frameworks can be violated by certain pieces of information or certain experiences. These meaning violations—having one's expectations, assumptions, or predictions disconfirmed—are followed by attempts to restore meaning in some way. Although theorizing on this process posits that people are motivated to restore their sense of meaning to reduce the state of aversive arousal that is triggered by meaning violations (e.g., Festinger, 1957; Heine et al., 2006; Van den Bos, 2009; see also Chapter 5, this volume), research has yet to empirically demonstrate the entire causal chain from meaning violations to aversive arousal to meaning restoration and reduced arousal. Potential reasons for this are that definitions of aversive arousal are relatively vague and the state itself can be difficult to measure.

In the present chapter, we defined this state of aversive arousal as the psychological experience of anxiety or threat and its embodiment. We described peripheral physiological measures that can serve as an index of threat and reviewed research using these measures that provides evidence for each link in the causal chain. The first link, that meaning violations lead to threat, is supported by evidence from a variety of different meaning violations—uncertainty, dissonance, violated self-views, violated worldviews, and violated category-based expectations. However, the second and third links, that threat motivates efforts to restore meaning and that the restoration of meaning results in decreased threat, enjoy much less support.

Future research, using peripheral physiological measures to index threat, should work to establish these latter two links in the causal chain, as well as examining the entire causal process at once.

Threat Motivates Meaning Restoration

Peripheral physiological measures offer an excellent way to provide more direct evidence that the threat triggered by meaning violations causes attempts to restore meaning. For example, after exposing participants to a meaning violation, researchers could assess their experience of threat using peripheral physiological measures such as those outlined in the BPS model of challenge and threat and then offer them an opportunity to restore their sense of meaning. Researchers could then test whether the degree to which participants experienced threat mediates their attempts at meaning restoration. An additional interesting possibility would be to examine whether manipulations shown to reduce meaning-making attempts have their effect through a reduction in threat. For example, recent work has shown that hand washing reduces attitude change in response to dissonance (Lee & Schwarz, 2010). Using physiological measures, researchers could test whether hand washing reduces threat, which in turn reduces attempts to resolve dissonance through attitude change.

Meaning Reduces Threat

Measures of peripheral physiological responses also provide a means with which to directly examine whether a restored sense of meaning diminishes threat. The most straightforward test of this link in the causal chain would be to allow participants to engage in some meaning restoration, either through assimilation, accommodation, or compensation, and to measure the effect of this on their physiological activity. For example, Kray and colleagues have shown that counterfactual thinking leads people to perceive greater meaning (see Chapters 16 and 17, this volume). Future work could expose participants to a meaning violation and then have them engage in counterfactual thinking or have them merely recall past events. Support for the third link in the meaning-violation-to-meaning-restoration chain would be provided if participants who engaged in counterfactual thinking showed less threat than those who did not. An additional interesting possibility for future research would be to compare the effectiveness of the three meaning restoration strategies, assimilation, accommodation, and compensation, by examining which leads to the largest decreases in threat.

Entire Causal Chain

Ideally, the entire causal process could be examined in single study. One way to examine the entire process would be to expose participants to a meaning threat such as interacting with an expectancy-violating partner or giving a counterattitudinal speech and then give participants the opportunity to restore meaning by endorsing an alternative meaning system or changing their original beliefs, all while measuring participants' physiological reactivity. If the predictions of meaning violation theories are correct, then physiological activity should mediate the relationship between meaning violation and meaning restoration such that participants exposed to a meaning violation should show greater physiological activity than participants not exposed to that violation and in turn should engage in greater meaning restoration. Furthermore, the more meaning restoration participants engage in, the lower their subsequent physiological activity should be.

CONCLUSIONS

Working hard in college will pay off with finding a good job after graduation; other people see me the same way I see myself; or Asian Americans do not speak with Southern accents—all of these are examples of meaning, and all can be violated. Such meaning violations are theorized to trigger a state of aversive arousal, which then motivates attempts to restore meaning in some way. By specifying this aversive arousal state as threat, our hope is that we may help to provide a way to integrate findings from a variety of different lines of research on responses to meaning violation and to reveal areas in which additional research is needed.

REFERENCES

Ayduk, Ö., Gyurak, A., Akinola, M., & Mendes, W. B. (2011). *Self-verification processes revealed in implicit and behavioral responses to feedback*. Manuscript submitted for publication.

Baumeister, R. (1991). *Meanings of life*. New York, NY: Guilford Press.

Blascovich, J. (2008). Challenge and threat. In A. J. Elliot (Ed.), *Handbook of approach and avoidance motivation* (pp. 431–445). New York, NY: Psychology Press.

Blascovich, J., & Kelsey, R. M. (1990). Using cardiovascular and electrodermal measures of arousal in social psychological research. In C. Hendrick & M. S. Clark (Eds.), *Review of personality and social psychology* (Vol. 11, pp. 45–73). Newbury Park, CA: Sage.

Blascovich, J., & Mendes, W. B. (2010). Social psychophysiology and embodiment. In S. T. Fiske, D. T. Gilbert, & G. Lindzey (Eds.), *The handbook of social psychology* (5th ed., pp. 194–227). New York, NY: Wiley.

Blascovich, J., Mendes, W. B., Hunter, S. B., Lickel, B., & Kowai-Bell, N. (2001). Perceiver threat in social interactions with stigmatized others. *Journal of Personality and Social Psychology*, *80*, 253–267. doi:10.1037/0022-3514.80.2.253

Blascovich, J., Vanman, E., Mendes, W. B., & Dickerson, S. S. (2011). *Social psychophysiology for social and personality psychology*. Thousand Oaks, CA: Sage.

Bruner, J. S. (1990). *Acts of meaning*. Cambridge, MA: Harvard University Press.

Cacioppo, J. T., Tassinary, L. G., & Berntson, G. G. (2007). Psychophysiological science: Interdisciplinary approaches to classic questions about the mind. In J. T. Cacioppo, L. G. Tassinary, & G. G. Berntson (Eds.), *Handbook of psychophysiology* (3rd ed., pp. 1–16). New York, NY: Cambridge University Press. doi:10.1017/CBO9780511546396.001

Cooper, J., Zanna, M. P., & Taves, P. A. (1978). Arousal as a necessary condition for attitude change following induced compliance. *Journal of Personality and Social Psychology, 36*, 1101–1106. doi:10.1037/0022-3514.36.10.1101

Croyle, R. T., & Cooper, J. (1983). Dissonance arousal: Physiological evidence. *Journal of Personality and Social Psychology, 45*, 782–791. doi:10.1037/0022-3514.45.4.782

Dickerson, S. S., & Kemeny, M. E. (2004). Acute stressors and cortisol responses: A theoretical integration and synthesis of laboratory research. *Psychological Bulletin, 130*, 355–391. doi:10.1037/0033-2909.130.3.355

Eliezer, D., Townsend, S. S. M., Sawyer, P. J., Major, B., & Mendes, W. B. (2011). System-justifying beliefs moderate the relationship between perceived discrimination and resting blood pressure. *Social Cognition, 29*, 303–321. doi:10.1521/soco.2011.29.3.303

Elkin, R. A., & Leippe, M. R. (1986). Physiological arousal, dissonance, and attitude change: Evidence for a dissonance-arousal link and a "don't remind me" effect. *Journal of Personality and Social Psychology, 51*, 55–65. doi:10.1037/0022-3514.51.1.55

Elliot, A. J., & Devine, P. G. (1994). On the motivational nature of cognitive dissonance: Dissonance as psychological discomfort. *Journal of Personality and Social Psychology, 67*, 382–394. doi:10.1037/0022-3514.67.3.382

Festinger, L. (1957). *A theory of cognitive dissonance*. Palo Alto, CA: Stanford University Press.

Fiske, A. P., Kitayama, S., Markus, H. R., & Nisbett, R. E. (1998). The cultural matrix of social psychology. In D. T. Gilbert, S. T. Fiske, & G. Lindzey (Eds.), *The handbook of social psychology* (4th ed., pp. 915–981). New York, NY: McGraw-Hill.

Galinsky, A. D., Stone, J., & Cooper, J. (2000). The reinstatement of dissonance and psychological discomfort following failed affirmations. *European Journal of Social Psychology, 30*, 123–147. doi:10.1002/(SICI)1099-0992(200001/02)30:1<123::AID-EJSP981>3.0.CO;2-T

Gerard, H. B. (1967). Choice difficulty, dissonance, and the decisions sequence. *Journal of Personality, 35*, 91–108. doi:10.1111/j.1467-6494.1967.tb01417.x

Greco, V., & Roger, D. (2003). Uncertainty, stress, and health. *Personality and Individual Differences, 34*, 1057–1068. doi:10.1016/S0191-8869(02)00091-0

Gunther Moor, B., Crone, E. A., & van der Molen, M. W. (2010). The heartbrake of social rejection: Heart rate deceleration in response to unexpected peer rejection. *Psychological Science, 21*, 1326–1333. doi:10.1177/0956797610379236

Heine, S. J., Proulx, T., & Vohs, K. D. (2006). The meaning maintenance model: On the coherence of social motivations. *Personality and Social Psychology Review, 10*, 88–110. doi:10.1207/s15327957pspr1002_1

Hogg, M. A. (2007). Uncertainty-identity theory. In M. P. Zanna (Ed.), *Advances in experimental social psychology* (Vol. 39, pp. 69–126). San Diego, CA: Academic Press.

Jennings, J. R., Averill, J., Opton, E., & Lazarus, R. S. (1970). Some parameters of heart rate change: Perceptual versus motor task requirements, noxiousness, and uncertainty. *Psychophysiology, 7*, 194–212. doi:10.1111/j.1469-8986.1970.tb02226.x

Jost, J. T., & Banaji, M. R. (1994). The role of stereotyping in system-justification and the production of false consciousness. *British Journal of Social Psychology, 33*, 1–27. doi:10.1111/j.2044-8309.1994.tb01008.x

Kay, A. C., Moscovitch, D. M., & Laurin, K. (2010). Randomness, attributions of arousal, and belief in God. *Psychological Science, 21*, 216–218. doi:10.1177/0956797609357750

Lazarus. R. S. (1966). *Psychological stress and the coping process*. New York, NY: McGraw-Hill.

Lee, S. W. S., & Schwarz, N. (2010, May 7). Washing away postdecisional dissonance. *Science, 328*, 709. doi:10.1126/science.1186799

Le Poire, B. A., & Burgoon, J. K. (1996). Usefulness of differentiating arousal responses within communication theories: Orienting response of defensive arousal within theories of expectancy violation. *Communication Monographs, 63*, 208–230.

Lerner, M. J. (1980). *The belief in a just world: A fundamental delusion*. New York, NY: Plenum Press.

Losch, M. E., & Cacioppo, J. T. (1990). Cognitive dissonance may enhance sympathetic tonus, but attitudes are changed to reduce negative affect rather than arousal. *Journal of Experimental Social Psychology, 26*, 289–304. doi:10.1016/0022-1031(90)90040-S

Major, B., Kaiser, C. R., O'Brien, L., & McCoy, S. K. (2007). Perceived discrimination as worldview threat or worldview confirmation: Implications for self-esteem. *Journal of Personality and Social Psychology, 92*, 1068–1086. doi:10.1037/0022-3514.92.6.1068

Markus, H. (1977). Self-schemata and processing information about the self. *Journal of Personality and Social Psychology, 35*, 63–78. doi:10.1037/0022-3514.35.2.63

Matheson, K., & Cole, B. (2004). Coping with a threatened group identity: Psychological and neuroendocrine responses. *Journal of Experimental Social Psychology, 40*, 777–786.

McGregor, I., & Little, B. R. (1998). Personal projects, happiness, and meaning: On doing well and being yourself. *Journal of Personality and Social Psychology*, *74*, 494–512. doi:10.1037/0022-3514.74.2.494

Mendes, W. B., Blascovich, J., Hunter, S., Lickel, B., & Jost, J. T. (2007). Threatened by the unexpected: Physiological responses during social interactions with expectancy-violating partners. *Journal of Personality and Social Psychology*, *92*, 698–716. doi:10.1037/0022-3514.92.4.698

Mendes, W. B., Blascovich, J., Lickel, B., & Hunter, S. (2002). Challenge and threat during interactions with White and Black men. *Personality and Social Psychology Bulletin*, *28*, 939–952.

Monat, A., Averill, J., & Lazarus, R. (1972). Anticipatory stress and coping reactions under various conditions of uncertainty. *Journal of Personality and Social Psychology*, *24*, 237–253. doi:10.1037/h0033297

O'Brien, L., & Major, B. (2005). System justifying beliefs and psychological well-being: The role of group status and identity. *Personality and Social Psychology Bulletin*, *31*, 1718–1729. doi:10.1177/0146167205278261

Plaks, J. E., Grant, H., & Dweck, C. S. (2005). Violations of implicit theories and the sense of prediction and control: Implications for motivated personal perception. *Journal of Personality and Social Psychology*, *88*, 245–262. doi:10.1037/0022-3514.88.2.245

Proulx, T., & Heine, S. J. (2008). The case of the transmogrifying experimenter: Affirmation of a moral schema following implicit change detection. *Psychological Science*, *19*, 1294–1300. doi:10.1111/j.1467-9280.2008.02238.x

Proulx, T., & Heine, S. J. (2010). The frog in Kierkegaard's beer: Finding meaning in the threat-compensation literature. *Social and Personality Psychology Compass*, *4*, 889–905.

Proulx, T., Heine, S. J., & Vohs, K. D. (2010). When is the unfamiliar the uncanny? Meaning affirmation after exposure to absurdist literature, humor, and art. *Personality and Social Psychology Bulletin*, *36*, 817–829. doi:10.1177/0146167210369896

Proulx, T., & Major, B. (2011) *A raw deal: Meaning affirmation in the face of trivial anomalies*. Manuscript in preparation.

Richards, J. E., & Casey, B. J. (1991). Heart rate variability during attention phases in young infants. *Psychophysiology*, *28*, 43–53.

Robinson, J. L., & Demaree, H. A. (2007). Physiological and cognitive effects of expressive dissonance. *Brain and Cognition*, *63*, 70–78. doi:10.1016/j.bandc.2006.08.003

Sapolsky, R. M. (2004). Social status and health in humans and other animals. *Annual Review of Anthropology*, *33*, 393–418. doi:10.1146/annurev.anthro.33.070203.144000

Sherman, D. K., & Cohen, G. L. (2006). The psychology of self-defense: Self-affirmation theory. In M. P. Zanna (Ed.), *Advances in experimental social psychology* (Vol. 38, pp. 183–242). San Diego, CA: Academic Press.

Swann, W. B., Jr. (2012). Self-verification theory. In P. Van Lang, A. Kruglanski, & E. T. Higgins (Eds.), *Handbook of theories of social psychology* (Vol. 2, pp. 23–42). London, England: Sage.

Swann, W. B., Jr., Rentfrow, P. J., & Guinn, J. (2002). Self-verification: The search for coherence. In M. Leary & J. Tagney (Eds.), *Handbook of self and identity* (pp. 367–383). New York, NY: Guilford Press.

Townsend, S. S. M., Major, B., Sawyer, P. J., & Mendes, W. B. (2010). Can the absence of prejudice be more threatening than its presence? It depends on one's worldview. *Journal of Personality and Social Psychology, 99*, 933–947. doi:10.1037/a0020434

Van den Bos, K. (2009). Making sense of life: The existential self trying to deal with personal uncertainty. *Psychological Inquiry, 20*, 197–217. doi:10.1080/10478400903333411

Vorauer, J. D. (2006). An information search model of evaluative concerns in intergroup interaction. *Psychological Review, 113*, 862–886. doi:10.1037/0033-295X.113.4.862

Zanna, M. P., & Cooper, J. (1974). Dissonance and the pill: An attribution approach to studying the arousal properties of dissonance. *Journal of Personality and Social Psychology, 29*, 703–709. doi:10.1037/h0036651

20

NEURAL AND MOTIVATIONAL MECHANICS OF MEANING AND THREAT

ALEXA M. TULLETT, MIKE S. PRENTICE, RIMMA TEPER, KYLE A. NASH, MICHAEL INZLICHT, AND IAN McGREGOR

Every action that we take is grounded in an elaborate web of beliefs and goals. Take the simple act of opening a door. Such an act depends on our beliefs about what lies beyond the door, as well as what is available to us in our current location. At an even more basic level, our attempt to open the door is rooted in a belief that we understand how a door works and are capable of using it. Furthermore, without the goal of pursuing something beyond the door, the act of opening the door would probably not take place. Of course, we are usually unaware of the precursors of our actions as we make them; we do not contemplate our presuppositions about the operation of doors or the contents of what lie beyond them before we open them. Nevertheless, when these presuppositions are challenged, their existence and importance come quickly into relief. Imagine that you open a door expecting a women's bathroom and you run into a man on his way out. In this case, your observation has come into conflict with your belief, and you are forced to pause and reconsider your course of action; the incoherence between your beliefs, goals, and observations has

DOI: 10.1037/14040-020
The Psychology of Meaning, Keith D. Markman, Travis Proulx, and Matthew J. Lindberg (Editors)

rendered you unable to act effectively until the discrepancy is resolved. The coherence that has been disrupted—what we refer to as *meaning*—is the basis for our effective interaction with the world.

The meaning of *meaning*, in both everyday parlance and scientific discourse, has been a perennial topic of discussion. Whereas the word is often equated with the value or significance of life events, Dilthey (1910/2002) proposed that meaning arises when we consider the connectedness between life events; "the individual moment has meaning through its connection with the whole, through the relation of past and future, of individual existence and humanity" (p. 253). Along these lines, meaning has been defined as "mental representations of relationships between committed propositions" (Proulx & Heine, 2010, p. 892) and as "consonance among the temporally extended and contextually distributed elements of the self" (McGregor & Little, 1998, p. 496). This basic human need for "systems of relations" (Camus, 1955, p. 10) is widely recognized, but what is its function?

The answer, we propose, is that meaning is required for action. As such, we define meaning as coherence between beliefs, salient goals, and perceptions of the environment that provides a foundation for our interactions with the world. Without this coherence, our actions would be ineffective, random, and disconnected from our surroundings. We further propose that meaning is not strictly a cognitive or perceptual phenomenon; there can be an identifiable affective experience as well. We can speak of a "feeling of meaning," much as we can speak of a feeling of satiety. In general, we pay more attention to our state of satiety when we are hungry. Similarly, we do not always notice a feeling of meaning, but we usually recognize when it has been disrupted, and we feel good when it is restored. This conceptualization of meaning draws heavily on the insights of others (e.g., Festinger, 1957) who have observed that disrupting the balance between these elements gives rise to feelings of distress and anxiety—a sense that "something isn't right"—followed by attempts to restore coherence (see Chapters 5 and 19, this volume).

Conflict among beliefs and actions is now widely recognized in social psychology as an important force guiding human behavior, in large part because of the influential work of Leon Festinger. Festinger (1957) was one of the first to investigate the mental state, termed *cognitive dissonance*, that we experience when our cognitions are not aligned with their actions. Consistent with the way we have talked about meaning threats as anxiety-producing events, cognitive dissonance is characterized by negative emotional arousal (Cooper, Zanna, & Taves, 1978; Elliot & Devine, 1994). This sense of dissonance, or imbalance, also arises when our attitudes do not accord with those of the people around us (Heider, 1958). For example, if a good friend scoffs at our favorite book, we question our beliefs (in either our friend or the book) in order to restore a sense of consistency. These ideas have received more recent treatment in various theoretical models that hold that we have an implicit drive to maintain meaning (Heine, Proulx, & Vohs, 2006; Peterson, 1999), certainty (McGregor, 2006b; Van den Bos, 2009), self-image (Steele, 1988), control (Kay, Gaucher, Napier, Callan, & Laurin, 2008), or symbolic immortality (Greenberg, Pyszczynski, & Solomon, 1986; see also Chapter 3, this volume). The common thread running through these fluid compensation models is that we have a desire to maintain order and consistency in our lives and that threats to this order are often met with reactive efforts to restore it (Proulx & Heine, 2010; Steele, 1988; see also Chapter 4, this volume). Although the lexicons used to describe these models vary, convincing evidence suggests that they describe the same fundamental process (e.g., McGregor, Zanna, Holmes, & Spencer, 2001; Proulx & Heine, 2010; Van den Bos, 2009). Consistent with this line of reasoning, there appear to be common brain mechanisms involved in the recognition of and response to conflict in these varied domains.

MEANING IN THE BRAIN

The various fluid compensation models of meaning share two features: (a) some kind of threat to meaning and (b) some process of ameliorating the threat. In this section, we focus on two corresponding processes in the brain: (a) the anterior cingulate cortex (ACC) becomes active when our meaning frameworks have been disrupted, and (b) approach motivational systems help to resolve incoherence and relieve distress (see Figure 20.1).

The Anterior Cingulate Cortex

The ACC, considered part of the brain's limbic system, has been implicated in a wide variety of cognitive and affective processes, including attentional control, emotion regulation, motivation, and error detection (see Bush, Luu, & Posner, 2000, for a review). Activity in the ACC is commonly assessed by observing event-related potentials (ERPs), distinctive patterns of electrical activity at the scalp. The ACC gives rise to two ERPs: the error-related negativity (ERN), which occurs when people make mistakes (Dehaene, Posner, & Tucker, 1994; Falkenstein, Hohnsbein, Hoorman, & Blanke, 1990; Gehring, Goss, Coles, Meyer, & Donchin, 1993), and the feedback-related negativity (FRN), which occurs when people are given negative or uncertain feedback about their response (Hirsh & Inzlicht, 2008; Miltner, Braun, & Coles, 1997). Here, we focus on the ACC as an important brain region for detecting threats to meaning, because of its role in identifying occasions when our actions have unexpected consequences.

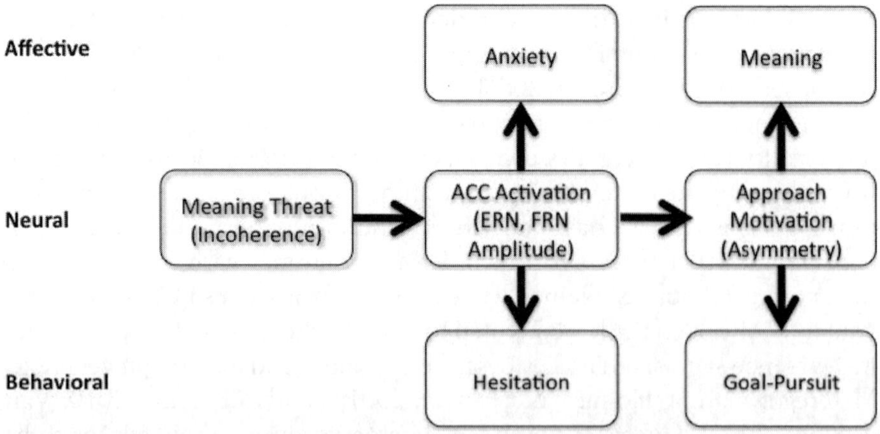

Figure 20.1. When we experience meaning threats to coherence we are warned about these inconsistencies by the ACC, which causes us to feel anxiety and to inhibit our actions (to hesitate). The prefrontal cortex then kicks in to help resolve the inconsistency (directly or indirectly) and to inhibit processing of dissonant information via goal shielding. As a result, we feel a restored sense of meaning and resume goal-pursuit. Meaning acts as the "go" signal for action. ACC = anterior cingulate cortex; ERN = error-related negativity; FRN = feedback-related negativity.

Traditional accounts of ACC function describe the brain region as a conflict monitor (Botvinick, Braver, Barch, Carter, & Cohen, 2001; Carter et al., 1998). According to this model, the ACC plays an important role in identifying when there is competition between multiple possible actions and thereby signaling the need for cognitive control. In other words, the ACC is responsible for indicating when we are unsure about what action to take. Evidence for this model comes from numerous studies demonstrating that the ACC becomes more active when people have to override prepotent response tendencies (Casey et al., 1997; Pardo, Pardo, Janer, & Raichle, 1990), when they have to choose between two equally desirable responses (Frith, Friston, Liddle, & Frackowiak, 1991; Petersen, Fox, Posner, Mintun, & Raichle, 1988), and when they make mistakes (Falkenstein et al., 1990; Gehring et al., 1993). Once the ACC has detected conflict, it recruits cognitive control resources that serve to prioritize one main goal and suppress distractors (e.g., focusing on the central symbol and ignoring peripheral symbols in the flanker task). Thus, the ACC notifies us when conflict occurs, so that coherence can be restored and we can continue to act effectively.

Emerging evidence, however, is beginning to show that the ACC is active in situations that go beyond response conflict and errors and may be more broadly viewed as an indicator that our actions are not having the effects that we expect. Gentsch, Ullsperger, and Ullsperger (2009) demonstrated that both self-generated errors and externally generated errors (resulting from a supposed "technical malfunction") increased ACC activity. This suggests that the ACC is not simply indicating when an error has occurred but is indicating when an outcome is unexpected. Additional compelling evidence that the ACC responds to expectancy violation rather than errors comes from research showing that the FRN can be elicited by positive feedback when the person is expecting negative feedback and vice versa (Oliveira, McDonald, & Goodman, 2007). These important lines of research highlight the role of the ACC in processing meaning threats: The ACC is active when our understanding of our relationship with the outside world is called into question, when our actions are not having the expected effects.

If ACC activity is involved in the detection of unanticipated action consequences, it should be linked with anxiety, a common affective response to expectancy violations (Barlow, 1988; Plaks & Stecher, 2007). Indeed, there is increasing evidence that the ERN is strongly associated with affect, particularly distress and anxiety (Bush et al., 2000). For example, the more we are bothered by failures on a task, the larger the ERN to those errors (Hajcak, Moser, Yeung, & Simons, 2005). Even when we have not made a mistake, if our response results in our losing money, we exhibit ACC activity (Gehring & Willoughby, 2002). ACC activity has been associated with a stronger skin conductance response (Hajcak, McDonald, & Simons, 2003) and a more pronounced defensive startle response (Hajcak & Foti, 2008), and ACC damage causes flat affect and a lack of distress (Corkin, Twitchell, & Sullivan, 1979; Critchley et al., 2003). For these reasons, the ERN has been labeled as a neural "distress signal" (Bartholow et al., 2005, p. 41).

In sum, converging evidence is beginning to highlight the ACC as a brain region that helps us monitor the consistency among our beliefs, observations, and goals. By detecting instances when there is incoherence, the ACC gives rise to distress, an emotion we are motivated to ameliorate. The ACC provides a signal—much like the feeling of hunger—that something is wrong, along with an unpleasant affective experience, and thus motivates us to make things "right."

Approach Motivational Systems

Once a meaning threat has been identified, our brain takes action to resolve the inconsistency. Here, we suggest, approach motivation plays a key role. In general, motivations can be classified into one of two categories: approach or avoidance. We want either to approach a desired goal or to avoid an undesirable outcome. Approach motivation involves goal pursuit, behavioral activation, and sensitivity to reward, whereas avoidance motivation is characterized by withdrawal, behavioral inhibition, and sensitivity to punishment (Amodio, Shah, Sigelman, Brazy, & Harmon-Jones, 2004; Coan & Allen, 2003; Davidson, Ekman, Saron, Senulis, & Friesen, 1990; Elliot, 1997; S. L. Gable, 2006; Gray & McNaughton, 2000; E. Harmon-Jones & Allen 1997; Higgins, Roney, Crowe, & Hymes, 1994; Wacker, Chavanon, Leue, & Stemmler, 2008). Moreover, these basic motivational directions are reflected in patterns of asymmetrical frontal cortical activation—left-frontal activity with approach and right-frontal activity with avoidance (Davidson, 1995; E. Harmon-Jones, 2004).

Two related models speak to the role of approach motivation in reactions to threat: the action-based model of dissonance (e.g., E. Harmon-Jones & Harmon-Jones, 2008) and reactive approach motivation (e.g., McGregor, Nash, Mann, & Phills, 2010). According to the action-based model, dissonance reduction serves to facilitate effective action (E. Harmon-Jones & Harmon-Jones, 2008). Thus, approach motivational states, which are associated with behavioral activation and action, should encourage threat reduction. Evidence stemming from this model demonstrates that putting people in an approach-motivated state facilitates greater efforts to change their beliefs to fit their behavior, thereby restoring consistency (C. Harmon-Jones, Schmeichel, Inzlicht, & Harmon-Jones, 2011; E. Harmon-Jones & Harmon-Jones, 2002; E. Harmon-Jones, Harmon-Jones, Fearn, Sigelman, & Johnson, 2008). For instance, in one study participants were put in an approach-motivated state by having them describe a project they wanted to complete and the steps they would take to complete it (E. Harmon-Jones et al., 2008). Participants in this condition, compared to control conditions, were more likely to say that an experiment in which they had previously chosen to participate was better than other alternatives that they had turned down. In other words, participants in an approach-motivated state were more likely to try to fit their beliefs (i.e., their attitude about the experiment) with their behaviors (i.e., their choice to do that experiment over the other options).

In the precursor to their reactive approach motivation model, McGregor et al. (2001) proposed that we react to meaning threats by turning to alternative goals or beliefs, a process termed *compensatory conviction*. Such compensatory responses appear to accompany a basic shift to approach motivation. For instance, threatening people with uncertainty was found to cause increases in implicit, explicit, and neural indices of approach motivation (McGregor, Nash, et al., 2010; McGregor, Nash, & Prentice, 2010). In this model, then, approach motivation helps people focus on and pursue new goals.

Common to the two models is a focus on approach motivation as a key component in anxiety-, threat-, and dissonance-reduction processes. Approach motivation serves to narrow our attentional focus, reducing the effect of distracting or conflicting information (P. A. Gable & Harmon-Jones, 2008, 2010). Recent research has demonstrated that brain measures reflecting dispositional or trait levels of approach motivation are associated with reduced ERN amplitude, corroborating the idea that when we are in approach motivational states, our responsiveness to inconsistent information and uncertainty is reduced (Nash, McGregor, & Inzlicht, 2010). Furthermore, trait approach motivation is associated with higher levels of well-being (Urry et al., 2004). Thus, approach motivation serves to reduce paralyzing feelings of uncertainty and anxiety by restoring effective action.

EVIDENCE FOR THE FUNCTION OF MEANING

So far, we have defined meaning as consonance among salient beliefs, goals, and perceptions of the environment and have reviewed ACC and approach motivation links to meaning-related processes. In this section, we provide support for the notion that such consonance is essential for effective action by summarizing evidence from the social psychology and social cognitive neuroscience literature. In particular, we outline research in support of three basic propositions that guide our theorizing: (a) coherence is generally related to effective goal pursuit, (b) threats to coherence are anxiogenic and interfere with goal-directed action, and (c) threats to coherence prompt ameliorative responses that allow for the resumption of effective activity toward goals (recall Chapter 1).

Coherence, Meaning, and Action

McGregor and Little (1998) drew on Dilthey's (1910/2002) theorizing that people will feel meaningful to the extent that there is coherence among self-elements (e.g., competencies, guiding values, defining memories) across time and context. In two studies, McGregor and Little demonstrated that self-reported meaning was positively associated with the extent to which people rated their personal projects (Little, 1983) as being important, being something to which they were committed, and reflecting their guiding values and own identity. McGregor and Little interpreted these personal project dimensions as reflecting the coherence of self-elements. Thus, to the extent that people's personal projects were consistent within the self-system, meaning was experienced.

In a similar line of research, Sheldon and Kasser (1995) assessed participants' personal strivings (Emmons, 1986) and asked them to rate the extent to which they perceived their strivings as helping them move toward six culturally valued possible futures (e.g., intimacy and friendship, attractive physical appearance). In their first study, Sheldon and Kasser found that vertical coherence, or the extent to which participants' goals were linked to bringing about desirable possible futures, was the sole significant predictor of vitality, a feeling of being globally alive and energized (Ryan & Frederick, 1997). In Study 2, vertical coherence of "intrinsic" possible futures (i.e., inherently satisfying futures) was positively related to engaging in "meaningful" (e.g., discussing one's life with another) versus "distracting" (e.g., watching television) daily activities. So, to the extent that people viewed their goals as helping them maintain a coherent link between current and desired states, they felt vital and engaged in purposive daily activities.

Some recent research suggests that consonance might be amenable to change in the laboratory. Recently, Kray et al. (2010; see also Chapter 16, this volume) demonstrated that counterfactual thinking about key life events increased the meaning in life derived from those events. They also found that the link between counterfactual thinking and meaning was mediated by perceptions of fate. In terms of the current theorizing, these results could be taken to suggest that counterfactual thinking increases coherence across time and context, creating a "meant-to-be-ness" in the self and its fit in the temporally distributed environment. This leads to increased feelings of meaning (see Chapter 17).

The research reviewed so far mostly speaks to the link between coherence and experienced meaning, but what does this integrity mean for behavior? Following Carver and Scheier's (1998) control theory of motivation, Sheldon (2004) proposed that actions are most likely to succeed when they concord with abstract goals (e.g., when the more concrete goal of "drive to work" functionally aligns with the more abstract goal of "be good at one's job"). In a test of this notion, Sheldon and Elliot (1999) examined goal attainment as a function of coherence, which they termed self-concordance, or the extent to which the goals participants were pursuing reflected enduring values and interests. They found that goal self-concordance was positively related to sustained effort toward the goal, which in turn predicted goal attainment. Self-concordance also seems to empower people to overcome obstacles when life gets difficult. Lydon and Zanna (1990) found persistence in the face of adversity only on goals that cohered with participants' most important personal values. In sum, these results support the claim that coherence provides a basis for effective action, as it sustains motivational energy to approach goals, which in turn leads to successfully attaining those goals.

Meaning Threats and Distress

Imagine that you are at home in your living room and have been reading most of the night on the couch. You now want to prepare to go to bed but have not been in your bedroom since you got home from work. You place your book on the end table and get up and open the bedroom door. Upon opening the door, you see that your room has been completely rearranged—your dresser is where your bed used to be, and your night table is upside down. Before you initiate behavioral or attributional efforts to lend coherence to the scene (e.g., verifying no one else is in the room, thinking about whether anyone might want to play a prank on you), what initial flicker of emotion might you be feeling?

If you imagined (or actually experienced) a pang of anxiety, then your response is in line with what numerous models of threats to meaning would predict. When people come across a situation that challenges beliefs about themselves, the environment, or their relation to the environment (Heine et al., 2006), particularly in ways that interfere with salient goals (Nash, McGregor, & Prentice, 2011), they become anxiously preoccupied with the meaning threat, at least until the deficit to meaning can be managed directly or ignored by engagement in a domain that is not as perilous.

Similarly, when goals are fraught with personal conflict, people tend to remain anxiously preoccupied with them until an avenue for meaning can found. Participants who completed an exercise that led them to ruminate about an uncertain dilemma in their lives remained highly preoccupied and anxiously aroused with the dilemma after completing other research materials. However, participants who were allowed to write about how they had acted consistently with a self-selected value and intended to continue to do so in the future were no more preoccupied or anxious than participants who had not been led to ruminate on their dilemma (McGregor et al., 2001). Writing about meaningful convictions, successes, and group identifications similarly eliminated anxious preoccupation with personal goal conflicts (McGregor, 2006b; McGregor & Marigold, 2003; McGregor, Niall, Marigold, & Kang, 2005).

Moreover, some support has recently been generated for the notion that disruptions to meaning are most poignant when they interfere with salient goals. Participants report feeling particularly anxious and uncertain when goals are first implicitly primed and then threatened, compared with when the same goal threats are faced without the relevant goal primes (Nash et al., 2011). Although there is some evidence to suggest that threats that are unrelated to goals can also cause compensatory reactions (e.g., Proulx & Heine, 2008), it appears that threats that specifically impair goal pursuit may be the most unsettling. This supports our contention that meaning is required for effective action. How, then, do people manage these feelings and return to effectively pursuing goals?

Responding to Threats to Resume Pursuit

People bother to deal with meaning threats because threats feel unpleasant and generate emotions like uncertainty and anxiety. We hold that to get rid of these negative feelings, people reengage approach motivation, a positively valenced state well suited to quell aversive emotions and allow for confident goal pursuit. We have begun to generate empirical support for the notion that when people respond to threats, they often enter an approach-motivated state that facilitates goal pursuit. Such reactions not only provide relief from an experiential standpoint but also facilitate goals.

In one study, participants high in self-esteem, who had been previously shown to be particularly reactive under threat (see McGregor, 2006a), exhibited greater approach-motivation-related brain activation (relative left frontal F7/F8 EEG activity) after a threat. Further, in a series of studies, McGregor, Nash, et al. (2010) provided evidence that people responded to threats by activating approach motivation, as measured by a line bisection task (Study 1), an approach-motivation implicit association test (Study 2), and approach motivation for personal projects (Study 3). These studies converge on the idea that people cling to their meaningful ideals and worldviews because doing so promotes approach motivation and relieves anxiety.

Other research converges on the notion that restoring coherence allows for effective action. For example, people who are dispositionally high in approach motivation appear to reduce cognitive dissonance more efficiently than those low in dispositional approach do (C. Harmon-Jones et al., 2011). These results further suggest that approach-motivated states might facilitate restoring coherence and running with one's decisions to achieve focal goals (cf. E. Harmon-Jones & Harmon-Jones, 2008; E. Harmon-Jones et al., 2008).

So far, we have seen that meaning can help people move effectively toward desired end states, that disrupting meaning can cause distress, and that people seek to manage threat-induced distress by throwing themselves into single-minded goal pursuit or idealism. One particularly interesting avenue of applying the theoretical perspective developed so far is provided by religion. Following James's (1902/1958) dictum that religion helps to make "the sand and grit of self-hood disappear" (p. 240), our laboratories have explored whether religion might provide an effective framework for obtaining and maintaining meaning. Next, we explore evidence that religion serves an anxiolytic function as a calming beacon of consonance.

RELIGION AND MEANING FRAMEWORKS

Religious systems are well suited to prescribe meaning. Most religious systems help believers to make sense of the world in the context of one's goals. And if one is uncertain what those goals should be, the religious system can be petitioned for guidance. Further, research has begun to uncover the apparent anxiolytic function that religion provides. Religious people live longer and healthier lives (Powell, Shahabi, & Thoresen, 2003; Seybold &

Hill, 2001), but what can psychological science tell us about these trends? We contend that it is through religion's meaning-providing function that its adherents benefit on a day-to-day and even moment-to-moment basis.

One key function of religion is its ordering of the perceptual world in ostensibly predictable ways. For example, invoking "God's will" as an explanation for an unexpected occurrence can reduce anxiety (Park, 2005; see also Chapter 13, this volume). Might religiosity lead to a sanguine state wherein everything appears to be right and good? And if so, how might we examine such a research question? As noted previously, the ACC acts as the brain's alarm system in response to uncertainty and conflict. Might it be, then, that religiosity increases the threshold for what the brain deems a conflicted state of affairs? This seems to be the case. In two studies, Inzlicht, McGregor, Hirsh, and Nash (2009) demonstrated that religion (as assessed by two measures) was negatively related to error-related negativity in the ACC. Extending this research in an experimental paradigm, Inzlicht and Tullett (2010) demonstrated that priming religion for believers decreased ERN amplitude. Together, these studies suggest that religious belief is generally negatively related to anxiogenic neurological processes and that engaging religious belief can situationally alter these processes (for believers).

This suggests that after meaning threats, religious ideals may help shelter people from anxiety. Indeed, McGregor, Nash, and Prentice (2010) demonstrated that, under threat, people navigated anxious uncertainty by increasing their endorsement of religiously zealous statements, such as "I would support a war that defended my religious beliefs." These results were specific to religious belief and not mere superstition (Study 1), and it was only participants who were dispositionally approach motivated who reacted to the threats with compensatory religious idealism (Study 2). Further, participants who already had avenues for channeling their approach motivation in their daily lives (i.e., being committed to their personal goals) did not respond in a religiously zealous manner (Study 3). Together, these findings suggest that people use religion to maintain meaning when it is challenged and are buffered against threats if they are already vigorously approaching their daily goals.

How might this research help to understand phenomena outside the laboratory? In a study of bereaved parents, Murphy, Johnson, and Lohan (2003) found that religious coping in response to the death of a child was a fairly strong predictor of making sense out of the negative events. This sense making, in turn, predicted better long-term adjustment both physically and psychologically. Similarly, anthropological studies during the Israel–Lebanon war of 2006 (Sosis, 2007) indicate that women who lived in the north of Israel turned to religion, by citing biblical psalms, when they faced the uncertainty of missile attacks; when they did, this relieved their feelings of anxiety and uncertainty. The lab-based research cited above can help shed light on findings like these. Although the loss of a child and the possibility of rocket attack are certainly traumatic and not easily managed, invoking religious explanations and coping strategies may help to efficiently restore predictability to the world and provide explanations for why the events occurred. This restored coherence, in turn, would allow for more optimal engagement with self and world and produce the optimal coping observed in the long term. Alternatively, a more palliative mechanism may be that religious ideals may reliably provide a haven of single-minded, motivational insulation from distress arising from incoherences in the temporal world. It is conceivable that such palliative uses of religion may provide anxiolytic value in the short term but become maladaptive if chronic use blinds individuals to broader temporal-social considerations (e.g., religious extremism).

CONCLUSION

In this chapter, we have attempted to provide an account of how people process threats to meaning. The ACC, serving to detect violations of consonance, is one brain region involved in signaling a lack or loss of meaning. Its activity is experienced as a feeling of anxiety—an uncomfortable uncertainty about what to do next—that motivates us to restore coherence. The subsequent threat-reduction process is characterized by approach-motivated processes and corresponds to left-frontal cortical asymmetry as our attention narrows and we prepare to act. More broadly, meaning frameworks—concrete systems of explanation that reduce the ambient uncertainty in the world around us—can help to buffer against the anxiety produced by meaning threats. These systems have been shown to be associated both with approach motivated processes and with the reduction of ACC activity and anxiety in the face of threat.

The ideas outlined here are a first step in providing a neural account of what happens when our beliefs, perceptions, and goals—the precursors of our actions—are out of sync and how our brain addresses these conflicts and repairs the foundation for our interactions with the world. Although work on the neurological consequences of meaning systems is still in its early stages, it should prove an interesting endeavor to discover which facets of these systems actually function to buffer from anxiety in the face of threat. Along these lines, recent research has hinted that one key component may be the assurance that we are actually capable of understanding the world around us and that we are not simply lost in a sea of randomness (Tullett, Inzlicht, & Kay, 2010). In addition, it will be important for future research to explore how other neural processes, for instance, the orienting response (Sokolov, 2002) or the P300 (Courchesne, Hillyard, & Galambos, 1975; Squires, Squires, & Hillyard, 1975), may be involved in identifying violations of coherence and perhaps also in recruiting approach motivational resources to bring about resolution. Such research would bring us closer to outlining a common mechanism—or perhaps a set of distinct mechanisms—that allows us to overcome the many sources of uncertainty in the world we live in.

REFERENCES

Amodio, D. M., Shah, J. Y., Sigelman, J., Brazy, P. C., & Harmon-Jones, E. (2004). Implicit regulatory focus associated with asymmetrical frontal cortical activity. *Journal of Experimental Social Psychology, 40*, 225–232. doi:10.1016/S0022-1031(03)00100-8

Barlow, D. H. (1988). *Anxiety and its disorders: The nature of treatment of anxiety and panic*. New York, NY: Guilford Press.

Bartholow, B. D., Pearson, M. A., Dickter, C. L., Fabiani, M., Gratton, G., & Sher, K. H. (2005). Strategic control and medial frontal negativity: Beyond errors and response conflict. *Psychophysiology, 42*, 33–42. doi:10.1111/j.1469-8986.2005.00258.x

Botvinick, M. M., Braver, T. S., Barch, D. M., Carter, C. S., & Cohen, J. D. (2001). Conflict monitoring and cognitive control. *Psychological Review, 108*, 624–652. doi:10.1037/0033-295X.108.3.624

Bush, G., Luu, P., & Posner, M. (2000). Cognitive and emotional influences in anterior cingulate cortex. *Trends in Cognitive Sciences, 4*, 215–222. doi:10.1016/S1364-6613(00)01483-2

Camus, A. (1955). *The myth of Sisyphus and other essays*. New York, NY: Vintage Books.

Carter, C. S., Braver, T. S., Barch, D. M., Botvinick, M. M., Noll, D., & Cohen, J. D. (1998, May 1). Anterior cingulate cortex, error detection, and the online monitoring of performance. *Science, 280*, 747–749. doi:10.1126/science.280.5364.747

Carver, C. S., & Scheier, M. F. (1998). *On the self-regulation of behavior*. New York, NY: Cambridge University Press.

Casey, B. J., Trainor, R. J., Orendi, J. L., Schubert, A. B., Nystrom, L. E., . . . Rapoport, J. L. (1997). A developmental functional MRI study of prefrontal activation during performance of a go-no-go task. *Journal of Cognitive Neuroscience, 9*, 835–847. doi:10.1162/jocn.1997.9.6.835

Coan, J. A., & Allen, J. J. B. (2003). Frontal EEG asymmetry and the behavioral activation and inhibition systems. *Psychophysiology, 40*, 106–114. doi:10.1111/1469-8986.00011

Cooper, J., Zanna, M. P., & Taves, P. A. (1978). Arousal as a necessary condition for attitude change following induced compliance. *Journal of Personality and Social Psychology, 36*, 1101–1106. doi:10.1037/0022-3514.36.10.1101

Corkin, S., Twitchell, T. E., & Sullivan, E. V. (1979). Safety and efficacy of cingulotomy for pain and psychiatric disorder. In H. R. Hitchcock, H. T. Ballantine, & B. A. Meyerson (Eds.), *Modern concepts in psychiatric surgery* (pp. 253–272). Amsterdam, Netherlands: Elsevier.

Courchesne, E., Hillyard, S. A., & Galambos, R. (1975). Stimulus novelty, task relevance, and the visual evoked potential in man. *Electroencephalography and Clinical Neurophysiology*, *39*, 131–143. doi:10.1016/0013-4694(75)90003-6

Critchley, H. D., Mathias, C. J., Josephs, O., O'Doherty, J., Zanini, S., Dewar, B.-K., . . . Dolan, R. J. (2003). Human cingulate cortex and autonomic control: Converging neuroimaging and clinical evidence. *Brain: A Journal of Neurology*, *126*, 2139–2152. doi:10.1093/brain/awg216

Davidson, R. J. (1995). Cerebral asymmetry, emotion, and affective style. In R. J. Davidson & K. Hugdahl (Eds.), *Brain asymmetry* (pp. 361–387). Cambridge: Massachusetts Institute of Technology.

Davidson, R. J., Ekman, P., Saron, C. D., Senulis, J. A., & Friesen, W. V. (1990). Approach–withdrawal and cerebral asymmetry: Emotional expression and brain physiology: I. *Journal of Personality and Social Psychology*, *58*, 330–341. doi:10.1037/0022-3514.58.2.330

Dehaene, S., Posner, M. I., & Tucker, D. M. (1994). Localization of a neural system for error detection and compensation. *Psychological Science*, *5*, 303–305. doi:10.1111/j.1467-9280.1994.tb00630.x

Dilthey, W. (2002). The categories of life. In R. A. Makreel & F. Rodi (Eds.), *The formation of the historical world in the human sciences* (pp. 248–265). Princeton, NJ: Princeton University Press. (Original work published 1910)

Elliot, A. J. (1997). Integrating the "classic" and "contemporary" approaches to achievement motivation: A hierarchical model of approach and avoidance achievement motivation. In M. Maehr & P. Pintrich (Eds.), *Advances in motivation and achievement* (pp. 243–279). Greenwich, CT: JAI Press.

Elliot, A. J., & Devine, P. G. (1994). On the motivational nature of cognitive dissonance: Dissonance as psychological discomfort. *Journal of Personality and Social Psychology*, *67*, 382–394. doi:10.1037/0022-3514.67.3.382

Emmons, R. A. (1986). Personal strivings: An approach to personality and subjective well-being. *Journal of Personality and Social Psychology*, *51*, 1058–1068. doi:10.1037/0022-3514.51.5.1058

Falkenstein, M., Hohnsbein, J., Hoorman, J., & Blanke, L. (1990). Effects of errors in choice reaction tasks on the ERP under focused and divided attention. In C. H. M. Brunia, A. W. K. Gallard, & A. Kok (Eds.), *Psychophysiological brain research* (pp. 192–195). Tilburg, Germany: Tilburg University Press.

Festinger, L. (1957). *A theory of cognitive dissonance*. Stanford, CA: Stanford University Press.

Frith, C. D., Friston, K. J., Liddle, P. F., & Frackowiak, R. S. J. (1991). A PET study of word-finding. *Neuropsychologia*, *29*, 1137–1148. doi:10.1016/0028-3932(91)90029-8

Gable, P. A., & Harmon-Jones, E. (2008). Approach-motivated positive affect reduces breadth of attention. *Psychological Science, 19*, 476–482. doi:10.1111/j.1467-9280.2008.02112.x

Gable, P. A., & Harmon-Jones, E. (2010). The motivational dimensional model of affect: Implications for breadth of attention, memory, and cognitive categorization. *Cognition & Emotion, 24*, 322–337. doi:10.1080/02699930903378305

Gable, S. L. (2006). Approach and avoidance social motives and goals. *Journal of Personality, 74*, 175–222. doi:10.1111/j.1467-6494.2005.00373.x

Gehring, W. J., Goss, B., Coles, M. G. H., Meyer, D. E., & Donchin, E. (1993). A neural system for error detection and compensation. *Psychological Science, 4*, 385–390. doi:10.1111/j.1467-9280.1993.tb00586.x

Gehring, W. J., & Willoughby, A. R. (2002, March 22). The medial frontal cortex and the rapid processing of monetary gains and losses. *Science, 295*, 2279–2282. doi:10.1126/science.1066893

Gentsch, A., Ullsperger, P., & Ullsperger, M. (2009). Dissociable medial frontal negativities form a common monitoring system for self- and externally caused failure of goal achievement. *NeuroImage, 47*, 2023–2030. doi:10.1016/j.neuroimage.2009.05.064

Gray, J. A., & McNaughton, N. (2000). *The neuropsychology of anxiety: An inquiry into the functions of the septo-hippocampal system*. New York, NY: Oxford University Press.

Greenberg, J., Pyszczynski, T., & Solomon, S. (1986). The causes and consequences of a need for self-esteem: A terror-management theory. In R. F. Baumeister (Ed.), *Public self and private self* (pp. 189–212). New York, NY: Springer-Verlag.

Hajcak, G., & Foti, D. (2008). Errors are aversive: Defensive motivation and the error-related negativity. *Psychological Science, 19*, 103–108. doi:10.1111/j.1467-9280.2008.02053.x

Hajcak, G., McDonald, N., & Simons, R. F. (2003). Anxiety and error-related brain activity. *Biological Psychology, 64*, 77–90. doi:10.1016/S0301-0511(03)00103-0

Hajcak, G., Moser, J. S., Yeung, N., & Simons, R. F. (2005). On the ERN and the significance of errors. *Psychophysiology, 42*, 151–160. doi:10.1111/j.1469-8986.2005.00270.x

Harmon-Jones, C., Schmeichel, B. J., Inzlicht, M., & Harmon-Jones, E. (2011). Trait approach motivation relates to dissonance reduction. *Social Psychological and Personality Science, 2*, 21–28. doi:10.1177/1948550610379425

Harmon-Jones, E. (2004). Contributions from research on anger and cognitive dissonance to understanding the motivational functions of asymmetrical frontal brain activity. *Biological Psychology, 67*, 51–76. doi:10.1016/j.biopsycho.2004.03.003

Harmon-Jones, E., & Allen, J. J. B. (1997). Behavioral activation sensitivity and resting frontal EEG asymmetry: Covariation of putative indicators related to risk for mood disorders. *Journal of Abnormal Psychology, 106*, 159–163. doi:10.1037/0021-843X.106.1.159

Harmon-Jones, E., & Harmon-Jones, C. (2002). Testing the action-based model of dissonance: The effect of action orientation on post-decisional attitudes. *Personality and Social Psychology Bulletin, 28*, 711–723. doi:10.1177/0146167202289001

Harmon-Jones, E., & Harmon-Jones, C. (2008). Action-based model of dissonance: A review of behavioral, anterior-cingulate, and prefrontal cortical mechanisms. *Social and Personality Psychology Compass, 2*, 1518–1538. doi:10.1111/j.1751-9004.2008.00110.x

Harmon-Jones, E., Harmon-Jones, C., Fearn, M., Sigelman, J. D., & Johnson, P. (2008). Left frontal cortical activation and spreading of alternatives: Tests of the action-based model of dissonance. *Journal of Personality and Social Psychology, 94*, 1–15. doi:10.1037/0022-3514.94.1.1

Heider, F. (1958). *The psychology of interpersonal relations*. Hoboken, NJ: Wiley. doi:10.1037/10628-000

Heine, S. J., Proulx, T., & Vohs, K. D. (2006). Meaning maintenance model: On the coherence of human motivations. *Personality and Social Psychology Review, 10*, 88–110. doi:10.1207/s15327957pspr1002_1

Higgins, E. T., Roney, C. J. R., Crowe, E., & Hymes, C. (1994). Ideal versus ought predilections for approach and avoidance: Distinct self-regulatory systems. *Journal of Personality and Social Psychology*, 66, 276–286. doi:10.1037/0022-3514.66.2.276

Hirsh, J. B., & Inzlicht, M. (2008). The devil you know: Neuroticism predicts neural response to uncertainty. *Psychological Science, 19*, 962–967. doi:10.1111/j.1467-9280.2008.02183.x

Inzlicht, M., McGregor, I., Hirsh, J. B., & Nash, K. (2009). Neural markers of religious conviction. *Psychological Science, 20*, 385–392. doi:10.1111/j.1467-9280.2009.02305.x

Inzlicht, M., & Tullett, A. M. (2010). Reflections on God: Religious affirmations can reduce neurophysiological response to errors. *Psychological Science, 21*, 1184–1190. doi:10.1177/0956797610375451

James, W. (1958). *The varieties of religious experience*. New York, NY: Mentor. (Original work published 1902)

Kay, A. C., Gaucher, D., Napier, J. L., Callan, M. J., & Laurin, K. (2008). God and the government: Testing a compensatory control mechanism for the support of external systems. *Journal of Personality and Social Psychology*, 95, 18–35. doi:10.1037/0022-3514.95.1.18

Kray, L. J., George, L., Liljenquist, K., Galinsky, A., Tetlock, P., & Roese, N. (2010). From what might have been to what must have been: Counterfactual thinking creates meaning. *Journal of Personality and Social Psychology*, 98, 106–118. doi:10.1037/a0017905

Little, B. R. (1983). Personal projects: A rationale and method for investigation. *Environment and Behavior, 15*, 273–309. doi:10.1177/0013916583153002

Lydon, J. E., & Zanna, M. P. (1990). Commitment in the face of adversity: A value-affirmation approach. *Journal of Personality and Social Psychology*, 58, 1040–1047. doi:10.1037/0022-3514.58.6.1040

McGregor, I. (2006a). Offensive defensiveness: Toward an integrative neuroscience of compensatory zeal after mortality salience, personal uncertainty, and other poignant self-threats. *Psychological Inquiry*, *17*, 299–308. doi:10.1080/10478400701366977

McGregor, I. (2006b). Zeal appeal: The allure of moral extremes. *Basic and Applied Social Psychology*, *28*, 343–348. doi:10.1207/s15324834basp2804_7

McGregor, I., & Little, B. R. (1998). Personal projects, happiness, and meaning: On doing well and being yourself. *Journal of Personality and Social Psychology*, *74*, 494–512. doi:10.1037/0022-3514.74.2.494

McGregor, I., & Marigold, D. C. (2003). Defensive zeal and the uncertain self: What makes you so sure? *Journal of Personality and Social Psychology*, *85*, 838–852. doi:10.1037/0022-3514.85.5.838

McGregor, I., Niall, P. R., Marigold, D. C., & Kang, S.-J. (2005). Defensive pride and consensus: Strength in imaginary numbers. *Journal of Personality and Social Psychology*, *89*, 978–996. doi:10.1037/0022-3514.89.6.978

McGregor, I., Nash, K., Mann, N., & Phills, C. (2010). Anxious uncertainty and reactive approach motivation (RAM). *Journal of Personality and Social Psychology*, *99*, 133–147. doi:10.1037/a0019701

McGregor, I., Nash, K., & Prentice, M. (2010). Reactive approach motivation (RAM) for religion. *Journal of Personality and Social Psychology*, *99*, 148–161. doi:10.1037/a0019702

McGregor, I., Zanna, M. P., Holmes, J. G., & Spencer, S. J. (2001). Compensatory conviction in the face of personal uncertainty: Going to extremes and being oneself. *Journal of Personality and Social Psychology*, *80*, 472–488. doi:10.1037/0022-3514.80.3.472

Miltner, W. H. R., Braun, C. H., & Coles, M. G. H. (1997). Event-related brain potentials following incorrect feedback in a time-estimation task: Evidence for a "generic" neural system for error-detection. *Journal of Cognitive Neuroscience*, *9*, 788–798. doi:10.1162/jocn.1997.9.6.788

Murphy, S. A., Johnson, L. C., & Lohan, J. (2003). Finding meaning in a child's violent death: A five-year prospective analysis of parents' personal narratives and empirical data. *Death Studies*, *27*, 381–404. doi:10.1080/07481180302879

Nash, K. A., McGregor, I., & Inzlicht, M. (2010). *Approach motivated neural activity predicts muted anterior cingulate cortex reactivity*. Unpublished manuscript, York University, Toronto, Ontario, Canada.

Nash, K. A., McGregor, I., & Prentice, M. (2011). *Threat and defense: Threats to implicitly primed goals cause aversive emotions and approach-motivated defenses*. Unpublished manuscript, York University, Toronto, Ontario, Canada.

Oliveira, F. T. P., McDonald, J. J., & Goodman, D. (2007). Performance monitoring in the anterior cingulate is not all error-related: Expectancy deviation and the representation of action–outcome associations. *Journal of Cognitive Neuroscience*, *19*, 1994–2004. doi:10.1162/jocn.2007.19.12.1994

Pardo, J. V., Pardo, P., Janer, K. W., & Raichle, M. E. (1990). The anterior cingulate cortex mediates processing selection in the Stroop attentional conflict paradigm. *Proceedings of the National Academy of Sciences, USA, 87*, 256–259. doi:10.1073/pnas.87.1.256

Park, C. L. (2005). Religion as a meaning-making framework in coping with life stress. *Journal of Social Issues, 61*, 707–729. doi:10.1111/j.1540-4560.2005.00428.x

Petersen, S. E., Fox, P. T., Posner, M. I., Mintun, M., & Raichle, M. E. (1988, February 18). Positron emission tomographic studies of the cortical anatomy of single-word processing. *Nature, 331*, 585–589. doi:10.1038/331585a0

Peterson, J. B. (1999). *Maps of meaning: The architecture of belief*. New York, NY: Routledge.

Plaks, J. E., & Stecher, K. (2007). Unexpected improvement, decline, and stasis: A prediction confidence perspective on achievement success and failure. *Journal of Personality and Social Psychology, 93*, 667–684. doi:10.1037/0022-3514.93.4.667

Powell, L. H., Shahabi, L., & Thoresen, C. E. (2003). Religion and spirituality: Linkages to physical health. *American Psychologist, 58*, 36–52. doi:10.1037/0003-066X.58.1.36

Proulx, T., & Heine, S. J. (2008). The case of the transmogrifying experimenter: Affirmation of a moral schema following implicit change detection. *Psychological Science, 19*, 1294–1300. doi:10.1111/j.1467-9280.2008.02238.x

Proulx, T., & Heine, S. J. (2010). The frog in Kierkegaard's beer: Finding meaning in the threat-compensation literature. *Social and Personality Psychology Compass, 4*, 889–905. doi:10.1111/j.1751-9004.2010.00304.x

Ryan, R. M., & Frederick, C. M. (1997). On energy, personality and health: Subjective vitality as a dynamic reflection of well-being. *Journal of Personality, 65*, 529–565. doi:10.1111/j.1467-6494.1997.tb00326.x

Seybold, K. S., & Hill, P. C. (2001). The role of religion and spirituality in mental and physical health. *Current Directions in Psychological Science, 10*, 21–24. doi:10.1111/1467-8721.00106

Sheldon, K. M. (2004). *Optimal human being: Towards integration within the person and between the human sciences*. Mahwah, NJ: Erlbaum.

Sheldon, K. M., & Elliot, A. J. (1999). Goal striving, need-satisfaction, and longitudinal well-being: The self-concordance model. *Journal of Personality and Social Psychology, 76*, 482–497. doi:10.1037/0022-3514.76.3.482

Sheldon, K. M., & Kasser, T. (1995). Coherence and congruence: Two aspects of personality integration. *Journal of Personality and Social Psychology, 68*, 531–543. doi:10.1037/0022-3514.68.3.531

Sokolov, E. N. (2002). *The orienting response in information processing*. Mahwah, NJ: Erlbaum.

Sosis, R. (2007). Psalms for safety: Magico-religious responses to threats of terror. *Current Anthropology, 48*, 903–911. doi:10.1086/523015

Squires, N. K., Squires, K. C., & Hillyard, S. A. (1975). Two varieties of long-latency positive waves evoked by unpredictable auditory stimuli in man. *Electro-encephalography and Clinical Neuropsychology, 38,* 387–401. doi:10.1016/0013-4694(75)90263-1

Steele, C. M. (1988). The psychology of self-affirmation: Sustaining the integrity of the self. In L. Berkowitz (Ed.), *Advances in experimental social psychology* (Vol. 21, pp. 261–302). San Diego, CA: Academic Press.

Tullett, A. M., Inzlicht, M., & Kay, A. C. (2010). *The comfort of predictability: Threats of randomness exacerbate anxious responding to errors.* Manuscript in preparation.

Urry, H. L., Nitschke, J. B., Dolski, I., Jackson, D. C., Dalton, K. M., Mueller, C. J., . . . Davidson, R. J. (2004). Making life worth living: Neural correlates of well-being. *Psychological Science, 15,* 367–372. doi:10.1111/j.0956-7976.2004.00686.x

Van den Bos, K. (2009). Making sense of life: The existential self trying to deal with personal uncertainty. *Psychological Inquiry, 20,* 197–217. doi:10.1080/10478400903333411

Wacker, J., Chavanon, M.-L., Leue, A., & Stemmler, G. (2008). Is running away right? The behavioral activation–behavioral inhibition model of anterior asymmetry. *Emotion, 8,* 232–249. doi:10.1037/1528-3542.8.2.232

21

STILL A THRILL: MEANING MAKING AND THE PLEASURES OF UNCERTAINTY

TIMOTHY D. WILSON, DIEYNABA G. NDIAYE, CHERYL HAHN, AND DANIEL T. GILBERT

Suppose that one day your boss ushers you into her office, saying that she has some good news. "Congratulations," she says. "Your promotion has come through, effective immediately!" How will you feel? As noted by appraisal theorists, your emotional reaction will depend on how you interpret the news: how important it is to you, how you explain why it happened, and the meaning you find in it (e.g., Frijda, 2007; Lazarus & Folkman, 1984; Ortony, Clore, & Collins, 1988; Scherer, 2001). If your job is the most important part of your life, and you know that you were the only one of 100 employees to be promoted, you will react quite differently than if you really couldn't care less about your job and you know that everyone in the company was promoted (not unlike the Society of Experimental Psychologists' recent elevation of all members to "Fellow" status).

Although years of research have illustrated the importance of the way in which we interpret emotional events (e.g., on appraisal theory and attribution theory), there has been less attention to the duration of those emotional

DOI: 10.1037/14040-021
The Psychology of Meaning, Keith D. Markman, Travis Proulx, and Matthew J. Lindberg (Editors)

reactions (Frijda, Mesquita, Sonnemans, & Van Goozen, 1991; Scherer, 2001). The latter depends largely on how quickly people adapt to emotional events, which, we suggest, is intimately related to the way in which people interpret and make sense of those events. In this chapter, we discuss the relationship between understanding emotional events and adapting to them, particularly positive events.

THE AREA MODEL OF AFFECTIVE ADAPTATION

Human beings need to find meaning in their experiences and are extremely good at doing so—as illustrated by the research discussed in the other chapters in this book. Indeed, one of the hallmarks of our species is the ability to use our huge brains to analyze and understand our environment in ways that allow us to predict and control it (Heider, 1958; Jones & Davis, 1965; Kelley, 1967). When we feel that we do not understand something important, we feel threatened and aroused and seek meaning from other sources (see Proulx & Heine, 2010).

The AREA model incorporates meaning making as a central part of affective adaptation (Wilson & Gilbert, 2008). AREA is an acronym that stands for attend, react, explain, and adapt. People's attention is drawn to events that are self-relevant but poorly understood, and the very same events tend to trigger strong emotional reactions. People then do their best to explain these events. We do not mean "explain" in the narrow sense of causal attribution but rather in the broader sense of trying to understand the event, place it in context, assimilate it to existing knowledge structures, or alter one's knowledge structures to accommodate it. In short, we mean "explain" as it is defined in the *Oxford English Dictionary*, namely, "to assign meaning to, state the meaning or import of, to interpret," which is similar to how others in this book have defined meaning making ("Explain," 1989).

To the extent that people succeed in explaining the event, they adapt to it. This process is captured by another definition of "explain" in the *Oxford English Dictionary: "to explain away:* to modify or do away with (a meaning, etc.) by explanation; to explain so as to deprive of force or significance." Once people feel that they understand an event, they no longer need to devote as much attention to it, and the intensity of their emotional reaction fades.

ADAPTATION TO NEGATIVE EVENTS

The AREA model shares with many other approaches the idea that making sense of negative life events speeds recovery from them (e.g., Bonanno & Kaltman, 1999; Janoff-Bulman, 1992; Joseph & Linley, 2005; Neimeyer,

2001; Taylor, 1983; Thompson & Janigian, 1988; Wortman & Silver, 1987). When life takes a turn for the worse, we do our best to understand and find meaning in the event, and if we succeed in doing so, we adapt quickly. If we are able to find some meaning in the death of a loved one, for example, we should recover from our grief relatively soon (Bonanno et al., 2002).

Research that has experimentally manipulated meaning making has found support for this hypothesis. Many studies have found, for example, that writing about traumatic events (typically for 20–30 minutes on 3 consecutive nights) has beneficial effects on physical and mental health (Pennebaker, 2004; Pennebaker & Chung, 2007). One explanation for these beneficial effects is that by writing about their experiences, people reach a better understanding of them and find meaning in the events (e.g., Rivkin, Gustafson, Weingarten, & Chin, 2006).

Research by Kross, Ayduk, and colleagues directly manipulated the way in which participants wrote about negative events and found support for the meaning-making hypothesis (Kross, 2009; Kross & Ayduk, 2008). In one study, for example, participants were asked to think about a time that they felt "overwhelming anger and hostility" toward another person (Kross, Ayduk, & Mischel, 2005, p. 711). Then, in a 2×2 design, participants were asked either to immerse themselves in the experience or to take a step back and view it from a distance and to focus on either their feelings or the reasons why they felt the way they did. Kross et al. (2005) hypothesized that one of the cells in the design—the one in which people distanced themselves and thought about reasons—would be particularly conducive to reconstruing the event and understanding it better, which would defuse feelings about it. Consistent with this prediction, participants in that cell reported the least amount of anger and negative affect. Further, a coding of the essays participants wrote revealed that participants in that cell expressed the most insight about the event and evidenced the most closure and that this increased understanding mediated the lowering of anger and negative affect. This research provides some of the best experimental evidence that understanding negative events speeds recovery from them and that specific kinds of writing exercises facilitate that process.

ADAPTATION TO POSITIVE EVENTS

Most approaches to affective adaptation, such as the literature on stress and coping, focus on people's reactions to negative events. The AREA model provides an understanding of adaptation to positive events as well. When something good happens to us, as in the opening example of receiving a job promotion, we attend to it and do our best to explain it. Indeed, if we want this event to happen again, it is to our advantage to understand it as best we can. But herein lies what we have called the *pleasure paradox:* By virtue of understanding the event we adapt to it, such that it no longer brings us the degree of pleasure it once did (Wilson, Centerbar, Kermer, & Gilbert, 2005).

As discussed earlier, our initial reaction to an event will be determined by our appraisal of it—whether the event is good or bad (e.g., are we really advancing in the company or is the promotion a gentle way of ushering us out to pasture?), how it relates to our goals, and why it occurred. But once we know what the event is (a promotion) and have appraised it to the point where we know what we feel (extreme joy, say), the time course of this emotional reaction is still an open question. Will the joy last for hours, days, weeks, or months? This will depend, we suggest, on whether people reach a sufficient understanding of the event to move on and think about other things or whether they need to do further cognitive work to understand it. At one extreme, Bob might know exactly who gave him the promotion (his immediate supervisor), why she did so (his exemplary work on the McNurtry project), and what it means for the future (he is now in charge of the McNurtry project). If so, the thrill of the promotion will fade relatively quickly, and Bob will not think about it that much. At another extreme, Bob might not know who gave him the promotion (was it his immediate supervisor or the president of the company?), why he got it (was it his work on the McNurtry project or the Aubrey account?), or what it means for his future (who is in charge of the McNurtry project, anyway?). In this case Bob will continue to think about the event, and to the extent that these thoughts are positive, his positive emotional reactions will persist.

To be clear, if these additional appraisals redefine the event such that it now seems less positive, the employee's emotions will change in a negative direction. If upon reflection, Bob is worried that his new job will interfere with his family life because of the extra travel it will entail, his unmitigated joy will be diluted with concern. Often, however, people know that an outcome is positive but do not fully understand why it occurred or what it means. Bob might be equally proud of his work on the McNurtry project and the Aubrey account, but not knowing which one led to his promotion keeps his thoughts on the event and thereby prolongs the joy he feels about it.

Note that this prediction is parallel to the one made in the stress and coping literature about adjustment to negative life events, namely, that the speed with which people adapt to such events depends on how easily they can make sense of them. Some negative life events are relatively easy to make sense of, and thus people adapt quickly to them, whereas others are difficult to understand and thus have a longer impact. The AREA model extends this reasoning to positive life events.

The model further specifies some of the variables that determine how easily people can understand an emotional event and thus how quickly they will adapt to it. One such variable is novelty. The first time something happens, we have fewer cognitive structures in place to understand it than we do the 20th time it happens. This is why novel events have more impact and are more memorable than repeated events (e.g., our first kiss as opposed to our 20th kiss). A second variable is surprise: When we expect an event to occur (e.g., that first kiss), we can do some of the explanatory work in advance, but when it happens unexpectedly, it takes longer to understand and explain (Wilson, Wheatley, Kurtz, Dunn, & Gilbert, 2004). A third factor is the variability of the event, namely, how much it changes over time. It is easier to understand and explain something that varies little over time, such as a painting of a sunset, than something that varies from one time to the next, such as actual sunsets. A fourth variable is uncertainty about the nature or cause of an event. It is easier to understand something when we know exactly what it is or why it occurred than when we are uncertain about what it entails, as in the example of the job promotion.

The Pleasures of Uncertainty

Our empirical research has focused primarily on the role of uncertainty on affective adaptation to positive events. In a series of studies on the *pleasures of uncertainty*, we have shown that withholding key details about a positive event prolongs the pleasure people receive from it. We have summarized these studies in Table 21.1 and discuss selected examples here (for earlier reviews, see Wilson & Gilbert, 2003, 2008).

First, a quick word about methodology: A difficulty in testing the pleasure of uncertainty hypothesis is ensuring that a positive event has the same meaning to participants in all conditions while manipulating their uncertainty about some aspect of it. If people are so uncertain about the nature of an event that they do not know whether to appraise it as good or bad (e.g., whether they have won or lost $500 in a bet), it is difficult to compare their reaction to that of people who know exactly what the event is (e.g., that they won $500). When we test our hypothesis that uncertainty prolongs adaptation, it is important to hold constant the valence of the event and show that people have the same initial positive reaction to it but that this positive reaction lasts longer among those who are uncertain about some aspect of it.

One way we have done this is to present participants with all possible meanings of the event, which are equally positive, and then resolve uncertainty in one group by telling these participants which meaning is true. For example, in Wilson et al.'s (2005) Study 2, participants watched an abridged version of the movie *Rudy*, which is a feature film based on the real story of a man who overcame many obstacles to attend Notre Dame University and then talked his way onto the football team, although he was not a very

TABLE 21.1
Studies of the Pleasures of Uncertainty and Surprise

Study	Positive event	Uncertainty manipulation	Uncertain condition, as compared to certain condition(s)
Wilson et al. (2005), Study 1	Unexpected gift of small amount of money	*Uncertain condition:* Did not know who gave them the gift or why *Certain condition:* Wording of text implied reasons	Better mood after a delay
Wilson et al. (2005), Study 2	Film with a happy ending about a real-life person	*Uncertain condition:* Did not know which of two stories was true about what happened to the person later in life *Certain condition:* Knew which story was true	Longer lasting positive mood
Wilson et al. (2005), Study 3	Positive written feedback from three opposite-sex peers	*Uncertain condition:* Did not know which person authored which message *Certain condition:* Knew which person authored each message	Longer lasting positive mood
Kurtz et al. (2007)	Receipt of one or two gifts worth $5	*Uncertain condition:* Did not know which of two gifts they would win *Certain conditions:* Knew which of two gifts they won or they won both gifts	Longer lasting positive mood
Koo et al. (2008), Studies 1–2	Thinking about a positive life event	*Uncertain condition:* Writing about how the event might not have occurred and how it was surprising that it did *Certain condition:* Writing about how the event occurred and how it was not surprising that it did	Better mood

Koo et al. (2008), Study 4	Thinking about a long-term romantic relationship	*Uncertain condition:* Writing about how they might have never met their partner *Certain condition:* Writing about how they did meet their partner	Increased satisfaction with their relationship
Bar-Anan et al. (2009)	Watching a 5-minute clip of movie depicting positive events	*Uncertain condition:* Read phrases connoting uncertainty (e.g., "I'm not sure what's happening") *Certain condition:* Read phrases connoting certainty (e.g., "I see what's happening")	Rated the film clip more positively
Lee & Qiu (2009)	Received gifts (worth $30 in Study 1, $10 in Study 2)	*Uncertain condition:* Did not know which gift they would receive *Certain condition 1:* Knew which gift they would receive	Better mood if in uncertain condition and gifts were easy to imagine
Whitchurch et al. (2011a)	Reading Facebook profiles of three men	*Uncertain condition:* Did not know whether the three men had all rated them highly or average *Certain condition 1:* Knew the three men had all rated them highly *Certain condition 2:* Knew the three men had all given them average ratings	Liked the men the most
Whitchurch et al. (2011b)	Participants told they might have a beneficial but rare hormone that helps people concentrate when under stress	*Uncertain condition:* Participants learned that they had a 70% chance of having the hormone *Certain condition:* Participants learned that they definitely had the hormone	Better mood
Ndiaye et al. (2011)	Watched a film clip with a positive ending	People either expected or did not expect the positive outcome and were either certain or uncertain why it occurred (2 × 2 design)	People in the unexpected/uncertain condition had the longest lasting positive mood

talented athlete. Rudy doesn't participate in any games until the last play of the last game of his senior year, when his teammates insist that he be inserted on defense, whereupon he breaks through the line and makes a spectacular tackle. It is a quintessential "feel good" movie, and most people are in a good mood after watching it.

After participants watched the film, we told them they might want to know what happened to Rudy after he graduated from college and that we had found two conflicting reports. In one, he was reported to have moved to New York City, where he became a successful community speaker. In the other, he was the vice president of a real estate company in Michigan, where he married and had three sons. These descriptions were pretested to be equally positive, though different in their details. In the uncertain condition we told participants that we were unable to determine which of the reports about Rudy was true. In the certain condition we told participants that we had been able to determine which one was true and told half that Rudy was the community speaker and half that he was the family man in Michigan. All participants then filled out a mood scale, worked on a filler task for 5 minutes, and filled out the mood scale again.

All participants thus knew the range of possible outcomes that Rudy had experienced. They differed only in whether they knew which one was true. As predicted, participants in both conditions were in a positive mood initially, but those in the uncertain condition maintained this positive mood longer than did those in the certain condition (see Figure 21.1). Uncertain participants also reported having thought more about what happened to Rudy, which is consistent with the AREA model's prediction that a lack of understanding of an event keeps attention on it.

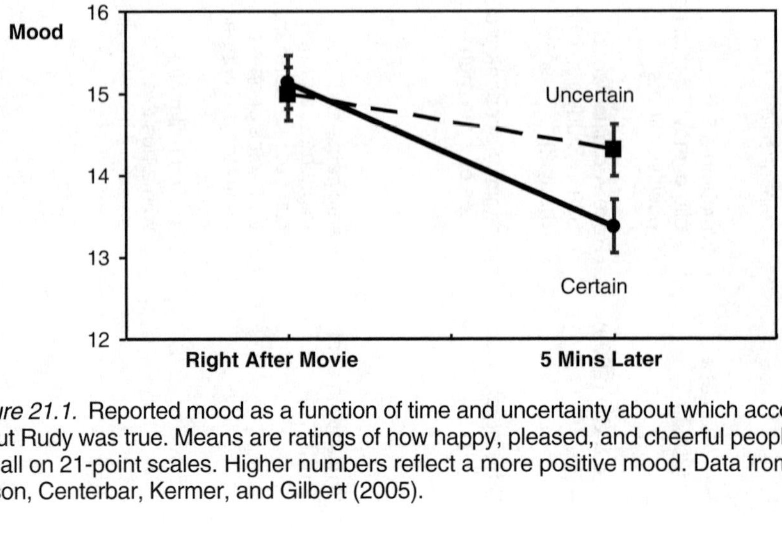

Figure 21.1. Reported mood as a function of time and uncertainty about which account about Rudy was true. Means are ratings of how happy, pleased, and cheerful people felt, all on 21-point scales. Higher numbers reflect a more positive mood. Data from Wilson, Centerbar, Kermer, and Gilbert (2005).

Subsequent studies have replicated the pleasures of uncertainty effect with different positive events and different manipulations of uncertainty. In Wilson et al.'s (2005) Study 3, for example, participants received very positive written feedback from three opposite-sex participants. Participants in the certain condition were told who had authored each message, whereas those in the uncertain condition received exactly the same feedback but did not know who had authored each message. Participants in both conditions were initially much happier than control participants who did not receive any feedback. But as predicted, those in the uncertain condition adapted to the positive feedback more slowly than did participants in the certain condition; that is, uncertain participants were in a better mood 15 minutes later than were certain participants.

Whitchurch, Wilson, and Gilbert (2011a) explored the interpersonal consequences of the pleasures of uncertainty, namely, whether there is some truth to the popular idea that keeping a partner guessing about one's feelings can increase his or her interest. Female college students learned that several male students from other universities had looked at their Facebook profiles, as well as those of several other college women, and had rated how much they liked each woman. The women then looked at the Facebook profiles of four of these men. In the "liked best" condition, participants believed that they were seeing the profiles of the four men who had given them the highest ratings; in the "average liking" condition, participants believed that they were seeing the profiles of the four men who had given them average ratings. In the uncertain condition, participants were told that the four men were either those who had given them the highest ratings or those who had given them average ratings, but that for reasons of experimental control, they would not be told which. The women in all three conditions then rated how attracted they were to the men.

Not surprisingly, given the power of reciprocity on attraction, women in the liked best condition were more attracted to the men than were women in the average liking condition. That is, the women liked the men more when they believed that the men had given them high ratings than when they believed that the men had given them average ratings. But the women in the uncertain condition were most attracted to the men—even more so than were the women in the liked best condition. Put differently, women were more attracted to the men when they believed that there was a 50% chance that the men liked them the best than when they believed there was a 100% chance that the men liked them the best, demonstrating the power of uncertainty. These results suggest that there may be something to the idea of "playing hard to get," if doing so creates uncertainty in a potential mate about how one feels about him or her.

Bar-Anan, Wilson, and Gilbert (2009) attempted to manipulate uncertainty more directly and show that it could influence participants' ongoing experience of a positive event. Participants watched 5-minute clips of movie scenes that were positive but not entirely understandable unless one had seen the entire movie, which participants had not (e.g., a scene in which a character wins an Olympic race from the movie *Chariots of Fire*). Ostensibly to simulate what it is like to chat while watching a movie, Bar-Anan et al. asked participants to say aloud designated phrases while watching the clips. Those in the certain condition read phrases that connoted certainty ("I see," "I understand," "I see what's happening"), whereas those in the uncertain condition read phrases that connoted uncertainty ("I wonder," "I'm curious," "I'm not sure what's happening"). This study had the advantage of keeping the stimulus event constant across conditions and manipulating only participants' feelings of uncertainty. As predicted, participants who uttered the uncertain phrases rated the film clips significantly more positively than did participants who uttered the certain phrases.

Uncertainty About the Valence of an Outcome

In most of the studies discussed thus far, all participants knew that something good had happened, though those in the uncertain conditions were kept in the dark about details of the event. In the Whitchurch et al. (2011a) study, for example, the women in all conditions knew that there were four men who liked them the best and four men who liked them an average amount; what varied was whether participants knew which set of men they were viewing. In Wilson et al.'s (2005) "Rudy" study, all participants knew that Rudy had done well in life in one of two ways; what varied was whether participants knew which life path he had actually taken.

In everyday life, of course, it is common to be uncertain about the valence of an outcome, that is, whether it will be good or bad. When we ask someone to marry us, the outcome can be good (he or she says yes and we go on a honeymoon cruise) or bad (he or she says no and leaves us for the cruise director). When our physician says, "I don't like the look of that mole on your arm," one possible outcome is good (the mole is benign) and the other is bad (you have skin cancer). What are the hedonic consequences of uncertainty in such instances? According to the AREA model, uncertainty keeps people's attention on the event—they think about it a lot—and their emotions depend on the valence of those thoughts. When one of the possible outcomes is negative—we might have cancer—it is hard to think of anything else and we experience worry and dread.

But what about the case in which we are pretty sure—though not certain—that a good thing will happen to us, and the alternative isn't so terrible? Maybe we're eligible for a professional award that would be nice to receive, but if we don't, well, there are plenty of other deserving people and plenty of other awards to win. Or maybe we buy a lottery ticket and dream of what we will do with the millions, knowing full well that we probably won't win. In such cases the undesirable outcome is the perfectly acceptable status quo, and people are thus able to think about and savor the positive outcome, even though they know it might not occur (Loewenstein, 1987).

This possibility leads to a counterintuitive hypothesis: There can be an affective cost to getting what we want. After something good happens to us, such as winning an award, our pleasure often fades quickly, because we make sense of the event and don't think about it much as time goes by. Before knowing whether we won, however, we might think about it a lot, and as long as the alternative isn't that bad, these thoughts are positive and bring us pleasure. In short, the pleasure of savoring a possible positive outcome might outweigh the pleasure of receiving it (for a related idea, see Chapter 9, this volume).

To test this hypothesis, Whitchurch, Wilson, and Gilbert (2011b) told college students that a new, rare hormone had recently been discovered that allows people to perform better when under stress, thereby providing them with an edge in professional and academic environments. Participants took a newly developed saliva test that supposedly tested whether they had the hormone. Participants in the certain condition learned that they definitely had it, whereas participants in the uncertain condition learned that there was a 70% chance that they had (i.e., the saliva test indicated that they had the hormone, but participants learned that the test was only 70% accurate). Participants in the control condition did not receive any feedback on the test.

It might seem that people who are certain that they have a beneficial hormone would be in a better mood than people who are only 70% certain that they have it, but in fact we found the reverse: Participants in the uncertain condition were in a significantly better mood than participants in the certain and control conditions. Surprisingly, participants in the certain condition were not in a better mood than were participants in the control condition. We did not measure mood until a few minutes after people in the certain condition received their feedback, and it may be that this was enough time for them to reach an understanding of the feedback and adapt to it. In any case, we did find that participants who were only 70% certain of a positive outcome were in a better mood than participants who were 100% certain.

The Pleasures of Surprise

People in long-term relationships tend to tell each other how they feel, rather than keep their partners guessing. Perhaps this is one reason that some people feel that the "magic is gone" in long-term relationships. There is no longer any novelty, surprise, variability, or uncertainty about one's partner, the very conditions that can prolong positive feelings. People know which television programs and movies their spouses will like, what they will order in restaurants, where they will want to spend their next vacation, and when they will be in the mood for sex. Some advice columnists in magazines recognize that such predictability can make a relationship seem stale, and they often recommend that couples interject novelty or surprise into their relationship, such as going to a bar separately and pretending that they are meeting for the first time or greeting their partner at the front door dressed in nothing but Saran Wrap.

Fortunately, there are ways of injecting surprise into a relationship without wasting good kitchen supplies. Koo, Algoe, Wilson, and Gilbert (2008) studied a sample of people who were in long-term, committed relationships. Some participants were randomly assigned to a factual condition in which they wrote about how their relationship began—how they met their partner, how they started dating, and how they ended up in a relationship with that person. Other participants were randomly assigned to a counterfactual condition in which they wrote about how they might never have met their partner, how they might never have started dating once they met, and how they might not have ended up in a relationship after they started dating. Participants in a control condition wrote about unrelated topics, such as their typical day.

We invite readers who are in long-term relationships to consider which would make them happier—writing about how they met their partner or about how they might never have met their partner. Koo et al. (2008) included a separate group of forecaster participants who answered this question, and almost all of them (88%) said that they would prefer to write about how they actually met their partner because that would make them happier. This seems to make sense; why rain on our own parade by thinking about all the ways that our relationship might never have begun or soured once it did?

But common sense is not always correct. In fact, among participants who actually did the writing exercise, those in the counterfactual condition reported more satisfaction with their relationship than did those in the factual or control conditions. Why? Mentally "subtracting" from our lives a positive thing to which we have adapted may make that thing feel novel and surprising again, thereby increasing how valuable it seems (e.g., "Wow, if I hadn't decided to go to Jane's party at the last minute I would never have met Phil; it's so amazing that we did meet").

Additional studies by Koo et al. (2008) revealed that mentally subtracting other positive events from one's life makes the events seem more surprising, which then increases positive feelings about them (see also Chapters 16 and 17, this volume). That is, unlike the previous studies on the pleasures of uncertainty, the Koo et al. studies examined the mediating role of another variable that can impede adaptation, namely, surprise. As mentioned earlier, surprise is one of the variables that the AREA model says can impede understanding of an event and thereby delay adaptation to it.[1]

Surprise vs. Explainability

The Koo et al. (2008) studies were designed to reinstate a feeling of surprise about past events to which participants had presumably already adapted. But what about the effects of surprise on events we are experiencing for the first time? Although it is a near truism that surprise intensifies reactions to emotional events—as evidenced by the frequency with which friends throw surprise parties for each other—the evidence for this phenomenon is surprisingly sparse. If an expectation about the likelihood of an event is active in memory (e.g., people are given the expectation a few seconds before the event occurs or are reminded of their expectations), then violations of those expectations do amplify people's emotional reactions to the event (e.g., Mellers, Schwartz, & Ritov, 1999; Shepperd & McNulty, 2002). The reason for this is that when people's expectations are accessible in memory, these expectations provide a salient counterfactual alternative to which people compare their actual experience (e.g., "I was going to spend the evening doing my laundry, yet here I am eating cake with all of my friends!").

Often, however, emotional events consume people's attention such that they are not thinking about the alternatives (Morewedge, Gilbert, Myrseth, Kassam, & Wilson, 2010). In such cases, unexpected events have no more impact than expected ones (Novemsky & Ratner, 2003). Further, there can be a cost to negative expectations before an event occurs. If people expect the worst, they will experience dread as the event approaches. True, they will pleasantly surprised if the worst does not happen, but the affective benefit that accrues when an event violates a negative expectation may not outweigh the

[1]Kray et al. (2010) found a different effect of counterfactual reasoning about life events (i.e., that it increased the extent to which people viewed those events as fated). In one study, for example, participants were asked to think about a turning point in their lives and to describe either how the event occurred (the factual condition) or how their life would be now if the event had never occurred (counterfactual condition). Participants in the latter condition rated the event as more the product of fate than did participants in the former condition, which is at odds with Koo et al.'s (2008) finding that counterfactual reasoning made a life event seem more surprising. There were a number of differences between the studies that might account for these discrepant results; for example, Koo et al. asked participants to think about events that were relatively easy to mentally undo and, in some of their studies, specifically asked people to describe all of the ways in which it was surprising that it occurred. In contrast, Kray et al. (2010) asked participants to "describe how your life would be now if the turning point incident had never occurred . . . write about who you would be, where you might be, the relationships you might have, the beliefs, values, and feelings that might characterize you, or any other details about this alternate world that you can imagine" (p. 110). It may be that it was more difficult to describe how one's entire life would be different, which thereby made participants think that the way things did turn out was meant to be. Subtle differences in how counterfactual questions are worded may lead people to think of life events as surprising in some cases but fated in others.

affective costs of holding that negative expectation before the event occurs (Golub, Gilbert, & Wilson, 2009).

Note that all of the research just reviewed concerns people's initial reactions to unexpected events, as opposed to how quickly people adapt to these events over time. According to the AREA model, surprise prolongs emotional reactions to an event to the extent that it impedes people's ability to understand and make sense of that event. Often this is the case, because people have spent more time thinking about events they expect to happen, giving them a head start in understanding and explaining them. If we know that our best friend is organizing a birthday party for us, for example, we spend time thinking about what it will be like, who the guests will be, and why our friend has chosen a Hawaiian theme when we are from Minnesota. But if the party is a surprise, and we arrive at our friend's house expecting a quiet dinner only to find our coworkers dressed in grass skirts and pineapple hats, it will take us longer to understand and explain the event (and hence the pleasure it brings us will last longer).

Even when an event is unexpected, however, there are times when people can understand it relatively quickly. Perhaps we know that our friend is from Honolulu and that he has always wanted to throw a Hawaiian party but never believed that he or she would actually throw one for us. Thus, we are surprised when we walk into the room but can reach an understanding of the event relatively quickly.

This raises the question of whether it is surprise per se that impedes adaptation to an emotional event or the inability to understand that event. In everyday life these two variables are typically confounded, but as in the example above, they are not identical. We conducted a study in which we separated these variables and examined their joint effects (Ndiaye, Ocker, Wilson, & Gilbert, 2011). Participants took part in a study that they thought was about reactions to real-life stories, especially ones that are accompanied by videos that people posted on websites such as YouTube.com. They learned that a man named Michael wanted to propose to his girlfriend, Molly, in a dramatic way. He did so by staging a spontaneous-looking performance at a train station where Molly commuted to work, videotaping it, and posting it on the web. He recruited dozens of friends and colleagues to pose as commuters, and when Molly entered the station they all sang a song from *The Sound of Music*, after which Michael dropped to one knee and proposed. After reading these details about the story, participants watched the video of the performance (the video was actually an improv performance staged in a train station in Belgium, but none of our participants were aware of this or had seen the video). After watching the video, participants learned that Molly had accepted Michael's proposal and that the couple was now happily preparing for their wedding. Pilot testing revealed that reading this story and seeing the video enhanced participants' moods.

In a 2 × 2 design, we independently manipulated participants' expectations about whether Molly would accept the marriage proposal and how easily they could understand why Michael proposed the way he did. Before watching the video and learning that Molly said yes, half of the participants read that Michael's friends were certain that Molly would accept, whereas half read that Michael's friends thought there was a good chance that Molly would say no. Thus, participants in the latter condition were more surprised than participants in the former condition when they learned that Molly had accepted the proposal.

In addition to manipulating expectations, we also manipulated how easily participants could explain why Michael chose to propose the way he did. Before watching the video, all participants were given two possible explanations, ostensibly based on conflicting reports on the Internet. According to some reports, they learned, Molly was a high school drama teacher and her favorite play was *The Sound of Music,* and according to other reports, Michael and Molly had met on vacation at the Frohnburg Palace in Austria, where the *The Sound of Music* movie had been filmed. Then, right after seeing the video and learning that Molly had accepted the proposal, participants in the explainable condition learned which one of the two reports was true (half were told that Molly was the high school drama teacher, and half were told that Michael and Molly had met in Austria). Participants in the unexplainable condition learned that it was unclear which of the two reports was true.

We then measured participants' moods, gave them a filler task for 7 minutes, and measured their moods again. As seen in Figure 21.2, participants in all conditions were in a positive mood at Time 1; the uplifting video and the news that Molly had accepted Michael's proposal made people happy. The question was, which group maintained this positive mood as time went by? By the time of the second mood measurement, 7 minutes later, mood had dropped in all four conditions, as people's thoughts turned to other things. However, people in the unexpected-unexplainable condition were least likely to show this drop (see Time 2 results in Figure 21.2). An Expectation × Explainability × Time between-within analysis of variance, on the Time 1 and Time 2 mood scores, revealed a significant three-way interaction. There were no significant differences in mood at Time 1, but the Expectation × Explainability interaction was significant at Time 2, as was a contrast that weighted the unexpected-unexplainable mean 3 and the other means −1.

In other words, reading about and seeing Michael's proposal enhanced participants' mood initially, but participants adapted to this relatively quickly, in that their mood was lower 7 minutes later—unless they had not expected Molly to accept the proposal *and* they could not explain why Michael had chosen to propose the way he did. Why were both of these factors necessary to delay adaptation? We speculate that is was because participants in this

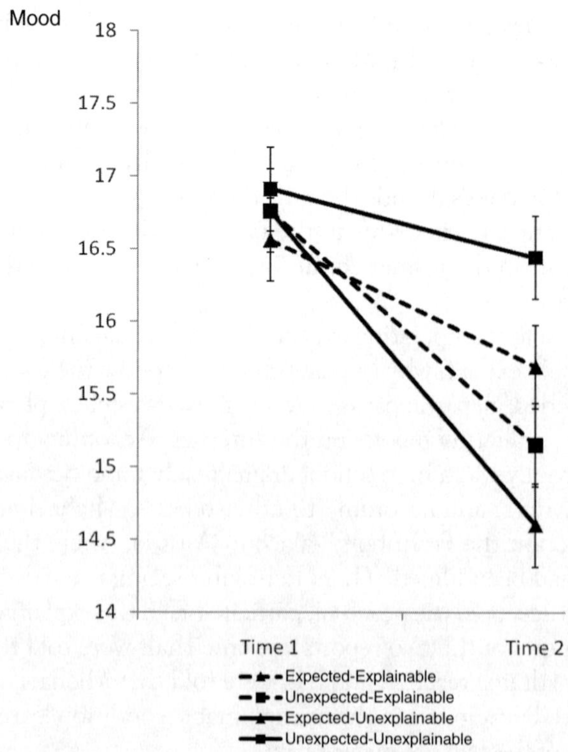

Figure 21.2. Reported mood as a function of time—how much people expected Molly to accept Michael's marriage proposal and whether they knew why he had proposed the way he did (explainability). Means are ratings of how happy, positive, sad (reverse scored), and disappointed (reverse scored) people felt, on 21-point scales. Data from Ndiaye, Ocker, Wilson, and Gilbert (2011).

cell of the design had the most difficulty understanding what happened and why, keeping their attention on the event. Because they were surprised that Molly accepted the proposal and did not know why Michael proposed the way he did, they may have spent the most time puzzling over and reliving the episode.

MEASURING MEANING MAKING

According to the AREA model, affective adaptation is caused by reaching an understanding of an emotional event, which leads people to stop attending to the event as much as they did initially. We have found substantial support for this prediction on the chief outcome measure of interest, people's affective states (e.g., mood). But what about evidence for the proposed mediators, namely, understanding of the event and attention to it? We have found support for these mediators in some studies; for example, as discussed above, participants in the certain condition of Wilson et al.'s (2005) "Rudy" study reported thinking about what had happened to Rudy significantly less than did participants in the uncertain condition, and there was some evidence that this reduced amount of thought mediated the decline in positive mood among people in the certain condition. Similarly, women in the certain condition of Whitchurch et al.'s (2011a) study of romantic attraction reported thinking about the men at other universities significantly less than did women in the uncertain condition. Here too there was some evidence that the reduced amount of thought mediated the drop in romantic attraction in the certain condition. In other studies, however, we have been less successful in finding evidence for the proposed mediating processes. In some we have included questions designed to tap directly how much people felt that they understood an event or had explained it, and these measures did not show the predicted results (i.e., people who were certain about an event did not report a greater understanding than people who were uncertain about it).

There is also conflicting evidence for meaning-making processes in the stress and coping literature, which has examined people's reactions to real-world negative events such as the death of a loved one. These studies use cross-sectional or longitudinal designs in which people are questioned about their emotional reactions and their attempts to make meaning of the negative event. Some studies have found, as predicted, that people who report that they have found meaning in the event recover more quickly than people who do not (e.g., McIntosh, Silver, & Wortman, 1993). Other studies, however, have found no relation between these measures or even the reverse, such that those who report attempts to make meaning are more distressed than are those who do not (e.g., Kernan & Lepore, 2009). In a review of the literature, Park (2010) concluded that the evidence that meaning making speeds adaptation to negative events is decidedly mixed.

One reason for this contradictory pattern of results, both in the stress and coping literature and in our laboratory studies on adaptation to positive events, is that meaning making involves a complex interplay of conscious and nonconscious processes that are difficult to measure. People are obviously aware of the events themselves; indeed, the AREA model assumes that people orient and attend to self-relevant, unexplained events, be they positive (a job promotion) or negative (the death of a loved one). But the process of understanding and explaining these events may not be entirely conscious. People often deliberate consciously about important life events, of course, but much of the cognitive work probably happens outside of conscious awareness in ways they can't report (Nisbett & Wilson, 1977; Wilson, 2002).

Consider, for example, Pennebaker's work on writing about traumatic events. As discussed earlier, people who write about something that has been troubling them show remarkable long-term benefits, especially if they succeed in understanding and finding meaning in the event. But does this sense making process happen consciously in a way that people can easily report? Clearly, it is partly conscious; the act of writing is a deliberate process that people are aware of doing. However, as any writer knows, writing stimulates nonconscious, generative processes, which might be doing the real work of meaning making. If so, then it is no surprise that asking people questions such as "How much sense would you say you have made of the event?" does not fully tap the process of meaning making and often does not correlate well with outcome measures of adjustment. Similarly, in our studies of adaptation to positive events, people probably reached an understanding of the events quickly and nonconsciously, particularly in our control conditions where we make it easy to do so (e.g., by resolving uncertainty about the event). Asking people global questions such as "How much have you reached an understanding of the event?" may not tap these nonconscious processes. This might be akin to trying to measure bacteria with a telescope instead of a microscope.

Unfortunately, we do not have the equivalent of a microscope to measure unconscious cognitive processes and are thus left in the uncomfortable position of not being able to provide direct evidence for the processes hypothesized to mediate our results. And, it might strike some as disingenuous to argue that our theory is correct but the mediating processes are unmeasurable. In response, we can only point out the same state of affairs exists in much of cognitive social psychology, where researchers do experiments to test theories about mental processes that are difficult to measure (Nisbett & Wilson, 1977). They do so not by measuring those processes directly (e.g., dissonance reduction, attribution processes) but rather by conducting experiments that manipulate variables that the theory says should trigger these processes in ways that influence measurable dependent measures, such as attitudes and behavior. The same state of affairs exists with tests of the AREA model, we suggest. We have demonstrated experimentally that uncertainty can prolong positive moods, which to our knowledge no other theory predicts. True, evidence for the cognitive processes mediating these effects is sparse. And ultimately, other theories might better account for these results. Until then, we maintain that what is happening in the black box of the mind is what the model says is happening.

One reason we bring up these issues is that they have stark implications for the literature on stress and coping and meaning making. To their credit, researchers in this area have attempted to study real-life events that are far more important to people than what could be studied experimentally, such as experiencing the death of loved ones and becoming seriously ill. The hazard of this approach, however, is that it hinges on the ability to measure cognitive processes that may be unmeasurable. That is, most studies in this area use correlational designs that measure meaning making and people's emotional reactions, assuming that there will be a link between these two variables. But given the difficulty of measuring meaning making, it is perhaps no surprise that after decades of research, there is still no definitive answer to the question of whether it speeds adjustment to real-life traumas (Park, 2010).

As difficult as it is to conduct experiments to test the effects of meaning making on adjustment to negative life events, it is not impossible, as research on the effects of expressive writing has illustrated (Kross, 2009; Pennebaker, 2004). As with our experimental tests of meaning making and positive events, this involves manipulating a variable (in this case, expressive writing) that is one step removed from the process that cannot be measured (meaning making) but that is thought to trigger that process. Other interventions designed to facilitate meaning making could be studied experimentally, rather than by relying solely on correlational designs that attempt to measure them directly.

CONCLUSION

As the chapters in this book demonstrate, this is an exciting time for the study of meaning making in psychology. There is an increasing recognition that human beings need to find meaning in their environments and are extremely good at doing so. In this chapter, we explored some of the ramifications of meaning making for adaptation to emotional events. We focused primarily on positive events, exploring what we have called the *pleasure paradox:* Understanding positive events allows people to predict and control them but also lowers the pleasure these events bring by speeding adaptation to them. We also argued that meaning making occurs largely outside of conscious awareness and is thus difficult to measure, which limits researchers' ability to test hypotheses directly. Nonetheless, progress is being made by experimentally manipulating variables thought to impede or promote meaning making.

REFERENCES

Bar-Anan, Y., Wilson, T. D., & Gilbert, D. T. (2009). The feeling of uncertainty intensifies affective reactions. *Emotion*, 9, 123–127. doi:10.1037/a0014607

Bonanno, G. A., & Kaltman, S. (1999). Toward an integrative perspective on bereavement. *Psychological Bulletin*, *125*, 760–776. doi:10.1037/0033-2909.125.6.760

Bonanno, G. A., Wortman, C. B., Lehman, D. R., Tweed, R. G., Haring, M., Sonnega, J., . . . Nesse, R. M. (2002). Resilience to loss and chronic grief: A prospective study from preloss to 18-months postloss. *Journal of Personality and Social Psychology, 83*, 1150–1164. doi:10.1037/0022-3514.83.5.1150

Explain. (1989). In *Oxford English Dictionary*. Retrieved from http://dictionary.oed.com

Frijda, N. H. (2007). *The laws of emotion*. Mahwah, NJ: Erlbaum.

Frijda, N. H., Mesquita, B., Sonnemans, J., & Van Goozen, S. (1991). The duration of affective phenomena or emotions, sentiments, and passions. In K. T. Strongman (Ed.), *International review of studies of emotion* (Vol. 1, pp. 187–225). Chichester, England: Wiley.

Golub, S. A., Gilbert, D. T., & Wilson, T. D. (2009). Anticipating one's troubles: The costs and benefits of negative expectations. *Emotion, 9*, 277–281. doi:10.1037/a0014716

Heider, F. (1958). *The psychology of interpersonal relations*. New York, NY: Wiley. doi:10.1037/10628-000

Janoff-Bulman, R. (1992). *Shattered assumptions: Toward a new psychology of trauma*. New York, NY: Free Press.

Jones, E. E., & Davis, K. E. (1965). From acts to dispositions: The attribution process in social psychology. In L. Berkowitz (Ed.), *Advances in experimental social psychology* (Vol. 2, pp. 219–266). New York, NY: Academic Press.

Joseph, S., & Linley, P. A. (2005). Positive adjustment to threatening events: An organismic valuing theory of growth through adversity. *Review of General Psychology, 9*, 262–280. doi:10.1037/1089-2680.9.3.262

Kelley, H. H. (1967). Attribution theory in social psychology. In D. Levine (Ed.), *Nebraska Symposium on Motivation* (Vol. 15, pp. 192–238). Lincoln: University of Nebraska Press.

Kernan, W. D., & Lepore, S. J. (2009). Searching for and making meaning after breast cancer: Prevalence, patterns, and negative affect. *Social Science & Medicine, 68*, 1176–1182. doi:10.1016/j.socscimed.2008.12.038

Koo, M., Algoe, S. B., Wilson, T. D., & Gilbert, D. T. (2008). It's a wonderful life: Mentally subtracting positive events improves people's affective states, contrary to their affective forecasts. *Journal of Personality and Social Psychology, 95*, 1217–1224. doi:10.1037/a0013316

Kray, L. J., George, L. G., Liljenquist, K. A., Galinsky, A. D., Tetlock, P. E., & Roese, N. J. (2010). From what might have been to what must have been: Counterfactual thinking creates meaning. *Journal of Personality and Social Psychology, 98*, 106–118. doi:10.1037/a0017905

Kross, E. (2009). When the self becomes other: Toward an integrative understanding of the processes distinguishing adaptive self-reflection from rumination. In S. Altran, A. Navarro, K. Ochsner, A. Tobeña, & O. Vilarroya (Eds.), *Annals of the New York Academy of Sciences: Vol. 1167. Values, empathy, and fairness across social barriers* (pp. 35–40). New York, NY: New York Academy of Sciences.

Kross, E., & Ayduk, O. (2008). Facilitating adaptive emotional analysis: Distinguishing distanced-analysis of depressive experiences from immersed-analysis and distraction. *Personality and Social Psychology Bulletin, 34*, 924–938. doi:10.1177/0146167208315938

Kross, E., Ayduk, O., & Mischel, W. (2005). When asking "why" does not hurt: Distinguishing rumination from reflective processing of negative emotions. *Psychological Science, 16*, 709–715. doi:10.1111/j.1467-9280.2005.01600.x

Kurtz, J. L., Wilson, T. D., & Gilbert, D. T. (2007). Quantity versus uncertainty: When winning one gift is better than winning two. *Journal of Experimental Social Psychology, 43*, 979–985. doi:10.1016/j.jesp.2006.10.020

Lazarus, R. S., & Folkman, S. (1984). *Stress, appraisal, and coping*. New York, NY: Springer.

Lee, Y. H., & Qiu, C. (2009). When uncertainty brings pleasure: The role of prospect imageability and mental imagery. *Journal of Consumer Research, 36*, 624–633. doi:10.1086/599766

Loewenstein, G. (1987). Anticipation and the valuation of delayed consumption. *Economic Journal, 97*, 666–684. doi:10.2307/2232929

McIntosh, D. N., Silver, R. C., & Wortman, C. B. (1993). Religion's role in adjustment to a negative life event: Coping with the loss of a child. *Journal of Personality and Social Psychology, 65*, 812–821. doi:10.1037/0022-3514.65.4.812

Mellers, B. A., Schwartz, A., & Ritov, I. (1999). Emotion-based choice. *Journal of Experimental Psychology: General, 128*, 332–345. doi:10.1037/0096-3445.128.3.332

Morewedge, C., Gilbert, D. T., Myrseth, K. O. R., Kassam, K. S., & Wilson, T. D. (2010). Consuming experience: Why affective forecasters overestimate comparative value. *Journal of Experimental Social Psychology, 46*, 986–992. doi:10.1016/j.jesp.2010.07.010

Ndiaye, D. G., Ocker, B. L., Wilson, T. D., & Gilbert, D. T. (2011). [The joint role of surprise and explainability on affective adaptation]. Unpublished raw data, University of Virginia, Charlottesville.

Neimeyer, R. A. (2001). The language of loss: Grief therapy as a process of meaning reconstruction. In R. A. Neimeyer (Ed.), *Meaning reconstruction and the experience of loss* (pp. 261–292). Washington, DC: American Psychological Association. doi:10.1037/10397-014

Nisbett, R. E., & Wilson, T. D. (1977). Telling more than we can know: Verbal reports on mental processes. *Psychological Review, 84*, 231–259. doi:10.1037/0033-295X.84.3.231

Novemsky, N., & Ratner, R. K. (2003). The time course and impact of consumers' erroneous beliefs about hedonic contrast effects. *Journal of Consumer Research, 29*, 507–516. doi:10.1086/346246

Ortony, A., Clore, G. L., & Collins, A. (1988). *The cognitive structure of emotions*. New York, NY: Cambridge University Press. doi:10.1017/CBO9780511571299

Park, C. L. (2010). Making sense of the meaning literature: An integrative review of meaning making and its effects on adjustment to stressful life events. *Psychological Bulletin, 136*, 257–301. doi:10.1037/a0018301

Pennebaker, J. W. (2004). *Writing to heal: A guided journal for recovering from trauma and emotional upheaval*. Oakland, CA: New Harbinger.

Pennebaker, J. W., & Chung, C. K. (2007). Expressive writing, emotional upheavals, and health. In H. S. Friedman & R. C. Silver (Eds.), *Foundations of health psychology* (pp. 263–284). New York, NY: Oxford University Press.

Proulx, T., & Heine, S. J. (2010). The frog in Kierkegaard's beer: Finding meaning in the threat-compensation literature. *Social and Personality Psychology Compass, 4*, 889–905. doi:10.1111/j.1751-9004.2010.00304.x

Rivkin, I. D., Gustafson, J., Weingarten, I., & Chin, D. (2006). The effects of expressive writing on adjustment to HIV. *AIDS and Behavior, 10*, 13–26. doi:10.1007/s10461-005-9051-9

Scherer, K. R. (2001). The nature and study of appraisal. In K. R. Scherer, A. Schorr, & T. Johnstone (Eds.), *Appraisal processes in emotion: Theory, methods, research* (pp. 369–391). New York, NY: Oxford University Press.

Shepperd, J. A., & McNulty, J. K. (2002). The affective consequences of expected and unexpected outcomes. *Psychological Science, 13*, 85–88. doi:10.1111/1467-9280.00416

Taylor, S. E. (1983). Adjustment to threatening events: A theory of cognitive adaptation. *American Psychologist, 38*, 1161–1173. doi:10.1037/0003-066X.38.11.1161

Thompson, S., & Janigian, A. (1988). Life schemes: A framework for understanding the search for meaning. *Journal of Social and Clinical Psychology, 7*, 260–280. doi:10.1521/jscp.1988.7.2-3.260

Whitchurch, E. R., Wilson, T. D., & Gilbert, D. T. (2011a). "He loves me, he loves me not . . . " Uncertainty can increase romantic attraction. *Psychological Science, 22*, 172–175. doi:10.1177/0956797610393745

Whitchurch, E. R., Wilson, T. D., & Gilbert, D. T. (2011b). *You shouldn't always get what you want: Uncertainty about the likelihood of a positive event can improve mood*. Manuscript submitted for publication.

Wilson, T. D. (2002). *Strangers to ourselves: Discovering the adaptive unconscious*. Cambridge, MA: Harvard University Press.

Wilson, T. D., Centerbar, D. B., Kermer, D. A., & Gilbert, D. T. (2005). The pleasures of uncertainty: Prolonging positive moods in ways people do not anticipate. *Journal of Personality and Social Psychology, 88*, 5–21. doi:10.1037/0022-3514.88.1.5

Wilson, T. D., & Gilbert, D. T. (2003). Affective forecasting. In M. P. Zanna (Ed.), *Advances in experimental social psychology* (Vol. 35, pp. 345–411). San Diego, CA: Academic Press.

Wilson, T. D., & Gilbert, D. T. (2008). Explaining away: A model of affective adaptation. *Perspectives on Psychological Science, 3*, 370–386. doi:10.1111/j.1745-6924.2008.00085.x

Wilson, T. D., Wheatley, T. P., Kurtz, J. L., Dunn, E. W., & Gilbert, D. T. (2004). When to fire: Anticipatory versus post-event reconstrual of uncontrollable events. *Personality and Social Psychology Bulletin, 30*, 340–351. doi:10.1177/0146167203256974

Wortman, C. B., & Silver, R. C. (1987). Coping with irrevocable loss. In G. R. VandenBos & B. K. Bryant (Eds.), *Cataclysms, crises, and catastrophes: Psychology in action. Master lectures series* (pp. 185–235). Washington, DC: American Psychological Association. doi:10.1037/11106-005

22

WHAT MAKES LIFE MEANINGFUL: POSITIVE MOOD WORKS IN A PINCH

MARC HALUSIC AND LAURA A. KING

To begin this chapter, we invite the reader, like a multitude of research participants, to rate the item "My life is very purposeful and meaningful" on a scale from 1 (*not at all*) to 7 (*extremely*). A vast literature on the important role of meaning in life (MIL) in human functioning would suggest that one's answer to this question is crucial to well-being, physical health, and survival itself (Wong & Fry, 1998). If judging one's life as meaningful is vital to human functioning, then understanding how individuals come to such a judgment is vital as well. Certainly, philosophers and psychologists (not to mention college students gathered for late night wine-soaked conversations) have puzzled over the existential dilemma of what makes life meaningful. In this sense, the meaning of human life has long persisted as one of life's great mysteries. Nevertheless, the mental calculus that underlies responses to the question of MIL may be deceptively simple. In this chapter, we outline some reasonable but ultimately only partial answers to the question of what makes life meaningful. Drawing on an emerging body of empirical research, we argue

DOI: 10.1037/14040-022
The Psychology of Meaning, Keith D. Markman, Travis Proulx, and Matthew J. Lindberg (Editors)

that although many of the deepest answers to the question may indeed provide life with a sense of meaning, failing these, a pretty good mood will do in a pinch.

We begin by briefly defining MIL and very briefly reviewing the literature that demonstrates that self-report judgments of MIL are, although potentially limited, quite important to human functioning. We next review a few candidate variables that likely feed into judgments of MIL, ultimately focusing on emerging experimental results that qualify those ideas and carve out a surprisingly large role for positive affect (PA) in MIL judgments. Finally, we argue for the adaptive or functional nature of the dynamic processes that may underlie judgments of MIL.

THE IMPORTANCE OF JUDGING LIFE AS MEANINGFUL

When we talk about MIL, what exactly are we talking about? Drawing on the vast theoretical and empirical literature on MIL, King, Hicks, Krull, and Del Gaiso (2006) defined MIL as follows: "Lives may be experienced as meaningful when they are felt to have significance beyond the trivial or momentary, to have purpose, or to have a coherence that transcends chaos" (p. 180). This definition captures three aspects of MIL that are common themes in the psychological literature. MIL has been defined in terms of the significance or a sense of mattering to the world, of the goals or life missions individuals are striving to accomplish, and, finally, in terms of the comprehensibility of one's existence (e.g., Antonovsky, 1988; Frankl, 1984; Yalom, 1980). Judging one's life as meaningful might, then, indicate that one has a sense of one's place in the broader universe that is provided by a sense of mattering, of purpose, or, essentially, of one's existence. Although most measures of MIL include items that tap into these components (and others), all of these measures also include items such as the one we noted at the opening of this chapter, essentially asking participants to rate themselves on how meaningful their lives are, whatever it is that they mean by that (Hicks & King, 2009a).

Evaluating the meaning of any experience or stimulus, in some sense, involves detecting a feeling of rightness about that experience (King, 2012). Similarly, judging life as meaningful involves evaluating the contents of mental life for a *phenomenological experience* or a *subjective feeling*, that life is, in essence, meaningful to the person living it (see, e.g., Klinger, 1977). Other notions of a meaningful life may involve more objective criteria. However, we argue that to the extent that the science of MIL is in large part based entirely on these subjective ratings, understanding the subjective feeling that life is meaningful is an important goal for research.

Perhaps the most exciting times to be a scholar of human nature involve the discovery of robust phenomena that fly in the face of conventional thinking (Deci, 1971; Festinger & Carlsmith, 1959; Milgram, 1963). That there are multitudinous benefits related to experiencing one's life as meaningful places us squarely *outside* such exciting times. MIL is theoretically and empirically important to human functioning. A number of scholars have argued for the central role of the experience of meaning in human life (e.g., Antonovsky, 1988; Yalom, 1980). Perhaps the most famous example is philosopher and psychoanalyst Viktor Frankl, who established logotherapy, his own variant of psychotherapy rooted in the attempt to aid patients in identifying meaning in their own life. Drawing on his personal experiences and observations as a prisoner in a Nazi concentration camp, Frankl contended that even in the most inhumane of circumstances, the capacity to weave the events of one's life into a coherent narrative is the key ingredient to retaining one's humanity and dignity. Frankl argued that all humans have an innate "will to meaning," or a driving need to explain one's existence in terms of a larger order to the universe (see Chapter 23, this volume).

Supporting this description of the importance of MIL are many empirical studies establishing that greater MIL correlates with a host of positive outcomes (see Steger, 2012, for a thorough review). For example, people who rate their lives as more meaningful are more satisfied with their lives (Chamberlain & Zika, 1988), have more hope about the future (Mascaro & Rosen, 2005; Zika & Chamberlain, 1992), and have better health outcomes following a serious illness (Chamberlain, Petrie, & Azariah, 1992). In addition, MIL is related to decreased levels of anxiety and depression (Crumbaugh, 1968), substance abuse, and suicide following depression (Harlow, Newcomb, & Bentler, 1986).

Once again, note that in this considerable literature, MIL has been measured with self-report questionnaires, suggesting that despite the acknowledged limits of such measures, a person's subjective rating of his or her life as meaningful is a judgment of some importance. How do individuals come to judge their lives as meaningful (or meaningless)? Next, we consider a variety of answers to this question.

WHAT MAKES LIFE (FEEL) MEANINGFUL?

Few, if any, authors assert that there exists any single source of all experienced MIL. MIL is, by necessity, a subjective judgment, and theorists tend to respect the notion that different sources of meaning are central to different people's lives (e.g., Baumeister, 1991; Frankl, 1984; Klinger, 1998). The literature does, nevertheless, include research investigating sources of meaning that theorists suspect to be especially impactful on MIL. In the present section, we provide an overview of theory and research in support of the notion that religious faith, social relationships, the satisfaction of basic psychological needs, and, finally (and perhaps somewhat surprisingly) PA are particularly important to the experience of MIL.

Religious Faith

Research has shown that religious faith is related to a strong sense of MIL (Emmons, 2005; Fry, 2000; Park, 2005). Furthermore, the relationship between religious faith and general well-being is mediated by the relationship between religiosity and MIL (Steger & Frazier, 2005; see also Chapter 11, this volume), supporting the notion that religious faith serves a meaning-making function. What explains the capacity of religion to make life meaningful?

Although many authors argue that there are qualitatively distinct ways to be religious that are likely to lead to divergent outcomes (e.g., Donahue, 1985; Pargament, 2002), such as the difference between viewing the divine as an unquestionable authority figure or as a partner in uncovering the mysteries of life, some research dealing with simple dimensions such as degree of religious commitment has suggested that religion/spirituality may be related to outcomes relevant to MIL.

One such research tradition couches meaning in terms of the Piagetian and cognitive constructs of schemata, assimilation, and accommodation. From this perspective, religious views constitute a cognitive structure, or schema, which acts as a lens through which people weave all manner of information, such as daily experience, into a self-consistent structure (McIntosh, 1995; Park, 2005; Silberman, 2005). From this perspective, as long as one's meaning system remains unchallenged by the environment, a sense of MIL ensues. McIntosh's (1995) religion-as-schema model draws on this general claim and garners much of its support from instances of coping with traumatic life events (Wuthnow, Christiano, & Kuzlowski, 1980). For example, in a study of bereaved parents, more elaborated religious schemas prior to the loss of a child predicted improved meaning- and well-being-relevant outcomes both immediately and 18 months after the event (McIntosh, Silver, & Wortman, 1993). Furthermore, Park (2005; see also Chapter 13, this volume) showed that the well-being benefits of religious commitment following trauma were partly mediated by greater engagement in meaning-making coping, a form of coping through active cognitive reappraisal of the traumatic event. Although this might contradict the earlier statement that greater religiosity leads to less frequent challenges to one's meaning system, it may be the case that religion gives people the empowerment and structure to seek satisfying answers to questions concerning the most difficult aspects of life.

Some scholars make the point that religion, though structured as a schema, is not just one among legions of possible frameworks that one might choose to make sense of the world (Myers, 2000; Pargament, 2002; Pargament, Magyar-Russell, & Murray-Swank, 2005; Silberman, 2005). Rather, religion and spirituality are uniquely capable of making sense out of the most important of life's questions, because only those schemas are tied to the sacred:

> The sacred refers to concepts of higher powers, such as the divine, God, or the transcendent, which are considered holy and set apart from the ordinary. As such, they are perceived as worthy of veneration and respect, and can become a unique source of significance in people's lives. (Silberman, 2005, pp. 645–646)

The assumption here is that, upon close enough inspection, a secular life ought to lead to nihilism from the recognition that any possible source of meaning is reducible to meaningless elements. Only if one's meaning system is attached to the sacred can one's life transcend the ephemeral and ordinary. Taking this line of reasoning even further, Geertz (1966) suggested that religion not only is uniquely able to function as a robust meaning system but was specifically created by human society to serve that purpose.

Social Relationships

Although there is strong evidence that religion can be a source of meaning in many people's lives, some researchers have argued that perhaps an even more fundamental source of meaning for people is the extent to which they feel a connection to close others, a sense of community, or a satisfaction of their need to belong (Baumeister & Leary, 1995). There are any number of reasons why this might be the case. If we accept the idea that the experience of an MIL is a fundamental human need, it would make sense that people would turn to close others to satisfy that need, as people tend to look to their community to satisfy most if not all of their fundamental needs (Baumeister, 2005). Communities help people feel a part of something greater than themselves. Others provide help in forming personal life narratives, and communities transfer beliefs and scripts that give order and a sense of predictability to the world.

Research demonstrates that participants spontaneously nominate family or friends as the single most important source of meaning in their lives in the vast majority of cases, regardless of whether the methodology employed is a free response format or a ranking of various theoretically generated sources of meaning (Lambert et al., 2010). Although such research may be criticized for its reliance on introspection, the presence and accessibility of cognitive constructs related to relationships with close others have been shown to be a unique predictor of MIL, even when controlling for other potential sources of meaning. For example, in one elderly sample, the strongest predictor of MIL was the belief that one's family or community would provide emotional support, should that prove necessary (Krause, 2007).

Convergent evidence for the thesis that feelings of closeness with others lead to enhanced MIL comes from studies that have investigated the effects of loneliness and social exclusion on MIL. In these studies, both individual differences in loneliness and experimentally manipulated social exclusion show negative relationships with MIL, and in the case of social exclusion, these effects are strongest and most long lasting for socially anxious participants (Zadro, Boland, & Richardson, 2006). What is remarkable about these experiments is that such a global and important dependent variable (MIL) can be undermined by clearly unimportant manipulations.

For example, the most typical manipulation involves a computer activity, called cyberball, in which a participant controls a character on a computer screen who passes a ball back and forth between himself and other characters, ostensibly controlled by other participants located elsewhere (though in truth, they are controlled by a computer program; Williams, 2007a, 2007b). Slowly, the other characters stop passing the ball to the participant, thus leading to a feeling of exclusion. That exclusion by strangers during a psychology experiment via a computer connection is sufficient to reduce feelings of personal MIL as well as the perception that life is meaningful is surprising. That these effects hold even when the interaction is over the Internet, when social *inclusion* in the task is financially costly, when the excluding others are members of a despised outgroup, or when the exclusion is attributable to a computer error (Stillman et al., 2009; Twenge, Catanese, & Baumeister, 2003; van Beest & Williams, 2006; Zadro, Williams, & Richardson, 2004) emphasizes the fundamental nature of this effect. In these studies, participants have generally been asked retrospectively about their feelings of meaningful existence during the manipulation. More recently, research has shown that the simple manipulation of being told that one was not remembered by an experimenter who ran a study 2 days prior led to lowered levels of general MIL (King & Geise, 2011).

Satisfaction of Basic Psychological Needs: MIL and Eudaimonia

Rather than linking MIL to one specific source of meaning, some scholars have argued that MIL is the product of psychological states suggesting personal growth that stems from the satisfaction of a small number of universal needs. When the social environment supports those needs, a person will identify and pursue whatever types of experiences he or she finds meaningful and satisfying. *Eudaimonic* well-being is a term derived from Aristotle's (trans. 1998) notion of the happiness that emerges from living a life of virtue. In the contemporary literature, research on eudaimonic well-being emphasizes growth and fulfilling one's potential over "hedonic" pleasure (Ryan & Deci, 2001; Ryff & Singer, 2008; Waterman, 1993). Theorists typically contrast this perspective on well-being with the hedonic perspective, which focuses on the experience of PA relative to negative affect and the cognitive evaluation of satisfaction with life (e.g., Diener, 2009). We note that, generally speaking, the experience of MIL itself is included in definitions of eudaimonic well-being (e.g., Ryff & Singer, 1998, 2008).

The eudaimonic perspective clearly has great appeal as a perspective on MIL. After all, people who have environments that support their growth and the realization of their potentials should have more frequent experiences with idiosyncratic sources of meaning and therefore should experience life as more meaningful. Theorists within this tradition vary in their proscriptions for exactly which life experiences ought to lead to this sort of organismic growth. The emphasis is that those experiences, sometimes called psychological needs, are not themselves idiosyncratic sources but instead are human universals.

For example, self-determination theory (SDT; e.g., Deci & Ryan, 1985b; Ryan & Deci, 2000) has identified the psychological needs of autonomy, competence, and relatedness as being crucial determinants of the sorts of self-growth, self-actualization, and experience of meaning that typify eudaimonic well-being. In theory, these psychological needs fuel the organismic processes of differentiation and integration, leading initially poorly differentiated aspects of the self, such as interests, tendencies, and preferences to expand and refine themselves as well as modify themselves to resolve structural self-conflicts (Deci & Ryan, 1991; Ryan, 1995; Ryan & Deci, 2002). As they do, they continually build toward a sense of self that is both multifaceted and coherent. Empirically, these psychological needs are associated with eudaimonically relevant variables, such as ego development, autonomous self-regulation, and intrinsic motivation (Deci, Koestner, & Ryan, 1999; Deci & Ryan, 1985a; Ryan & Deci, 2000).

Although there is definite overlap between the above literature that emphasized the role of close relationships as sources of MIL and the SDT psychological need "relatedness," a subtle distinction exists. The former construct could conceivably lead directly and mechanistically to enhanced MIL. By contrast, SDT eschews mechanistic models that cast the individual as passive or reactive; instead, it would suggest that the role of relatedness is not to make an individual experience MIL but rather to allow the individual to do so (Ryan & Deci, 1999).

Theorists in the SDT tradition argue that enhanced MIL should follow from the self-growth that is associated with psychological need satisfaction. Although these experiences may also lead to hedonic pleasure, they argue that any focus on affect and meaning misses the point (Ryan & Deci, 2001). It is to this focus that we now turn, arguing that, in fact, for MIL, PA may indeed often be the point.

Positive Affect

Although the definition of MIL may pose a particular challenge, PA bears no traces of such ineffability. PA simply refers to a person's experience of positively valenced mood states, including happy, cheerful, enjoyment, pleased, and so on. A great deal of evidence attests to a strong correlational relationship between MIL and the experience of positive feelings (see, e.g., King et al., 2006, for a review). It is easy to draw the conclusion from such a relationship that the experience of MIL is inherently pleasurable or satisfying (Csikszentmihalyi, 1990; Reker & Wong, 1988) and that the experience of MIL leads to happier feelings. Such a relationship is implied in the self-help literature, which is full of books offering the potential for a life of meaning and purpose in the service of becoming happier. We do not doubt that such a causal relationship may exist. However, current experimental evidence strongly suggests that the causal arrow certainly goes in the other direction as well: PA leads to greater reported MIL. In a number of studies, induced PA (e.g., using music, writing about positive personal memories or fictional scenarios, reading mildly amusing comic strips) has been shown to lead to higher ratings of MIL, relative to neutral (or negative) mood (Hicks & King, 2008, 2009b; Hicks, Trent, Davis, & King, 2012; King et al., 2006).

Thus, counter to the idea that perceptions of meaning must result from lives that are in some way objectively more meaningful, either in terms of life characteristics like religiosity or in terms of satisfaction of eudaimonic needs, accumulated data suggest that MIL judgments can be causally influenced by PA. Obviously, PA would seem to be a relatively trivial part of life compared with the other potential sources of MIL we have considered. How could the mundane experience of being in a pretty good mood possibly play a role in the grand judgment of life's meaning?

One way to approach this question is to consider PA as simply serving as a heuristic for MIL judgments. That is, when judging MIL, individuals may rely on PA as a shortcut guide for this complex judgment. A recent study casts doubt on this possibility. Trent and King (2010) assessed three sources of MIL—religious commitment, basic psychological need satisfaction (i.e., competence, autonomy, and relatedness), and PA—and had participants make MIL judgments under time constraints (i.e., as rapidly as possible) or with encouragement to take their time and think the judgment through. Given a perspective that eudaimonia is the ultimate source of MIL but hedonic mechanisms may be used as a heuristic, one might assume that PA would predict MIL in the rapid condition but not when cognitive resources were unencumbered. Similarly, such a perspective would predict that the eudaimonic variables of basic psychological need satisfaction would exert greatest influence on thoughtful MIL judgments but perhaps not when one is making unreflective, rapid judgments. Results were, in fact, the opposite of such predictions. Basic psychological need satisfaction related to MIL judgments only when participants rendered those judgments rapidly. Conversely, PA was most strongly associated with MIL judgments in the thoughtful condition. This research suggests that PA does not typically serve as a "quick and dirty" path to MIL judgments.

Another way to approach this question is to generate a list of potential mediators that might explain the relationship between PA and MIL. The sources of MIL we have reviewed thus far (e.g., religious faith, social relationships, psychological need satisfaction) share strong relationships to PA. Perhaps the relationship between PA and MIL can be explained by these less trivial variables. A series of studies has addressed these possibilities. These studies have involved measuring (or manipulating) PA along with other candidate sources of MIL and then asking participants to render judgments of MIL. These studies then evaluated the independent contribution of each of these predictor variables in MIL judgments. Studies have included religious commitment (Hicks & King, 2008), social relatedness and loneliness (Hicks & King, 2009b; Hicks, Schlegel, & King, 2010), global attentional focus (Hicks & King, 2007), and personal meaning system elaboration and salience (Hicks & King, 2012). In none of these studies have mediational predictions found support. Instead, a consistent pattern of moderation has emerged. Figure 22.1 illustrates this pattern.

As can be seen in the figure, if we plot a graph with PA on the *x*-axis and MIL on the *y*-axis and have one line indicate people high on the proposed mediator and a second line indicate people low on that variable, we end up with a graph that resembles a number 7. That is, for people who are high on a particular source of meaning, MIL is similarly high, regardless of their level of PA (or mood induction condition). However, for people low on the alternative source, their MIL depends on PA, leading to a diagonal line on the graph, with the "low, low" participants defining the bottom tip of the 7. These consistent results suggest that when other sources of meaning are lacking, PA can nevertheless lead to a commensurately high level of MIL. Thus, individuals can report very similar levels of MIL but for very different reasons, and PA (even when it emerges as a result of a mood induction) will apparently work in a pinch.

What processes might explain this pattern of effects? One possibility is to embed these results in more general processes of subjective judgments. Many judgments in life are performed with imperfect, ambiguous,

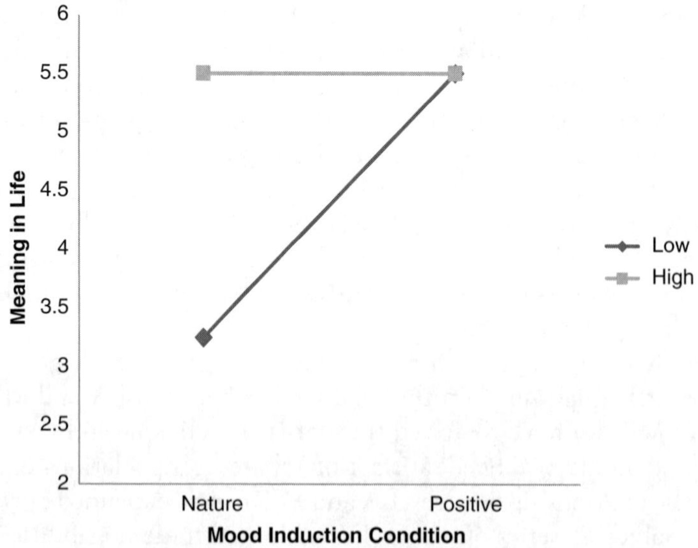

Figure 22.1. Meaning in life as a function of positive affect and an alternative source of meaning in life sample results.

or insufficient information. Furthermore, even given complete access to relevant information, people have limited cognitive resources and motivation to complete an exhaustive search of that information. In either case, the end result is that complex judgments often rely on an analysis of a limited subset of information that terminates as soon as it obtains an adequate response.

Models predicting reported subjective well-being judgments map well onto just such a general scheme. For instance, Schwarz and Strack (1991, 1999) proposed that when people report their subjective well-being, they rely both on their mood and on other relevant information that happens to be salient. A hypothetical model of MIL based on this framework would suggest that affect would directly influence MIL judgments but that effect would be diluted by other sources of information as they become salient (or more cognitively accessible). We might also posit that a very high level of a particular source of meaning implies chronic salience. In this sense, the MIL of individuals who are, for instance, highly religious reflects this chronic accessibility. For those who rely on PA, this source of meaning is, perhaps, less salient.

Evidence for the role of salience comes from research priming individuals with words that represent positive sources of meaning (e.g., heaven, positive social connections). Such primes, indeed, wiped out the effect of PA on MIL judgments (Hicks & King, 2008, 2009b). However, salience cannot fully explain the available data. Although positive primes generally result in the 7-shaped graph (with those primed with a positive source of meaning occupying the line at the top of the graph), negatively valenced primes (though presumably increasing the accessibility of constructs related to a source of meaning) do not disrupt the relationship between PA and MIL. For example, primes of loneliness increase reliance on PA in judgments of MIL (Hicks et al., 2010). The differential effects of primes of positive and negative valence suggest that motivational considerations may be at play, as Frankl's "will to meaning" would imply.

Motivational Biases

Given the personal importance that people ascribe to the meaningfulness of life, it would be naive to assume that personal MIL judgments are undertaken in a wholly impartial manner. Instead, when confronted with an item such as "My life is meaningful," all but the most reactive participants are likely to attempt to answer in the affirmative. Thus, when judging their own MIL, people typically have the goal to rally evidence for a meaningful life. To account for this motivational bias, Hicks and King (2008) proposed a "competition of cues" model for MIL judgments.

From this perspective, the sources of meaning that are used in MIL judgments should be those that are cognitively available, preferably relevant to the judgment, and perhaps most important, likely to provide the answer that "yes, life *is* meaningful." This model, then, suggests that MIL judgments are a product of a dynamic process in which sources of information may contribute to MIL judgments as a function of their availability, relevance, and confirming quality. This formulation notes that PA has an advantage over other sources of meaning in that it is rather easily accessed (e.g., by listening to music, eating chocolate) and, regardless of its source, generally offers an affirmative answer to whatever question is at hand. Thus, Hicks and King (2008) proposed that PA might provide a potentially affirming answer for MIL judgments, even in the absence of alternative supportive information.

Because it takes into account the motivational value of MIL judgments, this model proposes that patently relevant and salient sources of MIL will not be used as sources of information for the judgment if they are reminded that these might lead to a negative answer to the question of life's meaningfulness. Data from priming studies have supported this contention. In one study, Hicks and King (2008) primed Christian participants with words related to heaven (e.g., *god, heaven, salvation*) or to hell (e.g., *Satan, hell, damnation*) or with control words (e.g., *hubcap, ripple, violin*). They found that priming participants with words related to hell eliminated the relationship between religious commitment and MIL. Similarly, Hicks et al. (2010) found that primes of loneliness not only enhanced reliance on PA in MIL judgments but wiped out the relationship between social relatedness and MIL (even among individuals who had reported high levels of social relatedness). These results support the idea that people dynamically adjust the sources to which they refer when making MIL judgments. This dynamic adjustment appears to be a function of the extent to which that source of meaning is likely to provide an affirmative answer to the question of life's meaningfulness.

We suggest, based on the literature reviewed thus far, that the many sources of meaning are each potentially sufficient (but not necessary) for life to feel meaningful. In some sense, this research suggests that whatever works will be employed to garner a sense of MIL. Nevertheless, we note a few provocative findings that suggest a somewhat surprising role of PA in MIL judgments and the sources that contribute to that judgment.

First, we note that semantic primes that activate the concept of happiness but do not influence mood are sufficient to affect MIL reports. That is, subliminal presentations of words such as *happy*, *jovial*, *elated*, *content*, and *pleased* increased participant MIL even though the primes had no detectable effect on mood (King et al., 2006). This suggests that PA and MIL share a strong associative link.

Second, recent research suggests that the association between positive mood and MIL becomes stronger with age and limited time (Hicks et al., 2012). Drawing on socioemotional selectivity theory (e.g., Carstensen, 2006), Hicks et al. (2012) proposed that simple positive feelings should become increasingly associated with the experience of MIL with age and limited time. Socioemotional selectivity theory posits that with limited time, focus shifts from the experience of meaning as a function of the achievement of long-term life goals to emotion regulation in the present. In a series of studies, Hicks et al. (2012) found that, indeed, the relationship between PA and MIL was moderated by age and time perceptions, such that older individuals or those who perceived their life span as limited were more likely to rely on PA in judgments of life's meaning. The researchers suggested that although MIL may be a dilemma for young adults, it may become increasingly less problematic: As time on earth becomes short, the experience of MIL is more likely to be found in simple pleasures.

Finally, we return to the study by Trent and King (2010) described previously. Mediational analyses within the thoughtful condition are particularly telling. Recall that participants in that condition were instructed to think carefully about their MIL ratings and that these ratings were strongly predicted by PA. Mediational analyses revealed that although competence, autonomy, and relatedness all predicted MIL in that condition, these effects were fully mediated for autonomy and relatedness and partially mediated for competence by PA. Trent and King suggested that these results might indicate a kind of mental balance sheet, with PA as the likely bottom line. That is, they argued that a person judging MIL might, upon reflection, come to the conclusion "I have religious faith, friends, accomplishments, but am I happy?"—leading PA to be the final mental arbiter of MIL. This line of reasoning fits with the mood as information perspective (Schwarz & Clore, 2003), in which PA serves as a summary indicator of one's standing with regard to important life pursuits. PA may well be a valid indicator of life's meaning, to the extent that it reflects the many (and possibly unmeasured) sources of meaning that individuals draw upon in their lives. One of the qualities of mood is that we do not necessarily know where it comes from. In this sense, PA may serve as a proxy for a host of idiosyncratic and even nonconscious sources of meaning.

PA, MIL JUDGMENTS, AND ADAPTATION

Despite claims that MIL judgments ought to be rooted in a particular sort of experience, such as religion, close interpersonal relationships, or psychological need satisfaction, it appears that no one source of meaning is necessary to experience high MIL. Rather, even lacking a measured, objective source of MIL, people experiencing high levels of PA are often indistinguishable in terms of their MIL scores from people who have more concrete sources of personal meaning. Also, despite the normally defensible assumption that PA guides meaning judgments by providing a "quick and dirty" heuristic for MIL judgments, relevant research contradicts that guess. PA would appear to have a substantive role to play in the experience of MIL. This conclusion begs an important question. How could it be adaptive to base the experience of MIL on something as presumably unstable as PA? In this final section, we consider the implications of the research reviewed here for human adaptation.

PA may be viewed as relatively transient compared with other theoretically posited sources of MIL, but note that experimental studies using exclusion (as well as PA inductions) demonstrate that MIL judgments themselves are responsive to relatively subtle contextual manipulations. If MIL is vital to human existence, why should it also be flexible? One way to approach this question is to assume, as Baumeister (1991) did, that the experience of meaning leads to psychological benefits when supported and negative outcomes when thwarted. The theoretical dilemma of the notion of basic psychological needs is that such needs include not only the promise of strengths (when they are satisfied) but also liabilities (when they go unsatisfied). Thus, we can assume that a need for meaning evolved as a need because it confers some benefit on people that outweighs any possible liabilities (Baumeister & Leary, 1995; Ryan & Deci, 2000). This is not to say that the benefits from meaning have to be stronger than the deleterious consequences of having that need unmet, but rather, if there do exist extreme consequences to need deprivation (as we have already discussed), those deprivation experiences ought to be rare in everyday life.

The fact that MIL is malleable and responsive to situational shifts suggests an explanation for the role of PA in the feeling that life is meaningful. If MIL is, indeed, critical to survival, it ought not to be widely unavailable or attained only in the presence of particular or unusual psychological states (e.g., religious ecstasy). Perhaps it has become part of the mystique of MIL that it is portrayed, at times, as nearly unattainable, as if the meaningful life is a commodity earned by only a few rare and lucky souls. Such a conceptualization of MIL would seem to be at odds with the notion of the role of MIL in general human functioning. It is simply untenable that a resource that is necessary for survival should be impossible or even difficult to attain. Nothing that human beings require for survival should be unattainable. As such, the association between PA and MIL may provide a ready link to one of life's necessities. If the experience of MIL is truly an adaptive experience, it must be embedded in the quotidian circumstances of our existence.

We are not suggesting that PA is the ultimate source of meaning nor that it is optimal to routinely base one's MIL on PA. However, the research we have reviewed here indicates that the link between PA and MIL is likely strongest when other sources of meaning are absent or threatened, and, in this regard, PA may be serving a particularly important existential function. Increasingly, the role of positive emotional experiences in coping with negative life events (Folkman & Moskowitz, 2007) and resilience (Tugade & Fredrickson, 2004) has been recognized and demonstrated. PA appears to serve as a respite from difficult times and an avenue for recovery from negative emotion. To these benefits, we add the notion that PA may play a role in promoting a sense of MIL.

An illustration of this intriguing association is provided in an unlikely place, existentialist Jean-Paul Sartre's (1938/1964) *Nausea.* Sartre's protagonist, Antoine Roquentin, spends the novel in a state of existential angst, ruminating about a failed relationship and the utter meaninglessness of his existence. (It might be trivializing to describe Roquentin as low on PA, but at the very least one would note, in common parlance, that he is "riding a major bummer.") It is interesting that Roquentin finds respite from his utter disgust at his own purposeless existence as he listens to Sophie Tucker's rendition of "Some of These Days" (and, pointedly not in the more highfalutin Chopin pieces he encounters). This moment of simple pleasure (converging with his realization that he no longer desires his former lover), provides him, at last, a sense that life might well be worth living after all. The pleasure he gains from the song allows him to land on the goal of writing the book. He notes,

> Perhaps one day, thinking precisely of this hour, of this gloomy hour in which I wait stooping, for it to be time to get on the train, perhaps I shall feel my heart beat faster and say to myself, "That was the day, the hour when it all started." And I might succeed—in the past, nothing but the past—in accepting myself. (Sartre, 1938/1964, p. 178)

Amidst chaotic experience, the simple experience of a pretty good mood may serve as a sign that life, nevertheless, remains meaningful. Simple positive feelings, brought on by a piece of music, a good meal, or even a mood induction, may provide a foray into the feeling that one's existence, indeed, possesses significance, purpose, and coherence; in short, that life has meaning.

REFERENCES

Antonovsky, A. (1988). *Unraveling the mystery of health*. San Francisco, CA: Jossey-Bass.

Aristotle. (1998). *Nicomachean ethics* (J. L. Ackrill, J. O. Urmson, & D. Ross, Trans.). New York, NY: Oxford University Press.

Baumeister, R. F. (1991). *Meanings of life*. New York, NY: Guilford Press.

Baumeister, R. F. (2005). *The cultural animal: Human nature, meaning, and social life*. New York, NY: Oxford University Press.

Baumeister, R. F., & Leary, M. R. (1995). The need to belong: Desire for interpersonal attachments as a fundamental human motivation. *Psychological Bulletin, 117*, 497–529. doi:10.1037/0033-2909.117.3.497

Carstensen, L. L. (2006, June 30). The influence of a sense of time on human development. *Science, 312*, 1913–1915. doi:10.1126/science.1127488

Chamberlain, K., Petrie, K., & Azariah, R. (1992). The role of optimism and sense of coherence on predicting recovery following surgery. *Psychology & Health, 7*, 301–310. doi:10.1080/08870449208403159

Chamberlain, K., & Zika, S. (1988). Religiosity, life meaning, and wellbeing: Some relationships in a sample of women. *Journal for the Scientific Study of Religion, 27*, 411–420. doi:10.2307/1387379

Crumbaugh, J. C. (1968). Cross-validation of Purpose in Life Test based on Frankl's concepts. *Journal of Individual Psychology, 24*, 74–81.

Csikszentmihalyi, M. (1990). *Flow: The psychology of optimal experience*. New York, NY: Harper Perennial.

Deci, E. L. (1971). Effects of externally mediated rewards on intrinsic motivation. *Journal of Personality and Social Psychology, 18*, 105–115. doi:10.1037/h0030644

Deci, E. L., Koestner, R., & Ryan, R. M. (1999). A meta-analytic review of experiments examining the effects of extrinsic rewards on intrinsic motivation. *Psychological Bulletin, 125*, 627–668. doi:10.1037/0033-2909.125.6.627

Deci, E. L., & Ryan, R. M. (1985a). The General Causality Orientations Scale: Self-determination in personality. *Journal of Research in Personality, 19*, 109–134. doi:10.1016/0092-6566(85)90023-6

Deci, E. L., & Ryan, R. M. (1985b). *Intrinsic motivation and self-determination in human behavior*. New York, NY: Plenum.

Deci, E. L., & Ryan, R. M. (1991). A motivational approach to self: Integration in personality. In R. A. Dienstbier (Ed.), *Nebraska Symposium on Motivation: Perspectives on motivation* (pp. 237–288). Lincoln: University of Nebraska Press.

Diener, E. (2009). *The science of well-being: The collected works of Ed Diener*. New York, NY: Springer.

Donahue, M. J. (1985). Intrinsic and extrinsic religiousness: Review and meta-analysis. *Journal of Personality and Social Psychology, 48*, 400–419. doi:10.1037/0022-3514.48.2.400

Emmons, R. A. (2005). Striving for the sacred: Personal goals, life meaning, and religion. *Journal of Social Issues, 61*, 731–745. doi:10.1111/j.1540-4560.2005.00429.x

Festinger, L., & Carlsmith, J. M. (1959). Cognitive consequences of forced compliance. *Journal of Abnormal and Social Psychology, 58*, 203–210. doi:10.1037/h0041593

Folkman, S., & Moskowitz, J. (2007). Positive affect and meaning-focused coping during significant psychological stress. In M. Hewstone, H. A. W. Schut, J. B. F. de Wit, K. van den Bos, & M. S. Stroebe (Eds.), *The scope of social psychology: Theory and applications* (pp. 193–208). New York, NY: Psychology Press.

Frankl, V. E. (1984). *Man's search for meaning* (3rd ed.). New York, NY: Washington Square Press.

Fry, P. S. (2000). Religious involvement, spirituality and personal meaning for life: Existential predictors of psychological wellbeing in community-residing and institutional care elders. *Aging & Mental Health, 4*, 375–387. doi:10.1080/713649965

Geertz, C. (1966). Religion as a cultural system. In M. Banton (Ed.), *Anthropological approaches to the study of religion* (pp. 1–46). London, England: Tavistock.

Harlow, L. L., Newcomb, M. D., & Bentler, P. M. (1986). Depression, self-derogation, substance use, and suicide ideation: Lack of purpose in life as a mediational factor. *Journal of Clinical Psychology, 42*, 5–21. doi:10.1002/1097-4679(198601)42:1<5::AID-JCLP2270420102>3.0.CO;2-9

Hicks, J. A., & King, L. A. (2007). Meaning in life and seeing the big picture: Positive affect and global focus. *Cognition & Emotion, 21*, 1577–1584. doi:10.1080/02699930701347304

Hicks, J. A., & King, L. A. (2008). Mood and religion as information about meaning in life. *Journal of Research in Personality, 42*, 43–57. doi:10.1016/j.jrp.2007.04.003

Hicks, J. A., & King, L. A. (2009a). Meaning in life as a judgment and lived experience. *Social and Personality Psychology Compass, 3*, 638–653. doi:10.1111/j.1751-9004.2009.00193.x

Hicks, J. A., & King, L. A. (2009b). Positive mood and social relatedness as information about meaning in life. *Journal of Positive Psychology, 4,* 471–482. doi:10.1080/17439760903271108

Hicks, J. A., Schlegel, R. J., & King, L. A. (2010). Social threats, happiness, and the dynamics of meaning in life judgments. *Personality and Social Psychology Bulletin, 36,* 1305–1317. doi:10.1177/0146167210381650

Hicks, J. A., Trent, J., Davis, W. E., & King, L. A. (2012). Positive affect, meaning in life, and future time perspective: An application of socioemotional selectivity theory. *Psychology and Aging, 27,* 181–189. doi:10.1037/a0023965

King, L. A. (2012). Meaning: Ubiquitous and effortless. In M. Mikulincer & P. Shaver (Eds.), *Meaning, mortality, and choice: The social psychology of existential concerns* (pp. 129–144). Washington, DC: American Psychological Association. doi:10.1037/13748-007

King, L. A., & Geise, A. C. (2011). Being forgotten: Implications for the experience of meaning in life. *Journal of Social Psychology, 151,* 696–709.

King, L. A., & Hicks, J. A. (2012). Positive affect and meaning in life: The intersection of hedonism and eudaimonia. In P. T. Wong (Ed.), *The human quest for meaning: Theories, research, and applications* (2nd ed., pp. 125–142). New York, NY: Routledge.

King, L. A., Hicks, J. A., Krull, J., & Del Gaiso, A. K. (2006). Positive affect and the experience of meaning in life. *Journal of Personality and Social Psychology, 90,* 179–196. doi:10.1037/0022-3514.90.1.179

Klinger, E. (1977). *Meaning and void.* Minneapolis: University of Minnesota Press.

Klinger, E. (1998). The search for meaning in evolutionary perspective and its clinical implications. In P. P. Wong & P. S. Fry (Eds.), *The human quest for meaning: A handbook of psychological research and clinical applications* (pp. 27–50). Mahwah, NJ: Erlbaum.

Krause, N. (2007). Longitudinal study of social support and meaning in life. *Psychology and Aging, 22,* 456–469. doi:10.1037/0882-7974.22.3.456

Lambert, N. M., Stillman, T. F., Baumeister, R. F., Fincham, F. D., Hicks, J. A., & Graham, S. M. (2010). Family as a salient source of meaning in young adulthood. *Journal of Positive Psychology, 5,* 367–376. doi:10.1080/17439760.2010.516616

Mascaro, N., & Rosen, D. H. (2005). Existential meaning's role in the enhancement of hope and prevention of depressive symptoms. *Journal of Personality, 73,* 985–1014. doi:10.1111/j.1467-6494.2005.00336.x

McIntosh, D. N. (1995). Religion-as-schema, with implications for the relation between religion and coping. *International Journal for the Psychology of Religion, 5,* 1–16. doi:10.1207/s15327582ijpr0501_1

McIntosh, D. N., Silver, R. C., & Wortman, C. B. (1993). Religion's role in adjustment to a negative life event: Coping with the loss of a child. *Journal of Personality and Social Psychology, 65,* 812–821. doi:10.1037/0022-3514.65.4.812

Milgram, S. (1963). Behavioral study of obedience. *Journal of Abnormal and Social Psychology, 67*, 371–378.

Myers, D. G. (2000). The funds, friends, and faith of happy people. *American Psychologist, 55*, 56–67. doi:10.1037/0003-066X.55.1.56

Pargament, K. I. (2002). The bitter and the sweet: An evaluation of the costs and benefits of religiousness. *Psychological Inquiry, 13*, 168–181. doi:10.1027/S15327965PLI1303_02

Pargament, K. I., Magyar-Russell, G. M., & Murray-Swank, N. A. (2005). The sacred and the search for significance: Religion as a unique process. *Journal of Social Issues, 61*, 665–687. doi:10.1111/j.1540-4560.2005.00426.x

Park, C. L. (2005). Religion as a meaning-making framework in coping with life stress. *Journal of Social Issues, 61*, 707–729. doi:10.1111/j.1540-4560.2005.00428.x

Reker, G. T., & Wong, P. P. (1988). Aging as an individual process: Toward a theory of personal meaning. In J. E. Birren & V. L. Bengtson (Eds.), *Emergent theories of aging* (pp. 214–246). New York, NY: Springer.

Ryan, R. M. (1995). Psychological needs and the facilitation of integrative processes. *Journal of Personality, 63*, 397–427. doi:10.1111/j.1467-6494.1995.tb00501.x

Ryan, R. M., & Deci, E. L. (1999). Approaching and avoiding self-determination: Comparing cybernetic and organismic paradigms of motivation. In C. Carver & M. Scheier (Eds.), *Perspectives on behavioral self-regulation: Advances in social cognition* (pp. 193–215). Mahwah, NJ: Erlbaum.

Ryan, R. M., & Deci, E. L. (2000). Self-determination theory and the facilitation of intrinsic motivation, social development, and well-being. *American Psychologist, 55*, 68–78. doi:10.1037/0003-066X.55.1.68

Ryan, R. M., & Deci, E. L. (2001). On happiness and human potentials: A review of research on hedonic and eudaimonic well-being. *Annual Review of Psychology, 52*, 141–166. doi:10.1146/annurev.psych.52.1.141

Ryan, R. M., & Deci, E. L. (2002). Overview of self-determination theory: An organismic dialectical perspective. In E. L. Deci & R. M. Ryan (Eds.), *Handbook of self-determination research* (pp. 3–33). Rochester, NY: University of Rochester Press.

Ryff, C. D., & Singer, B. (1998). The contours of positive human health. *Psychological Inquiry, 9*, 1–28. doi:10.1207/s15327965pli0901_1

Ryff, C. D., & Singer, B. (2008). Know thyself and become what you are: A eudaimonic approach to psychological well-being. *Journal of Happiness Studies, 9*, 13–39. doi:10.1007/s10902-006-9019-0

Sartre, J. (1964). *Nausea* (A. Lloyd, Trans.). New York, NY: Laughlin. (Original work published 1938)

Schwarz, N., & Clore, G. L. (2003). Mood as information: 20 years later. *Psychological Inquiry, 14*, 296–303. doi:10.1080/1047840X.2003.9682896

Schwarz, N., & Strack, F. (1991). Evaluating one's life: A judgment model of subjective well-being. In F. Strack, M. Argyle, & N. Schwarz (Eds.), *Subjective well-being: An interdisciplinary perspective* (pp. 27–47). Oxford, England: Pergamon.

Schwarz, N., & Strack, F. (1999). Reports of subjective well-being: Judgmental processes and their methodological implications. In D. Kahneman, E. Diener, & N. Schwarz (Eds.), *Well-being: The foundations of hedonic psychology* (pp. 61–84). New York, NY: Russell Sage.

Silberman, I. (2005). Religion as a meaning system: Implications for the new millennium. *Journal of Social Issues, 61*, 641–663. doi:10.1111/j.1540-4560.2005.00425.x

Steger, M. F. (2012). Experiencing meaning in life: Optimal functioning at the nexus of spirituality, psychopathology, and well-being. In P. T. P. Wong (Ed.), *The human quest for meaning: Theories, research, and applications* (2nd ed., pp. 165–184). Mahwah, NJ: Erlbaum.

Steger, M. F., & Frazier, P. (2005). Meaning in life: One link in the chain from religion to well-being. *Journal of Counseling Psychology, 52*, 574–582. doi:10.1037/0022-0167.52.4.574

Stillman, T. F., Baumeister, R. F., Lambert, N. M., Crescioni, A. W., DeWall, C. N., & Fincham, F. D. (2009). Alone and without purpose: Life loses meaning following social exclusion. *Journal of Experimental Social Psychology, 45*, 686–694. doi:10.1016/j.jesp.2009.03.007

Trent, J., & King, L. A. (2010). Predictors of rapid vs. thoughtful judgments of meaning in life. *The Journal of Positive Psychology, 5*, 439–451. doi:10.1080/17439760.2010.534106

Tugade, M. M., & Fredrickson, B. L. (2004). Resilient individuals use positive emotions to bounce back from negative emotional experiences. *Journal of Personality and Social Psychology, 86*, 320–333. doi:10.1037/0022-3514.86.2.320

Twenge, J. M., Catanese, K. R., & Baumeister, R. F. (2003). Social exclusion and the deconstructed state: Time perception, meaninglessness, lethargy, lack of emotion, and self-awareness. *Journal of Personality and Social Psychology, 85*, 409–423. doi:10.1037/0022-3514.85.3.409

van Beest, I., & Williams, K. D. (2006). When inclusion costs and ostracism pays, ostracism still hurts. *Journal of Personality and Social Psychology, 91*, 918–928. doi:10.1037/0022-3514.91.5.918

Waterman, A. S. (1993). Two conceptions of happiness: Contrasts of personal expressiveness (eudaimonia) and hedonic enjoyment. *Journal of Personality and Social Psychology, 64*, 678–691. doi:10.1037/0022-3514.64.4.678

Williams, K. D. (2007a). Ostracism. *Annual Review of Psychology, 58*, 425–452. doi:10.1146/annurev.psych.58.110405.085641

Williams, K. D. (2007b). Ostracism: The kiss of social death. *Social and Personality Psychology Compass, 1*, 236–247. doi:10.1111/j.1751-9004.2007.00004.x

Wong, P. T. P., & Fry, P. S. (Eds.). (1998). *The human quest for meaning: A handbook of psychological research and clinical application*. Mahwah, NJ: Erlbaum.

Wuthnow, R., Christiano, K., & Kuzlowski, J. (1980). Religion and bereavement: A conceptual framework. *Journal for the Scientific Study of Religion, 19*, 408–422. doi:10.2307/1386134

Yalom, I. D. (1980). *Existential psychotherapy*. New York, NY: Basic Books.

Zadro, L., Boland, C., & Richardson, R. (2006). How long does it last? The persistence of the effects of ostracism in the socially anxious. *Journal of Experimental Social Psychology*, *42*, 692–697. doi:10.1016/j.jesp.2005.10.007

Zadro, L., Williams, K. D., & Richardson, R. (2004). How low can you go? Ostracism by a computer lowers belonging, control, self-esteem, and meaningful existence. *Journal of Experimental Social Psychology*, *40*, 560–567. doi:10.1016/j.jesp.2003.11.006

Zika, S., & Chamberlain, K. (1992). On the relation between meaning in life and psychological well-being. *British Journal of Psychology*, *83*, 133–145. doi:10.1111/j.2044-8295.1992.tb02429.x

23

PSYCHOTHERAPY AND THE RESTORATION OF MEANING: EXISTENTIAL PHILOSOPHY IN CLINICAL PRACTICE

PETER ZAFIRIDES, KEITH D. MARKMAN, TRAVIS PROULX, AND MATTHEW J. LINDBERG

The chapters in this final part of the volume examine how individuals respond to meaning violations, all of which appear to share a common feature—the violation of expectation (see Wilson, Ndiaye, Hahn, & Gilbert, Chapter 21, this volume, for an extensive discussion regarding how individuals adapt and react to expectancy violation). Indeed, van den Bos's "flabbergasted self" (see Chapter 18) experiences anxiety, even in situations where the expectancy violation is advantageous to the self. Of critical importance, and as highlighted by Townsend, Eliezer, and Major (see Chapter 19) and Tullett et al. (see Chapter 20), any given violation of expectation, however trivial, appears to provoke a physiological threat response that in turn motivates efforts to restore meaning and reduce anxiety. What, then, is the nature of these meaning restoration attempts? As Peterson notes quite powerfully in Chapter 2, "life is the forthright challenging of the insufficiencies that confront us, and the powerful, life-affirming existential meaning that such pursuit instinctively produces." Thus, in its most palliative form, meaning

DOI: 10.1037/14040-023
The Psychology of Meaning, Keith D. Markman, Travis Proulx, and Matthew J. Lindberg (Editors)

restoration takes the form of approach behaviors that are aimed at actively constructing and reconstructing meaning when understandings and expectations have been violated.

Given the sheer and sometimes overwhelming complexity of life, it is not surprising that many individuals suffer so profoundly when dealing with the chronic uncertainties and persistent meaning violations that suffuse the fabric of their day-to-day lives. In many cases, they become emotionally dysregulated. Lacking any sort of adaptive compensatory strategies that might point them in the right direction, the result is often anxiety and depression. Fortunately, psychotherapy provides possible short- and long-term solutions to such chronic feelings of fear and despair.

In this final chapter, we explore how themes of existential philosophy have been used to develop a formal orientation of psychotherapy, and we discuss the main principles of existential psychotherapy and their application in practice. We also draw upon case examples to specifically illustrate how the approach of existential psychotherapy is utilized in clinical practice. In the case examples, each patient's identify has been disguised to maintain confidentiality.

EXISTENTIAL PSYCHOTHERAPY

Historically, existential psychotherapy grew as "European psychiatrists took issue with many of the basic tenets of Freud's psychoanalytic approach" (Yalom, 1980, p. 16). Specifically, Freud's theories on human behavior were thought to be too reductionist in nature. Additionally, it was felt that Freud relied too heavily on the principle of determinism:

> The various existential analysts agreed on one fundamental procedural point: the analyst must approach the patient phenomenologically; that is, he or she must enter the patient's experiential world and listen to the phenomena of that world without presuppositions that distort understanding. (Yalom, 1980, p. 17)

Although existential psychotherapy was growing, it was doing so in relative obscurity and in a most disparate way. Many of its main thinkers—including Ludwig Binswanger, Melard Boss, and Viktor Frankl—"were almost entirely unknown to the American psychotherapeutic community until Rollo May's highly influential book Existence . . . introduced their work into this country" (Yalom, 1980, p. 17).

Building upon the contributions of existential psychotherapy's early thinkers, Irvin Yalom's *Existential Psychotherapy* (1980) is considered by many to be the most influential and elegant contribution to the field of existential psychotherapy. It should be noted, though, that existential psychotherapy "is not a specific technical approach that presents a new set of rules for therapy. It asks deep questions about the nature of anxiety, despair, grief, loneliness, isolation, and anomie" (May & Yalom, 1995, p. 262). It is within the contextual framework of Yalom's view of existential psychotherapy that we describe its application in clinical practice.

Ultimate Concerns

Yalom (1980) identified four basic conflicts that drive both adaptive and pathological human behavior. Yet it is important to understand what is meant by "conflict" within the context of existential psychotherapy. "The existential position emphasizes a different kind of basic conflict: neither a conflict with suppressed instinctual strivings nor one with internalized significant adults, but *instead a conflict that flows from the individual's confrontation with the givens of existence* [emphasis added]" (Yalom, 1980, p. 8). Yalom referred to these givens of existence as "ultimate concerns."

There are four ultimate concerns: *death, freedom, existential isolation,* and *meaninglessness*. The therapist's goal in existential psychotherapy is to partner with and help guide individuals in their journey as they confront these universal facts of life. Through the process of therapy, individuals gain a deeper awareness of themselves. Many aspects of therapy focus on the development of this newly acquired knowledge.

From the existential perspective, anxiety originates from the *awareness* of these ultimate concerns. Awareness may be conscious or unconscious, but anxiety results. One's behavior (both healthy and unhealthy) represents the actions taken to mitigate these core existential givens. At first glance, the four ultimate concerns may seem overwhelming or futile, but Yalom (1980) stressed that these are universal concerns that represent the very essence of the human condition. Every one of us, through our actions—but not necessarily through our awareness—faces these concerns. As Yalom noted, *we* must, because we *are*.

Death

One of the most obvious existential concerns is the theme of death. The gift of human consciousness also places upon us the responsibility to bear the somber awareness of our eventual death (for a more extensive discussion of this idea, see Arndt, Landau, Vail, & Vess, Chapter 3, this volume). We constantly (though not necessarily consciously) face the undeniable reality of our finiteness. It is an inescapable truth. The theme of death is perhaps one of the most common to arise in the therapy setting. Some therapists use the analogy of an "existential onion" to illustrate to clients the layers of defense mechanisms (adaptive and maladaptive) used in the service of basic existential concerns. Depression and anxiety are very effective in their ability to peel away the layers of defense mechanisms and, hence, expose the core givens of our existence to an acutely aware client. This awareness can cause confusion, uncertainty, and profound distress: "A core existential conflict is the tension between the awareness of the inevitability of death and the wish to continue to be" (Yalom, 1980, p. 8).

Freedom

Throughout history, human beings have sought to be free. So strong has been this belief in freedom that men and women have been willing to sacrifice their lives in its attainment. Yet in its existential sense, *freedom* refers "to the absence of external structure" (Yalom, 1980, p. 8). It is not always easy to conceptualize the potentially negative aspects of freedom. Although it is somehow quintessentially human to desire freedom, one does not always stop to consider the responsibility inherent in freedom itself. This responsibility—namely, that an individual is fully responsible for the entirety of one's life—can be quite anxiety provoking. Within the therapy setting, many situations hint at this underlying distress. For example, the struggle involved in this conflict may manifest itself in the form of a seemingly random but pronounced increase in emotional distress during the less structured days of the weekend. In his book, *Man's Search for Meaning,* Viktor Frankl (1959; recall that Proulx, Markman, & Lindberg, in Chapter 1 of this volume) referred to this phenomenon as the "Sunday neurosis" (p. 112). The distress resulting from one's freedom (and responsibility) of choice may manifest itself as depression, anxiety, or—in a less clinical but much more pervasive way—boredom. To be the author of our lives means that "below us there is no ground, a void, an abyss. A key existential dynamic, then, is the clash between our confrontation with groundlessness and our wish for ground and structure" (Yalom, 1980, p. 9).

Existential Isolation

Existential isolation refers to the individual's true "aloneness" in the world. This sense of aloneness is quite different from that of interpersonal isolation. It refers to the reality that all of us enter and depart from existence alone, regardless of our relationships or how close we feel to one another. In the clinical setting, this sense of isolation is one of the most common presentations of emotional distress. In addition to the literal suffering, emotional pain can also bring to awareness this fundamental, unbridgeable gap of aloneness. A common theme in depression, anxiety (and even physical pain) is this sense of isolation, which no one but the individual can feel. We are truly alone in our suffering. "The existential conflict is thus the tension between the awareness of our isolation and our wish for contact, for protection, our wish to be part of a larger whole" (Yalom, 1980, p. 9).

Meaninglessness

Why do we exist? What is the meaning of life? Can it possibly be that there is no true meaning other than the one we must create? If the path of our life is not predetermined, then the responsibility for creating all meaning and purpose falls squarely upon our shoulders (see also Peterson, Chapter 2, and Steger, Chapter 11, this volume). This is an awesome yet terrifying concept for one to reconcile, especially today. We are prone to anxiety within contemporary society, as "no instinct tells [man] what he has to do, and no tradition tells him what he ought to do; sometimes he does not even know what he wishes to do" (Frankl, 1959, p. 111). Frankl (1959) believed the primary motivation in life was one's search for meaning. He referred to "the striving to find a concrete meaning in personal existence" (p. 106) as the *will* to meaning. Issues of meaning and purpose are very common themes within the psychotherapy setting. Within the framework of existential psychotherapy, conflict arising from the issue of meaning "stems from the dilemma of a meaning-seeking creature who is thrown into a universe that has no meaning" (Yalom, 1980, p. 9).

The Existential Onion

The ultimate concerns of our existence make up the very core of the existential onion. Like layers of onionskin, various psychological defense mechanisms are used throughout the course of one's life to protect the self from these core existential anxieties. Resulting behaviors may be healthy (e.g., mitigating the anxieties of aloneness and mortality, for example, by marrying and raising children) or quite unhealthy (e.g., using alcohol or drugs to mitigate the anxieties of meaning and purpose), depending on the psychological health of the individual. Consistent with the assumptions of terror management theory (e.g., see Arndt et al., Chapter 3, this volume), much of this anxiety exists unconsciously, hidden from daily awareness. The closer one gets to this existential core, however, the more one gains conscious awareness of the ultimate concerns of existence. It is only when the levels of psychological defenses begin to peel away—like the layers of onionskin—that one begins to feel increasing levels of psychological distress.

It is important to emphasize the ubiquity of this psychological process. The awareness of—and reaction to—the ultimate concerns of existence is not an indication of psychopathology. Rather, one's confrontation with these ultimate concerns is a basic part of the human condition, and confronting the basic dilemmas of our existence (death, freedom, isolation, and meaning) need not be an exercise filled with dread. "The confrontation with the givens of existence is painful but ultimately healing" (Yalom, 1980, p. 14). Thus, one should not approach the therapeutic process with trepidation, for there is great wisdom to be gained, both about one's self and about one's individual place in the world.

EXISTENTIAL PSYCHOTHERAPY IN PRACTICE

Although the ultimate concerns of existence are part and parcel of the human condition, they truly come to the fore in the psychotherapeutic milieu. The core issues of existence manifest themselves in the lives of the individuals whom clinicians are privileged to treat. Existential conflicts of meaning, isolation, freedom, and mortality are clearly evident in the daily struggle of those who suffer from depression and other forms of emotional illness.

Existential Anxiety Manifested Through Emotional Symptoms

Existential themes are clearly evident in the individuals who seek treatment for their emotional problems. Manifestations of existential conflict appear in many forms. Existential anxiety can be especially prominent in the individual during times of transition. Whether these transitions represent change that is positive (marriage, childbirth, retirement) or negative (death of a loved one, divorce, effects of military action), existential conflict arises. In addition, an individual's thoughts, feelings, and comments expressed during an episode of depression or anxiety are often dominated by existential themes. From the clearly overt presentation to the less obvious, once the existential onion begins to peel, the givens of existence (death, meaning, isolation, and freedom) begin to fundamentally alter one's emotional landscape.

One of the most commonly presenting existential themes in the depressed and anxious patient is that of existential isolation—*aloneness*. Patients who are depressed will often acknowledge a feeling of "separation" from the rest of the world. Impairment in the ability to engage in activities of daily living (e.g., work and family obligations) may become quite pronounced, further adding to the feelings of isolation. In therapy, the anxiety of existential isolation is exemplified by comments such as "I feel so alone," "No one can understand how I feel right now," and "No one cares."

Questioning the meaning and purpose of one's life represents another example of existential anxiety during these negative mood states. Fundamental beliefs and important goals may completely lose their motivational energy and relevance. Emotionally, individuals feel as if they are a hapless floating object, desperately trying to find footing on solid ground once again.

In therapy, the existential conflict of meaning and purpose is exemplified in comments such as "There really is no purpose to my life," "Why should I even try anymore?" and "Is this all there is?"

Finally, existential themes of death are quite common in depressed and anxious states, and fantasies of death may serve as an emotional relief valve that mitigates one's constant pain and suffering. In therapy, the existential theme of death is exemplified in comments such as "I am not sure how long I can go on like this" and "I wish I could go to sleep and not wake up," or "Why does life have to be so painful?" and "I am better off dead."

Case Example

Michael is a 38-year-old veteran of Operation Iraqi Freedom who had multiple tours of duty during his service. On several occasions, he engaged in direct combat with enemy forces. Although he was not personally involved in any combat fatalities (and he had not directly witnessed any deaths), several members of his unit were killed in the course of the conflict, including one who was a close friend.

Michael presented to the therapist for treatment of his depression and anxiety. Symptoms of posttraumatic stress disorder (including bad memories, flashbacks, nightmares, and hypervigilance) were also present. In addition to being prescribed medications, Michael was interested in psychotherapy. Beyond the overt symptoms of depression and anxiety, what bothered Michael the most was a sense of being "disconnected from the rest of the world." He could never remember at any previous time in his life experiencing this kind of "detached" feeling. He was an extravert by nature, but since returning from the war, he had found it quite hard to relate to family and friends. He did not "see the point."

As therapy continued, multiple existential conflicts clearly became evident. Most prominent was Michael's loss of meaning and purpose. In returning home after the war, it was hard for him to find relevant meaning in the daily routine of life. He anguished over trying to reconcile the disparity between his daily existence in wartime combat—literally fighting for his life—and the relative peace of his existence now, safe at home.

Existential themes of death were evident, as he was greatly conflicted between feelings of happiness for having made it home alive and feelings of guilt for that happiness, because several of his fellow soldiers died in combat. As he stated, "How do I deserve to be happy when I know [my friends] died back there? Why did I make it out alive? How do I make any sense of all of this?"

Themes of existential isolation and aloneness were evident as well. Michael became increasingly depressed and withdrawn, which was once again a significant departure from his extraverted personality prior to the war.

He felt very alone in his personal struggle. He did not want to be a burden to his friends and family. He felt they could never truly understand what he was going through: "How could they know what I am feeling? They weren't there. They don't know." This further added to his sense of isolation and despair.

As the sessions progressed, Michael's existential understanding and acceptance grew. He was able to see how his struggle was but his unique manifestation of the human condition. He was able to understand that although his specific struggles were uniquely his, the core existential concerns—death, meaning, isolation, and freedom—were universal. As a result, Michael's mood slowly began to improve. He began to reconnect with his family and reclaim friendships without being burdened by guilt. He realized that he possessed the freedom to decide how he reconciled the war deaths of his fellow soldiers. In addition to seeing their deaths as a symbol of ultimate bravery, Michael began to realize that it was his duty to reclaim his life (and happiness) in their honor. In an authentic and genuine way, he found meaning—not only in their deaths but in his life as well. More generally, and in a related vein, Halusic and King (Chapter 22) would suggest that to the extent that Michael's search for meaning, itself, gives rise to positive affect, his sense of meaning in life will be enhanced.

Existential Anxiety Manifested Through Physical Symptoms

In addition to the psychological manifestations discussed in this chapter, existential conflict can manifest itself as physical symptoms. One way emotions can be somatically expressed is through pain and physical discomfort. To be clear, there are many medical disorders of various etiologies—infectious, neurologic, and cancerous, to name a few—where physical pain is part of the symptomatology. Here we are referring to pain that either has no obvious etiology (i.e., all causes have been ruled out) or presents in an anatomically inconsistent fashion (e.g., pain that migrates across the midline of the body or skips from one anatomical area to the next). In these patients, the *originating cause* of their physical symptoms typically has an emotional basis.

Why might emotions manifest themselves as painful physical symptoms? Stanley J. Coen of Columbia University's College of Physicians and Surgeons first suggested that psychosomatic physical symptoms were "in all likelihood a defense against noxious unconscious emotional phenomena" (Sarno, 2006, p. 92). Inspired by Coen's research, John Sarno (2006) of New York University developed an important theory of tension myositis syndrome (TMS). According to the theory, the pain of TMS serves as a dramatic and purposeful distraction when unwanted negative emotions threaten to escape into conscious awareness. Sarno noted that "the altered physiology in TMS appears to be a mild, localized reduction in blood flow to a small region or a specific body structure, such as a spinal nerve, resulting in a state of mild oxygen deprivation. The result is pain" (p. 15). The pain is very real, but its origin lies in an internal emotional trauma, not in a physical injury or a disease process.

Although the initial psychological explanation of TMS derived from psychoanalytic (Freudian) theory, existential anxiety can often be at the root cause of pain in these patients. Although not overt, existential themes—mortality, meaning, isolation, and freedom—dominate the emotional landscape of these individuals. Existential psychotherapy often results in profound relief of both emotional and physical symptoms.

Case Example

Matthew is a married 62-year-old microbiology professor with full tenure at a local university. He sought treatment from a therapist for his worsening mood, brought about from years of chronic, severe neck pain. In the 2 years prior to beginning therapy, he had been seen by a variety of medical professionals, but the diagnostic studies (X-ray, EMG, CAT scan, and MRI) done during that time revealed no significant pathology. His neck pain persisted despite courses of physical therapy, traction, exercise, yoga, and even steroid injections. He was so frustrated that at one point he was even willing to consider spinal surgery. "But the surgeons told me there was nothing 'wrong' with my neck as far as they could see," said Matthew. "They said there was nothing in my neck that needed surgery." Frustration was turning into depression and despair. It was at that point that he chose to enter into therapy.

When treatment began, Matthew was approximately one year away from retirement. He had spent the prior 34 years of his life teaching, doing research, and publishing in the field of microbiology. He acknowledged the stress earlier in his career to gain tenure, but he was pleased overall with his professional life. He took a great deal of pride in his ability to consistently bring in the most research grant money to his department. About three years ago, anticipating his retirement, Matthew decided to stop doing research and refocus his energies solely on teaching. Other colleagues were now bringing in much larger research grants than he, and thus he felt it was "the right time" to make this change.

As the therapeutic sessions progressed, he was able to recall (after some considerable retrospection) the first time he remembered feeling the pain in his neck. It was during the first semester of teaching classes after he had made the decision to stop doing research. At first, he thought the pain was due to the increased teaching load. He stated, "I figured since I was teaching more classes, maybe I was holding my head and neck the wrong way." At first, he did not think much about it. But his pain persisted and proceeded to worsen over the next few months. Worried, he began to seek out medical help. "I never thought my pain would last for this long," he said as he described his course of treatment over the past few years. He was exhausted, both physically and emotionally.

The therapist asked Matthew if he thought there might be a relationship between his neck pain and the decision to no longer do research, noting that his neck pain began in the semester *after* he chose to stop his research. Although Matthew voluntarily made the choice to no longer do research and focus on teaching, it was quite conceivable that his decision might have evoked some profound existential anxieties relating to mortality, meaning, and purpose that were creating his anxiety. In response, he first acknowledged feeling as if "things were really changing in the department" as the younger faculty on tenure track began to bring in much larger grants, and then admitted that he missed doing his research over the past 3 years. He was then asked to consider the possibility that in response to the existential anxieties evoked, his mind may have created his neck pain as a defense against bringing those existential givens to conscious awareness. In this way, the mind determines that it is "less painful" to have physical pain than to suffer emotional pain.

Although somewhat skeptical, Matthew agreed to read up about the basics of TMS and existential approaches to treatment. In the following weeks, the therapist and the patient continued to explore these existential anxieties and their role in Matthew's physical symptoms. After continuing treatment for several more weeks, Matthew announced during therapy that for the first time in nearly two years he had no neck pain. "I am not sure what happened, but I just woke up a few days ago and it was gone," he said. That was two years ago, and Matthew has continued to be pain-free. On occasion he will get a brief flare, but he is able to see the connection it has to his psychological stress. By acknowledging the existential anxieties, Matthew properly equipped himself with the tools he needed to prevent these psychophysiologic symptoms from dominating his life in the future.

CONCLUSION: RESTORING MEANING IN PSYCHOTHERAPY

Existential psychotherapy is a dynamic approach based upon the ubiquitous and universal concerns that are an inexorable part of the human condition. Throughout our lives, and with different levels of awareness, we courageously confront the questions of our existence. As Peterson (Chapter 2) notes, "The fundamental problem of life is the overwhelming complexity of being," and Peterson urgently recommends, "When chaos threatens, confront it, as quickly as possible, eyes open, voluntarily." In so doing, meaning can be both constructed and restored.

Meaning: What and Why

At the outset of this volume, we argued that a global understanding of meaning making involves "the ways that we *make sense* of ourselves and our environment, the feelings that are aroused when these understandings are constructed or violated, and the common ways in which we respond to these violations" (Proulx et al., Chapter 1). Furthermore, we focused on a general distinction within the notion of meaning—a sense of *what* is and a sense of *why* this should be so. The *what* of sense making refers to an epistemic concern with understanding (e.g., "What does it all mean?"), whereas the *why* refers to a teleological exploration of value and purpose (e.g., "Why should I go on?"). As Proulx (Chapter 4) argues, epistemic and values motivations are understood as being both distinct and complementary.

Meaning: What

In Chapter 5 of this volume, Higgins makes the case that a core concern for individuals is truth motivation—our general motivation to determine what is real—and that we often feel "confused and bewildered" when our truth motivation goes unsatisfied. Similarly, Burton and Plaks (Chapter 6) note that people feel anxious if their lay epistemic theories are violated by unexpected experiences. In psychotherapy, the client is guided by an objective therapist who can point out different means by which truth can be ascertained—means, importantly, that the client has heretofore not entertained. Conversely, the therapist can also urge the client to let go of the search if a given truth seems unknowable or obscured from view. Either way, the client derives a sense of efficacy—mastery, predictability, and control—from engaging in the therapeutic process (see Waytz, Chapter 7).

Meaning: Why—A Guide for Living

In Chapter 1, we noted, "While a sense of the *what* organizes our epistemic understanding of reality, a sense of the *why* directs us in how we should conduct our lives, and provides explanations for the events that constitute our life story." Indeed, the telling and framing of one's life story is absolutely central to psychotherapy. As Wachtel (2011) described it:

> When successful, psychotherapy helps the patient to retell his life story, to provide a different frame and give a different moral to the story. Hence, it enables him to give different *meaning* to events and experiences that had previously been a source of hopelessness and blockage and had contributed to a demeaning or depressing view of himself and of his life. (p. 27)

The means by which individuals tell their life stories and create progress narratives (i.e., suggesting that one will be flourishing in the future) are explored in great detail in the chapters by Walker and Skowronski (Chapter 8) and McAdams (Chapter 9). In particular, Walker and Skowronski describe how progress narratives created about negative events are effective in reducing lingering anxiety about those events, whereas McAdams notes that such narratives often converge on a redemptive self that allows one to understand past suffering as functional and a precondition for future success. Moreover, the redemptive self often adopts a moral code by which to live in the future (Janoff-Bulman, Chapter 10). Psychotherapists would seem well equipped to guide the construction of adaptive progress narratives for their clients. Of course, therapists should also keep in mind that there is such a thing as "enough meaning" (Steger, Chapter 11) and that it is important to maintain a homeostatic view of meaning-making and maintenance behaviors.

Meaning: Why—Explanations for Events

As Silver and Updegraff note in Chapter 12, when unexpected tragedies short-circuit the progress we believe we are making toward satisfying long-term goals, we often compensate by generating explanations for why a given traumatic event occurred. Likewise, Park (Chapter 13) describes how threats to our global life commitments evoke anxiety that, in turn, activates sense-making efforts. To this end, individuals often turn to religion and spirituality for the purpose of addressing both epistemic and teleological concerns. Likewise, Anderson, Kay, and Fitzsimons (Chapter 14) discuss how unexpected and negative events can elicit compensatory searches for silver linings that help offset feelings of sadness and anxiety. The psychotherapist should encourage this search for explanations but also remain attuned to biases and distortions of perceptions that might lead clients to be unrealistically optimistic and make poor choices in the future.

Finally, the chapters by Routledge, Sedikides, Wildschut, and Juhl (Chapter 15); Kray, Hershfield, George, and Galinsky (Chapter 16); and Lindberg, Markman, and Choi (Chapter 17) all focus on how individuals construe the past in a way that allows them to derive retrospective understanding and, perhaps, prospective purpose. More specifically, Routledge et al. describe how thinking back to prior meaningful experiences evokes feelings of nostalgia that can often soften emotional reactions to negative life experiences. Whereas nostalgia seeking represents more of a compensatory reaction to meaning violations, counterfactual thinking (Chapters 16 and 17)—imagining that our lives could have easily turned out differently—appears to be an active attempt to view the past deterministically. Contemplating how an event could have turned out differently—but also acknowledging that it did not, in fact, turn out differently—appears to give rise to a sense that the event was "meant to be," guided perhaps by the hands of Fate. Although counterfactual thinking has been shown in certain contexts to enhance retrospective control perceptions and intensify goal pursuit, therapists should be wary of encouraging overly deterministic worldviews, as such mind-sets may actually diminish feelings of mastery, predictability, and control.

The *new science of meaning*, represented by the chapters in this volume, not only offers therapists a deep conceptual framework within which to practice older, more established techniques but should also suggest new approaches. By recognizing the centrality of meaning as sense making, and acknowledging the distinction between the *what* and the *why* of sense making, therapists should be armed with a variety of epistemic and teleological tools with which to fashion therapy strategies that are unique for each individual.

REFERENCES

Frankl, V. L. (1959). *Man's search for meaning*. New York, NY: Simon & Schuster.

May, R., & Yalom, I. D. (1995). Existential psychotherapy. In R. J. Corsini & D. Wedding (Eds.), *Current psychotherapies* (5th ed., pp. 262–292). Itasca, IL: Peacock.

Sarno, J. E. (2006). *The divided mind: The epidemic of mindbody disorders*. New York, NY: HarperCollins.

Wachtel, P. L. (2011). *Inside the session: What really happens in psychotherapy*. Washington, DC: American Psychological Association. doi:10.1037/12321-000

Yalom, I. D. (1980). *Existential psychotherapy*. New York, NY: Basic Books.

INDEX

Abdollahi, A., 62
Abelson, Robert, 104–105
Abilities, malleability of, 117–119
Abnormal counterfactuals, 319
Absurdity
in existentialist theories of meaning, 72–73
inauthentic responses to, 75
and meaning reinstatement, 64–65
of mortality, 76
and violations of understanding, 6
ACC (anterior cingulate cortex), 403–405
Accessibility
of death-related thoughts, 305
of memories, 161–162
Accommodation processes, 78, 268
Accuracy, of memories, 160–163
Action-based model of dissonance, 406
Action identification, mortality salience and, 58–59
Actions. *See also* MAP (motivation, action, perception) schemas
and coherence restoration, 410
as function of meanings, 402, 407–408
and goals/beliefs, 401
Actors, social
meaning in life for, 173–176
meaning makers as, 172
Adams, J. S., 361
Adams, M. J., 161
Adaptation. *See also* AREA model of affective adaptation
AREA model of, 422
autobiographical memories about, 162
and construction of life stories, 320
counterfactual thinking in, 325–326
and meaning in life, 457–459
to negative events, 422–423
to positive events, 423–436
rate of, 424–425, 434–436
Adaptive sequencing, 326–327
Addiction, 95–96
Adjustment
of cancer survivors, 264–266
and meaning making, 249, 267
and religious coping, 267–268
of trauma victims, 240–241, 243–244
Adolescents
as autobiographical authors, 180–182
formal operational thought of, 181
pursuit of goals by, 178
reminiscence bumps for events experienced as, 158–159
Advantageous inequity, reactions to, 361–362, 369–370
Adversity
counterfactuals for coping with, 325
and self-concordance/goal attainment, 408
Affect. *See also* Negative affect; Positive affect
and anterior cingulate cortex activation, 405
and counterfactual thinking, 340
fading affect bias, 155–156
fixed, flexible, and flourishing, 156
homeostasis beliefs and forecasting of, 128
in human judgment, 199
MAP schema in regulation of, 31
Affective adaptation. *See* AREA model of affective adaptation
Affordances, 18n1, 161
Age
and nostalgia, 300
and perceptions of events, 159–160
and positive mood/meaning in life, 456
Agents, motivated
meaning in life for, 176–179
meaning makers as, 172
Aggression, dominance and, 25–26
Aknin, L. B., 205
Algoe, S. B., 342, 432
Almost counterfactuals, 319, 327
Aloneness, 468–472

Alternate realities, in counterfactual thinking, 319
Altruistic acts
in eudaimonic approach to well-being, 205–206
by trauma survivors, 198, 206
Alzheimer's patients, teleological bias of, 140
Ambiguity, in consolidate/augment model, 224–225
Ancient cultures, personal memory in, 149–150
Anderson, B., 265
Anderson, J. E., 287, 290
Angst, 74–75
Anomalous events, MAP schemas from, 33–34
Antecedent-consequent relationships, 347–348, 351
Anterior cingulate cortex (ACC), 403–405
Anthropocentric thinking, by children, 140
Anthropomorphic knowledge, elicitation of, 137
Anthropomorphism, 135–143
and dehumanization, 142–143
and desire for meaning, 137–138
future research on, 142–143
and mastery motivation, 139–142
mechanisms of, 138–139
terminology for, 136
Anxiety
and anterior cingulate cortex activation, 405
in aversive arousal, 382
and behavioral inhibition system activation, 363, 366
from challenges to theories of personality, 122–124, 127–128
and death salience/nostalgia, 306
emotional symptoms of, 470–472
existentialist perspective on, 467, 469
physical symptoms of, 472–474
and religious ideals, 411
from theory replacement vs. violation, 126
from threats to meaning, 409
and understanding, 5
Appraisals. *See also* Reappraisals
behavior inhibition system in, 362
by cancer survivors, 265–266
redefining events with, 424
Approach motivational systems
and MAP schemas, 34–35
for threat resolution, 405–407, 409–410
Area F5 (cerebral cortex), 29
AREA model of affective adaptation, 422
attention in, 428
meaning making in, 436
for negative events, 422–423, 437
for positive events, 423–425, 437
surprise in, 433, 434
tests of, 438
uncertainty in, 428, 430
Aristotle, 203–205, 216, 450
Arndt, J., 55–56, 58, 60, 62
Arousal. *See also* Aversive arousal
and cognitive compensation, 79
optimal arousal model, 222, 223
and SAM activation, 385
Asch, S. E., 106, 360–361, 369
Asian cultures, autobiographical memory in, 153
Asian tsunami (2004), 325
Assimilation, of experiences and schemata, 78
Associate-relevant behavior, 121
Assumptions
about reality, 280–281
in counterfactual thinking, 349–350
Astigarraga, E., 328
Atheism, mortality salience and, 62
Attachment, nostalgia and, 302–303
Attachment theory, beliefs in, 279
Attend, react, explain, adapt model. *See* AREA model of affective adaptation
Attention
in approach motivational systems, 406
for emotional events, 433–434
global attentional focus, 453–454

and rate of adaptation, 434–436
for stereotype-consistent information, 120–121
and uncertainty about events, 428, 430
and understanding of events, 437–438
Attitudes
lay theories vs., 116
revision of, 80
Attraction, 429
Attributions
of arousal, 392
of behavior, 101–102
by cancer survivors, 265–266
cognitive load and uncertainty about, 140
counterfactual thinking in, 320–321, 348–349
and moral judgments, 200–201
Audience tuning, 108–110
Autobiographical authors
meaning in life for, 180–184
meaning makers as, 172
Autobiographical experiences. *See also* Life stories
counterfactual thinking about, 333
nostalgic vs., 305, 307–308
Autobiographical memory(-ies), 149–165
content of, 156–159
intrinsic meaning of, 160–163
meaning making from, 155–160
in scientific psychology, 149–151
self-relevant meaning of, 153–155
self/social context for, 151–153
value of, 163–164
Autobiographical reasoning, 181
Autokinetic effect, 107
Autonoetic consciousness, 150
Aversive arousal
meaning restoration after, 381–384
from meaning violations, 383–384
measurement of, 382, 384
psychological indexes of, 384–387
self-reports of, 384
Aversive (avoidance) motivational systems, 365, 405–406
Ayduk, O., 390, 423
Balance theory, 104, 105
Bandura, A., 195
Bar-Anan, Y., 427, 429–430
Barreto, M., 194
BAS (behavioral activation system), 359, 363
Baumeister, R. F., 163–164, 172, 173, 218, 457
Bear, D. M., 163
Becker, E., 38, 53, 63, 84, 332
Beer, J. S., 119
Beginnings, in life stories, 322–323
Behavior(s)
anthropomorphic perception of, 142
associate- vs. trait-relevant, 121
attributions of, 101–102
and belief conflicts, 401–403
concordance of goals and, 408
exploratory, 34–35
justification of, 8
in lay theories of personality, 117
and mental state, 138, 139
predictability of, 102–104
rationalization of, 195
social situational factors of, 360
Behavioral activation system (BAS), 359, 363
Behavioral disinhibition
manipulation of, 371–372
and proself values, 372–373
and sense making, 366–370
Behavioral inhibition system (BIS), 359–375
and genuine self, 372–374
overactivation of, 375
psychological function of, 370–372
and sense making by disinhibited individuals, 366–370
and sense making by flabbergasted individuals, 360–362
and sense making by inhibited individuals, 362–366
Beldarrain, M. G., 328
Belief(s)
and actions, 401
conflicts in, 401–403
disconfirmation of, 106
in fate, 329–330
global, 258, 261, 264

Belief(s), *continued*
homeostasis, 128
incongruence of, 287–289
justice, 279–281, 283–284
in meaning maintenance, 38–39
religious, 140, 262, 285
resolving dissonance by changing, 406
shaping of reality by, 279
stereotypic, 109–110
in synchronicities, 328
in system justification theory, 280
threats to, 281–282, 290
universal, 279–280
and well-being of cancer survivors, 264–267
Belief in Ultimate Justice Scale (BUJ), 284
Belongingness, 82, 310
Belson, K., 206
Benefit finding
mechanisms for, 351
as type of meaning, 341–343
Benevolence, assumptions about, 280
Benign disinhibition effect, 366–368, 372–373
Bentham, Jeremy, 94
Bereavement
meaning making after, 243–244
reappraisals in coping with, 285
religious coping with, 411–412
religious faith and meaning in life during, 448
Berkowitz, K., 97–98
Berridge, Kent, 95
Betz, A. L., 159
Biases
cognitive, 280–281
fading affect, 155–156
hindsight, 343–344
ingroup, 305–306
motivational, 455–457
Big Five personality dimensions
and differences in counterfactual thinking, 331
and dispositional traits, 175–176
and lay theories of personality, 126
Binswanger, Ludwig, 466
Biological motivations
for morality, 193
for seeking meaning, 220–222
Biological needs, truth motivation and, 94–95
Biological structures, conservation of, 21–22
Biopsychosocial (BPS) model, 386
BIS. *See* Behavioral inhibition system
Black Americans, uncertainty in intergroup interactions for, 388
Blame, 240, 250
Blascovich, J., 388
Blood pressure, as measure of threat, 386, 389
Bluck, S., 156, 181
Boon, C., 241
Bosnian refugees, memories of, 158
Boss, Melard, 466
BPS (biopsychosocial) model, 386
Bradley, S. L., 265
Bratslavsky, E., 163–164
Brewer, M. B., 194
Brown, J. D., 325–326
Bruner, Jerome, 77, 81
BUJ (Belief in Ultimate Justice Scale), 284
Bulman, R. J., 239
Burgess, A. W., 342
Burgoon, J. K., 393
Burrus, J., 330
Burton, C., 128
Bush, George W., 332
Butler, R., 118
Bystander effect, 367–368

Calling, autobiographical authors' view of their, 183
Campbell, D. T., 194
Campbell, Joseph, 326
Camus, A., 5–8, 74, 75, 216
Cancer survivors, 257–270
appraised meaning for, 265–266
counterfactual thinking by, 342
defined, 263
future research on, 269–270
global meaning for, 264–265
meaning discrepancies for, 266–267
meaning-making model of coping for, 258–262
meaning-making process for, 267–268
meaning revision by, 268–269

phases of survivorship, 263–264
religion as source of meaning for, 264–268
Carder, B., 97–98
Carver, C. S., 363, 365, 370
Category-based expectancies, violation of, 391–392
Caudal segment (hypothalamus), 24, 34
Causal attributions
by cancer survivors, 265–266
cognitive load and uncertainty about, 140
counterfactual thinking in, 320–321, 348–349
and moral judgments, 200–201
Central neurophysiological processes, 384
Cerebral cortex, 29
Certainty, 5, 330
Challenge(s)
biopsychosocial model of, 386
entity vs. incremental theorists' views of, 118–119
to lay theories of personality, 122–125, 127–128
Childhood sexual abuse, 241–242
Children
anthropocentric thinking by, 139
dominance hierarchy for, 36
lay theories of personality by, 118–119
MAP schemas of, 25
memory research in, 150
morality in, 27
play as social cognition by, 26–27
pursuit of goals by, 178
schemata of, 78
symbolic perceptions of, 52–53
teleological reasoning of, 140
truth effectiveness for, 98
Chomsky, N., 193
Christians, mortality salience of, 54, 62
Closure
and emotional responses to memories, 155
and meaning making for negative events, 423
need for, 56, 331
and Openness to Experience, 332
Coen, Stanley J., 472
Cognitive biases, justice beliefs and, 280–281
Cognitive compensation, 79, 82–83. *See also* Compensatory responses
Cognitive consistency
in meaning frameworks, 72–73
and reality, 104–106
in terror management, 55–56
Cognitive dissonance
aversive arousal from, 383
and behavior, 402
and hand washing, 395
meaning restoration after, 392–394
in social psychology, 78–79
as trigger for threat, 388–389
Cognitive dissonance theory, 79–80, 104
Cognitive load, causal uncertainty and, 140
Cognitive maps, 35
Cognitive processes
conscious, 438–439
construals of mortality salience in, 58
morality in, 199–201
social-, 55–57
for truth motivation fulfillment, 100
unconscious, 83, 438–439
Cognitive restructuring, after collective trauma, 246–247
Coherence
as function of meaning, 407–408
and religious coping, 412
restoration of, 410, 412
Collective traumas
Columbine High School shootings as, 245–246
meaning-making after, 245–250
natural disasters as, 246–247
September 11 terrorist attacks as, 247–250
as violation of expectations, 237–238
Columbine High School shootings, 245–246
Commitment, 82, 323, 324
Communication
autobiographical memories in, 157
goals of, 107–110, 157
interpersonal, 107
and shared reality, 107–110
Community, sense of, 449–450

Community-shared stereotypic beliefs, 109–110
Comparator theory, 30–31
Compensatory control, 286–287
Compensatory conviction, 406
Compensatory responses, 279–290. *See also* Cognitive compensation
  and belief incongruence, 287–289
  to challenges of personality theories, 123, 128–129
  and justice beliefs, 280–281
  to meaning threats, 224
  to negative experiences, 281–282
  not involving self or death, 82–83
  and personal control, 82, 284–287
  to positive outcomes, 282–284
Competition, cooperation and, 39–40
Competition of cues model, 455–456
Complete objective modeling, hypothesis of, 31
Complexity, meaning making to deal with, 39
Comprehensibility, meaning as, 192, 239
Concepts, relation of objects to, 20
Concordance, 28–29, 408
Confidence
  epistemic, 116–117
  prediction, 124–125
Conflict(s)
  and ACC activation, 404
  of beliefs, 401–403
  in existential psychotherapy, 467
  of social pressure and personal values, 368
Conflicts of interest, 39
Conscientiousness, 176
Conscious cognitive processes, in meaning making, 438–439
Consciousness, autonoetic, 150
Conservation tasks, 81
Conservatives, values of, 179
Consolidate or augment model, 223–230
  predictions from, 225–230
  and value of search for meaning, 223–224
Constructive meaning making, 332–333
Consummatory rewards, 24–25
Contamination sequences, 326
Content, of autobiographical memories, 156–159
Control
  compensatory, 286–287
  and counterfactual thinking about meaning, 350
  desire for, 141
  and fate in meaning making, 330
  and meaning-focused coping, 260
  and meaning making after traumas, 282
  of motor systems, 24n4
  and pattern completion, 138–139
  personal, 82, 284–287
  and situational meanings, 258, 265
  and uncontrollability as threat, 285
  vicarious, 285
Control effectiveness, truth motivation and, 97–98
Control estimation tasks, 122
Control motivation, 92–93, 408
Conviction, compensatory, 406
Cooper, J., 392
Cooperation, 26, 39–40
Coping
  autobiographical memories about, 162
  by cancer survivors, 266
  with collective traumas, 248–249
  downward social comparisons in, 325
  and meaning making after personal trauma, 240–241
  meaning-making model of, 258–262, 448
  and meaning making/stress, 438
  nostalgia in, 308–309
  with personal traumas, 243
  reappraisals in, 285
  religious, 411–412
Core details, of event memories, 158
Cornblat, M. W., 268
Cortisol, as measure of aversive arousal, 386, 388
Cosmides, L., 194
Costanzo, E. S., 265
Counterfactual fallacy, 345
Counterfactual thinking, 317–333, 339–351
  abnormal counterfactuals, 319
  about negative experiences, 289–290

almost counterfactuals, 319, 327
and constructive vs. defensive meaning making, 332–333
creating coherence with, 408
defined, 318, 340
deliberate counterfactuals, 328
downward, 324–325, 340, 342, 345, 350
and fate, 329–330
individual differences in, 331–332
in mechanisms for meaning making, 350–351
personal meaning from, 320–329
and pleasures of surprise, 432–433
problem solving with, 318–320
sense-making function of, 346–350
spontaneous, 327–329
and threat, 395
and types of meaning, 341–345
upward, 324–326, 340, 350
Crawley, R. A., 155
Creeping determinism, 343
Cuddy, A. J., 202
Cultural value, of life, 186
Cultural worldview
defending, 54–55, 80
and mortality salience, 80
in multilevel meaning-making, 51–53
Culture
audience-tuned memories in, 109–110
in narrative identity, 181–183
universal morality in, 192
Cybernetic framework, for MAP schemas, 30

Damasio, A. R., 163
Darley, J. M., 360, 369, 371
Dasein, 75
Davis, C. G., 244, 341, 351
Davis, W., 58
Death
accessibility of thoughts about, 305
in existentialist theories of meaning, 75–76
in existential psychotherapy, 467–468, 471
meaning compensation not involving, 82–83
in psychology of meaning, 79–81
in terror management theory, 64
Death awareness, 54–65. *See also* Mortality salience
as catalyst for meaning, 64–65
and consolidate/augment model, 225
and ingroup bias, 305–306
and macro-level strategies for meaning maintenance, 54–55
and micro-level strategies for meaning maintenance, 55–57
and perceptual shifts, 57–59
and self-esteem, 59–61
Deci, E. L., 203
Decision making, counterfactual thinking in, 327–328
Defense mechanisms, in existentialism, 459, 467–470
Defensive meaning making, 332–333
Defying-the-odds accounts, 351
Dehumanization, 142–143
Del Gaiso, A. K., 203, 341, 446
Deliberate counterfactuals, 328
Demaree, H. A., 389
Democritus, 19
Dennett, Daniel, 17, 137, 138
Depression
and existential anxiety, 470–472
worldview defending by depressed individuals, 55
Descartes, Rene, 5
Desire
for control, 141
for meaning, 137–138
as motivation, 31
Destiny, 322. *See also* Fate
Determinism, 466
in counterfactual thinking research, 347–348
creeping, 343
fatalistic, 344–346
scientific, 345
Development
autobiographical memory during, 152–153
personal value during, 52–53
Devine, P. G., 393
De Waal, F., 26, 191
Dewhurst, S. A., 158

Dichotic listening paradigm, 120
Dickerson, S. S., 386, 388
Diener, Ed, 95
Dilthey, W., 402
Diogenes Laertius, 18
Discomfort, psychological, 393–394
Discrimination, 390–391
Discussion, for meaning making, 252
Disengagement, moral, 195–196
Disequilibrium, of schemata and experiences, 78, 81
Disinhibition
activation of disinhibition system, 368
behavioral, 366–367, 371–373
benign disinhibition effect, 366–368, 372–373
online disinhibition effect, 373–374
sense making by disinhibited individuals, 366–370
toxic, 374
Dispositional skills/traits, of social actors, 175–176
Distress
after traumas, 241, 242, 244, 247
of cancer survivors, 266
in equity theory, 361
from expectancy violations, 77
freedom as source of, 468
from global/situational meaning conflicts, 260–261
meaning making in response to, 238, 241, 242, 244, 247
religion and isolation from, 412
and searching for meaning, 219
from threats to beliefs, 281
from threats to meaning, 408–409
Dodes, Lance, 95
Dominance hierarchy, 25–27, 36
Downey, G., 243
Downward counterfactual thinking, 340
about pivotal moments, 324–325
assumptions in sense making and, 350
benefit finding with, 342
and fatalistic determinism, 345
Downward social comparisons, 325
Drive theories, 97, 221
Dual processing models, 199
Dunn, E. W., 205
Dweck, C. S., 119

Eastern cultures, search for meaning in life in, 220–225
Ebbinghaus, H., 150, 165
Ecological optics, 19
Effectance motivation, 137–138
Effectiveness
control, 97–98
truth, 97–99
value, 96–97
Efficacy, of social actors, 173
Effort, usefulness of, 117–119
Ego threats, 333
Eisenberger, N. I., 364
Eliezer, D., 391
Eliot, T. S., 317
Elkin, R. A., 394
Elkind, D., 181
Ellemers, N., 194
Elliot, A. J., 393, 408
Ellis, S., 345
Emerging adulthood, autobiographical authors in, 180–182
Emotional dysregulation, meaning restoration and, 466
Emotional events, attention paid to, 433–434
Emotional responses
of cancer survivors, 263
duration of, 421–422
to memories, 155–156
Emotion-focused coping, 260
Emotions
and extraversion, 176
and MAP schemas, 32
memories associated with, 163–164
negative, 32, 163–164
neutral, 164
and nostalgia, 300
positive, 32, 163–164, 176, 300
Empathy, 26
Endings, in life stories, 323–324
Entity theory of personality, 115–129
defined, 115
as framework for prediction, 125–126
implicit benefits of, 129

individual differences in theorists of, 126–128
malleability of traits and abilities in, 117–119
measuring endorsement of, 116
self-preservation of, 119–125
value of behavior in, 117
Epinephrine, 385
Episodic memory, 150
Epistemic confidence, lay theories of, 116–117
Epistemic perspective
on meaning, 5–7
on sense making, 374
Epstein, Greer, 339
Equity theory, 361–362
Erikson, E. H., 180–182
ERPs (event-related potentials), 402–403
Error-related negativity, 403, 405, 411
Errors
and anterior cingulate cortex activation, 404–405
in autobiographical memories, 160
Ersner-Hershfield, H., 324, 327, 329
Eudaimonia, 204, 216
Eudaimonic approach to well-being, 203–206, 450–452
Event age, 159–160
Event order, event age and, 159
Event-related potentials (ERPs), 402–403
Evolutionary approach to perception, 22–24
Evolutionary theory
mortality salience and acceptance of, 63
social role performance in, 174–175
Exclusion, social, 450
Existential fear, 63
Existential isolation, 468–472
Existential psychotherapy, 456–477
clinical practice of, 470–474
history of, 466–470
layers of defense mechanisms in, 467–470
restoring meaning in, 474
Existential Psychotherapy (Irvin Yalom), 466–467
Existential theories of meaning, 71–76
the absurd in, 72–73
angst in, 74–75
and existentialists as psychologists, 76–77
self and death in, 75–76
Existential threat, counterfactual thinking as, 332
Expectancy disconfirmation, 105–106
Expectancy violation(s), 12–13, 383, 465–477
category-based, 391–392
and meaning making, 360
and meaning restoration, 465
for self, 75–76
self-image-based, 389–390
surprise as, 433
traumas as, 237–238
as triggers for threat response, 389–392
and violations of lay theories, 116–117, 122
worldview-based, 390–391
Expectations
and anterior cingulate cortex activation, 404–405
in consolidate or augment model, 224
and counterfactual thinking, 327, 349
and experiences, 30
Experiences
assimilation of schemata and, 78
autobiographical, 305, 307–308, 333
and expectations, 30
in nostalgia narratives, 303
perception of past, 59
phenomenological, 446
reinterpretation of, 77–78
transience of, 149
Experimental psychology, measures of meaning in, 4
Explainability, 433–436
Explanations, for events, 422
Explanatory coherence account, 351
Exploratory behavior, in MAP schemas, 34–35
External justification, of negative experiences, 288–289

External sources of meaning, 172
Extrapersonal causes, 345–346, 350. *See also* Fate
Extraversion, 176
Extreme sports, pleasure as motivator in, 95–96
Extrinsic goals, 64
Eysenck, H. J., 18

Fading affect bias, 155–156
Faith
- absurdity of, 72
- and meaning in life, 448–449
- and mortality salience, 54–55, 62
- and multilevel meaning-making, 54

False hope syndrome, 129
Family, 162, 297
Fatalistic determinism, 344–346
Fate, 329–330
- in counterfactual thinking, 342, 346–348
- in meaning making after traumas, 239
- and need for closure, 331
- in reappraisals of negative experiences, 285

Fear, existential, 63
FedEx, 322
Feedback
- about morality and meaning in life, 205–206
- entity vs. incremental theorists' views of, 119, 124–125
- and mortality concerns, 60

Feedback-regulated negativity potential, 403, 405
Festinger, L., 55, 78, 105, 106, 288, 289, 402
Finkenauer, C., 163–164
Fischhoff, B., 343, 344
Fiske, S. T., 202
Fitzsimons, G. M., 287
Fixed affect, 156
Flabbergasted individuals, 360–362, 465
Flexible affect, 156
Flourishing affect, 156
Fluid compensation models of meaning, 402–403
Fogassi, L., 28
Formal operational thought, by adolescents, 181
The Foundations of Hedonic Psychology (Kahneman, Diener, & Schwarz), 95
Frame problem, 17
Frameworks for meaning, 17–42
- considering multiple forms of meaning, 20–21
- at intersection of the known and unknown, 38–42
- the known as, 21–29
- and nature of reality, 18–20
- and reality, 18–20, 383
- in sense making, 14
- the unknown as, 29–38

Frankl, Viktor, 6–8, 74, 216, 218, 221, 447, 466, 468, 469
Frantz, C. M., 192
Frazier, P., 218
Frederickson, B. L., 164, 176
Freedom, 217, 468
Freezing function, of need for closure, 331
Freud, Sigmund, 94, 466
Friedman, R. S., 56
Friends, 162, 297
Frontal cortex, 406
Future
- counterfactual thinking and narratives about, 323–324
- mortality awareness and perception of, 59
- motivated models of present and, 31

Galinsky, A. D., 319–320, 333
Gall, T. L., 268
Gallese, V., 28
Games
- competition and cooperation in, 39–40
- joint schemas in, 27–28

Garcia-Monco, J. C., 328
Geertz, C., 449
General Electric, 361
Generative roles, meaning in life from, 174
Generativity
- and construction of life stories, 320

and early blessings/advantages, 322–323
and life trajectory, 326
and redemptive narratives of Americans, 182–184
Gentsch, A., 404–405
Genuine self, 372–374
Gerard, H. B., 389
Gibson, J. J., 18, 19, 161
Giffords, Gabrielle (attempted assassination), 329
Gilbert, D. T., 342, 429–432, 434–435
Gist memory, 161–162
Gladwell, Malcolm, 317–318
Glick, P., 202
Global attentional focus, 453–454
Global beliefs, 258, 261, 264
Global goals, 258, 261, 264–265
Global meaning, 257
for cancer survivors, 264–265
defined, 258
discrepancy of situational and, 260–261
in meaning-making model of coping, 259
meanings made as changes in, 261–262
reappraisals of, 268
Goals
and actions, 401
behavior and, 408
extrinsic, 64
global, 258, 261, 264–265
and MAP schemas, 22
meaning in life from pursuit of, 176–179
personal, 177, 184–186
pursuit of, 409–410
in religious systems, 410
salience of, 409
threats to, 409–410
vertical coherence of, 407–408
Goal theories, 97
Goffman, E., 51, 175
Goldenberg, J. L., 55
Gonzalez, A., 328
Grafman, J., 328
Gray, J. A., 17, 30–32, 363, 365, 370
Greco, V., 388
Green, Christina Taylor, 329
Green, J. D., 205
Greenberg, J., 54–56, 60
Group-based sociality, morality from, 191–192
Groups, social roles in, 174–175
Growth
in narrative identity, 154–155
personal, 269
self-, 451
stress-related, 269

Habermas, T., 181
Habits, 37, 75
Haidt, J., 193n1, 199
Hand washing, 395
Happiness, 203, 216, 452–455
Hart, J., 62
Hawkins, N. A., 245–246
Hedonic approach to well-being, 203
Hedonism
and eudaimonic well-being, 451
as heuristic for meaning in life, 452–453
and truth effectiveness, 98
and truth motivation, 91–92, 94–95
and value effectiveness, 97
Hegel, Georg Wilhelm, 77
Heidegger, M., 74–76
Heider, Fritz, 55, 104, 105, 137–139
Heine, S. J., 82, 222–223, 329, 384, 402
Herlihy, J., 158
Herman, C. P., 129
Hero's journey, 41, 184, 326
The Hero With a Thousand Faces (Joseph Campbell), 326
Hershfield, H. E., 333
Hicks, J., 203
Hicks, J. A., 341, 446, 455–456
Hierarchies
dominance, 25–27, 36
of MAP schemas, 25–29, 32
Higgins, E. T., 107–108
High points, in life stories, 324–326
Hindsight bias, 343–344
Hippocampus, 34–36
Hirsch, J. B., 411
Hofer, Johannes, 298
Holman, E. A., 245–246, 248

Holmes, T. H., 162
Holmstrom, L., 342
Homeostasis, 221–222
Homeostasis beliefs, 127–128
Homesickness, nostalgia vs., 299
Hope, schema maintenance and, 33
Howsepian, B. A., 266
HPA activation. *See* Hypothalamic-pituitary-adrenal cortical activation
Human alarm system, 363–364
Human functioning, meaning in life in, 445, 446, 458
Humans
  dominance hierarchies of, 25–26, 36
  methods of dealing with complexity for, 39
  perception by, 23–24
Hume, David, 136, 138, 143
Husserl, Albrecht, 77
Hydra, perception by, 23
Hyperthymesia, 160–161
Hypothalamic-pituitary-adrenal cortical (HPA) activation
  assessment of, 385–386
  in BPS model of challenge and threat, 386
  as peripheral neurophysiological process, 385
Hypothalamus, 23–24, 34

Identity. *See also* Narrative identity
  in emerging adulthood, 180–181
  MAP schemas in, 25
  of social actors, 174
Ideology, mortality and, 62–63
Imbalances, cognitive, 104–105
Imitation, 28–29
Implicit Theories Questionnaire, 116
Impression formation, 201–202
Improvement, entity vs. incremental views of, 117–119
Inauthentic responses, 75
Incongruence, of beliefs, 287–289
Incremental theory of personality, 115–129
  defined, 115
  as framework for prediction, 125–126
  implicit benefits of, 128–129
  individual differences in theorists, 126–128
  malleability of traits and abilities in, 117–119
  measuring endorsement of, 116
  self-preservation of, 119–125
  value of behavior in, 117
Individual differences, in personality, 126–127
Inductive reasoning, 139
Inequity, 361–362, 369–370
Infants, as social actors, 175
Information processing, counterfactual thinking in, 319
Ingroup bias, death salience and, 305–306
Ingroup morality, 193–196
Inhibited individuals, sense making by, 362–366
Inhibition, public, 367
Instrumental values, 179
Insufficiency, MAP schemas and, 22
Intelligence
  lay theories of, 123–124
  malleability of, 118–119
Intelligent design theory, 63
Intentionality
  in establishing reality, 101–102
  in moral judgments, 200–201
  and negative outcomes, 140–141
The Intentional Stance (Daniel Dennett), 137
Interconnectedness, 74
Intergroup interactions, 388, 390
Intergroup prejudice, 61
Internal sources, of meaning in life, 172
Internet, online disinhibition effect on, 373–374
Interpersonal communication, shared reality and, 107
Interpersonal interactions
  category-based expectancies in, 391–392
  pleasures of uncertainty in, 429
Interpersonal isolation, 468
Interpersonal relationships, surprise in, 431–432
Intervention, nostalgia as, 311

Intrinsic meaning, of autobiographical memories, 160–163
Intuitive decision making, counterfactuals in, 328
Intuitive moral judgments, 199–202
Inzlicht, M., 411
Iraq war, 332
Irrationality, of faith, 72
Isolation, existential, 468–472
Israel–Lebanon war, 411–412

James, William, 98, 100, 177, 410
Janoff-Bulman, R., 77, 192, 196, 197, 238, 251, 280, 283, 290, 349
Japanese earthquake and nuclear disaster, 206
Japanese students, meaning seeking models for, 229
Jennings, J. R., 387
Jensen, T. K., 325
Jobs, as sources of meaning, 173–174
Johnson, L. C., 411
Judgmentalism, search for meaning and, 220
Judgments
- establishing reality with, 101–102
- intuitive moral, 199–202
- of well-being, 453–454

Juhl, J., 58
Jung, C. G., 176
Justice, need for structure and, 57
Justice beliefs, 279–280
- and compensatory responses, 280–281
- and offsetting of positive outcomes, 283–284

Justification
- of behaviors, 8
- for negative experiences, 288–289

Just world theory, 77–78

Kahneman, D., 95, 327
Kaler, M., 218
Kant, I., 77, 366
Kashdan, T. B., 219
Kasser, T., 407
Kawabata, Y., 220
Kay, A. C., 287, 392
Kemeny, M. E., 386, 388
Keynes, John Maynard, 96
Kierkegaard, S., 71–73, 75, 77
King, L. A., 176, 203, 341, 446, 452–453, 455, 456–457
Klinger, E., 218
Knobe, J., 199–202
The known
- as framework for meaning, 21–29
- intersection of unknown and, 38–42

Kohlberg, L., 199
Koo, M., 342, 426, 427, 432, 433
Kosovo refugees, memories of, 158
Kramer, R. M., 201–202
Kray, L. J., 289–290, 319–320, 322, 324, 325, 329–331, 333, 342, 350, 395, 408, 433n1
Kross, E., 423
Kruglanski, A. W., 331
Krull, J., 203, 341, 446
Kuhn, Thomas, 77
Kurtz, J. L., 426

Landau, M., 57, 60
Larson, J., 341
Latané, B., 360, 361, 364, 367, 369, 371
Lay theories of personality, 115–129
- as framework for prediction, 125–126
- function of, 115–117
- implicit benefits of, 128–129
- individual differences of theorists, 126–128
- malleability of abilities in, 117–119
- modes of social thought in, 117–129
- self-preservation of, 119–125
- terminology for, 116

Leach, C. W., 194
Learning
- entity vs. incremental views of, 118
- negative, 37–38

Lee, Y. H., 427
Leippe, M. R., 394
Le Poire, B. A., 393
Lerner, M. J., 77
Levine, L. J., 156
Lewin, Kurt, 97
Liberals, values of, 179
Lichtman, R. R., 342
Lieberman, M. D., 364
Life, meaning in. *See* Meaning in life

Life pursuits, effectiveness in, 96–99
Life stages, 159
Life stories. *See also related topics, e.g.:* Autobiographical memory(-ies)
beginnings in, 322–323
construction of, 318, 320–327
endings in, 323–324
high and low points in, 324–326
trajectories and redemptive themes in, 326–327
turning points in, 321–322
Life trajectories, narratives about, 326–327
Liking, wanting vs., 95
Listening, dichotic, 120
Little, B. R., 402, 407
Living beyond cancer stage, 263
Living through cancer stage, 263
Living with cancer stage, 263
Loftus, E. F., 151
Logotherapy, 447
Lohan, J., 411
Loneliness
and meaning in life, 450, 453–454
as nostalgia trigger, 301
and positive affect, 453–454
Long-term memories, accuracy and accessibility of, 161
Long-term relationships, surprise in, 431–432
Low points, in life stories, 324–326
Luria, A. R., 30–32
Lutgendorf, S. K., 265
Lydon, J. E., 408
Lyon, D., 54

Macro-level meaning-making, 50, 53
and cultural worldview, 51
and death awareness, 54–55
self-esteem in, 53
Maddi, S. R., 172, 218
The Mahabharata, 217
Maintain or restore models
predictions from, 225–230
and value of search for meaning, 222–223
Major, B., 390, 391
Maladaptive response, meaning making as, 240–241
Malleability
of abilities, 117–119
of meaning in life, 458
of personality traits, 117–119. *See also* Incremental theory of personality
Maniar, D., 344
Man's Search for Meaning (Viktor Frankl), 216
MAP (motivation, action, perception) schemas, 22–29
components of, 22
and consummatory rewards, 24–25
disruptions in, 29–38
and evolutionary approach to perception, 22–24
joint construction of, 28–29
shattering of, 37
in social groups and hierarchies, 25–29
Marlborough, M., 158
Martens, J. P., 63
Mastery, perceived vs. real, 143
Mastery motivation, 139–142
May, Rollo, 466
McAdams, D. P., 320, 322, 326, 332
McCrae, R. R., 332
McGregor, I., 402, 406, 407, 409–411
McIntosh, D. N., 245–246
McLean, K. C., 153, 154
McNaughton, N., 363, 370
Meaning
conceptualization of, 383
considering multiple forms of, 20–21
desire for, 137–138
epistemic perspective on, 5–7
function of, 407–410
measures of, 4
new science of, 477
nostalgia as provider of, 306–310
purpose vs., 7–8
and reduction in threat, 395
restoring, after violations of, 12–13
and sense making, 13–14
situational, 239
teleological perspective of, 6–7
terminology for, 50, 341, 402
types of, 192, 341–345
variety of research on, 4

Meaning compensation, 82–83.
See also Compensatory responses; Violation compensation
Meaning consolidation, 222
Meaningful living, 216
Meaningfulness
of autobiographical memories, 162–163
in global meaning, 258
Meaning in life, 171–186, 445–459.
See also Search for meaning in life
and adaptation, 457–459
for autobiographical authors, 180–184
defined, 446
and eudaimonia, 450–452
from family and friends, 297
importance of, 446–447
in meaning-making model of coping, 261
and morality, 196, 202–206
and mortality salience, 304–305
for motivated agents, 176–179
motivational biases in, 455–457
negative experiences in, 286
and nostalgia proneness, 306–307
and positive affect, 203, 452–455, 457–459
presence of vs. search for, 341
and rationalization of negative experiences, 286–289
re-creation of, by trauma survivors, 198
religious faith in, 448–449
for social actors, 173–176
social relationships in, 449–450
sources of, 171–172, 447–448
for victims, 283
Meaninglessness
as in existential psychotherapy, 469
feelings of, 52–54
in history of philosophy, 216, 217
as nostalgia trigger, 308
of trauma victims, 197
Meaning maintenance, 38–39, 382
Meaning maintenance model, 222–223
Meaning makers, positions of, 172–173
Meaning making
in affective adaptation, 422, 423
and autobiographical memory, 155–160
and changes in situational/global meaning, 261–262
constructive vs. defensive, 332–333
counterfactual thinking in, 350–351
and expectancy violations, 360
mechanisms for, 350–351
from nostalgia, 303–310
with religion, 267–268
and uncertainty, 436–439
Meaning-making model of coping, 258–262, 448
Meaning of Life Questionnaire (MLQ), 218–219, 226–229, 288
Meaning restoration. See also Maintain or restore models
after expectancy violations, 465
after meaning violations, 12–13, 393–394
after threats, 392–393, 403
future research on, 395
for low-PNS individuals, 62
in system justification theory, 282–283
Meaning revision, by cancer survivors, 268–269
Meaning seeking process
and experiencing meaning, 225–230
experiencing meaning and, 219–220
motivation for, 215–216
reasons for, 218–219
Meanings made, 259, 261–262
Meaning violations, 381–396
aversive arousal from, 383–384
for cancer survivors, 266–267
defined, 381
and interconnectedness, 74
and meaning restoration after threats, 392–393
and psychological indexes of aversive arousal, 384–387
restoring meaning after, 12–13, 393–394
for self, 73
as triggers for threat, 387–392
Melville, H., 329
Memory(-ies). See also Autobiographical memory(-ies)

Memory(-ies), *continued*
in ancient cultures, 149–150
emotional responses to, 155–156
gist, 161–162
reconstruction errors in, 160
and rehearsal, 151
Memory bias, 108
Mendes, W. B., 391
Mentalistic concepts, 138
Mental state, behavior and, 138, 139
Meritocracy, 390
Merluzzi, T. V., 266
Messick, D. M., 201–202
Meta rules for moral conduct, 193–194
Micro-level meaning-making, 50, 53
and perceptions of social environment, 51–52, 58
self-esteem in, 53
Milgram, S., 360, 361, 369
Miller, G. A., 19
Mirror neurons, 28–29
Missions, of autobiographical authors, 183
MLQ. *See* Meaning of Life Questionnaire
Molden, D. C., 117
Monat, A., 387
Mood. *See also* Positive affect
after meaning violations, 75
and meaning in life, 446, 456, 459
as nostalgia trigger, 301–302
and surprise, 435–436
and uncertainty, 431
Mood as information perspective, 457
Moral disengagement, 195–196
Moral inversion, 196–198
Morality, 191–207
aspects of, 192–194
in children, 27
ingroup, 193–194
at intersection of the known and unknown, 41
and intuitive moral judgments, 199–202
and meaning in life, 196, 202–206
and meaning maintenance, 39
and "moral universe," 194–198
and well-being, 202–206
Moral judgments, intuitive, 199–202
Moral philosophy, search for meaning in, 217–218
"Moral universe," 194–198
Mortality concerns
absurdity of, 76
ideology as buffer against, 62–63
self-esteem as buffer against, 60–61
Mortality salience, 54–62
cognitive compensation without, 82–83
and defense of cultural worldview, 80
effect of nostalgia on, 304–306
and ingroup bias, 305–306
in macro-level meaning maintenance, 54–55
in micro-level meaning maintenance, 55–57
perceptual shifts in, 57–59
and self-esteem, 59–61
Motivated agents
meaning in life for, 176–179
meaning makers as, 172
Motivated models of present and future, 31
Motivation. *See also* Truth motivation
for autobiographical storytelling, 152
biological, 193, 220–222
control, 92–93, 408
desire as, 31
effectance, 137–138
mastery, 139–142
for multilevel meaning-making, 50
reality and motivational mechanisms, 100–101
sociality, 137
value, 92–93
will to meaning as, 74
Motivation, action, perception schemas. *See* MAP schemas
Motivational biases, 455–457
Motivational systems
approach, 34–35, 405–407, 409–410
avoidance/aversive, 365, 405–406
Motor systems, control of, 24n4
Mowrer, Orval Hobart, 94–95
Multilevel meaning-making, 49–65
death awareness as catalyst for, 64–65
and importance of feeling valued, 52–54
maintaining multilevel meaning, 54–57

open-minded thinking in, 61–64
perceptual shifts in, 57–59
self-esteem in, 59–61
for sustaining personal value, 50–52
Mumon, 215, 230
Murphy, S. A., 411
Music, nostalgia evoked by, 307
Muslims, open-mindedness of, 62
Mythology
as intersection of the known and unknown, 40–41
life stories in, 326

Narrative identity
and autobiographical memory, 153–155
meaning in life from, 180–184
selection of memories for, 164–165
turning points in, 322
Narratives, redemptive, 182–184, 326–327
Nash, K., 410, 411
National Coalition for Cancer Survivorship, 263
Natural disasters
meaning-making in, 246–247
moral inversions from, 197
Naturalism, 63
Nausea (Jean-Paul Sartre), 458–459
Ndiaye, D. G., 427, 434–435
Near-loss mind-sets, 324
Need for closure, 56, 331
Needs, meaning in life from, 172
Negative affect
and emotional responses to memories, 155
and fading effect bias, 155–156
and meaning making for negative events, 423
and nostalgia, 300, 301
Negative emotions
memories associated with, 163–164
and obstacles to MAP schemas, 32
Negative events
adaptation to, 4, 422–423, 437–439
counterfactual thinking about, 324–325
emotional responses to, 155
meaning making for, 437–439
in narrative identity, 154–155
role of, 281–282
self enhancement with recalling of, 157–158
Negative learning, 37–38
Negative outcomes, intentional agency and, 140–141
Negative valuation, of memories, 163
Negativity
error-related, 403, 405, 411
self-processing and minimization of, 158
Neisser, Ulric, 162
Nervous system, complexity and reaction time of, 22–24
Nestler, S., 344
Neurological condition, nostalgia as, 298–299
Neuroticism, 127, 176
Neutral emotions, memories associated with, 164
Newcomb, Theodore, 104
Nichomachean Ethics (Aristotle), 204
Nickerson, R. S., 161
Nida, S., 361, 364, 367
Nietzsche, F., 77, 218
Nolen-Hoeksema, S., 341
Nonrelations, 74
Norton, M., 205
Nostalgia, 297–312
content, triggers, and functions of, 300–303
future research on, 310–311
historical research on, 298–299
meaning making from, 303–310
and mortality salience, 59
Novelty, rate of adaptation and, 425
Novelty seeking, 224–225
Nussbaum, D. A., 119
Nussbaum, M., 204

Objects
perceptions of, 18–20
relation of concepts to, 20
Obstacles, MAP schema, 32
Ocker, B. L., 434–435
Oishi, S., 218
Old Testament, 217
Online disinhibition effect, 373–374
Open-mindededness, 61–64
Openness to Experience, 331–332

Operational thought, by adolescents, 181
Optimal arousal model, 222, 223
Order, in representations of reality, 19
Orienting response, 30–31, 34, 37–38, 393
Origin stories, 322–323
Outcomes
negative, 140–141
positive, 282–284, 342, 447
uncertainty and valence of, 430–431

Pain
and existential anxiety, 472–474
as motivator, 94–96
social, 364
Pals, J. L., 154
Paradigms
dichotic listening, 120
and experience of reality, 77
revision of, 77–78
spreading of alternatives, 389
Paralysis, meaning making by patients with, 240
Pargament, K. I., 262
Park, C. L., 281, 437, 448
Park, M., 339
Parkinson's patients, counterfactual thinking by, 319
Past events
counterfactual thinking about, 318. *See also* Counterfactual thinking
perception of, 59
reflections on. *See* Nostalgia
Pattern completion, loss of control and, 138–139
Peck, M. Scott, 328
Peirce, C. S., 18
Pennebaker, J. W., 438
Pepitone, A., 330
Perceived mastery, real vs., 143
Perception. *See also* MAP (motivation, action, perception) schemas
evolutionary approach to, 22–24
frameworks for, 17–18
limits of, 21
multilevel meaning-making and shifts in, 57–59
of objects, 18–20
of positive outcomes, 282–284
of social environment, 51–52
Peripheral details, of memories, 158
Peripheral neurophysiological processes
associated with threat, 384–387
future research on, 394–396
measuring orienting response and vigilance with, 393
Personal control, compensatory responses and, 82, 284–287
Personal fables, 181
Personal goals, 177, 184–186
Personality traits. *See also* Lay theories of personality
Big Five personality dimensions, 126, 175–176, 331
and counterfactual thinking, 331
malleability of, 117–119
and narrative identity, 182
Personal meaning
from counterfactual thinking, 318, 320–329, 351
in narrative identity, 182
and positive affect/meaning in life, 453–454
Personal memories, in ancient cultures, 149–150
Personal need for structure (PNS)
and meaning restoration, 62
and mortality salience, 56–57
and rationalization of negative experiences, 288–289
Personal traumas, 238–245
early studies of meaning-making with, 239–242
longitudinal studies of meaning making with, 243–244
as violation of expectations, 237–238
Personal value(s)
conflict of social pressure and, 368
importance of feeling valued, 52–54
sustaining, 50–52
Peters, F., 366
Phenomenological experiences, 446
Philosophy, search for meaning in life in, 216–218
Physical reality, social vs., 106–107
Physical symptoms, of existential anxiety, 472–474

Piaget, Jean, 30, 32, 78, 81, 181
Pivotal moments, 324–326, 330
Plaks, J. E., 119–126, 128, 392
Play, as social cognition, 26–28
Playing hard to get, 429
Pleasure
and eudaimonic well-being, 204–205
as motivator, 94–96
from possible positive outcome, 431
from surprises, 431–433
from uncertainty, 425–430
Pleasure paradox, 424
PNS. *See* Personal need for structure
Poignancy, 323–324
Political values, 179
Polivy, J., 129
Pope, B., 63
Positive affect
in competition of cues model, 455
from counterfactual thinking, 342
and fading effect bias, 155–156
and meaning in life, 203, 452–455, 457–459
Positive emotions
associated with MAP schemas, 32
and extraversion, 176
memories associated with, 163–164
and nostalgia, 300
Positive events
adaptation to, 423–437
counterfactual thinking about, 432–433
meaning making for, 436–437
pleasure from possibility vs. reality of, 431
Positive illusions, 325–326
Positive mood, meaning in life and, 456
Positive outcomes
and meaning in life, 447
mental undoing of, 342
offsetting of, 283–284
perception of, 282–284
Positive reappraisals, of traumas, 285
Positive reframing, of traumas, 239, 241, 243, 249, 250
Positive valuation, of memories, 163
Postevent processing, of autobiographical memories, 151–153
Posttraumatic stress, 249
Posttraumatic stress disorder (PTSD), 37, 195–196
Power, dehumanization of others and, 143
Predictability, of behavior, 102–104
Prediction confidence, 124–125
Predictions
from lay theories of personality, 125–126
from maintain/restore and consolidate/augment models, 225–230
Prefrontal cortex, counterfactual generation and, 328
Prejudice, intergroup, 61
Presence of Meaning scale, 226, 229
Present, motivated models of, 31
Primacy of evaluation, 199
Primates
dominance hierarchies of, 25–26
MAP schema hierarchies of, 35
Proactive sense making, disinhibition in, 374
Problem-focused coping, 260
Problem solving, 318–320, 374
Productive growth, in narrative identity, 154–155
Progress, motivated agents' view of, 178
Progress narratives, 476
Proself values, 372–373
Prosocial acts, by trauma survivors, 198
Proulx, T., 82, 222–224, 384, 402
Psychological discomfort, 393–394
Psychological health, nostalgia and, 309, 311
Psychological illness, nostalgia as, 299
Psychological indexes of aversive arousal, 384–387
Psychological needs, satisfaction of, 450–453, 457–458
Psychologists, existentialists as, 76–77
Psychology of meaning, 8–12, 76–84
as discipline, 4–5
and meaning compensation without self or death, 82–83
and relational perspective on violation compensation, 83–84
self and death in, 79–81
theory of, 77–79

Psychosomatic physical symptoms, of existential anxiety, 472–474
Psychotherapy, existential. *See* Existential psychotherapy
PTSD (posttraumatic stress disorder), 37, 195–196
Public inhibition, 364, 367
Punishment, behavioral inhibition and, 365–366
Purpose
  and meaning in life, 177
  meaning vs., 7–8
  as necessity, 6–7
  and search for meaning, 218
Pyszczynski, T., 54–56

Qiu, C., 427
Qur'an, 217

Rahe, R. H., 162
Randles, D., 224
Rape victims, counterfactual thinking by, 342
Rationalization
  and external justification, 288–289
  of immoral behavior, 195
  for injustices to self, 284–287
  of negative experiences, 287–289
  and personal need for structure, 287–288
Rats
  exploratory behavior in, 35
  reaction to unexpected threats in, 36
RCOPE measure, 267
Reactive approach model of dissonance, 406
Reactive sense making, inhibition in, 374
Reality, 100–110
  alternate, 319
  beliefs in shaping of, 279
  and cognitive consistency theories, 104–106
  empirical verification of, 52
  and frameworks for meaning, 18–20
  fundamental assumptions about, 280–281
  and intention, 101–102
  and meaning frameworks, 383
  memory as representation of, 160–161, 163
  and motivational mechanisms, 100–101
  paradigms and experience of, 77
  perceptions of objects in, 19–20
  physical, 106–107
  and predictability of behavior, 102–104
  social and shared, 106–110
  subjective experience of, 72–74, 77
Real mastery, perceived vs., 143
Reappraisals
  by cancer survivors, 268
  of negative experiences, 281–282
  religious meanings in, 268
  by trauma victims, 285
Reconstruction, of autobiographical memories, 156–157, 160
Redemptive narratives
  and generativity of Americans, 182–184
  life stories as, 326–327
Redemptive self, 183–184
Rehearsal, memory, 151, 164–165
Reinterpretation, of experiences, 77–78
Relatedness, meaning in life and, 451
Relational perspective on violation compensation, 83–84
Relational processing style, 319–320
Relationships
  counterfactual thinking about origins of, 323
  counterfactual thinking to understand, 318–320
  and meaning in life, 449–450
Religion
  anthropomorphism in, 137
  and appraised meaning, 265–266
  for cancer survivors, 264–266
  and global meaning, 264–265
  meaning frameworks in, 410–412
  and meaning making, 239, 242, 267–268
  moral worldviews in, 196
  and mortality salience, 62
  and search for meaning, 217
Religiosity
  and error-related negativity, 411
  and meaning making after trauma, 252

and personal growth, 269
spirituality vs., 262
Religious beliefs
anthropomorphism in, 140
and meaning in life, 448–449
in reappraisals of negative experiences, 285
U.S. prevalence of, 262
Religious commitment, positive affect and, 453–454
Religious meaning making, 259, 267–268
Religious values, meaning in life and, 179
Reminiscence bump, 158–159
Repetition, as inauthentic response, 75
Responsibility, 367, 468
Restored meaning. *See* Meaning restoration
Revision
of attitudes, 80
of paradigms, 77
of worldviews, 77–78
Rewards, consummatory, 24–25
Rholes, W. S., 107–108
Risk assessment, in reaction to unexpected threats, 36
Rizzolatti, G., 28
The Road Less Traveled (M. Scott Peck), 328
Robinson, J. L., 389
Robinson, Terry, 95
Roese, N. J., 330, 344, 349
Roger, D., 388
Rose, S. L., 265
Rosenblatt, A., 54
Ross, M., 157, 158
Rostral segment (hypothalamus), 24, 34
Routledge, C., 55, 58, 63
Rules of social interaction, 37
Ruminations, 240–242
Ryan, R. M., 203

The sacred, 449
Saffiotti, L., 330
SAM (sympathetic adrenal medullary) activation, 385–387
Sarno, John, 472
Sartre, Jean-Paul, 216–217, 458–459
Satisfaction, relationship, 432
Sawyer, P. J., 391
Saying-is-believing effect, 108, 109
Schemas, 78, 448–449
Scheuchzer, J. J., 298
Schizophrenia patients, counterfactual thinking by, 319
Schwarz, N., 95, 454
Scientific determinism, 345
Scientific psychology, autobiographical memory in, 149–151
Scragg, P., 158
SDT (self-determination theory), 63, 451
Search for meaning in life, 215–230
empirical research on, 218–220
in history of philosophy, 216–218
predictions from maintain/restore and consolidate/augment models, 225–230
presence of meaning in life vs., 341
in Western vs. Eastern cultures, 220–225
Search for Meaning scale, 226
Security, MAP schema maintenance and, 33
The self
in autobiographical memory creation, 151–153, 160
coherence of elements in, 407–408
in existentialist theories of meaning, 75–76
genuine, 372–374
in inductive reasoning, 139
meaning compensation not based on, 82–83
meaning violations for, 73
morality of ingroup and, 194–196
in narrative identity, 153–154
in nostalgia narratives, 300, 302
protection of, 157–158
in psychology of meaning, 79–81
in reconstruction of autobiographical memories, 157–158
redemptive, 183–184
social roles as presentation of, 175
temporal orientation for, 186
as victim of negative experiences, 284–287
Self-concordance, goal attainment and, 408

Self-context, for autobiographical memory, 151–153
Self-determination theory (SDT), 63, 451
Self-enhancement
with autobiographical memories, 157–158
and mortality salience, 60–61
Self-esteem
and approach motivation systems, 410
and lay theory of personality, 126
and mortality concerns/salience, 54, 60–61
in multilevel meaning-making, 59–61
and nostalgia, 302, 310
and personal value, 53
and pursuit of goals, 177
and self-enhancement, 60–61
Self-growth, meaning in life from, 451
Self-image-based expectancies, violation of, 389–390
Self-preservation, of lay theories of personality, 119–125
Self-regulation, function of, 375
Self-relevant meaning, 153–155
Self-threat/self-affirmation studies, 84
Self-verification theory, 389
Self-worth
fundamental assumptions about, 280
and meaning in life, 186
for social actors, 173
Senior citizens, meaning making by, 242
Sensation seeking, biological motivations for, 222
Sense making
anthropomorphism as means of, 136
BIS activation in, 359–360
with counterfactual thinking, 346–350
by disinhibited individuals, 366–370
and event age, 159–160
by flabbergasted individuals, 360–362
as impulse, 5–6
by inhibited individuals, 362–366
as meaning, 4–5, 13–14, 343–346
mechanisms for, 351
morality in evaluations of, 199–202
threat as motivator of, 392–393
Sensory memories, accuracy and accessibility of, 161
September 11 terrorist attacks
counterfactual thinking about, 339–340
meaning-making after, 247–250
Serotonin selective reuptake inhibitors, 37
Shared reality
and audience tuning, 108–110
establishing reality from, 106–110
Sheldon, K. M., 407, 408
Sherif, M., 106–107
Sherman, S. J., 344
Shyness, entity vs. incremental views of, 119
SIDS (sudden infant death syndrome), 243–244
Significance, meaning as, 192
Silberman, I., 449
Silver, R. C., 242, 245–246, 248
Silver, R. L., 240–242
Simmel, M., 137–138
Simon, L., 55
Situational information
in incremental theory of personality, 117
predicting behavior from, 103–104
recounting of memories based on, 157
Situational meaning, 257–262
after traumas, 239
for cancer survivors, 265–266
global and, 260–261
in meaning-making model of coping, 259
meanings made as changes in, 261–262
reappraisals of, 268
of stressful encounters, 258
Skills, of social actors, 175–176
Skin conductance, as measure of threat, 389
Skowronski, J. J., 156, 157, 159, 164
Smith, Fred, 323
Social actors
meaning in life for, 173–176
meaning makers as, 172
Social being, 25
Social-cognitive processes, 55–57

Social comparisons, 119, 325
Social competence, 125
Social context, for autobiographical memories, 151–153
Social environment
  and meaning making after trauma, 251–252
  multilevel meaning-making in, 51–52
  and narrative identity of emerging adults, 181
Social exclusion, 450
Social groups, MAP schemas in, 25–29, 35
Social influence, 367
Social interaction, rules of, 37
Social intuition, 199
Sociality, as source of morality, 191–192
Sociality motivation, 137
Social norms, shared reality and, 107
Social pain, 364
Social pressure, personal values and, 368
Social psychology
  behavioral inhibition in, 360–361
  cognitive dissonance in, 78–79
  self and death in, 79
  violation compensation in, 84
Social reality, 106–110
Social relatedness, positive affect and, 453–454
Social relationships
  and meaning in life, 449–450
  nostalgia and strengthening of, 302–303, 310
  in nostalgia narratives, 300
Social roles
  meaning in life from, 173–176
  and personal goals, 177
Social situational factors, of behavior, 360
Social support, 249, 252, 270
Social thought, 117–129
  and malleability of traits, 117–119
  predictions and lay theories in, 125–129
  self-preservation of lay theories in, 119–125
Socioemotional selectivity theory, 456
Sokolov, E. N., 30–32
Solomon, S., 54–56
Somatic markers, for autobiographical memories, 163
Southern California firestorm, 246–247
Sperling, G., 161
"Spinal" animals, perception and action in, 23n1
Spinal cord injuries, meaning making by patients with, 239–241
Spirituality
  of cancer survivors, 257
  and meaning in life, 449
  and meaning making after trauma, 252
  religiousness vs., 262
Sponges, perception by, 22–23
Spontaneous counterfactual reflection, 327–329
Spreading of alternatives paradigm, 389
Status, MAP schema and, 36–37
Status ideology, 390
Stecher, K., 123–125
Steger, M. F., 218–220, 227, 341
Stereotype content model, 202
Stereotypes
  compensatory responses to, 283–285
  and lay theories of personality, 120–122
Stimuli, framing of, 17
Stones, M. H., 241
Strack, F., 454
Stress
  from collective traumas, 248–249
  and coping, 268, 438
  meaning making as reaction to, 248–249, 261–262, 438
  nostalgia as intervention for, 309
  from situational–global meaning discrepancies, 260–261
  situational meaning of stressful encounters, 258
  from uncertainty, 388
Structure-seeking, 56, 225. *See also* Personal need for structure (PNS)
Subjective experience, reality as, 72–74, 77
Subjective feelings
  in assessment of meaning in life, 446–447
  in global meaning, 258

Subjective judgments, of well-being, 453–455
Sudden infant death syndrome (SIDS), 243–244
Suffering
global beliefs about, 264
and lack of meaning, 6–7
and stress-related growth, 269
Suicide, 8
Suler, J., 373–374
Sullivan, D., 60
Sunday neurosis, 468
Support, social, 249, 252, 270
Surprises
explainability vs., 433–436
pleasure from, 426–427, 431–433
and rate of adaptation, 425
Survival, 74, 93–94
Swanson, L. W., 22, 27, 32, 34, 37–38
Symbolic value, multilevel meaning-making and, 50–51
Sympathetic adrenal medullary (SAM) activation, 385–387
Synchronicities, 328–329
System justification theory
beliefs in, 280
injustices to self in, 284–285
meaning restoration in, 282–283

Tait, R., 242
Task performance, counterfactual thinking and, 320
Taves, P. A., 392
Taylor, S. E., 325–326, 342
Teasing, 25
Technology, anthropomorphism of, 141–142
Teigen, K. H., 325, 345
Teleology, 6–7, 58, 140–141
Temporal landmarking, 159–160, 162
Temporal recategorizations, 157
Tension myositis syndrome (TMS), 472–473
Terminal values, 179
Territories, cognitive mapping of, 35
Terror management theory (TMT), 55–57, 62–64
cognitive consistency in, 55–56
and consolidate or augment model, 225
and need for closure, 56
and nostalgia in meaning making, 304–306
and personal need for structure, 56–57, 62–63
and symbolically transcending death, 64
Theodicies, 264
Theories of Cognitive Consistency (Robert Abelson), 104
Theory of mind, 199–201
Theory replacement, theory violation vs., 126
Thompson, C. P., 158, 159, 164
Thompson, S. C., 252
Threat(s), 401–413
and anterior cingulate cortex activation, 403–405
approach motivational systems for resolving, 405–407
and aversive arousal, 384
belief conflict as, 401–403
to beliefs, 281–282, 290
biopsychosocial model of, 386
consolidate/augment model and responses to, 224–225
and counterfactual thinking, 332, 395
and function of meaning, 407–410
and human alarm system, 364
meaning and reduction in, 393–395
meaning violations as triggers for, 387–392
as motivator of meaning restoration, 392–393, 395
religion-based meaning frameworks for, 410–412
unexpected, 36
Tiberius, V., 217
TMS (tension myositis syndrome), 472–473
TMT. *See* Terror management theory
Todorov, A., 201, 202
Townsend, S. S., 391
Toxic disinhibition, 374
Tracy, J. L., 62
Trait-relevant behavior, 121
Traits
in entity theory of personality, 117
malleability of, 117–119
of social actors, 175–176

Transitions
existential anxiety during, 470
in life stories, 321
Transitive associations, 35
Traumas, 237–252
collective, 245–250
future research in, 251–252
meaning making and adaptation to, 438
moral inversion from, 196–198
personal, 238–245
reappraisals after, 281–282, 285, 290
revision of worldviews after, 77–78
writing about, 423
Trent, J., 452–453, 456–457
Trier Stress Test, 309
Trope, Yaacov, 102
Trust, ingroup morality and, 193
Trustworthiness, 201–202
Truth
as concept, 98
as outcome, 93
Truth effectiveness, 97–99
Truth motivation, 91–110
control and value motivation vs., 92–93
definition of, 92
and effectiveness in life pursuits, 96–99
for establishing reality, 101–110
and hedonism, 91–92
mechanisms for fulfilling, 100–101
and pleasure/pain as motivator, 95–96
and survival as motivator, 94–95
Tulving, E., 150
Turner, S., 158
Turning points
counterfactual thinking about, 329, 342–343, 433n1
fate in, 329
in life stories, 321–322

Ullsperger, M., 404–405
Ullsperger, P., 404–405
Ultimate concerns, in existential psychotherapy, 467–470
Uncertainty, 421–439
and adaptation to negative events, 422–423
and adaptation to positive events, 423–436
and AREA model of affective adaptation, 422
aversive arousal from, 383–384
and explainability, 433–436
and fate, 330
measuring meaning-making from, 436–439
pleasures of, 425–430
and rate of adaptation, 425
and religious ideals, 411
and surprises, 431–436
as trigger for threat, 387–388
and valence of outcomes, 430–431
Unconscious cognitive processes
in meaning compensation, 83
in meaning making, 438–439
Uncontrollability, as threat, 388
Understanding
and adaptation, 437–438
and anxiety, 5
violations of, 6
United States
belief in synchronicities in, 328
cancer survivors in, 263
generativity and redemptive narratives in, 182–184
intergroup interactions in, 388
meaning making after collective trauma in, 247–250
meaning seeking models in, 228–229
political values of liberals vs. conservatives, 179
prevalence of religious beliefs in, 262
status ideology in, 390
Unity, will to meaning and, 74
Universal beliefs, 279–280
Universal moral grammar, 193–194
The unknown
intersection of known and, 38–42
as meaning framework, 29–38
Unpredicatability, 141
Updegraff, J. A., 248
Upward counterfactual thinking, 340, 350
about pivotal moments, 324
and well-being, 325–326

Uslaner, E. M., 202
Utility
Jeremy Bentham's definition of, 94
of memories, 160–161

Vail, K. E., 58, 62
Vallacher, R. R., 58
Value(s)
of autobiographical memories, 162–164
instrumental and terminal, 179
personal, 50–54, 368
and personal goals, 179
political, 179
religious, 179
symbolic, 50–51
Value effectiveness, 96–97, 99
Value motivation, 92–93
Van den Bos, K., 361, 362, 367–370
Van Lange, P. A. M., 361, 362, 368–370, 373
Van Tongeren, D. R., 205
Variability (of event), rate of adaptation and, 425
Ventral tegmental dopaminergic system, 34
Vertical coherence, of goals, 407–408
Vess, M., 55, 58, 63, 302
Veterans, moral disengagement by, 195–196
Vicarious control, 285
Victim-blaming
and mortality salience, 57
relieving threats to beliefs with, 281–282, 290
Victim derogation, 61
Vigilance, meaning restoration and, 393
Vinogradova, O., 30–32, 34, 37
Violation(s). *See also* Expectancy violation(s)
of beliefs, 267
of commitment, 82
of lay theories of personality, 126–127
theory replacement vs., 126
of understanding, 6
Violation compensation. *See also* Compensatory responses
and cognitive dissonance theory, 79–80
and meaning compensation, 82–83
not related to self or death, 81–83
relational perspective on, 83–84
Virtue, eudaimonic well-being and, 204–205
Vision, goals and values in, 179
Vitality, nostalgia and, 309
Von Collani, G., 344

Wachtel, P. L., 475
Walker, W. R., 156, 157, 164
Wanting, liking vs., 95
Waytz, A., 142–143
Webster, D. M., 331
Wegner, D. M., 58
Well-being
and belief violation, 267
of cancer survivors, 264–268
and content of goals, 178–179
eudaimonic approach, 203–206, 450–452
and fate, 330
and global beliefs, 264–265
and morality, 202–206
nostalgia as protection of, 308, 309
and religious faith, 448
and religious/spiritual coping, 268
and situational beliefs, 266
subjective judgments of, 453–454
and upward counterfactual thinking, 325–326
Western cultures
autobiographical memory in, 153
mortality salience in, 59
search for meaning in life in, 220–225
When Prophecy Fails (Leon Festinger), 105–106
Whitchurch, E. R., 427, 429–431, 437
White, R. W., 137
White, T. L., 363, 370
White Americans, uncertainty in intergroup interactions for, 388
Wiener, Norbert, 30
Will to meaning, 221, 447, 469
Wilson, A. E., 157, 158
Wilson, T. D., 342, 425, 429–432, 434–435, 437
Wisdom, 217

Wojciszke, B., 195
Wolf, S., 205–206
Wong, E. M., 319–320
Wood, J. V., 342
Woodworth, Robert, 96, 97
Worldview-based expectancy violations, 390–391
Worldviews
defined, 390
reconciling trauma with, 250
revision of, 77–78
self-esteem and threats to, 60–61
Worldview verification theory, 390
World War II, autobiographical memories of, 151–152
Worry, uncertainty and, 430
Wortman, C. B., 239

Xu, J., 202

Yalom, Irvin, 466–470
Yopyk, D., 197
Young adults
as autobiographical authors, 180–182
pursuit of goals by, 178

Zajonc, R. B., 199
Zanna, M. P., 392, 408
Zinnbauer, B. J., 262

ABOUT THE EDITORS

Keith D. Markman, PhD, is an associate professor of psychology at Ohio University, where he is a member of the social judgment and behavioral decision-making program. Dr. Markman received his doctorate in 1994 at Indiana University and completed a 3-year postdoctoral fellowship at The Ohio State University. He conducts research in the areas of counterfactual thinking, creativity, and psychological momentum and has published over 40 articles and book chapters in these areas. Dr. Markman is currently an associate editor of *Social and Personality Psychology Compass*, was nominated for the 2003 Theoretical Innovation Prize in social and personality psychology, and won the Outstanding Junior Faculty Award at Ohio University in 2004. His edited volume, *The Handbook of Imagination and Mental Simulation*, was published in 2009.

Travis Proulx, PhD, is an assistant professor in the Department of Social Psychology at Tilburg University's School of Social and Behavioral Sciences in Tilburg, Netherlands. Dr. Proulx received a master's degree in interdisciplinary studies at the University of British Columbia and went on to receive a doctorate in developmental psychology. He subsequently completed a postdoctoral fellowship in social psychology at the University of California, Santa Barbara. Drawing from these diverse perspectives, Dr. Proulx has worked in collaboration on the meaning maintenance model—a discipline-spanning framework that offers an integrated account of inconsistency compensation phenomena. His research focuses on the common ways that people respond to a wide array of meaning violations, ranging from absurdist humor to the absurdity of human mortality.

Matthew J. Lindberg, PhD, is a visiting researcher in the Department of Psychological Sciences at Case Western Reserve University in Cleveland, Ohio. Dr. Lindberg received his doctorate in 2010 at Ohio University and subsequently joined the Department of Psychology at Fayetteville State University as an assistant professor. His research focuses on how people think about the world and people around them and how such thoughts affect their emotions, motivations, and behaviors. Dr. Lindberg has conducted research on counterfactual thinking, creativity, meaning, conscious and unconscious thinking, and jury decision-making.